The Routledge Handbook of Green Social Work

Green social work espouses a holistic approach to all peoples and other living things – plants and animals, and the physical ecosystem; emphasises the relational nature of all its constituent parts; and redefines the duty to care for and about others as one that includes the duty to care for and about planet earth.

By acknowledging the interdependency of all living things it allows for the inclusion of all systems and institutions in its remit, including both (hu)man-made and natural disasters arising from the (hu)made ones of poverty to chemical pollution of the earth's land, waters and soils and climate change, to the natural hazards like earthquakes and volcanoes which turn to disasters through human (in)action. Green social work's value system is also one that favours equality, social inclusion, the equitable distribution of resources, and a rights-based approach to meeting people's needs to live in an ethical and sustainable manner. Responding to these issues is one of the biggest challenges facing social workers in the twenty-first century which this *Handbook* is intended to address.

Through providing the theories, practices, policies, knowledge and skills required to act responsibly in responding to the diverse disasters that threaten to endanger all living things and planet earth itself, this green social work *Handbook* will be required reading for all social work students, academics and professionals, as well as those working in the fields of community development and disaster management.

Lena Dominelli holds a Chair in Applied Social Sciences in the School of Applied Social Sciences and is Co-Director at the Institute of Hazards, Risk and Resilience Research at Durham University, where she has particular responsibility for work on vulnerability and resilience. She has undertaken research through major large projects including those funded by the United Kingdom Research Councils – the ESRC ('Internationalising Institutional and Professional Practices'), EPSRC ('Climate Change, the Built Infrastructure and Health and Social Care Provisions for Older People'), and NERC (Earthquakes without Frontiers); and DfID (Department of International Development) and Wellcome Trust (Health Interventions during Volcanic Eruptions). Lena has published extensively in the fields of sociology, criminology, community development and social work. She has received a number of honours for her contributions to the profession including a medal from the Social Affairs Committee of the French Senate (2002); the Katherine A Kendall Memorial Award (2012) and two honorary doctorates (KwaZulu-Natal, 2008; and Malmö, 2017). Lena has been active internationally for many years, including having served as President of the International Association of Schools of Social Work (IASSW) 1996–2004, chairing a number of committees, representing it at the United Nations, including the UNFCCC meetings on climate change, served on various editorial boards and been an Editor of *International Social Work*, 2009–2017.

The Routledge Handbook of Green Social Work

Edited by Lena Dominelli

(with Bala Raju Nikku and Hok Bun Ku)

LONDON AND NEW YORK

First published 2018
by Routledge
2 Park Square, Milton Park, Abingdon, Oxon OX14 4RN

and by Routledge
711 Third Avenue, New York, NY 10017

Routledge is an imprint of the Taylor & Francis Group, an informa business

© 2018 selection and editorial matter, Lena Dominelli; individual chapters, the contributors

The right of Lena Dominelli to be identified as the author of the editorial material, and of the authors for their individual chapters, has been asserted in accordance with sections 77 and 78 of the Copyright, Designs and Patents Act 1988.

All rights reserved. No part of this book may be reprinted or reproduced or utilised in any form or by any electronic, mechanical, or other means, now known or hereafter invented, including photocopying and recording, or in any information storage or retrieval system, without permission in writing from the publishers.

Trademark notice: Product or corporate names may be trademarks or registered trademarks, and are used only for identification and explanation without intent to infringe.

British Library Cataloguing-in-Publication Data
A catalogue record for this book is available from the British Library

Library of Congress Cataloging-in-Publication Data
A catalog record for this book has been requested

ISBN: 978-1-138-74079-2 (hbk)
ISBN: 978-1-315-18321-3 (ebk)

Typeset in Bembo
by Apex CoVantage, LLC

Printed and bound in Great Britain by
TJ International Ltd, Padstow, Cornwall

This Handbook is dedicated to Planet Earth, that sustains all animate beings and inanimate things.

Disclaimer: Each author assumes full responsibility for the words in their particular chapter and obtaining all necessary permissions. The views contained therein are those of each author and not those of the editor or the publishers.

Contents

Acknowledgements   *xiii*
Contributors   *xiv*
Preface   *xxxii*
ROBERT GLASSER
Foreword: Green social work: a new direction for social work   *xxxiv*
LENA DOMINELLI

Introduction: why green social work?   1
Lena Dominelli, Bala Raju Nikku and Hok Bun Ku

PART I
Green social work theory   7

1 Green social work in theory and practice: a new environmental paradigm for the profession   9
Lena Dominelli

2 Transdisciplinary collaboration between physical and social scientists: drawing on the experiences of an advisor to Earthquakes without Frontiers (EwF)   21
Peter Sammonds

3 Disasters, health impacts and the value of implementing the *Sendai Framework for Disaster Risk Reduction 2015–2030*   35
Virginia Murray, Lorcan Clarke and Rishma Maini

4 The critical role of social work in disaster response: experiences in the United Kingdom   51
David N. Jones

Contents

5 Rebuilding lives post-disaster: innovative community practices for sustainable development 63
Julie Drolet, Haorui Wu, Robin Ersing, Margaret Alston, Desley Hargreaves, Yen Yi Huang, Chao Hsing Huang and Golam Mathbor

6 Green social work for environmental justice: implications for international social workers 74
Meredith C. F. Powers, Jennifer Willett, John Mathias and Anna Hayward

PART II
Natural disasters 85

7 Promoting public interest design: green social work interventions during the post-Ya'an earthquake reconstruction and recovery in Sichuan, China 87
Haorui Wu

8 Solidarity in times of disaster: the case of Chile 99
Rosemary A. Barbera

9 Social work response to Himalayan disasters: insights from green social work 110
Bala Raju Nikku

10 Dissecting a Himalayan disaster, finding pathways 121
Malathi Adusumalli and Soumya Dutta

11 A post-Morakot environmentally friendly reconstruction solution: reflections from a green social work perspective 132
Yen Yi Huang, Chiau Hong Chen, Shu Ching Chang and Shu Yuan Hsiao

12 Dominica – Tropical Storm Erika and its impacts 144
Letnie F. Rock, Debra D. Joseph and Ayodele O. Harper

PART III
Green agricultural practices 157

13 Developing green social work in a participatory small watershed management programme in China's tourism city of Lijiang 159
Tak Chuen Luk

14 Reflections on a Tribal Kitchen Project: a case study about green social work in Taiwan   171
    Ying-Hao Huang

15 Community gardening: the nexus for community, social work and university collaboration   182
    Robin Sakina Mama

PART IV
Food (in)security   193

16 Food insecurity: where social injustice meets environmental exploitation   195
    Cheryl Molle

17 The food security crisis and CSA movement in China: green social work practice in Yunnan Province   206
    Hok Bun Ku and Hairong Yan

PART V
(Hu)man-made disasters   217

18 Environmental issues and controversies in Latin America: a challenge for social work   219
    Nilsa Burgos Ortiz

19 Green social work requires a green politics   231
    Carolyn Noble

20 Green social work within integrated coastal zone management: Mauritius and Barbados   242
    Komalsingh Rambaree and Letnie F. Rock

21 Social protection options for women farmers in the face of climate change: a case study of women farmers and agriculture in Goromonzi, Zimbabwe   254
    Mildred T. Mushunje and Vishanthie Sewpaul

22 Climate justice, capabilities and sustainable livelihoods: insights from an action research project   267
    Sunil D. Santha, Sowmya Balasubramaniam, Anup Shenai, Asha Banu Soletti, Sharvan Verma, Jaydip Solanki and Rupali Gaikawad

PART VI
Extreme weather events — 279

23 The 2015 Chennai Floods: green social work, an emerging model for practice in India — 281
Miriam Samuel, Prince Annadurai and Sowndarya Sankarakrishnan

24 Mitigating the impact of drought in Namibia: implications for social work practice, education and policy — 293
Peggie Chiwara and Antoinette Lombard

PART VII
Disaster-driven migration — 307

25 Understanding poverty through the experiences of women who are forced migrants: considerations for a social work response — 309
Mehmoona Moosa-Mitha, Feinula Bhanji and Fariyal Ross-Sheriff

26 Positioning Social Workers Without Borders within green social work: ethical considerations for social work as social justice work — 321
Lauren Wroe, Bridget Ng'andu, Matthew Doyle and Lynn King

PART VIII
Health disasters — 333

27 Intersectionality in health pandemics — 335
Susan A. Taylor

28 The arrival of chikungunya on the Caribbean island of Curaçao: the important role of social workers — 347
Odette van Brummen-Girigori and Auronette Girigori

29 The challenge of maintaining continuity in health and social care during extreme weather events: cross-sectoral and transdisciplinary approaches — 359
Sarah Curtis, Lena Dominelli, Katie J. Oven and Jonathan Wistow

PART IX
Industrial and urban issues — 371

30 Sowing the seeds: a green social work project in Sri Lanka — 373
Yasmin Perera

31 The ecological hazards of nuclear waste disposal: tensions between aspirations for economic prosperity and community sustainability in a small Croatian municipality   385
    Nino Žganec and Ana Opačić

32 Integrating green social work and the US environmental justice movement: an introduction to community benefits agreements   397
    Amy Krings and Hillary Thomas

PART X
Practicing green social work   **407**

33 Historical trends in calls to action: climate change, pro-environmental behaviours and green social work   409
    Erin Kennedy

34 Community resistance and resilience following an environmental disaster in Aotearoa/New Zealand   420
    Heather Hamerton, Sonya Hunt, Kelly Smith and Rebecca J. Sargisson

35 Human-made disasters and social work: a Ukrainian perspective   431
    Tetyana Semigina

36 Strategies used by activists in Israeli environmental struggles: implications for the future green social worker   442
    Ariella Cwikel and Edith Blit-Cohen

37 Working with children in disasters   454
    Ines V. Danao

38 Persons with disabilities in the Great East Japan Earthquake: lessons learnt and new directions towards evidence-based empowering just practices   464
    Shigeo Tatsuki

39 Social work and terrorism: voices of experience   478
    Marilyn Callahan

40 Personal reflections on the *Prevent* programme   489
    Neil Denton and Kate Cochrane

41 Reflecting on the 2015 Gorkha earthquake, tread carefully   500
    Hanna A. Ruszczyk

Contents

PART XI
Education   **511**

42 Making connections with survivors of a catastrophic flood in West Virginia: a green social work approach to climate change adaptation   513
   Willette F. Stinson and Larry D. Williams

43 Towards a curriculum in disaster risk reduction from a green social work perspective   522
   Carin Björngren Cuadra and Guðný Björk Eydal

44 Greening social work education in Aotearoa/New Zealand   535
   Lynsey M. Ellis, Ksenija Napan and Kieran O'Donoghue

45 Greening Australian social work practice and education   547
   Sharlene Nipperess and Jennifer Boddy

46 Greening social work education: transforming the curriculum in pursuit of eco–social justice   558
   Peter Jones

   Conclusions: towards a green society and mainstreaming green social work in social work education and practice   569
   Lena Dominelli, Bala Raju Nikku and Hok Bun Ku

Name index   *573*
Subject index   *586*

Acknowledgements

A book is never the undertaking of one person. It involves hosts of people whose willingness to share their stories is a wonderful gift that contributes to other people's learning directly and indirectly. But everyone gains from the interaction. Your names and contributions remain anonymous but your numbers are legion. Your words had diverse aims but were united in one common goal: looking after the planet that nurtures us all. You are also those with the courage to use green social work and move it in new directions. Special thanks go to indigenous peoples across the world who have inspired me enormously, particularly those among the First Nations of Canada that shared insights with me.

To the participants whose knowledge and wisdom are the pillars of this *Handbook*, gratitude is given beyond measure. The contributors to this book, academic colleagues, practitioners, friends and relatives who helped me along this journey; the students who inspire me daily with their questions, insights and support; and the colleagues whose courage to transgress and challenge given nostrums, to guide others; to all of them many thanks are owed. The words of Robert Glasser, Head of UNISDR, encouraging green social workers to engage fully with the sustainable development and disaster risk reduction agendas, are particularly heart-felt.

I gratefully acknowledge Bala Raju Nikku and Hok Bun Ku whose enthusiasm in the early days led to a proposal that we co-edit a reader, but it morphed into a much larger *Handbook* under my editorship. I warmly acknowledge their assistance.

Finally, a huge debt of thanks is owed David for helping to get this book through during the silent hours of the night and morning. Thank you for being there when no one else was.

Lena Dominelli
Editor

Contributors

Malathi Adusumalli is Associate Professor in the Department of Social Work, University of Delhi. She has over two decades of teaching experience and grassroots experience of working with civil society groups in the disaster-affected areas of Andhra Pradesh. She has worked in the areas of Jogin the Reform and Rehabilitation Programme there. She follows anti-oppressive practice and has been associated with the atheist and humanist movements of the world. Her current research interests are working with mountain communities for sustainable development in the light of climate crisis, improving gender relations and disaster response.

Margaret Alston is Professor of Social Work, Head of Department and founder of the Gender, Leadership and Social Sustainability (GLASS) Research Unit at Monash University. She was awarded an Order of Australia for her work with rural women in 2010. Margaret has an extensive record in research and publications covering gender relations, farming communities in Australia, Bangladesh and other Asian countries, and in disaster management. She has served with UNESCO, FAO, UN Habitat and UNEP. She has also given a number of keynote addresses in her profession.

Prince Annadurai is Assistant Professor, Department of Social Work, Madras Christian College in Chennai, India. He has 22 years of teaching and research experience in social work. He was a Visiting Faculty Member in Appalachian State University, NC, US (2007) and Department of Public Health at the National Institute of Epidemiology, ICMR, Chennai (2008–2014). He has acted as Consultant to several INGOs in the US, Canada, Australia and UK and to various Government of India Projects and NGOs. His areas of interests are public health, health and social work, environmental social work and social work research.

Sowmya Balasubramaniam is an early career action researcher working in the field of sustainable livelihoods and empowerment at the grassroots. By training, she is an engineer and also has a postgraduate degree in social work. In the past two years, she has been striving towards promoting and establishing women-led collective enterprises in the tribal villages of Maharashtra. Currently, she is contributing towards livelihood promotion for marginalised groups in the hill ranges of Uttarakhand. Her research interests are in sustainable agriculture, women's empowerment and reproductive health.

Rosemary A. Barbera is Associate Professor and Director of Field Education in the Department of Social Work at La Salle University. She has been working in human rights since the 1980s in the US and Latin America. Her areas of practice include human rights, surviving torture, community rebuilding after human rights violations and disaster, participatory action research and social work in Latin America. Current research examines the role memory plays in post-dictatorship society, community resilience after disaster and building human rights social movements. She has also worked with Juntos/Casa de los Soles, the Agrupación de Familiares de Detenidos Desaparecidos, and the Junta de Vecinos Concierto y Cultura. For more than 20 years, she has brought students to the población La Pincoya in Santiago, Chile where they learn about past and present human rights issues and learn from human rights activists.

Feinula Bhanji is pursuing a Master's of Science in Applied Economics at Johns Hopkins University with a focus on Development and Regional Economics. As the Global Program Coordinator, she assisted a team of researchers in several countries to examine the causes and consequences of ultra-poverty and develop capacity to redress poverty using a participatory development model. Her contributions include designing, monitoring and evaluation, resulting in best practices for service provision. Her interests include making an impact on poverty alleviation through sustainable development, public–private partnerships, strengthened civil society and institutional infrastructure. She has co-authored journal articles related to poverty and displaced populations.

Guðný Björk Eydal is Professor of Social Work at the University of Iceland. Guðný has served as Head of Faculty of Sociology and Social Work. Her main research field is family and care policies in Iceland and the Nordic countries and she directs a project in disaster social work. Among her recent work is a book *Fatherhood in the Nordic welfare states: Comparing policies and practice*, co-edited with Professor Tine Rostgaard. Guðný is also leading a long-term research project on the outcome of the paid parental leave legislation in Iceland which includes within it a comparative study on the parental practices of parents born in Poland and Iceland.

Carin Björngren Cuadra is Associate Professor in Social Work at the Department of Social Work at the University of Malmö, Sweden. Her interests involve migration and health including human services' responses to diversity and the distribution of security and welfare, precarity, risk and vulnerability. She is currently undertaking research on the role of social work in disaster management and the Swedish contingency system.

Edith Blit-Cohen is the Head of the Joseph J. Schwartz M.A. Programmes (Early Childhood Studies and Management of NGOs and Community Organisations), and Head of the Community Social Work Track, Paul Baerwald School of Social Work and Social Welfare, Hebrew University of Jerusalem. She is a consultant and facilitator of community work for the Ministry of Social Affairs. As a community social work expert, she combines fieldwork and academia. Her research and activism are focused on excluded populations, human rights, social change and community practice.

Jennifer Boddy is a Senior Lecturer and Programme Director of the Master of Social Work at Griffith University, Gold Coast, Australia. Jennifer holds the values of social justice, human rights and integrity at the forefront of her research and teaching. Her research spans several areas including hope, gender and the creation of healthy, sustainable environments. Jennifer is particularly interested in understanding and addressing the impacts of climate change on disadvantaged populations such as older people, women and those living in poverty. She is also Treasurer of the Australian and New Zealand Social Work and Welfare Education and Research (ANZSWWER) association.

Contributors

Nilsa Burgos Ortiz has a PhD from Columbia University School of Social Work in New York. She worked as a professor and researcher at the University of Puerto Rico, Graduate School of Social Work, Río Piedras Campus from 1983–2014. She is an internationally recognised scholar whose publications on gender, violence and work have been widely used in universities throughout the Caribbean, Central America and South America. In September 2015, she was elected President of the Latin America Association of Academic and Research in Social Work (ALAEITS in Spanish). This position allows her to hold a position as a Vice-President in the International Association of Schools of Social Work.

Marilyn Callahan is a Professor Emeritus at the University of Victoria, School of Social Work in Victoria, BC, Canada. She has taught for over 25 years in the areas of social welfare, human service organisations and child welfare. Her research and publications focus on women and child welfare, with attention to the gendered, racist and class-based bias of child welfare systems. She was awarded the 2009 Canadian Association for Social Work Education Award for Excellence, given annually to a Canadian academic in social work. Her most recent book, *At Risk: Social Justice in Child Welfare and Other Human Services*, co-authored with Karen Swift, examines how risk assessment has infiltrated many human services, including child welfare, and how the science and application of risk assessment tend to protect organisations rather than the individuals they serve.

Shu Ching Chang is a staff member of the Kaohsiung Community Vision Empowerment Center and Secretary of The Alliance of Small Communities in Kaohsiung. She was a housewife who was recruited as a local disaster worker to participate in the reconstruction following Typhoon Morakot. Since being a disaster worker, she has attended Social Work Continuing Education Credit Courses and will graduate this year. Shu-Ching's involvement allowed her to extend her horizon and accumulate community knowledge. She hopes to continue a career in community work while forming solid and sustainable partnerships with local communities.

Chiau Hong Chen has a major in Taiwanese Literature and Traditional Arts, and is a Supervisor of the Kaohsiung Community Vision Empowerment Centre and a part-time Lecturer at the Department of Life and Death at Nanhua University, Taiwan. He participated in the reconstruction following Typhoon Morakot. Since 2014, Chiau-Hong has devoted himself to developing a community-based organisation, The Alliance of Small Communities, in Kaohsiung. After governmental reconstruction resources had left, the Alliance with existing local networks and organisations continued to undertake local disaster workers training and building collaboration while addressing long-term reconstruction issues.

Peggie Chiwara is a Zimbabwean social worker, living and working in Namibia. She holds a Master's of Social Work in Social Policy and Development (Distinction) from the University of Pretoria. She is currently in the process of enrolling for a PhD in Social Work with the same institution. Her proposed PhD research topic is entitled, 'Green social work in Namibia: Implications for social work policy, education and practice'. Peggie's research interests include developmental social work, green social work, social welfare policy and social development.

Lorcan Clarke joined the Global Disaster Risk Reduction team at Public Health England (PHE) in February 2017 to assist with the development of technical guidance notes for disaster loss data. Prior to working with PHE, Lorcan was a Consultant in Sustainable Development and Health Equity, and a Graduate Intern in Research Promotion and Development, at the Headquarters of the Pan American Health Organisation (PAHO), Region Office of the Americas for the World Health Organisation, in Washington D.C., US. Lorcan is particularly interested in the economic aspects of community resilience, and has a Bachelor's of Arts in Economics and History from Trinity College Dublin, Ireland.

Kate Cochrane is an emergency planner within Newcastle City Council with specific responsibilities for planning for the recovery from major and critical Incidents, the response to flooding and security hazards and the support of people whose everyday lives are interrupted by significant emergencies. She is a Subject Matter Expert within the UK's Emergency Planning College, acts as an advisor to the Institute of Hazard Risk and Resilience at Durham University, sits on the governmental Local and National Recovery Advisory Groups, the Communities Prepared National Group and the Emergency Planning Society's Human Aspect Group.

Sarah Curtis is Professor Emeritus at Durham University, UK, where she previously held the position of Professor of Health and Risk, directing the interdisciplinary Institute of Hazard, Risk and Resilience. A specialist in health geography, she has led a range of research focusing on the social and physical environmental factors that are important for health inequality. She has worked collaboratively with a number of non-academic agencies, making a significant contribution in various fields of health policy.

Ariella Cwikel is a teacher and instructor at the Hebrew University of Jerusalem, Paul Baerwald School of Social Work and Social Welfare, where she teaches communication skills in community work. She is Head of the Community Sustainability Unit at the Jerusalem Municipality. Combining environment and community work has been her professional focus since 2008. She conducted qualitative research for her Master's of Arts focusing on communities engaged in environmental struggles. She is a founder and volunteer board member of the Jerusalem African Community Centre (R.A.), a grassroots NGO working with African refugees and asylum seekers in Jerusalem.

Ines V. Danao is former Vice-President of the Board of Directors of the National Association for Social Work Education, Inc (Philippines) and current Vice-President of the Society of Filipino Family Therapists. She has been a social work educator in the Philippines for 23 years, including two years in Vietnam. She has also been a trainer and resource person in social work, mental health and child welfare in the Philippines, Hong Kong, Vietnam and Japan in order to work with Filipino migrants in Japan over a period of 30 years. Her main interests are social work practice in urban human settlements, international refugee work, residential care for street children, working with survivors of violence including in disasters, Filipino Family Therapy, children in conflict with the law and persons with mental disorders. She received a Bachelor's of Science in Social Work, *Magna Cum Laude* from Concordia College and Master's of Science in Social Work at the Asian Social Institute.

Neil Denton is an experienced practitioner in community mediation and conflict transformation. For 12 years he led the work to challenge hate crime, manage community tensions and prevent violent extremism on behalf of Safe Newcastle (a partnership of the City Council, Probation, Health, Fire and Rescue and the Police). He now works with a range of organisations promoting dialogue about difficult issues between communities.

Lena Dominelli holds a Chair in Applied Social Sciences in the School of Applied Social Sciences and is Co-Director at the Institute of Hazards, Risk and Resilience Research at Durham

University, where she has particular responsibility for work on vulnerability and resilience. She has undertaken research through major large projects including those funded by the United Kingdom Research Councils – the ESRC ('Internationalising Institutional and Professional Practices'), EPSRC ('Climate Change, the Built Infrastructure and Health and Social Care Provisions for Older People'), and NERC (Earthquakes without Frontiers); and DfID (Department of International Development) and Wellcome Trust (Health Interventions during Volcanic Eruptions). Lena has published extensively, and received a number of honours for her contributions to the profession.

Matthew Doyle is a student member and activist in Social Workers Without Borders (SWWB). He is also a volunteer in Gaza.

Julie Drolet is an Associate Professor in the Faculty of Social Work at the University of Calgary. In 2009 she was awarded a prestigious Canadian Foundation for Innovation (CFI) Leaders Opportunity Fund grant in recognition of research excellence in the field of disasters, climate change, and sustainable development. Julie has published extensively in international social work and social development with a particular focus on climate change and disasters, gender and development, international social protection initiatives, and international migration and Canadian immigration. Her current interests focus on social work and disasters, social protection initiatives, relational well-being, and immigrant settlement and integration in smaller communities. She teaches courses on social work and research, social work and sustainable social development, international social work and field education. She collaborates with several interdisciplinary teams of scholars on various research initiatives and employs numerous students as research assistants.

Soumya Dutta is the convener of Climate and Energy, Beyond Copenhagen Collective. He has extensively engaged with the UN System, National and Sub-National Policy level and engaged with a large number of CSOs on issues of energy and climate justice interfaces with water agriculture and forests. He has written several books, many papers and critical reviews, as well as delivered a number of lectures in academic and non-academic fora in many universities in different countries, contributing immensely to the debates on climate change and energy nationally and internationally. He has advised a number of national collectives on climate change adaptation and disaster risk reduction.

Lynsey M. Ellis is a PhD student and a Registered Social Worker with 19 years of social work practice experience within clinical mental health, primarily with homeless and transient populations, in both the UK and Aotearoa/New Zealand. Since 2010 she has worked in an academic position as a Professional Clinician and Field Education Coordinator within the School Social Work, College of Health at Massey University Albany, Auckland. This position gives her connections and access to both students and staff within the social work practice and education sector. She has been studying the connection between social work, climate change and sustainability since 2012. During this time, in her role as Professional Clinician, she has developed and delivered workshops on sustainable social work as part of the field education training at Massey University Albany campus on the Bachelor's and Master's of Social Work curriculum. She has been instrumental in introducing sustainable principles to Massey's social work field education programme in response to the Global Agenda for Social Work and Social Development (IASSW, ICSW, IFSW, 2012).

Robin Ersing is Associate Professor in the School of Public Affairs with a joint appointment in the School of Social Work at the University of South Florida (USF). She conducts research on adaptive capacity and community resilience within the context of natural hazards. She has been funded by the National Science Foundation and is a co-investigator on a multi-national research study on rebuilding lives post-disaster. Her research has been disseminated through international conferences in Australia, Canada, Austria, and Japan. Robin has published the book, *Surviving Disaster: The Role of Social Networks*, and is a certified Community Emergency Response Team member.

Rupali Gaikawad is a committed social worker striving towards the empowerment of marginalised tribal groups in Maharashtra, India. She considers her strengths as the ability to interface with marginalised groups and co-create meaningful livelihood enhancement initiatives. As a postgraduate in social work, she continues her research interests in community development and sustainable livelihoods.

Auronette Girigori graduated with a Bachelor's in Management and Business Communication and Master's of Science in Business Management. She has worked as a Coordinator of Research projects at the University of Curaçao, Dr Moises da Costa Gomez. Currently she has her own practice for communication, data-collection and processing. She has plenty of experience in collecting and coordinating research projects regarding oral health and obesity among the youth, the development of toddlers, father absence, being prepared for natural disasters and observation studies. Therefore she has been acknowledged locally and internationally for her participation and collaboration in several research projects.

Heather Hamerton is a Pākehā New Zealander and a registered community psychologist. She is Research Manager at the Tauranga Campus of Waiariki Bay of Plenty Institute of Technology. She regularly undertakes research that investigates social and human behaviour from an ecological viewpoint. She resides in the Bay of Plenty and considers the coastal region as home. As one member of a multidisciplinary team of researchers, she shares the dedication to responding to the challenges of protecting and supporting this world and addressing issues of environmental justice in all peoples' lives and throughout professional practice.

Desley Hargreaves gained a PSM from the University of Queensland, Australia and worked in both federal and state government and the non-government sector. She headed the National Social Work Service in the federal Department of Human Services with responsibility for approximately 700 social workers delivering services across Australia. Desley has had extensive experience in disaster recovery including for Australians impacted by terrorism or natural disasters in other countries. She was awarded the Public Service Medal in the Bali Honours for work undertaken during the Bali bombings.

Ayodele O. Harper is a counselling psychologist who works as the Clinical Supervisor and Internship Coordinator for the M.Sc. Counselling Psychology Programme and as part-time Lecturer in the Department of Government, Sociology and Social Work at the University of the West Indies, Cave Hill Campus. Her research interests span several areas in psychology including bereavement, trauma and crisis intervention (e.g. natural disasters, sudden deaths, sexual abuse, rape, domestic violence, teenage pregnancies). She is a member of the Barbados Society of Psychology and Barbados Association of Professional Social Workers.

Anna Hayward is an Associate Professor at Stony Brook in NY, US. Her areas of interest include children and family services, father involvement, juvenile justice, and the implementation and evaluation of evidence-based interventions. She is also particularly interested in environmental and ecological justice, as well as environmental social work. She recently served as a Fulbright Visiting Scholar to Jamaica.

Xin Hou is Associate Dean of the School of Social Work, Associate Professor of Social Work, School of Social Work at the China Youth University for Political Science and holds a Master's of Social Work from Hong Kong Polytechnic University. His research interests include youth social work, mentoring programmes, and positive youth development.

Shu Yuan Hsiao is Director of Living Stone Foundation for Social Welfare and Charity and previously a Social Worker Supervisor for women and community empowerment at the Bureau of Social Affairs in the Kaohsiung City Government. She organised training programs for front-line disaster workers, human resources and empowerment mechanisms in response to Typhoon Morakot. She advocated for a reconstruction program that valued local organisations' and workers' input and channelled governmental resources into building capacity and collaborative networks in local organisations.

Chao Hsing Huang is Assistant Professor in the Centre for Social Empowerment Taiwan (COSET) at the Chang Jung Christian University in Taiwan. He works on disasters and empowering service users.

Yen Yi Huang is a Professor in the Department of Social Policy and Social Work at the National Chi-Nan University in Puli, Taiwan and has a major in Community Work. She has long-term experience in working with women in community groups to address issues of care and gender. She also co-operates with theatre workers to train social work students in creativity, self-expression and sensitivity to gender issues. During the last four years, she has been involved in the following research projects: 'Empowerment and Community Work: In and Against the State'; 'Rebuilding Lives Post-Disaster: Innovative Community Practices for Sustainable Development of 921 earthquake'; 'Women Leaders' Agency in Environment-Friendly Businesses and Organisations: The Study of 921 earthquake and Typhoon Morakot'; and 'Indigenous Women Use Ecology to Reconstruct Their Tribes after the Strike of Typhoon Morakot in Taiwan'.

Ying-Hao Huang is the Founder of the Taiwan Indigenous Dmavun Development Association (TIDDA) and is now its General Secretary. Before holding this position, he was the Social Worker Supervisor. Currently, he is also an Assistant Professor of the National Dong Hwa University in Taiwan.

Sonya Hunt is a New Zealand Registered Social Worker and Lecturer on the Social Work Programme at the University of Waikato, Tauranga campus. She resides in the Bay of Plenty and considers the coastal region as home. As one member of a multidisciplinary team of researchers, she shares the dedication to responding to the challenges of protecting and supporting this world and addressing issues of environmental justice in all peoples' lives and throughout professional practice.

David N. Jones is a Qualified Social Worker with over 40 years' experience in local, national and international social work practice and policy. He was President of the International Federation of Social Workers 2006–2010 and is the Coordinator of the Global Agenda for Social Work and Social Development process. He has held various national positions, including General

Secretary of the British Association of Social Workers, Head of the association representing Chairs of Local Safeguarding Children Boards (2014–2016) and advisory roles in central government, one of which included being the Department of Health social care lead on pandemic flu emergency planning. He is a trustee of Children and Families Across Borders (International Social Services UK). David has written about social work responses to disasters and has been personally involved in a civil emergency.

Peter Jones is a Senior Lecturer in Social Work and Human Services at James Cook University, Australia. He has been involved in environmental activism and education for over 30 years and has been teaching and developing materials around social work and the environment since 1997. He has twice been awarded with an Australian Office of Learning and Teaching 'National Citation for Outstanding Contribution to Student Learning', and is a Fellow of the Higher Education Research and Development Society of Australasia (HERDSA). In addition to eco-social work education, his research and practice concerns include transformative learning and international social work.

Debra D. Joseph is a Lecturer in the Social Work Unit at The University of the West Indies (UWI), Faculty of Social Sciences, Cave Hill, Barbados. Her nationality is that of Trinidad and Tobago. She has been a clinical social worker for over 10 years. Her research specialty is in HIV/AIDS, disaster management and sustainable development. She has worked previously in the technical field of meteorology for 20 years and has working knowledge of weather systems, clouds and weather observations. A deliberate career switch to the social field culminated in a Bachelor's of Science in Social Work with a minor in Psychology, a Master's in Social Work (Clinical) and a PhD in Social Work. She is using her past working experience in meteorology in combination with her current social work profession to explore avenues of research and scholarly output with respect to climate change and sustainable development in the Caribbean.

Erin Kennedy is a PhD Candidate in the School of Social Work at Lund University. She is interested in the low-carbon development and community level climate change action in China and Japan. The focus of her thesis research remains in China wherein Erin is exploring community-engagement strategies that enable stakeholder involvement in planning local community-level climate change action. In China Erin is based at the Tyndall Centre at Fudan University in Shanghai. Erin has another project in Japan where she is collaborating with the National Institute of Environmental Studies (NIES) to provide an analysis of stakeholder involvement in planning local community-level climate change actions and facilitating dialogue between engaged participants who represent different societal groups within the community. She hopes to contribute to the discussion on collaborative, participatory and network governance in the area of community-level climate change resilience-building, which may provide some analytical frameworks for how to involve non-public bodies, actualise the role of social work in sustainable development, and address social and environmental changes.

Lynn King is a Co-Founder of Social Workers Without Borders (SWWB). She is also an experienced social worker in adult social care, a qualified Best Interest Assessor and Practice Educator. Lynn currently works as a Professional Development Educator in the county of Kent, England.

Amy Krings is an Assistant Professor of Social Work at Loyola University Chicago. Her research interests include environmental justice, community organising, urban politics and social justice education. Her dissertation research included a four-year (2010–2014) political ethnographic study of a Southwest Detroit campaign to secure a community benefits agreement as a means to promote environmental justice.

Hok Bun Ku is an Associate Professor in the School of Social Sciences at Hong Kong Polytechnic University. He is also the Deputy Director of the Peking U-PolyU Social Work Research Center, Associate Editor of *Action Research*, and Executive Editor of *China Journal of Social Work*. Hok Bun was 2007 Fulbright Scholar at Washington University, St. Louis; and Senior Research Fellow at Durham University, UK. He has held honourable positions in China at Minzu University, Yunnan University, Sun Yat-sen University, China Youth University for Political Sciences, Shandong Youth University for Political Sciences, Central China Agriculture University; Taiwan National Central University; and York University, Canada. He wrote *Moral Politics in a South Chinese Village: Responsibility, Reciprocity and Resistance* (2003).

Antoinette Lombard is Professor in Social Work and Head of Social Work and Criminology at the University of Pretoria, South Africa. Her research interests include developmental social work and welfare, and social development. An established researcher, she holds C1 rating from the National Research Foundation in South Africa and a national award from the Minister of Science and Technology, Researcher of the Year award in the Cluster Applied Social Sciences in the Faculty of Humanities, University of Pretoria, and was second runner-up for the 2015 Distinguished Women in Science Award (WISA) in Humanities and Social Sciences, alongside other awards. Antoinette is IASSW's Chair of the Global Agenda for Social Work and Social Development and Coordinator of the Global Agenda in the Africa Region, on the Board of the International Consortium for Social Development (ICSD), and served on various South African professional bodies over the years, including work leading to the first registered minimum standards for the Bachelor's of Social Work. On the international front, she represented the Association of South African Social Work Education Institutions (ASASWEI) on the Board of the International Association for Schools of Social Work (IASSW) from 2012 to 2015.

Tak Chuen Luk is Associate Professor in the Department of Applied Social Sciences in the Institute of Higher Education in the College of Technology of Hong Kong. He was trained as a professional social worker at the Chinese University of Hong Kong and obtained a PhD from the Department of Sociology at the University of Chicago. He has taught in the Department of Sociology at the Baptist University and established the Centre for Research and Development of Oxfam Hong Kong in Beijing. His professional career is characterised by inter-sectoral collaboration of practice and research between social work and development work. His expertise includes action research, developmental social work, rural social work, working with migrant communities, poverty reduction, NGOs and the philanthropic sector in China.

Rishma Maini qualified in medicine from the University of Edinburgh in 2005 and worked as a junior doctor in Scotland and Australia. In 2009, she joined the UK Public Health training scheme and gained a Master's in Public Health. Between 2012 and 2015 she worked in Kinshasa, the Democratic Republic of Congo, initially as a Health Adviser for 1.5 years with the Department for International Development, and latterly as a PhD student enrolled at the London School of Tropical Medicine and Hygiene. Rishma is currently working with the Global Disaster Risk Reduction team at Public Health England (PHE).

Robin Sakina Mama is Professor and Dean of the School of Social Work at Monmouth University, West Long Branch, New Jersey. She received her Bachelor's of Social Work degree from College Misericordia in Dallas, PA, Master's of Social Service, Master's of Law and Social Policy, and PhD in Social Work and Social Research degrees from Bryn Mawr College. For 10 years, Robin worked at the Philadelphia Area Project on Occupational Safety and Health where she was responsible for providing technical assistance to unions on workers compensation, contract language for health and safety, and right-to-know information. At Monmouth, Robin teaches in the International and Community Development concentration of the Master's of Social Work programme. Her teaching and research interests are in human rights, field education, international social development and international social work. In 2009 the School began the Monmouth University Community Garden with Master's of Social Work intern, Sean Foran.

Golam Mathbor is Professor of Social Work at Monmouth University in the US where he also served as Associate Dean of the School of Humanities and Social Sciences from 2006 to 2014. He was the founding Chair of the Department of Philosophy, Religion, and Interdisciplinary Studies and served as Chair for two terms: 2007–2010 and 2013–2016. He is now President of the American Institute of Bangladesh Studies (AIBS), and a member of the Board of Directors of the Council on American Overseas Research Centers (CAORC). He has published widely, especially in the field of social development.

John Mathias is a doctoral candidate in the Joint Program in Social Work and Anthropology at the University of Michigan. He has conducted research on environmental justice organising and environmental policy in the US and South India. He has also engaged in several international environmental advocacy collaborations. His current project examines the ethical dimensions of diverse efforts to promote environmental change in Kerala, India.

Cheryl Molle holds a Master's of Social Work in Practice with Communities and Policy Arenas from Temple University, Philadelphia, Pennsylvania, US. She is a Licensed Master of Social Work in the Commonwealth of Pennsylvania. Recognising the magnitude of food insecurity as a social and ecological injustice, she has dedicated her time and skills to a number of Philadelphia hunger relief programmes and towards raising awareness of food insecurity. As a macro-practice social worker, she has worked in research and programme evaluation and development and communications at Philadelphia-based non-profit organisations dedicated to promoting health and well-being, affecting social policy, and facilitating community and economic development.

Mehmoona Moosa-Mitha is an Associate Professor at the University of Victoria, School of Social Work, Victoria, Canada. Mehmoona has extensive research experience in the study of global poverty as well as in analysing children's citizenship rights. She has also published and researched in the area of transnational citizenship and social work practice, particularly as it affects Muslim populations living in the West.

Virginia Murray was appointed as Consultant in Global Disaster Risk Reduction for Public Health England (PHE) in April 2014. This appointment is to take forward her work as Vice-Chair of the UN International Strategy for Disaster Reduction (ISDR) Scientific and Technical Advisory Group and as the Chair of the Science and Technology Organising Committee for the UNISDR Science and Technology Conference on the implementation of the *Sendai Framework*. Prior to this, she was appointed as Head of Extreme Events and Health Protection, PHE. With the Extreme Events team, she helped to develop evidence-based information and advice on flooding, heat, cold, volcanic ash, and other extreme weather and natural hazards events. She was appointed as Visiting Professor in Health Protection, MRC-HPA Centre for Environment and Health, Imperial College and King's College, London (2004) and Honorary Professor at University College London (2013), and has published widely.

Mildred T. Mushunje is a social worker with experience in gender, social protection and child welfare. She has worked for the Social Services Ministry, international and national NGOs and the UN. She holds a Bachelor's degree in Social Work from the University of Zimbabwe, Master's degree in Gender and Development Studies from Manchester University, and a Diploma in Women's Rights from the University of Raoul Wallenberg (Sweden). She is reading for her PhD in social work with a focus on women in agriculture at the University of KwaZulu Natal.

Ksenija Napan is an Associate Professor at Massey University in Aotearoa/New Zealand. Her main research interests are in inquiry, intercultural communication and 'whole people' learning. She developed two teaching methods based on principles of cooperative and dialogic teaching and learning for beginning and advanced social workers which are applicable in a range of other disciplines. Ksenija values social justice, academic relevance, sustainability and kaitiakitanga (sustainable guardianship) expressed in a context of collaborative and respectful relationships. Her passion is in the integration of seemingly opposing polarities like research and practice, science and spirituality, internal and external, tertiary education and fun, individual and communal, fear of change and love for transformation, sustainability and transformation of unsustainable political systems.. She believes in human-caused climate crisis providing an opportunity for improvement of the quality of life of communities, families and individuals, the continuous improvement of educational processes for social workers, and engagement with communities, inquiry and research.

Bridget Ng'andu is a Tutor in Social Work at Ruskin College, Oxford. She is also a member of Social Workers Without Borders (SWWB). She has a social work background in working with children and families, including unaccompanied asylum seekers.

Bala Raju Nikku is Assistant Professor in Social Work at Thompson Rivers University, Canada. He was a founding director of the Nepal School of Social Work (NSSW) in Kathmandu, Nepal. Bala Raju was Senior Research Fellow, Durham University, UK in 2015. He was on the Boards of the International Association of Schools of Social Work (IASSW) and the Asian and Pacific Association of Social Work Education (APASWE). He was also a visiting senior lecturer at Universiti Sains Malaysia (USM) and Thammasat University, Thailand. His research interests include social work education in post conflict and transition countries, disasters, children, age care, international social work, comparative social policy in Asia and university community engagement. He is a member of the Editorial Advisory Boards of *International Social Work; Journal of International Social Issues; Practice: Social Work in Action* and Associate Editor of *Social Work Education: The International Journal*.

Sharlene Nipperess is a Lecturer and Program Manager of the Undergraduate Social Work Programmes at RMIT University, Melbourne, Australia. Her research and teaching interests are diverse and include critical human rights-based practice, social work ethics, critical multicultural practice, and practice with refugees and asylum seekers. She is also interested in the notion of place in relation to environmental issues and the connection with human rights. She is

President of the Australian and New Zealand Social Work and Welfare Education and Research (ANZSWWER) association and is a Member of the Australasia-Pacific Board of the international journal *Ethics and Social Welfare*.

Carolyn Noble is Foundation Professor of Social Work at NPI/ACAP in Sydney, Australia and Emerita Professor of Social Work, School of Social Sciences and Psychology at Victoria University, Melbourne, Australia. She has been involved with International Association of Schools of Social Work (IASSW) and Asia Pacific Schools of Social Work (APASWE) since 1988 in various executive positions. She has published widely in her areas of research and continues to present her work nationally and internationally. She is co-editor of two APASWE books on social work education and supervision across the Asia Pacific and a book for IASSW focusing on social work education across the globe. She is Editor-in-Chief of IASSW's social dialogue magazine www.social-dialogue.com. Her research interests include: social work philosophy and ethics, work-based learning, professional supervision, community engagement, critical theory and practice development in social work, gender democracy, and equal employment opportunity for women in higher education and human services.

Kieran O'Donoghue is an Associate Professor and Head of the School of Social Work at Massey University, New Zealand. His research interests and publications are in social work theory and practice, clinical supervision and field education. He is a co-editor of *Social Work Theories in Action* published by Jessica Kingsley and has had articles published in leading international social work journals.

Ana Opačić is a social worker who received her PhD on the topic of underdeveloped communities in Croatia in 2015. She has worked at the Social Work Department in Faculty of Law, University of Zagreb as a teaching assistant with special preference towards community work and theory in social work since 2009. So far she has published several articles and a textbook regarding this topic, and is currently actively involved in a research project regarding educational and employment transitions among youth living in poverty. She has also practised as an Evaluator, Field Educator and Group Social Worker in delivering numerous projects in vulnerable communities.

Katie J. Oven is Research Associate at Durham University with leading responsibility for work packages in major interdisciplinary research projects. A geographer working at the interface between physical and social science, her interests include disasters and development in the Global South, in particular the social production of vulnerability and resilience to natural hazards. Katie is engaged in applied research and works closely with a number of government and non-government partners within the UK and internationally.

Yasmin Perera is a social work and sociology graduate of Monash University, Melbourne, Australia. She worked in community development in a Melbourne municipality. After working in Australia for 25 years, Yasmin returned to Sri Lanka, her birth country, to work for World Vision in some 2004 tsunami-affected areas as a Trainer in Child Protection. With a desire to contribute to the development of social work in Sri Lanka in her retirement, she has been involved with the Social Work Programme of the National Institute of Social Development in Colombo as a Lecturer, Consultant and External Supervisor for their students. As a passionate environmentalist she is involved in working towards creating a love of nature and fostering environmental protection in Sri Lanka and is currently running a project on recycling garbage.

Contributors

Meredith C. F. Powers is an Assistant Professor at the University of North Carolina at Greensboro, US. Her current research includes the professional socialisation of social workers, ecological justice and university–community partnerships for sustainability. Meredith serves on the Environmental Justice Committee for the Council on Social Work Education (CSWE), US. She also established and administers the growing, online network 'Green/Environmental Social Work Collaborative Network' for social workers around the world who are committed to ecological justice.

Komalsingh Rambaree is an Associate Professor of Social Work at the University of Gävle, Sweden. He has been actively involved in ICZM projects, in Western Indian Ocean Islands, funded by the European Unions and World Bank. He is actively involved in teaching, learning and researching related to social work for sustainable development. His recent publications include eco-social work for sustainable development in Mauritius.

Letnie F. Rock is Senior Lecturer in Social Work and a former Head of the Department of Government, Sociology and Social Work at the University of the West Indies (UWI) Cave Hill Campus, Barbados. Her research interests are in the areas of child abuse and neglect, domestic violence and disaster management. She is the immediate Past President of the Association of Caribbean Social Work Educators (ACSWE) and a member of the Sustainability, Climate Change and Disaster Intervention Committee, the Human Rights and International Projects Committees of the International Association of Schools of Social Work (IASSW).

Fariyal Ross-Sheriff is a graduate Professor of Social Work at Howard University. Her area of specialisation is displaced populations, with a focus on refugee and immigrant women. As a leader of an international team of researchers, Fariyal examined the experiences, causes, consequences and service implications of addressing poverty using a grounded research approach to create alternative models of social service delivery. As a globally engaged scholar, she has worked extensively with Muslim refugees in Pakistan to investigate challenges facing refugees and service providers, and in Afghanistan to facilitate the repatriation and resettlement of refugee families.

Hanna A. Ruszczyk is currently submitting her PhD thesis for examination (2017) on the topic of 'Urban risk perceptions, events and problematising community resilience'. She has been a Researcher in the Department of Geography and the Institute of Hazard, Risk and Resilience at Durham University. Hanna has been investigating rapidly urbanising concepts and learning how people perceive risk both in the everyday and when events occur. Through this research, she is engaging with the concept of disaster community resilience and the manner in which the international aid community has framed its work under the rubric of resilience. For Hanna, this PhD was an opportunity to explore and engage critically with a wide range of subjects including resilience, community, urbanisation, risk, power, natural hazards, linking research to practice, Bihar State, India and Nepal. Hanna has spent most of her career living and working in countries that are rapidly changing and urbanising. Her international development work (ILO, UNDP, USAID) focusing on micro- and small-enterprise development has taken her to 10 countries and she has lived in several of them. Hanna has recently co-edited a book on the Gorkha earthquake and has also published on her PhD research.

Peter Sammonds is Professor of Geophysics at University College London and Director, UCL Institute for Risk and Disaster Reduction. He is Strategic Advisor to UK Natural Environment Research Council (NERC) and Economic and Social Research Council (ESRC) Increasing

Resilience to Natural Hazards (IRNH) research programme. The Earthquake without Frontiers consortium project is part of that programme. He is interested in transcending disciplinary boundaries between the physical and social sciences. He has worked extensively in this field.

Miriam Samuel is Associate Professor and Head of the Department of Social Work, Madras Christian College, Chennai, India since 1989 and took office as Head from 1993. Her specialisation is in the field of Medical and Psychiatric Social Work and Gender. She worked as an Intake Counsellor at TTK Hospital – Addiction Treatment Centre in Chennai from 1987 to 1989 before joining MCC in 1989. Her accomplishments in MCC includes, among many others: redesigning of curriculum into a credit-based system; Consultant; Resource Person and Trainer in Gender, Women's Empowerment, Mental Health and Research; designing and establishing the Centre for International Social Work, Member Curriculum Development Committee; and responsible for introducing the Service-Learning Programme. She served as Dean of Humanities and the Coordinator of the Internal Quality Assurance Cell of the College. Miriam is actively involved in research and serves as Co-investigator in various projects funded by World Health Organisation, Indian Council for Medical Research, Social Sciences and Humanities Research Council of Canada (SSHRC), and Canadian International Development Agency (CIDA). Her recent work has been in the area of disasters. She has travelled widely to attend and present papers in conferences and in relation to her research work.

Sowndarya Sankarakrishnan is a graduate student in the School of Social Policy at the University of South Australia in Adelaide.

Sunil D. Santha, Associate Professor at the TATA Institute of Social Sciences, has a keen interest in the fields of environmental risks, climate justice and livelihood uncertainties. He strives towards understanding the role of social institutions and participatory action in reducing vulnerabilities and strengthening just adaptation practices. He also believes in action research towards innovating participatory methods of entrepreneurial action and livelihood promotion among the poor and marginalised sections of the society. Some of his research and teaching interests include: a) action research; b) climate justice, vulnerability and adaptation; c) disaster risk reduction and livelihood recovery; d) inclusive value chain analysis and development; and e) local knowledge systems, livelihoods and environment. He has published more than 25 peer-reviewed articles in journals of international repute in his interest areas.

Rebecca J. Sargisson is a psychologist who lectures at the University of Waikato's Tauranga campus. She resides in the Bay of Plenty and considers the coastal region as home. As one member of a multidisciplinary team of researchers, she shares the dedication to responding to the challenges of protecting and supporting this world and addressing issues of environmental justice in all peoples' lives and throughout professional practice.

Tetyana Semigina is a Professor at the Academy of Labour, Social Relations and Tourism (Ukraine) and at the National University of Kyiv-Mohyla Academy (Ukraine). She is the author of more than 300 publications on social work and social policy, including monographs and textbooks. Her area of research interests and activities covers such topics as HIV/AIDS and health policy, history of social work and innovative practices of social work. Tetyana was an expert and consultant for the various international projects aimed at strengthening social policy and social services in Ukraine (sponsored by UNDP, EU, USAID, World Bank, among others). Tetyana served as a Member-at-Large of the Board of Directors of the International Association of Schools of Social Work (IASSW) in 2011 and was elected Secretary of the IASSW from 2012–2016.

Vishanthie Sewpaul is Senior Professor (Social Work), School of Applied Human Sciences and Emeritus Professor at the University of KwaZulu Natal and was Professor at Zayed University, Dubai. Her research interests include globalisation, social justice, human rights, vulnerable groups, community work and international social work. Her teaching interests include emancipatory/critical/radical social work, social justice, human rights, social work ethics and values, and international social work. She has also published extensively on the same.

Anup Shenai is passionate about the conservation of water resources in extremely drought-prone regions of India. He is a social innovator cum entrepreneur who has been striving towards developing sustainable innovations towards water conservation and resource management. He has a deep critique of redundant and obsolete water conservation practices. By training, he is an engineer and also has a postgraduate degree in Social Work. His research interests are in watershed management, sustainable agriculture and social entrepreneurship development.

Kelly Smith is a social worker registered in New Zealand and lectures on the Social Work Programme at the University of Waikato, Tauranga Campus. She resides in the Bay of Plenty and considers the coastal region as home. As one member of a multidisciplinary team of researchers, she shares the dedication to responding to the challenges of protecting and supporting this world and addressing issues of environmental justice in all peoples' lives and throughout professional practice.

Jaydip Solanki is a grassroots-level social entrepreneur. Currently, he is involved in setting up fishworkers' collectives and enterprises along the coast of Gujarat and Maharashtra in India. By training, he is an expert in commerce and management and also has a postgraduate degree in Social Work. His research interests are in community organisation and social entrepreneurship development.

Asha Banu Soletti is Professor and Chairperson at the Centre for Health and Mental Health. She teaches Master's of Arts social work courses in public health and mental health. Her research interests include children affected by HIV/AIDS, ageing and health, homelessness and tribal elders. She practices in community health, mental health, community mental health and development, HIV/AIDS, gerontology, cancer care and palliative care. She has extensive field engagement in urban and rural contexts through field action projects and other community-level interventions. She currently coordinates a field action project, *Integrated Rural Health and Development Project*, which is located in a tribal belt and caters to the health needs of the Konkana, Warli and Katkari tribes through a social determinants framework. She has actively responded and contributed to the disaster relief work operations of the Institute. She is also actively involved in training and capacity-building of diverse stakeholders in her fields of practice.

Willette F. Stinson has a PhD in Library and Information Studies from Florida State University, an MLS degree from University of Pittsburgh, and a Bachelor's of Arts degree in Political Science and Communications from Saint Vincent College, where in 1987 she became one of its first women graduates. In her college teaching experience, she has taught at Florida State University, La Roche College and Antioch College. She is an innovative and service-driven Director of Library Services employed at West Virginia State University. She was honoured with US Congressional recognition, formally sent by Congresswoman Sheila Jackson-Lee, and serves on the National Committee on Diversity of the American Library Association. Her recent publications pertain to copyright and fair use, as well as assessments of student learning outcomes.

Shigeo Tatsuki is Professor of the Sociology of Disaster at Doshisha University in Kyoto, Japan. He has worked with survivors of natural disasters in Japan and across the globe for 30 years. His first encounter with victim–survivors of disasters occurred when he managed student volunteers during the 1995 Kobe earthquake (Japan). This led to a lifetime of work conducting community-based participatory research to promote survivors' resilience. In addition to Japanese victims of disasters such as floods, earthquakes and typhoons, he has also worked with those affected by Hurricane Katrina (US) and other global disasters.

Susan A. Taylor is a Professor in the College of Health and Human Services, Division of Social Work at California State University, Sacramento. Her teaching and research involves environmental health, health systems, public health and ocean environments, and collaborative interdisciplinary practice. In social work, she teaches health policy and practice at graduate level and undergraduate interdisciplinary classes with social work in environmental health, public health, climate change and zoonotic disease as the primary foci. At the Davis School of Medicine (University of California), she is involved in interdisciplinary practice and field research that has immersed her in a veterinary science environment, doing a hospital rotation at an internationally recognised marine mammal rehabilitation and research. She has worked with seals and sea lions especially affected by trauma related to illness directly connected to climate change, mass morbidity events due to habitat destruction and food scarcity, and the effects of ocean pollution. She has written 'Social science research in ocean environments: A social worker's experience' in *Environmental Social Work*, edited by Mel Gray, John Coates and Tiani Hetherington.

Hillary Thomas is a Master's of Social Work candidate at Loyola University Chicago, where she works as a Research Assistant with Amy Krings. She co-facilitated a discussion on environmental justice and social work at the 2016 Social Justice Forum hosted by Loyola's School of Social Work.

Odette van Brummen-Girigori is Associated Professor at the University of Curaçao, Dr Moises da Costa Gomez. She was graduated in Child Psychology and Social Psychology, received her PhD in Psychology, and is registered as ZKM Consultant of Education, Child and Youth Psychologist (NIP) and Euro-Psychologist. She has worked as Program Director and Dean. Currently, she is Research Coordinator at the Faculty of Social and Behavioral Sciences. She has a wealth of experience as an educator in psychology, but focuses also on research topics such as father absence, jealousy, body image, learning disabilities, green social work and being prepared for natural disasters.

Sharvan Verma has laid out his commitment towards the promotion of sustainable livelihood initiatives among marginalised and vulnerable communities in India. His action research interests include the innovation of just financial inclusion practices among poor segments of the population. Currently, he is involved in strengthening grassroots-level livelihood support groups in the state of Rajasthan. By training, he is an expert in commerce and management and has a postgraduate degree in social work. His research interests are financial inclusion, project management and social entrepreneurship development.

Contributors

Jennifer Willett is an Assistant Professor at the University of Nevada, Reno, US. Her areas of expertise include environmental justice, community support and formal aid processes. Her most current research explored the impacts of slow violence in poor communities in Kenya and how affected community members adapted together in lieu of aid.

Larry D. Williams is the Director of the Master's of Social Work Program and Assistant Professor in the Department of Social Work at the North Carolina Central University. He received his PhD in Policy Analysis, Planning and Organisation Development and a Cognate in Education Leadership from Clark Atlanta University and received his Master's degree in Social Work from the University of Georgia. In addition, he has completed a six-month internship in addiction medicine at the Morehouse School of Medicine (Cork Institute), a Postdoctoral Certificate in Integrative Health from the West Chester University, and Postdoctoral studies in Global Health from the University of Texas and in Social Epidemiology and International Maternal and Child Health from the University of North Carolina at Chapel Hill. Upon completing his PhD, he served as a faculty member at Texas A&M University System and West Chester University before accepting a position at North Carolina Central University. In 2005, he was awarded the prestigious Fulbright-Group Abroad Project to China, where he conducted extensive research on the implications of the one child policy. In 2008, he joined the faculty at North Carolina Central University, where he developed the children and family programme. His research interests include power and oppression among minority populations and sustainability.

Jonathan Wistow is Lecturer in the School of Applied Social Sciences at Durham University, UK. His interest in health inequalities centres on the implications of both methodological and ideological framings for how this issue is understood and addressed. His research in this area focuses on the application of both complexity theory and qualitative comparative analysis to health inequalities and links to broader debates about governance and public policy implementation.

Lauren Wroe is a Co-Founder of Social Workers Without Borders (SWWB) in the UK. She is a practicing social worker with experience of working with adults and children in the statutory and voluntary sectors. Her research interests are identity, social work advocacy and the movement of people across borders.

Haorui Wu is a Postdoctoral Fellow in the Faculty of Social Work at the University of Calgary, Alberta, Canada. With the interdisciplinary background of architecture, urban planning and design, and social work, he focuses on applying interdisciplinary knowledge and methods into community-engaged design (public interest design), ethics, theory and the practice of sustainable development. Given the global context of climate change and disaster, his humanitarian architectural teaching, research and practice examine the post-disaster reconstruction and recovery of built environment through the lens of social and environmental justice, aiming to provide the benefits of architecture to underserved individuals, families and communities in order to assist them in the fulfilment of their social requirements, the improvement of their well-being, the advancement of their social capacities and the achievement of sustainable development.

Hairong Yan is Associate Professor in the Department of Applied Social Sciences at Hong Kong Polytechnic University. She is the author of *New masters, new servants: migration, development and women workers in China* (2008).

Nino Žganec is from Croatia, where he finished social work study and obtained his PhD. Since 1991 he has worked at the Faculty of Social Work and currently is Associate Professor and Head of the Social Work Department at Faculty of Law, University of Zagreb. His writings, research interests and practice are in community social work, human rights and organisation of social services. He introduced several new social work subjects in the curriculum of the social work study such as ethics in social work, social work and human rights. Since 2015 he has been the President of the European Association of Schools of Social Work and Vice President of the International Association of Schools of Social Work. He was Assistant Minister and State Secretary in the Ministry of Labour and Social Welfare in the government of Republic of Croatia from 2000–2005. During his term in the office he initiated and led the reform of the Croatian social welfare system. He is the President of the Croatian Anti-Poverty Network and member of the Executive Committee of the European Anti-Poverty Network.

Preface

We live in a world where there is increasing recognition that the human condition and the condition of the planet on which we depend are inextricably linked. The emergence of the concept of green social work is an inevitable consequence of the realisation that environmental crises and extreme weather events have profound effects on people's well-being.

By some estimates, there are today over 100 million people whose lives have been turned upside down by a wide range of natural hazards which include tropical storms, heavy rains and floods, landslides and mudslides, extreme heat and cold, earthquakes and tsunamis. No region on earth has been spared from such visitations.

We live in an era when more and more people are aware of the existential threat posed by climate change and on a daily basis they can witness the results on their television screens that show people marooned in the floodwaters of Houston or Mumbai, or in a state of shock following the loss of hundreds of lives from a mudslide in Sierra Leone or Peru. There are also the soul-destroying consequences of long-term drought which drive people from their home place, strip them of their dignity and take away their means of making a living.

Inevitably, this has an impact on a profession which began many years ago with a commitment to the "person-in-the environment." It is clear that disaster management has to be about much more than the delivery of food, shelter and household goods, and green social work can play a major role in both disaster preparedness and post-disaster recovery.

Social workers have a profound role to play in helping communities exposed to both extensive and intensive risks through the establishment of relationships with vulnerable families that help them cope with the daily challenges of life and to survive traumatic events in an intelligent and focused manner.

One practical example would be helping a family to ensure that an older person or a child living with a disability are adequately catered to in the case of a tropical storm warning which required an evacuation or other protective measures to be taken. All too often it is the weakest members of society who end up on lists of missing and dead in the wake of a major disaster.

Beyond that, it seems to me that the great truth which lies at the heart of green social work is the re-definition of "the duty to care for and about others as one that includes the duty to care for and about the planet," as alluded to in the introduction to this fascinating *Handbook*, a volume full of deep reflection on the place of environmental justice within the overall concept of social justice.

The *Sendai Framework for Disaster Risk Reduction 2015–2030* seeks the following outcome: "The substantial reduction of disaster risk and losses in lives, livelihoods and health and in the economic, physical, social, cultural and environmental assets of persons, businesses, communities and countries."

It is difficult to see how this outcome which is so essential to the achievement of the Sustainable Development Goals, particularly the eradication of poverty, can be achieved without the meaningful engagement of social workers, particularly those attuned to the concerns aired so well in this *Handbook*.

The truth of the matter is that we are consuming the planet's resources at an unsustainable rate. Green social work promotes a value system which is inclusive, sustainable and based on an equitable distribution of resources rather than one based on reckless disregard for the obvious links between environmental catastrophes and the creation of disaster risk in the pursuit of short-term financial gains.

Robert Glasser,
UN Secretary-General's Special Representative
for Disaster Risk Reduction,
UNISDR, Geneva, Switzerland

Foreword
Green social work:
a new direction for social work

I wrote *Green Social Work* (Dominelli, 2012) to open a new dimension in social work's approaches to environmental issues and it is unique in the following respects. The green social work (GSW) perspective is holistic; reconfigures critical theory in the environment by embedding the notion of environmental justice within the concept of social justice; is transdisciplinary; challenges models of industrialisation that treat the earth as a means to be exploited primarily to meet neoliberal industrialisation's end of producing profits for the few; questions the inequitable and unsustainable distribution of resources and short-termism in political structures; and argues for locality-specific, culturally relevant approaches to risk mitigation and disaster interventions. Green social work has challenged the narrow focus on the physical environment displayed by environmental social work because it disregards much of the social, political, economic and cultural contexts within which its concerns have been embedded. This is not to reduce the significance of the questions raised by authors such as Rogge (1994) and Besthorn (2008, 2011) who resurrected social work's wider concern for the person-in-their-environment, and challenged ecological social work's prime focus on social and cultural institutions ranging from the family to the community. However, the 'deep' ecology movement in social work failed to transcend the limitations of the physical dimension and engage with neoliberalism's exploitation of planet earth for profit. Indigenous perspectives (Davis, 1998) have sought to introduce the importance of the relationship between people, other living things and the physical environment (Simpson, 2009). For example, First Nations' people in Canada have considered neo-colonial relationships and their separation of physical environments from people's lives and highlighted their traditional worldviews which argued the unity of people and the physical environment. Both need each other, and many First Nations' claims to their land rights are rooted in their concern to fulfil their responsibilities as custodians of the earth. In Canada, The Assembly of First Nations has made 'Honouring Earth' part of its mandate, and advocates a minimal footprint for existence.

Green social work's claims to be an innovative approach to environmental issues as practised in the social work profession. These innovations include: its holistic approach to all peoples, other living things – plants and animals, and the physical ecosystem; emphasising the relational nature of all its constituent parts; redefining the duty to care for and about others as one that includes the duty to care for and about planet earth. A healthy planet earth can look after living things more easily than one that people treat as a means to an end – modernity and industrial development that exploit the earth's resources – its flora, fauna, minerals and other physical elements of the environment alongside labour power, to earn profits for the few who enjoy luxurious and wealthy lifestyles (Oxfam, 2014). Thus, green social work incorporates a critique of neoliberal models of development and its governance structures for destroying the environment in the search for profits. Green social work's holistic critical approach acknowledges the interdependency of all living things; focuses on the inclusion of all systems and institutions in its remit; includes both (hu)man-made and natural disasters arising from the (hu)made ones of poverty to chemical pollution of the earth's land, waters and soils and climate change, to the natural hazards like earthquakes and volcanoes which turn to disasters through human (in)action. Green social work's value system is also one that favours equality, social inclusion, the equitable distribution of resources, the obligation not to destroy resources so that these can be conserved or sustained for future generations of people, animals, plants and planet earth, and a rights-based approach to meeting people's needs to live and develop their talents in an ethical and sustainable manner. Or, as First Nations peoples would say, 'Without leaving a footprint to show where they have been'. Responding to these issues is one of the biggest challenges facing contemporary social workers which this *Handbook* is intended to address.

This *Handbook*, therefore, covers a wide remit so as to provide the practitioners of the 21st century with the theories, practices, policies, knowledge and skills they require to act responsibly in responding to the diverse disasters that threaten to endanger all living things and planet earth itself. This breadth of coverage is indicated in the table of contents and abstracts for each chapter. Thus, *The Routledge Handbook of Green Social Work* has a critical contribution to make in delivering a step-change in social work education, research and practice. The issues green social work addresses are global, and so it is relevant in all countries, although the individual chapters indicate that it has been developed more in some countries than others, and must be locality specific and culturally relevant wherever it is found. There is no 'one size fits all' response in green social work, although some essential values and principles may be shared. Foremost among these is respecting and valuing the world and all that it contains. Moreover, green social work is transdisciplinary, working across the physical and social sciences and arts and humanities. And, it encourages diverse disciplines to work with community residents to coproduce action plans and sustainable projects that will protect the physical environment while meeting people's needs. The *Handbook* is crucial in mainstreaming holistic approaches to environmental considerations in social work curricula across the globe. Ensuring that this occurs is a responsibility of all those who care about this beautiful planet of ours. Let us safeguard it to meet the needs of future generations as well as ours and incorporate that into caring for all living things and inanimate objects.

Lena Dominelli

References

Besthorn, F. (2008). Environment and social work practice. In Mizrahi, T. and Davis, L. (Eds.) *Encyclopedia of social work*, 2nd ed. Oxford: Oxford University Press.

Besthorn, F. (2011). The deep ecology's contribution to social work: A ten year perspective. *International Journal of Social Welfare*. Online version, 9 December.

Davis, M. (1998). *Biological and indigenous knowledge* (Research Paper 17, 1997–98). Canberra: Australian Parliament, Science, Technology and Resources Group. Also on www.aph.gov.au/About_Parliament/Parliamentary_Departments/Parliamentary_Library/pubs/rp/RP9798/98rp17#MAJOR [Accessed 12 July 2016].

Dominelli, L. (2012). *Green social work*. Cambridge: Polity Press.

Oxfam (2014). *Economy for the one per cent*. Oxford: Oxfam.

Rogge, M. (1994). Environmental justice: Social welfare and toxic waste. In M. D. Huff and J. G. McNutt (Eds.), *The global environmental crisis: Implications for social work and social welfare*. Aldershot: Ashgate.

Simpson, L. (2009). *Lighting the eighth fire: The liberation, resurgence and protection of indigenous nations*. Winnipeg: Arbeiter Ring Publishing.

Introduction
Why green social work?

Lena Dominelli, Bala Raju Nikku and Hok Bun Ku

Introduction

The world is undergoing numerous environmental crises, both 'natural' and (hu)man-made which are increasing in frequency and damage caused to people and their social systems, other living beings and the physical environment (UNISDR, 2016). Social workers are often engaged in responding to these, providing practical assistance and psychosocial care. They have been less visible at the top decision-making tables in the United Nations (UN) and its organisations because the discipline and profession are quite erroneously considered as vocational in their orientation, instead of being research-led just like other disciplines and professions. One of the exciting dimensions of this volume, *The Routledge Handbook of Green Social Work* (the *Handbook*), is that it clearly demonstrates that there is a theory and a practice behind the work that social workers do in the environment, responding to people and environmental issues in their totality. Additionally, it is transdisciplinary in its approach and has much to contribute to others committed to valuing planet earth. Social work is also morally and philosophically attuned to protecting the environment as it considers humanity as part of the environment, of nature, not outside it as advocated by the exponents of modernity.

Social work, therefore, is a discipline embedded in the realities of people's lives and has a holistic, social justice approach to social problems and a value-base which makes it easy to integrate environmental justice issues into its remit (Dominelli, 2002). The profession began with a commitment to the 'person-in-the environment' (Hollis, 1967). Today, green social work reminds the profession of its origins and seeks to transcend the limitations of those early beginnings to include the duty to care for the environment within its jurisdiction. As a result, green social work opens new doors in dealing with environmental crises.

This introductory chapter argues the urgent need to develop green social work theory and practice further. It also makes the case for the inclusion of green social work in the discipline's mainstream curriculum. The points made within this contribution are elaborated upon throughout the chapters of the *Handbook*. Consequently, we present the volume's structure to reveal that a diverse conglomeration of settings, contexts, themes and approaches to similar types of issues come together in *green social work*, to provide a model that constitutes a new development in the social work repertoire, and contributes to innovations in theory, practice and policies that affect the interactions between people's everyday lives and the entirety of the environments within which they operate. The contributors to this book come from different countries, but all their contributions provide material that demonstrates that green social work has vital roles to play in shaping policy and practice responses to increased levels of environmental degradation, climate change and disasters. The *Handbook* as a whole achieves its aim of 'bridging a gap' in social work scholarship on the environment, and for the first time, brings together a global coverage that reveals the breadth and depth of social work interest in this subject. Additionally, the chapters are written by a range of social work educators, researchers and practitioners. But, it also includes people from non-social work disciplines who have important contributions to make to this *Handbook*. Particularly important in this regard are Sammonds (Chapter 2) and Murray et al. (Chapter 3).

Green social work: a new approach to environmental issues

Green social work opens a new dimension in social work's approaches to environmental issues and is unique in the following respects. It is holistic; it has reconfigured critical theory in the environment by embedding the notion of environmental justice within the concept of social justice; it emphasises the connectivities and relational nature of all the earth's constituencies; it highlights the interdependencies between animate and inanimate realities; it is transdisciplinary; it redefines the duty to care for and about others as one that includes the duty to care for and about planet earth; it challenges models of industrialisation that treat the earth as a means to be exploited by industrialists whose prime relationship with nature aims to meet their goal of producing profits for the few while the many are pauperised in ways that uproot them from their physical environment and treat them as means to an end; it rejects hyper-urbanisation as depicted by the growth of monolithic megacities that degrade and destroy the environment as they expand; it questions the inequitable and unsustainable distribution of resources and technologies; it is critical of short-termism in political structures; and it argues for locality-specific, culturally relevant approaches to risk mitigation and disaster interventions (Dominelli, 2012: 25). Thus, green social work lays claim to being an innovative approach to environmental issues as traditionally practised in the social work profession.

Green social work as a theory and a practice seeks to transform the socio-political and economic forces that have a deleterious impact upon the quality of life of poor and marginalised populations and secure the policy changes and sustainable social transformations necessary for enhancing the well-being of people and the planet today and in the future. Green social work has challenged the narrow focus of much environmental social work on the anthropomorphic dominance of the physical environment for disregarding much of the social, political, economic and cultural contexts within which its environmental concerns were based. This is not to reduce the significance of the questions raised by authors such as Rogge (1994, 2003; Hoff and Rogge, 1996) and Besthorn (2008, 2012) who resurrected social work's wider concern for the person-in-their-environment, and challenged ecological social work's prime focus on social and cultural institutions ranging from the family to the community. However, the 'deep' ecology movement in social work failed to transcend the limitations of their positionality and engage with neo-liberalism's exploitation of planet earth for profit. Indigenous perspectives (Davis, 1998) have sought to introduce the importance of the relationship between people, other living things and the physical environment into the profession. For example, First Nations' people in Canada have considered neo-colonial relationships and their separation of the physical environment from people's lives and highlighted their traditional worldviews which postulated the unity between people and the physical environment. Both need each other, and many First Nations' claims to their land rights are rooted in their concern to fulfil their responsibilities as custodians of the earth. In Canada, The Assembly of First Nations has made 'Honouring Earth' part of its mandate, and is key to green social work values.

A healthy planet earth can look after living things more easily than one in which both people and the planet are treated as a means to an end. Neoliberalism, the current expression of modernity and industrialisation, earns profits for elites enjoying luxurious lifestyles at the expense of the rest (Oxfam, 2016). Thus, green social work incorporates a critique of neoliberal models of development and its governance structures to highlight its destruction of the environment in the search for profits, as witnessed by contributions to this *Handbook*. Green social work seeks to include all systems and institutions within its remit; and both (hu)man-made and natural disasters. The boundaries between these two types of disasters are becoming increasingly blurred and dominated by (hu)man-made ones ranging from poverty to chemical pollution of the earth's land, waters and soils, alongside climate change because natural hazards like earthquakes and volcanoes turn into disasters through human (in)action.

Green social work's value system favours equality, social inclusion, the equitable distribution of resources, sustainability as the obligation not to destroy resources so that these can be conserved for future generations of people, animals, plants and planet earth, and a rights-based approach to meeting people's needs to live and develop their talents in an ethical and sustainable manner. Or, as Canada's First Nations peoples would say, 'Without leaving a footprint showing where they have been'. Responding to these issues is one of the biggest challenges facing social workers in the 21st century which this *Handbook* is intended to address.

The chapters in the book contribute to theory-building by addressing environmental issues from both social work and social justice perspectives, advocating for and strengthening the voices of marginalised communities and those of green social workers who support communities before, during and after disasters at policy-making and practice levels, however and wherever, they take place. As editor and assistants we have enjoyed and immensely benefited from reading and reviewing the collection of chapters in this book. We have tried to ensure that the chapters follow a basic framework to give the book coherence. But each chapter also stands on its own so that readers can read individual chapters at their own pace and compare the strategies used by social workers in one particular country with those in another.

The *Handbook* covers a wide range of environmental issues ranging from green social work's theory-building to putting theory into practice and curriculum development. Natural disasters, green agricultural practices, food (in)security, (hu)man-made disasters, disaster-driven migration and curriculum innovation are topics considered within the volume's many pages. Practicing green social workers have written about their work to provide the practitioners of the 21st century with inspiration as they read about the theories, practices, policies, knowledge and skills they require to act responsibly in responding to the diverse disasters that threaten to endanger all living things and planet earth itself. This breadth of coverage is indicated in the table of contents and abstracts for each chapter. Readers will find that each chapter in this *Handbook* is accessible and full of skills and insights. The breadth and depth of these contributions allow for critical reflection and provide useful ideas for thinking about what might be done in one's own context, including in identifying areas for further research. Finally, *The Routledge Handbook of Green Social Work* aims to make a critical contribution to delivering a step-change in social work education, research and practice.

Structure of the *Handbook*

In the foreword, Lena Dominelli sets the tone for the *Handbook* by building on why and how green social work has become a new direction for social work. In this introductory chapter, the authors provide further compelling arguments and examples for why green social work, suitably adapted for cultural relevance and locational specificity, should be adopted by the profession across the globe. This introductory chapter enables the reader to navigate this *Handbook* by giving the reader a quick overview of its contents. The *Handbook* can also be used as a critical social work reference or resource book by educators and practitioners in their own teaching, research, practice and policy advocacy work. Each contribution is independent from the others and can be read alone.

For easy referencing and reading, the *Handbook* is divided in to 11 parts with a few chapters in each. Part I begins with green social work theory to set the context for the rest of the *Handbook*. This section provides insights into reconfiguring the environmental landscape in which social work as a transdisciplinary collaborative endeavour engages with other disciplines, especially those in the physical sciences, to communicate scientific and local expertise across and between scientists and local and indigenous communities to coproduce knowledge and skills that address current environmental disasters and encourage future planning that draws upon community capabilities. This section also provides insights on how to deal with disasters and the consequent health impacts. Of particular importance here is the crucial role of green social workers' involvement in facilitating the political will to implement the *Sendai Framework for Disaster Risk Reduction 2015–2030*, not only globally, but also in their own countries.

Part II includes chapters that discuss dealing with different types of 'natural' disasters across the globe, including countries such as China, India, Nepal, Taiwan. These contributions show how green social work frameworks have been implemented in practice and what the results were. Part III is about green agricultural practices. It is followed by Part IV which covers food (in)security. In these two sections, readers can explore why food inequalities exist and how food inequality can be addressed through social justice initiatives that address environmental exploitation. Interesting case studies from Zimbabwe and China provide evidence on how green social work promotes food security by addressing agro-environmental crises. In one, a collective approach in China led to a CAS movement in Yunan Province.

In Part V the *Handbook* returns to a critical (hu)man-made disaster that is beginning to impinge on all others – climate change. Readers will find compelling arguments in this section about how can green social work can be a vital force in addressing climate change concerns. The contributing authors argue that green social work requires a green politics to make climate change policies work for communities and not for multi-national corporations. This section also presents case studies from Mauritius and Barbados to demonstrate the usefulness of doing green social work within the integrated coastal zone management plans and programmes. The Zimbabwean case shows that social protection can provide options for farmers facing extreme weather events (floods and droughts) caused by climate change. Moreover, the case study of women farmers in Goromonzi, Zimbabwe reveals that politics and discourses on climate change are gendered. The example from India reveals the urgent need to re-imagine social work practice and how to nurture social work graduates and practitioners about issues concerning climate change, vulnerability and adaptation that enhance community resilience.

Part VI continues the theme of extreme weather events as specific issues in particular locations (e.g. floods in India, droughts in Namibia). The chapters not only explain the causes of these extreme weather events, but also help readers understand the politics of managing floods and droughts. These chapters provide insights on the implications of such events for social policy, social work responses and how social work education and practice should respond to the increasingly mismanaged extreme weather events which are causing great human suffering and environmental devastation. These consequences can be reduced and minimised through social work advocacy, policy changes and community organising.

Part VII focuses on disaster-driven migration and how green social work is being applied to respond to the immense suffering experienced by those displaced by such calamities. Environmentally induced human displacement and migration are exacerbating risk and having increasingly severe implications for human mobility. The chapters in this section help the reader to further understand poverty through the experiences of women who have become forced migrants many times over.

Part VIII considers health disasters and highlights the importance of health issues in any environmentally degraded situation. Part IX is on industrial and urban issues. Its contributions explore the practices of reducing waste, recycling and reusing materials. They also highlight how these practices are further complicated by ethnicity and gender status. This section also comments on the differentiated experiences of industrial pollution, an issue rarely considered in the profession's current environmental discourses.

Part X focuses on how to practice green social work. In this section, readers will encounter interesting contributions about the ecological hazards of nuclear waste disposal policies and practices that are further affected by political aspirations, economic prosperity (or lack of it) and community activism. This section also provides lessons for practice when raising human consciousness about environmental disasters. Additionally, the reader will gain valuable insights of the strategies used by activists in Israeli environmental campaigns and human-made disasters and social work interventions in conflict situations from a Ukrainian perspective.

Part XI is about social work education. This section provides insights on the imperative of reflexive ecological thought, action and ethics in the social work curriculum, past, present and future. It provides specific case studies on how social work educators in particular countries (for example, Aotearoa/New Zealand) have made efforts to green their social work education to meet the country's societal challenges and community aspirations. Similarly, examples from Australian social work practice and education explore different responses to the integration of green social work when pursuing eco-social justice issues. This section also has contributions on integrating disaster risk reduction within the social work curriculum. This section is followed by a concluding chapter written by the three of us, calling for movement towards a green society and the mainstreaming of green social work in social work education and practice.

In concluding, we welcome the contributions to this work from all the authors. Thank you for embarking on an exciting and critical journey with us. We benefitted immensely from reading the range of ideas and evidence that you presented in your writings. This *Handbook* makes an important contribution to developing social work scholarship around holistic approaches to environmental considerations in social work education and practice across the globe. In it, the authors demonstrate that green social work is transdisciplinary, albeit defined differently for specific locales. But they have highlighted the significance of bringing together the work of physical sciences, social sciences, arts and humanities to enhance resilience and sustainability across the world. Such interaction encourages innovation by having diverse disciplines engage fully with community residents to coproduce action plans and sustainable projects that will protect the physical environment while meeting people's needs.

By engaging in this project, we were encouraged to see the evidence that the authors have provided to demonstrate that the issues that green social work are both local and global. From this, we were heartened to learn that by engaging with local issues in culturally specific ways, the principles of greening social work are relevant to all countries. However, the individual chapters also indicate that green social work is better developed in some countries than others, although it is always locality specific and culturally relevant. There is no 'one size fits all' response (Dominelli, 2012). Some essential values and principles may be shared, but for us, the first and foremost is that of respecting and valuing the world and all that it contains.

References

Besthorn, F. H. (2008). The environmental restoration movement as an issue of justice. In K. van Wormer (Ed.), *Restorative justice across the East and West*. Hong Kong: Casa Verde Publishing, pp. 205–229.

Besthorn, F. (2012). Deep Ecology's contributions to social work: A ten-year retrospective, *International Journal of Social Welfare*, 21(3): 248-259. First published online in 2011.

Davis, M. (1998). *Biological and indigenous knowledge* (Research Paper 17, 1997–98). Canberra: Australian Parliament, Science, Technology and Resources Group. Also on www.aph.gov.au/About_Parliament/Parliamentary_Departments/Parliamentary_Library/pubs/rp/RP9798/98rp17#MAJOR [Accessed 12 July 2016].

Dominelli, L. (2002). *Anti-oppressive social work theory and practice*. New York: Palgrave Macmillan.

Dominelli, L. (2012). *Green social work: From environmental crises to environmental justice*. Cambridge: Polity Press.

Hoff, M. D. and Rogge, M. E. (1996). Everything that rises must converge: Developing a social work response to environmental justice. *Journal of Progressive Human Services*, 7(1): 41–58.

Hollis, F. (1967). *Casework: A Psychosocial Therapy*. New York: Random House.

Oxfam (2016). *An economy for the one percent*. Oxford: Oxfam.

Rogge, M. E. (1994). Field education for environmental hazards: Expanding the person-in-environment perspective. In M. D. Hoff and J. G. McNutt (Eds.), *The global environmental crisis: Implications for social welfare and social work*. Aldershot, England: Avebury Books, Ashgate Publishers, pp. 258–276.

Rogge, M. E. (2003). The future is now: Social work, disaster management, and traumatic stress in the 21st century. *Journal of Social Service Research*, 30(2), 1–6.

UNISDR (United Nations Office for Disaster Risk Reduction) (2016). *UNISDR Annual Report 2016*. Geneva: UNISDR.

Part I
Green social work theory
Scene setting section

1
Green social work in theory and practice
A new environmental paradigm for the profession

Lena Dominelli

Introduction

Green social work (GSW) is a transdisciplinary, holistic approach to environmental crises that has challenged the social work profession to incorporate its principles, values and concern over environmental degradation, and the disasters associated with this into daily, routine, mainstream practice. Whether arising through air, water and soil pollution caused by industrial contaminants or 'natural' hazards, these have damaged people's health and well-being, and exploited the environment for the gain of the few. Thus, environmental crises perpetrate environmental injustices that must be eradicated before their deleterious effects become irreversible. The green in green social work highlights the imperative of caring for the beautiful living planet human beings inhabit. The earth that sustains us has its bounty currently exploited by 1 per cent of the population for itself. Its destruction impacts heavily on the 99 per cent.

Poor people live and work in the degraded environments that feed the industrial system. Adults simultaneously struggle to obtain basic necessities including food, clothing, housing, healthcare, social services, and education for themselves and their children; and sustain their communities and geographical spaces. This calls for a rethinking of the economy – how it distributes goods and services; how it uses the earth's physical resources; how it uses and treats human labour, animals and plants; how the products of human labour are distributed; and what economic alternatives can be developed to meet the need of each human being now to enjoy a decent standard of living, without destroying the earth for future generations. Neoliberalism, the current socio-economic system, is not fit for purpose within countries or globally. Neoliberalism is steeped in inegalitarianism. Thus, a new system has to be redistributive and regenerative. It has to ensure that every human being has his/her share of the earth's goods and services, and that the earth's capacity to regenerate itself is maintained. The global trends towards hyper-urbanisation and hyper-industrialisation, and creation of ugly urbanity for people to live in, must stop.

Why are these concerns a matter for all social workers? The answer is simple. Social workers are the professionals responsible for the health and well-being of those with whom they work. Their practice engages those whose lives are undermined by the lack of access to resources and opportunities in myriad settings. Thus, they have a professional and moral responsibility to examine why service users are in such situations and work with them for transformative change. Also, social work services should be universal. Within this framework, social workers should also work with the 1 per cent who own more than they can possibly use, and engage them in thinking about how they can contribute to the development of new, alternative economic systems that do not exploit people or the earth – its flora, fauna, minerals and physical environment.

Consequently, green social workers can ask awkward questions about the direction of humanity's travel: Who benefits from the current socio-economic arrangements and governance systems? Who loses? How can the earth's bounty be shared more equitably? How can the geographic spaces within which people's sense of identity and belonging reside be enhanced and preserved? To contribute to answering these questions, green social work includes the incorporation of environmental justice within the profession's social justice agenda, alongside that of critiquing neoliberal socio-economic forms of development and highlighting the duty to care for the earth in sustainable ways so that it can meet the needs of contemporary and future generations. Such commitment is embedded in acknowledging and addressing the interconnectedness and interdependencies that exist between living beings and inanimate things and maintaining a sustainable planet.

Addressing environmental concerns allows social workers to adopt a number of diverse roles ranging from being coordinators of practical assistance to developing community and individual resilience in responding to disasters throughout the disaster cycle – prevention, preparedness, immediate relief, recovery, and reconstruction. And, it challenges social workers to understand the porous borders between 'natural' and (hu)man-made disasters and include environmental rights in their conceptual framework of social justice at the local, national, regional and international levels (Dominelli, 2012). There is no area of human life that is beyond the remit of green social workers. Their interventions are based on engaging victim–survivors of disasters to coproduce solutions to problems that are defined by those in the communities within which they are working. These should be inclusive and innovative. Green social work has initiated a paradigm shift in conceptualising environmental social work, away from leaving knowledge in the hands of environmental scientists into mutual sharing of scientific and lay expertise and embedding the coproduction of disaster action plans in mainstream social work values and empowering practice.

In this chapter, I describe the beginnings of green social work, its theoretical framework and value-base for practice, and its commitment to social change, including at the policy level, especially as it concerns the elimination of poverty and equitable distribution of resources from the local to the global. This aim is central to reducing vulnerabilities among the world's poorest and most marginalised peoples before, during and after their differentiated experiences of disasters. I conclude with a call for social workers to include environmental concerns in their routine practice and social work curriculum for training and practice.

Developing the Green Social Work Framework

The absence of social workers' voices during the 2004 Indian Ocean Tsunami when 250,000 people were killed in the 12 countries affected by its destructive waves spurned me to contemplate collective social work responses through the International Association of Schools of Social Work (IASSW) to change this state of affairs. A week after this disaster, IASSW established the Rebuilding People's Lives After Disasters Network (RIPL) to do this (Dominelli, 2013). I became its first chair and later RIPL turned into IASSW's Disaster Intervention, Climate

Change and Sustainability Committee, which I currently head. Strengthening social work's visibility in disaster interventions also led me to undertake research in this arena, and produced the 'Internationalising Institutional and Professional Practice' (IIPP) research project (Dominelli, 2015) funded by the UK's Economic and Social Science Research Council (ESRC).

When I was appointed a co-director in the Institute of Hazards, Risk and Resilience (IHRR) at Durham University, I started to work with physical scientists including geologists, earth scientists, volcanologists and geographers to think about the science underpinning natural hazards such as earthquakes and volcanoes and the (hu)man-made ones including climate change, floods and poverty in projects that were funded by the Engineering and Physical Sciences Research Council (Wistow et al., 2015) and the Natural and Environmental Research Council (Dominelli et al., 2015). The ensuing research interactions made me realise how little social workers knew about how natural hazards became disasters, and highlighted the importance of thinking differently about the social dimensions of disasters, and in appreciating the intricate connections between the animate and inanimate elements of the ecosphere, and between the so-called 'natural' aspects of a disaster and its 'social' ones.

Social justice is an integral part of social work, and strongly embedded in its value of equality. The inclusion of struggles for environmental justice within an environmental framework is a critical and significant part of green social workers' activities. It surfaces when redressing complex issues involving environmental degradation, vulnerability among marginalised populations, and disaster responses. Contributing to these involves green social workers in highlighting the:

- Human rights violations that go hand-in-glove within degraded environments.
- Socio-economic political systems that fail to hold multinational corporations accountable for destroying environmental resources and perpetuating structural inequalities.
- Inadequate governance structures that discourage local communities from acting as co-producers of solutions to the environmental problems they encounter.
- The global, inequitable distribution of the world's physical resources and conflicts that ensue among those seeking to acquire a share of the earth's 'natural' resources.
- Neglect of cultural diversity including the undermining of aboriginal, indigenous and/or nomadic lifestyles, knowledges and expertise.
- Lack of environmentally friendly, sustainable socio-economic developments.
- Absence of local environmentally friendly community relationships that acknowledge interdependencies between people and the environment.
- Inadequate care of natural resources and poor environment-enhancing regional and national policies.
- Lack of universal publicly funded provisions for health and social care services that promote the well-being of people and their capacity to prevent, mitigate and recover from disasters.
- Lack of care for the physical environment in its own right (i.e. as an end in itself).
- Disregard of the environmental damage caused by armed conflicts including the carbon dioxide discharged and ensuing environmental degradation.
- Lack of recognition of the interdependencies among peoples, and between people and the biosphere/ecosystem.
- Absence of resilient built infrastructures, resources and communities (Dominelli, 2012).

Addressing these issues requires social workers to engage with the knowledge and expertise held by other disciplines and community residents. Accordingly, green social workers have sought to develop transdisciplinarity to highlight the links between the physical and social sciences in 'doing science differently' (Lane et al., 2011) with local communities. In Dominelli (2016), I differentiate between multidisciplinarity, interdisciplinarity and transdisciplinarity as follows:

- *Multidisciplinarity* consists of a group of disciplines working together, but with little or no attempt to develop a coherent team ethos of working together, learning from each other or developing new approaches as a result of their interactions.
- *Interdisciplinarity* comprises of a number of disciplines working together as one team in a specific project with specific aims that all those involved are aiming to fulfil, with a limited focus on how their work can be facilitated through some common approach or theoretical framework.
- *Transdisciplinarity* involves a number of disciplines working together on a specific project using a common holistic theoretical and practice framework. Specific endeavours are made to develop joint understandings about a problem that draws on the: local, indigenous, and expert knowledges; development of new approaches; considerations about how an issue might be resolved through coproduced solutions that engage with all forms of expertise; and that provides for changes in current policies and practices.

Physical scientists had highlighted the dangers of human activities on the environment some time earlier (e.g. Rachel Carson's [1962] *Silent Spring*). She spelt out the dangers that chemicals in everyday artefacts such as pesticides in farming and cleaning fluids in the household were causing by polluting the soil and water. Some people's behaviour changed as a result of reading it. President J. F. Kennedy initiated a scientific committee to investigate pesticides. I read the book as a teenager shortly after publication, and it engaged my interest in the topic. At that point, I was more intrigued by chemistry's capacity to solve the problem, rather than understanding that changing people's socio-economic behaviour was possibly a much better solution.

On one level, social work's concern with the environment is not new. It is a thread deeply embedded in its professional foundations. Social work began with a focus on the person-in-the-environment with the Settlement Movement in Victorian London's East End (Younghusband, 1978). However, its emphasis on the physical environment, especially built infrastructures such as housing, was lost with the ecological school of thought that followed Brofenbrenner (1979) who emphasised social systems as the environment within which people were located. By the 1990s, a number of American social work academics (Rogge, 1994, 2000; Besthorn, 2012; Besthorn and Meyer, 2010) and Canadian scholars (Coates, 2005; Ungar, 2002) had again raised the physical environment as an issue for social workers to take seriously. In the UK, I (Dominelli, 2002) had tried to include the physical environment in holistic, anti-oppressive approaches to social work, depicting it the anti-oppressive social work chart I devised. But, at that point, the holistic, transdisciplinary approach to the theory and practice of green social work had yet to be developed. Moreover, these strands have begun to come closer together as more authors collaborate on environmental theory development (Coates and Gray, 2012; Coates et al., 2013; Drolet et al., 2015; Alston and McKinnon, 2016).

While the social work academy saw a general narrowing of the profession's wider remit, individual practitioners, particularly those embedded in community action, had responded to environmental concerns by supporting poor communities ravaged by different polluting agents released by chemical and nuclear explosions (e.g. Bhopal, India in 1984 and Chernobyl in the Ukraine in 1986, respectively). In 2010, with the support of Angie Yuen, then-president of IASSW, I initiated and completed the process whereby IASSW joined the United Nations Framework Convention on Climate Change (UNFCCC). This venture was a response to increased academic interest in social work's roles in the environment (Dominelli, 2011). To promote green social work in the UK, I returned to community social work traditions to engage a local community in Durham in renewable energy as a way of exiting fuel poverty and unemployment through transdisciplinary green social work approaches (Dominelli, 2012).

Green social workers also support people who are inured physically and psychosocially during disasters and provide practical help such as water, food, medicine, clothing, shelter and family reunification. They also assist in repairing damaged environments and facilitate longer-term transformative initiatives that develop environmentally just, sustainable, life-enhancing forms of being and doing throughout the disaster cycle. Doing this in the reconstruction phase when preventative measures are being considered is especially important because most external actors and civil society organisations leave a site within six months of a disaster. Also, for those whose mental health is undermined by disasters, social workers provide psychosocial support (IASC, 2007). Indeed, this dimension is the area of social work intervention most often embedded in public consciousness. Although when the appropriate time to engage psychosocial workers and how this service should be provided is contested (Sim and Dominelli, 2016), the IASC (Inter-Agency Standing Committee) has developed guidelines, the *IASC Guidelines on Mental Health and Psychosocial Support in Emergency Settings*, for these practitioners.

Additionally, in completing community-based coproduced actions, green social workers carry out duties such as:

- Assessing need among victim–survivors and disaster-affected communities.
- Coordinating and delivering goods and services to alleviate individual suffering and rebuild communities.
- Assisting family reunification, and ensuring children's rights are safeguarded and that they are well-cared for, preferably in families and communities with whom they already have a relationship or they know.
- Supporting individuals and communities in rebuilding their lives, developing resilience and building individual and community capacities to minimise future risks and better prepare people to survive future calamitous events.
- Advocating, lobbying and mobilising for changes that protect the environment and all other living things, mitigate future disasters and reduce losses in this sphere.

The Green Social Work Framework encourages practitioners to become involved with confidence in environment-enhancing activities, because green social work is not completely outside their knowledge-base. It draws on generic social work skills known to all social workers. Additionally, it is:

- Transdisciplinary.
- Evidence based, including undertaking its own social work-based research.
- Community based and participative throughout action and research processes.
- Social change oriented because it links its research analyses to changing policy, practice, socio-economic systems and identifying future research questions.
- Coproduces community-based social action throughout the disaster cycle.
- Coproduces solutions/action plans to grow resilience at local, national and international levels.

Green social work reshapes social work's generic skills by emphasising the coproduction of knowledge and action in transdisciplinary, empowering processes that operate before a disaster, throughout it and afterwards in reconstruction endeavours. It does so by engaging local residents in the development of resilience as people and communities recover from the impact of a disaster. Green social workers are driven by egalitarian values and have the capacity to intervene in all types of disasters, adding to their personal knowledge-base by forming transdisciplinary partnerships.

The steps that green social workers undertake in their interventions are visually encapsulated in the green social work model. Its framework for practice is an iterative one in which interventions are constantly being co-evaluated through reflective thought and community engagement, and altered as appropriate after collective co-evaluation involving practitioners and local residents. The steps undertaken in this process are expressed in Figure 1.1.

Green social work is a form of community social work that addresses both (hu)man-made disasters including poverty because that condition exacerbates vulnerabilities, and natural hazards which lead to disasters such as earthquake-induced ones. The green social worker engages community residents and other relevant stakeholders. These can include local government officials, elected representatives, civil servants, civil society organisations and businesses to coproduce research, documents and solutions to the issues they face. Together, they begin by identifying and then assessing the hazards and vulnerabilities which are evident in their social, cultural, political, economic and physical environments to compile their risk assessments. Having done that, they then focus on coproduced resilience-building exercises. Risk assessments should include self-care.

The science behind risk assessments in social work is imperfect, and has to be used with caution (Swift and Callahan, 2010). However, used carefully, risk assessments are important in responding to current and future disasters because they assist in mitigation planning, especially around people's safety and security. Mitigation planning is part of reducing the risk of hazards, 'natural' and (hu)man-made, and hence constitute an important element in the formation of preventative strategies and their subsequent implementation. Engaging local residents in risk assessments is an interesting process that requires green social workers to use an array of communication tools ranging from audio-visuals to games, depending on age and capacities, including literary skills among those individuals involved.

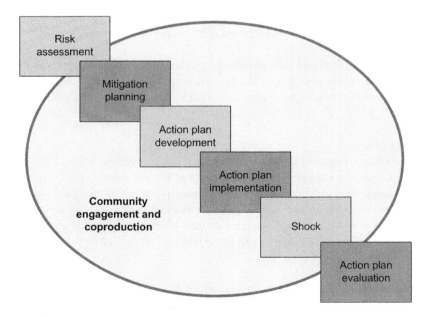

Figure 1.1 The green social work model: a framework for practice

These risk assessments form the basis of action plan developments which are locality based. Engaging residents in co-formulating solutions is not the prerogative of social workers alone. Lane et al. (2011) describe their community engagement in devising solutions to flooding in Pickering, England. Their efforts have prevented flooding in that location since, and expose the advantages of good community work practice in bringing physical and social science knowledges together with community-based expertise. Discussing this example with Stuart Lane contributed to my conceptualising green social work as transdisciplinary.

Action plans should be forward-looking and contain preventative dimensions that mitigate future risks. If this were to be the case, when a shock turns into a disaster, people would be better prepared to survive it. A shock is caused by an adverse event that undermines a person's or community's sense of stability and causes them to feel less able to cope than usual (i.e. they experience a reduction in their capacity to respond with resilience). Resilience in social work terms is an emergent property with fractured characteristics aimed at 'rebalancing a system and refocusing . . . [that] involves preventative measures, crisis responses, and long-term reconstruction and is essential in tackling structural inequalities' (Dominelli, 2012: 65). When a shock occurs, it creates an emergency that cannot be solved purely at the local level. Individuals and diverse communities and organisations from the local to the global respond to re-examine risks, devise risk-proofing measures and plans for immediate responses and their implementation, and develop future resilience locally.

Resilience strategies became a resource and foundation for action plan implementation. These have to be contextualised; adjusted for scale, locality and culture; and disaster specific. Once implemented, it is crucial that the action plan is evaluated constantly. Evaluation should not be treated as a one-off event. Coproduced action plan evaluations are important activities at the community scale. Evaluation is also a dimension of generic social work practice. This should make it easier for practitioners to understand the processes involved, although they will be exercising their skills in a new arena – the environment. These include key social work concepts that green social workers comprehend already (e.g. risk, vulnerability, adaptation and resilience). The usefulness of generic social work skills in green social work means that mainstream social workers do not have to feel intimidated by moving into a new area of practice.

Furthermore, practitioners working for environmental justice aim to uphold the duty to care for others and in turned be cared for by them. This is a relationship that includes the duty to care for the planet that humanity inhabits – earth, to ensure its sustainability. In carrying out this task green social workers seek to:

- Support people endeavouring to affirm their human, social and environmental rights.
- Support people in protecting the environment; enhancing the well-being of humans and the flora, fauna and physical ecosphere; and securing environmental justice.
- Mobilise people in diverse local, national, regional and international partnerships and alliances to promote residents' well-being and the earth's health.
- Empower marginalised individuals, communities and groups, especially those aiming to influence commercial interests, institutional routines, policymakers and other decision-makers engaged in determining environmental policies and practices that impact upon the environment, especially how it is exploited and misused.
- Mobilise residents to protect their local environment (Dominelli, 2012).

The support of social workers, their managers and government is critical to mainstreaming green social work in the social work curriculum in both the academy and fields of practice. The roles that green social workers can play in reducing environmental degradation and mitigating environmental and social vulnerabilities are those that they are also familiar with:

- *Protectors*. This involves not harming people or the planet's flora, fauna or physical environment.
- *Consciousness-raisers*. Practitioners can share scenarios about reducing greenhouse gases, developing alternative models of sustainable socio-economic development and acting as cultural interpreters conveying information across diverse settings, disciplines, professions, organisations, and societies and their different cultures.
- *Lobbyists*. Practitioners can promote preventative measures locally, including built infrastructures (e.g. housing and health facilities) while incorporating local conditions, traditions and resources; advocating at national and international levels for policy changes that facilitate access to green technologies, and equitable sharing of resources regardless of country boundaries; and tackling (hu)man-induced climate change.
- *Coordinators*. Practitioners can coordinate residents, multiple stakeholders, opinion-formers, resources and activities.
- *Mobilisers*. Green social workers can assist communities to reduce carbon emissions and care for the physical environment.
- *Translators*. Green social workers can translate and make easily accessible local knowledges to scientific experts, and scientific expertise to local communities.
- *Co-producers*. Green social workers can engage scientific experts and local residents in sharing their respective knowledges to find new solutions to identified environmental problems.
- *Dialogue agents*. Green social workers, physical scientists, other professionals and local policymakers can work with residents to engage opinion-formers in the media in dialogues that aim to change environmental policies locally, nationally and internationally.
- *Curriculum changers*. Green social work academics can engage in research and argue for curricula changes that cover climate change, sustainable development and disaster interventions to build resilience within individuals and communities (adapted from Dominelli, 2011: 438).

Environmental issues have to become integrated into mainstream social work curricula. Carrying this out effectively requires the training of social work educators, managers and practitioners, most of whom are unaware of these concerns. Once these changes occur, they can act as advocates for the sustainable care of the environment in research, teaching and practice. Additionally, it would enable them to undertake the consciousness-raising that has to occur to change behaviour among local residents and society more generally.

Creating the green social work curriculum for community-based disaster risk reduction and sustainable development

Community-based disaster risk reduction and sustainable development is high on the policy agenda of the UNISDR (United Nations International Strategy on Disaster Reduction). UNISDR agreed the *Sendai Framework for Disaster Risk Reduction 2015–2030* at Sendai, Japan in 2015 as the successor to the *Hyogo Framework for Action* (HFA) 2000–2015. IASSW was represented at Sendai and social work researchers including myself presented papers there. In the next 15 years, the UNISDR seeks to use the *Sendai Framework* to achieve substantial reductions of disaster risk and losses in lives, livelihoods and health; and protect the economic, physical, social, cultural and environmental assets of persons, businesses, communities and countries. The

Sendai Framework aims to reduce existing disaster risks through seven targets and four priorities for action. Its four priorities are to:

- Understand disaster risk.
- Strengthen disaster risk governance better to manage disaster risk.
- Invest in disaster reduction to build resilience.
- Enhance disaster preparedness for effective responses and 'building back better' expressed as resilience in recovery, rehabilitation and reconstruction.

The green social work curriculum has a role to play in enabling students, practitioners and local residents to understand the provisions of the *Sendai Framework* and engage in its implementation. This they can do through local practice initiatives which they can utilise to co-formulate solutions that advance local objectives. Green social work facilitates this ambition through its holistic and transdisciplinary framework that enables green social work practitioners to:

- Work in empowering community-based partnerships to resolve environmental issues with coproduced solutions that local residents feel that they own, control and manage.
- Understand disasters, their nature, causes and associated secondary hazards. Much of these knowledges, especially the physical science behind it, have to be made easily accessible to non-specialists.
- Know the spatial contours or geographic particularities of each disaster. Communities are located in specific physical settings. Understanding their specific vulnerabilities and strengths are important in caring for the physical environment and not stressing it with inappropriate demands (e.g. building housing on floodplains).
- Understand the social, cultural, economic, political and historical contexts of the locality in which the disaster has occurred. These aspects are central to individuals' sense of identity and belonging. People's attachment to space and place is usually under-rated in traditional models of community-based disaster risk reduction strategies. This approach is eschewed by green social workers who understand that attachment issues are deep, profound and critical in explaining people's sense of security and safety in a specific place and space.
- Appreciate the physical environment as an end in itself, not only as the context in which people live and acquire the resources they need to survive and thrive.

The green social work curriculum has to be mainstreamed for every social work student to engage service users in the coproduction of locality-specific and culturally relevant solutions to the environmental issues that undermine their health and well-being. To facilitate this endeavour, the mainstream curriculum should be mined for materials that involve transferable knowledge and skills of use in green social work practice. These include: the generic knowledge contained within practice theories and methods; the skills associated with communication, interviewing people, and coordinating agencies and activities; organisational cultures; group work; community action; social development; and an understanding of human relationships and development, and human interactions with social and material systems and structures. These elements ought to be linked to disaster legislation and procedures from micro- to macro-level to ensure relevance to any new developments and disaster interventions within which they may participate.

McKinnon (2008: 10) argues that the 'university curriculum and continuing professional development program[mes] for social workers [have to] raise these [environmental] issues and consider processes for sustaining reflexive and relevant social systems alongside mediating economic and ecological factors'. The curriculum can include elements already covered by existing pedagogic processes (e.g. its value-base of anti-oppressive, socially and environmentally just, empowering practice). This is central to empowering local residents in environmentally degraded areas, including those enduring 'environmental racism' or the dumping of pollutants in marginalised neighbourhoods (Rogge, 1994), poor African American communities (Bullard, 2000) and low-income households with children (Rogge and Coombs-Orme, 2003). Moreover, large-scale hydro-projects are significant in undermining indigenous peoples' lives by destroying the biosphere in tropical rainforests (Liebenthal, 2005), such as those owned by the Mapuche tribes in Chile (Carruthers and Rodriguez, 2009). Covering indigenous perspectives in the curriculum can help social work students understand connections between people and their living environments and the responsibilities that they have for their use of the earth's resources (Grande, 2004). Unlike the exploitation of the earth's resources favoured by multinational corporations, indigenous worldviews promote those who ask people to act as custodians of the earth now and into the future to ensure that there is a healthy physical environment for future generations of living beings to enjoy.

According to Adger (2006), vulnerability highlights a tendency to succumb to harm in the context of a disaster. He argues that the degree of vulnerability is shaped by exposure to a shock, a sensitivity to stress, and the capacity to react and adapt. Each of these dimensions can mitigate or reduce vulnerability. No country is immune from environmental disasters. However, countries in the global South are more vulnerable than those in the global North, primarily because the former have larger numbers of poor people, and inadequate built infrastructures including housing, health and social care facilities, schools, power utilities, water supplies, sanitation, transportation and communication networks. Consequently, the Global South bears 76 per cent of damages caused by disasters; 92 per cent of people affected by disasters live in countries located there; and 65 per cent of economic losses occur in these locations (IFRC, 2009). Additionally, it is important that green social workers consider differentiated vulnerabilities, particularly among older people, women and children, because they are seldom heard in pre-disaster planning or in post-disaster reconstruction (Alston, 2002; Pittaway et al., 2007; Seballos et al., 2011). Their differentiated experiences are a critical dimension and ought to be included in the curriculum. Essential to this consideration are economic questions about paid employment and workplace organisation. Low-paid jobs increase vulnerabilities by impacting upon people's income levels and social status. When these are low, people are more likely to live in environmentally vulnerable areas and have fewer resources with which to survive disasters and build resilience.

Transdisciplinarity encourages student engagement with a wide range of expertise necessary for operationalising social, economic and environmental justice into disaster interventions, and include people from other disciplines and professions in their multi-stakeholder partnerships for sustainable social development and disaster interventions. Additionally, their curriculum has to cover advocacy, lobbying skills, knowledge about how to form wide-ranging and strong alliances, the development of strategic thinking and non-violent conflict resolution skills. The green social work curriculum is, therefore, multi-dimensional and has to include items that ensure it is relevant to the environmental and life challenges of the 21st century.

Conclusions

Green social work envisages a world that meets the needs of all people, the earth's flora, fauna, other living things and the physical environment today and in the future. To achieve this aim, green social work provides a new paradigm for environmental issues to be tackled by social workers. It asks them to go beyond their traditional comfort zone by becoming engaged in sustainable, coproduced transformative social change that creates a living, viable earth with equitably shared and distributed resources and opportunities. Thus, green social work is redistributive and regenerative. Green social workers endeavour to develop preventive and responsive emergency services before, during and after disasters. Like other responders, their overall objective is to reduce the number of deaths and casualties among people, animals and plants; and to assess the needs of people. It transcends these by including other living things with which people share the physical environment and the inanimate world itself within its remit. Green social work, therefore, is conducted to promote a healthy and sustainable physical environment and biosphere; enhance resilience in the social, physical and built environments; and enable disaster survivors to flourish in the future.

Green social workers engage local residents and experts in holistic approaches that bring people together to protect their physical, social, political, economic and cultural environments across all phases of disasters. These dimensions are part of an integrated whole, and not separate from it. To pursue the cause of environmental justice, endorse social justice in environmentally degraded communities, undertake reconstruction tasks and intervene effectively, green social work practitioners ought to understand the complex power dynamics and relationships that underpin the entrenched views that people hold about their involvement in ending the exploitation of the physical environment and its resources, and elimination of environmental injustice. Its complexity highlights the significance of green social workers engaging all stakeholders – 100 per cent of the earth's population, in developing the new socio-economic alternatives needed, and raising questions to ensure that no one group is privileged above another.

References

Adger, W. N. (2006). Vulnerability. *Global Environmental Change*, 16(3): 268–281.

Alston, M. (2002). From local to global: Making social policy more effective for rural community capacity building. *Australian Social Work*, 55(3): 214–226.

Alston, M., and McKinnon, J. (Eds.) (2016). *Ecological social work: Towards sustainability*. London: Palgrave Macmillan.

Besthorn, F. (2012). The contributions of deep ecology to social work: A ten year perspective. *International Journal of Social Welfare*, 21(3), 248–259.

Besthorn, F. and Meyer, E. (2010). 'Environmentally displaced persons Broadening social work's helping imperative', *Critical Social Work*, 11(3), pp. 123–138.

Brofenbrenner, U. (1979). *The ecology of human development*. Cambridge, MA: Harvard University Press.

Bullard, R. (2000). *Dumping in Dixie: Race, class, and environmental quality*. 3rd ed. Boulder, CO: Westview Press.

Carruthers, D. and Rodriguez, P. (2009). Mapuche protest, environmental conflict and social movement linkage in Chile. *Third World Quarterly*, 30(4): 743–760.

Carson, R. (1962). *Silent spring*. Greenwich, CT: Fawcett Publications Inc.

Coates, J. (2005). The environmental crisis: Implications for social work. *Journal of Progressive Human Services*, 16(1), 25–49.

Coates, J. and Gray, M. (2012). The environment and social work: An overview and introduction. *International Journal of Social Welfare*, 21(3), 230–238. doi: 10.1111/j.1468–2397.2011.00851.x

Coates, J., Gray, M., and Hetherington, T. (Eds.) (2013). *Environmental social work*. London: Routledge.

Dominelli, L. (2002). *Anti-oppressive social work theory and practice*. London: Palgrave Macmillan.

Dominelli, L. (2011). Climate change: Social workers' contributions to policy and practice debates. *International Journal of Social Welfare*, 20(4), 430–439. doi: 10.1111/j.1468–2397.2011.00795.x

Dominelli, L. (2012). *Green social work: From environmental crises to environmental justice*. Cambridge: Polity Press.

Dominelli, L. (2013). Empowering disaster-affected communities for long-term reconstruction: Intervening in Sri Lanka after the Tsunami. *Journal of Social Work in Disability and Rehabilitation*, Special Edition on Disaster management and social work: Asian Pacific experiences in recovery and rehabilitation, 12(1–2), 48–66. doi: 10.1080/1536710X.2013.784175

Dominelli, L. (2015). The opportunities and challenges of social work in disaster situations. *International Social Work*, Special edition on disaster interventions, 58(5): 659–672, September. doi: 10.1177/0020872815598353

Dominelli, L. (2016). Greening Social Work: linking social and environmental justice in social work theory and practice. Translated as Grõnt Socialt Arbete (Greening Social Work)', in Knutagård, M., Meeuwisse, A., Sunesson, S. and Swärd, H., eds., Socialt Arbete: En Grundbok. Stockholm: Natur och kultur, chapter 22, pp 445-462.

Dominelli, L., Sim, T., and Cui, K. (2015). Community-based approaches to disaster risk reduction in China. In *Pathways to earthquake resilience in China: A report*. London: Overseas Development Institute, pp. 30–41.

Drolet, J., Dominelli, L., Alston, M., Ersing, R., Mathbor, G. and Wu, H. (2015). Women rebuilding lives post-disasters: Innovative community practices for building resilience and promoting sustainable Development. *Gender and Development*, 23(3): 433–448.

Grande, S. (2004). *Red pedagogy: Native American and political thought*. Lanham, MD: Rowman & Littlefield.

IASC (Inter-Agency Standing Committee (2007). *The IASC Guidelines on Mental Health and Psychosocial Support in Emergency Settings*. Available on www.who.int/mental_health/emergencies/guidelines_iasc_mental_health_psychosocial_june_2007.pdf [Accessed 21 April 2017].

IFRC (International Federation of the Red Cross and Red Crescent Societies) (2009). *World disaster report 2009: Focus on early warning and early action*. Geneva: IFRC.

Lane, S. N., Odoni, N., Landström, C., Whatmore, S. J., Ward, N. and Bradley, S. (2011). Doing flood risk science differently: An experiment in radical scientific method. *Transactions*, 36, 15–36.

Liebenthal, A. (2005). *Extractive industries and sustainable development*. Washington, DC: World Bank.

McKinnon J. (2008). Exploring the nexus between social work and the environment. *Australian Social Work*, 61(3): 268–282.

Pittaway, E., Bartolemei, L. and Rees, S. (2007). Gendered dimensions of the 2004 tsunami: and a potential social work in post-disaster. *International Social Work*, 50(3): 307–319.

Rogge, M. (1994). Environmental justice: Social welfare and toxic waste. In M. D. Hoff and J. G. McNutt (Eds.), *The global environmental crisis: Implications for social welfare and social work*. Aldershot, Hants: Ashgate.

Rogge, M. (2000). Social development and the ecological tradition. *Social Development Issues*, 22(1): 32–41.

Rogge, M. and Coombs-Orme, T. (2003). Protecting children from chemical exposure: Social work and US social welfare policy. *Social Work*, 48(4): 439–450.

Seballos, T., Tanner, M., and Gallegos, J. (2011). *Children and disasters: understanding impact and enabling agency*. Brighton, UK: Save the Children, UNICEF.

Sim, T., and Dominelli, L. (2016). When the mountains move: A Chinese post-disaster psychosocial social work model. *Qualitative Social Work*, 1–8. doi: 10.1177/1473325016637912

Swift, K., and Callahan, M. (2010). *At risk: Social justice in child welfare and other human service*. Toronto: Toronto University Press.

Ungar, M. (2002). A deeper, more ecological social work practice. *Social Services Review*, 76(3): 480–497. doi: 10.1086/341185

Wistow, J., Dominelli, L. Oven, K., Dunn, C. and Curtis, S. E. (2015). The role of formal and informal networks in supporting older people's care during extreme weather events. *Policy and Politics*, 43(1): 119–135. doi.org/10.1332/030557312X655855

Younghusband, E. (1978). *Social work in Britain: 1950–75*. London: Allen and Unwin.

2

Transdisciplinary collaboration between physical and social scientists

Drawing on the experiences of an advisor to Earthquakes without Frontiers (EwF)

Peter Sammonds

Introduction

The UK government's £1.5 billion Global Challenges Research Fund (GCRF) launched in 2016 supports 'cutting-edge research that addresses the challenges faced by developing countries' and represents a major research shift in UK research. It emphasises 'challenge-led interdisciplinary research and strengthening research capacity within both the UK and developing countries' (RCUK, 2017). GCRF's significance, reflected in its share of the total government R and D budget of £4.7 billion annually (BIS, 2017), is evident in Figure 2.1. GCRF, as part of the UK's Official Development Assistance (ODA) commitment, is monitored by the Organisation for Economic Cooperation and Development (OECD). ODA-funded activities aim to promote long-term sustainable growth in developing countries (RCUK, 2017). UK research councils have previously funded transdisciplinary research that addressed these challenges, such as Earthquakes without Frontiers (EwF). This has never been on the scale now envisaged.

The science budget, flat in real terms, is dropping sharply as a percentage of gross domestic product. The GCRF represents significant new funding for research (BIS, 2017). GCRF is administered through the UK Research Councils (RCUK) and national academies (e.g. Royal Society of London and British Council). RCUK has responded by calling for transdisciplinary projects. The call in summer 2017 aims to establish a cohort of large-scale Global Challenges Interdisciplinary Research Hubs, which are expected to deliver integrated and innovative international research programmes meeting ODA aims and 'incorporate new collaborations and partnerships and be transformative for development challenges and inter-disciplinary in approach' (RCUK, 2017). UK universities' responses to GCRF have been corporate in nature, setting up high-level university committees with members drawn from several faculties, under directors of research, to coordinate action across a university.

GCRF funding was announced in the 2015 UK government spending review. Its substantial value and rapidity of the spending have taxed the capacity of funder organisations (research

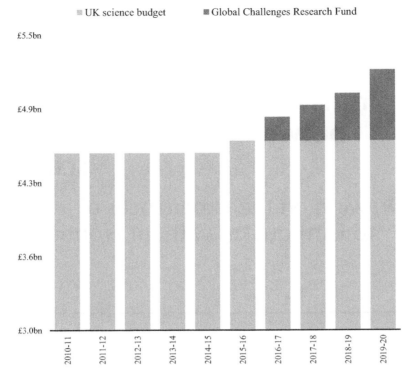

Figure 2.1 Comparison of UK science budget and Global Challenges Research Fund (GCRF)

councils and academies) and research organisations (universities and research centres) to respond. Additionally, neither funder nor research organisations have drawn on existing institutional knowledge regarding interdisciplinary working and engaging with ODA countries. This is exemplified by the Natural Environment Research Council (NERC), Economic and Social Research Council (ESRC) and Arts and Humanities Research Council (AHRC) Programme on Building Resilience (NERC, 2017). Most funded projects have investigators who have not previously collaborated and/or undertaken research in ODA countries. Researchers who have led successful transdisciplinary teams on ODA-linked projects did not apply for funding because the call was too complex. High-level committees in funders' and research organisations do not draw on those with the most experience in transdisciplinary working in the development context (e.g. the prominence given to working with development organisations in the Building Resilience Programme). In some ODA countries, working with international development NGOs is anathema in influencing policymakers. Senior scientists with long experience in transdisciplinary research in ODA countries have raised concerns that these factors will either waste GCRF research funds or produce poor outcomes.

Thus, experiences of transdisciplinary research that address challenges faced by developing countries should be described and analysed. Only a few across research councils had been funded. One of these, the NERC–ESRC Increasing Resilience to Natural Hazards in Earthquake-prone and Volcanic Areas (IRNH) Programme, funded two research consortia: Earthquakes without Frontiers (EwF) and Strengthening Resilience in Volcanic Areas (STREVA). EwF (2012–2017) offers a paradigm for transdisciplinary research in ODA countries in central Asia. EwF has produced high-quality research and achieved significant impact. STREVA (2017) has also produced new ways of transdisciplinary working in geo-hazards, but is not considered here. A successor programme to IRNH, Increasing Resilience to Natural Hazards in China, was launched in 2016. This chapter draws on published research, publicly available documents from the research councils, online programme reports, formal and informal interviews with international physical scientists and social scientists as well as professionals and practitioners in government, research funders, NGOs, a Community Survey, and the outputs of transdisciplinary working groups. The challenges of how to work across disciplinary boundaries with different cultures, expectations and professional norms; how to communicate science to local communities; and how to innovate and keep everyone on board provide important lessons for others embarking on such enterprises.

Structure of transdisciplinary working

Hoffmann-Riem et al. (2008) in the *Handbook of Transdisciplinary Research*, argue that transdisciplinary research aims to overcome the mismatch between knowledge production in academia, and knowledge requests for solving societal problems. They suggest that developing a state of the art for transdisciplinary forms of research is best done by learning from experience.

> In a world characterised by rapid change, uncertainty and increasing interconnectedness there is a growing need for science to contribute to the solution of persistent, complex problems, which include not only some of the now broadly known environmental issues such as climate change and biodiversity loss, but also related issues such as poverty, security and governance.
>
> *(Jäger, J., ibid.)*

The division between expert scientific knowledges and local, indigenous knowledges is unfortunate from the point of view of 'doing science differently' (Lane et al., 2011). Yet, there are disciplines within the academy that make it their business to engage with local residents and bring these two knowledges together to initiate changes in behaviour and institutional structures. Among these are social work and community development. EwF included social workers and community development workers in its consortium, and is unique for this reason. Additionally, the research undertaken in EwF contributed to the further development of green social work (Dominelli, 2012). Although reaching similar conclusions as Hoffmann-Reim et al. (2008), green social work arrived at these from a different perspective, namely coproducing them from the ground up. Using participative action-research methodologies (PAR), the marginalised peoples who form the majority among the service users of these social science disciplines have their knowledge valorised and validated alongside that of the scientific experts (Dominelli, 2012). PAR, used in social work since the 1960s, enables researchers to hold the tensions and disagreements between diverse participants, and seek common objectives for avoiding being trapped in the 'them–us' binary, thereby persuading them to coproduce solutions that work for the common good (Dominelli, 2012).

As Hirsch Hadorn et al. (2008) point out, while methodological divisions characterised the emergence of modern scientific disciplines from the 17th century, for society to benefit from scientific progress, a figure as prominent as Francis Bacon (1561–1626) was convinced that collaboration among scientists was crucial. Division within science continued with the 19th-century emergence of the social sciences which were strongly influenced by the severe conditions experienced by the working class (*ibid.*). Professional social work emerged at that time to solve the then-pressing social problems, especially poverty, unemployment and housing among disenfranchised populations in London's East End (Gilchrist and Jeffs, 2001). The drive to solve real-world problems has promoted transdisciplinarity whereby different academic disciplines work jointly with practitioners (Klein et al., 2001).

Transdisciplinary research generally shows four characteristics:

1   Focus on real-world problems;
2   Transcending and integrating of disciplinary paradigms;
3   Participatory research; and
4   Search for unity of knowledge beyond disciplines (Hirsch Hadorn et al., 2008).

These characteristics of the IRNH programme and EwF research consortium are at the heart of green social work theory and practice. So it is worth examining in some detail the mechanisms for how the IRNH research programme was initiated, the working methods employed to keep everyone on board and focus on increasing resilience as a transdisciplinary theme.

Structuring the Increasing Resilience to Natural Hazards (IRNH) research programme

The IRNH programme was initiated in 2009 as the Natural Hazards Theme Action Plan by NERC (NERC, 2009). Its grand challenge was: 'Reducing societal exposure to natural hazards by better forecasting, integrated risk assessment and scientific advice'. The programme was to stimulate areas where science was internationally immature, thus providing the UK with opportunities to lead research in new science areas and be closely aligned with the wider international disaster reduction agenda. It had three thematic research drivers: 1) effectively forecasting natural hazards and their consequences; 2) improving considerably the communication and application of scientific knowledge and understanding of natural hazards; and 3) emphasising mitigation strategies and investing significant financial resources in them.

Among the programme's actions was Action 1, increasing resilience through improved hazard forecasting and take-up of scientific advice in earthquake-prone and volcanic regions, with a proposed budget of £7 million. Hazards are only a component of risk, and vulnerability is the element that can be managed most effectively. NERC science was to be developed with partners in the social and economic sciences. This produced an integrated research programme between NERC and ESRC (funding ratio 4:1 approximately). Although including other important partners, particularly the Engineering and Physical Sciences Research Council, Medical Research Council and UK Department for International Development (DfID), was strenuously pursued from the outset, it was not possible to persuade these funders to take this broad transdisciplinary approach. Researching vulnerability without engineering and health disciplines, and key relevant government departments, were setbacks, which were addressed in other ways. On the other hand, their absence raised the importance of social science in the programme. Sister NERC programmes in the Action Plan covered uncertainty, risk and scientific advice, and hydro-meteorological hazards.

The action was to address research areas where the science was 'internationally immature and so provide the UK with the opportunity to lead research in new science areas'. However, the novelty of a transdisciplinary approach for UK research required a programme of integration activities, which NERC and ESRC introduced. These were:

- Appointment of a Strategic Advisor (the author) responsible for the strategic direction and alignments of the programme, providing overall intellectual leadership and ensuring

progress against the delivery of the programme's objectives. Tasks included ongoing liaison and advice to the research councils through the Programme Executive Board (PEB), research consortia and knowledge exchange (KE) fellows, writing the programme calls (Announcement of Opportunities or AOs) and scientific leadership for programme meetings.
- Establishing a programmatic Natural Hazards Advisory Group (NHAG), chaired by the strategic advisor, tasked with advising the PEB on the strategic direction of the programme, recommending the award of research funds (but not making specific project-funding decisions) and integration of the programme science. NHAG was composed of four research council staff, six researchers (two international), one member from a government agency and one from an NGO. Areas of expertise covered physical sciences (earthquake and volcanoes), social science, public health, economics and humanitarian response. These formed an effective team with international experience. The involvement of colleagues from the Instituto Nazionale di Geofisica e Vulcanologia, Rome, was particularly valuable.
- The commissioning of six scoping studies in a competitive process. An additional earthquakes-focused Scoping Study and report on resilience thinking in health protection were independently produced. Their reports are publicly available through the NERC website. Three of these studies fed directly into the two successful consortia research projects.
- Professional survey of nine in-depth interviews undertaken by the strategic advisor over a one-month period in May 2011 with representatives of the UK government, and professionals employed in finance, engineering, humanitarian agencies and NGOs engaged in disaster risk and reduction work. Participants were contacted beforehand with information about the programme and indicative interview questions. All discussions were noted and written up.
- Community online survey prepared by Oxford Innovation in April 2011 in two phases totalled 104 online visits. Of 59 respondents answering the Phase 1 questionnaire, 19 had been involved in the programme scoping studies. Phase 2 resulted in 44 respondents completing the survey. This survey aimed to: 1) gather a breadth and diversity of perspectives on the challenges that the scientific community foresaw in this transdisciplinary area; and 2) encourage individuals to view the topic from various perspectives (Oxford Innovation, 2011). The survey comprised two phases: Phase 1 asked individuals to contribute their thoughts and ideas to set questions; Phase 2 took responses from Phase 1 questions and asked individuals to evaluate and comment upon these responses.
- Programme meetings included an open one-day Town Hall Meeting in London that brought together physical and social scientists; an open three-day meeting in Chengdu, China; and a two-day integration workshop in Windsor for the IRNH-in-China programme.

I have provided considerable details because my reflections suggest that these are necessary components in successfully launching a transdisciplinary research programme in a research community with limited experience of either transdisciplinary working or engaging with ODA governments and communities around the geo-hazards theme. Other research communities in the natural environment (e.g. climate change) had far more experience.

Defining resilience

The IRNH Programme's high-level goal is to increase economic and social resilience to earthquake, volcanic and related hazards based on reliable knowledge of the fundamental physical and social processes involved, and full understanding of prevention and mitigation of the associated risks. An early issue for NHAG to address was what was meant by increasing resilience. The definitions and etymology of resilience had previously and subsequently been much studied (Thywissen, 2006; Bahadur et al., 2010; Castleden et al. 2011; Alexander, 2013).

The professional survey showed that their organisations had dealt with this issue, and some like the UK Cabinet Office, in-depth (Cabinet Office, 2017). The Community Survey revealed a spread of opinion about the definition of resilience. But, a common reaction to the question was to request that NERC–ESRC provide their definition (Oxford Innovation, 2011). What the Community Survey also revealed was a minority who did not accept resilience as a suitable topic for a NERC research theme.

An outcome of the Scoping Study by a transdisciplinary team led by Densmore (2011) was the recommendation that: 'Resilience must be defined in the broadest possible context, to allow for the multi-faceted nature of the ways that populations engage with and adapt to earthquake-related hazards. Resilience is fundamentally a dynamic concept, rather than a static or conservative one.' The Scoping Study consultations also highlighted that meaningful resilience with respect to livelihoods may not necessarily predicate re-establishment of the pre-disaster state. Importantly, changes to pre-disaster arrangements involving livelihood, location and mobility may 'enhance future resilience'. Members of the EwF consortium involved in this Scoping Study are currently using green social work principles to enhance individual and community resilience in post-Gorkha community-based developments, including sustainable income-generation projects and recording these developments for further research purposes and changes in policy and practice. Dominelli (2017) discusses the implementation of green social work post-disaster in Nepal.

A definition, adapted from the United National International Strategy for Disaster Reduction (UNISDR), was adopted for the IRNH programme as it encompassed the spread of opinion and encouraged a transdisciplinary approach:

> Increasing societal resilience requires that the society, community, economies or system exposed to these natural hazards has the ability to resist, absorb, accommodate to and recover from their effects in a timely and efficient manner, including through the preservation and restoration of its essential basic structures and functions, determined by the degree to which the society has the necessary resources and is capable of organising itself both prior to and during times of need.

Science excellence versus societal co-benefits

Physical hazards are only one component of risk. Significant amplification of the impact of the research programme, including reductions in mortality rates and economic loss, would be achieved through the broader interdisciplinary characterisation of risk and resilience. As the IRNH Programme Announcement of Opportunity stated (NERC, 2017), one of the principal goals:

> is the integration of natural and social science research across the programme to enhance the potential for impact on those affected by natural hazards, in the short and long-term. To that end a co-productive approach to research was required [of the project consortia] involving a framework for the sharing in parallel of knowledge and values between natural and social scientists and by consultation with policy makers, civil society and other stakeholders throughout the research programme.

In reaching this point, there had been considerable discussion within NHAG. It took the view that the programme delivering scientific excellence and societal co-benefits were of equal value.

So, the natural science research needed to be undertaken in conjunction with social science (co-designed, produced and delivered) that addressed issues including decision-making under conditions of uncertainty, vulnerability analyses to increase resilience; translating assessment into policy, and policy into action; exploring knowledge relationships and reflective learning across disciplines; and recovery management. The position was strongly endorsed by physical scientists who had direct experience of dealing with similar issues. Co-production of the research was not envisaged in the NERC Theme Action Plan, so approval from members of NERC Council was necessary for the AO to be approved. This required unanimity in NHAG.

The Community Survey revealed that co-produced programmes between natural and social sciences were not popular. When the IRNH programme questioned what should be the balance between commissioning science publishable in the highest quality journals versus science with 'impact' in increasing resilience, comments indicated some resistance that suggested transdisciplinary research should be a priority – rather studying the fundamentals of the physical process. In response to the question, 'what would be your main suggestions to the IRNH interdisciplinary research programme', community responses indicated that a sizeable proportion were unwilling to engage in research outside the physical sciences domain. Figure 2.2 summarises the Phase 2 Community Survey output showing the mix of opinions and perceived role of social

High relevance, low disagreement
1. Education
2. Increase use of scientific knowledge by NGOs/responder
3. Knowledge and its effective use in risk mitigation
4. Increasing knowledge of the hazard in the developing world
5. Making the right choices in selecting research questions
6. Resilience requires good governance and societal awareness
7. Capacity and resilience in developing countries
8. Improve early warning/forecast and communication
9. Collaborations between scientist across international lines
10. Improve monitoring and engage with community

High relevance, high disagreement
1. Complexity of the problem
2. Working with communities and local governments
3. Focus
4. Understanding precursors / producing good hazard maps
5. Imperative to do science rather than monitoring
6. Mitigating damage before and after the event
7. Forecasting hazardous events
8. To make them relevant for the people effected

Low relevance, low disagreement
1. These hazards are global
2. Cost for human townships etc. unknown for marine systems
3. Providing aid
4. There are already well-developed international programs
5. Unpredictable point location events - disbursed impacts
6. Insuring consistency across boundaries
7. Money and understanding communities

Low relevance, high disagreement
1. Predictability - big problem for volcanoes
2. Unpredictability
3. Coordination and use of geographic information
4. Some mechanisms for volcanic eruptions need research
5. High-density urban populations
6. Getting the right things into a disaster zone
7. Integrating bottom-up / top-down knowledge and actions
8. Securing understanding of the potential threats in advance
9. Co-operation - share knowledge, expertise and equipment
10. Livelihood protection and stimulation of the economy

RELEVANCE (MEAN)

DISAGREEMENT (STANDARD DEVIATION)

Figure 2.2 Community Survey Phase 2 outputs: challenges to produce the best research excellence and societal co-benefits

Source: Oxford Innovation, 2011

science in the programme. There was low disagreement that education, increasing the use of scientific knowledge by NGOs as responders and increasing knowledge in the developing world were highly relevant. There was high disagreement over working with communities and local governments, mitigating damage and making science relevant for the people affected. This supports the view that many physical scientists regard the role of social sciences as communicating the science, rather than engaging in a co-designed, co-produced and co-delivered programme.

Natural hazards remit

As part of the broader NERC Natural Hazards Theme Action Plan and to avoid overlap with other programmes, the IRNH Programme was prescribed a range of natural hazards in geo-hazards. This excluded a multi-hazard approach which would have been the best approach if the increasing resilience had been addressed primarily through vulnerability. However, as highlighted in the Theme Action Plan, earthquakes, volcanoes and related hazards – such as landslides, tsunamis and lahars – cause enormous human and economic losses and disruption which continue to grow worldwide. Lack of preparedness in major urban conurbations (e.g. Teheran) makes the million-death earthquake seem inevitable (Musson, 2012). The sudden onset of an extreme natural event can have catastrophic, regional-scale, long-term social and economic effects. For example, the 2010 Haiti earthquake had high levels of mortality and morbidity, and economic losses that exceeded annual GDP. The societal disruption caused may require a generation to overcome and this can be superimposed on existing poor development and health.

Earth is a dynamic planet, as the IRNH AO pointed out (NERC, 2017). Slow forcing from the underlying mantle drives both volcanism and earthquakes. Resulting crack growth in the crust is highly non-linear, making individual earthquake or volcanic events difficult to predict. Long inter-event times result in standard hazard assessments that can be grossly misleading, such as for the 2011 Tohoku Japan earthquake and tsunami, 2010 Haiti earthquake and 2010 Eyjafjallajökull eruption. The direction of recent UK research into the physical processes that control the occurrence and magnitude of natural hazards in earthquake-prone and volcanic regions has the potential markedly to contribute to increased resilience (NERC, 2017). For instance, recent research has made significant contributions to the forensic studies of earthquakes in the determination of spatial patterns of inter-seismic strain rates, on fault interactions and subsequent migration of seismic activity, which together allow quantitative assessments of the zones of greatest earthquake hazard. A very high proportion of losses in earthquake-prone regions are caused by related hazards of landslides, and tsunamis activated during earthquakes. Advances in their spatial characterisation have considerable potential for development within risk management.

Earthquakes without Frontiers (EwF) is a five-year transdisciplinary consortium project funded from the IRNH Programme, involving Cambridge, Durham, Hull, Leeds, Northumbria and Oxford universities, the Overseas Development Institute, British Geological Survey and National Centre of Earth Observation in the UK. The consortium aims to provide transformational increases in knowledge of the primary and secondary earthquake hazards in the continental interiors (EwF, 2017). Frequent, devastating, large magnitude (M_w = 7~8) earthquakes occur in continental interiors. As England and Jackson (2011) argue, the networks of faults within the continents are not well mapped out. The fault zones are commonly hundreds or thousands of kilometres in width and contain many separate faults, each slowly straining. A large earthquake is caused by a fault slipping a few metres so the time required for the necessary strain to accumulate is a few hundred to a few thousand years. This makes assessing the hazard from widely dispersed continental faults with long inter-event times particularly challenging. EwF employ a range of advanced scientific methodologies to understand continental faulting. These include: 1) measurement of strain in Earth's crust from satellite, combined with seismology; and 2) forensic analyses of faults (including hidden faults), combining established field mapping techniques, trenching across faults and Quaternary dating with innovative survey techniques to produce high-resolution topographic models. For example, in Kazakhstan, EwF have uncovered and surveyed the ruptures from a great earthquake in 1889 that destroyed the then-town, and now-major city, of Almaty, and have also discovered the ruptures from another unknown large earthquake that occurred 300–400 years ago. Analysing seismically triggered landslides through field surveys and satellite remote sensing to understand temporal and spatial distributions is a key part of this enquiry (EwF Report, 2015; NERC, 2017).

Vulnerability to geo-hazards

As stated in the IRNH Programme AO:

> understanding vulnerability is at the heart of increasing economic and social resilience, and increasing the impact of physical science advances. Vulnerability can be social, economic, technical and infrastructural, and understanding vulnerability historically can help inform approaches to each of these areas. Components of vulnerability that require research include well-being, self and social protection, governance, the strength of livelihoods, resolve to survive, modelling techniques and methods which use social and spatial data to develop indices of vulnerability and community risk maps.
>
> *(NERC, 2017)*

The developed world is characterised by societies relatively highly resilient to geo-hazards. This is illustrated by the low death tolls from significant recent earthquakes such as 2011 Christchurch where only 0.1 percent among those exposed to shaking of intensity VIII+ were killed (England and Jackson, 2011). By contrast in the developing world, for example, even relatively small events may cause large death tolls that have huge social and economic impacts. ODA countries also provide the best opportunity for UK science to make significant impact. So the IRNH AO contained a clear steer in that direction. EwF research addresses the Alpine–Himalayan belt, which stretches from the Mediterranean to the Pacific, with specific focus on Northeast China, Iran and Central Asia (including the Tian Shan mountains in Kazakhstan, Figure 2.3), and the Himalayan mountain front (including Nepal). The project's second objective is to identify pathways to building resilience in populations affected by earthquake hazards (EwF, 2017).

Community Based Disaster Risk Reduction

To translate science into resilience and impact of the IRNH programme, effective exchanges of knowledge between scientists and communities at risk, local governments and regional organisations, including through the dissemination of scientific ideas, education, training and building of local capacity, was required. The IRNH programme required that this be undertaken in the appropriate context and in collaboration with and understanding of communities at risk, supported by partnership-building with scientific organisations, government agencies, policymakers, and industry and commerce. At the community level, how capacity, resilience and agency can be increased while avoiding the imposition of a 'top-down' model of hazard assessment and risk management was an important consideration (NERC, 2017). It was a concern that externally generated scientific expert knowledge (like hazard maps) may not be appropriate

Figure 2.3 Kazakhstan. Cattle are walking up a hidden earthquake fault close to the Tian Shan mountain front

Source: photograph by author

for communities at risk in the developing world, with the result that such knowledge may not contribute to resilience-building. But as Densmore claimed:

> The findings from the Scoping Study challenge the binary view of scientific/indigenous knowledge often reported within the literature. In reality, people's understanding of earthquake hazards is far more nuanced than this simple distinction suggests. Also, different knowledge types can come together in surprising ways, such that people may hold quite different explanations for geophysical hazards at any one time with little tension between these opposing world-views.
>
> *(2011: 2)*

Encouragingly, the low death toll in some Tohoku coastal towns demonstrates the importance of successful mitigation measures of communication, preparedness and flexibility, even when the magnitude of the event was significantly under-predicted (EEFIT, 2011).

EwF employed a method for Community Based Disaster Risk Reduction by using sets of scenarios, co-developed by communities, civil society organisations and local government officials working closely in teams with scientists. This is described by Davies et al. (2015). These scenarios were based on the impacts of realistic high-magnitude earthquakes and landslides on a community and provided a basis for further work by community/scientist/local government teams to devise mitigation strategies for reducing the impacts. In China, the government policy required that people would be exposed to scenarios that would not worry them, so EwF had to focus on the 1556 earthquake. They emphasised the need for long-term partnerships between the different stakeholder groups including government, to build trust and develop in-depth understanding of the social and natural systems and their changing vulnerability over time. This approach is a substantial departure from much current practice. Its implementation requires local governments, civil society organisations, scientists and communities to work equitably and constructively with each other (Sim et al., 2017).

Translating assessment into policy and policy into action

There is commonly a disjuncture between the evolution and provision of expert knowledge and its effective utilisation. Research needs to assess how scientific knowledge and risk reduction strategies can be most effectively developed and communicated. Working across Central Asia, EwF have found that there is no universal approach across the diverse countries. These countries range from middle-income former Soviet republics to low-income democracies. Only by understanding the political, cultural and socio-economic context of the country can strategies that make policy impact be devised. An important common strand is the importance of gaining trust among and working with local scientists (*ibid.*). EwF's first goals were to: (i) organise meetings with stakeholders in individual countries, and (ii) establish links with the scientific communities in partner countries. Their approach was to organise a three-day meeting in Cambridge in October 2012, bringing together stakeholders from Europe, the Middle East, Asia, and the Indian sub-continent. This led to in-country meetings in Nepal and India, China and Central Asia (EwF Report, 2013; NERC, 2017). These in-country meetings were frequently linked to fieldwork where a range of stakeholders, and early career scientists, were invited (Figure 2.4).

Figure 2.4 The Geological Institute, Almaty, Kazakhstan. The somewhat austere Soviet location for a meeting of international physical and social sciences, practitioners and government officials in September 2016

Source: photograph by author

EwF's use of science in earthquake risk reduction efforts in Nepal exemplifies its work. They established that: 1) there is a high level of knowledge around earthquakes among physical scientists, although earthquake-triggered landslides were a critical unknown; 2) important gaps exist between scientists, practitioners and engineers, such that current scientific knowledge is poorly taken up; and 3) scientific knowledge is useful for practitioners as an advocacy tool but plays little role in disaster risk reduction, given their focus on spatial variations in vulnerability (EwF Report, 2014; NERC, 2017).

The EwF programme actively engages and supports scientific and technical communities to inform decision-making and capacity-building. For example, EwF ran a two-week summer school/workshop on Earthquake Tectonics and Hazards on the Continents in Trieste, Italy, in association with the International Center for Theoretical Physics. This involved 50 students from partnership countries (including Iran, Kazakhstan, Kyrgyzstan, China, India, Pakistan and Mongolia) and other developing countries in Africa, Indonesia and Asia. Highly successful, it raised the level of knowledge and skills among participating students and scientists (EwF, 2017). This is an essential component of EwF, but funding for in-country capacity-building has to come from other sources.

EwF response to the Nepal Gorkha Earthquake, 25 April 2015

During the EwF project, a significant major earthquake occurred in Nepal: the Gorkha earthquake of 25 April 2015 (M_w=7.8). This killed almost 9000 people, destroyed hundreds of thousands of homes and damaged the rich cultural heritage of Nepal. The earthquake and its aftermath are an important test of the IRNH experiment, to observe the outcome of transdisciplinary research and its practical impact. EwF's engagement with this earthquake is described in EwF Reports (EwF, 2017). The Gorkha earthquake became the major focus of the EwF team (EwF, 2017).

Ten days before the Gorkha earthquake, EwF had held a three-day meeting in Kathmandu with colleagues in the National Society for Earthquake Technology in Nepal. EwF had well-established collaborations in Nepal and strong trust relations (Oven et al., 2016). The response to the earthquake and its aftermath included:

- Media engagement. EwF PIs and others engaged in the IRNH programme gave over 60 interviews on television and radio.
- Advice to UK government. EwF researchers were involved in briefing chief scientists of the UK government and DfID, and provided direct daily inputs to UK government briefing committees, SAGE and COBR, on what happened in the main shock, implications for the humanitarian relief effort, significance of aftershock activity and possibility that future large earthquakes will occur adjacent to the region.
- EwF researchers collaborated with the British Geological Survey to deliver a series of maps of coseismic and postseismic landslides. These were made freely available through the Humanitarian Data Exchange and MapAction, which used the data to prepare outputs for the UN Logistics Cluster and Nepal Red Cross to plan relief activities.
- EwF researchers provided advice to the UN Resident Coordinator's office.
- EwF monitored landsliding through the 2015 monsoon, providing important scientific insights.
- EwF interacted with colleagues in Nepal (National Seismic Center), India and California to monitor the areas adjacent to the 2015 rupture, which are thought to be particularly vulnerable to future large earthquakes.

- EwF scientists contributed to several high-profile publications on the Gorkha earthquake, including in *Science* and *Nature Geoscience*.
- EwF social scientists were involved in supporting earthquake victim–survivors throughout the disaster cycle from relief and recovery to income generation as part of reconstruction.
- EwF were invited to carry out two substantial reviews: a review of the '9 Minimum Characteristics of a Disaster-Resilient Community', led by the International Federation of the Red Cross and Red Crescent and the Ministry of Foreign Affairs and Local Development, supported by the DfID South Asia Research Hub, to inform future Community Based Disaster Risk Reduction policy and practice in Nepal.
- EwF was invited by the UN to prepare an earthquake scenario led by social scientists for use in contingency planning by the Humanitarian Country Team (consisting of major UN organisations and major NGOs).

Conclusion

The NERC–ESRC Increasing Resilience to Natural Hazards Programme funded bold experiments in transdisciplinary research. Looking back, the level of distrust revealed by the Community Survey was exaggerated. UK science has worked out new ways of transdisciplinary working to increase resilience to natural hazards in ODA countries. With substantial large-scale funding for challenge-led transdisciplinary research from GCRF, the IRNH programme seems remarkably prescient. The wisdom gained in transdisciplinary working needs be taken up by research councils, universities and government.

The success of the IRNH programme was revealed following the 2015 Gorkha earthquake. The EwF consortium delivered not only high-quality research, but also significant and long-lasting societal benefits locally and nationally in Nepal and other ODA countries, high-level science advice to the UK government, and internationally in the United Nations (UN). This lends to great optimism: GCRF projects can bring significant societal benefits to ODA countries.

References

Alexander, D. E. (2013). Resilience and disaster risk reduction: An etymological journey. *Natural Hazards and Earth System Sciences*, 1, 1257–1284.

Bahadur, A., Ibrahim, M., and Tanneret, T. (2010). *The resilience renaissance? Unpacking of resilience for tackling climate change and disasters*, 1, IDS, University of Sussex.

BIS (2017, April 29). *The allocation of science and research funding*. Available on www.gov.uk/government/uploads/system/uploads/attachment_data/file/505308/bis-16-160-allocation-science-research-funding-2016-17-2019–20.pdf

Cabinet Office (2017, May 1). *Resilience in society: Infrastructure, communities and businesses*. Available on www.gov.uk/guidance/resilience-in-society-infrastructure-communities-and-businesses

Castleden, M., McKee, M., Murray, V. and Leonardi, G. (2011). Resilience thinking in health protection. *Journal of Public Health*, 33, 1–9. doi: 10.1093/pubmed/fdr027

Davies, T., Beaven, S., Conradson, D., Densmore, A., Gaillard, J. C., Johnston, D., Milledge, D., Oven, K., Petley, D., Rigg, J., Robinson, T., Rosser, N., Wilson, T. (2015). Towards disaster resilience: A scenario-based approach to co-producing and integrating hazard and risk knowledge. *International Journal of Disaster Risk Reduction* 13: 242–247. doi: dx.doi.org/10.1016/j.ijdrr.2015.05.009

Densmore, A. (2011). *Building rural resilience in seismically active regions: Scoping study final report*. Available on www.nerc.ac.uk/research/funded/programmes/resilience/densmore/ Accessed 4 November 2017, page 2.

Dominelli, L. (2012). *Green social work: From environmental crises to social justice*. Cambridge: Polity Press.

Dominelli, L. (2017). Green social work and the uptake by the Nepal school of social work: Building resilience in disaster stricken communities. In L. Bracken (Ed.), *The Gorkha Earthquake*. London: Palgrave Macmillan.

EEFIT, Pomonis, A., Saito, K., Fraser, S., Chian, S. C., Goda, K., Macabuag, J., Offord, M., Raby, A., and Sammonds, P. (2011). *The M_w 9.0 Tohoku earthquake and Tsunami of 11th March 2011: A field report by EEFIT*. London: UK Institution of Structural Engineers, Earthquake Engineering Field Investigation Team.

England, P. and Jackson, J. (2011). Uncharted seismic risk. *Nature Geoscience*, 4: 348–349. doi: 10.1038/ngeo1168

EwF (Earthquake without Frontiers) (2013). *Earthquake without Frontiers Annual Report 2013*. London: Overseas Development Institute.

EwF (Earthquake without Frontiers) (2014). *Earthquake without Frontiers Annual Report 2014*. London: Overseas Development Institute.

EwF (Earthquake without Frontiers) (2015). *Earthquake Science and Hazard in Central Asia*. London: Overseas Development Institute.

EwF (2017, May 1). *Earthquakes without Frontiers*. Available on www.cam.ac.uk/research/news/earthquakes-without-frontiers/ Accessed 30 October 2017.

Gilchrist, R., and Jeffs, T. (2001). *Settlements, social change and community action: Good neighbours*. London: Jessica Kingsley Publishers.

Hirsch Hadorn, G., Biber-Klemm, S., Grossenbacher-Mansuy, W., Hoffmann-Riem, H., Joye, D., Pohl, C., Wiesmann, U. and Zemp, E. (2008). Idea of the handbook. In Hirsch Hadorn, G., Hoffmann-Riem, H., Biber-Klemm, S., Grossenbacher-Mansuy, W., Joye, D., Pohl, C., Wiesmann, U. and Zemp, E. (Eds.), *Handbook of transdisciplinary research*. Berlin: Springer, p. 3.

Hoffmann-Riem, H., Biber-Klemm, S., Grossenbacher-Mansuy, W., Hirsch Hadorn, G., Joye, D., Pohl, C., Wiesmann, U. and Zemp, E. (2008). Idea of the Handbook. In Hirsch Hadorn, G., Hoffmann-Riem, H., Biber-Klemm, S., Grossenbacher-Mansuy, W., Joye, D., Pohl, C., Wiesmann, U. and Zemp, E. (Eds.), *Handbook of transdisciplinary research*. Berlin: Springer, pp. 19–39.

Klein, J. T., Grossenbacher-Mansuy, W., Häberli, R., Bill, A., Scholz, R. W. and Welti, M. (2001). *Transdisciplinarity: Joint problem-solving among science. An effective way for managing complexity*. Birkhäuser Verlag: Basel.

Lane, S., Odoni, N., Landström, C., Whatmore, S., Ward, N. and Bradley, S. (2011). Doing flood risk science differently: An experiment in radical scientific method. Transactions of the Institute of British Geographers, 36, 15–36. doi: 10.1111/j.1475-5661.2010.00410.x

Musson, R. M. W. (2012). *The million death quake*. London: Palgrave Macmillan.

NERC (2009). *Natural hazards theme action plan 2009*, Swindon: Natural Environment Research Council.

NERC (2017). *Building resilience*, April 30. Available on www.nerc.ac.uk/research/partnerships/international/gcrf/news/brnh/

Oven, K. J., Milledge, D. G., Densmore, A. L., Jones, H., Sargeant, S. and Datta, A. (2016). *Earthquake science in DRR policy and practice in Nepal*. Working Paper. London: Overseas Development Institute.

Oxford Innovation (2011). *Community survey report for the IRNH programme*, Oxford: Oxford Innovation.

RCUK (2017). *Global challenges research fund*, April 29. Available on www.rcuk.ac.uk/funding/gcrf/

Sim, T., Dominelli, L. and Lau, J. (2017). A pathway to initiate bottom-up community-based disaster risk reduction within a top-down system: The case of China. *International Journal of Safety and Security Engineering*, 7, 283–293.

STREVA (2017). *Strengthening resilience in volcanic areas*, April 30. Available on http://streva.ac.uk

Thywissen, K. (2006). Core terminology of disaster reduction: a comparative glossary. In J. Birkmann (Ed.), *Measuring vulnerability to natural hazards – towards disaster resilient societies*. Hong Kong: United Nations University Press, pp. 448–496.

3

Disasters, health impacts and the value of implementing the *Sendai Framework for Disaster Risk Reduction 2015–2030*

Virginia Murray, Lorcan Clarke and Rishma Maini

Introduction

Disasters disrupt the functioning of communities, involving widespread human, health, material, economic or environmental losses and impacts. Disasters may result from natural or man-made causes, and have serious implications for health (including deaths, injuries, infectious diseases, chemical contamination and psychosocial effects) (UNISDR, 2015). Disasters, by definition, are events that exceed the ability of the affected community to cope using its own resources. The health effects that occur will depend on the type of disaster, where the disaster took place and the population's capacity to cope.

According to Dominelli:

> the aim of green social work is to work for the reform of the socio-political and economic forces that have a deleterious impact upon the quality of life of poor and marginalised populations, secure the policy changes and social transformations necessary for enhancing the well-being of people and the planet today and in the future and advance the duty to care for others and the right to be cared by others.
>
> *(Dominelli, 2012: 25)*

This chapter seeks to link green social work and its implementation to the urgent need for disaster risk reduction that is so clearly articulated by the UN member states' voluntary adoption of the *Sendai Framework for Disaster Risk Reduction 2015–2030* in UN General Assembly resolution 69/283 (UNGA, 2015a).

The emergence of UN frameworks on disaster risk reduction and their links to social vulnerability

The United Nations (UN) has formally recognised the need to address the issues of disasters and their implications on social, health and environmental factors, and sustainable development over the last four decades with relevant instruments adopted at the General Assembly. A summary of these by timeline is shown in Figure 3.1.

Structured programmes displayed in Figure 3.1 began with the 1989 launch of the IDNDR or *International Decade for Natural Disaster Reduction* (UNGA, 1989). From the outset, the IDNDR programme sought inclusion for resource-constrained and marginalised populations. At an international level, the IDNDR acknowledged: 'the need for the United Nations system to pay special attention to the least developed, land-locked and island developing countries in that regard' (UNGA, 1989: 2). Furthermore, the IDNDR included in its national policy recommendations the need to consider facilities which are crucial to the infrastructure of green social work. This was noted as follows:

> To pay due attention to the impact of natural disasters on health care, particularly to activities to reduce the vulnerability of hospitals and health centres, as well as the impact on food storage facilities, human shelter and other social and economic infrastructures.
>
> *(UNGA, 1989: 3)*

Five years later, the First Global Platform for Disaster Risk Reduction was held in Yokohama, Japan in 1994, the outputs of which formed the *Yokohama Strategy and Plan of Action for a Safer World: Guidelines for National Disaster Prevention, Preparedness and Mitigation* (UNGA, 1994). Within the document's 20 pages was a coherent outlining of priorities and concerns for action in the context of disasters, with specific reference made to the same concerns addressed by green social work. This is clear from the document's outset, as immediately following the introduction is the first point of affirmation that 'those usually most affected by natural and other disasters are the poor and socially disadvantaged groups in developing countries as they are least equipped to cope with them' (World Conference on Natural Disaster Reduction, 1994: 4). This is compounded by the concern that 'some patterns of consumption, production and development have the potential for increasing the vulnerability to natural disasters, particularly of the poor and socially disadvantaged groups' (World Conference on Natural Disaster Reduction, 1994: 9).

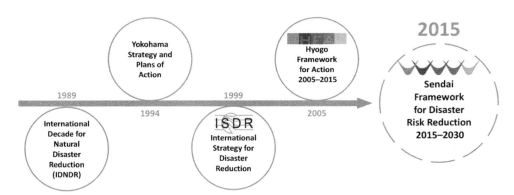

Figure 3.1 Timeline of establishment of disaster-related instruments by the UN. Instruments referenced: International Decade for Natural Disaster Reduction (IDNDR), Yokohama Strategy and Plan of Action for a Safer World: Guidelines for National Disaster Prevention, Preparedness and Mitigation, International Strategy for Disaster Reduction, Hyogo Framework for Action 2005–2015: Building the Resilience of Nations and Communities to Disasters, Sendai Framework for Disaster Risk Reduction 2015–2030

Source: adapted from Maskrey (2015) (reproduced with permission)

Addressing this was kept in mind in national policy recommendations, which also extended to the need to 'stimulate genuine community involvement and empowerment of women and other socially disadvantaged groups at all stages of disaster management programmes in order to facilitate capacity building, which is an essential precondition for reducing vulnerability of communities to natural disasters' (World Conference on Natural Disaster Reduction, 1994: 15). In 1999, the UN agreed to set up the International Strategy for Disaster Reduction (UNGA, 1999). This formalised global efforts to address disasters in a specific UN body, the United Nations International Strategy for Disaster Reduction (UNISDR). In the founding of UNISDR, previous social concerns ratified with 'deep concern' were expressed as: 'massive losses of life and long-term negative social, economic and environmental consequences for vulnerable societies worldwide, in particular in developing countries' (UNGA, 2000: 2).

UNISDR supported continued progression and global engagement in 2005 at the Second World Conference on Disaster Reduction in Kobe, Japan. This resulted in the adoption of the *Hyogo Framework for Action 2005–2015: Building the Resilience of Nations and Communities to Disasters* (UNGA, 2006). Concern for outcomes of vulnerable communities continued and was augmented in the Hyogo Framework, with an increased focus on engagement processes. Of particular note were broader aspects of resilience included in the reduction of underlying risk factors, such as to:

> Strengthen the implementation of social safety-net mechanisms to assist the poor, the elderly and the disabled, and other populations affected by disasters. Enhance recovery schemes including psycho-social training programmes in order to mitigate the psychological damage of vulnerable populations, particularly children, in the aftermath of disasters.
> *(UNISDR, 2005: paragraph 19(g))*

The Hyogo Framework's 'General considerations' were coherent with green social work goals, advocating that 'a gender perspective should be integrated into all disaster risk management policies, plans and decision-making processes, including those related to risk assessment, early warning, information management, and education and training'. Importantly, the Hyogo Framework included a common accepted definition for vulnerability, defining it as 'The conditions determined by physical, social, economic, and environmental factors or processes, which increase the susceptibility of a community to the impact of hazards' (UNISDR, 2009: 16). In sum, coherence with the aims of green social work has existed within disaster risk reduction mechanisms for some time, and will continue to do so under the current guidance provided by the *Sendai Framework for Disaster Risk Reduction 2015–2030 (Sendai Framework)*. This successor to the *Hyogo Framework* was produced in March 2015 at the Third UN World Conference on Disaster Risk Reduction hosted in Sendai, Japan (UNGA, 2015a). The following section outlines in further detail the aspects of the *Sendai Framework* which apply to and support the aims of green social work programmes.

Green social work in the context of the *Sendai Framework for Disaster Risk Reduction 2015–2030*

From the outset, the *Sendai Framework* recognises the complex and uneven impact of disasters and the non-uniform distribution of risk within and between societies. This is a worrying reality, compounded further by exposure to disaster risk which is greater than the effect of measures that reduce vulnerability:

> Disasters, many of which are exacerbated by climate change and which are increasing in frequency and intensity, significantly impede progress towards sustainable development.

> Evidence indicates that exposure of persons and assets in all countries has increased faster than vulnerability has decreased, thus generating new risks and a steady rise in disaster related losses, with a significant economic, social, health, cultural and environmental impact in the short, medium and long term, especially at the local and community levels. Recurring small-scale disasters and slow-onset disasters particularly affect communities, households and small and medium-sized enterprises, constituting a high percentage of all losses. All countries – especially developing countries, where the mortality and economic losses from disasters are disproportionately higher – are faced with increasing levels of possible hidden costs and challenges in order to meet financial and other obligations.
>
> *(UNISDR, 2015: Paragraph 4)*

Within this context, the goal of the *Sendai Framework* is to:

> prevent new and reduce existing disaster risk through the implementation of integrated and inclusive economic, structural, legal, social, health, cultural, educational, environmental, technological, political and institutional measures that prevent and reduce hazard exposure and vulnerability to disaster, increase preparedness for response and recovery, and thus strengthen resilience.
>
> *(UNISDR, 2015: Paragraph 17)*

The stated aim of the *Sendai Framework* is all-encompassing by design. In this respect, it is similar to the goal of green social work (Dominelli, 2012).

In the section on Guiding Principles (Section III), the *Sendai Framework* notes that the implementation of the *Framework* will be guided by principles, which take into account national circumstances, and that these should be consistent with domestic laws as well as international obligations and commitments. Within this section, the need to promote and protect all human rights including the right to development is recognised:

> Managing the risk of disasters is aimed at protecting persons and their property, health, livelihoods and productive assets, as well as cultural and environmental assets, while promoting and protecting all human rights, including the right to development.
>
> *(UNISDR, 2015: Paragraph 19c)*

By taking into account the experience gained through the implementation of the *Hyogo Framework for Action*, and in pursuance of the expected outcome and goal, the *Sendai Framework* identified four priorities for action within and across sectors by UN States at the local, national, regional and global levels. These priorities are:

> **Priority 1:** Understanding disaster risk.
> **Priority 2:** Strengthening disaster risk governance to manage disaster risk.
> **Priority 3:** Investing in disaster risk reduction for resilience.
> **Priority 4:** Enhancing disaster preparedness for effective response and to 'Build Back Better' in recovery, rehabilitation and reconstruction.
>
> *(UNISDR, 2015: Paragraph 20)*

Within each priority are statements requiring actions that are applicable to the green social work model. In *Priority 1: Understanding disaster risk* at national and local levels, the *Framework* has identified the need to systematically document disaster losses and understand their social and health impacts:

> To systematically evaluate, record, share and publicly account for disaster losses and understand the economic, social, health, education, environmental and cultural heritage impacts, as appropriate, in the context of event-specific hazard-exposure and vulnerability information.
>
> *(UNISDR, 2015: Paragraph 24 d)*

Thus in *Priority 2: Strengthening disaster risk governance to manage disaster risk* at national and local levels, the *Framework* has identified that governance itself is essential. Within green social work and other domains such accountability is of import if the following call for action is to be implemented:

> To adopt and implement national and local disaster risk reduction strategies and plans, across different timescales, with targets, indicators and time frames, aimed at preventing the creation of risk, the reduction of existing risk and the strengthening of economic, social, health and environmental resilience.
>
> *(UNISDR, 2015: Paragraph 27 b)*

In *Priority 3: Investing in disaster risk reduction for resilience* at national and local levels, the *Framework* has identified the need for inclusive policies and social safety-net mechanisms that need to be inclusive. It advocates:

> To strengthen the design and implementation of inclusive policies and social safety-net mechanisms, including through community involvement, integrated with livelihood enhancement programmes, and access to basic health-care services, including maternal, newborn and child health, sexual and reproductive health, food security and nutrition, housing and education, towards the eradication of poverty, to find durable solutions in the post-disaster phase and to empower and assist people disproportionately affected by disasters.
>
> *(UNISDR, 2015: Paragraph 30 c)*

Additionally in *Priority 3: Investing in disaster risk reduction for resilience* at global and regional levels, the *Framework* has identified that it is necessary to develop social safety nets, such as social development and welfare programmes, in order to ensure resilience at household and community levels:

> To promote and support the development of social safety nets as disaster risk reduction measures linked to and integrated with livelihood enhancement programmes in order to ensure resilience to shocks at the household and community levels.
>
> *(UNISDR, 2015: Paragraph 31 g)*

In *Priority 4: Enhancing disaster preparedness for effective response and to 'Build Back Better' in recovery, rehabilitation and reconstruction* at national and local levels, the *Framework* has identified the crucial need for socially and culturally relevant early warning systems:

> To invest in, develop, maintain and strengthen people-centred multi-hazard, multi-sectoral forecasting and early warning systems, disaster risk and emergency communications

mechanisms, social technologies and hazard-monitoring telecommunications systems; develop such systems through a participatory process; tailor them to the needs of users, including social and cultural requirements, in particular gender; promote the application of simple and low-cost early warning equipment and facilities; and broaden release channels for natural disaster early warning information.

(UNISDR, 2015: Paragraph 33 b)

In Section VI of the *Sendai Framework*, addressing international cooperation and global partnership, it is important that green social workers note the similarities in the call for improving the social, health and economic well-being of individuals, communities and countries by using partnerships across the world. It is articulated as follows:

North-South cooperation, complemented by South-South and triangular cooperation, has proven to be key to reducing disaster risk and there is a need to further strengthen cooperation in both areas. Partnerships play an additional important role by harnessing the full potential of countries and supporting their national capacities in disaster risk management and in improving the social, health and economic well-being of individuals, communities and countries.

(UNISDR, 2015: Paragraph 44)

The *Sendai Framework* places unprecedented emphasis on the role of science and technology and the building of partnerships and networks including health in disaster risk reduction and calls for a strengthening of platforms, and research summarised as follows:

To enhance the scientific and technical work on disaster risk reduction and its mobilization through the coordination of existing networks and scientific research institutions at all levels and in all regions, with the support of the United Nations Office for Disaster Risk Reduction Scientific and Technical Advisory Group, in order to

- strengthen the evidence base in support of the implementation of the present *Framework*;
- promote scientific research on disaster risk patterns, causes and effects;
- disseminate risk information with the best use of geospatial information technology;
- provide guidance on methodologies and standards for risk assessments, disaster risk modelling and the use of data;
- identify research and technology gaps and set recommendations for research priority areas in disaster risk reduction;
- promote and support the availability and application of science and technology to decision-making;
- contribute to the update of the publication entitled *2009 UNISDR Terminology on Disaster Risk Reduction*;
- use post-disaster reviews as opportunities to enhance learning and public policy;
- disseminate studies.

(UNISDR, 2015: Paragraph 25 g)

The emphasis on health and science and technology evidence and partnerships building is applicable for demonstrating the value of green social work and offers an opportunity and challenge as a valuable outcome.

The *Sendai Framework* also includes for the first time in 25 years of international commitments to disaster risk reduction, a series of global targets. Each country's national targets and indicators will contribute to the achievement of the outcome and goal of the present *Framework* and will feed into the determination of the seven global targets, which are:

(a) Substantially reduce global disaster mortality by 2030, aiming to lower the average per 100,000 global mortality rate in the decade 2020–2030 compared to the period 2005–2015;
(b) Substantially reduce the number of affected people globally by 2030, aiming to lower the average global figure per 100,000 in the decade 2020–2030 compared to the period 2005–2015;
(c) Reduce direct disaster economic loss in relation to global gross domestic product (GDP) by 2030;
(d) Substantially reduce disaster damage to critical infrastructure and disruption of basic services, among them health and educational facilities, including through developing their resilience by 2030;
(e) Substantially increase the number of countries with national and local disaster risk reduction strategies by 2020;
(f) Substantially enhance international cooperation to developing countries through adequate and sustainable support to complement their national actions for implementation of the present *Framework* by 2030;
(g) Substantially increase the availability of and access to multi-hazard early warning systems and disaster risk information and assessments to people by 2030.

(UNISDR, 2015: Paragraph 18)

Science and technology are needed to deliver the agreed global targets and their indicators. Of the seven targets, four address disaster losses (A, B, C and D), which in an overarching sense are coherent with the goals of green social work. Target B is particularly relevant, due to its focus upon the reduction of the number of people affected by disasters globally. The component indicators by which progress will be assessed were confirmed by the UN General Assembly in February 2017, following working group efforts in 2015 and throughout 2016 (UNGA, 2017). These are as follows:

B-1 (compound) Number of directly affected people attributed to disasters, per 100,000 population.
B-2 Number of injured or ill people attributed to disasters, per 100,000 population.
B-3 Number of people whose damaged dwellings were attributed to disasters.
B-4 Number of people whose destroyed dwellings were attributed to disasters.
B-5 Number of people whose livelihoods were disrupted or destroyed, attributed to disasters.

(UNGA, 2016: 5)

Given that the term *'affected'* encompasses a large swathe of eligible variables, it is emphasised that no indicator can provide an absolutely precise, accurate and exhaustive measure of affected populations.

In the agreed terminology summarised in the recommendations of the open-ended intergovernmental expert working group on terminology relating to disaster risk reduction (UNGA, 2017), 'affected' is defined as:

> **Affected**
>
> 'People who are affected, either directly or indirectly, by a hazardous event. Directly affected are those who have suffered injury, illness or other health effects; who were evacuated, displaced, relocated or have suffered direct damage to their livelihoods, economic, physical, social, cultural and environmental assets. Indirectly affected are people who have suffered consequences, other than or in addition to direct effects, over time, due to disruption or changes in economy, critical infrastructure, basic services, commerce or work, or social, health and psychological consequences.
>
> *Annotation:* People can be affected directly or indirectly. Affected people may experience short-term or long-term consequences to their lives, livelihoods or health and to their economic, physical, social, cultural and environmental assets. In addition, people who are missing or dead may be considered as directly affected' (UNGA, 2016: 11).

Individual estimations of directly affected can be subjective, dependent on the methodology and criteria used in data collection. For these reasons, 'directly affected' is assessed rather than 'indirectly affected', as a proxy for the number of persons impacted by disasters.

Furthermore, it is important to note that the *Sendai Framework* adopted an 'all-hazards' approach to disaster risk reduction (UNISDR, 2015). This implies that hazards of all types and scales are included in vulnerability reduction practices, a strategy which encompasses the plethora of projects which fall under the banner of green social work. Any efforts that directly affect the well-being of individuals are present in Target B of the *Sendai Framework*.

Indicator B-5 provides the strongest hook for aligning the purposes of the *Sendai Framework* with support for green social work practices. It is consistent with the people-centred approach of the Sustainable Development Goals (UNGA, 2015b). It addresses one of the long-term multiplier effects of disasters and offers a proxy for individuals' well-being. It also offers project funders and policymakers a global standard against which to assess progress.

The *Sendai Framework* and health impacts

Though general themes have clear roots in the disaster risk reductions frameworks and strategies that have been put in place since 1989, connections made to health have been scarce. Of the original strategy documents prior to the *Sendai Framework* there is little, if any, direct reference made to 'health'. However by 2015, following sustained and significant effort to do so, 'health' has taken up a far greater role in disaster risk reduction strategy; 'health' appears 38 times in the published version of the *Sendai Framework for Disaster Risk Reduction 2015–2030*, and is specifically targeted within two of the seven global targets, namely Targets A and B.

This weight of inclusion of 'health' in the *Sendai Framework* is in recognition of the need for a holistic approach to the management of risks associated with natural and human-induced hazards. This approach ensures that individuals and societies are resilient to shocks of all kinds. Furthermore, in keeping with the *Sendai Framework's* focus upon actionable statements, the following excerpts are noted for their relationship with health and also to ensure that such actions are effectively carried out within green social work:

Paragraph 18: Inclusion of health related global targets – Target A and Target B – for monitoring and reporting on disaster risk management.

Paragraph 30(i): Recommended at national and local levels:

> To enhance the resilience of national health systems, including by integrating disaster risk management into primary, secondary and tertiary health care, especially at the local level; developing the capacity of health workers in understanding disaster risk and applying and implementing disaster risk reduction approaches in health work; promoting and enhancing the training capacities in the field of disaster medicine; and supporting and training community health groups in disaster risk reduction approaches in health programmes, in collaboration with other sectors, as well as in the implementation of the International Health Regulations (IHR, 2005) of the World Health Organization (WHO).

Paragraph 30(j): Recommended at national and local levels:

> To strengthen the design and implementation of inclusive policies and social safety-net mechanisms, including through community involvement, integrated with livelihood enhancement programmes, and access to basic health-care services, including maternal, newborn and child health, sexual and reproductive health, food security and nutrition, housing and education, towards the eradication of poverty, to find durable solutions in the post-disaster phase and to empower and assist people disproportionately affected by disasters.

Paragraph 30(k): Recommended at national and local levels:

> People with life-threatening and chronic disease, due to their particular needs, should be included in the design of policies and plans to manage their risks before, during and after disasters, including having access to life-saving services.

Paragraph 33(c): Recommended at national and local levels:

> To promote the resilience of new and existing critical infrastructure, including water, transportation and telecommunications infrastructure, educational facilities, hospitals and other health facilities, to ensure that they remain safe, effective and operational during and after disasters in order to provide live-saving and essential services.

Paragraph 33(o): Recommended at national and local levels:

> To enhance recovery schemes to provide psychosocial support and mental health services for all people in need.

Paragraph 33(n): Recommended at national and local levels:

> Establishing a mechanism of case registry and a database of mortality caused by disaster in order to improve the prevention of morbidity and mortality.

(UNISDR, 2015)

Strengthening and integrating public health and disaster management measures will increase the resilience of those at risk. Health strategies must be developed to reduce the health impacts of disasters, both before (preparedness), during and after (response) an event occurs. Issues associated with the stages of the disaster management cycle in: prevention, preparedness, early warning and detection, response and recovery all require planning for disaster prevention. Health planning and relief measures are essential in order to minimise the impacts of disasters on vulnerable populations.

Ensuring that green social work is recorded and reported

Opportunity to implement coherence in action has been ever-present in global agreements that preceded the *Sendai Framework*. The founding document of the International Decade for Natural Disaster Reduction stressed the need for *'concerted international action'* (UNGA, 1989). Through the lens of history, green social work has coherence with themes outlined in the common goals and priorities of the international disaster risk reduction community for almost three decades. The *Sendai Framework* offers more than the most recent iteration of this. Rather, it coherently outlines the strategy for disaster risk reduction and areas to address which can lead to goals that can be assessed. Though a voluntary agreement, it has been signed up to by heads of UN member states, and activities ensuring its completion are to the benefit of domestic prosperity and international reputation.

Efforts to improve community resilience and response to disasters fall closely in line with green social work, and it is important to understand the impact that these efforts have. This makes technical guidance for collating activities absolutely critical. In turn, a lack of agreed standards prevents the sharing and reliable comparison of information and evidence. Thus, it is recommended that common data principles are used in implementation and assessment by green social work, and that a common database of projects is developed and maintained to ensure due assessment and understanding can take place to ensure effective efforts are sustained and augmented. To ensure the protection and augmentation of information quality, it is recommended that National Statistics Offices are functionally autonomous, and independent of sector ministries and political influence.

In light of this call to action, it is recommended that green social work projects are carried out with common reporting principles and characteristics including, but not limited to being:

- *Useful* – Data collected must be applicable to any country in the world and, to the maximum degree possible, allow comparison among countries or regions. Results should be usable not only for measuring achievement, but also for strategy planning and related policies. It should meet the needs of users in a timely manner (ONS, 2017).
- *Feasible* – Data should be easy to collect regardless of the level of development or income of each country. Data collection should not pose an impossible burden to countries. Existing systems should be used as much as possible to maximise efficiency (ONS, 2017).
- *Transparent* – The method used for collecting data should be well established, with any caveats or limitations declared. Underlying design of sampling, methods, tools and datasets should be explained and published alongside findings (IEAG, 2014). Moreover, this extends to data being 'open by default' when projects are carried out using public funds, with narrow exemptions for genuine security or privacy concerns. This implies both technical and legal openness being present with respect to accessibility and sharing protocols. Ultimately this will enable greater scrutiny, understanding and independent analysis of information as it produced.
- *Consistent* – In order to robustly compare interventions over time and across countries, data must be recorded and reported in a consistent way. A continuous view of implementation effects is essential to avoid biases and other inconsistencies that can reduce the reliability of information (ONS, 2017).
- *Relevant* – In order to ensure data are relevant, users and their expectations need to be identified (UNSTATS, 2002).
- *Complete* – Areas for which statistics are available should reflect the needs and priorities expressed by the users (UNSTATS, 2002). Completeness is an extension to relevance, for

completeness does not only mean that statistics should serve user needs but also they should serve them as completely as possible, taking restricted resources into account.

Furthermore, it is recommended that green social work reporting adopts a clear definition of standards in coordinating efforts at national and international levels. Definition standards would take the form of taxonomies in this field of work, which are established and controlled vocabularies of precise and agreed terms, ideally structured in a hierarchical relationship. Data standards such as these extend to the use of common terminologies (controlled vocabularies) and constructing agreements as to how the data are represented and encoded in reporting.

Green social work shares a core aim of the international frameworks and agreements developed to guide practice in the Sustainable Development Era, that local, poor and marginalised populations are actively engaged in the production and carrying out of policy platforms. Data disaggregation is therefore essential to reporting of activities. Just as established taxonomies are needed for data reporting in general, they are of further importance and coherence in the disaggregation of data. Example categories for disaggregation include: hazard type, geography, income, sex, age, disability, type of subject of impact (i.e. livelihoods, specific types of livelihoods).

With these principles in mind, common issues with data sources and data collection should also be taken into account in reporting green social work practices in the context of disasters. The following framing principles are listed to provide an insight into the considerations necessary for practitioners to make to ensure that the health and wider impacts of their work is efficiently recorded, analysed and reported:

- *Temporal* – Periods of time need to be clearly defined for which disaster loss and damage data is recorded and reported. This accounts for improvements in loss estimates over time following disasters, augmented through increased amounts of information and more accurate data. Defining time periods is critical, especially in the accurate recording of slow-onset disasters losses (e.g. drought).
- *Thresholds* – There is no common international standard used for reporting thresholds in metadata (i.e. disaggregation by age). This needs to be taken into account in reporting practices.
- *Attribution* – Indirect and multiplier effects from disaster losses can make attribution challenging (Stanke et al., 2013).
- *Coverage* – Systematic collection of data is not a given, and methods to assess impact may need to be developed to understand baseline data from which impact can be assessed. Furthermore, gaps in coverage offer clear indications of where strengthening is required.
- *Precision* – Uncertainty and bias can arise in data collection. Basic but systemic problems such as double-counting (between disaggregated groups), should be accounted for and have verified methods of address (ONS, 2017).
- *Reporting lag* – The time between registration and reporting of data can decrease data validity. It is also connected with other reporting challenges such as temporal and threshold framing, whose validity are connected closely with time of record.

Way forward for green social work

Collaboration between green social work and the work to implement the three landmark UN 2015 agreements, a group which includes the *Sendai Framework*, will help ensure more rapid progress. By leveraging global support for capacity development, the green social work community along with healthcare professional partners, academia, and a range of other stakeholders will help ensure that all countries can produce, access and effectively use scientific information for disaster risk reduction in terms of lives, livelihoods and health.

The *Sendai Framework* puts unprecedented emphasis on the role of science and building partnerships in understanding and delivering risk reduction. It reflects shifts in scientific thinking over the last 20 years, with a powerful message that disasters are not natural events against which human societies are powerless, but are the result of the interaction between hazards (natural and human-made), exposure levels and pre-existing vulnerability, some of which may be related to human behaviours and actions.

Important recommendations of the *Sendai Framework* to the scientific community and its partners, including emerging groups such as the green social work community, are to improve the scientific and public understanding of risk and optimise the use of science for decision-making. The *Framework* highlights the importance of outbreaks and epidemics, chronic disease management, psychosocial interventions and rehabilitation as part of disaster recovery and makes several references to the International Health Regulations (IHR). The IHR have been designed to assist the global community in preventing and responding to acute public health risks that have the potential to cross borders and threaten people worldwide (WHO, 2005).

The *Sendai Framework* is a strong call to action for improving decision-making through a stronger science–policy–practice nexus with one expected outcome: 'The substantial reduction of disaster risk and losses in lives, livelihoods and health', and one goal to: 'Prevent new and reduce existing disaster risk through the implementation of integrated and inclusive measures that prevent and reduce hazard exposure and vulnerability to disaster, increase preparedness for response and recovery, and thus strengthen resilience'.

Some consider that reconnecting science and emerging groups such as the green social work community with policy and practice are among the important tasks in implementing the *Sendai Framework*, particularly to support people in low- and middle-income countries and especially minority groups and women. A large body of research exists to support political and financial investment in the eradication and disruption of both the intergenerational transmission of poverty and the perpetuation of socioeconomic inequalities. With rising vulnerability and exposure through urbanisation and demographic change, the importance of disaster preparedness can no longer be ignored, and the green social work community are needed to help us deliver on this vital agenda.

References

Dominelli, L. (2012). *Green social work: From environmental crises to environmental justice.* Cambridge: Polity Press.

Independent Expert Advisory Group on a Data Revolution for Sustainable Development (IEAG) (2014). *A world that counts.* Available on www.undatarevolution.org/wpcontent/uploads/2014/11/A-World-That-Counts.pdf [Accessed 20 April 2017].

Maskrey, A. (2015). Twenty five years of international commitments to disaster risk reduction. *Launch of the 2015 Global Assessment Report on Disaster Risk Reduction.* Geneva, Switzerland: UNISDR.

Office for National Statistics UK (ONS) (2017). *Guidelines for measuring statistical quality.* Available on https://unstats.un.org/unsd/dnss/docs-nqaf/UK-Guidelines_Subject.pdf [Accessed 20 April 2017].

Stanke, C., Kerac, M., Prudhomme, C., Medlock, J. and Murray, V. (2013). Health effects of drought: A systematic review of the evidence. *PLOS Currents Disasters.* doi:10.1371/currents.dis.7a2cee9e980f91ad7 697b570bcc4b004 [Accessed 20 April 2017].

United Nations Department of Economic and Social Affairs Statistics Division (UNSTATS) (2002). *Interagency meeting on coordination of statistical activities: Dimensions of statistical quality.* Available on https://unstats.un.org/unsd/accsub/2002docs/sa-02-6add1.pdf [Accessed 28 February 2017].

United Nations General Assembly (UNGA) (22 December 1989). *International decade for natural disaster reduction*, A/RES/44/236. Available on www.un.org/documents/ga/res/44/a44r236.htm [Accessed 20 April 2017].

United Nations General Assembly (UNGA) (13 December 1994). *International decade for natural disaster reduction [International framework for action and operationalisation of the Yokohama strategy]*, A/RES/49/22. Available on www.unisdr.org/files/resolutions/N9460117.pdf [Accessed 20 April 2017].

United Nations General Assembly (UNGA) (1 December 1999). *Environment and sustainable development: International decade for natural disaster reduction: Report of the second committee*, A/58/588/Add.2. Available on www.unisdr.org/files/resolutions/N9936925.pdf [Accessed 20 April 2017].

United Nations General Assembly (UNGA) (3 February 2000). *International decade for natural disaster reduction: Successor arrangements*, A/RES/54/219. Available on www.unisdr.org/files/resolutions/N0027175.pdf [Accessed 20 April 2017].

United Nations General Assembly (UNGA) (2 March 2006). *International strategy for disaster reduction*, A/RES/60/195. Available on www.unisdr.org/files/resolutions/N0549930.pdf [Accessed 20 April 2017].

United Nations General Assembly (UNGA) (23 June 2015a). *Sendai framework for disaster risk reduction 2015–2030*, A/RES/69/283. Available on www.preventionweb.net/files/resolutions/N1516716.pdf [Accessed 20 April 2017].

United Nations General Assembly (UNGA) (25 September 2015b). Transforming our world: The 2030 agenda for sustainable development, A/RES/70/1. Available on http://undocs.org/en/A/RES/70/1 [Accessed 20 April 2017].

United Nations General Assembly (UNGA) (1 December 2016). *Report of the open-ended intergovernmental expert working group on indicators and terminology relating to disaster risk reduction*, A/71/644. Available on http://undocs.org/A/71/644 [Accessed 20 April 2017].

United Nation General Assembly (UNGA) (2 February 2017). Report of the open-ended intergovernmental expert working group on indicators and terminology relating to disaster risk reduction, A/RES/71/276. Available on http://undocs.org/A/RES/71/276 [Accessed 20 April 2017].

United Nations Office for Disaster Risk Reduction (UNISDR) (2005). *Hyogo framework for action 2005–2015: Building the resilience of nations and communities to disasters*. Available on www.unisdr.org/files/1037_hyogoframeworkforactionenglish.pdf [Accessed 20 April 2017].

United Nations Office for Disaster Risk Reduction (UNISDR) (2009). *2009 UNISDR terminology on disaster risk reduction*. Available on www.unisdr.org/we/inform/terminology [Accessed 20 April 2017].

United Nations Office for Disaster Risk Reduction (UNISDR) (2015). Sendai Framework for Disaster Risk Reduction 2015-2030. Available on http://www.unisdr.org/files/43291_sendaiframeworkfordrren.pdf [Accessed 21 October 2017].

World Health Organization (WHO) (2005). *International health regulations 2005*. Available on http://apps.who.int/iris/bitstream/10665/246107/1/9789241580496-eng.pdf?ua=1 [Accessed 17 March 2017].

World Conference on Natural Disaster Reduction (1994). *Yokohama strategy and plan of action for a safer world: Guidelines for national disaster prevention, preparedness and mitigation*. Available on www.unisdr.org/files/8241_doc6841contenido1.pdf [Accessed 20 April 2017].

Theory into practice section

4

The critical role of social work in disaster response

Experiences in the United Kingdom

David N. Jones

Introduction

The United Kingdom (UK), not generally exposed to serious natural disasters like major earthquakes and extreme weather events, but experiences flooding, landslides, terrorist incidents, major fires, accidents and flood risk which could increase fourfold by 2080 (Kapucu, 2009). The national 'civil protection and emergency response' strategy specifies who is responsible for: identifying and mitigating risks; responding to emergencies when they arise; and how responses are delivered. The Social Market Foundation suggests that disaster management will be one of the six key challenges for local government over the next 20 years, resulting mainly from climate change (Corfe and Keohane, 2017).

'Social workers' skills and experience are highly relevant for multidisciplinary disaster work. Of particular significance are their understanding of human behaviour, emphasis on 'person-in-environment', experience in community work and programme planning, and recognition of the value of advocacy and social justice' (Cronin and Jones, 2015: 753). Senior local authority social work managers in the UK are invariably involved in developing local disaster strategies and social work practitioners have key roles in providing post-disaster support, advice, counselling and coordinating practical assistance. Social workers in less developed countries can be among the few professional people 'on the ground' with effective links to local communities; they have a key role in disaster response (Bragin, 2010). The personal experience of being caught up in an emergency or disaster has long-lasting impact on people; personal reflection can highlight issues of general significance.

This chapter provides a brief overview of the UK's disaster response strategy and considers examples of responses to some recent disasters including a brief personal account of being caught up in a disaster. The Grenfell Tower fire happened while writing this chapter. Some of the challenges it poses to national and local government and questions to be answered by the public enquiry are identified. This is set within the context of the evolving understanding of the significance for social work of the 'natural' and built environment, and 'green social work' (Coates and Gray, 2012; Dominelli, 2012).

UK statutory framework for civil protection, emergencies and disaster responses

The UK has recognised the need for preparation for disasters and emergencies in order to mitigate the risks, prevent events from happening, respond quickly and appropriately to those which do occur, and ensure effective recovery. The nationwide framework for managing emergencies and disasters is the Civil Contingencies Act 2004 (CCA) and related statutory guidance. There is a statutory duty to keep the Act under review (Cabinet Office, 2017b). A comparison of the disaster policies of six European nations, including the UK, is summarised by Christensen et al. (2014).

An emergency (or disruptive challenge) is defined as

> a situation or series of events that threatens or causes serious damage to human welfare, the environment or security in the United Kingdom. This definition covers a wide range of scenarios including adverse weather, severe flooding, animal diseases, terrorist incidents and the impact of a disruption on essential services and critical infrastructure.
>
> *(Cabinet Office, 2013, para 1.1)*

The guiding principles, developed to capture the core characteristics of effective emergency responses and which should be applied to the management of any emergency are preparedness, continuity, subsidiarity, direction, integration, communication, co-operation and anticipation (Cabinet Office, 2013, para 1.3).

The central government mechanism for handling major national and international emergencies is coordinated by the Civil Contingencies Committee, a Cabinet committee usually chaired by the home secretary or minister from the lead department, but sometimes by the prime minister. It deals with major crises such as terrorism or major natural disasters and is supported by the Civil Contingencies Secretariat, which is part of the Cabinet Office. The Committee is generally referred to as COBRA, after the room in which it meets (Cabinet Office Briefing Room A). Relevant local officials attend. The UK Resilience website is a central source of public information on British civil defence and disaster preparedness (Cabinet Office, 2017a).

The arrangements place specific responsibilities on 'category 1 responders' – local authorities, fire and rescue services, police, health and environment agencies, with a local duty to involve all other relevant partners, such as transport and utility companies, businesses and community groups, in a 'local resilience forum' (England and Wales) (and equivalent provisions for Scotland).

The CCA sets out the local arrangements for civil protection, including:

- the definition of 'Emergency';
- the duties of the organisations covered by the CCA to assess risks, maintain plans in case of an emergency occurring, and maintain arrangements to advise and warn the public;
- requirements on organisations covered by the CCA to put in place business continuity management arrangements;
- ministerial powers to monitor and enforce the CCA's provisions; and
- lists of the Category 1 ('core') and Category 2 ('cooperating') responders. The latter includes social workers.

The CCA Regulations describe the extent of the duties imposed on organisations under the CCA and how those duties are to be performed. The main provisions cover the following:

- the requirement to cooperate in a 'local resilience forum' (England and Wales) (and equivalent provisions for Scotland), including the ability to identify lead responsibilities among responders;

- the duty of responders to assess risk and maintain a 'community risk register';
- the nature of response plans, including the requirement to have regard to the role of voluntary sector agencies and to include arrangements for exercising and training;
- the requirement to publish risk assessments and plans, and to have regard to the importance of not alarming the public unnecessarily;
- arrangements for discharging the duty to warn and inform the public;
- arrangements for the provision of advice and assistance to the public on business continuity (applies to local authorities);
- information sharing between responders, including the conditions in which information can be requested and shared;
- particular arrangements for London and Northern Ireland; and
- the requirement to conduct a review of the regulations.

The most recent systematic review of the arrangements by the Cabinet Office concluded:

> There is no specific evidence, anecdotal or from the RCS [Resilience Capabilities Survey], to suggest that major legislative change is required. In practice – based on our regular conversations with interested parties, exercises and lessons learned from real incidents – the legislative framework appears fit for purpose.
>
> *(Cabinet Office, 2017b, para 19)*

An independent review of the arrangements also claimed that the CCA arrangements 'offer a more comprehensive approach to all-hazards management of disaster' (Rogers, 2011: 91). Some elements of this conclusion may be called into question by the experience of the Grenfell Tower fire (see the 'Grenfell Tower fire (2017)' section later in this chapter) (Alexander, 2017).

Examples of responses to major incidents in the UK

Flooding

Widespread flooding in the winter of 2014–2015 affected many parts of the UK. The county of Somerset was badly hit, with some low-lying homes and villages under water for months (*BBC News*, 2014; Somerset County Council, 2014; BBC documentary, 2015). The disaster response required temporary accommodation for hundreds of households, intervention to limit flooding and action to prevent a repeat. Some argued that the flooding was made worse by failure to dredge sections of rivers and drainage ditches and environmental changes which resulted in greater water run-off. A government commissioned report argued that:

> The increase in the risk of flooding as a result of extreme weather and climate change makes it essential for local authorities and communities to engage with this issue. . . . The measures being developed include property-level protection, flood resilience groups, volunteer flood wardens and community champions, engagement with more vulnerable groups and efforts to increase financial resilience.
>
> *(Twigger-Ross et al., 2014: 1)*

Media reports suggest that flooded communities recovered quite quickly (Norwood, 2015), thanks to insurance, community action and local government support.

Crowd disasters at sporting events

A top-level football match being played at Hillsborough in Sheffield in 1989 had to be abandoned when people standing in a fenced area were crushed by too many people trying to crowd into the space. The gates were not opened to enable people to escape the crush and 96 people died. The initial police account, headlined in *The Sun* newspaper, was that deaths were the result of drinking and hooligan behaviour.

The disaster response involved arrangements for receiving and identifying the dead, providing medical treatment for those with injuries, making arrangements for formal identification of bodies, providing immediate and longer-term support to families of the deceased, and reviewing the incident for lessons to be learnt and changes made. Some have since commented that the behaviour of the first responders was disrespectful and insensitive; for example, failing to express condolences and demanding to know whether the dead person had been drinking. They also suggested that initial approaches by social workers were not welcome. People assumed that they were being assessed for whether they were a risk to their own children. Some have argued that social worker visits to family homes were too soon or not done in the right way (Professional Social Work, 2016).

A 'determined and dignified' campaign by Hillsborough Family Support Group, supported by Members of Parliament (MPs) and others, refused to accept the 'establishment' narrative and eventually persuaded the government to set up an independent enquiry (Harrison, 1999; see also Scraton, 2004; Hillsborough Independent Panel, 2012: 1). The enquiry found that events had been misrepresented and was critical of the police and other officials. The Crown Prosecution Service subsequently announced formal trials of six officials. Steen (2016: 254) compares Hillsborough with other stadium tragedies.

Distant disasters

The 2004 Pacific Tsunami resulted in the death, injury or disruption of a significant number of tourists (Masters, 2005; Pittaway et al., 2007; Larson et al., 2015). A West Sussex Social Services Department team at Gatwick airport met returning tourists and provided support and assistance. Distant disasters can have local impacts which need to be anticipated.

Terrorism

A number of terrorist incidents, usually involving bombs, have occurred in the UK over the past 30 years. The chance of any individual being involved is very slight, but hundreds of people can be affected by any one incident and a speedy response is essential to contain the incident and provide support to those affected. Emergency services and hospitals have well-rehearsed procedures. The longer-term follow-up is more complex, especially when incidents involve people from scattered populations.

The Manchester lorry bomb (1996) was preceded by an Irish Republican Army (IRA) official warning. Attempts to defuse the bomb were unsuccessful and it created massive physical damage. Over 200 people were injured but there were no fatalities largely due to the fast response of emergency services and evacuation of thousands from the area (Scheerhout, 2016; Williams, 2016). The response was coordinated from the city council incident room. Social workers were involved. The bombing came to be seen as the springboard for the rebuilding and renaissance of the city (King, 2006). Manchester suffered an earlier bombing in 1992, when two

IRA bombs exploded, wounding 65 people and damaging many buildings (Foster and McKittrick, 1992).

On 22 May 2017, a suicide bomber detonated a homemade bomb at the Manchester Arena as crowds were leaving a concert by American singer Ariana Grande, killing 23 adults and children, including the bomber, and injuring 250 (Rawlinson and Ross, 2017). The tragedy happened during the General Election campaign, which was briefly suspended. Responding to survivors' needs in the aftermath created challenges (e.g. getting them home, contacting families some distance away).

London also suffered several incidents during the IRA campaign and others recently linked to Middle East conflicts. The 7/7 bombings involved three explosions on underground trains and one bus explosion, killing 52 people and injuring nearly 800 (See 'Reflections on a personal experience of a major incident' below). The London Assembly report on the bombings and the aftermath is a comprehensive analysis of the management of disasters affecting millions of people in a major conurbation. It concluded:

> What is clear is that all the relevant statutory organisations have their emergency plans in place, as indeed do many of the large non-statutory institutions. These plans have been tested, practised against and refined. However, the thread that links them all together is that in the event they proved service-specific, meeting the needs of the services, and lacked an outward focus that took into account the needs of their client groups.
>
> *(London Assembly, 2006)*

The report investigated all aspects of the immediate response and support given to those affected. It found that there had been no plans for psychological support to large numbers of people following a terrorist attack and made several recommendations about how such services, including survivor self-help groups, should be organised (London Assembly, 2006: 109–115). A follow-up report commented positively on the response to most of the recommendations but raised concerns about support for survivors, an issue dramatically highlighted by the inadequate response to the Grenfell Tower fire (see the 'Grenfell Tower fire (2017)' section later in this chapter):

> The responding organisations have acknowledged the need to establish survivor reception centres close to the scenes of major incidents, but further work may be required to ensure that this will be done in the event of a future major incident. This will enable survivors' details to be collected, which will help to ensure that they receive the immediate and ongoing support they need.
>
> *(London Assembly, 2007: 7)*

A more recent form of terrorism has used motor vehicles and/or knives to attack large, gathered populations. The 2017 Westminster Bridge (*BBC News*, 2017a) and London Bridge (*BBC News*, 2017b) attacks in London involved a car and van respectively, driven purposely at pedestrians at speed, followed by random knife attacks. In France, the attack in Nice involved a heavy lorry driven at crowds of people. In all cases, hundreds of people were affected – deaths, major injuries and large-scale psychological impacts.

The response to major incidents in other cities, such as the Boston Marathon (Gates et al., 2014), where the effective, pre-rehearsed emergency response minimised loss of life (Biddinger et al., 2013), and the Bataclan in Paris (Catto, 2016), highlight the need for preparation, co-ordination and a focus on survivor needs. Jerusalem is well used to serious incidents. Yanay and Benjamin (2005: 263) report that:

> during city emergencies, Jerusalem municipality social workers are assigned to the disaster site, and with them hospitals, police services, the forensic institute and notification units form the Jerusalem Emergency Team (JET). Using formal and informal ties, social workers establish a professional, closely-knit helping network ... [and they] should be trained to deal with relief work and its traumatic outcomes.

Disaster response always generates ethical and emotional responses and dilemmas (Sweifach et al., 2010). This includes who should receive assistance when numbers are overwhelming and to what extent should the political context influence who receives help.

Grenfell Tower fire (2017)

This is probably the worst fire disaster in Europe in the past 20 years. A small refrigerator fire on the fourth floor of a 24-storey block of flats spread to the external structure of the building and within minutes the flames had shot up the exterior insulation and cladding, engulfing the whole building. The standard advice to people caught in a tower block fire is to retreat to their flats, close all doors and windows and wait for rescue, on the assumption that modern building regulations inhibit the spread of fire and give time for evacuation. However, the Grenfell external cladding was not fire-proof and facilitated the very rapid spread of the blaze. Within minutes it was impossible for emergency services to reach areas of the building. At least 80 people died and hundreds were made homeless.

In contrast to some of the other disasters discussed, the perception of those affected was that local authority co-ordination of the response was inadequate or virtually non-existent. Long (2017) suggests that this perception is not supported by the facts. Whatever the reality, and this will be explored by a public enquiry, the widely accepted narrative is that there was no effective leadership of the humanitarian effort to support residents; the slowness in providing alternative accommodation; and an apparent lack of support and information for those affected. Yet, the official account was 'that every family has a family liaison officer or social worker if they want one' (Long, 2017). The leader of the council was forced to resign in the days following the disaster and new managers appointed.

The prime minister set up a public enquiry to consider not only the building structure and regulations but also the effectiveness of the disaster response (Grenfell Tower Inquiry, 2017). There was great bravery by teams of firefighters but should the fire service have had better equipment, especially to fight fires in tower blocks from the outside? Why was there an apparent lack of co-ordination on the ground? Why was it apparently necessary for local religious groups to mediate between angry residents and the perceived distant and unresponsive authorities (Sherwood, 2017)? Why did the disaster plan prove ineffective, including the apparent breakdown in co-ordination between the council and voluntary organisations such as Red Cross? Was there sufficient planning for alternative emergency accommodation and for liaison with survivors as recommended in the 7/7 report? Did the government's austerity policy, substantial reductions in local authority funding, poorly enforced building regulations and changes in social housing policy contribute to the disaster?

Recent disasters have also prompted reconsideration of the best strategy for post-disaster messaging (Easthope, 2017). Leaders are advised to stress resilience and determination to 'carry on'. However, experience of media activity following individual child abuse tragedies has taught me that acknowledging the legitimacy of strong emotions and pain has to come before, or at least at the same time, as a commitment to 'carrying on'.

Reflections on a personal experience of a major incident

I was commuting to London by train as usual on 7 July 2005. It seemed a very ordinary day, but arriving at the London terminus, I found the Underground closed and people pouring up the escalators out of the tube station. I went to catch a bus and found large crowds outside and the main road being closed by police. I caught a bus, along with many others, and went onto the upper deck. Something major was obviously happening so I phoned my daughter who worked for *BBC News* to ask if there was a major incident. She found no reports, but as the bus left Russell Square, there was a loud bang behind us. I looked round to see the roof of the bus behind flying through the air. People on my bus screamed and rushed forward. I feared people would be pushed down the stairs so shouted 'don't panic'. The bus stopped suddenly and everybody got out. I then heard my daughter on the phone – it had been live throughout – shouting, 'Dad, what's happened?' I said that there had been a bomb. She said she would phone me back from a studio, which is how I came to do the first *BBC News* interview about the Russell Square bus bomb (*BBC News*, 2005). Others were more closely involved and suffered serious injury and psychological damage (e.g. Tulloch, 2008).

People in the UK have become accustomed to the reality of terrorist incidents over several decades (see 'Terrorism' above). During my younger years, the main threat was from the IRA. They gave coded warnings of bombs, although that did not always enable areas to be cleared, and many people were murdered by these bombs. The more recent threat has come from attacks linked to Middle East conflicts, where there usually *is* an intention to kill. However, while unpredictable and scary, the risk of death from a terrorist incident is infinitesimally small; there are far greater risks from accidents in the home or on the roads (Drury and Cocking, 2007; Allouche and Lind, 2010).

Finding oneself in a major incident is a disruptive experience. There are now several studies of differential recall after major incidents (e.g. Drury and Cocking, 2007; Brown and Hoskins, 2010). The transcript of my radio interview shows I said very little, partly because the interview was cut short because the studio was needed almost immediately for a live broadcast, and partly because I was in shock. The public mobile phone system shut down soon after, so I was not able to reconnect with my daughter to continue. Mobile smart devices with news feeds did not exist then and, in any event, the decision to close the mobile phone network (because it was overloaded) cut off communication. Within minutes the whole area was alive with police and emergency vehicles; more roads were closed and taped off. There was suddenly a deathly quiet. The eerie silence was punctuated only by the blare of sirens – which still brings back immediate memories of that morning.

My next decision was whether to go back to see what had happened and whether I could help. I knew that I had no first aid skills but my main, somewhat selfish thought was to get away from the risk of another explosion. People around me then began to say that they had heard there were other bombs in London. Suddenly, the whole city seemed risky – was anywhere safe? The feeling of being unsafe lasted for some hours and effectively glued me to the spot. It later emerged that there had been three bombs on underground trains one hour earlier. It is thought the suicide bomber on the bus had originally intended to explode the bomb on a fourth tube train, but was thwarted and chose the bus as an alternative.

All public transport in the city had been withdrawn – there were no trains or buses and major rail termini had been closed. I walked to the next city square and consciously decided to wait in the middle of the green space feeling it was a 'safe' place away from any new risk. Other people were standing round and began to share news and experiences; more news about other bombs began to filter through. Somebody was seen walking through the square with soot on his face. People gathered round. 'What had happened?' He had been on one of the bombed tube trains, had walked out of the tunnel and was walking home as he had not been injured. No official had offered him any help.

Journalists arrived, keen to talk with anybody who had experienced the explosion. After about an hour I decided to risk going into a café for a cup of tea. As I was waiting to pay, still anxious about risks, a policeman shouted to evacuate the square. Adrenalin rose again. I paid for the tea and walked quickly to the next square, where I noticed a rucksack left on a bench – was it another bomb? I asked if anybody claimed the bag and somebody immediately ran to it and apologised. I then became aware that heavy traffic *was* moving on the main road outside the cordon. Life was continuing as normal for most people. I got a phone signal and my daughter invited me to her offices for lunch. She arranged another live radio interview on the World Service programme covering the bombings. I said that I identified with people living in cities which experienced daily bombings and called on the G7 leaders then meeting in Scotland to work harder to stop conflicts.

Around five hours had passed since the explosions and I was still in limbo, insecure and uncertain what to do next. Was there transport home? Should I stay with family in London – but with no transport that also presented a challenge. News came through that the main railway lines were re-opening. I decided to go for a train and return home. The only option was a 20-minute walk to the station through silent streets, lots of people walking down the centre of normally jammed roads. I caught an almost empty train. An hour later, I arrived to find station staff offering bottles of water; I was grateful for the kindness. Suddenly, I was out of London and people were carrying on as though nothing had happened. I wrote a 'blog' about the experience which I shared with colleagues around the world as a form of therapy. I slowly returned to normal but am still sometimes 'spooked' by unexpected sirens.

Social work in action – emergencies and disasters

Social work has always been concerned about the person in their environment, 'based on the notion that an individual and his or her behaviour cannot be understood adequately without consideration of . . . that individual's environment (social, political, familial, temporal, spiritual, economic, and physical)' (Kondrat, 2011). Concern for the relationship between people and their natural and physical environment has not received the attention it deserves (Marlow and Rooyen, 2001). This is being corrected with the emergence of green social work (Dominelli, 2012; Leung, 2015).

Social workers' skills and experience are very relevant for disaster work (Dominelli, 2015). They are well placed to make a distinctive contribution at all stages of disaster work – preparation and prevention, initial response, long-term follow-up and recovery (Cronin and Ryan, 2010; Cronin and Jones, 2015). Concerns for human rights, protection of children and vulnerable people, and social inclusion are distinctive and valuable in a disaster context. The response to disasters is a priority in the Global Agenda for Social Work and Social Development (International Federation of Social Workers, International Association of Schools of Social Work et al., 2012; Jones and Truell, 2012a; 2012b; 2017). One disaster specialist commented: 'the ideal situation is one in which those whose decisions and actions caused the [tragic disaster] 'own' the problem, while those who survived it 'own' the solution' (Alexander, 2017).

Social work is at its best when emphasising self-determination and working 'with' people, rather than doing things to them, as emphasised in green social work. This encourages the active involvement of those involved in planning and deciding actions or 'social inclusion'. UN agencies recognise that this has frequently been absent in disaster response (Cronin and Jones, 2015). There is growing evidence that active involvement of disaster survivors in the recovery process and planning for the future facilitates quicker recovery (Christensen et al., 2014; Truell, 2014), always taking account of local culture and social systems (Dominelli, 2012).

The impact of disasters on workers is significant. Their needs are often similar to those they are supporting; they may be survivors themselves. These needs must be addressed through support and professional supervision (Chan et al., 2010; Ramon and Zavirsek, 2012; Dominelli, 2012; Boulanger et al., 2013).

Conclusion

UK social work needs to rediscover the value of including the physical and 'natural' environment in the curriculum, assessments and practice. UK disaster legislation and planning appear to be effective, although support for survivors needs improvement. The response to the Grenfell fire tragedy has provoked concerns about disaster arrangements which will be examined in the public enquiry. There are good examples of social work involvement in disaster responses. Disaster preparedness should be a part of continuing development and practice, and the educational curriculum as advocated by green social workers.

Acknowledgements

I thank Philip Gray, Northamptonshire County Council, for assistance with technical aspects of this chapter.

References

Alexander, D. E. (2017). The Tinder-Box Tower: Fire and the neo-liberal model of disasters. *Disaster e planning and emergency management*. Available on http://emergency-planning.blogspot.co.uk/2017/06/the-tinder-box-tower-fire-and-neo.html [Accessed 12 July 2017].

Allouche, J. and Lind, J. (2010). *Public attitudes to global uncertainties – a research synthesis exploring the trends and gaps in knowledge*. Brighton: Institute for Development Studies. Available on www.esrc.ac.uk/files/public-engagement/public-dialogues/full-report-public-attitudes-to-global-uncertainties [Accessed 19 July 2017].

BBC documentary (2015). Somerset after the floods. *YouTube.com, BBC*. Available on www.youtube.com/watch?v=0jm18rfECnE [Accessed 12 July 2017].

BBC News (2005). Witnesses tell of bomb blast hell. London, BBC. Available on http://news.bbc.co.uk/1/hi/england/london/4659243.stm [Accessed 19 July 2017].

BBC News (2014). Somerset floods crisis: How the story unfolded. Available on www.bbc.co.uk/news/uk-england-somerset-26157538 [Accessed 12 July 2017].

BBC News (2017a). London attack: Four dead in Westminster terror attack. Available on www.bbc.co.uk/news/uk-39359158 [Accessed 19 July 2017].

BBC News (2017b). London attack: Seven killed in vehicle and stabbing incidents. Available on www.bbc.co.uk/news/uk-40146916 [Accessed 19 July 2017].

Biddinger, P. D., Baggish, A., Harrington, L., d'Hemecourt, P., Hooley, J., Jones, J., Kue, R., Troyanos C. and Dyer K. S. (2013). Be prepared: The Boston Marathon and mass-casualty events. *New England Journal of Medicine*, 368(21): 1958–1960.

Boulanger, G., Floyd, L. M., Nathan, K. L., Poitevant, D. R. and Pool, E. (2013). Reports from the front: The effects of Hurricane Katrina on mental health professionals in New Orleans. *Psychoanalytic Dialogues*, 23(1): 15–30.

Bragin, M. (2010). *United Nations International Strategy for Disaster Reduction* (UNISDR) – *the critical role of social work*. Council on Social Work Education – Katherine A. Kendall Institute for International Social Work Third International Seminar on Disasters. Hong Kong, China: (unpublished).

Brown, S. D. and Hoskins, A. (2010). Terrorism in the new memory ecology: Mediating and remembering the 2005 London Bombings. *Behavioral Sciences of Terrorism and Political Aggression*, 2(2): 87–107.

Cabinet Office (2013). *Responding to emergencies: The UK central government response – concept of operations*. London, HM Government. Available on www.gov.uk/government/uploads/system/uploads/attachment_data/file/192425/CONOPs_incl_revised_chapter_24_Apr-13.pdf [Accessed 11 July 2017].

Cabinet Office (2017a). *Emergency planning*. London, HM Government. Available on www.gov.uk/government/policies/emergency-planning [Accessed 12 July 2017].

Cabinet Office (2017b). *Report of the post implementation review of the Civil Contingencies Act (2004) (Contingency Planning) Regulations 2005*. London: HM Stationery Office. Available on www.gov.uk/government/uploads/system/uploads/attachment_data/file/607045/post_implementation_review_civil_contingencies_act__print.pdf [Accessed 30 April 2017].

Catto, K. D. (2016). The Paris attacks: Government responses, scholarly reactions and social solidarities. *Critical Studies on Security*, 4(2): 222–224.

Chan, S. S., Chan, W., Cheng, Y., Fung, O. W., Lai, T. K., Leung, A. W., Leung, K. L., Li, S., Yip, A. L. and Pang, S. (2010). Development and evaluation of an undergraduate training course for developing international council of nurses disaster nursing competencies in China. *Journal of Nursing Scholarship*, 42(4): 405–413.

Christensen, T., Danielsen, O., Lægreid, P. and Rykkja, L. H. (2014). *The governance of wicked issues: A European cross-country analysis of coordination for societal security*. Bergen, Norway: Stein Rokkan Centre for Social Studies, University of Bergen. Available on http://dspace.uib.no/handle/1956/9383 [Accessed 12 July 2017].

Coates, J. and Gray M. (2012). The environment and social work: An overview and introduction. *International Journal of Social Welfare*, 21(3): 230–238.

Corfe, S., and Keohane, N. (2017). *Local public services 2040*. London: Social Market Foundation. Available on www.smf.co.uk/wp-content/uploads/2017/06/2040-report-web.pdf [Accessed 12 July 2017].

Cronin, M. and Jones, D. N. (2015). Social work and disasters. In J. D. Wright (Ed.), *International encyclopedia of the social & behavioral sciences*, 2nd ed. Oxford: Elsevier, pp. 753–760.

Cronin, M. and Ryan, D. (2010). Practice perspectives of disaster work. In D. Gillespie and K. Danso (Eds.), *Disaster concepts and issues: A guide for social work education and practice*. Alexandria, VA: Council on Social Work Education, pp. 163–188.

Dominelli, L. (2012). *Green social work: from environmental crises to environmental justice*. Cambridge: Polity Press.

Dominelli, L. (2015). The opportunities and challenges of social work interventions in disaster situations. *International Social Work*, 58(5): 659–672.

Drury, J. and Cocking, C. (2007). *The mass psychology of disasters and emergency evacuations: a research report and implications for practice*. Brighton: University of Sussex. Available on www.sussex.ac.uk/affiliates/panic/Disasters%20and%20emergency%20evacuations%20(2007).pdf [Accessed 6 May 2017].

Easthope, L. (2017). I'm an emergency planner. Manchester shows we need new ways to heal. *Guardian*, London, 24 May 2017. Available on www.theguardian.com/commentisfree/2017/may/24/emergency-planner-manchester-heal-terror-hurts [Accessed 19 July 2017].

Foster, J. and McKittrick, D. (1992). IRA widens bomb campaign: Manchester shoppers hurt as attacks on commerce switch away from London. *Independent*, London, 4 December 1992. Available on www.independent.co.uk/news/ira-widens-bomb-campaign-manchester-shoppers-hurt-as-attacks-on-commerce-switch-away-from-london-1561326.html [Accessed 19 July 2017].

Gates, J. D., Arabian, S., Biddinger, P., Blansfield, J., Burke, P., Chung, S., Fischer, J., Friedman, F., Gervasini, A., Goralnick, E., Gupta, A., Larentzakis, A., McMahon, M., Mella, J., Michaud, Y., Mooney, D., Rabinovici, R., Sweet, D., Ulrich, A., Velmahos, G., Weber, C. and Yaffe, M. B. (2014). The initial response to the Boston Marathon Bombing: Lessons learned to prepare for the next disaster. *Annals of Surgery*, 260(6): 960–966.

Grenfell Tower Inquiry (2017). *Terms of Reference*. https://www.grenfelltowerinquiry.org.uk/about/terms-of-reference [Accessed 19 October 2017].

Harrison, S. (Ed.) (1999). *Disasters and the media: Managing crisis communications*. Basingstoke: Palgrave Macmillan.

Hillsborough Independent Panel (2012). *The report of the Hillsborough Independent Panel*. London: The Stationery Office. Available on http://hillsborough.independent.gov.uk/repository/report/HIP_report.pdf [Accessed 12 July 2017].

International Federation of Social Workers, International Association of Schools of Social Work and International Council on Social Welfare (2012). *The global agenda for social work and social development: Commitment to action*. Available on http://cdn.ifsw.org/assets/globalagenda2012.pdf [Accessed 20 March 2012].

Jones, D. N. and Truell, R. (2012a). The global agenda for social work and social development: A place to link together and be effective in a globalized world. *International Social Work*, 55(4): 454–472.

Jones, D. N. and Truell, R. (2012b). Social work rises to a new level. *Guardian*, London, 26 March 2012. Available on www.guardian.co.uk/social-care-network/2012/mar/26/world-social-work-day-2012?INTCMP=SRCH [Accessed 26 March 2012].

Jones, D. N. and Truell, R. (2017). Global Agenda for Social Work and Social Development. In C. Franklin *Encyclopedia of social work*. Oxford: Oxford University Press. Available on http://socialwork.oxfordre.com/view/10.1093/acrefore/9780199975839.001.0001/acrefore-9780199975839-e-1158 [Accessed 20 July 2017].

Kapucu, N. (2009). *Emergency and crisis management in the United Kingdom: Disasters experienced, lessons learned, and recommendations for the future*. Washington, DC: FEMA. Available on www.training.fema.gov/emi-web/edu/Comparative%20EM%20Book [Accessed 12 July 2017].

King, R. (2006). *Detonation: Rebirth of a city*. Warrington, UK: Clear Publications.

Kondrat, M. E. (2011). Person-in-environment. In *Oxford bibliographies*. Oxford: Oxford University Press. Available on www.oxfordbibliographies.com/view/document/obo-9780195389678/obo-9780195389678-0092.xml [Accessed 31 December 2012].

Larson, G., Drolet, J. and Samuel, M. (2015). The role of self-help groups in post-tsunami rehabilitation. *International Social Work*, 58(5): 732–742.

Leung, T. T. F. (2015). Harmony and social work practice. In J. D. Wright (Ed.), *International encyclopedia of the social and behavioral sciences*, 2nd ed. Oxford, Elsevier, 529–535.

London Assembly (2006). *Report of the 7 July Review Committee*. London: London Assembly. Available on www.london.gov.uk/about-us/london-assembly/london-assembly-publications/7-july-review-committee-follow-report [Accessed 19 July 2017].

London Assembly (2007). *7 July Review Committee – Volume 4: Follow-up report*. London: London Assembly. Available on www.london.gov.uk/sites/default/files/gla_migrate_files_destination/archives/assembly-reports-7july-follow-up-report.pdf [Accessed 19 July 2017].

Long, J. (2017). Pain, distrust and competing 'truths': The stark immediate legacy of Grenfell. *Guardian*, London, 16 July 2017. Available on www.theguardian.com/commentisfree/2017/jul/16/grenfell-tower-legacy-pain-distrust-and-competing-truths [Accessed 19 July 2017].

Marlow, C. and Rooyen, C. V. (2001). How green is the environment in social work? *International Social Work*, 44(2): 241–254.

Masters, S. (2005). Response to human tragedy of Asian tsunami. *Professional Social Work*, Birmingham (February 2005).

Norwood, G. (2015). 2014 floods: How have Britain's towns recovered? *Telegraph*, London, 17 January 2015. Available on www.telegraph.co.uk/finance/property/11350709/2014-floods-how-have-Britains-towns-recovered.html [Accessed 12 July 2017].

Pittaway, E., Bartolomei, L. and Rees, S. (2007). Gendered dimensions of the 2004 tsunami and a potential social work response in post-disaster situations. *International Social Work*, 50(3): 307–319.

Professional Social Work (2016). BASW UK annual conference and annual general meeting 2016, *Professional Social Work* (June 2016) 14–17.

Ramon, S. and Zavirsek, D. (2012). Editorial – special issue: Armed conflict. *International Social Work*, 55(5): 609–611.

Rawlinson, K. and Ross, A. (2017). What happened in Manchester? What we know so far about the attack. *Guardian*, London, 24 May 2017. Available on www.theguardian.com/uk-news/2017/may/23/manchester-arena-attack-what-we-know-so-far [Accessed 19 July 2017].

Rogers, P. (2011). Resilience and civil contingencies: Tensions in northeast and northwest UK (2000–2008). *Journal of Policing, Intelligence and Counter Terrorism*, 6(2): 91–107.

Scheerhout, J. (2016). The 999 heroes who made sure nobody died in the IRA bomb. *Manchester Evening News*, Manchester, 15 June 2016. Available on www.manchestereveningnews.co.uk/news/greater-manchester-news/ira-bomb-manchester-emergency-services-11451352?service=responsive [Accessed 19 July 2017].

Scraton, P. (2004). Death on the terraces: The contexts and injustices of the 1989 Hillsborough disaster. *Soccer and Society*, 5(2): 183–200.

Sherwood, H. (2017). Grenfell: Faith groups step in to mediate between officials and community. *Guardian*, London, 19 July 2017. Available on www.theguardian.com/uk-news/2017/jul/19/grenfell-faith-groups-step-in-to-mediate-between-officials-and-community [Accessed 19 July 2017].

Somerset County Council (2014). *The Somerset levels and Moors flood action plan*. Taunton, Somerset County Council. Available on https://somersetnewsroom.files.wordpress.com/2014/03/flood-action-plan-final.pdf [Accessed 12 July 2017].

Steen, R. (2016). Interwoven tragedies: Hillsborough, Heysel and denial. *Sport in Society*, 19(2): 254–266.

Sweifach, J., LaPorte, H. H. and Linzer, N. (2010). Social work responses to terrorism: Balancing ethics and responsibility. *International Social Work*, 53(6): 822–835.

Truell, R. (2014). The Philippines social workers who are still battling typhoon Yolanda. *Guardian*, London, 17 February 2014. Available on www.theguardian.com/social-care-network/2014/feb/17/social-workers-philippines-support-community [Accessed 19 July 2014].

Tulloch, J. (2008). Becoming iconic. *Criminal Justice Matters*, 73(1): 33–34.

Twigger-Ross, C., Kashefi, E., Weldon, S., Brooks, K., Deeming, H., Forrest, S., Fielding, J., Gomersall, A., Harries, T. and McCarthy, S. (2014). *Flood resilience community pathfinder evaluation: Rapid evidence assessment*. London: Department for Rural Affairs. Available on http://eprints.mdx.ac.uk/13837/ [Accessed 12 July 2017].

Williams, J. (2016). The man in charge of town hall's emergency response to the IRA bomb in 1996. *Manchester Evening News*, Manchester, 15 June 2016. Available on www.manchestereveningnews.co.uk/news/greater-manchester-news/manchester-bomb-emergency-response-council-11426118 [Accessed 19 July 2017].

Yanay, U. and Benjamin, S. (2005). The role of social workers in disasters: The Jerusalem experience. *International Social Work*, 48(3): 263–276.

5
Rebuilding lives post-disaster
Innovative community practices for sustainable development

Julie Drolet, Haorui Wu, Robin Ersing, Margaret Alston, Desley Hargreaves, Yen Yi Huang, Chao Hsing Huang and Golam Mathbor

Introduction: Rebuilding Lives Post-Disaster (RLPD) partnership

Social workers have an important and unique contribution in disaster relief work – specifically, working with marginalised people in supportive and compassionate ways, and considering a social and structural analysis of oppression and inequality. The number and impacts of natural and human-made disasters have increased substantially in recent years and social workers are being called upon to use their skills for disaster preparedness, relief and recovery. Recent disasters such as the Indian Ocean tsunami, Hurricane Katrina, the Australian bushfires, Fort McMurray wildfires and other events highlight the need to examine how social workers might be better equipped to respond and prepare for disasters.

Nationally and internationally, the frequency of natural disasters is increasing (Public Safety Canada, 2008). Floods, wildfires, tropical cyclones and hurricanes are natural hazards that affect communities, and the cumulative effect of these events produce significant personal, material and economic strain on individuals, communities and the fiscal capacity of all levels of governments. Previous research on social work and disasters has focused predominantly on the need to prepare social work practitioners in disaster recovery efforts, with far less attention paid to the long-term consequences (Streeter and Murty, 1996; Coates, 2005; Zakour, 2010). Yet disaster reconstruction is crucial to the survival and vitality of many communities affected by natural disasters, including small cities and rural communities, because of their need to boost local economies, offset labour shortages, and address crucial sustainable development and environmental issues as green social workers advocate (Dominelli, 2012). The Rebuilding Lives Post-Disaster (RLPD) Partnership aims to advance knowledge in long-term disaster recovery and reconstruction by exploring community-based disaster mitigation that includes sustainability, equity and livelihoods in disaster-affected small city and rural communities in Canada, the US, Australia, India, Pakistan and Taiwan (RLPD, 2015). The Partnership brings together academic researchers, practitioners, educators, social work associations, research institutes and community-based partners active in disaster recovery processes.

The International Disaster Database indicates that 'the incidence of flood and windstorm disasters has not only increased markedly since the 1960s, but the events themselves are more intense, last longer and affect more people' (Dow and Downing, 2006: 26). Most countries, as signatories to the United Nations Framework Convention on Climate Change (UNFCCC), have committed to preventing dangerous anthropogenic [human-induced] climate change (UNFCCC, 2016a). There were 196 international parties in attendance at the 2015 United Nations Climate Change Conference (COP21) where the Paris Agreement was adopted to reduce greenhouse gas emissions and global warming (Sutter et al., 2015). In the 11th Summit of the Group of 20 major economies (G20) in Hangzhou, China (September 2016), G20 leaders agreed to actively participate in the Paris Agreement and the 2030 Agenda for Sustainable Development to deal with global climate change and achieve sustainable development for all (UNFCCC, 2016b). Communities with limited capacity to prepare for, respond to and rebound from such natural catastrophes have been especially hard hit. It is well documented in the literature that disasters strike hardest at the most vulnerable groups – poor people, especially women, children and older people, and the most vulnerable disproportionately experience the negative effects (Thomas and Twynam, 2006). This project was initiated in response to the reconstruction challenges faced by affected communities impacted by disasters such as wildfires in Canada and Australia, the 2004 Indian Ocean Tsunami, hurricanes in the US, extensive flooding in Pakistan and earthquakes in Taiwan.

It is well known that the effects of a disaster last a long time. Disaster-affected countries deplete much of their financial and material resources in the emergency response phase. However, there is a pressing need to consider longer-term needs for sustainability, equity and livelihood options that are not being adequately addressed in long-term recovery. Within the reconstruction process after a disaster, there is an opportunity to 'build back better', ensuring disaster risk reduction, resilience and community participation that are designed into redevelopment. For those affected by disasters, following the immediate trauma and shock, the urgent question is how to rebuild lives and livelihood options (Ruwanpura, 2008; Enarson, 2009). The partnership considers this complexity between the changing social, economic and natural environment. International conventions have increasingly recognised the need to engage resource users to achieve their desired aims, as part of more holistic approaches to sustainable development (Thomas and Twynam, 2006), and explicit aim of green social work (Dominelli, 2012).

Literature review

Global climate change and disasters have catastrophically influenced various essential aspects of human lives (Drolet et al., 2015). According to the Internal Displacement Monitoring Centre (IDMC), from 2010 to 2015, disasters propelled 159.2 million people worldwide to be relocated from their original homes (IDMC, 2016; IDMC, 2015). Migration or displacement triggered by climate change and disaster is understood as one of many 'complex household-level livelihoods strategies to minimise risks and optimise economic, social, political gains' (Sudmeier-Rieux et al., 2017: 1). According to the *Sendai Framework on Disaster Risk Reduction*:

> it is urgent and critical to anticipate, plan for and reduce disaster risk in order to more effectively protect persons, communities, and countries, their livelihoods, health, cultural heritage, socioeconomic assets and ecosystems, and thus strengthen their resilience.
>
> *(United Nations, 2015: 10)*

Green social work recognises human beings' efforts to reduce vulnerability, enhance adaptation, and advance resilience in the context of climate change and disasters (Dominelli, 2012). Disaster vulnerability mainly refers to social and gendered construction of vulnerability (Enarson, 2001; Adger and Kelly, 1999). All dimensions of disaster vulnerability are affected by gendered patterns of access, and control over resources, and gender roles (Enarson and Morrow, 1998; Pacholok, 2009). There is a need to further understand the interconnections between vulnerability, resilience and adaptation to develop strategies for mitigating the effects of climate change and disasters on human lives (Nunes, 2016).

There is a strong connection between climate-related humanitarian crises and human activities, as they inform the policy-making process and require policy support (Lu and Schuldt, 2016). Schipper et al. (2016) argue that the insufficient coherence of political action regarding climate change adaptation and disaster risk reduction has dramatically increased vulnerability to environmental disasters. And, a recent American-based case study indicates that public awareness and political acceptance towards climate change are very slow (Carlson and McCormick, 2015). The United Nations Office for Disaster Risk Reduction has built a global platform for governments, NGOs, and UN organisations, to share their experience, innovations, and successful implementations of climate change adaptation and disaster risk reduction (UNISDR, 2015). Human experience of climate change and disaster reflects structural social and environmental inequalities (Dominelli, 2012; Gray and Coates, 2015). The social dimension is critical for community resilience post-disaster (Thompson-Dyck et al., 2016).

'Social work's reticence [in] embrac[ing] the environment as a domain of practice has led to the profession's lack of visibility in environmental and climate change planning and decision-making' (Alston, 2015: 361). Social work proficiency in enhancing human wellbeing holistically and advancing social justice and social equity qualify social work practitioners to potentially contribute to community-based post-disaster reconstruction, recovery and rehabilitation (Dominelli, 2015). It is critically important to build knowledge in 'green social work' approaches. Social work education continues to lack curricula and training that reflect the complexities associated with community and disaster-related human service (Cooper and Briggs, 2014). Humanistic values and sustainability theories must be embedded into social work practice relating to climate change and environmental degradation (Drolet et al., 2015). Green social work interventions especially must raise local residents' awareness regarding climate change and disaster and enhance their capacities to deal with environmental crisis in various ways, such as mitigation, preparedness, response, reconstruction and recovery (Dominelli, 2012; Mathbor, 2016). Social workers must fight against social inequalities, promote social justice, build social capital, and assist individuals, families and communities to rebuild their lives. Social workers are responsible for creating community-based innovative strategies in post-disaster recovery, sharing them with international communities affected by climate change and disaster, and informing related decision-making processes (Dominelli and Ioakimidis, 2015).

Research partnership

The rationale for the Rebuilding Lives Post-Disaster Partnership originates in the range and complexity of the issues facing small cities and rural communities affected by disasters, and discussions with Lena Dominelli about the need for social work research to build new green social work knowledge and understanding about long-term disaster recovery. This research partnership recognises the importance of local community-based factors, and aims to foster participatory action and change through community-based research. Members of the research team draw from a range of universities and build upon local community–university research partnerships. Practitioners create new connections with university researchers, both locally and internationally. At the field site level, researchers engage local interests and focus on issues and concerns of importance to promote engagement between university and community partners for mutual benefit.

The Partnership builds on a number of formal bilateral and multilateral formal collaboration agreements between social work researchers and partners. The International Association of Schools of Social Work (IASSW), Council on Social Work Education (CSWE) and Canadian Association for Social Work Education (CASWE) are among leading professional social work associations that promote the development of social work education throughout the world, develop standards to enhance quality of social work education, encourage international exchanges, provide fora for sharing social work research and scholarship, and promote human rights and social development through policy and advocacy activities. The Partnership is designed to make a significant contribution to the advancement of knowledge and understanding in green social work by focusing on the lived realities in disaster-affected communities.

Methods

The RLPD study employed qualitative research methods, and the sample for all six countries included over 70 interviews with community leaders, government officials and disaster responders, and 18 focus group meetings with over 250 affected women and men to learn about the social and economic effects of disasters, and in particular their impact on gender roles and power relations. In-depth face-to-face interviews were conducted in each field site with key informants in the community such as NGO representatives, community leaders, government specialists, managers and practitioners. Focus group meetings were held with local residents to assess differential impacts of exposure to disaster events in terms of social, economic and gender impacts. Qualitative data was analyzed using grounded theory that guided data analyses and interpretations using open coding and axial coding (Strauss and Corbin, 1998) for developing categories and themes (Glaser and Strauss, 1967) in each field site and across the six countries. Nvivo 10.0 was used to explore potential relationships between the codes.

The research was guided by the principles of community-based research in diverse cultural contexts, which holds that it is appropriate to learn from the perspectives of disaster-affected individuals and community members in disaster recovery processes. An international comparative approach allowed for the same interview and focus group questions to be adopted in each field site, with some modifications to account for diverse cultural contexts.

Each co-investigator was responsible for overseeing all aspects of research activities including assigning responsibilities to student researchers, hiring and supervising students, submitting a detailed methodological design, preparing and obtaining ethics approval in their post-secondary institution, drafting and revising reports, and overseeing their budget allocation. Research assistants were hired locally in each field site. The community-based research methodology is reflective of diverse cultural contexts, and appropriate for learning from community members affected by disaster.

Case studies

By considering the socio-economic, political and cultural context in four countries, and the intervention at the community level, the next section presents case studies on lessons learned for disaster recovery from Taiwan, Australia, Pakistan and the US.

921 earthquake in Nantou, Taiwan

On 21 September 1999, an earthquake measuring 7.6 on the Richter Scale hit Nantou County in central Taiwan. Known as the 921 Earthquake, it was the deadliest natural disaster to hit Taiwan in 50 years. The Taiwan country team conducted field research in Puli Town, Nantou County, where nearly 50 percent of buildings were completely or partially destroyed. Nantou County had been under-funded and under-staffed prior to the 921 earthquake, and the results of the quake reflect the link between poverty and vulnerability to disaster.

Immediately after the earthquake, the government set up two emergency response systems to organise the recovery and reconstruction processes: (1) Community Empowerment Projects (CEPs) sponsored by the central government's Council of Culture Affairs, which comprised workers from various fields and concentrated on community-based recovery efforts; and (2) Life Reconstruction Service Centres (LRSCs), which were facilitated by the Nantou County government and the 921 Reconstruction Council. These centres focused on emergency and related services where most social workers were stationed. The findings from the focus groups revealed that the CEPs focused on community redevelopment issues and supported community-based organisations to rebuild the livelihoods of residents. For example, the CEPs introduced eco-tourism and eco-friendly farming to local farmers to help them re-establish their livelihoods and related income. After several years, some of the CEP's programmes that were originally managed by community practitioners were transformed into initiatives managed by local organisations that contributed to broader issues, such as greenbelt planning and environmental preservation, and quality-of-life matters. These initiatives engaged sustainable strategies by balancing development and conservation.

The interview participants explained that social workers from the LRSC were casework oriented and agency based, and were effective at helping local vulnerable and marginalised populations. They were less directly involved with long-term development initiatives than their community-practitioner counterparts. However, some social workers worked with local residents to develop community-based approaches to seek an alternative approach that might enhance the quality of life of residents and conserve the environment. They believed the standard industrialisation model contributed to the local environmental degradation and affected the local dwellers' well-being. Their experience with the LRSC over two years empowered the younger social workers to discover critical issues in disaster social-work practice, although their efforts were not recognised by Taiwan's mainstream professional social workers at the time.

The Taiwan case provides several insights on building post-disaster resilience. Conserving the ecological environment can be a livelihood option for victim–survivors in Puli, a city affected by the earthquake; sustainability and outmigration issues can be addressed in the long-term recovery plan. It is important to note the networking and interdisciplinary collaboration between the CEP and LRSC. This resulted in the enhancement of the capacity of communities to recover faster from the earthquake and of social workers to address the well-being of residents in long-term community recovery efforts. Social workers also need to transcend their traditional repertoire, to be sensitive to market-led developments, and to take a more proactive role in grassroots activities that aim to address problems in both the social and physical environments.

2009 bushfires in Victoria, Australia

In February 2009 the Australian State of Victoria experienced one of its worst disasters. Devastating bushfires ravaged the State resulting in 173 lives lost; communities and towns were destroyed; schools and businesses, bushland and farmland, stock, native animals and fencing burned; livelihoods disappeared. This case study reflects research undertaken almost five years after the event in one of the small communities affected. Ten interviews were conducted with service providers, Commonwealth (national government in Australia), and state and local government managers integrally involved in the response – five of whom were social workers. Two focus groups were also conducted with men and women impacted by the bushfires.

Based on the data collected in Australia, the participants felt that recovery was not possible and that the focus needed to be on shaping a 'new normal'. The importance of place, and its destruction, significantly affected people's sense of well-being and identity. Many felt that the agency and autonomy of individuals and the local community was not recognised or supported, and indeed was undermined by post-disaster responses. Those affected felt that they were disempowered by the response efforts and that this contributed greatly to their capacity to adapt, and had a significant impact on mental health problems.

> People are still very – we're very angry – and that's about exacerbated trauma and communities were not listened to.

Politics at and within all levels impacted the renewal process. This included tensions between various levels of government as well as within the local community and between individuals. Timelines for accessing assistance, and especially financial assistance, were seen to be unrealistic. This affected the ability of local people to have a say in how their community recovered, including how the money raised from public appeals was directed to what the community felt was most needed, such as critical community infrastructure such as schools. The rush to restore 'place' reinforced inherent inequalities. A number of those in the focus groups articulated the view that the response itself created secondary trauma for those affected by the bushfires.

> We might have recovered from the disaster but we are now recovering from the process of what was done in the name of recovery after that.

> We used to joke about wearing badges that said 'total loser' you know, like speed dating.

Data from our focus groups indicate significant differences in the gendered responses to the disaster and respondents noted that some case managers tended to 'welfarise' their experience – that is to treat people as welfare recipients rather than survivors. This was a particular issue for those people who had had no contact with the welfare system previously.

Based on the lessons learned, a number of promising practices emerged for community-based social work practice. These include:

- Social work's core focus is to intervene at the interface between people and their social, cultural and physical environments. Place really matters.
- Starting where the client or community is and staying the journey wherever possible is good practice.
- Social workers need to have an understanding of both the theory and language of trauma and how this impacts their relationships and interventions with individuals, families and communities.
- Understanding and managing the politics of post-disaster interventions where governments, NGOs and other organisations rush to assist is an important strategy for social workers in this setting.
- Social workers as change agents have a key role in community development interventions before, during and after disasters.

Promoting the notion of the need to assist people to a 'new normal' rather than recovery holds resonance with affected people and can be a key role for social workers in influencing understanding of others involved in the post-disaster policy and service delivery decision-making.

- Staff support, professional supervision and self-care are non-negotiable requirements in any disaster situation. Social workers too can be impacted by vicarious trauma and it is important to have strategies to address and minimise these impacts.

Flooding in the Bodin District of Sindh, Pakistan

Pakistan has experienced 13 major floods since 1947 as reported in the National Monsoon Contingency Plan of 2013. The 2010 super-floods that affected the Thatta District were unprecedented, while the 2011 rains and floods severely affected lives and livelihoods in the Bodin District of Sindh Province of Pakistan. People in the devastated communities reported having no information on climate change. However, they claimed to be experiencing longer and colder winter seasons (Focus Group with Females, Baksho Dero, 11 January 2014). As a result of extreme weather in the locality, there are profound impacts on their cultivation practices. The cotton and rice production in the area is being delayed as a result of extreme weather (Focus Group with Males, Baksho Dero, 11 January 2014). This has had a serious impact on their lives and livelihood.

There is no history of this severity of flood affecting the region, and as a result, people and the government were not prepared to tackle the consequences of such a disaster. No formal early warnings were given before the flood. However, radio broadcasts did provide some early warning information to the public. Some local, national and international organisations provided food and non-food items by plane and helicopter to the affected areas in the response phase. As a result of the 2011 floods in Bodin district, there was a breakdown in communication and people could not contact each other or emergency services for help. INGOs or NGOs supported them after the disaster by providing food and non-food items. Affected people in Bodin District received help from neighbouring communities. NGOs participated in the recovery activities and solicited community involvement in the process. Some social welfare organisations like UNDP, Save the Children and Strengthening Participatory Organisations (SPO) supported them immediately after the flood. National Rural Support Program (NRSP) supported affected people by repairing the roads in their villages. Save the Children provided training regarding the precautions of disasters and they trained local people to cope with the situation.

Regarding innovations and promising practices, respondents expressed their desire to receive training on emergency management and early warning systems. It was recommended that emergency kits should be provided prior to disasters. Rebuilding the infrastructure has to occur immediately after a disaster so that transportation facilities are functional to deliver commodities. Skills provided by the neighbouring community Thatta District played an important role in post-disaster recovery in Bodin District. People in the locality must find ways to maintain their livelihoods by exploring other sources of cultivation practices such as switching from rice production to cultivating various types of vegetables which requires shorter harvesting seasons. This will enable them to harvest their essential crops before winter begins. Residents in the affected communities must adopt these new practices in order to cope with climate change and its impact on their livelihoods.

Hurricanes in Volusia County, Florida, US

In 2004, the State of Florida experienced one of its worst hurricane seasons of all time. Four major hurricanes measuring Category 3 or 4 in strength, made landfall in just 44 days, leaving behind an estimated US$45 billion dollars in physical destruction and changing the lives of thousands of people forever (Federal Emergency Management Agency [FEMA], 2009). Volusia County, situated on the eastern Atlantic coast of the state, was directly impacted by three of those storms: Charley, Frances and Jeanne. The county is known for its vibrant agricultural industry including field and orchard harvesting and horticultural work. As a result, the area has a large concentration of migrant farm labourers.

Data collected from the focus groups suggested the importance of social ties and networks within the farm labourer communities to support their recovery post-disaster. This was significant given reports of obstacles encountered when attempting to gain resources after the storms due to lack of trust between migrant families, law enforcement and emergency service providers. Issues of documented legal status and language barriers were most often described. The frequency of storms, which resulted in a high level of destruction in the agricultural industry, forced some workers to leave the area in search of employment.

> If I'm undocumented, then I do not have legal status to reside in the U.S. For example, if I went to FEMA for assistance, I needed to show my son's social security number to them but my children were not born here.

> My home smelled like fish and it had flies. At the time, my children were very young and we did not have any light or water and it was awful. I asked FEMA for assistance but they did not provide assistance because [I] did not qualify.

Some stakeholders also acknowledged these obstacles between the migrant community and those providing emergency assistance:

> Up in the far west of Volusia County there is a lot of immigrants, undocumented immigrants . . . they were afraid to come and get the help so that was a challenge we took care of it you know . . . that was the biggest thing and again they didn't speak English . . . they did not trust people.

> Everyone is impacted by the disaster but we have to make sure that the people who have the resources know how to get it out there to everyone that's affected not just the people who speak English but to everyone in the community gets the information.

Overall, stakeholders tended to view the disaster recovery process as an opportunity to acknowledge shortcomings in service delivery and engage with the farm-worker community as a way to mitigate vulnerability. In this regard, despite issues of immigration politics, some saw the disaster as a first step in bridging relationships between non-English-speaking labourers and local agencies which would advance efforts to mutually prepare for and recover from future hazard events.

> Well I think certainly the organizations learned what their boundaries and limits were and had to work together to come into a community and kind of work side by side . . . there were a number of overlapping responsibilities things like you know who provided water where the water distribution came from . . . I think there were some ethnic relationships that were established uh from some of our pockets in Volusia county . . . like our Mexican farm workers and all that have different needs from some of the general public had. And some of the organizations that help each other there I think grew and established some long term relationships such that now they have some ethnic people on some of these disaster recovery teams to enable communication right at the beginning.

The importance of social networks and leveraging local assets emerged as a promising strategy to promote post-disaster community resilience within a marginalised population. The concept of *collective action*, particularly through grassroots organising, was identified among focus group participants and stakeholders as a central response which pulled people together in a unified effort of recovery.

> In 2004, Maria opened a distribution site there on her front yard.... People started to bring food to her house and we started supporting her so we can distribute food into the community. We united so she can continue working. There were people that gave donations and with her, we would distribute them into the community while we look[ed] for people who were in need.

> People come together when there's a disaster when they are all hurting and they start helping each other and that's when they get to know each other better on a personal basis in their communities.

Conclusion

The importance of knowledge and skills grounded in local communities is repeatedly found across the field sites in this international study. Community work is seen as a powerful means of highlighting the link between poverty, environmental quality and the human impacts of natural disaster (Dominelli, 2012). The importance of locally based community organisations participating in disaster recovery efforts is evident across the case studies.

The lessons from 921 Earthquake highlight the importance of the government's role in deploying resources and setting up reconstruction schemes. Long-term disaster recovery can take a decade, or longer, and requires a holistic development plan to address environmental protection, local infrastructures, livelihoods and community redevelopment. The Australian case recommends that social work education include disaster and trauma theory and practice if social workers are to be appropriately equipped to respond, points also emphasised in green social work. It is critical to enhance government support for disaster recovery efforts in collaboration with affected communities. Green social work approaches need to bridge government interventions with community rebuilding efforts.

Disaster social workers need to help disaster survivors to re-establish their new social connections and social networks. The Pakistan case reports NGOs' critical role in emergency response and suggests that swift reconstruction of infrastructural systems is necessary for post-disaster reconstruction and recovery. Green social work must facilitate relationship building and social connections to foster a sense of belonging. The US case examines the perceptions and experiences of migrant workers, along with reflections from disaster services stakeholders, 10 years post-disaster. This case recommends that emergency services consider the status of undocumented workers and language issues in order to address their vulnerabilities and build their social networks. Green social work approaches must recognise diversity including immigration status and language among other factors. The importance of collective action, seen in the US case with grassroots organising, builds community resilience through participation and a unified effort of recovery. Green social work advocacy and collectivist approaches need to be integrated into social work education and training in order to foster transformative change. This Project is significant because it provides a range of community perspectives on sustainability, equity and livelihoods in post-disaster situations that are of interest to emergency service volunteers, educators, social workers and community practitioners, particularly in the relationship between the social construction of disasters, climate change adaptation and mitigation, the environment and sustainable development.

References

Adger, W. N. and Kelly, P. M. (1999). Social vulnerability to climate change and the architecture of entitlements. *Mitigation and Adaptation Strategies for Global Change*, 4(3–4): 253–266.

Alston, M. (2015). Social work, climate change and global cooperation. *International Social Work*, 58(3): 355–363.

Carlson, K. and McCormick, S. (2015). American adaptation: Social factors affecting new developments to address climate change. *Global Environmental Change*, 35, 360–367.

Coates, J. (2005). The environmental crisis: Implications for social work. *Journal of Progressive Human Services*, 16: 25–49.

Cooper, L. Z. and Briggs, L. (2014). Do we need specific disaster management education for social work? *Australian Journal of Emergency Management*, 29: 58–65.

Dominelli, L. (2012). *Green social work: From environmental crises to environmental justice*. Cambridge: Polity Press.

Dominelli, L. (2015). The opportunities and challenges of social work interventions in disaster situations. *International Social Work*, 58(5): 659–672.

Dominelli, L. and Ioakimidis, V. (2015). Social work on the frontline in addressing disasters, social problems and marginalization. *International Social Work*, 58(1): 3–6.

Dow, K. and Downing, T. E. (2006). *The Atlas of climate change. Mapping the world's greatest challenge*. London: Earthscan and Stockholm: Stockholm Environment Institute.

Drolet, J., Alston, M., Dominelli, L., Ersing, R., Mathbor, G. and Wu, H. (2015). Women rebuilding lives post-disaster: Innovative community practices for building resilience and promoting sustainable development. *Gender and Development*, 23(3): 433–448.

Drolet, J., Wu, H., Taylor, M. and Dennehy, A. (2015). Social work and sustainable social development: teaching and learning strategies for 'green social work' curriculum. *Social Work Education: The International Journal*, 34: 528–543.

Enarson, E. (2001). What women do: Gendered labor in the Red River Valley flood. *Global Environmental Change Part B: Environmental Hazards*, 3(1): 1–18.

Enarson, E. (2009). Gendering disaster risk reduction: 57 steps from words to action. In E. Enarson and P. G. Dhar Chakrabarti (Eds.), *Global issues and initiatives*. New Delhi, India: SAGE, pp. 320–336.

Enarson, E., and Morrow, B. (1998). *The gendered terrain of disaster*. New York: Praeget. Available on www.ops.org.bo/textocompleto/ide18245.pdf

Federal Emergency Management Agency (FEMA) (2009). *Fact sheet: Hurricane Charley recovery by the numbers*. State Emergency Response Team. Washington, DC: U.S. Department of Homeland Security.

Glaser, B. S., and Strauss, A. (1967). *The discovery of grounded theory*. Hawthorne, NY: Aldine Publishing Company.

Gray, M. and Coates, J. (2015). Changing gears: Shifting to an environmental perspective in social work education. *Social Work Education*, 34(5): 502–512.

Internal Displacement Monitoring Centre (IDMC). (2015). *Global figures*. Available on www.internal-displacement.org/global-figures/#natural [Accessed 23 June 2016].

Internal Displacement Monitoring Centre (IDMC). (2016). *GRID 2016: Global report on internal displacement*. Available on from www.internal-displacement.org/globalreport2016/ [Accessed 9 September 2016].

Lu, H. and Schuldt, J. P. (2016). Compassion for climate change victims and support for mitigation policy. *Journal of Environmental Psychology*, 45: 192–200.

Mathbor, G. M. (2016). Local capacity building in humanitarian crises: An effective dealing strategy for Bangladesh. *Sociology and Anthropology*, 4(5): 408–415.

Nunes, A. R. (2016). *Assets for health: Linking vulnerability, resilience and adaptation to climate change*. Available on www.tyndall.ac.uk/sites/default/files/twp163.pdf

Pacholok, S. (2009). Gendered strategies of self: Navigating hierarchy and contesting masculinities. *Gender, Work and Organization*, 16(4): 471–500.

Public Safety Canada (2008). *Canada's national disaster mitigation strategy*. Available on www.publicsafety.gc.ca/cnt/rsrcs/pblctns/mtgtn-strtgy/mtgtn-strtgy-eng.pdf

Rebuilding Lives Post-Disaster (RLPD) (2015). *Project*. Available on www.rlpd.ca/project/

Ruwanpura, K. N. (2008). Temporality of disasters: The politics of women's livelihoods 'after' the 2004 tsunami in Sri Lanka. *Singapore Journal of Tropical Geography*, 29(3): 325–340.

Schipper, E. L. F., Thomalla, F., Vulturius, G., Davis, M. and Johnson, K. (2016). Linking disaster risk reduction, climate change and development. *International Journal of Disaster Resilience in the Built Environment*, 7(2): 216–228.

Strauss, A. and Corbin, J. (1998). *Basics of qualitative research. Techniques and procedures for developing grounded theory*. Thousand Oaks, CA: SAGE.

Streeter, C. L., and Murty, S. A. (1996). *Research on social work and disasters*. New York, NY: The Haworth Press.

Sudmeier-Rieux, K., Fernández, M., Gaillard, J. C., Guadagno, L., and Jaboyedoff, M. (2017). Introduction: Exploring linkages between disaster risk reduction, climate change adaptation, migration and sustainable development. In K. Sudmeier-Rieux, M. Fernández, I. M. Penna, M. Jaboyedoff, and J. C. Gaillard (Eds.), *Identifying emerging issues in disaster risk reduction, migration, climate change and sustainable development*. Cham, Switzerland: Springer International Publishing, pp. 1–11.

Sutter, J. D., Berlinger, J., and Ellis, R. (2015, December 14). Obama: Climate agreement 'best chance we have' to save the planet. @ *CNN News*. Available on www.cnn.com/2015/12/12/world/global-climate-change-conference-vote/

Thomas, D. S. G. and Twynam, C. (2006). Adaptation and equity in resource dependent societies. In W. N. Adger, J. Paavola, S. Huq, and M. J. Mace (Eds.), *Fairness in adaptation to climate change*. Cambridge, MA: The MIT Press, pp. 223–228.

Thompson-Dyck, K., Mayer, B., Anderson, K. F., and Galaskiewicz, J. (2016). Bringing people back in: Crisis planning and response embedded in social contexts. In Y. Yamagata and H. Maruyama (Eds.), *Urban resilience*. Cham, Switzerland: Springer International Publishing, pp. 279–293.

UN Framework Convention on Climate Change (UNFCCC). (2016a, September 9). *Citizens' climate pledge encourages citizens around the globe to make personal contributions to climate action*. Available on http://newsroom.unfccc.int/climate-action/citizens-climate-pledge-encourages-citizens-around-the-globe-to-make-personal-contributions-to-climate-action/

UNFCCC (2016b, September 6). *G20 leaders commit to join Paris agreement soon as possible*. Available on http://newsroom.unfccc.int/paris-agreement/g20-leaders-commit-to-boost-global-growth/

United Nations Office for Disaster Risk Reduction (UNISDR) (2015). *2017 global platform for disaster risk reduction*. Available on www.unisdr.org/conferences/2017/globalplatform

United Nations (2015). *Sendai framework for disaster risk reduction*. Available on www.unisdr.org/files/43291_sendaiframeworkfordrren.pdf

Zakour, M. J. (2010). Vulnerability and risk assessment: Building community resilience. In D. F. Gillespie and K. Danso's (Eds.), *Disaster concepts and issues: A guide for social work education and practice*. Alexandria, VA: Council on Social Work Education, pp. 15–33.

6

Green social work for environmental justice

Implications for international social workers

Meredith C. F. Powers, Jennifer Willett, John Mathias and Anna Hayward

Introduction

Green social work is a holistic perspective that seeks to secure the well-being of people and the planet through reforming socio-political power structures (Dominelli, 2012). It is an eco-centric perspective that respects not only humans, but also values the natural environment in its own right within the ecosystem. Humans are in a symbiotic relationship with the environment, but the impact humans have on the ecosystem often put the environment and humans at great risk and have created a global, ecological crisis. Unrestricted, environmental problems often lead to more complex ecological crises. For example, the production and use of toxins contaminate soil, air, and water, causing insufficient and/or unsafe access to food and water for all living species. Such ecological problems also create social and political conflicts as people try to access and control what is left of the viable, natural resources; these can lead to unprecedented levels of human suffering and forced migration (Basher, 2008; Besthorn and Meyer, 2010; Dominelli, 2012; Willett, 2015b). The ecological crisis is complex, requiring global, interdisciplinary, and community-based responses (Schmitz et al., 2012). While the ecological crisis affects the whole ecosystem, the specific impacts these hazards have on vulnerable and historically marginalised people are the focus of environmental justice work (Dominelli, 2012).

Environmental justice highlights the linkage between environmental degradation and power imbalances as the mainly human victims of environmental degradation also must contend with injustices related to class, gender, race, ethnicity, and locale (Bullard, 1994; Nixon, 2011). Environmental injustice occurs at the macro-level as global economic and political inequalities unjustly shift environmental hazards and burdens away from wealthier countries and onto poorer countries (Healy, 2008). Environmental injustice also occurs at the micro/local level, particularly within developing countries, as poor people bear a disproportionate burden of environmental degradation (Besthorn, 2003; Coates, 2005; Dominelli, 2012; Hoff and Rogge, 1996; IPCC, 2014; McKinnon, 2008; Zapf, 2009). These injustices exist because of global systems of inequality, and global collaboration is necessary to confront them.

Social workers are increasingly being called upon to engage in the global response to address environmental injustices, as these problems affect the clients and communities they already serve (Weick, 1981; Soine, 1987; Berger and Kelly, 1993; Estes, 1993; Hoff and Rogge, 1996; Besthorn, 2003; Coates, 2005; Gitterman and Germain, 2008; Mary, 2008; McKinnon, 2008; Zapf, 2009; Jones, 2010; Dominelli, 2012; Peeters, 2012; Närhi and Matthies, 2016; Powers, 2016). In fact, many of the early pioneers in social work focused on holistic community practices that involved environmental justice issues such as creating improvements in sanitation and waste management, developing parks, and working to decrease the spread of communicable diseases (Addams, 1970; Kelley, 1970). In addition, national and international social work associations have identified environmental justice as a core issue within the profession (e.g. inclusion within several standards including in the new Educational Policy and Accreditation Standards for the Council on Social Work Education, 2015; in the 10th Grand Challenge of the American Academy of Social Work and Social Welfare, 'Create Social Responses to a Changing Environment', see Kemp and Palinkas, 2015; and earlier internationally as the third agenda item in Global Agenda for Social Work and Social Development: Commitments to Action, 'Working Toward Environmental Sustainability', see IASSW, ICSW, and IFSW, 2012). Due to environmental injustices being disproportionately found in the developing world, social workers from the US and other developed nations may often engage in international, cross-cultural practice and research contexts. Thus, the profession has to develop ways to equip and train social workers to not only become better prepared to address environmental injustices, but also to learn how to address the unique challenges of working in international, cross-cultural settings (Dominelli, 2000; Healy, 2008; Mary, 2008; Dominelli, 2012).

In this chapter, three cases of research and practice will illustrate three social workers' contributions to and challenges within international, cross-cultural contexts as they worked alongside multiple stakeholders to address environmental injustices. These cases include: (1) Willett's work in a collaborative research role alongside an Advisory Board in impoverished rural communities in Kenya which have been impacted by climate change; (2) Hayward's identification of the need for long-term work with local community members to preserve land and address destruction of natural resources in Jamaica; and (3) Mathias's work to build trusting relationships within a campaign to stop factory pollution in a village in India. To understand the lessons of these cases, two points must be noted. First, Willett, Hayward, and Mathias are American (US) social workers. While they present their cases from an international point of view, social workers from other nations may have different experiences of working in cross-cultural, international contexts. Second, in the communities in which they worked, there was little to no local social work presence and their collaborators had no social work training, thus there may be different lessons in communities that are actively working with local social workers. The conclusion of this chapter includes a discussion related to how green social work can serve as a mechanism to meet challenges and opportunities when working in international, cross-cultural settings on environmental justice issues.

Case examples of green social work in international, cross-cultural contexts exploring the impacts of climate change in Kenya: collaborative research using a local Advisory Board

Kenya is among the countries most affected by climate change and yet the first-hand impacts of climate change on vulnerable people and communities have not been explored fully. This case offers brief findings from an international social worker's research exploring the impacts of climate change in two rural communities in Kenya – Mutito and Wamunyu, alongside a collaborative model for exploring green social work issues in local communities (Willett, 2015a).

Mutito and Wamunyu are semi-arid, rural, and impoverished locations. The predominant livelihood strategies for community members are based on access to productive land. Prior to climatic changes experienced in recent decades, the communities were semi-arid with two rainy seasons, which allowed community members to farm consistently. However, due to climatic change, survival in these areas has become increasingly challenging. Community members in Wamunyu and Mutito spoke of increased drought and desertification since their childhoods, and explained that instead of two rainy seasons, they are fortunate if they see one period of consistent rain annually. The relatively wealthy community members have been able to adapt through installing irrigation systems and boreholes, but the livelihoods of poor residents have been decimated. Food insecurity and famine have increasingly become the norm. Businesses are shut and children are pulled out of school to gather water during periods of drought, which impacts long-term opportunities for the impacted community members.

In addition to droughts, community members detailed that rather than a steady rainy season, there are now short bursts of heavy rain which often result in flash floods. These flood waters sweep away the top layer of fertile soil, further decreasing land productivity. Again, the relatively wealthy community members are able to adapt through buying fertilizers to mitigate flash flood-induced soil depletion. The poor community members struggle to survive with decreasing farm yields.

Climate change is a global environmental injustice as the wealthy countries contribute more to the causes of the crisis while, as this case demonstrates, poor communities in the least developed countries bear the brunt of the consequences and must adapt to volatile climate changes locally. In addition, as seen in this case, climate change can exacerbate local inequality within affected communities as the wealthy are able to adapt to changes while the poor community members cannot, and consequently become even more impoverished.

Despite minimal responsibility for the global climate crisis, affected communities in developing countries receive little support to mitigate and cope with the problems resulting from this crisis (IPCC, 2014). In Mutito and Wamunyu, poor community members struggled to identify key players who were willing to consistently work on these issues with them. They reported that the Kenyan government provides food aid only on an ad hoc basis. Aid from foreign or international organisations was rarely available. When it was, it was often provided in exchange for work, a practice that most local community members considered an abuse of their desperate position with respect to basic human needs for food and water. Community members were upset with these measures but did not know how to navigate local, national, and international aid systems to advocate for their communities. They also lacked experience organising their communities to pressure aid actors. These gaps present opportunities for support from green social workers, including social workers from outside of Kenya.

International social workers should take an inclusive, participatory approach to promoting green social work within communities that have historical legacies of marginalisation and exclusion – histories which are often the source of ill feelings towards national and international actors. In this case, this was done by forming an Advisory Board of people in the communities who were poor and impacted by the severe climate changes in their local environment. All members were rural to urban migrants who fled droughts in Mutito and Wamunyu. Advisory Board members and the international social worker met through work on a separate project and developed their relationship over a period of several years to build trust and understanding. Advisory Board members agreed to guide the project after negotiating what they would need to be successful partners (e.g. payment, hours of work, location of work). Tangible benefits were stressed over theoretical or trickle-down benefits by the international social worker and were the key to the successful forming of the Advisory Board.

The Advisory Board ensured that the international social worker (and the project) benefitted from a local viewpoint and that the Advisory Board benefitted from the international social worker's contributions. To ensure a local viewpoint, members introduced the international social worker to local community members, explained the study to community members, included topics within the study that were important to community members (which were often different from those assumed by the international social worker), helped develop culturally competent methods, and promoted the trustworthiness of the data. In turn, the Advisory Board members gained paid work experience through the project and worked on developing skills they desired, such as when the international social worker trained the Advisory Board members on basic computer skills. At least one Advisory Board member obtained a job later based on the work experience gained.

The Advisory Board model has many positives but it is not without challenges. The inclusion of female participants was limited in this project, despite the fact that the international social worker was a woman. This was attributed to the all-male membership of the Advisory Board. As is common with this situation of internal, drought-based migration in Kenya, the Advisory Board members were young men whose home communities had sent them to urban areas to earn money for their families. Despite discussion about the need for gender diversity, they were reluctant to value female inclusion in the study when a male was available for participation. Relatedly, there were limitations regarding the ethnic breakdown of participants as well. The Advisory Board members were all of a single ethnic group, and they wanted the study to focus on their ethnic group only, which was attributed to enduring ethnic tensions in Kenya. In contrast to requesting more female participation, the international social worker largely agreed to adhere to these inclusion criteria.

While green social work aims to protect the well-being of people and the planet through reforming socio-political power structures, these end goals are difficult to accomplish as an individual social worker. Variations in the Advisory Board model could be used with social work on environmental justice issues in cross-cultural situations to shift socio-political power structures at a micro-level through the empowerment and self-determination of local community members. However, it is important to acknowledge that while the model may successfully challenge certain inequities, it may also perpetuate other inequities, such as the exclusion of women and people of diverse ethnicities in this case.

Crisis in the cockpit: identifying long-term engagement to address bauxite mining in Jamaica's protected lands

Jamaica, like other developing, small island nations, faces immense pressure for development and the extraction of limited natural resources. International Monetary Fund (IMF) and World Bank development mandates, limited land, and rare mineral resources have created ecological crises for such nations. Environmental and community groups in Jamaica continue to face challenges related to (mostly foreign) development projects. Coupled with the effects of climate change, including rising sea levels, protected areas in Caribbean nations are increasingly at risk and land-use issues in these developing nations are of increasing importance. The need for employment in economically struggling communities further complicates efforts for land and community conservation. Jamaica has a long history of both environmental injustice and social movements, and there are several organisations working to preserve protected land and space as well as fight for environmental justice. However, these conservation organisations and community members often face conflicting interests and claims to protected areas. Indigenous groups residing on potential sites for bauxite mining are but one constituency, along with nature conservationists and other community groups, who usually have complementary, but sometimes competing agendas.

One current issue in Jamaica is the potential siting of bauxite mines in Cockpit Country, which is of paramount concern to both environmental and community groups. Cockpit Country is an area of rural Jamaica with sparse human population but a dense and complex ecology of rare indigenous plants and animals. Cockpit Country is also an historic Maroon tribal territory (a politically independent and sovereign tribal nation of Africans who escaped and resisted slavery by using the rugged terrain to their advantage and successfully hiding from their oppressors). The area is approximately 1,100 square kilometres and is mostly inaccessible by major roads, which has afforded the area some protection from most types of development. A recent ecosystem evaluation noted several important features that the area contributes including: gas and climate regulation (carbon mitigation), water regulation (the unique topography mitigates flooding) and water quality (filtrations through the limestone and underground caves), soil stability, pollination of local species, habitat for indigenous plants and animals, timber and forest provision for local communities, and recreation and cultural uses (Edwards, 2011).

Several groups have coalesced to address the threat of mining in these protected areas including conservation groups, local community groups, representatives from the Maroon nation tribes, the University of the West Indies, and other smaller groups interested in protecting various species (e.g. bird watching groups). Social workers are not often present at the table in large numbers but could contribute to these efforts in various ways.

Using a green social work perspective with its environmental justice framework, the international social worker interviewed stakeholders to identify the key roles that social workers could potentially play in efforts to address potential threats to this area. An identified important role for social workers was working with local communities to collect data for community profiles. Little information is available regarding the census and socio-demographic makeup of more secluded rural areas. Social workers, in partnership with local community leaders and community members, could collect important data such as population demographics, access to water, food availability, and the number of households affected by any local or upstream mining. Despite an overall commitment to protecting the land, the most important motivators for local residents may be economic. Without alternative mechanisms for livelihood, buy-outs from mining companies may represent economic stability for families that have few other options, despite the immediate and long-term ecological hazards they would face as a result of mining. Another important issue in Cockpit communities is access to fresh water for farming and living. Without addressing the concrete needs (food, water, shelter) and economic needs (alternative mechanisms for generating income), environmental education programmes maybe offer only superficial solutions and prove to be ineffective.

The work of protecting these lands ultimately falls to Jamaicans and outside help is often (rightly) perceived as intrusive. To work with local communities and understand their economic and social challenges, a green social work perspective can serve as a framework to navigate the power and socio-political structural dynamics within environmental justice problems in an international context. International social workers, foreign NGOs, and Peace Corps volunteers, for example, would benefit from spending several years in communities to engage with stakeholders in order to address power imbalances, establish rapport, and understand better the ways of helping effectively. Hiring research staff from within local communities is necessary as a first step in developing a culturally competent research or community organising agendas. With these approaches social workers can engage in environmental justice work in international, cross-cultural contexts, as green social work advocates.

Being the international outsider: building relationships with the Gandhamur factory campaign, Kerala, India

Whereas the first two cases describe how American social workers contributed to environmental justice interventions, this case explores the complex positionality of social workers engaged in such work. Between 2010 and 2014, the American social worker conducted ethnographic fieldwork on a campaign to shut down a gelatine factory in the village of Gandhamur, in the southern Indian state of Kerala. In contrast to the cases described earlier in the chapter, the village of Gandhamur was a mixed-class, mixed-caste community that, taken as a whole, does not easily wear the label 'vulnerable'. Nonetheless, village residents were in a vulnerable position vis-à-vis the gelatine factory, which was jointly owned by a Japanese corporation and the Kerala state government. According to village residents, when the factory opened 30 years earlier, it had been welcomed as a boon to the local economy, particularly by those from lower castes and socio-economic strata. However, by-products of the gelatine production process included a blackish sludge that the factory dumped into a nearby river and a stench that spread throughout the village at night. The smell kept people awake coughing and many complained of itching and rashes from the river water. In 2008, some residents formed an action council to demand an end to the pollution. Upon its inauguration, this local action council immediately began to collaborate with environmental activists from across Kerala.

These environmentalists were part of a network of Kerala activists who provided support for environmental justice campaigns in the forms of scientific expertise, media support, and legal contacts. They had been looking for an opportunity to take action against the Gandhamur gelatine factory since the mid-1990s. Thus, when the local action council formed in 2008, they were ready and waiting to assist. These environmental activists introduced the social worker to the Gandhamur action council in 2010, and he observed their collaboration intermittently between 2010 and 2013.

In the summer of 2013, the campaign against the gelatine factory intensified after police charged protesters gathered at the factory gates and beat them with wooden batons. Both local and non-local activists were injured, and the campaign against the factory became a major story in state-wide newspapers and TV news. Many politicians and civil society figures expressed their support. Both leading up to and in response to this event, support from non-local environmental activists increased greatly, with some taking up residence with action council members to work on the campaign full-time.

The social worker's position in this collaboration was in many respects more that of an observer than a participant. As a foreigner, there were strict legal limits on supporting such campaigns, and he was careful to stay within those limits. Nonetheless, his past experience working on environmental justice issues in the US and India was crucial to his relationship with both the Gandhamur action council and environmental activists. It was through contacts from this past experience that he had been introduced to the Kerala environmental activist network, and through that network, he had arrived in Gandhamur. Despite his being legally barred from supporting the campaign in any way, action council members invited him to participate in whatever ways he could. Moreover, in conversations with other village residents, they often claimed him as a supporter. Similarly, key figures within the environmental activist network invited him to events, included him in discussions, and requested that he evaluate their work. The social worker accepted these invitations, but also accepted those from opponents of the campaign to maintain the neutrality required by law. Also, he was open about his past participation in environmental justice work and broader concerns about these issues. Thus, while participation in the campaign against the factory was limited, the research relationship between campaign participants and the social worker was grounded in mutual recognition of a common commitment to environmental justice.

The social worker's position became more complicated shortly after a beating by police, which opened a rift between the local action council leaders and the environmental activist network. The company that owned the factory claimed that Maoists, who were leading armed rebellions in other parts of India, had incited the violence. The environmental activists demanded that the leaders of the Gandhamur action council refute these claims loudly and publicly, but local leaders made no move to do so. Many environmental activists felt betrayed by this silence and began to withdraw their support for the campaign. The specifics of why and how the collaboration between the action council and the environmental activist network came apart are analysed elsewhere (Mathias, in press). In this section, we explore the challenges that this breakdown in collaboration created for the social worker as an international outsider.

If members of the environmental activist network were outsiders in the Gandhamur campaign, then the social worker was doubly an outsider. He had been introduced to the leaders of the action council by members of the network and was, at least initially, only 'a friend of a friend'. Thus, as environmental activists began to withdraw from the campaign and cut ties with the action council, it was unclear whether his connection with the action council would also be severed. As the conflict between the two groups became more severe, the social worker found his own alliances and commitments called into question by some local leaders in the action council. At one point, it seemed the action council might end the research relationship altogether.

That is not what happened. Instead, the more that locals and outside activists withdrew from the collaboration, the more the social worker found himself in a limbo, neither in one camp nor the other. This ambiguous position brought its own challenges. Some members of the environmental activist network teased or chided him for continuing to study the Gandhamur campaign, which they increasingly talked about as corrupt. Local action council members were not so explicit, but some seemed more guarded around him, particularly when they were speaking about the solidarity organisers. Nonetheless, both groups continued to invite him to attend events, observe their work, and participate to the extent that he could.

With the collaboration over, the social worker had to find his footing again with both groups; this did not make him more of an outsider in Gandhamur. Over the ensuing 10 months, he continued to build deeper relationships with members of both groups. He continued to accept invitations to attend meetings and campaign actions as well as religious festivals, rice harvesting events, school plays, and afternoon teas. In Gandhamur, he was no longer 'a friend of a friend', and this was in part because his participation in the everyday life of the village formed the basis of many new friendships. But it was also because the environmental activists were no longer around to mediate his relations with the action council. Instead of arriving in Gandhamur in the company of these 'outside' activists, he was now arriving alone, and this opened up new possibilities for more direct relationships. Over time, the social worker became a mediator between the Gandhamur residents and members of the environmental activist network, each of whom would ask him for updates about the others.

This is not to say that the American social worker ceased to be an outsider. Nor that he was less of an outsider than the Kerala-based environmentalists. In many ways, they were still more on the inside. For example, environmentalists may have chosen not to participate in the campaign anymore, but the social worker *could not* participate in the campaign because of his lack of citizenship. In addition, he remained marked as an outsider by his accented Malayalam, his American wealth, and his whiteness. None of these things had changed. Moreover, one might say that his position with respect to the campaign had not changed much either. What had changed most were the positions of everyone else relative to each other.

Being from outside India did not simply make the social worker more of an outsider than those who were Kerala-based. It made him an outsider in qualitatively different ways. Distinctions between insiders and outsiders are neither binary nor fixed (Cui, 2014; Edmonds-Cady, 2011). Being from the US made the social worker something of an anomaly with respect to the dominant insider/outsider distinctions in environmental justice campaigns in Kerala, which concerned relations between locals and members of the all-Kerala environmental activist network. This anomalous position foreclosed certain kinds of participation in the Gandhamur campaign, but also opened up forms of relationship that were not available to others. Moreover, the researcher's position with respect to local insider/outsider distinctions shifted over time. While these shifts resulted in part from the researcher's own efforts to build alliances and friendships, they were largely out of the researcher's control. In particular, the researcher's position changed as the result of changing relations between others involved in the campaign.

Discussion and conclusion

The three cases we provide in this chapter serve as tools for understanding the green social work perspective as it relates to how to negotiate collaborations as social workers in international, cross-cultural contexts when addressing environmental justice issues. Each case demonstrates ways to engage with marginalised communities with few resources, ways to navigate relationships at multiple levels, and appropriate roles for a green social worker engaging in environmental justice issues.

As illustrated in these three cases, social workers can engage in culturally appropriate work when engaging with environmental justice issues, such as the use of participatory methods for practice and research. This means promoting social work values of inclusivity and empowerment of self-determination in order to avoid 'colonising' local initiatives to address environmental injustices, as green social workers advocate (Dominelli, 2012). For example, the social workers in the cases presented each supported community-driven actions, rather than top-down decisions made by outsiders to the communities. The green social worker's role was often to listen, value local expert knowledges, help all voices to be heard, and assist in bringing resources to the table. Through participatory research and practice methods the social worker can also encourage the community members to identify problems and potential solutions, teach advocacy skills, and link community members to resources that support their goals. This type of work allows for outcomes that the community finds more beneficial for their desires, and equips and empowers them to continue their work on their own.

Importantly, green social workers must recognise that while environmental issues are often discussed in scholarly scientific arenas using technical jargon, marginalised communities are experts in understanding these problems as they live with the severe impacts of environmental degradation in their daily experiences. Their voices should not be discounted due to an inability to engage in the technical discourses. Social workers in international settings can approach from a stance of partner and look to the locals as experts in their own communities.

Social workers addressing environmental issues in international settings also often must contend with conflicts between varying conceptions of environmental injustice and local values regarding the environment and social justice. They must practice diplomatic skills and help different perspectives and voices to all be heard.

Relatedly, social workers must also recognise their own position of power and privilege when operating across political boundaries in international, cross-cultural settings, so as to be a collaborative advocate in their work, rather than reinforce the unfair global power dynamics that affect such communities. Also, green social workers must identify the structural and sociopolitical power dynamics within the groups who are working on environmental justice issues and within the local communities in order to understand the holistic contexts at play.

In international settings, social work on environmental issues is compounded with the challenges of navigating relationships on multiple levels with a variety of local and non-local actors. In each case presented in this chapter, the authors found that these insider/outsider collaborations cannot happen overnight. Thus, social workers must be willing to dedicate the time needed in communities to develop such relationships, especially when many non-governmental organisations and local projects are not long-lasting; perseverance is key.

Another lesson to be drawn here is that being an outsider is not simply a matter of degree. There are qualitatively different ways to be an insider or an outsider with respect to the organising process. In the community organising literature, it is common to think of insiders and outsiders spatially, in terms of metaphorical distance from the centre of a campaign or issue (e.g. Rivera and Erlich, 1992). This mode of thinking seems particularly natural when considering insiders and outsiders in grassroots environmental movements, which are often geographically localised. However, spatial metaphors obscure the many kinds of relationships involved in the organising process and, by the same token, the qualitatively different ways whereby one can be more or less 'inside' a community, campaign, or movement. In addition, social workers pursuing grassroots collaborations internationally should be prepared to face such complexities and ambiguities, in which the inside and outside of a movement are constantly reforming themselves, and fluid.

From the cases presented in this chapter, the green social work perspective enabled these social workers to serve a supporting role in addressing climate change in Kenya, to identify a potential role for social workers in long-term community-based work to address land preservation in Jamaica, and to be flexible and build trusting relationships in an anti-pollution campaign in India. The cases provide examples that can be used as a teaching tool to explore environmental injustices, and to humanise and understand the local impacts of climate change. These cases can also be used to understand better community organisation and community development.

Green social workers must learn how to work within and reform local and global systems of inequalities; and to become part of the global collaboration that works alongside marginalised communities, such as the ones presented in this chapter. The social work roles presented offer lessons on engaging in collaborative practice when working for environmental justice in international, cross-cultural settings. They are also relevant for working with domestic communities affected by similar issues. Green social work promotes environmental justice within a larger framework of promoting human and non-human well-being and addressing both global and local impacts of ecological crises.

References

Addams, J. (1970). *Hull-House maps and papers* (R. C. Wade, Ed.). New York: Arno Press.
Basher, R. (2008). Disasters and what to do about them. *Forced Migration Review: Climate Change and Displacement*, 31: 35–36.
Berger, R. M. and Kelly, J. J. (1993). Social work in the ecological crisis. *Social Work*, 38(5): 521–526.
Besthorn, F. H. (2003). Radical ecologisms: Insights for educating social workers in ecological activism and social justice. *Critical Social Work: An Interdisciplinary Journal Dedicated to Social Justice*, 3(1): 66–106.

Besthorn, F. H. and Meyer, E. E. (2010). Environmentally displaced persons: Broadening social work's helping imperative. *Critical Social Work*, 11(3): 123–138.
Bullard, R. (ed). 1994. *Unequal protection*. San Francisco: Sierra Club.
Coates, J. (2005). *Ecology and social work: Toward a new paradigm*. Black Point, Nova Scotia: Fernwood.
Council on Social Work Education (CSWE) (2015). The *2015 Educational Policy and Accreditation Standards (EPAS)*. https://www.cswe.org/getattachment/Accreditation/Standards-and-Policies/2015-EPAS/2015EPASandGlossary.pdf.aspx [Accessed 9 March 2016].
Cui, K. (2014). The insider – outsider role of a Chinese researcher doing fieldwork in China: The implications of cultural context. *Qualitative Social Work*, 14(3): 356–369.
Dominelli, L. (2000). International comparisons in social work. In R. Pearce and J. Weinstein (Eds.), *Innovative education and training for care professionals: A providers' guide*. London: Jessica Kingsley, pp. 25–40.
Dominelli, L. (2012). *Green social work: From environmental crises to environmental justice*. Malden, MA: Polity Press.
Edmonds-Cady, C. (2011). A view from the bridge: Insider/Outsider perspective in a study of the Welfare Rights Movement. *Qualitative Social Work*, 11(2): 174–190.
Edwards, P. (2011). Ecosystem service valuation of Cockpit Country. *Windsor Research Centre*. Available online on www.cockpitcountry.com/LFMP/Cockpit_NRV.pdf
Estes, R. (1993). Toward sustainable development: From theory to praxis. *Social Development Issues*, 15(3): 1–29.
Gitterman, A. and Germain, C. (2008). *The Life Model of social work practice: Advances in theory and practice*, 3rd ed. New York: Columbia University Press.
Healy, L. M. (2008). *International social work: Professional action in an interdependent world*. New York, NY: Oxford University Press.
Hoff, M. D. and Rogge, M. E. (1996). Everything that rises must converge: Developing a social work response to environmental injustice. *Journal of Progressive Human Services*, 7(1): 41–57.
Intergovernmental Panel on Climate Change (IPCC) (2014). Summary for policymakers. In C. B. Field, V. R. Barros, D. J. Dokken, K. J. Mach, M. D. Mastrandrea, T. E. Bilir, M. Chatterjee, K. L. Ebi, Y. O. Estrada, R. C. Genova, B. Girma, E. S. Kissel, A. N. Levy, S. MacCracken, P. R. Mastrandrea, and L. L. White (Eds.), *Climate Change 2014: Impacts, Adaptation, and Vulnerability*. Part A: Global and Sectoral Aspects. Contribution of Working Group II to the Fifth Assessment Report of the Intergovernmental Panel on Climate Change. Cambridge: Cambridge University Press and New York, NY, pp. 1–32.
International Association of Schools of Social Work, International Council on Social Welfare, International Federation of Social Workers (2012). *The global agenda for social work and social development: Commitment to action*. Available on www.globalsocialagenda.org/ [Accessed 17 November 2015].
Kemp, S. P. and Palinkas, L. A. (2015). *Strengthening the social response to the human impacts of environmental change*. Working paper No. 5 for the Grand Challenges for Social Work initiative. American Academy of Social Work and Social Welfare. Available on http://aaswsw.org/wp-content/uploads/2015/03/Social-Work-and-Global-Environmental-Change-3.24.15.pdf [Accessed 17 November 2015].
Jones, P. (2010). Responding to the ecological crisis: Transformative ways for social work education. *Journal of Social Work Education*, 46(1): 67–84.
Kelley, F. (1970). *Hull-House maps and papers* (R. C. Wade, Ed.). New York: Arno Press.
Mary, N. (2008). *Social work in a sustainable world*. Chicago, IL: Lyceum Books.
Mathias, J. (in press). Scales of Value: Insiders and Outsiders in Environmental Organizing in South India. *Social Service Review*.
McKinnon, J. (2008). Exploring the nexus between social work and the environment. *Australian Social Work*, 61(3): 256–268.
Närhi, K. and Matthies, A. L. (2016). Conceptual and historical analysis of ecological social work. In J. McKinnon and M. Alston (Eds.), *Ecological social work: Toward sustainability*. London: Palgrave Macmillan, pp. 21–38.
Nixon, R. (2011). *Slow violence and the environmentalism of the poor*. Cambridge, MA: Harvard University Press.

Peeters, J. (2012). The place of social work in sustainable development: Towards ecosocial practice. *International Journal of Social Welfare*, 21(3), 287–298.

Powers, M. C. F. (2016). Transforming the profession: Social workers' expanding response to the environmental crisis. In A.-L. Matthies and K. Narhi (Eds.), *Ecosocial transition of societies: Contribution of social work and social policy*. London and New York: Routledge.

Rivera, F. G., and Erlich, J. (1992). *Community organizing in a diverse society*. Boston, MA: Allyn and Bacon.

Schmitz, C. L., Matyók, T., Sloan, L. M. and James, C. (2012). The relationship between social work and environmental sustainability: Implications for interdisciplinary practice. *International Journal of Social Welfare*, 21(3): 278–286.

Soine, L. (1987). Expanding the environment in social work: The case for including environmental hazards content. *Journal of Social Work Education*, 23(2): 40–46.

Weick, A. (1981). Reframing the person-in-environment perspective. *Social Work*, 26(2): 140–143.

Willett, J. (2015a). *Experiences of slow violence in poor Kenyan communities: Micro-disasters, formalized aid responses, and community support through social networks* (Doctoral dissertation, University of Connecticut). Available on http://digitalcommons.uconn.edu/dissertations/776/

Willett, J. (2015b). The slow violence of climate change in poor rural Kenyan communities: 'Water is life. Water is everything'. *Contemporary Rural Social Work*, 7(1): 39–55.

Zapf, M. K. (2009). *Social Work and the Environment: Understanding People and Place*. Toronto, ON: Canadian Scholars Press.

Part II
Natural disasters

7

Promoting public interest design

Green social work interventions during the post-Ya'an earthquake reconstruction and recovery in Sichuan, China

Haorui Wu

Introduction

The catastrophic effect of global disasters and climate change has had dire consequences within social, economic, and ecological environments at individual, family, and community levels (Gillespie and Danso, 2010). According to the Internal Displacement Monitoring Centre (IDMC), from 2010 to 2014, disasters have forced approximately 131.4 million people worldwide to be relocated from their original homes (IDMC, 2015). Following these enormous disaster-caused displacements, almost all evacuated communities have had to endure the different stages of post-disaster reconstruction and recovery. On the brighter side, this has provided valuable redevelopment opportunities, especially for vulnerable and marginalised communities (Wu, 2014). The United Nations' (UN) 2015 *Sendai Framework for Disaster Risk Reduction* established new requirements for post-disaster reconstruction and recovery, which 'more effectively protect persons, communities, and countries, their livelihoods, health, cultural heritage, socioeconomic assets and ecosystems, and thus strengthen their resilience' (United Nations, 2015: 10).

Disasters continue to threaten environmental justice in both developing and developed nations (Dominelli, 2012). 'Environmental justice is the social justice expression of environmental ethics' (Warner and DeCosse, 2009, para. 1). Environmental justice ensures that environmental protection is to be afforded to all people equally, and all stakeholders are comprehensively included in the process of environmental policy decision-making, so that no one is unfairly and/or disproportionately exposed to environmental hazards (Dominelli, 2012; Nesmith, 2015). Post-disaster reconstruction and long-term recovery offer a critical opportunity for affected areas to 'build back better' (UN, 2015); thus strengthening the communities' resilience and achieving goals of sustainable development (Thompson-Dyck et al., 2016).

Sustainable development requires that economic, social, and environmental dimensions are equally addressed (World Commission on Environment and Development, 1987). Community sustainable development requires synchronisation of social development within physical environment renewal (Oliver-Smith, 2010). Political and economic forces that drive international disaster initiatives have prioritised addressing short-term, emergency responses, and physical reconstruction, without allowing for equal or enough attention to be given to long-term, social reconstruction and recovery (Dominelli, 2012; Wu, 2014). This disproportionate emphasis causes environmental and social injustice because disaster survivors' social requirements are not adequately addressed. Since the built environment is not able to offer a solid platform to support social development, this potentially negatively influences community resilience and community sustainable development. Consequently, the UN's (2015) *Sendai Framework for Disaster Risk Reduction 2015–2030* has made social protection and social resilience top priorities within the post-disaster initiatives, an imperative of green social work too.

The post-disaster initiatives require cooperation among architects, planners, social workers, engineers, economists, anthologists, and other professionals to guarantee that the final results achieve sustainable development goals by balancing the social, economic, and environment dimensions (Ackerly, 2016). Transdisciplinary approaches are advocated by green social work (Dominelli, 2012). Using the post-Lushan earthquake reconstruction as an example, this chapter considers the collaborative efforts of two professional groups: (1) the social recovery group of social work practitioners; and (2) the built environment reconstruction group of architects and planners, who concentrated on the reconstruction of the built environment, including housing, public buildings, and infrastructural systems. This chapter reveals how these professionals took advantage of this post-disaster reconstruction to create opportunities to practice social justice and social equity by embedding social protection and social resilience into the reconstruction of the built environment.

Human-centered participatory design

Post-disaster reconstruction generally commences when the initial planning and architectural design of the new built environment begins. The UN's mandate is that post-disaster reconstruction must consider long-term sustainable issues by balancing the social, economic, and environmental dimensions throughout the entire planning and architectural designing stages. These requirements have created a new trend in community planning and community design called public interest design (PID). The PID employs a human-centered, participatory approach that addresses ecological, economic, and social issues to reach sustainable achievement (Cary and Martin, 2012). The PID compels the community-based architects, planners, and other designers to utilise human-centered design and planning approaches to guarantee local residents' living requirements and other rights by stimulating grassroots participation in the planning and design process itself. The PID aims to improve the quality of the physical residential living environment, and build a solid physical platform to support ongoing social-economic and social-cultural development, which ultimately would ensure that all the residents may enjoy the benefits of community planning and/or design. However, community-based architects and planners have been slow to recognise the significance of built environmental forces on fulfilling local residents' social requirements, and have not on the whole been proficient at applying the relevance of this to their profession (Bell, 2004).

'Social work engages people and structures to earnestly attempt to address life challenges and enhance wellbeing' (International Association of School of Social Work [IASSW], 2015, para. 4). Social workers have been making significant contributions towards post-disaster initiatives through various means, from the day-to-day community-based social services of psychological intervention, consulting service, and community resources mapping that are provided during the emergency response stage, to addressing long-term social development issues, such as advocating for social equity, reducing social vulnerabilities, building local inhabitants' social competency, and enhancing community social resilience (Gillespie and Danso, 2010; Zakour, 2010; Dominelli, 2012; Alston, 2015; Dominelli and Ioakimidis, 2015). Social work expertise regarding respect for social diversities, promoting social justice, and protecting human rights increases local residents' capacity to achieve sustainable social development in the context of global climate change and disaster (IFSW et al., 2012). Dominelli (2012: 8) has developed the terminology of green social work to define social work interventions in the midst of climate change and disaster, by arguing it is:

> part of practice that intervenes to protect the environment and enhance people's well-being by integrating the interdependencies between people and their socio-cultural, economic and physical environments, and among peoples within an egalitarian framework that addresses prevailing structural inequalities and unequal distribution of power and resources.

Green social workers offer evidence-based strategies to inform the governmental post-disaster reconstruction-related policies, plans, and instruments to better serve marginalised and vulnerable groups, advancing their long-term well-being and resilient competencies (Drolet et al., 2015). More importantly, green social workers glean opportunities from the disasters to help develop marginalised and vulnerable groups' social capacities by stimulating their participation in the post-disaster activities being conducted in their communities (Alston, 2015). Hence, green social workers' expertise enables them to cooperate with, or at least provide suggestions to other professionals, especially the planners and architects in the post-disaster reconstruction field, to help these professionals to better recognise the local residents' various requirements that they may have of the community's built environment (mainly housing and civic infrastructure) and to facilitate these social demands within the planning and architectural design. If that is fulfilled, all the residents would enjoy the benefits from the newly built communities and quickly resume their daily lives, which are the main achievements of PID. Meanwhile, green social workers promote civic participation in planning and design of built environment and advance their leadership in community-based decision-making process (Dominelli, 2012). How could disaster social work contribute to the community's physical reconstruction? The post-Lushan earthquake efforts provide valuable evidence-based strategies for addressing this question.

Post-Lushan earthquake reconstruction and recovery

Reconstruction during the economic boom

In 1978, China's Open Door Policy swiftly accelerated the economic transformation of modern China (Hu, 1995). Since then, the entire world has been witnessing the super swift economic boom in China (Hu, 1995). Under the government's powerful control, the extremely rapid economic development produced an economy-concentrated development model, which guarantees abundant material sources for redevelopment of built environment (He, 2016). Both the 2008 Wenchuan earthquake and the 2013 Lushan earthquake occurred during this boom period. This strong economic thrust guaranteed swift and successful physical reconstruction following these two earthquakes (Wu and Hou, 2016). The government-led, massive-project and short-term post-Wenchuan earthquake reconstruction was successful in accomplishing immense tasks (United Nations Office for Disaster Risk Reduction [UNISDR], 2010). The infrastructure-oriented physical reconstruction outcomes after the Wenchuan earthquake astonished the entire world, which, to some extent, set the basic tone for what followed after the Lushan earthquake, during reconstruction and recovery (Wu, 2014). However, the infrastructural-oriented reconstruction model has continued to trigger a number of social problems, such as exclusion of civic participation, destruction of local ecological and cultural milieus, and the widening gap between rich and poor people in certain communities (Wu, 2014).

The Lushan earthquake was seen as a sub-quake of the Wenchuan earthquake (Broadbent, 2014). With a magnitude of 7.0, the earthquake caused 196 deaths, 21 missing persons, and over 15,000 reported injured (Vervaeck, 2013). With the knowledge gained from the previous crisis response after the Wenchuan earthquake, the central government conducted Lushan's emergency response smoothly (Demick, 2013). The lessons learned from Wenchuan switched the government's concentration from its previous predominately economic focus to a more balanced connection among economic re-stimulation, social redevelopment, and environmental protection. Accordingly, after the Lushan disaster, the central government increased its investment in the reconstruction of the social protection system (Wu and Hou, 2016).

Disaster social work initiatives

The history of Chinese professional social work originated at the beginning of the 20th century (Leung and Tam, 2014). Prior to 1949, only a few Chinese universities had social work programmes (Yan and Cheung, 2006). The modern social work post-secondary education for social workers was resumed during the mid-1980s (Leung and Tam, 2014). The increasing demands of social issues that accompanied the rapid economic development in China urgently called for more social work practitioners (Yan and Cheung, 2006). In 2010, the State Council released the National Development Mid- and Long-Term Framework on Human Capital 2010–2020, announcing that 3 million professional social workers would be trained by 2020. Influenced by the Chinese Communist political environment, social work in China primarily focuses on the maintenance of societal stability by addressing existing urgent social problems and crises, such as, poverty reduction, left-behind children in remote and rural communities, and the flood of migrant workers from the rural areas into urban areas (Chen and Chan, 2016; Hopkins et al., 2016; Hurst, 2009). Rarely have social work interventions been included in the planning and design of the built environment by generating a human-centered, participatory approach, on which PID focuses. Green social workers Ku and Dominelli (2017) are exceptions.

Immediately after the Wenchuan earthquake, and prior to governmental recognition and funding, Chinese social workers were, for the first time, to conduct disaster social work intervention (Zheng and Han, 2009). They became involved in emergency responses, psychological services, and community development, as well as developed and facilitated a special domestic post-disaster psychosocial work model (Sim and Dominelli, 2016). Social work practitioners' significant contributions during the Wenchuan event propelled the Chinese central government to formally include disaster social work as one of the eight essential streams of the National Social Work Education and Practice Regulation (Zheng and Han, 2009). The government went on to recognise and financially support research, education, and practice of disaster social work (Zheng and Han, 2009). This transformative step enabled Chinese social workers, immediately following the Lushan earthquake, to engage into post-disaster efforts.

Green social work and sustainable post-disaster reconstruction

Green social workers utilise eco-social interventions to deal with environmental crises, establish environmental and social justice, improve people's well-being, and achieve sustainable development goals (Dominelli, 2012). In additional to traditional disaster social work interventions, green social workers help to resolve environmental conflicts and economic injustice (Dominelli, 2015). In the context of the post-disaster environment, green social work intervention should be embedded within the holistic built environment reconstruction. As mentioned in the section on 'Human centered participatory design', having the social needs reflected in the design process and utilising the design outcomes to support social development, enhancement of stakeholders' well-being, and achieve sustainable development goals also comprise the main thrust of PID. Moreover, this was explicitly aligned with the Chinese central government's ultimate goal in the post-Lushan earthquake reconstruction.

The post-Lushan earthquake reconstruction and recovery were designed and directed by urban planners and architects. Under the influence of the economic boom, the primary focus was on swiftly reconstructing the built environment. However, professional designers were not equipped with the capacity to address social issues and, therefore, did not connect the physical environment and the local residents' well-being or address these within the physical reconstruction process. Furthermore, social workers' promotion of social rights and residents' well-being includes making suggestions that will improve governmental policies that protect human rights. Since disaster social work was not included as one of professional fields in the Post-Earthquake Provincial Reconstruction and Recovery Committee, Chinese social workers' voices were not heard and they were unable to become deeply involved in the government decision-making process. Hence, green social work interventions were barely visible in the government's key top-down policies, regulations, and plans.

The Chinese disaster social workers involved in the Wenchuan event were known to have established very solid community-based cooperation with local residents (Zheng and Han, 2009). At grassroots level, their long-term, firmly established engagement with local communities enabled them to offer evidence-based suggestions to the on-site professional designers (Wu, 2014). This is a constituent element of green social workers' mission. Hence, how did the green social workers cooperate with the community planners and architects during the Lushan event?

Methodology

Immediately after the Lushan earthquake, the author served on the provincial post-disaster reconstruction and recovery committee. The committee was directed by an interdisciplinary professional team, conducting field trips into the earthquake-hit area, to obtain first-hand information from the local communities affected by the calamity for application in the reconstruction efforts. Professors who came from the School of Architecture and Urban-Rural Development at Sichuan Agricultural University (SAU), who served in the provincial post-Lushan earthquake reconstruction and recovery committee, conducted several villages' overall planning and reconstruction in the worst-hit areas. Social workers (as research collaborators) and social work undergraduate students (as research assistants), who came from the SAU's Department of Social Work, participated in the built environment reconstruction projects in the relevant villages. These social workers and social work students also conducted other community-based social service projects, such as community mapping, coordinating related training programmes, and long-term consulting services, with cooperation of local governments and other domestic and international social work organisations.

Leading some the planning and architectural reconstruction projects, the author had good opportunities to build trust with local survivors and social workers, and gained an in-depth understanding of the green social workers' contribution during the post-disaster reconstruction and recovery processes. Qualitative research was employed in this research by conducting two focus groups and 10 individual interviews within a two-year period following the earthquake. All the participants in both the focus groups and the individual interviews were directly involved in the community reconstruction efforts after the Lushan earthquake. One of the two focus groups was designed for local inhabitants (seven participants), and the other one recruited five undergraduate social work programme students, who served as community-based research assistants and directly worked with local residents to obtain first-hand experience regarding their social demands. The individual interviewees included four local social worker practitioners from SAU, two governmental officials, two community designers, one community planner, and one architect. The transcriptions from audiotaped focus groups and interviews were imported into the qualitative data analysis software NVivo 10, through a process of coding and theming (QSR International, 2015).

Green social work interventions in PID

With official support given by central government, green social work practitioners were actively engaged in the reconstruction and recovery activities after the Lushan earthquake. This section focuses on what the green social workers accomplished during that time and how it contributed towards the practice of PID in the planning and design of the built environment reconstruction. It involved three aspects: (1) stimulating civic participation, (2) improving professional design, and (3) promoting long-term social and economic recovery.

Facilitating informal civic participation

Engaging the local inhabitants into the post-disaster decision-making process is considered the most essential step necessary to improve the quality of built environment and enhance community resilience (Aldunce et al., 2015). This type of participation establishes social equity, guarantees the local residents' social rights, and further enhances their leadership competencies. China's traditional top-down political system, however, to some extent, limits grassroots involvement in the decision-making process. Green social workers have the capacity to stimulate civic participation at grassroots level. Sim and Dominelli (2016) call this the bottom-up and top-down approach to community-based disaster reduction (CBDRR). A woman from one of the residential focus groups described her experience as:

> We watched the central government's reconstruction policies on TV. . . . My village leader announced all the information on the Internet and asked us to check [by ourselves]. Our [rural community] doesn't like the city, we are farmers, we don't know how to use [Internet]. The students from SAU brought us some pictures and talked with us [about the reconstruction plan of our village]. [After that], we know what the new village will look like and we feel good about the design.

The tense relationship that has existed for a long time between grassroots organisations and the government has restrained local residents in expressing their wishes and desires, and they disregard their rights to obtain further information from government. The social worker's consultation with the residents, based on the photos and other visual materials, guaranteed the local residents' right to know the information about potential developments in their communities, and built a fundamental step for participation.

A social worker, who was also a faculty member in the Social Work Department at SAU described the process:

> Local residents did have a lot of very good ideas [regarding planning and design of their new community]. The students collected some [reconstruction ideas] from the residents

and gave them to [interviewee]. You know that referring them [local residents to some professionals or governmental department] is useless. I must personally talk with upper level governmental officials (the major architects and community planners), to let them know [the residents'] wishes. That is a good start though!

In the rural communities, green social work practitioners protect the local people's right to know. And, they convey the desires and opinions of grassroots people to the community planner and designers. Although the top-down political system limits the local dwellers' direct and formal participation in the decision-making process, the green social workers' endeavours enable their indirect and informal participation in the reconstruction stage. Having the local residents' desires and wishes made known and even utilised in their communities' reconstruction, architects and planners value the residents' experience as the essential community-based place-making skills and knowledge, which is not only required by PID, but also fundamentally improves the quality of the planning and architectural design to fit better the local social, cultural, and environmental surroundings. These communities would fundamentally stimulate and effectively support the disaster survivor's daily activities. These would help the earthquake survivors become familiar with the new built and natural environments, and re-establish their social relationships and social networks in the new communities. These activities potentially accelerate the earthquake survivors' process of becoming attached to their new place in a smooth fashion, the ultimate aim of PID.

Improving the professional design

The planners and architects the government appointed for Wenchuan came from provinces throughout China. Their limited knowledge regarding the local natural and social environments resulted, in many instances, in their design projects not being suitable to the local surroundings and residents' needs. Some projects were not welcomed by local residents and even triggered certain problems, including the use of building materials, styles, and construction methods that did not match the local climate, inappropriate cultural processes and high maintenance expenditure for maintaining the incongruous structures. The government-appointed planners and architects involved in Lushan also came from provinces outside of Sichuan. However, the experience of Wenchuan enabled them to realise this issue and seek solutions. An architect narrated his experience as:

> Lushan County does not have enough archival documents [regarding] the local ecological, hydrological, cultural and social backgrounds. We all know that local residents have plenty of very good knowledge. But, you know, because we talk to the government, [local residents] didn't want to talk with us and did not trust us. I found that they love talking with the social workers [who provide consulting service and other types of community service].... I requested the help of social workers; that really worked very well.

A social work undergraduate student, who came from one of the worst-hit areas, discussed the reconstruction that had been conducted in her home village as:

> Some designers came to my village. Most people in my village don't like them and think they were government officials because they speak Mandarin.... Most of my neighbours are not able to speak Mandarin and the designers don't understand the Sichuan dialect. I helped translate. We told them [designers] that we needed storage space for farming tools,

> a plaza for traditional festivals and drying grain [in the harvest season]. Some elder villagers told them that the north side of our old village flooded almost every year and not to build there. Some elders said that they did not like stairs because their legs were not good. The [local] carpenter told them how to choose the right kind of wood because the humidity here is very high.

The lack of trust that the local citizens had for the local government initially blocked the way for the non-local professionals to obtain an understanding of local residents' expertise. The non-local architects and planners were eager to utilise local expertise to improve their planning and design. Social workers consulted with local residents, collected their traditional skills and knowledge, and helped local residents to open their hearts and offer their suggestions to the non-local designers. This green social work intervention built bridges between the professional designers and local residents so that the local residents' traditional knowledge and skills regarding the use of space and putting up appropriate and sturdy housing could be utilised during the reconstruction. The social work student quoted earlier in this paragraph clarified that the residents did not expect that any of their requirements would be accepted but, at the same time, all the villagers had a positive feeling about their new homes. The new village was a place for all of them. A small plaza provided an area where children and elders could have a place to socialise. The green social workers assisted the professional designers to understand deeply the relationship between the local residents' well-being and their built environment. Their efforts built a daily living platform, where local residents' daily activities could be conducted and they could enjoy the newly built communities rather than complain about how the insufficient planning and design strategies gave their post-disaster lives more trouble. Hence, the improvement in the built environment, brought about by the green social workers, supported and augmented the recovery and redevelopment of the disaster survivors' well-being.

Promoting long-term community sustainable development

Social work expertise in holistically enhancing human well-being potentially contributes to the humanitarian development in post-disaster reconstruction and recovery (Dominelli, 2015). As mentioned in the introduction section, the UN clearly highlighted the importance of the social dimension in the *Sendai Framework for Disaster Risk Reduction 2015–2030* (UN, 2015). Balancing the social and economic dimensions with the physical reconstruction enhances the community's resilience by building the community's social capacities and stimulating the community's economic development (Weisz and Taubman, 2011). Social and economic recovery will, in turn, stimulate the improvement of the built environment, protect the ecological landscape, and better facilitate sustainable development (LaMore et al., 2006). The following two examples demonstrate two approaches regarding how green social workers promoted social and economic development in the physical reconstruction.

A village leader described how social workers engaged with community-based designers and utilised his village's physical reconstruction to stimulate long-term social and economic recovery:

> The earthquake destroyed several very old, special places in our village. We all thought they were gone. They [social workers] brought in some designers and they decided to rebuild all these places. They said our village would become a tourist village. They helped us to understand that these very old places had a lot of history and were important.

> The adult men in my village are migrant workers in the cities. They [social workers] brought teachers from SAU to train the wives how to start up the tourism and how to begin some small businesses at home. . . . Embroidery is one of our traditional skills. Almost all the adult women are good at it. [Social workers] suggested that the women make some embroidery in their spare time and sell it to the tourists. And also cook some local food [for tourists]. Now, they not only have income from farming, but also from tourism and family businesses. [Women] no longer need to completely rely on their husbands.

A social worker expressed their effort of long-term social and cultural service in the earthquake-hit area:

> We proposed that the planners include a community centre in their planning. . . . Our social service stations were located in these community centres. Social work students and practitioners offered regular service in those stations, such as family or individual consulting, information regarding job opportunities in the urban areas, information about the new rural social insurance policies. We contacted other professionals to come and give lectures and training, such as new farming technologies and new agricultural seed varieties. We also focused on the very current, recent issues important in rural communities, such as left-behind children, stay-behind elders, and poverty reduction. . . . The designers also visited our station to know the feedback from local residents about how they were using their new community.

Physical reconstruction could only be completed swiftly. The positive influence of the new built environment could last for a very long period. Green social workers undertook various activities. They (1) cooperated with the professional designers to discover the local heritage and traditional customs and culture, in order to raise their awareness of the importance of their heritage; and (2) trained the local residents on new skills based on their traditions and the new landscape to strengthen their attention towards protecting their cultural and natural heritage, which potentially could support their new livelihood. The improved built environment was able to better fulfil the residents' daily requirements and support their well-being by developing new income resources and even addressed some gender-related inequity issues. Additionally, the green social workers engaged their social service in the community's long-term development process by dealing with the emerging social issues on an ongoing basis. The green social workers' effort combined social, cultural, economic, and environmental aspects into the planning and design of the new community, which further facilitated the community's long-term sustainable development.

Conclusion

The green social workers' novel approaches stimulated cooperation with planners, architects, and other community-based designers and promoted the practice of public interest design over the course of the post-disaster reconstruction and recovery cases in China. This facilitated informal civic participation and improvement of the professional design, as well as promoted long-term community sustainable development. Green social work interventions of motivating civic participation, as the primary initiative, opened a way for the disaster survivors to understand the government's reconstruction-related polices, plans, and regulations. This not only served to protect the dwellers' right to know, but also built a basic communication platform, from which the inhabitants could understand their rights and potentially have the opportunity to offer their input into the reconstruction and recovery decision-making process of their homes and lives. Furthermore, this platform might also provide an opportunity to repair or improve the very tense relationship that has existed between the local dwellers and their governments. Green social workers provided a bridge between the government-appointed designers and local residents, allowing these professionals to obtain access to the local residents' valuable, accumulated traditional place-making knowledge and construction skills. Obviously, their efforts improved the quality of the newly built environment by facilitating the local traditions to be reflected in it. This accelerated the earthquake survivors' process of attaching to their new communities and established a solid daily living platform, enabling them to recover a regular daily life and supporting the development of their well-being.

Building on the improvement of communication and daily living platforms, green social work strategies further created a sustainable development platform by embedding social and economic dimensions into the long-term recovery process. Green social workers helped the local inhabitants realise the importance of their cultural and historical heritage and to discover the value of their traditional skills. They then helped the people to utilise their heritage and skills to re-establish the local economy and address some social inequity and social injustice. The long-term community-based social service continually targets on the emerging social problems and offers practical suggestions to improve these social issues. These three platforms fundamentally improved the physical reconstruction outcomes, supported the earthquake survivors' well-being, and are still being put into practice in the long-term sustainable development of the place where they the people, the survivors, live.

Margareta Wahlström (2015), the special representative of the UN secretary-general for disaster risk reduction, made a special call to planners, architects, and other related designers which, in addition to launching an appeal that every citizen should be provided with a safe living shelter that reduces exposure to disasters, the post-disaster built environment must also support citizens' social resilience and development, by reducing their social vulnerability, enabling them to recover their social lives, and thus empowering them to exercise their social right of participating in community-related decision-making.

Dominelli (2011) and Alston (2015: 361) argue that 'social work's reticence to embrace the environment as a domain of practice has led to the profession's lack of visibility in environmental and climate change planning and decision-making'. Representing the solid community-based knowledge and skills of the rural survivors, green social workers must, ever increasingly, stand up and liaise for these people with professional designers to practice and improve the social reconstruction and recovery that accompanies physical reconstruction after disaster. This is, for both professional designers and green social workers, a social responsibility. They have to promote environmental justice and social justice in the reconstruction of the built environment and guarantee that environmental protection is provided to all residents equally.

References

Ackerly, B. A. (2016). Hidden in plain sight: Social inequalities in the context of environmental change. In R. McLeman, J. Schade, and T. Faist (Eds.), *Environmental migration and social inequality*. Cham, Switzerland: Springer International Publishing, pp. 131–149.

Aldunce, P., Beilin, R., Howden, M. and Handmer, J. (2015). Resilience for disaster risk management in a changing climate: Practitioners' frames and practices. *Global Environmental Change*, 30: 1–11.

Alston, M. (2015). Social work, climate change, and global cooperation. *International Social Work*, 58(3): 355–363.

Bell, B. (2004). *Good deeds, good design: Community service through architecture*. New York, NY: Princeton Architectural Press.

Broadbent, N. (2014). *Longmanshen fault zone still hazardous, suggest new reports*. Available on www.seismosoc.org/Society/press_releases/SRL_85-1_Lushan_Focus_Press_Release.pdf

Cary, J. and Martin, C. E. (2012, October 6). *Dignifying Design @ The New York Times*. Available on www.nytimes.com/2012/10/07/opinion/sunday/dignifying-design.html?pagewanted=all [Accessed 25 January 2015].

Chen, M. and Chan, K. L. (2016). Parental absence, child victimization, and psychological wellbeing in rural China. *Child Abuse and Neglect*, 59: 45–54.

Demick, B. (2013, April 20). China earthquake death toll reaches 156; more than 3,000 hurt. Available on http://articles.latimes.com/2013/apr/20/world/la-fg-wn-china-earthquake-death-toll-reaches-156-20130420

Dominelli, L. (2011). Climate change: Social workers' contributions to policy and practice debates. *International Social Work*, 20(4): 430–439. doi:10.1111/j.1468-2397.2011.00795.x

Dominelli, L. (2012). *Green social work: From environmental crises to environmental justice*. Cambridge: Polity Press.

Dominelli, L. (2015). The opportunities and challenges of social work interventions in disaster situations. *International Social Work*, 58(5): 659–672.

Dominelli, L. and Ioakimidis, V. (2015). Social work on the frontline in addressing disasters, social problems and marginalization. *International Social Work*, 58: 3–6.

Drolet, J., Dominelli, L., Alston, M., Ersing, R. Mathbor, G. and Wu, H. (2015). Women rebuilding lives post-disaster: Innovative community practices for building resilience and promoting sustainable development. *Gender and Development*, 23: 433–448.

Drolet, J., Wu, H., Taylor, M. and Dennehy, A. (2015). Social work and sustainable social development: teaching and learning strategies for 'green social work' curriculum. *Social Work Education: The International Journal*, 34: 528–543.

Gillespie, D. and Danso, K. (Eds.). (2010). *Disaster concepts and issues: A guide for social work education and practice*. Alexandria, VA: Council on Social Work Education.

He, C. (2016). Economic transition, urban dynamics, and economic development in China: An introduction to the special issue. *Growth and Change*, 47(1): 4–8.

Hopkins, E., Bastagli, F. and Hagen-Zanker, J. (2016). *Internal migrants and social protection: a review of eligibility and take-up*. Available on www.odi.org/sites/odi.org.uk/files/resource-documents/10473.pdf

Hu, S. (1995). *Stanley K. Hornbeck and the open door policy, 1919–1937 (No. 48)*. Westport, CT: Greenwood Publishing Group.

Hurst, W. (2009). The Chinese worker after socialism. *The China Quarterly*, 198: 459–493.

IFSW, IASSW, and ICSW. (2012). *The global agenda for social work and social development commitment to action*. Available on www.iassw-aiets.org/uploads/file/20121025_GA_E_8Mar.pdf. [online]. [Accessed 8 December 2015].

Internal Displacement Monitoring Centre (IDMC). (2015). *Global figures*. Available on www.internal-displacement.org/global-figures/#natural [Accessed 23 June 2016].

International Association of School of Social Work (IASSW). (2015). *Global definition of social work/Review of the global definition*. Available on www.iassw-aiets.org/global-definition-of-social-work-review-of-the-global-definition [Accessed 20 June 2016].

Ku, H. B. and Dominelli, L. (2017). 'Not just eating together': Space and green social work intervention in hazard affected areas in Ya'an, Sichuan, China. *British Journal of Social Work*, bcx071, https://doi.org/10.1093/bjsw/bcx071

LaMore, R. L., Link, T. and Blackmond, T. (2006). Renewing people and places: Institutional investment policies that enhance social capital and improve the built environment of distressed communities. *Journal of Urban Affairs*, 28(5): 429–442.

Leung, T. T. F. and Tam, C. H. L. (2014). The 'person-centered' rhetoric in socialist China. *British Journal of Social Work*, bct192, 1–19. doi:10.1093/bjsw/bct192

Nesmith, A. (2015, June 17). *Environmental justice in our backyard: Environmental hazards affecting vulnerable Minnesota communities* [PowerPoint slides]. Available on http://umacs.org/wp-content/uploads/2013/09/EnvironmentalJusticeInOurBackyard_AndeNesmith.pdf [Accessed 27 December 2015].

Oliver-Smith, A. (2010). *Defying displacement: Grassroots resistance and the critique of development*. Austin, TX: University of Texas Press.

QSR International. (2015). *What is NVivo?* Available on www.qsrinternational.com/what-is-nvivo

Sim, T. and Dominelli, L. (2016). When the mountains move: A Chinese post-disaster psychosocial social work model. *Qualitative Social Work*, 16: 594–611.

Thompson-Dyck, K., Mayer, B., Anderson, K. F., and Galaskiewicz, J. (2016). Bringing people back in: Crisis planning and response embedded in social contexts. In Y. Yamagata and H. Maruyama (Eds.), *Urban resilience*. Cham, Switzerland: Springer International Publishing, pp. 279–293.

United Nations Office for Disaster Risk Reduction (UNISDR). (2010). *Wenchuan earthquake 2008: Recovery and reconstruction in Sichuan province*. Available on www.unisdr.org/we/inform/publications/16777

United Nations. (2015). *Sendai framework for disaster risk reduction*. Available on www.unisdr.org/files/43291_sendaiframeworkfordrren.pdf

Vervaeck, A. (2013, April 27). *Deadly earthquake Sichuan (Ya'an), China – Death toll now at 196 (21 missing)*, April 26 update. Available on http://earthquake-report.com/2013/04/20/very-strong-earthquake-sichuan-china-on-april-20-2013/

Wahlström, M. (2015). *New Sendai Framework*. Keynote address presented at Sixth annual roundtable on disaster risk reduction: Charting the future of disaster risk reduction in Canada, Calgary, AB, Canada, November 2.

Warner, K. D. and DeCosse, D. (2009). *Lesson five environmental justice*. Available on www.scu.edu/ethics/practicing/focusareas/environmental_ethics/lesson5.html [Accessed 22 November 2015].

Weisz, A. and Taubman, A. (2011). Emerging concerns for international social work and disaster response: From relief to development and sustainability. *Columbia Social Work Review*, 2: 37–48.

World Commission on Environment and Development. (1987). *Our common future*. Oxford: Oxford University Press.

Wu, H. (2014). *Post-Wenchuan Earthquake Rural Reconstruction and Recovery, in Sichuan China: Memory, Civic Participation and Government Intervention* (Doctoral Dissertation). Available on http://circle.ubc.ca/handle/2429/50340

Wu, H. and Hou, C. (2016). Community social planning: The social worker's role in post-earthquake reconstruction and recovery planning, Sichuan China. *Social Dialogue*, 4: 26–29.

Yan, M. C. and Cheung, W. K. (2006). Politics of indigenization: A case study of development of social work in China. *Journal of Sociology and Social Welfare*, 33(2): 63–84.

Zakour, M. J. (2010). Vulnerability and risk assessment: Building community resilience. In D. F. Gillespie and K. Danso (Eds.), *Disaster concepts and issues: A guide for social work education and practice*. Alexandria, VA: Council on Social Work Education, pp. 15–33.

Zheng, L. and Han, Y. (2009). Post-disaster reconstruction and social work development in the Chinese mainland. *China Journal of Social Work*, 2(3): 221–223.

8
Solidarity in times of disaster
The case of Chile

Rosemary A. Barbera

Introduction

When disaster strikes, people become off-balance, confused, dazed, overwhelmed and shocked. During times of great stress such as disasters, people may be supported by their community and engage in profound acts of solidarity. Thus, the experience of disaster is one of incredible stress, but it is also one of deep community, solidarity, support and courage, especially in the Global South. Here, community ties and collective well-being are often more important than individual success or status.

Chile is a country known for its seismic activity. Some of the world's strongest earthquakes have occurred there. In February 2010, Chile experienced an earthquake that measured 8.8 on the Richter Scale. The earthquake was so strong that it changed the world's rotation slightly. In the following weeks, the press showed numerous photos of intense destruction caused by the earthquake and the so-called post-earthquake looting. While some people do take advantage of the chaotic aftermath of a disaster, this is often an outcome of inequality. In societies that are unequal, violence is more pervasive (Houle, 2016) than in poor societies. Certain things may be expected to happen. Often the media show us pictures and relate stories that confirm that perception. But that is not the whole story (Tierney, 2003).

The press was covered with images of people who were bereft, needy, powerless and alone. However, many people react altruistically (Solnit, 2009) in communities during and after disasters due to their existing social ties and commitment to others. The press did not report the incredible acts of solidarity that were evident throughout Chile. After the Chilean disaster of the military coup on Tuesday, 11 September 1973, similar acts of solidarity and resiliency were demonstrated throughout Chile. These responses are not atypical and are often overshadowed by the responses of large international NGOs that rob common people of their agency and take over as elite panic sets in.

This chapter examines community responses to disaster, both human-made and natural, from a perspective of solidarity and resiliency. It shares the responses of some of the most affected Chileans during the disaster and tells their stories of survival and community and contextualises these within the long tradition of brave acts of solidarity of ordinary Chileans. The chapter builds on 29 years of work and study in Chile examining the immense solidarity of ordinary people in the face of death and destruction, whether a dictatorship or a natural disaster. The examples of ordinary Chileans can teach social workers a good deal about resiliency, solidarity, community building, and relationships of partnership and mutuality.

This chapter does not claim that disasters do not produce suffering. They do. And, they exacerbate already tenuous living situations for so many in the world. At the same time, disaster 'relief' often ignores the community and does not build on already-existing community resources.

Background

On 18 September 1810, Chile began a 10-year war that resulted in independence from Spain. However, its relationship with Spain and the influence of Spanish culture and society did not end there. The new country of Chile was heavily influenced by Spanish custom, culture, religion and government. The Spanish colonisers based the state on their view of Catholicism as hierarchical and a strong oligarchy (Salazar and Pinto, 1999). This tradition of oligarchical power in the hands of an elite group persisted throughout the 19th and 20th centuries (Vitale, 1992). And, it compelled 19th-century miners of the nitrate mines in northern Chile to forge an alliance and seek better working conditions. This was the first of many examples of the working class standing up for themselves and organising to improve the quality of their work and lives. This led to the formation of the first unions in Chile and the start of a 'long march' (Winn, 1986) that 140 years later would culminate with the 1970 election of Salvador Allende Gossens, a socialist, as president of the Republic.

Allende ran for president at the head of a coalition of political parties known as the *Unidad Popular* (Popular Unity – UP), promising to redistribute the wealth of Chile – the largest exporter of copper in the world – to improve the quality of life of all. Allende was supported by the working-class and poor people of Chile, but he faced significant opposition from within the country, and from Washington, D.C. (Petras and Morley, 1975; Verdugo, 2004). The Cuban Revolution was only 11 years old and the Nixon Administration feared that if Chile 'fell to communism' there would be radical changes throughout the Americas (Kornbluh, 1998; National Security Archive, n.d.; Uribe and Opaso, 2001). Nixon and Kissinger developed a plan to 'make the Chilean economy scream' and defeat Allende (Kornbluh, 2003). The United States (US) intervened economically and militarily to destabilise the country. On Tuesday, 11 September 1973, the Chilean military, headed by Augusto Pinochet Ugarte, staged a military coup, supported by the Chilean elites, and ushered in over 17 years of state terrorism.

During the first years of the dictatorship, the principal aim was to 'cure Chile of its communist cancer' (quote attributed to General Pinochet). The military regime focused on eliminating leaders in the *poblaciones* (shantytowns), factories and political parties associated with the UP. The military claimed that they were waging an internal war against the threat of godless communism, and they established massive concentration camps in soccer stadiums in Santiago, on remote islands in the South and old mining towns in the North. In these concentration camps, they brutally tortured and killed prisoners. From these camps, thousands of persons disappeared; the majority of their remains are still missing. Some of the bodies of the disappeared were thrown into the sea; others were buried in clandestine graves. According to the Truth Commission Report, 'the system of disappearances was systematically applied during the first four years of military rule. Detention of the victims was not acknowledged' (*Comisión Nacional*, 1991: xxv).

During this time, all organisations and meetings, including church meetings, were outlawed by the military junta, especially in poor areas. Political meetings were banned, as was all neighbourhood organising. Anyone found organising or engaging in communal activities was subject to arrest, torture and worse. The military police and armed forces patrolled the country and decreed a state of siege so that people could not be on the streets after dusk. Despite these consequences, resilient *pobladores* (people living in shantytowns) throughout Chile continued to organise. They organised in different ways, and under different auspices, but, 'the citizens had learned to participate and wanted to participate, and they did not accept, at this point in their own development, to be excluded' (Salazar and Pinto, 1999: 49). The numbers of persons participating dramatically decreased, but there was still activity throughout the country.

The resilience that ordinary Chileans demonstrated immediately after the coup and for over 17 years of military dictatorship is a strong indicator of the resilience of Chileans, and solidarity as a societal value. This ensured everyone had access to food, especially if family members were being pursued by the military. Acts of solidarity became less numerous as the regime dragged on and people became fearful for themselves. These are the same characteristics that led so many Chileans to assist their neighbours after the earthquake in 2010.

Earthquakes and reactions to disaster

Seismic activity has led to many disasters around the world. In places where there is little infrastructure and high levels of poverty, the devastation can be massive and lead to already-precarious living conditions becoming threatening.

> Earthquakes, tsunamis, hurricanes, and other natural disasters shed light on social cracks and fissures invisible in everyday life. These disasters provoke social crises that states tend to resolve with militarization, which in turn shows the profound crises that our societies have been undergoing.
>
> *(Zibechi, 2010: 1)*

The fissures in the Earth seem to mirror the fissures in society, or vice versa. This does not mean that the people most affected are unable to respond and are reduced to rubble like the buildings around them. Examples from around the world – San Francisco, CA in 1906, and Mexico City in 1985 (Solnit, 2009) – demonstrate the resilience of people who in the midst of disaster save the lives of others. '[T]he prevalent human nature in disaster is resilient, resourceful, generous, empathic, and brave' (Solnit, 2009: 8), reaching out to neighbours, known and unknown, to offer assistance and work together to survive. This is particularly true in more collectivist societies or among immigrant populations from collectivist societies. 'What you believe shapes how you act. How you act results in life or death, for yourself or others' (Solnit, 2009: 2). So, if one believes in the goodness of humanity and if they see their well-being tied to the well-being of others, they respond accordingly.

Elite panic

While those most affected are responding to disaster, government organisms and non-governmental organisations are also mobilising. While they often lend needed assistance and have the ability to provide tangible goods such as food and temporary housing, they often impose their assistance on those affected without incorporating people who have already been mobilised. In many instances, governmental and non-governmental organisations dismantle the organic forms of organising and assistance that emerge during disasters. Their articulated concern is the wish to deal with panic and chaos in the community, but research reveals that panic is relatively rare and is more pervasive in situations where social bonds do not exist. However, panic exists in the plans of those who prepare the responses to disaster (Clarke and Chase, 2008). To a certain measure, perpetuating the myth of panic also serves the interests of the elites in that they can impose their model of relief and maintain their importance in the hierarchy (Tierney, 2003). This is often discussed in the literature as 'elite panic'.

Elite panic underestimates the ability of people to organise and provide assistance and safety for themselves and their community. Elite panic emerges from the belief that the organising that occurs after disaster will usurp the role of the state and of powerful NGOs. 'Planners and policy makers sometimes act as if the human response to threatening conditions is more dangerous than the threatening conditions themselves' (Clarke and Chase, 2008: 994). So, they quickly move in to squash work that has sprung up organically and do not recognise that 'in the wake of an earthquake, a bombing, or a major storm, most people are altruistic, urgently engaged in caring for themselves and those around them, strangers and neighbours as well as friends and loved ones' (Solnit, 2009: 2). These planners doubt the good intentions of those who have mobilised and see themselves as the rightful 'saviours'.

Research has demonstrated that this image of people in a chaotic panic is not accurate (see Clarke and Chase, 2008; and Solnit, 2009).

> Decades of meticulous sociological research on behaviour in disasters, from the bombings of World War II to floods, tornadoes, earthquakes, and storms across the continent and around the world, have demonstrated this, but belief lags behind, and often the worst behaviour in the wake of a calamity is on the part of those who believe that others will behave savagely and that they themselves are taking defensive measures against barbarism.
>
> *(Solnit, 2009: 2)*

Elite panic is based on a fallacy that is perpetuated by those who have built a reputation for action after disasters and who can disseminate their message quickly through press and state channels. But, like the Chileans that continued to organise under threat during the military regime, in the aftermath of disasters many people continue to organise and engage in profound solidarity work. The next section will discuss this.

Protagonists and protagonism

The epicentre of the 2010 earthquake was in the final weekend of summer in the south of Chile, close to the coast. Many people were at the coast. Residents, accustomed to earthquakes and increased sea levels, were able to escape. Tourists, however, were not as lucky because they did not know to flee to higher ground. The tsunami left boats more than a kilometre inland after the sea receded. The earthquake toppled historic buildings and new constructions. It did not affect constructions from the Allende years, however, since they were built to withstand earthquakes, a policy that the Pinochet regime repealed.

Amidst all that destruction were courageous acts of solidarity among people who knew each other and people who did not. Disaster requires that:

> we act, and act altruistically, bravely, and with initiative in order to survive or save the neighbors, no matter how we vote or what we do for a living. The positive emotions that arise in those unpromising circumstances demonstrate that social ties and meaningful work are deeply desired, readily improvised, and intensely rewarding.
>
> *(Solnit, 2009: 7)*

In Chile the history of people acting bravely in the face of disaster and political violence surfaced after the earthquake to show that 'the prevalent human nature in disaster is resilient, resourceful, generous, empathic, and brave' (Solnit, 2009: 9).

A defining characteristic of outside groups responding to disasters is a focus on work with individuals to help them deal with trauma. While these events are indeed traumatic, in collective cultures, the individual approach is not helpful. Survivors of torture and disaster, for example, talk about their need to be connected to others in order to heal. The assistance they need is in rebuilding what was damaged so that they can return to some semblance of normality. When survivors of torture return to their communities, they are able to reintegrate well when they have a community group, political party or religious organisation that welcomes them back. It is only when their ties to the community have been broken – because community members are scared to associate with them, for instance, that they fare poorly and need therapeutic assistance. They need to be reconnected to community for the 'language of therapy speaks almost exclusively of the consequence of disaster as trauma, suggesting a humanity that is unbearably fragile, a self that does not act but is acted upon, the most basic recipe of the victim' (Solnit, 2009: 9). The following examples demonstrate the resilience and power that many survivors embody.

La Pincoya

The *población La Pincoya* emerges within the context of land taken by poor people without a home of their own, taking over unused land and establishing squatters' settlements. These land takeovers were well-organised by community groups actively working to find a solution to a lack of adequate housing in poor areas (Lagos, et al., 2002). *La Pincoya* was formed through a series of *tomas* (land takeovers) in the late 1960s. Neighbours had been meeting and saving money to work with the government to find housing.

When the government became unresponsive, they searched for suitable spaces themselves. They found these and talked with the owners who agreed to sell the land to the government to build low-income housing. Government disinterest led people to engage in a series of land takeovers, with the permission of the owners of the land to call attention to their situation and force the government to work with them. When Allende was campaigning for president he visited these *tomas* and promised that if he were elected, he would work with them to construct their new houses. Shortly after his election Allende returned to *La Pincoya* and fulfilled his promise. He and his administration worked closely with the residents to plan and build their neighbourhood. The people themselves worked closely with the architects to design the size and layout of their homes, including what kind of materials would be used in their construction.

Starting a new neighbourhood with more than 500 families was an awesome task that required high levels of organisation. The leaders of *La Pincoya* were up to the challenge and mobilised the residents to work in committees to establish schools, public transport and healthcare, as well as bringing plumbing and electricity to the neighbourhood. They continued to organise to build homes, schools and health centres. On the morning on 11 September 1973, residents awoke to helicopters circling overhead and tanks in their streets. Because this area was known to be one of significant organisation, it was one of the first areas to suffer the repression of the military regime. On that day, and in the weeks to follow, men and boys were rounded up and taken to a nearby soccer field where they stood for hours on end in the rain, without food or water. While they remained in the field, houses were searched. This happened not once, but repeatedly in the first year of the dictatorship. Neighbourhood leaders were also rounded up and taken to military barracks.

Luzmenia Toro remembers being taken and held *incomunicada* for days, away from her three young children and husband. She was released, only to be rearrested a number of times. Hers is not the only case. The residents' work of building their lives and their homes stopped dead in its tracks since any collective work was now considered subversive or terrorist activity. According to Luzmenia:

> We had continued to battle for our houses. We were lucky because our homes, in this sector (of *La Pincoya*) were completed before the military coup – other sectors were not so lucky. Our houses were stable, built of brick and designed by us. They may have been small, but they met our needs. Neighbours from other *tomas* saw how we had designed our homes and decided they wanted the same. However, after the coup, all advancement in building the houses ceased, and our neighbours were left living in shacks. You can still see the difference today, nearly 40 years later.
>
> *(Personal communication, June, 2010)*

The military coup interrupted the social processes and collective life of *La Pincoya*. While much had been accomplished through ongoing collective struggle and sacrifice, much remained to be done. The collective life of this *población*, and so many others, was brutally curtailed by outside forces that used military might to control them. Residents were left terrorised and scared; their leaders were jailed, and tortured. Some leaders were assassinated; others disappeared; and still others fled for their lives. According to one leader, 'The social leaders were persecuted by the government of Pinochet; many were disappeared, others killed' (Personal communication, June, 2010), but they did not stop their work. This is the miracle of *La Pincoya*.

Participation in popular organisations dropped after the coup. Despite the devastating terror that was overwhelming the country, some leaders in *La Pincoya* continued to meet and organise clandestinely. The leaders of the *población* began *comedores infantiles* to distribute food to children in the *población*. After the coup, unemployment levels were high because factories were closed and people who had any relationship to the UP or unions were repressed. Since *La Pincoya* had a high concentration of residents who supported the UP, this *población* was hit especially hard by the military. These *comedores* first focused on the children of people who were detained or had to flee the country, and then on other children. Eventually they became *comedores populares*, providing food to children and adults, without distinction.

Aside from the *comedores*, residents organised *bolsas de cesantes* (groups of unemployed workers) and workshops to train people in labour-oriented skills such as sewing. They worked closely with the pastor of the local Catholic Church, and formed women's groups, health committees and youth groups. In the wake of the dictatorship disaster, these neighbours demonstrated incredible resilience and protagonism.

When the earthquake of 2010 occurred, residents of *La Pincoya* once again mobilised. Although the epicentre was far to the south of *La Pincoya*, the earthquake and tsunami affected the electrical grid of most of Chile. Consequently, people were left without electricity and unable to get water since the pumps were not functioning. Leaders worked with youth leaders to organise brigades to walk the two kilometres to get water and walk back uphill to distribute it. They also took cell phones to be charged at the police barracks over one kilometre away. Likewise, they distributed food to people since many stores were not functioning and people without work could not afford to purchase food. Finally, the health committees that saved lives during the military regime and continued to work to put pressure on the government to fulfil the human right to health offered healthcare to neighbours since health clinics were barely functioning. Once again, *Pincoyanos* were the protagonists of their own lives. As neighbourhood leader Luzmenia Toro explained, 'La Pincoya is a testament to the pursuit of human rights. Its creation is due to the resiliency of the people and the effects that people can have when they unite and work together for a common goal' (Personal communication, June, 2010).

Agüita de la Perdiz

In the South of Chile, in the city of Concepción, close to the epicentre of the earthquake, the damage and devastation from the powerful quake was very severe. Tall buildings were reduced to rubble and entire neighbourhoods swallowed by the sea. Water and electricity were cut off everywhere and many streets were impassable because they had buckled or were filled with debris. In this context, neighbours of *población Agüita de la Perdiz* organised to take care of one another.

Like *La Pincoya*, *Agüita de la Perdiz* is an emblematic *población* whose roots are tied to a land takeover and whose residents actively opposed the military regime. Precariously situated on the side of hill, houses seem placed in a haphazard way, looking like they might tumble down the hill at any moment. Most residents are working class and have seen their ability to earn a liveable wage deteriorate over more than 30 years with the imposition of a savage form of neoliberalism in Chile.

The first priority of leaders of *Agüita de la Perdiz* was to care for survivors and search for those missing. After the initial search, some leaders began to organise getting food to residents and finding clean water. At this point, the story of *Agüita de la Perdiz* becomes more interesting. The press in Chile and beyond was focusing on the immense damage caused by the earthquake and tsunami. Pictures of destruction abounded in news reports; the images were not pleasant. In the midst of these images of destruction, the press began to show images of a couple of stores being looted by people in Concepción. The same images were shown over and over, as if to argue that large-scale looting was occurring. The stories focused on one man who stole a television set and others who ransacked the local supermarket. What the media stories did not show was that the leaders of *Agüita de la Perdiz* used that food and water to feed the people of the community. The news continued to call out the 'looters' and condemn them on live television, but no one bothered to ask the 'looters' what they planned to do with these supplies.

Moreover, not only did the leaders from *Agüita de la Perdiz* reach out to others in Concepción from middle- and upper-class neighbourhoods, but also asked them if they needed supplies. As one woman, a university professor at nearby *Universidad de Concepción*, stated:

> I live close to a shantytown (*Agüita de la Perdiz*). I saw with my own eyes what happened to the supposedly looted boxes – they were immediately distributed outside of the local school, and packages were made for those who were hardest hit. In fact, days after the hurricane, when the government had not yet responded and there was nothing else around, the people of the shantytown came to us to see if we were OK and to offer us, the middle-class, help. They were not trying to sell us anything, they offered help for free and they left a package for me with candles and batteries.
>
> *(Personal communication, June, 2010)*

Once again, people in dire circumstances demonstrated their resilience and reached out to others to share what they had available. This provides a lesson for social workers who are concerned with ensuring that all persons can live a life of dignity.

Application to social work

Stories like those from *La Pincoya* and *Agüita de la Perdiz* appear regularly throughout the world. People share what little they have with people who have even less. The lesson is not that we need little to survive, as some would have us believe. The real lesson is that through solidarity we improve our lives and the lives of those around us. This lesson is an important one. Green social workers can take away significant lessons from these stories and apply these to work with vulnerable populations. They can learn to: see beyond mainstream accounts of what is happening; question theories including those of elite panic; and accept people as protagonists who take charge of their own lives when appropriate conditions exist. They can pursue justice, not charity, and integrate vicarious resilience into their practice.

Believe in the power of the people, not those in power

One of the central lessons exemplified by *La Pincoya* and *Agüita de la Perdiz* is that real change can come from below. Paraphrasing Margaret Mead, change can only happen when people themselves organise to make it happen. While affecting policy is an important commitment of social work, it is woefully insufficient. Even the most honest of politicians must be backed by the people to propose legislation that can make significant change. Opposition to them has vast reserves of money. Those struggling for social and economic justice do not have those resources so they have to be loud and persistent, as well as allow those most affected by injustice to lead. This means giving up the tired slogan of 'being a voice for the voiceless'. That statement robs people of their agency. Vulnerable and oppressed groups are not voiceless; their voices are just not listened to. Social workers have to use the power and privilege afforded by their education and professional status in society, not to be ventriloquists, but to make sure those voices are heard. Rather, we can help open doors of power and then step aside to let the people enter first.

Given the fear that the elite have, making sure people's voices are heard is not insignificant. As seen in disasters, those in power fear the potential power of their constituents (Solnit, 2009). People's responses of generosity and solidarity to political violence and natural disasters, demonstrate that even in the face of great danger, significant social change can be achieved if these were permitted to continue. Fearful elites truncate those processes. One factor is that:

> Elites fear disruption of the social order, challenges to their legitimacy. . . . Fear of social disorder; fear of poor [people], minorities and immigrants; obsession with looting and property crime; willingness to resort to deadly force; and actions taken on the basis of rumor.
> *(Tierney, 2003: 34)*

This fear is about losing control, stature and power in society. Thus, control and order are imposed from above. The people themselves have many of the answers to social problems and with further resources, could be the engines of social change. Movements for social change begin by building community and green social workers can play a role in making that happen. 'People at that moment [of disaster] felt a solidarity and an empathy for each other that they did not feel at other times' (Solnit, 2009: 28) since they were facing a crisis together. Green social workers can help that cooperation and community continue and grow.

Believe in people – vicarious resilience

Another powerful lesson from people who organise to meet their needs in times of crisis, disaster and danger refers to the power of vicarious resilience. Social workers often experience vicarious trauma because they work with people who have suffered greatly. This vicarious trauma is real since the stories many social workers hear and witness can be profoundly harmful. However, by only focusing on trauma, social workers ignore one of the profession's tenets – to believe in the innate strength and resilience of human beings rather than its pathologies and weaknesses. Many people with whom practitioners work have suffered greatly, but they have survived despite those circumstances. The trauma can be both acknowledged and work with to overcome it, while simultaneously celebrating their resilience and integrating that resilience into social workers' own lives (Enstrom, Hernández, and Gangsei, 2008).

Likewise, the Northern World's interpretations of what is needed must be left behind because those interpretations can strip communities of their resiliency and solidarity and cause long-term damage rather than healing. After the massive tsunami that hit Asia in 2004, people from helping professions from the Northern World arrived *en masse* to places like Sri Lanka to offer psychological support. They never asked whether a network of professionals already engaged in this work existed in Sri Lanka because the country was in the midst of a long-standing civil war. Nor did they know the local languages or cultures. They just assumed that their model of healing after disaster would be useful. It was not, and the Psychosocial Working Group of Sri Lanka published a brochure kindly asking the foreigners to leave as they were doing more harm than good (Araceli Garcia del Soto, Personal communication, May, 2005), a concern echoed by green social workers (Dominelli, 2012).

Social workers can also learn from those who worked with people affected by significant political violence, including torture, assassination and disappearance. They have noted how inspired they were by the people with whom they worked. The way people 'overcame adversity affected or changed the therapist's own attitude and emotions' (Hernández, Gangsei, and Engstrom, 2007: 234). The therapists' vicarious learning was positive – they were able to integrate the resilience of the people and not be held down by traumatic experiences. In at least one case, the therapist was affected to the extent that she was able to regain hope for the future (Hernández, Gangsei and Engstrom, 2007).

Pursue justice and liberation, not charity

Another powerful lesson for practitioners to learn from these examples of solidarity and mutual aid is that what is being done is not charity, which perpetuates the status quo and unjust social structures. Rather, these call upon the profession to ensure that practice advances social and economic justice and leads to liberation. Charity is short term and does not ask the hard questions that go to the root of the problem. Thus, charity is often welcome in the face of disaster because it does not upset the structures already in place. Justice, as green social workers argue, makes us question those structures, recognise that they are inherently unjust and have been put in place to benefit a few.

Charity can also be humiliating. In the south of Chile, for example, government shacks began to arrive to house those most affected by the earthquake and tsunami months later. Winter was coming and the crisis was worsening because the Chilean winter in the South is harsh. The housing that the government sent had gaping holes in the sides of the structures. The wind close to the coast can be fierce in winter and the cold whipped through these shacks. The wood used to construct the homes was nothing more than particleboard which had already begun to swell and develop mould with the winter rains. The people clearly understood that they were not a priority. They were living in shacks that were so poorly constructed they would not last through the month. However, these same shacks came with electric metres already installed so that they could be charged for using electricity right away. People who I spoke with (May, 2010) were humiliated and indignant. Some even decided to burn the shacks, preferring to build their own structures with their neighbours in order to survive the winter. 'The difference between citizens feeding themselves and each other and being given food according to a system involving tickets and outside administrators is the difference between independence and dependence, between mutual aid and charity' (Solnit, 2009: 47). Solidarity, or mutual aid, should be the priority of social workers committed to social transformation and individual and community empowerment according to green social work principles (Dominelli, 2012).

Conclusion

Responses to natural and political disasters, including the earthquake/tsunami and military coup/dictatorship in Chile, offer examples of how best to support the organic work that communities of vulnerable populations have always performed for their survival. Because that work is ongoing, these communities are well prepared to respond to disasters by continuing with their assistance and support of each other. These moments give a glimpse into how society might be better organised. 'It is present immediately, instantly, when people demonstrate resourcefulness, altruism, improvisational ability and kindness. A disaster produces chaos immediately, but the people hit by that chaos usually improvise' (Solnit, 2009: 95) to respond in solidarity with one another and provide for and with one another.

The kinds of responses of ordinary people are those of people who care about others and are concerned for their collective future. These are people who, in the moments after disaster, embody what it means to be civically active for the betterment of society. Rather than expending so much energy trying to control them, social workers should be asking how to cooperate to strengthen and recreate this type of civic action all the time. This action is democracy in action: 'Here the people govern and the government obeys' (Los Zapatistas, as cited by Solnit, 2009: 180). Luzmenia Toro, who at 18 was one of the principal organisers of the *toma* that became *La Pincoya* sums it up well: 'Resistimos, y seguiremos resistiendo, porque la historia nuestra es una de protagonismo'. 'We have resisted, and will continue resisting because our history is a history of protagonism' (Personal communication, July, 2010, author's translation). Social workers are faced with the challenge: Do they obstruct such protagonism and become agents of social control, or do they follow the lead of the people to become true agents of change as advocated by green social workers?

References

Clarke, L. and Chase, C. (2008). Elites and panic: More to fear than fear itself. *Social Forces*, 87(2): 993–1014.
Comisión Nacional de Verdad y Reconciliación. (1991). *Informe* [Report]. Santiago: Ercilla.
Dominelli, L. (2012). *Green social work: From environmental crises to environmental justice*. Cambridge, UK/Malden, MA: Polity Press.
Engstrom, D., Hernández, P. and Gangsei, D. (2008). Vicarious resilience: A qualitative investigation into its description. *Traumatology: An International Journal*, 14(3): 13–21.
Hernández, P., Gangsei, D. and Engstrom, D. (2007). Vicarious resilience: A new concept to work with those who survive trauma. *Family Process*, 46(2): 229–241.
Houle, C. (2016). Why class inequality breeds coups but not civil wars. *Journal of Peace Research*, 53(5): 680–695.
Kornbluh, P. (1998). *Chile and the United States: Declassified Documents Relating to the Military Coup*, 11 September 1973. Available on George Washington University, National Security Archive Web site: www.gwu.edu/~nsarchiv/ [Accessed 18 July 2001].

Kornbluh, P. (Ed.). (2003). *The Pinochet file: A declassified dossier on atrocity and accountability*. New York: The New Press.

Lagos, J., González, J. M, Núnez, N., Rodríguez, G., and Finn, J. (2002). *La Victoria: Rescatando la historia* [La Victoria: Reclaiming History]. Santiago, Chile: Junta de Vecinos de La Victoria.

National Security Archive. (n.d.). *Chile and the United States*. Retrieved as updated between 1997 and present, from www.gwu.edu/~nsarchiv/NSAEBB/NSAEBB8/nsaebb8i.htm

Petras, J. and Morley, M. (1975). *The United States and Chile: Imperialism and the overthrow of the Allende government*. New York: Monthly Review Press.

Salazar, G. and Pinto, J. (1999). *Historia contemporanea de Chile I: Estado, Legitimidad, ciudadanía* [The Contemporary history of Chile I: State, Legitimacy, Citizenship]. Santiago, Chile: Lom Ediciones.

Solnit, R. (2009). *A Paradise Built in Hell: The Extraordinary Communities That Arise in Disaster*. New York: Penguin Group.

Tierney, K. (2003). Disaster beliefs and institutional interests: Recycling disaster myths in the Aftermath of 9–11. In L. Clarke (Ed.), *Research in Social Problems and Public Policy*. Bradford, UK: Emerald Group Publishing Limited, pp. 33–51.

Uriba, A. and Opasa, C. (2001). *Intervención Norteamericana en Chile: Dos textos claves* [North American Intervention in Chile: Two key texts]. Santiago de Chile: Editorial Sudamericana.

Verdugo, P. (2004). *La Casa Blanca contra Salvador Allende: Los orígenes de la Guerra preventive* [The White House against Salvador Allende: The origins of preventative war]. Madrid: Tabla Rasa.

Vitale, L. (1992). *Interpretación Marxista de la historia de Chile* [Marxist Interpretation of Chilean History]. Santiago, Chile: Ediciones CELA.

Winn, P. (1986). *Weavers of revolution: The Yarur workers and Chile's road to socialism*. New York: Oxford University Press.

Zibechi, R. (2010). *Eathquake and tsunami in Chile: The militarization of natural disasters*. Retrieved from http://upsidedownworld.org/archives/chile/earthquake-and-tsunami-in-chile-the-militarization-of-natural-disasters/

9
Social work response to Himalayan disasters
Insights from green social work

Bala Raju Nikku

Introduction

The Himalayan region is very susceptible to disasters. The North Indian State of Uttarakhand, with abundant perpendicular slopes, ample water and turbulent rivers has a history of ecological chaos. A multi-day cloud burst (sudden violent rainstorm) centred on the Uttarakhand from 14 to 17 June 2013 caused devastating floods and landslides which became India's worst natural disaster since the 2004 Indian Ocean Tsunami. The enormity was exceptional in 130 years of Indian meteorological records. More than 6,000 people and thousands of animals lost their lives; many were stranded for days before being rescued. Tens of thousands of houses, public buildings and over 15,000 kilometres of roads got damaged and 4,000 villages were affected.

In Nepal, two mega-earthquake disasters during April and May 2015 shook Nepal's social, economic, political and cultural fabric. More than 10,000 lives were lost, 500,000 houses buckled and another 250,000 schools and hospitals and other vital infrastructures collapsed.

Were these Himalayan disasters caused by climate change coupled with reckless human greed and corrupt governance practices? What has been the social work response? Taking concepts from Dominelli's (2012) *Green Social Work*, this chapter builds on the Himalayan disasters research project in India and Nepal supported by the International Association of Schools of Social Work (IASSW). The chapter, divided into four sections, discusses how social workers used green social work perspectives in Nepal and India; prepared for and responded to disasters; and assisted in building resilient communities. It concludes that green social work offers a model relevant to these disasters.

Himalayan disasters and development

The Himalayas or Himalaya are a mountain range in Asia separating the plains of the Indian subcontinent from the Tibetan Plateau. The Himalayan range has the Earth's highest peaks, including the highest, Mount Everest (8,848 metres). The Himalayas include over 100 mountains exceeding 7,200 metres (23,600 ft) in elevation. The Himalayas are spread across five countries: Bhutan, India, Nepal, Pakistan (from the South Asian region) and China. Some of the world's major rivers – the Indus, the Ganges, and the Tsangpo-Brahmaputra – rise in the Himalayas, and their combined drainage basin is home to some 600 million people. The Himalayas have profoundly shaped the cultures of South Asia; many Himalayan peaks are sacred in Hinduism and Buddhism (https://en.wikipedia.org/wiki/Himalayas).

The Himalayas as a region has always been susceptible to disasters like earthquakes, landslides, floods and lake outbursts, due to the neo-tectonic mountain building processes. The Himalayas are heavily glaciated, due to their high altitude (and consequent low temperatures) and snowfall brought by the summer monsoon (in the central and eastern Himalayas) and winter storms (mainly in the western Himalayas). The Himalayas are tectonically active and the combination of earthquakes and long steep slopes is particularly worrying. Some parts of the Himalaya are more active than others (www.st-andrews.ac.uk).

To understand the nature of Himalayan disasters, one should also be aware of the three main Himalayan river systems and their impact on the livelihoods of millions of people in the Hindu-Kush Himalayan region. The three river systems are the: Indus (Sindhu) – Sutlaj, Byans, Chenab, Jhelum, Nubra, Syok, Kabul (covering Tibet, India, Pakistan, Afghanistan); Ganga – Yamuna, Kali, Karnali, Ghaghra, Kosi (Tibet, India, Nepal, Bangladesh); and Brahmaputra – Teesta, Siang, Subarnsiri, Lohit, Manas (Tibet, India, Bhutan, Bangladesh).

The spread of reckless developmental activities in this region coupled with unchecked, corrupt governance practices have transformed many natural hazards into human-made disasters. Two of the most populous nations in Asia and the world, China and India, are building hundreds of dams in a violently active geologic zone, possibly causing more earthquakes in the Himalayas. Earthquakes could fracture hydro-dams and cause secondary disasters placing a heavy toll on life, property and development infrastructures. The aftershocks that follow such quakes also crack or damage other smaller hydropower projects resulting in dam bursts. Landslide disasters are another major source of damage and destruction in the region and are associated with other calamities like earthquakes, floods or volcanoes, involving movements of the earth.

The Himalayan region is a diverse and complex region, prone to both natural and political disasters. Communities in the Himalayan region maintain a close relationship with livestock, because animal husbandry forms part of a livelihood strategy and culture. It plays a vital role for the survival of people especially in the 'drier parts where production systems usually are based on some form of pastoralism, which involves seasonal mobility of herds and people between grazing areas' (Anderson et al., 2010: 204).

The research sites: Uttarakhand (India) and Nepal

Uttarakhand

The Indian state of Uttarakhand shares borders with Tibet (China) and Nepal. Uttarakhand is the 27th state of India, newly carved in the year 2000 by joining a number of districts from the northwestern part of Uttar Pradesh and a portion of the Himalayan mountain range. The state is mostly known for its natural and scenic features and riches of the Himalayas, the *Terai* and the *Bhabhar*. The autonomous territory of Tibet is situated to the north of this state. Uttarakhand has about 11 million people and is known as the '*Dev Bhumi*' or 'Land of Gods' because it houses various Hindu religious places of worship that are regarded as the most sacred and propitious areas of devotion and pilgrimage.

The 13 districts in the state are grouped into two administrative divisions, namely Kumaun and Garhwal. Out of the 13 districts, three are plain and the remaining 10 are hill districts. Geographically, the state can broadly be divided into three zones, namely the upper hills (Uttarkashi, Chamoli, Rudraprayag, Pithoragarh and Bageshwar); middle hills (Tehri-Garhwal, Garhwal,

Almora, and Champawat, the hill regions of Nainital and Chakrata tehsil of Dehradun); and foothills (the remaining area of Dehradun, Haridwar, Udham Singh Nagar and the remaining area of Nainital). The concentration of population is quite high in the middle and foothills as compared to the high/upper hills. The state is predominantly rural with 16,826 rural settlements, of which 12,699 or 81 per cent have a population of less than 500. The small size of settlements and their widespread distribution is reported as one of the main challenges for the delivery of services including that of social work (www.ukhfws.org). Agrawal (2013: 16) observes that:

> Uttarakhand remains largely rural with 69.45 per cent of its population living in villages and 58.39 per cent of its workforce engaged in agriculture. But agricultural land in the state has decreased. . . . One can imagine how many more people will lose their primary livelihood if all the 558 proposed dams and Hydro Electric Projects (HEPs) are constructed. Although at 1.91 per cent, the population growth rate is not alarming, large-scale migration of people from the hilly regions to the plains has been a constant factor and will only increase . . . given the daily energy consumption in rural Uttarakhand, how much of people's displacement, their loss of land and livelihood and the destruction of natural resources like land, water and forests is justified to produce power for the plains?

Nepal

Nepal is known as a landlocked country with three geographically distinct areas. However, it could be considered a land-linked country linking China and India. It has the highest mountain range in the world in the north; hills and mountains in the middle; and the lowland plains of the *Terai* (plains) in the south. The population of over 29 million recorded at the last census covers 125 caste/ethnic groups, 123 languages and 10 religions. Hinduism is the dominant religion (81.3 per cent) and the Chhetri (16.6 per cent) and Brahman (12.2 per cent) are the dominant castes (CBS, 2012).

Nepal, declared a federal republic when the institutional Monarchy was abolished in 2008, is a socially, culturally and environmentally diverse country. Nepal is one of the poorest countries in South Asia with a per capita income ranging from $700 to $1260 per head by different organizations (World Bank, 2013). It is ranked as 157 on the Human Development Index (HDI) and, despite economic growth, absolute inequalities persist with two out of three Nepalese living in poverty (HDR, 2011).

> In Nepal development is rarely a cumulative process, evolving indigenously through its symbiotic interaction with the expanding base of local knowledge and resources. It is predefined and predetermined in accordance with the Westerners' assumption of superiority of their economic rationality, imbued with techno-fetishism. It is this overt emphasis on the presumed superiority of Western economic rationality that has led to the total devaluation of the local modes of life and economics, consequently breeding and nurturing the culture of dependency and dependent development in Nepal.
>
> *(Shrestha 1997: 22)*

The work of scholars like Shrestha amply captures the dynamics of Nepalese society, polity, the ongoing community conflicts, disasters and the role of foreign aid, and role of China and India vying for influence (see Malone, 2011; Nikku and Azman, 2014). Life expectancy in Nepal has risen by more than 20 years in the past three decades and is currently 68 years of age. Until recently, Nepal was one of the few nations where men, on average, outlived women (Nikku, 2010).

Social work responses to Himalayan disasters

The nature and frequency of disasters is on the rise worldwide. Disasters have always threatened human communities and their resilience. The more recent disasters and destruction have become global mass media spectacles dramatically delivered to living rooms throughout the world (Rosenberg, 1997). Disasters are now defined as the outcome of hazards that are income neutral and colour-blind. However, their impact is not (Cutter et al., 2003). Leading disaster researchers have revised their conceptualizations of disasters to include ideas about the 'social amplification of disasters and crisis' and the existence of 'trans-system social ruptures' (Quarantelli et al., 2006).

The Himalayan region within the Asian region is prone to both natural and political disasters. Social work in Himalayan countries is diverse, dynamic and also disjoined. The nature, scale and impact of disasters in this region are also increasing and are having differential impacts on the livelihoods of the communities that live in this region.

Professional social work responses and contributions to the reconstruction and rebuilding communities after disasters have not been well documented, particularly for Asian societies (Tang and Cheung, 2007; Dominelli, 2015). Only a limited literature is available to understand the social work's contribution to disasters, such as the 1993 Latur earthquake (India), 1999 earthquake in Taiwan, 2001 Bhuj earthquake (India), 2004 Asian Tsunami, 2005 Kashmir earthquake (Pakistan), 2008 Wenchuan earthquake (China), 2011 Japan tsunamigenic earthquake and 2015 Nepal earthquakes (Nikku, 2015; 2014). Social work as a human rights-based profession claims to intervene to enhance people's well-being. To achieve this goal within disaster settings, Lena Dominelli (2012) argues that a 'green social work model' is necessary to address social inequalities, change socio-economic models of development rooted in neoliberalism and the environmental degradation that impacts adversely primarily on disadvantaged communities.

The Uttarakhand floods

Floods and other disasters are recurring events in the state of Uttarakhand. Communities are highly vulnerable to multiple hazards and their associated risks and unprepared to cope with recurring disasters. Uttarkashi is one of the more disaster-prone districts in Uttarakhand, having faced earthquakes in 1991 and 1999, a cloud burst in 2012 and floods in 2013. The Chamoli district faced an earthquake in 1999 and Okhimath in the Rudraprayag District was devastated by a cloud burst in 1998.

On 17 June 2013, the river Mandakini flooded Rudraprayag around 2 o'clock in the morning. The National Highway 107 was washed away and many hotels along the road were destroyed. Buildings and other infrastructures built on the banks of the Alaknanda, Mandakini, Bhagirathi and Kalinadi rivers were swept away as many of them were built without applying building codes and safety measures. Hundreds of buildings along the banks of the Alaknanda and the Bhagirathi have been swept away in Rudraprayag district alone. Downstream, the Ganga, Yamuna and other rivers have reached levels not seen in years, posing difficulties for the officials responsible for disasters in Delhi, India's capital. This tragedy had the makings of a national calamity (*The Hindu*, 21 June 2013). Initial estimates showed that more than 100,000 people needed to be evacuated from Rudraprayag, Chamoli and Uttarkashi districts. To carry out this enormous task about 10,000 defence and paramilitary personnel and volunteers aided by 83 aircraft were deployed to search for survivors and deliver relief (*Bloomberg News*, 26 June 2013).

The flash floods also caused a massive flood in the Mahakali River of Nepal on 16 June 2013. It claimed many lives and weakened the livelihoods of people in the Darchula, Baitadi districts of the far western development region of Nepal. Thousands of Nepalese, mainly from western Nepal, were working in Uttarakhand (India) as porters, palanquin bearers and manual labourers. Alongside these labourers, a majority of those reported missing in the 16 June disasters were pilgrims visiting the Hindu shrines of Kedarnath, Badrinath, Gangotri and Yamunotri.

Within the first week of the Uttarakhand flood disaster, Bala Raju Nikku, author of this chapter and member of the International Association of Schools of Social Work (IASSW) Disaster Committee headed by Lena Dominelli were able to contact a few social work colleagues from the states of Uttarakhand, Himachal Pradesh in India and Nepal to learn about disasters and offer possible support. They also reached out to the Nepalese social workers in 2013 and after the mega-earthquakes in 2015. Using ICT tools and personal contacts, Bala Raju Nikku collected and collated brief information about the scale of these disasters, their impact on communities and potential social work interventions in the two sites. This was accompanied by a short status report on the social work response and community needs. Further discussions with the social work colleagues from Kathmandu (Nepal) and Uttarakhand (India) illustrated the lack of skills and resources to respond to the needs of the disaster victims. The need for capacity-building in disaster social work became clear. To address this gap, a disaster social work research capacity-building proposal was developed and submitted to IASSW's small grants committee in the latter half of 2013. The proposal (led by Bala Raju Nikku, Lena Dominelli and Vimla Nadkarni) subsequently secured a small budget of US$4000 to carry out work with social work educators from India and Nepal.

A two-day capacity-building research training workshop for social work educators and practitioners was organised during 4–5 September 2014 with a theme 'Social Work Responses to Himalayan Disasters' with the local support from Uttarakhand Open University, Department of Social Work, Haldwani, India. About 25 social work educators and practitioners and two Nepalese educators took part, presented their work with the disaster-affected families and communities, and identified challenges. Expert lectures, some delivered by Skype, were arranged in addition to actual field visits to the post-flood recovery communities.

Shekhar Pathak, a former professor of history at Kumaun University, Nainital and founder of People's Association for Himalaya Area Research (PAHAR), delivered an orientation on understanding Himalayan disasters. He provided a brief overview of Himalayan diversity and a landscape that spans many countries (i.e. Afghanistan, Bangladesh, Bhutan, Tibet (China), India, Myanmar, Nepal and Pakistan). Known as the water tower of Asia, the Himalayan region represents nearly about 40 million people. The Hindus of Indian origin mainly dominate the Sub-Himalayan and Middle-Himalayan valleys. The Great Himalayan region in the north is populated largely by Tibetan Buddhists who are seen from Ladakh to northeast India. In central Nepal, both Indian and Tibetan cultures have blended together, producing a mixed culture of Indian and Tibetan traits (www.himalaya2000.com). Thousands of peaks and glaciers (about 15,000) originate from the Himalayas to provide a source of water for drinking, irrigation, water mills, hydro-electricity and the water-packaging industry.

Lena Dominelli of Durham University gave an online presentation about green social work and the framework that could be further applied to analyse the socio-economic power structures and governance mechanisms that were threatened by the Uttarakhand flood disaster. Participants were encouraged to share their practice and reflect upon the challenges this highlighted to understand what social work models could be applied to strengthen the families affected by the devastation.

According to their feedback forms, the online lectures, presentations, field visits and sharing of local knowledge practices, enhanced participants' understanding about Himalayan ecology, diversity and disaster social work concepts and tools that can be applied in such situations. The reflections and self-narratives influenced social work thinking about the disasters for the future, as well as enhanced understanding of how to intervene in a holistic way and what aspects to include in the social work curriculum in India and Nepal.

Mandakini River Valley, Rudraprayag District

Two community organisers from Mountain Shepherds, a community-owned and operated eco-tourism company that grew out of the Nanda Devi campaign for cultural survival and sustainable livelihoods, shared their flood responses and challenges in working with communities. According to them, many volunteers and guides came from local communities, all over the upper reaches of the Himalayas, to extend helping hands, especially during the rescue phase. A few staff members of this NGO were also trained at the Nehru Institute of Mountaineering and were equipped with mountaineering skills like making rope bridges. Zip-line (Tyropean Traverse) was one of these methods used to cross the rivers and/or connect two high points for ferrying members and supplies across ravines. These skills were used during the flood disaster and rescued many lives in the district. The participants suggested that basic training in mountaineering and disaster rescue techniques should be made available to all the young people from the state, as it is a mountainous and disaster-prone area.

In their presentation, the participants shared how Ziplines were being used elsewhere and can be installed within few hours of flood to rescue people by evacuating them from their villages to safer and higher altitudes using high-quality mountaineering equipment such as static mountaineering rope, tandem pulleys, carabiners and jumars. These tools are lightweight and hence easy to carry to remote locations. The presenters concluded that if a few sets of these materials are made available to technically trained human beings, especially young people, in each of these flood-prone villages, many lives could be saved during emergencies. The presenters highlighted the need for providing training opportunities to women and young people to receive training in basic mountaineering, eco-tourism and life-saving skills during disasters. Not only can they obtain employment in the tourism industry, but also contribute to livelihood regeneration. It became clear in the ensuing discussions that preventive measures and prior training would minimize disaster risks in the communities. Helping communities to deal with the risks is an important aspect of disaster management and social workers can play an important role in helping communities to access these resources and facilitate training.

The 2015 Nepal earthquakes

Across the Earth each day there are hundreds of earthquakes. Most of them are too small to be detected without monitoring equipment, but some are powerful enough to destroy villages, cities, vital infrastructures like schools and hospitals, cultural artefacts, hundreds of families and communities in a few seconds. Two devastating earthquakes struck Nepal on 25 April and 12 May 2015 followed by hundreds of tremors. The many aftershocks following these events continued for many months and brought international attention and support to Nepal. There were thousands of stranded people, many of whom were evacuated and saved by rescue teams that came from other countries. Those wounded and rescued were transported to temporary shelters, mobile clinics and local hospitals which were also damaged by the earthquake. Many local non-governmental organizations, civil society groups and international agencies appealed for immediate relief and rescue support to the communities with whom they were working. This assistance was additional to the rescue and relief efforts of the Government of Nepal. Despite all these efforts more than 10,000 lives were lost, thousands injured and over 250,000 buildings were destroyed including many of the Kathmandu Valley's historical architectural treasures. The economic losses were estimated at anything between US$1–10 billion, with the second most probable scenario showing that damages may reach US$100 billion. The country's GDP stood at $19.29 billion in 2013. These figures tell the tale that Nepal, as an economically weak state, will take many more years to recover from the human, economic and cultural losses of these disasters.

Nepal witnessed the more conventional responses to disasters such as that of the Nepal Red Cross which responded immediately with its wide network of volunteers. However, its assistance is very short term in nature. Organizations like the Red Cross, with their years of experience in disaster management and know-how, make a difference to the lives of disaster victims. Similarly, the Nepal situation indicates that the international aid agencies and their practices are good for short-term responses: sending in relief and rescue teams, distributing medical supplies, and setting up temporary shelters. This kind of assistance only addresses the symptoms of an earthquake and the problems of built environment. Disaster relief and management interventions that focus only on meeting victims' immediate emergency disaster survival needs enabled some victims to resume their activities, in some cases to rebuild their lives independently. It also became evident that emergency-focused relief work only was not enough as these approaches failed to answer critical questions about how to respond to the long-term needs of survivor–victims. All those affected communities need additional psychosomatic services that are culturally appropriate and financial inputs for the long term in order to rebuild their livelihoods, and restore family ties and community cohesion.

The pressing questions then are: What are the sustainable ways to respond to such devastating disasters in Nepal, a country that is located in a seismically active zone of the Alpine-Himalayan subduction belt? Earthquakes are common at subduction zones, points where one plate moves below another. How can communities be nurtured to build their resilience to disasters? Examining these questions from a green social work perspective developed by Lena Dominelli followed her introduction of it to the Nepal School of Social Work (NSSW) students and faculty a week before the 25 April 2015 earthquake on her visit to Kathmandu yielded some pathways for Nepalese social workers involved in disasters. These were built upon subsequently through the Nepal Earthquake Virtual Helpline which helped to deliver training and support through the internet and Skype.

By mobilizing immediate internal resources and self-care methods, a small NSSW team took its first and crucial step in disaster social work. Very soon, the school became a small hub for providing information related to disaster management, a place giving shelter to community members, and a space in which local police could plan and discuss relief activities. After two weeks the school also started serving as the reference institution for a few other (foreign) agencies who came to deploy their medical and other psychosocial teams. These were well intentioned and trained, but had problems in terms of local cultural sensitivities, language and communication skills.

The students of NSSW had volunteered, and in some cases, were hired immediately by these organizations. Their reactions illustrated that collectively the social work educators and students were able to perceive opportunities, needs to be met and the importance of self-care while extending help to other survivors. They have shown a deep conviction that 'disasters often create a political and economic atmosphere wherein extensive changes can be made more rapidly than under normal circumstances. The collective will to take action is an advantage that should not be wasted' (UNDRO, 1992: 202). As a relatively new school of social work, NSSW successfully demonstrated the use of collective leadership despite a lack of resources and the required disaster social work skills. When disasters occur irrespective of whether a country is developed or developing, social workers and other health service professionals often prioritize post-disaster counselling that includes trauma and grief management, critical incident stress debriefing (CISD), possibly because this is where the skills and funding are available. Offering such support is not always appropriate and highlights an issue that the 'green social work model' questions, particularly with regards to timing. Psychosocial support for many people is a matter for response later. And then, it has to be culturally relevant and fit in with traditional rituals (Dominelli, 2012).

Consequently, NSSW started its work with practical relief and support activities with 913 families in the Sipapokhari Village Development Committee of Sindupalchowk District. The team quickly realised that the need for help is huge and that all requests for help cannot be handled by NSSW alone. In this process it became difficult to locate sufficient funding to organize the disaster-devastated families in this district. Resources external to the community are required, and speedily (Dominelli, 2012). The NSSW team also became aware that relief materials alone cannot help as there are politics involved in aid distribution. The disaster-affected communities have to become empowered to become involved in disaster policy formulation and post-disaster implementation so as to access the resources required to overcome their vulnerabilities. The traditional disaster management model often only encompasses the physical hazard component and the social vulnerability component is often ignored. The same situation was observed by the Nepal earthquake disaster management. Reducing or addressing social vulnerabilities (stress, poor coping, isolation, exclusion, to name a few) can decrease both human suffering and economic losses, but much neglected by disaster bureaucracies.

Like in any other country in the region, social work education in Nepal is influenced by risk perceptions, traditional human behaviour theories, and group and community organization methods despite of the lack of coherence in the curriculum. After the one month of disaster work, the NSSW faculty started to discuss the need for more focus and content on understanding community dynamics, needs assessment skills, policy advocacy and group work skills, all materials that are necessary to build robust grassroots organizations. Such reflections on the mega-earthquakes of Nepal are marking a beginning for disaster social work to be developed and integrated into all levels of education in the country. Being aware of these issues, NSSW focused on reducing social vulnerabilities by working with communities, schools, youth groups and green social work interventions that are aimed at enhancing family and community resilience.

Conclusion and way forward

What social work lessons can be derived from these two research sites? The United Nations Development Programme (UNDP) in 2004 reported that about 75 per cent of the world's population was affected *at least once* by natural disasters during the 20-year period from 1980 to 2000. This situation suggests that there lies huge need for disaster social workers and a responsibility for education systems to provide them. Increasingly, there is a necessity for a paradigm shift that reorganizes the environment for social work as a more holistic, global one, rather than a mainly Western-dominated, anthropocentric and social arena (Dominelli, 2012; Gray, Coates, and Hetherington, 2012). Dominelli (2012: 25) defines green social work as:

> a form of holistic professional social work practice that focuses on the: interdependencies amongst people; the social organisation of relationships between people and the flora and

fauna in their physical habitats; and the interactions between socio-economic and physical environmental crises and interpersonal behaviours that undermine the well-being of human beings and planet earth. It proposes to address these issues by arguing for a profound transformation in how people conceptualise the social basis of their society, their relationships with each other, living things and the inanimate world.

There is urgency about greening social work education in the region as is evident from the two research sites (Uttarakhand, India) and Kathmandu (Nepal) discussed in this chapter. The focus of most disaster management programmes in the Himalayan countries remains external because the resources, both physical and human, that are deployed come from outside the disaster zone and produce delays in disaster mitigation and recovery efforts, with a consequent loss of human lives and economic resources.

The modernization of education in Himalayan countries started only after the end of the Second World War in 1945 and continued over the last few decades, but the process is far from complete due to the failure of higher education policies. Out of the five countries of the Himalayan region, two countries are landlocked (Nepal and Bhutan) and both are included in the list of least developed countries (LDCs). The political, economic, social and cultural milieu of the Himalayan region offers vast potential and abundant challenges for disaster social work. The cultures and philosophies that exist in this region are rich, complex and diverse. Professional social work, like the diversity of the region, is not a homogeneous entity in the region. Different models of social welfare and social work have developed over many decades.

The existing literature on disaster risk, rescue and rehabilitation informs social workers that the scale and complex nature of disasters in the Himalayan region requires knowledge and practical evidence from more than one form of science, as advocated by green social work. It is crucial that the natural sciences, social sciences, medical and health sciences, law, arts, humanities, social work, social policy and engineering, to name a few, should come together in interventions as a comprehensive, integrated whole (Dominelli, 2012) and not as separate disciplines that examine one aspect of the disaster and its devastating impact on human lives. The need for inter- and trans-disciplinarity is more than ever necessary for designing and implementing sustainable disaster management practices in the region. This requires reforms in higher education policies and the allocation of budgets to incubate innovations that can answer the wicked problems encountered in disaster management and community action.

The concept of 'disaster resilience' has been frequently used and cited in both scientific and social science literature but has been explored less in social work. The concept of resiliency is both problematic and refreshing. It is problematic when used loosely by many and refreshing when opening new areas for further interdisciplinary research. When disasters occur and threaten communities and their livelihoods, they pose challenges not only to the physical but also the social and ecological resiliency of communities. They tear at the fabric of economies, democracies and citizenship (Abel et al., 2006; Dominelli, 2012; Hayward, 2013; Nikku, 2013). Adger (2000) has used the term social resilience to highlight ways whereby human communities withstand a variety of external shocks to their social infrastructure. Other concepts like coherence, social memory, community and family coping, shared vulnerability and elements of compassion are useful to develop further the concept of social resilience in the region. Curriculum reforms that integrate disaster science as a cross-cutting theme in the higher education institutions in the region and social work are also essential, and not insulated from this process.

The exploitation of rivers in the region by building mega-dams with their resulting negative environmental and livelihood impacts are not well evidenced and are a cause of concern for green social workers. In-depth studies about the construction activities in several river valleys (including the Narmada, Alaknanda and Bhagirathi) have exposed the corruption, unethical practices of several construction companies and ineffective state monitoring (*The Hindu*, 16 December 2014). Green social workers should make use of these studies to understand the links between ecological devastation, corruption and the violation of human rights, and to use these findings in their advocacy and lobbying efforts to ensure safe livelihoods.

Solas (1990: 149) identified criteria for effective teaching that indicated that students felt 'the most important component of overall teaching effectiveness was the relationship between the educator and themselves'. Now the questions before the social work educators of the Himalayan region are: how to ensure the relationship and connectedness that ensures effective social work teaching? Which methods of teaching will encourage autonomy within social work students' learning so as to motivate them to work for themselves and significant others during disasters? How can disaster social workers ensure that the students have the required knowledge and skills to be able to work with disaster-prone communities and be successful in their own terms?

This chapter has shown how, working in collaborative partnerships with local and overseas contributors, it is possible for local schools of social work to enhance their capacities to deliver assistance in difficult circumstances and develop models of social work that can address the complex needs that arise in disasters. A holistic, green social work approach was one of these because it covered immediate needs and long-term reconstruction goals alongside caring for the physical environment. NSSW's interventions also highlighted the importance of distributing scarce relief resources to local populations using equity principles yielded in making the best use of limited resources. There is much evidence that it is not the disasters *per se* but the way they are managed that presents the crux of the problem. There are bound to be conflicts in accessing these meagre resources warranting the crucial role for green social workers to facilitate this. The green social work framework provides social workers with the knowledge, skills and understandings, not only for applying appropriate interventions during the post-disaster period, but also for preparing communities to respond to disaster vulnerabilities before and after disasters strike.

References

Agrawal, R. (2013). Hydropower projects in Uttarakhand: Displacing people and destroying lives. *Economic and Political Weekly*, XLVIII(29): 14–16.

Adger, W. N. (2000). Social and ecological resilience: are they related? *Progress in Human Geography*, 24: 347–364.

Abel, N. D., Cumming, H. M. and Anderies, J. M. (2006). Collapse and reorganization in social-ecological systems: questions, some ideas, and policy implications. *Ecology and Society*, 11(1): 17.

Anderson, S., Morton, J. and Toulmin, C. (2010). Climate change for Agrarian societies in drylands: Implications and future pathways. In R. Means and A. Norton (Eds.), *Social dimensions of climate change*. Washington, DC: The International Bank for Reconstruction and Development/The World Bank, pp. 259–275.

Central Bureau of Statistics (CBS). (2012). *National population and housing census 2011*. National Report to the Government of Nepal by the Central Bureau of Statistics, November 2012.

Cutter, S. R., Voruff Bryan, J. and Lynn Shirley, W. (2003). Social vulnerability to environmental hazards. *Social Science Quarterly*, 84(1): 242–261.

Dominelli, L. (2012). *Green social work: From environmental crises to environmental justice*. Cambridge: Polity Press.

Dominelli, L. (2015). The opportunities and challenges of social work interventions in disaster situations. *International Social Work*, 58(5): 659–672.

Gray, M., Coates, J. and Hetherington, T. (2012). *Environmental social work*. London: Routledge.

Hayward, B. M. (2013). Rethinking resilience: Reflections on the earthquakes in Christchurch, New Zealand, 2010 and 2011. *Ecology and Society*, 18(4): 37.

http://dx.doi.org/10.5751/ES-05947-180437.

Human Development Report (HDR). (2011). *Nepal Country Profile*. Available on http:/hdrstats.undp.org/eng/countries/profiles/NPL.html

Malone, D. (2011). *Does the elephant dance? Contemporary Indian foreign policy*. Oxford: Oxford University Press.

Nikku, B.R. (2010). A triangle of peace, politics, and people's voice: Nepal. In H. Moksnes and M. Melin (Eds.), *Power to the People? (Con)Tested civil society in search of democracy*. Uppsala, Sweden: Uppsala Centre for Sustainable Development, Uppsala University.

Nikku, B. R. (2013). Children rights in disasters: Concerns for social work – insights from South Asia and possible lessons for Africa. *International Social Work*, 56(1): 51–66.

Nikku, B.R. (2014). Disaster, displacement and social work in 21st century: Turning devastation in to development. In P. Norvy (Ed.), *Development, displacement and marginalisation*. India: Vincentian Service Society.

Nikku, B.R. (2015). Editorial: Living through and responding to disasters: Multiple roles for social work. *Social Work Education*, 34(6): 601–606.

Nikku, B. R. and Azman, A. (2014). Politics, policy and poverty in Nepal. *International Journal of Social Work and Human Services Practice*, 2(2): 1–9.

Quarantelli, E. L., Lagadec, P. and Boin, P. (2006). A heuristic approach to future disasters and crises: New, old and in-between types. In H. Rodríquez, E. L. Quarantelli, and Dynes, R. R. (Eds.), *Handbook of disaster research*. New York: Springer.

Rosenberg, D. (1997). *Folklore, myths and legends: A word perspective*. New York: McGraw-Hill Professional.

Shrestha, N. R. (1997). *In the name of development: A reflection on Nepal*. Kathmandu: Educational Enterprises.

Solas, J. (1990). Effective teaching as construed by social work students, *Journal of Social Work Education*, 26: 145–154.

Tang, K.-L. and Cheung, C.-K. (2007). The competence of Hong Kong social work students in working with victims of the 2004 tsunami disaster. *International Social Work*, 50: 405–418.

United Nations Disaster Relief Organization (UNDRO). (1992). An Overview of Disaster Management. UNDRO Disaster Management Training Programme, 2nd edn. Geneva: UNDRO

World Bank. (2013). *Nepal*. Available on http://data.worldbank.org/country/nepal [Accessed 12 May 2017].

10
Dissecting a Himalayan disaster, finding pathways

Malathi Adusumalli and Soumya Dutta

Introduction

The massive climate-triggered disaster in Uttarakhand (and parts of Himachal Pradesh) in June 2013 is categorised as one of the biggest climate-related disasters in India's recorded history. The four worst affected districts of *Pithoragarh*, *Chamoli*, *Rudraprayag* and *Uttarkashi* were devastated in all respects. The economy of the entire state, which depended upon tourism for nearly a quarter of its GDP and a large part of employment, also collapsed for a few months, making any recovery response that much more difficult. Large amounts of agricultural and forest lands were washed away and nearly 15,000 kilometres of roads were damaged. Skewed government and media priorities focused most attention on the richer tourist population that got stranded, while nearly 4 million affected local residents received little attention. Additionally, the devastation and massive human lives lost in the *Mandakini* valley *(Kedarnath* area) drew government and NGO resources to that area, while other affected areas languished. This was the context when the authors made preliminary visits to the *Uttarkashi* district to understand the impact of the disaster and community concerns.

This chapter examines how the 2013 disaster in Uttarakhand has affected the lives of the affected communities and seeks to understand community responses, while locating these within their natural and social contexts. The chapter describes the nature of the interventions undertaken in the disaster-affected villages, with implications for social and environmental justice, in accordance with the principles of the green social work model. Focusing on the impacts of the disaster and the initiatives undertaken in 20 villages of Uttarkashi, this chapter raises important concerns and related to sustainability of natural resource-based livelihoods, disaster preparations and forest rights, suggesting a strong reliance on local governance structures and community participation. Green social work supports advocacy for forest rights, sustainable use of the lands discussed in this chapter and the promotion of community resilience after disasters as advocated by Dominelli (2012).

Demographic, socio-economic and cultural conditions

The approximately 8000 square kilometres of Uttarkashi district has about 400,000 people, giving a population density of 50 persons/per Km^2. This is significantly fragile by mountain standards. The entire upper *Bhagirathi* valley comprises of deep valleys, fast flowing rivers and steep forested mountain slopes, with snow covered peaks and ridges nearby. It is dominated by temples and religious places and depends for total income and employment opportunities largely on religion, adventure (to a lesser extent) and nature tourism. Three large hydro-electricity projects under construction on the Bhagirathi river in this area were halted in 2010 when the Ministry of Environment and Forests (MOEF, n.d.) served an Eco-Sensitive Zone (ESZ) notice. The declaration of the 135-kilometre stretch from Uttarkashi to Gaumukh as ESZ has curtailed any industrial activity, severely limiting local employment opportunities. This has created high levels of resentment in more than 85 villages and small towns in the region, but no significant alternative arrangement(s) have been attempted by government at different levels. However, the state government with the active support of both main political parties (the Congress and Bharatiya Janata Party) is now actively seeking to restart hydro-electricity projects in this fragile belt and proactively encouraging people to protest the ESZ notification and demand that it be scrapped.

The social structure is heavily influenced by the caste system, giving caste norms and networks a strong hold over communities. The population is mostly Hindu, with upper castes numerically dominant. A small minority of Muslims and migratory buffalo-rearing Gujjar populations also live there. A large part of the population is deeply religious and patriarchy rules with women often not getting a share in property (land or houses) or decision-making, while undertaking a major share of work on the farms and at home. There is a small growing migrant Nepali population and migrant workers from other Indian states. Along with the phenomenon of out-migration from mountain villages, this in-coming 'foreign' population is settling in several less accessible and remote areas, and sometimes causes tensions locally. Primary incomes among higher altitude villages stem from horticulture (apples) and tourism while the lower altitude villages have economic activities tied to budget-tourism along with the cultivation of cash crops – potatoes, kidney beans and vegetables. Although poverty is not as acute as in some eastern states, people are not secure in their incomes primarily due to the uncertainties and unpredictability of the weather and climate. Almost everything can get disrupted, even destroyed with a particularly bad climatic event, as has happened repeatedly at an increasing frequency over the past two decades. This possibility has induced a trend of people abandoning their mountain villages and settling in lower altitude towns at the first available opportunity. Nonetheless, among the registered population, 90 per cent remains rural. As the private/agricultural land holding is extremely small, measured in *Nalis* (about 240 square yards or 1/20th of an acre), people are mostly subsistence farmers, except in the upper reaches where apple growing is a big source of livelihoods. Sheep and goat rearing and their by-products provide supplementary incomes.

The work with village communities is important in the light of preliminary assessments (Adusumalli et al., 2013) that showed a clear tendency of the government to focus on rescuing stranded pilgrim tourists. A major question remained as to what happened to the village communities. Based on visits to the village communities of Gajoli (Assiganga area), Bhatwari, Sainj and Malla near Bhatwari Block Headquarters and of eight border villages near Gangotri in the *Upla Taknore* area, we initiated work using participatory assessments to focus on livelihoods, food security and disaster preparedness as indicated in the green social work model (Dominelli, 2012). Twenty villages became the focus of three clusters – *Bhatwari, Assiganga* and Border villages. The selected villages in the Bhatwari cluster, *Bhatawri, Sainj, Malla, Athali Dilsaud* and *Chamkot*, are quite close to the road. In the Assiganga Cluster, seven villages were chosen: *Gajoli, Seku, Agoda, Dasda, Dandalka, Bankholi and Nau Gaon*. These lay close to the *Sangam Chatti* Area which is 15 kilometres away from Uttarkashi, the main town, and would take a sturdy trek uphill

Dissecting a Himalayan disaster

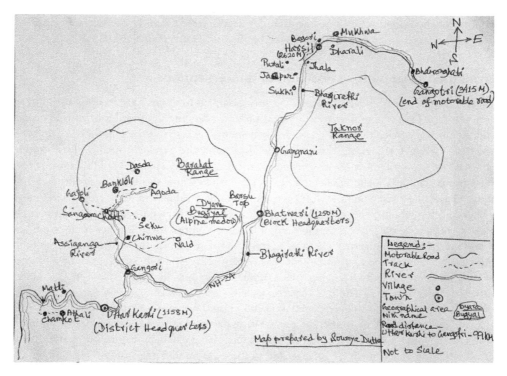

Figure 10.1 Map showing some of the project villages prepared by S. Dutta (2017)

of two to three hours. The Upla Taknore border villages enroute to Gangotri consisted of: *Sukki, Jhala, Jaspur, Purali, Dharali, Bagori, Harsil and Mukhwa* (see Figure 10.1 for details).

The initiatives

Participatory assessments became the basis for commencing the work as it meant that the results could be shared at once and action initiated by community members. These formed the basis of initiating and sharing responsibility for action. Macchi (2011) and Dominelli (2012) emphasise the contextual issues underpinning vulnerability and the need to take account of the institutional and social contexts in developing effective steps to combat extreme climate events. Furthermore, mountain communities are subject to specific vulnerabilities that are both biophysical and socio-economic, and recognise gendered vulnerability (Adger and Kelly, 1999; Brodnig and Prasad, 2010; MacGregor, 2017).

Assessments regarding their livelihoods and how these are being affected by disasters were mapped and analysed in a shared manner. For this purpose, village-level meetings were held at 20 villages with the project team having repeated interactions with them. Rapport was built through the initial interactions wherein field investigators who spoke the local dialect shared the purpose of these interactions and what it could mean for the villagers. They also sought the participation of the village community especially that of the *Gram Sabha* (which is empowered under the 73rd Act of the Indian Constitution to deal with village-level issues and oversee the implementation of central sector schemes). Village became the basis for interaction – the minutes of the various discussions held with villagers were taken. This effort was facilitated through a research grant from Indian Council of Social Science Research (ICSSR).

Livelihoods mapping, assessment and interventions

Agriculture and livestock rearing were the major occupations of the villagers in these mountain communities. Thus, the project team focused on understanding the impacts of climate change and disasters on agriculture and the socio-demographic features associated with it. This work entailed holding focus group discussions to understand the gendered nature of agricultural work. While it is well known that women bear the brunt of the work and hold a major share in the agricultural work, there has been difference in terms of how this work pans out in each of these villages, depending on how close their sources of fuel, fodder and water are located to their village and households. The villagers face issues of pest attacks, wild boar attacks and monkey attacks on their fields. There is an increasing tendency to move towards other occupations and abandon agriculture altogether. Disasters in terms of floods and landslides have made this more difficult to practice. The first assessments from seven villages in the Assiganga cluster pointed to dwindling productivity over the years alongside insect attacks. This resulted in seeking the support of the district agricultural department who readily collaborated in participating in a one-day agricultural meeting organised at Gajoli village. Participation at the meeting included around 70 farmers and 25 women's representatives, facilitating an open discussion on farming concerns, including protection from pest attacks, increasing yields, protecting crops and sharing information on government schemes related to these. Regarding the quality of soil conditions, the Agricultural Department suggested checking soil health conditions. The work initiated was in line with the green social work principles of co-producing solutions (Dominelli, 2012) by engaging scientific experts (here agricultural experts) and local communities in participatory dialogues. The follow-up involved taking soil samples to the Agricultural Department. However, the follow-up did not materialise as desired for a variety of reasons including physical distance and the dominant perceptions about receiving support. These had been shaped by prior experience with NGOs, whose actions of 'providing material benefit' nurtured a sense of dependency.

Suggestions arising from the meeting concerned raising vegetables in poly-tunnels to avoid pest attacks. These were taken up in earnest by the project team who explored subsidy-based schemes from the government's agricultural department. Critical concerns included the government's inability to reach remote and inaccessible village communities (Assiganga Cluster) and those communities' incapacity to respond. Other reasons government departments typically gave for their failure included the exhaustion of funds for that year or that their programmes had already reached the required number of participants.

Forest resources are integral to the agricultural work practised in these communities. There are a number of species of plants that are used as fodder, fuelwood and food sources. The communities, especially the women, possess local knowledge related to these. They are also aware of how climate change is affecting these resources much better than the men. The region boasts a substantial presence of medicinal and aromatic plants. The strong presence of the Forestry Department in controlling access to and the utilisation of these resources to prevent commercial exploitation, while retaining its role in auctioning these resources to major *Ayurvedic* pharmaceutical companies, meant the erosion of community authority. Historically, there has been a tussle for the control and commercial exploitation of these resources between the forest-dependent communities and Forestry Department since British colonial times (Guha, 1991). Numerous community struggles, including violent ones, to wrest their rights from the authorities have led to the recognition of their usufructuary rights to forests. The State Medicinal Plants

Board and the District Administration promote licensing and training for those farmers desiring to diversify into cultivation of medicinal and aromatic plants, actively encouraging such efforts by farmers. The opposite holds for the Forestry Department. Instances of Forestry Department officials harassing these farmers and seizing their produce at the time of harvest and even sending them to prison on the pretext of illegal exploitation of the government's resources were brought to light during the project's interactions with the villagers. This led to discussions as to who owns the forests and what is the nature of their ownership. The suggestion of one of the authors to seek a legal basis from the Scheduled Tribes and Other Forest Dwellers (Recognition of Forest Rights) Act (FRA), 2006 to develop their livelihoods. The sanctions of the Forestry Department and the legacy of controlling forests generated from British colonial times impacting upon the regulation of forest-dependent lives, was shared in meetings held with the project team. Green social work encourages local use and ownership of land and its resources and the FRA work restores community ownership of natural resources.

The project team then began to disseminate the FRA in earnest. To access rights under this Act which came into force in 2008, there are set procedures, which begin with the formation of the Forest Rights Committees under an open Gram Sabha Meeting (composed of all adults 18 years and over). The constitution of the committee ensured that the voices of those traditionally marginalised in decision making were represented by mandatorily requiring that one-third of the committee members was composed of women, one-third from tribal communities (if any) and one-third from the remaining villagers. Requiring a specific gendered representation will ensure that their voice is heard. Further as per the FRA, the traditional rights of usage of forests are assured unhindered only when the claims for individual rights and community rights are submitted with evidence to the Sub-Divisional Level Committee (SDLC). The SDLC is one of the three tiers for the implementation of the FRA, the other two are the District Level Committee (DLC) and State Level Monitoring Committee (SLC). The work could be described in these broad steps, sometimes overlapping with each other: dissemination and formation of Committees for Forest Rights; evidence gathering for forest usage at village level including official documents such as working plans and revenue records; resolving forest usage disputes between contiguous villages; preparation of claim documents; submission of claim documents to the Sub-Divisional Level Committee; engaging with government officials at the SDLC and DLC. While these appear to be neat steps, in accessing rights, the work entailed tremendous efforts by both the project team and villagers. In line with the green social work model, the work entailed building capacities among both project staff and communities, especially in understanding and developing confidence in accessing these governance structures to safeguard their rights. The project team partook of training at Bilaspur (Chattisgarh) to acquire a first-hand understanding of these.

This meant understanding the various procedures in accessing rights under the FRA and disseminating it to the village communities through a series of community-based workshops, focus group discussions and wall posters with clearly written messages. Many villagers questioned their powerlessness vis-à-vis the Forestry Department. A major concern expressed often was how to secure the Forest Department's agreement. Developing village community confidence in having their rights of usage respected was a major challenge. This was slowly overcome as continuous interactions and sharing success stories from other states where the FRA was implemented were undertaken in the village gatherings and through the *Bhagirathi Jan Samvad*, the project newsletter. Evidence of customary usage of the forest resources was also collected in each village with women as local knowledge providers. Archival records were sought from both the Revenue and Forest Departments to be used as evidence for claiming the rights of usage of these forest resources. Evidence of usage was also collected in each village. The Act stipulated that older people's statements duly approved by Gram Sabha could be cited as evidence of usage, as they would know how their community has been using the forests. Further evidence of usage available at village level (collecting receipts of usage permitted by government officials including the Forestry Department) or any receipts of paying fines for infringement were also collected for each of the villages. The FRA stipulates that evidence in the form of government documents, revenue records and working plans which speak of the usufructuary rights of communities could be utilised; this evidence was sought among the archival records of the Forestry Research Institutes at Dehradun and the Forest Training Institute at Haldwani. Further delineating the community claims through GPS marking was another task accomplished with the support of the project team. Also, the FRA resource persons from Maharashtra and Himachal Pradesh who had positive experience of realising people's rights under the FRA were invited to share their success stories at various meetings both at village level and at a larger meeting with representatives of the Forestry Rights Committees (FRCs) at Uttarkashi.

Of the 18 FRCs that were formed in the 20 project villages, five have been able to follow the necessary procedure to submit the claim documents to the SDLC. Inspired by these developments, one more village contacted and consulted the project team to help support its claims to dwelling in the forest land under the FRA, resulting in the submission of the required documents. Recently our effort has brought to light that there has been no SDLC meeting at Bhatwari Block since the FRA came into existence. This exposes a serious lack of concern regarding the implementation of the FRA by government officials. Its realisation carries a strong possibility of increasing villagers' stake in the forest and ensuring ecological and intergenerational sustainability, issues inherent in green social work approaches to post-disaster reconstruction (Dominelli, 2012). Increasingly, as a modernising state being driven by a development agenda, the state's proclivity to protect natural resources is diminishing. The ruling of the High Court of Uttarakhand to treat Ganga and Yamuna as living entities and also the water streams, forests and meadows fuels hope that communities' concerns related to their rights and stakes in protecting and accessing forests will be realised (Livelaw Network, 2017).

Disaster mapping, assessments, preparedness and organisation

Assessments also covered disaster preparedness, as advised by green social work. These entailed mapping physical vulnerability areas within and around the villages and preparing action plans for dealing with these. The actions were shared within the Gram Sabha and resolutions were passed regarding mitigation actions which allocated responsibility with either the local administration or the villagers. Accordingly, action was taken to submit request letters to improve the administration. Some of the actions initiated were the construction of a cut-off pathway between Chamkot village and Dilsor village to prevent landslides protect water sources, protective walls around the gullies/streams and pathways. It also included identifying potential landslide zones and sending information to and requesting action from the authorities. Many small bridges were washed away in the Assiganga cluster of villages. This required action from the authorities. These issues were highlighted through appeals for action to the authorities duly endorsed by the Gram Sabha and items in the Newsletter *Bhagirathi Jan Samvad*, in the local language Hindi, which was circulated to both civil society and the administration. Some impacts included pathways being built, especially between the Dilsor and Chamkot villages; water points at Dilsor village were repaired; and sanctioned bridges across Bhagirathi at Chamkot and Athali were raised with the authorities. During the June 2013 disaster the bridge connecting the villages of Chamkot and Athali disappeared when the highway was washed away. Before the bridge and highway were rebuilt, the authorities sanctioned the use of a trolley to ferry people across the river. However this entailed great difficulties as a trolley had to be pulled with strong iron ropes. Doing this could be particularly difficult when a sick person had to be taken to hospital. Also trolleys could not ferry villagers' animals across even if they needed veterinary services, thereby requiring villagers to incur huge costs if they had to pay veterinary officials to visit them. The trolley system to ferry people is commonly adopted by the administration whenever they must provide quick relief and arrange some form of transport. Trolleys are never a preferred mode as it means that one needs to crouch or sit in the trolley and have strong arms to pull the iron ropes to propel oneself forward. These difficulties mean that sick, older people or young people cannot use the trolley without the help of others. Furthermore, many loads had to be carried out from the road head in Bazar to the village to fetch goods to meet daily requirements. All these had to be carried in the trolley which meant delays and waiting. Also, the ropes need to be greased regularly to run smoothly, but usually they were not. In Chamkot, a groom's wedding party had to cross over in a trolley, making several trips until the entire group could reach the village, evoking comic scenes. The transport of goods to and fro by trolley causes delays and becomes burdensome. Now that that bridge has been built, it has been easier for the villagers to commute. Issues of connectivity affect the daily routines of villagers and can increase their vulnerability, which can be reduced through effective post-disaster responses to restore communication and connectivity as advocated by green social workers.

The disaster had major impacts on livelihoods based on subsistence agriculture. The villagers grew potatoes which they transport to the lower hills. The assessment pointed out that pathways from the Assiganga villages were destroyed during the 2012 floods when the Assiganga River also washed away a mini-hydropower plant that was built close to its banks. The main marketplace serving 15 villages at Sangam Chatti was affected as a major portion was submerged by the river. The villagers' livelihoods depended on the pathways connecting them to the Sangam Chatti area which is 15 kilometres from Uttarkashi main town. The villagers depend on these fragile pathways to ferry goods and services to and fro. *Asadi Aloo* (the potato grown during the rainy season) is harvested in late August and September, and has been a major crop that villagers rely upon for their incomes. Standing water on their lands arising from the incessant rains of June 2013 prevented them from retrieving their crops. However, even harvested crops could not be transported to Uttarkashi due to the damaged pathways.

The bridge connecting pathway to Agoda village from Sangam Chatti was also washed away. Replacing it was taken up in earnest, but the new bridge was destroyed by the next rainy season. Another bridge has been constructed subsequently. Participatory assessments were initiated by the project to highlight community grievances and find facilities for storing food grains in their own villages. Doing this required submitting resolutions from Gram Sabha to the administration. Part of the assessment included the identification of the 'landslide zones', where cracks were appearing on the hillsides, and how these were affecting villagers' shelter, given the threat of rocks and debris falling on their houses, making it dangerous to live there. This was a particular hazard in Bankholi, Dasda and Dandalka. The project team and villagers mapped these hazards and followed up on issues with the administration, giving green social workers an advocacy role.

Major issues related to compensation for losses suffered, especially the loss of crops and cattle, emerged. Lack of clear guidelines for assessment and difficulties in reaching villages to make loss assessment during disasters led to many compensation claims being rejected. Sometimes, low values are placed on losses suffered and paltry amounts were offered along with associated costs for processing. Discussions with villagers revealed that asset mapping had to be undertaken with each individual household to enable their claims to be certified by the *Pradhan* (elected village Head as per the 73rd Amendment), to legitimise their asset status. Certified asset assessments could be leveraged to claim insurance or to estimate losses and determine compensation because these assessments were more reliable and transparent. Accordingly, all the 20 villages compiled Asset Registers. *Having been duly certified by the Pradhan*, each household and the *Gram Panchayat* were given a copy.

Issues related to losses suffered due to lack of transportation, especially in the apple belt of the eight villages of *Upla Taknore* region, and growing demand for cold storage were also shared with the government in a report. The long-standing demand of the apple growers in these eight border villages has had some results because cold storage is being developed in the region. In the village of *Dharali* in the *Upla Taknore region* (border villages close to Gangotri pilgrim centre), the *Kheerganga* stream washed away farmlands and toilets constructed on either side of its banks. A major demand for walling the embankment to prevent further erosion led to the construction of a wall which was begun in 2014 and is now completed. *Bagori* village was affected by the mountain stream, *Purkha Nala*. This flooded and the ensuing volumes of water destroyed fields. The village now has protection walls. Consistent efforts by the project team and villagers enabled them to demand the requisite amount to be sanctioned for the Gram Sabha to undertake these works.

Working with committees

To provide a forum to raise the collective voice of the villagers on disasters and their concerns related to preparedness on various fronts with government officials, a joint meeting of 66 villages affected by the disaster was called for. The meeting took place on 30 October 2015 at Bhatwari, the Block Headquarters. The villagers articulated critical issues and concerns. The meeting involved a fair representation of women. The larger meeting formed a coordination committee with the backing of the villagers to speak on disaster preparedness with one voice. In December 2015, a committee to work at the cluster level was formed with the cooperation of the 20 villages at Uttarkashi. However, the mode of representation for this committee has thrown up major dilemmas like how are the members to be chosen, on what basis? It was then realised that such a committee had to be built from the bottom-up instead of relying on those traditionally seen as representing villagers' interests. This required working to initiate village-level disaster preparedness and response teams/committees. Inclusivity and bottom-up approaches are encouraged by green social work (Dominelli, 2012).

Village-level disaster committees had already been formed by the government with some of the village governance council members and other officials who were the village contact persons. However, these village communities had not been trained on disaster preparedness. During December 2015, the project team sought answers from the district administration. In January 2016, the government initiated the process of seeking expressions of interest and giving disaster preparedness training to villagers with the help of local NGOs. Since committees had already been formed at the behest of voluntary organisations at the village level (with abysmally low training aspects), the duplication of efforts was avoided by not forming yet another committee at this level. Work with these members continued at the village level and during the forest fires in March 2016. The villagers of Chamkot and Athali informed and worked with the Forestry Department in stopping the fire from spreading. Each collective effort is intended to build more effective efforts in preparing for and responding to future disasters.

Responding to the needs of the villagers, building on their skills and working with the administration were undertaken alongside disaster preparation initiatives. The newsletter which ran 12 issues from the second year of the project highlighted significant progress in these areas. Villagers' key concerns were associated with disaster preparedness, livelihoods and forest rights.

The rationale for the initiatives of the project team has always been to build collaborative efforts, share information, listen carefully and prepare to work with government officials. Government has the reach and resources to reach the remote communities. The project team's principle aim has been to prepare communities for their rightful share in decision-making and ensure access to these. The combined efforts of the civil society, government and communities will enable for a just and sustainable development (Dominelli, 2012).

Some important insights and lessons

Selection and preparation of personnel

Field investigators were selected from the local communities. However, it was soon realised that their involvement has both positive and negative connotations. In the highly entrenched caste system, social networks are formed mainly on caste lines. Identity issues affected the method and outcome of participatory assessments. Social groups perceive and relate to each other differently. Consequently, villagers' familiarity with the caste identity of local researchers through their surnames impacted upon their willingness to share information. Cultural sensitivity is an issue in green social work, but changing existing social relations is for villagers to initiate (Dominelli, 2012).

The culture impact on the villagers' work and migratory patterns

Culture is an important aspect of community development (Dominelli, 2012). The planning of the work had many ups and downs as pathways remained blocked, especially in the Assiganga cluster where villagers could not be reached. Many of the households had migrated to the *Channis* (the higher altitudes where they move with their animals in the summer and farm from June to October). This absence affected significant numbers of villagers and their absence posed problems for village gatherings when Gram Sabha meetings were called. The eight villages in *Upla Taknore*, the high-altitude villages near Gangotri, practice transhumance. Thus, these villagers live in a high-altitude village for the six months of summer and move down to villages at lower altitudes close to the district headquarters during the winter months, moving their schools with them. As all meetings must be held during this short time-span, opportunities for holding community-level meetings and initiatives are restrained. The wedding season dominates March and April, so villagers are busy visiting relatives and attending weddings. This also curtails collective efforts. That young people leave their villages in search of jobs in the plains, leaving older people to practice agriculture, limits their involvement in disaster preparedness. Split families exist in Chamkot and Athali. Older parents remain in the village while the rest of the family lives across river in the *Bazar* (market area) to pursue their children's education. Fewer 'family hands' to work on agriculture pose concerns about losing the 'culture of agriculture'.

Complexity of civil society interventions and the location of work

Civil society initiatives have enabled a culture that is at once seen as 'receiving' and not participating. There are narratives of disaster relief efforts and cases where the relief materials were distributed many times to the same individuals and families. There have been number of agencies working in the communities. A strong NGO presence in these communities results in two to three being in the villages. However, these NGOs have inculcated a strong receiving attitude rather than promoting participation. The Uttarakhand Livelihood Support Programme (ULSP) was initiated with substantial World Bank funding for community mobilisation. The presence of multiple agencies, all catering to the same village community with no coordination between them, means that everyone is busy completing their targets. While the climate promotes 'receiving' aid, the struggle for justice or rights under the FRA has invoked queries as to why the project team is pursuing participatory goals rather than focusing on 'distribution'. It took almost a year to clarify and make the communities understand that the project work would require strong participation from them. Having multiple players in the civil society arena, offering different services under diverse motivations creates their own challenges.

Work at the Gram Sabha level is essential

The local system of governance under the Constitution of India is secular. However, it is caught in a highly skewed social space that practices hierarchy. This entails challenges in making the Gram Sabha a practicing democratic institution. The key to community development in these mountain communities is strengthening democratic processes at the Gram Sabha level. This entails capacity-building for decision-making, encouraging a democratic spirit, developing a climate for sharing and collaboration between and among villagers. Democratic processes need to become daily routines.

Working with government officials

In accessing services and ensuring rights, working with government officials is necessary. Success in enlisting local administrative support is always precarious, as matters change a lot. The disaster preparation work or livelihoods related Forest Rights Work brings in a number of challenges and Eureka moments. There have been frequent changes to the district administrative leadership, with the work of verifying claims under the FRA pending at the Sub-Divisional Level. Thus, advocacy and lobbying for rights with the duty bearers is crucial and has to be undertaken simultaneously.

Conclusions: theory and practice innovations, current and future, and new research questions

This work raises critical questions for the future. These relate to theoretical questions about governance and participatory processes – instilling a democratic spirit and the right to receive services efficiently. How is it possible that villages with a history of protest from British times to the Chipko movement now accept this governance or the lack of it without raising a voice or fighting for their rights to forests and protecting their farms? During relief distribution after the disaster, many villagers participated in a protest march against the unjust distribution of relief. They sought '*sadak, samman aur suraksha*' (roads, respect and protection), and were clearly against charity. Many villagers rescued pilgrims who were caught in the disaster and provided shelter and food from their own stocks (Nichenametla, 2013). However, once the initial hardships were overcome, there has been a meek acceptance of the situation and no demand for their rights. Is there democratic fatigue? One wonders. And how can a culture of democracy be built in a social set-up that is highly iniquitous?

The Gram Sabha processes following the Panchayati Raj Act require all adult members to participate in village affairs. However, participation is often lacking and the Panchayat secretary (representative of Panchayati Raj Department from state government) whose responsibilities are to oversee and ensure democratic processes at the Gram Sabha level performs lip service to the idea of participation. Hence, the work of Forestry Rights Committees needs to be watched and hand-holding is required to ensure democratic processes in decision-making. The democratic ethos contrasts with the everyday reality of patriarchy and stark caste hierarchies. Hence, future research could focus on how the democratic processes can be assured and strengthened. How can women's voices be represented and what mechanisms could be put in place to ensure their participation in the Forestry Rights Committees? Can their participation in household-level work continue alongside their farm work and governance work? What could drive and sustain such participation? Further questions could focus on what mechanisms government must put in place to guarantee forest rights and how these coalesce, contradict or conflict with the other government actions and policies like the promotion of van panchayats (or forest regeneration with funds received from multilateral agencies). Green social workers, with their commitment to environmental justice, can carry this objective forward and simultaneously develop the model further.

References

Adger, W.N. and Kelly, P.M. (1999). Social Vulnerability to Climate Change and the Architecture of Entitlements. *Mitigation and Adaptation Strategies for Global Change* 4, 253-266

Adusumalli, M., Dutta, S. and Jha, A. (2013). *Climate extremes and loss and damage: Lessons from Uttarakhand Disaster*. New Delhi: Beyond Copenhagan.

Brodnig, G. and Prasad, V. (2010). *A view from the top: Vulnerability in mountain systems*. (Social development notes No. 128). World Bank, June 2010. Available on http://siteresources.worldbank.org/EXTSOCIALDEVELOPMENT/Resources/244362-1164107274725/3182370-1164201144397/3187094-1277143060338/Vulnerability_Mountain_Systems_June_2010.pdf [Accessed 2 May 2017].

Dominelli, L. (2012). *Green social work: From environmental degradation to Environmental Justice*. Cambridge: Polity Press.

Guha, R. (1991). *The unquiet woods: Ecological change and peasant resistance in the Himalaya*. New Delhi: Oxford University Press.

Livelaw news network (2017). Uttarakhand HC declares air, glaciers, forests, springs, waterfalls etc. As legal persons on 1 April. Available on www.livelaw.in/uttarakhand-hc-declares-air-glaciers-forests-springs-waterfalls-etc-legal-persons/ [Accessed 14 May 2017].

MacGregor, S. (2017). Moving Beyond Impacts: more answers to the 'gender and climate change question', In *Understanding Climate Change through Gender Relations*. (Eds.) Susan Buckingham and Virginie Le Masson Oxon, New York: Routledge.

Macchi, M. (2011). *Framework for community-based climate vulnerability and capacity assessment in mountain areas*. Kathmandu: ICIMOD.

MOEF (n.d.). Bhagirathi eco sensitive zone notification. www.moef.gov.in/sites/default/files/Bhagirathipercent20Ecopercent20zonepercent20-percent20ZMPpercent20comments_0.pdf [Accessed 10 March 2017].

Nichenametla, P. (2013). Uttrakhand: A tiny village does what a state fails to do. *Hindustan Times*, 25 June 2013.

11
A post-Morakot environmentally friendly reconstruction solution

Reflections from a green social work perspective

Yen Yi Huang, Chiau Hong Chen, Shu Ching Chang and Shu Yuan Hsiao

Introduction

Disasters trigger reflections on human–environment relations. Taiwan's Typhoon Morakot dropped copious rain during a short period, causing diverse people to reflect on the factors that had aggravated the disaster. These included climate change, the impact of larger storms, soil erosion, landslides, inappropriate large-scale developments and construction projects in environmentally inappropriate areas. In the Typhoon's aftermath, greater attention was placed on environmental protection and environmentally friendly projects. However, the question remained: have such reflections produced actions and changes in the field? After the disaster, survivors were offered generous government resources. After funding ran out, some sponsored programmes were sustained; others were suspended. Many factors yielded these outcomes. This chapter analyses four post-Morakot environmentally friendly reconstruction cases to consider the contextual requirements for sustainable, local, long-term community reconstruction programmes. Then, it will reflect upon local green social work practices in Taiwan.

Typhoon Morakot

In 2009, Typhoon Morakot's long-lasting, heavy rains in the mountains and plains of Chiayi, Tainan, Kaohsiung, Pingtung and Taitung devastated southern Taiwan with landslides, large amounts of driftwood, flooding and waterlogging. This was the deadliest typhoon in Taiwan for 50 years (Lee et al., 2011). Much of the serious damage resulting from Typhoon Morakot was associated with global warming and increases in severe weather stemming from a changing climate in combination with the absence of a long-term national land conservation plan. The resultant devastation was also attributed to traditional capitalist land management wherein interrelated political and commercial interests produced the environmental degradation of mountains, forests and coastal lands (Chiang, 2010).

Fan (2012) indicated that failure to consider local characteristics and lay knowledge in risk assessments by excluding local communities in reconstruction decision-making processes resulted in further environmental injustices. For example, the Tzu-Chi Foundation (TCF) suggested that a permanent housing policy to reduce the cost of building pre-fabricated houses. This view was supported by central government (Shao, 2012; Chiang 2013). Also, TCF advocated for a 'total evacuation of interior settlement and reforestation of the mountains' which the government enacted as 'Forced Resettlement or Village Relocation', a pivotal point of post-disaster reconstruction policy (Shieh et al., 2012: 43).

Indigenous peoples' areas were most seriously affected by Typhoon Morakot (MTPDRC, 2011). Accordingly, dozens of indigenous Taiwanese villages were relocated from the mountainous interior to the foothills. Removing indigenous people from ancestral lands destroys their traditional territory, livelihoods, interpersonal relationships, material culture and collective memory (Taiban, 2013: 59). This reconstruction policy caused multiple protests and resistance activities, further increasing victim–survivors' anxiety including mental and physical stresses. The man-made disaster caused by government policy may have had a greater impact than the natural disaster (Hsieh et al., 2011:159; Dominelli, 2012).

Typhoon Morakot's devastation is associated with many issues that green social workers address, such as the impact of physical and ecological environments on humans (and vice versa), environmental and ecological justice, and environmental damage induced by capitalism and neoliberalism (Dominelli, 2012). The experiences of several local workers and their practices in confronting this environmental disaster will be discussed in this chapter through case studies.

Sources of information

Memory work was used to obtain source information (Haug, 2000, 2008). This method, based on group research, brings together a group of people to engage actively in the research process and share thoughts, knowledge and analyses with each other. Adjustments were made to Huag's (2000) models to fit local conditions. The steps taken were:

1 The authors formed a group to develop research questions collectively.
2 Issues were first clarified, and then discussions were held with local workers. Discussions were recorded and transcribed verbatim for the first author to conduct the initial analysis.
3 Brainstorming within the group of researchers identified similarities, differences, contrasts or inconsistences in the transcripts, leading to further discussions and revisions.

Several discussion groups were held. Those that occurred on 22 August 2015 and 26 April 2016 involved seven and three local workers, respectively. They had participated in post-Typhoon Morakot reconstruction responses. The transcript was emailed to co-authors for three rounds of review. Another group discussion on 18 November 2016 revised the manuscript. Additionally, a two-hour interview to clarify items was held with a local worker in Dakanua Village on 17 December 2016. The first author also visited reconstruction sites during the research period, and field observations were recorded for further analysis.

The transcripts were analysed to generate themes and categories from repeatedly comparing and contrasting the differences and similarities found within the texts. A further analysis linked these dialogues with theory and related concepts in the literature. Koutroulis (2001) argues that *memory work* is a form of meta-analysis in which participants share, record and analyse each other's memories during the research process, placing participants in an equal position as co-researchers. With this collective, participatory approach, the authors worked with the participants to coproduce knowledge as green social work advocates.

Local participants remain anonymous, and informed consent was obtained. Participants also reviewed the final draft of this chapter. The seven members of the first group are identified as M1, M2, M3, M4, M5, M6 and M7. The second and third groups included M2, M6 and M7. Since M8 was unable to participate in group discussions, the first author visited for a one-on-one interview.

Cases of environmentally friendly reconstruction

Typhoon Morakot represented a crisis and opportunity for change. After the disaster, some communities proposed different ideas on how to structure their communities' economies, switching from a consumption-oriented approach that attracted many tourists to a model based on local agricultural assets and characteristics. Although this transition has not been globally applied, the current case studies exemplify a good start.

A. Jiasian Community Association

The Jiasian Community Association (JCA) was extensively dedicated to rural education and actively advocated on issues pertaining to public farmland and agricultural topics before Morakot. JCA continues to make adjustments and shift its direction as a result of hands-on experimentation. It has promoted cultivation of Indica Rice and integrated their advocacy efforts with the Typhoon Morakot Temporary Work Programme within the existing Public Farmland System. The planting of organic rice is executed in conjunction with the Wild Peanut Family, formed by students at Chi-Mei Community College. They also participate in food and farming education at elementary schools and advocate environmentally friendly farming techniques developed through working with independent farmers. JCA organises farming events for children, expecting hands-on experiences to enable young students to connect with the land.

The Jiasian region is famous for taro ice cream. Even though taro is the key ingredient in the ice cream, people in this area bought taro from other regions. During the post-Typhoon Morakot reconstruction process, JCA and other local organisations encouraged large numbers of farmers in Jiasian to grow taro. The Agriculture Bureau then started investing in Jiasian taro farming. Local taro ice cream makers are now using local taro to support local agriculture.

Usage of local products has boosted the income of local farmers, created more work opportunities and lowered carbon footprints. Previously, business owners in Jiasian competed with each other and fought over business opportunities. After the Typhoon, the community engaged in discussions on how best to showcase Jiasian's unique features and come together for joint marketing in new collaborations and connections.

JCA provides a dependable platform that informs independent farmers about sustainable farming. It organises small local excursions, which have led to better care of the smallest corners of the community, wherein local stories are highlighted. These excursions entail more than just promotion and smart packaging. The management and maintenance of each destination depends on discovering new attractions in the community's accumulated history, and community-building processes. They allow consumers of farm products to experience farming and interact with farmers. These excursions have shifted conceptions of and reframed farmers as knowledge holders, not merely labourers. Furthermore, these excursions have created diverse educational opportunities and greater awareness of community values.

B. Duona Tribal Village

Duona Tribal Village, located in Maolin District, is composed of indigenous peoples from the Rukai Tribe. Its tourism, based on hot springs, was previously this community's major source of income. M6 says:

> It used to be that when neighbours in the hot springs region of Duona ran into each other they would ask how many customers they had that day. Because the hot springs were damaged after the Typhoon, the locals started developing other jobs locally, so now they would greet their neighbours by asking, 'Have *you* eaten yet? Have *you* been sleeping well?'

Thus, the Typhoon altered relationships among residents.

After the hot springs were buried by landslides, residents thought about other local assets to survive. The tribe invited tribal elders to elder care locations and traditional weaving workshops to develop and teach the craft of traditional weaving to women and young people. Tapakadrawane, or the 'Black Rice Festival', has been revived after a two-decade hiatus. Environmentally friendly farming methods are used to cultivate a type of black rice that is unique to this region. Children are guided by the tribal elders to plant rice and learn about the history of their tribe. After the disaster, a restaurant owner began growing herbs on a long-abandoned piece of land and served food cooked with home-grown organic ingredients. The restaurant offers guided tours and invites children with mental disorders to gain hands-on gardening experiences. This serves as a form of therapy. Underprivileged people are also employed in the herb garden.

These exemplify that people are thinking beyond making money as green social workers suggest. They develop their businesses and help underprivileged people. Land is no longer solely linked with production or considered a good for trading. It is now connected with important issues including provision of local ingredients, food safety, job opportunities and care for less fortunate people.

Different organisations present in Duona Tribal Village include a patrol team, women's association and youth association. These groups quickly organise to form a support system in times of disaster. The village office becomes an emergency response centre, the village chief serves as the commander-in-chief, and villagers are divided into groups to handle different tasks during emergency scenarios. As M2 says, 'They can proudly say that even without air-dropped relief supplies, they can still survive for two weeks'.

C. Small-Town Community Empowerment Alliance of Kaohsiung City

The Small-Town Community Empowerment Alliance of Kaohsiung City (Small Town) was founded in September 2014. After the conclusion of post-Typhoon Morakot rebuilding, a group of local staff that participated in rebuilding formed a regional cross-township organisation to carry on mid- to long-term rebuilding. As M6 states, 'We can't leave and won't leave because our home is here, and it doesn't feel like the disaster was that long ago, so we need to continue to gain more experiences'.

Small Town now serves as a connective platform for community resources and information distribution and acts as a consulting team for the community. M2 claims, 'Whenever resources are made available for the region, we can quickly help with allocating the resources to the groups with the most urgent needs'. This group has also organised a cross-generational education programme with donated cameras to record participants' lives and efforts during both recovery and reconstruction periods.

Its core focus is to bring locals together in an alliance of companionship to inspire, provoke and engage other local inhabitants in discussions with one another and devise collective solutions for potential problems. The alliance hopes to ignore one-time carnival-like events that entail passive participation and traditional community development models. Rather, it brings people together to face regional problems collectively and form a pathway towards local, sustainable solutions.

Community work is being neglected in Taiwanese social work education, and many young social workers are unsure of what to do when they arrive in a community. Small Town acts as a bridge for social workers coming from outside the community, helping them understand and learn how to work with the community. Small Town recruits student interns majoring in social work, who are trained in post-disaster reconstruction. The alliance anticipates continued participation in training future social workers.

D. Dakanua

After Typhoon Morakot, Dakanua Village located in Namasia, Kaoshiung opted for in-situ reconstruction instead of moving people into the government's permanent housing. As described by M8:

> When some tribal members and I came back here, each one chose a tree. When the flood came or the government forced us to relocate, we decided to tie ourselves against the tree. We would prefer being washed away with the tree in the flood than become homeless in cities.

After the disaster, maintaining livelihoods was the main priority. Dakuna's women grew traditional crops using natural farming methods, restored endangered golden taros, raised chickens and baked breads. They called it *Usuuru*, or 'the women's farm', where women used their knowledge and resources to restore plant species that had nearly been lost and connected farming with their lives and livelihoods. Tribal farmers had been growing cash crops as their main source of income, utilising chemical fertilisers and pesticides to increase yields. The products were high in production costs, yet low in market price. Environmentally friendly ways of farming have now been adopted to reconstruct the tribe through the rediscovery of wisdom from their own culture.

'A tribe does not imply solidarity or collaboration. It did, perhaps. Yet under the impact of globalisation, the interpersonal cooperation in a tribe is not as close as we imagined anymore', said one woman of the tribe (fieldwork note). Therefore, a group of women returned to the tribe and founded a network to provide mutual help, offering a communal kitchen and after-school programme. These women urged other women to take their children to the after-school programme and invited older people to teach children about their traditional culture and diet. An hourly rate paid to those providing instruction fosters a sense of accomplishment and source of income.

After Typhoon Morakot, numerous mental health specialists came to provide treatment for post-traumatic stress disorder. This was of little help for older people. Instead, Dakanua villagers' creation of space for older people to share their cultural wisdom became an important healing mechanism (Apu'u Kaaviana, 2015). The Usuuru provides women and older people with income and a chance to see how different life can be when working together and using their collective power and wisdom. Women of the tribe are committed to restoring endangered traditional crops and teaching children the tribe's traditional culture. This restoration ensures diversity of agricultural seeds and a supply of quality food for disaster preparedness (e.g. planting crops resistant to heavy rain). As M8 explained, 'canned food is provided by the government for disaster preparedness. But canned food has expiration dates, which no one checked. We do not dare to eat those'.

Small Town and Usuuru in Dakanua were founded after Typhoon Morakot, while the organisations in Duona Village and the JCA had been operating before the disaster. During the government's five-year reconstruction period, many resources were provided by public and private sectors. Both M7 and M6 noted:

> Some organisations were set up to accept such resources. However, most of these organisations are out of operation now and some of the buildings are left vacant or have become 'mosquito halls' where insects are the only occupants. Those organisations left nothing but problems. Those continuing to take root after the end of reconstruction period are often local organisations with a basis that had already been developed.
>
> *(M7)*

> Some . . . community organisations have had a plan and strategies for local empowerment but have suffered due to scarce resources [prior to] Morakot. The resources provided for recovery . . . allowed such organisations to step-up, advance and expand . . . their original basis.
>
> *(M6)*

The observations of M6 and M7 show that certain levels of existing local capacities are required. The communities that had mutual help organisations involved in community and environmental issues before Typhoon Morakot were more likely to continue these trajectories and become more sustainable afterwards. Nevertheless, growing local organisations and empowering human beings are very important in the vast and complex mid- and long-term reconstruction efforts.

Significance of local organisation and human resources

The centres and work stations of disaster reconstruction following Typhoon Morakot were generally planned by central government. As the right to commission organisations nationwide belongs to central government, NGOs are geographically and socially closer to central government. Consequently, local NGOs were less favoured in the competition for the resources following the disaster. After field visits, the first author discovered that when national or large institutions left a site at the end of the reconstruction period, their work or experiences were not always transferred to local organisations. Consequently, sustaining the reconstruction endeavours of a service network for fundamental necessities was difficult. Having been closed, these stations dismissed many capable and enthusiastic local workers.

Unlike other impacted counties and cities, Kaohsiung started to implement the 'Human Resources Supporting Plan' (HRSP) in 2010 to involve local workers in reconstruction and provide them with training. Unlike the projects of central government, local organisations were made eligible to apply for second phase projects. As M3 pointed out, 'granting funding to high-profile NGOs or to local associations that are willing to engage and take responsibility, I think, will lead to two different outcomes'. Local organisations often play more critical roles during times of emergency (Lin, 2010). As M5 said:

> It was mainly because at the early stage of reconstruction, the stricken areas were in disarray. The place and people as a whole were in such an unstable state that the locals were the only ones who were capable of managing the logistics. They also had more and better ideas and solutions throughout the entire intervention.

Organisations operating in a community when a disaster strikes can act as a self-help relief force until formal rescue units arrive. For example, an elder care service existed in the Baolai community. When Typhoon Morakot struck, frightened local older people were kept company by community leaders and given instructions on how to evacuate, prevent or prepare for disasters. Now, when a Typhoon warning is issued, their community disaster prevention plans become activated.

In the early aftermath of Typhoon Morakot, many external teams providing services in stricken places were unfamiliar with local characteristics and cultural particularities and spent time on mutual adjustments (Wang et al., 2014). M1 and M3 noted that language barriers or short time frames made it hard for external professional helpers to fit into the community, making it difficult to establish trusted relationships and have smoothly running services. In contrast, local workers who knew the environment and community situation were able to pass on information and distribute resources to affected residents. Additionally, they were in the same situation as the victim–survivors, making it easier to develop a sense of trust.

The HRSP aims to train local women and young people to be semi-professional reconstruction workers. However, 'because no immediate effect could be produced and no results were demonstrated by the person in charge, the project ended up being regarded a waste of money', said M7. Projects that do take root and foster the long-term empowerment of human resources and community may not show results after the reconstruction period ends. The experience shared by M7 shows that recovery programmes that empower local people ensures a deep-rooted, locally relevant and more visionary means of post-disaster follow-up. According to opinions in the focus groups, the community needs substantial, long-term support. Organisations founded in response to specific resourcing are usually unsustainable. This reflects the importance of local organisations in long-term reconstruction work, when external organisations withdraw.

The government's role

The central government's decision to force relocation and permanent housing was the most controversial policy following Typhoon Morakot. Researchers criticised government for ceding disaster management and the direction of reconstruction programmes to large NGOs (Tseng, 2010; Chen, 2012). Indigenous people, most affected by forced relocation, endured benevolent violence (Awi, 2009: 38), which implies that the provision of housing is a form of help while denying indigenous people their perspective or self-determination.

One researcher questioned whether the state executed village relocation to create a suitable environment for capitalist development (Cheng, 2009). The forced relocation policy also implies that the government prioritised 'convenience in management' or refused to waste resources on 'mountainous areas with no economic benefits' (Chen, 2010: 419). These studies highlight issues of environmental justice, as does green social work (Dominelli, 2012). According to Kapucu (2005), a policy without coordination, communication and comprehensive planning that is formed without listening to survivors can intensify the impact of a natural disaster and create an even worse man-made one.

The lengthy process from initial emergency responses to reconstruction requires enormous quantities of material and human resources. Therefore, community empowerment and participation are highly valued. Dominelli (2012) emphasises the significant role played by the community in providing local knowledge, collaboration efforts and decision-making. M1 mentioned that local workers often strongly opposed inadequate governmental policies and measures that put massive limitations in practices involving local knowledge and wisdom. Habitual ways of thinking and practising ensure that governmental reconstruction projects are composed of countless performance reports, repetitive achievement presentations and incessant payment requests and verifications (Hung, 2015). Sponsored community organisations were busy with extensive paperwork. Performance-focused reconstruction projects made life in the community unusual, rendering it more difficult for the community to return to life as usual (ibid). M7 argued that after five years many community workers were trained experts in writing project plans to obtain funding and considered 'success' by mainstream values. M2 mentioned:

> The absence of a comprehensive community economy development plan that would comprise the establishment of a marketing platform led to overproduction [of community generated products] in many cases. People were working and working like crazy, but no one was buying. No one buys. In fact, it was wearing down the community. In the end, it was the grandpas and the grandmas who bought the produce or products themselves.

Without comprehensive planning and carefully used resources to guide community reconstruction, many governmental measures became formalised routine work rather than attending to community needs. If the care of people and the land are not included and reconstruction plans remain short term, then reconstruction programmes are nothing more than a series of activities or projects. This makes it impossible to use resources wisely or generate new ways of thinking to guide appropriate avenues for development and reconstruction.

All local workers in the focus group sessions claimed that both central and local governments were eager to erase memories of disasters after their arbitrary recovery period of five years, after which any hints of Typhoon Morakot would disappear. The government also dismissed disaster workers' wish to symbolically mark the accomplishment of the recovery mission.

Reflections on green social work

Landslides caused by Typhoon Morakot devastated agricultural and indigenous tribal communities of southern Taiwan following heavy rainfalls. These were attributed to climate change, continual development efforts and neglect of national land conservation. Like a magnifying glass, the disaster exacerbated disadvantage among deprived groups, agricultural villages and rural Taiwan. Working to reduce these in the cases of Jiasian Community Association, Duona Tribal Village, Small-Town and Dakanua stimulated the following reflections on green social work.

A. The importance of the state's role

Quarantelli (1960) noted the myth of the state's almighty response to disaster. Government is expected to control everything. However, during Typhoon Morakot, local workers experienced the state's operational failures including its exclusion of local groups in favour of designing the framework and sharing reconstruction work with large, national NGOs.

Rather than encouraging nation-states to support neoliberalism, green social workers advocate for nation-states to act in partnership with local communities to coproduce solutions devised, agreed and owned by the local populace (Dominelli, 2012). One lesson highlighted by Typhoon Morakot was that local organisations and interpersonal neighbourhood networks provide the cornerstones of reconstruction when external aid groups have gone. However, the state controls most disaster relief resources and reconstruction programmes. These should be utilised to reduce vulnerability, support high-risk populations and include disaster risk factors like gender, poverty and inequality in mitigation efforts, endorsed by green social workers. Strong social and state institutional support is critical in disaster responses, providing social security and

B. Value of long-term reconstruction

The five-year reconstruction period set for Typhoon Morakot was inadequate. Many issues did not emerge until later according to local workers. Therefore, government agencies should plan resource distribution and allocation from a long-term perspective, establishing mechanisms to sustain human resources, empower organisations, and channel resources into organisations founded after the disaster. Long-term coproduced reconstruction is advocated by green social workers.

C. Significance of local organisation and dedicated personnel

Another concern is how to achieve constant, long-term, sustainable effects given the abundant resources made available after Typhoon Morakot. This study found that community organisations with experience in community empowerment and participation before the disaster sustained their activities, while those established specifically to capture new resources usually suspended their operations when funding ceased. Disaster relief and reconstruction efforts should build and consolidate relationships with existing local social networks and organisations (Dominelli, 2012).

Instead, central government commissioned successful bidders for Morakot disaster reconstruction centres under the Government Procurement Act. This favoured large institutions and national NGOs at the expense of small local organisations who could not compete. Yet, national NGOs operate badly in unfamiliar localities and lack cultural sensitivity (Lin and Lin, 2014). Hence, this privatisation mechanism excluded participation from local organisations, residents and indigenous people (Wang, 2010).

To showcase the achievements of reconstruction, the government dismissed disaster workers as soon as reconstruction projects ended. Furthermore, these workers were marginalised as recipients of social assistance or a low-wage backup workforce. Short-term or volunteer positions are disadvantageous in developing human resources: a decent position and stable wage can support local workers through long-term reconstruction efforts. So, reconstruction programmes should value local organisations and workers. Valuing locality emphasises decentralised, collaboration-oriented and place-based projects, and engages grassroots organisations, as proposed in green social work.

D. Environmental justice

Environmental problems and human right issues are gaining attention in social work. Dominelli (2012) advised making environmental justice a core element of social work's social justice framework. Schlosberg (2007) suggests that environmental justice includes local communities or those affected by environmental issues in decision-making and choice-making and recognises community culture, traditional lifestyles and knowledge.

Numerous studies on Typhoon Morakot demonstrated that inadequate public policies and industrial capitalism turned indigenous peoples into victims most affected by environmental disasters (Lu, 2010; Chen and Kuo, 2011). Additionally, indigenous peoples are excluded from the formation of reconstruction policies, and their cultural and regional particularities are ignored in decision-making processes (Wang, 2010). A disaster is socially constructed, and individuals from different groups or social status have differing levels of vulnerability. Environmental justice should be addressed in disaster impact assessment and national land-use planning (Guo, 2009).

E. Responding to climate change

Before the Morakot disaster, local livelihoods depended mainly on crop cultivation, tourism, Bed and Breakfast hotels, and hot-spring tourism. Although central and local governments formulated tourism-oriented reconstruction programmes, some local organisations considered alternative economic development options to respond to the severe challenges and unpredictability of climate change.

This chapter illustrates attempts to change dominant frameworks and strike a balance between conserving livelihoods and local environments. A capitalist approach reproduces the vulnerabilities of agricultural villages and tribes. Current economic activities dominated by neo-liberalist ideology that prioritise profits over people and the environment were rejected locally, as in green social work. The cases discussed in this chapter indicate that organisations following individualistic economic development endeavours avoid their environmental impact without mitigating neoliberalism's negative influences on disadvantaged groups or communities, especially tribes. Focus group interlocutors reiterated that reconstruction no longer solely implies economic restoration. It involves emotional elements, enhancing connections between people and land, fresh perspectives on the relationship between humans and nature, and acknowledgement of ecological justice.

F. Value of physical and ecological environments

Green social work emphasises the social, physical and ecological environments (Dominelli, 2012). The physical space and permanent housing for Morakot survivors reflect a lack of sensitivity towards indigenous agriculture, lifestyles and culture. Some indigenous survivors rebuilt their homes at their tribe's original site because the land was relevant not only to their livelihoods but also their cultural heritage. Some community organisations became aware that their community's future relies on conserving the ecological environment and implemented a more locally relevant or place-conscious reconstruction.

Townsend and Weerasuriya (2010) identified the effects of the natural environment on health and welfare. This study revealed that new rice cultivation workshops in Jiasian and the Usuuru of Dakanua exemplify nature-compatible solutions. People living in rural areas are generally reluctant to permit children and teenagers to receive psychological counselling. The rice cultivation workshop organised by the Jiasian Community Association provided a subtle and localised solution for improving students' mental health (Ho, 2010). Dakanua's experience showed that tribe members regained serenity through interaction with the land and nature, and self-reflection during crop planting and animal farming. These activities also calmed older people and children. In addition, the Usuuru collaboration of women provided a space where local women could give and receive support.

Conclusion

The post-Typhoon Morakot reconstruction experience highlights the importance of incorporating physical, ecological and social environments alongside local experiences and place-based concepts in reconstruction plans. Post-disaster reconstruction should not simply restore the past, but develop networks and connections between residents and organisations and inter-organisational alliances to face the future impacts of disasters on land, livelihoods and the environment together. In this framework, long-term post-disaster reconstruction should be substantial and address issues like sustainability, environmental justice and ecological justice. Disadvantaged individuals and communities suffer most in climate change-induced disasters (Wisner et al., 2003). The areas most severely stricken by Typhoon Morakot illustrate the problems of structural inequality within Taiwan. Individual resilience to disaster risks are determined by ethnic background, class, gender, age and other social divisions (Huang, 2014).

Community organisations and empowered human resources are potential assets to emerge from the aftermath of a disaster. Environmental justice issues should be considered during national decision-making and land-use planning. Reconstruction represents more than mobilisation or organisational activities. It is a joint effort in finding means for returning affected peoples to normal livelihoods. In the case of Taiwan, the government did not commemorate or recognise the experience of disaster, but focused instead on the achievements of reconstruction. Local wisdom and strategies during the reconstruction process should be more systematically documented. Researchers and practitioners must collaborate and coproduce knowledge to ensure that future disaster relief and reconstruction practices can rely on databases and recorded information rather than memory alone. Green social workers can facilitate these tasks and affirm local knowledge, skills and innovations.

References

Apu'u Kaaviana (2015). *Finding a way back home: An aboriginal woman's life story* (Unpublished master's thesis). National Kaohsiung Normal University, Taiwan. (In Chinese)

Awi, M. (2009). Post-Morakot reconstruction and human rights protection: An indigenous culture-based reflection. *Taiwan Democracy Quarterly*, 6(3): 179–193. (In Chinese)

Chen, H. M. (2012). Some issues of community empowerment in the advent of post-disaster period. *Journal of Environment and Art*, 11: 31–48. (In Chinese)

Chen, Y. L. (2010). Subjectification, movement, and tribe re-establishment in indigenous area of southern Taiwan after Morakot Flood. *Taiwan: A Radical Quarterly in Social Studies*, 78: 403–435. (In Chinese)

Chen, Y. T. and Kuo, H. J. (2011). The concept of modern environmental citizenship and apocalypse for education: The case study of Tseng-Wen reservoir trans-basin water. *Far East Inquiry*, 28(2): 169–181. (In Chinese)

Cheng, W. N. (2009). Section report: Taiwan aborigines' traditional environmental wisdom and settlement migration: Comparison between autonomous migration and compulsory relocation. In R. L. Chu (Chair), *Climate change, homeland conservation and Taiwan aborigines' socio-cultural vision conference*. Symposium conducted at Institute of Ethnology, Academia Sinica, Taipei, Taiwan. (In Chinese)

Chiang, B. (2010). Disaster, culture and 'subjectivity': Reflections after typhoon Morakot. *Si Xiang*, 14: 19–32. (In Chinese)

Chiang, B. (2013). Legal limbo and homeland blues: The case of Prilayan Paiwan in post-disaster relocation plan. In J. Weiner (Chair), *Legal ground: Land and law in contemporary Taiwan and the pacific*. Symposium conducted at Institute of Ethnology, Academia Sinica, Taipei, Taiwan. (In Chinese)

Dominelli, L. (2012). *Green Social Work: From environmental crises to environmental justice*. Cambridge: Polity Press.

Fan, M. F. (2012). Exploring the Tseng-Wen reservoir trans-basin water diversion project from the perspective of environmental justice. *Taiwan Political Science Review*, 16(2): 117–173. (In Chinese)

Haug, F. (2008). Memory work. *Australian Feminist Studies*, 23(58): 537–541.

Haug, F. (2000). *Memory-work as a method of social science research: A detailed rendering of memory-work method*. Available on www.friggahaug.inkrit.de/documents/memorywork-researchguidei7.pdf [Accessed 27 May 2016]

Hsieh, W. C., Cheng, F. S. and Cheng, C. W. (2011). This is just a house, not our home: The immigration and life-shock's experience of Taiwanese indigene after typhoon Morakot through an interpretive interactionism perspective. *NTU Social Work Review*, 24: 135–166. (In Chinese)

Huang, Y. Y. (2014). Shifting perspectives on environmental issues in social work and some implications for social work education. *Social Policy and Social Work*, 18(2): 1–32. (In Chinese)

Hung, H. L. (2015). The limitations and creative capacity of community empowerment in a disaster society: Paper presented at 2015 Annual Conference of Cultural Studies Association, March. Available on www.

csat.org.tw/paper/d2-3%E6%B4%AA%E9%A6%A8%E8%98%AD%E3%80%88%E7%81%BD%E9%9B%A3%E7%A4%BE%E6%9C%83%E4%B8%AD%E7%A4%BE%E9%80%A0%E4%B9%8B%E4%B8%8D%E8%83%BD%E8%88%87%E5%89%B5%E8%83%BD%E3%80%89.pdf (In Chinese) [Accessed 25 May 2016]

Ho, S. J. (2010). *The legend of Jiasian rice*. Available on http://museum02.digitalarchives.tw/teldap/2010/88news/www.88news.org/index202a.html?p=5975&cpa Persp ge=12010/08/21 (In Chinese) [Accessed 24 May 2016]

Kapucu, N. (2005). Intergovernmental coordination in dynamic context: Networks in emergency response management. *Connections*, 26(2): 33–48.

Koutroulis, G. (2001). Soiled identity: Memory-work narratives of menstruation. *Health*, 5(2): 187–205.

Lee, C.Y., Lai, W. C., Chen, C.Y., Huang, H.Y. and Kuo, L. H. (2011). The reconstruction of the processes of catastrophic disasters caused by the 2009 typhoon Morakot. *Journal of Chinese Soil and Water Conservation*, 42(4): 313–324. (In Chinese)

Lin, J. J., and Lin, W. I. (2014). A study on the service networks of typhoon Morakot post-disaster reconstruction in the south Taiwan: A governance approach to disaster. *Thought and Words: Journal of the Humanities and Social Science*, 52(3): 5–52. (In Chinese)

Lin, J. R. (2010). Does only masculinity fulfil rescue work: Silenced voices of women in disaster discourse. *Gender Equity Education Journal Quarterly*, 51: 16–19. (In Chinese)

Lu, L. T. (2010). Environmental colonialism to environmental refugee: The story of Xiaolin village. *Journal of State and Society*, 9: 1–31. (In Chinese)

MTPDRC (Morakot Typhoon Post-Disaster Reconstruction Council, Executive Yuan) (2011). *Rebuilding a sustainable homeland with innovation and united efforts*. Kaohsiung: Morakot Typhoon Post-Disaster Reconstruction Council.

Quarantelli, E. L. (1960). Images of withdrawal behavior in disasters: Some basic misconceptions. *Social Problems, 8:* 68–79.

Guo, P. Y. (2009). Section report: Climate change and the difficulties for global aborigines: Comparison among Taiwan aborigines, Austronesian aborigines and others. In B. Chiang(Chair), *Climate change, homeland conservation and Taiwan aborigines' socio-cultural vision conference*. Symposium conducted at Institute of Ethnology, Academia Sinica, Taipei, Taiwan. (In Chinese)

Schlosberg, D. (2007). *Defining environmental justice: Theories, movements, and nature*. New York: Oxford University Press.

Shao, P. C. (2012). Cooperative states and issues between public and private sectors for post-disaster relocating reconstruction: In a case of Morakot typhoon. *Society for Social Management Systems Internet Journal*, Retrieved from http://kutarr.lib.kochi-tech.ac.jp/dspace/bitstream/10173/993/1/sms12-6422.pdf [Accessed 27 May 2016]

Shieh, J. C., Fu, T. S., Chen, J. S., and Lin, W. I. (2012). A road far away from the aboriginal hometown? – Rethinking the post-disaster relocation policy of typhoon Morakot. *NTU Social Work Review*, 26: 41–86. (In Chinese)

Taiban, S. (2013). From Rekai to Labelabe: Disaster and relocation on the example of Kucapungane. *Anthropological Notebooks*, 19(1), 59–76.

Townsend, M., and Weerasuriya, R. (2010). *Beyond Blue to Green: The benefits of contact with nature for mental health and well-being*. Melbourne: Beyond Blue Ltd.

Tseng, S. C. (2010). The issues of community reconstruction after the strike of Typhoon Morakot. *TAHR PAS Fall*. 10: 12–13. (In Chinese)

Wang, T. Y. (2010). Helping relations and subjectivity of indigenous peoples in post-disaster recovery: Returning to whose home? *Taiwan: A Radical Quarterly in Social Studies*, 78: 437–449. (In Chinese)

Wang, M.Y., Lin, D. L. and Lu, T. (2014). The experience of local service of a psychiatric medical team to execute the project of psychological rehabilitation after typhoon Morakot, and reflection on the role of the psychiatric social worker. *NTU Social Work Review*, 29: 91–148. (In Chinese)

Wisner, B., Blaikie, P., Cannon, T., and Davis, I. (2003). *At risk: Natural hazards, people's vulnerability, and disasters*. London: Routledge.

12
Dominica – Tropical Storm Erika and its impacts

Letnie F. Rock, Debra D. Joseph and Ayodele O. Harper

Introduction

The Commonwealth of Dominica, the nature island of the Caribbean, is situated 15 25 N, 61 20 W of the equator, with a land area of 750sq km, 47km long, and 26km wide. Its coastline is 148km. The most mountainous of the Lesser Antilles, it experiences heavy rainfall. Dominica's diverse physical habitats include nine active volcanoes, dense rainforest, hundreds of rivers, woodland and varied fauna and flora. There are natural resources of timber, hydropower and arable lands (CIA, 2016). The island has a sub-tropical climate and is prone to natural disasters having experienced earth tremors, volcanic eruptions, mudslides, floods, cyclones and ravages of hurricanes like Hurricane David in 1979 and Hurricane Maria in September 2017. The country's population is 73,757 (CIA, 2016); 29 percent live below the poverty line; and 23 percent were unemployed in 2000 (CIA, 2016). A small population of indigenous people – the Kalinago, whose descendants predate European colonisation – live in their own territory on the northeast coast and are virtually the only survivors of the region's first peoples (Crask, 2016).

Dominica was first settled by the Spanish, later the French and then the English. It attained political independence from Britain in 1978 (CIA, 2016) and is a member of the Caribbean Community (CARICOM) and Commonwealth of Nations. The main industries of Dominica are agriculture and tourism. The main exports are agricultural products including bananas, coffee, cocoa and citrus fruits. Dominica's main environmental issues include deforestation, soil erosion, untreated sewage disposal, and pollution of the coastal zone by chemicals used in farming and the soap industry (The Commonwealth, 2017).

In August 2015, the weak 50 mph Tropical Storm Erika unexpectedly hit the island, dumped 380 mm of rain in seven hours, causing catastrophic mudslides and flooding. In its aftermath, hundreds of homes were destroyed and entire villages flattened. Erika left over 30 people dead and until Maria, a category 5 hurricane that recently devastated the island, Erika was regarded as the deadliest natural disaster to hit Dominica since Hurricane David in 1979. The total damage from Erika was around US$482.8 million. The country's socio-economic development was set back approximately 20 years (Pash and Penny, 2016).

When social workers consider Dominica's history of vulnerability to natural disasters, its physical size and characteristics as a nature island, source of peoples' livelihoods and the social, economic and psychological impact of disasters on the well-being of its people and communities, their strategic interventions must include a green social work perspective. Dominelli defines green social work (GSW) as:

> A form of holistic professional social work practice that focuses on: the interdependencies among people; the social organisation of relationships between people and the flora and fauna in their physical habitats; and the interaction between socio-economic and physical environmental crises and interpersonal behaviour that undermine the well-being of human beings on Planet Earth.
>
> *(2012: 25)*

This chapter discusses the social, cultural, economic and political impact of Erika on the people of Dominica. An example of post-disaster social work intervention in Dominica by the authors is considered. It concludes with: lessons that might be useful for others building a GSW perspective; theoretical and practice innovations relevant to individuals and communities post-disaster; and questions that can be answered by further research.

Socio-cultural impacts of Tropical Storm Erika

> The residents of Dominica were totally unprepared for Tropical Storm Erika. Its death toll created a sense of loss for families and friends. The dead included persons who drowned in the storm's surge, rough seas, and fresh water floods alongside those who died from causality effects including lightening, wind-related events, and collapsing structures. Erika also left 574 persons homeless, and created a crisis of unprecedented proportion in Dominica.
>
> (Pash and Penny, 2016)

The Jungle Bay Resort, a popular tourist destination, sustained catastrophic damage from Erika's landslides and flooding (Raphael, 2015). Surrounding villages also suffered tremendous damage. Petite Savanne had the greatest loss with the death of 20 persons. The survivors of Petite Savanne were evacuated as the government declared the area unstable, and a disaster zone unfit for residents (Dominica News Online, 2015). This devastated families through loss of community life, culture and family support. Personal experiences of separation and loss were grave. Loss of homes, loved ones and land space that supported their entire livelihoods intensified feelings of hopelessness. Families were initially housed in shelters (schools designated for this purpose) but later many displaced families were temporarily split up to provide adequate accommodation elsewhere for all survivors. Other rural communities including Delices, Boetica and La Plaine were affected. Petite Savanne, a community of about 750 residents, had 538 persons evacuated in September 2015. Below, an 85-year-old resident expresses her views:

> I don't even know what to say. I am feeling very bad about the entire situation. I have cried so much already. . . . Right now my heart is just pounding and I am afraid. . . . From where I was living, I have never seen a landslide like that. . . . I now have to start all over again. I don't know where that will be. I will miss Petite Savanne, the unity, the koudmen, the cultural aspects, the people. We all lived together as one, the bay-leaf, and the quietness in the community.
>
> *(The Sun, 2015a, para. 3–8)*

Bay-leaf is a popular spice and an export of Dominica. 'Koudmen' is a Creole term of French origin, meaning a 'coupe de main'. One of the meanings in English is 'a helping hand'. Koudmen helped to build Dominica and its communities in the past. During natural disasters community residents spontaneously lend a helping hand. Such practices are formidable in places where finances are deficient, as many receive help and are helped in return. In Dominica, Koudmen are the *social glue* that keeps communities together (Gabriel, 2015). The disruption of the community's Koudmen support system compounded the sense of loss.

The Dominica Grammar School (DGS) near Bath Estate in Roseau, the capital, housed residents from Petite Savanne instead of admitting new students in September 2015. Residents included babies, teenagers, middle-aged people, fishermen, housewives and teachers – the displaced individuals of Petite Savanne for whom DGS became a new, temporary home (*The Sun*, 2015b). One survivor stated:

> My house wasn't damaged because I live lower down Petite Savanne. But next morning after the storm I went to help, looking for those buried, and helping families to cross over landslides to move them from the bad areas in case more rain fell.
>
> *(The Sun, 2015b, para. 8)*

The Sun (2015b) reported that the number of persons in the shelter would change as family and friends (Koudmen) would house some people in their homes, demonstrating the community spirit of togetherness and 'we-ness' that exists among the people of Dominica.

Erika greatly impacted the socio-cultural environment of Dominica. The deaths, injuries, displacement, unemployment and grief will continue to impact the residents for months and years post-disaster. It is fortuitous that the informal networks built by community residents in Dominica proved to be a source of resilience and empowerment for survivors in the immediate aftermath of Erika. However, the government and its agencies must actively address the mental health of the people and their livelihoods as part of their disaster management and relief plans post-disaster. Social workers played a crucial role in crisis intervention post-Erika. However, with very limited social work resources not all residents received professional help. Dominelli (2012) suggests that in such situations social workers work alongside specific communities to promote their well-being. When one considers the direct interdependencies of human life, the natural environment, human relationships and well-being, the application of a GSW approach in working with affected individuals and communities in Dominica is underscored.

Economic and political impacts of Tropical Storm Erika

An architect's view on Erika (*The Sun* 2015c) is that construction building practices in Dominica were compounded by a general lack of understanding of the vulnerability of housing stock to dangerous environmental conditions and contributed significantly to the havoc wreaked by Erika. The architect believes that the populace had forgotten lessons from Hurricane David's destruction and recommendations for vulnerability assessments of all housing in Dominica. In his professional opinion, bad practices, specifically the widespread building of walls along river banks which narrowed waterways encroached dangerously on the natural courses of the rivers and worsened Erika's impact. In many badly affected and other areas, people had constructed buildings much too close to rivers, and utility lines commonly passed under bridges. These utility lines blocked debris borne by the surging waters of rivers during the storm. The architect expressed concern about the destruction of bridges and concluded that Erika's flood waters clearly mapped out Dominica's flooding danger zones and water courses (*The Sun*, 2015c).

Estimated damages from Erika ranged up to US$500 million; about $1.35 billon Eastern Caribbean Currency (EC) (Pash and Penny, 2016). With a 2015–2016 national budget of $563 million EC, it was impossible for Dominica to cover the rebuilding costs post-disaster. The prime minister announced an estimated $612.7 million EC to repair the infrastructural damage, and a further $39.5 million EC to rebuild the country's airport (Caribbean 360, 2016). This financial estimate excluded the rebuilding of Petite Savanne (James, 2015). The country needed to borrow money to help with reconstruction. However, one Dominican environmentalist noted that funding the reconstruction of the island post-Erika extended beyond aid-hunting and required judicious social planning that would take the country's environment and topography into account (James, 2015).

After a natural disaster, the infrastructure requires urgent repairs to make roads, bridges and other services functional for daily living. The economy of Dominica will recover slowly because of its weak economic resource base and its strong dependence on tourism. Dominica, a small island developing state (SIDS), will require financial aid from local, regional and international sources to aid its economic recovery. Funding has been forthcoming to assist with reconstruction and recovery (Government of the Commonwealth of Dominica, 2015).

Socio-economic interventions that utilise a GSW approach as defined earlier are key in positioning Dominica to recover economically and socially from the effects of disasters such as Erika and empower the country and its people to prepare for future disasters. Social workers and other social planners must acknowledge that a people's way of life is intertwined with the natural environment. Many of the vulnerabilities that can disrupt people's lives in the event of a natural disaster exist in Dominica. These include poorly constructed bridges and roads, poor housing stock, inadequate drainage systems, buildings sited along river banks and foothills of mountains that increase susceptibility to flooding and landslides. Within poor, rural communities the livelihoods of people who are employed in sectors such as agriculture, tourism and fishing are greatly dependent on natural resources and environmental conditions. When these are disrupted their well-being is also directly affected. Fortunately, Dominica's residents have resilient and empowering informal networks that served them well post-disaster. Dominelli (2012: 25) notes that 'the interactions between socio-economic and environmental crises and interpersonal behaviours that undermine the well-being of human beings and planet earth' are critical factors to be considered when using a GSW approach to interventions post-disaster. Efforts at rebuilding must also ensure social justice including the equal distribution of power and resources and conservation of the natural resources for enjoyment by all.

Social work intervention in Dominica post-disaster

Intervening in the aftermath of a disaster requires that social workers are trained and skilled to deal with the issues that survivors present (Rock and Corbin, 2007). Survivors are usually concerned about immediate or ongoing danger to the self, the safety and whereabouts of loved ones, and the loss of homes, jobs, personal property, pets, neighbourhoods and schools (James and Gilliland, 2013). Psychosocial counsellors including social workers need to be attuned to the traumatic experiences, immediate needs, coping strategies and resilience of survivors.

Following natural disasters in the Caribbean region, the mental health of those impacted is likely to be overlooked due to the scarcity of psychosocial professionals. However, psychosocial support is necessary to reduce the heightened feelings of anxiety of survivors. Failure to address adequately the negative psychological effects of post-traumatic stress disorder (PTSD), depression, panic attacks, acute stress disorder, and alcohol and substance abuse among survivors can be detrimental to their recovery if they adopt inappropriate coping strategies.

Erika's devastation necessitated psychosocial help for survivors. A counselling team comprised of the authors visited Dominica to assist residents. The team aimed to provide psychosocial support to survivors who had suffered extreme trauma and losses due to the disaster and to work collaboratively with mental health professionals in Dominica to assess needs in disaster-affected communities.

Dominica has few psychosocial professionals who can provide psychosocial support to assist in recovery following a disaster. Rock and Corbin note that:

> Disasters can have a severe impact on the socio-economic bases of small developing states with fragile economies such as those of the Caribbean. Many of these countries already lack an adequate public health infrastructure and structured emergency planning, efficient communication and transportation systems and the human and material resources to mitigate a major disaster and/or ensure recovery.
>
> *(2007: 383)*

Erika disrupted transportation by air, sea and road. Residents accepted help from anyone willing to assist. The visiting social workers linked up with participating in-country psychosocial and mental health professionals, 'and become incorporated into their aid services' (Javidian, 2007: 242). The visiting team linked with a mental health team (doctors and nurses) from Dominica to tour affected areas. Ironically, on that day the mental health team was celebrating World Mental Health Day under the global theme, 'Dignity in Mental Health: Recovery Happens'. The local mental health team had planned the tour and day's events to begin their week's activities. The joint team of visiting psychosocial professionals including social workers, a psychologist and mental health personnel from Dominica worked in groups and toured two communities: Colihaut and Coulibistrie. These were farming communities that were seriously impacted by Erika's flooding and landslides. Team members spoke with survivors and heard from men, women, teenagers and children about the severity of their disaster experiences, current plight and needs. Many survivors shared heroic stories about their escape from flood waters. They credited this to being able to 'think quickly on their feet' (flight syndrome) (Dictionary.com, 2017). They narrated stories of damage to homes and property, and of how they were working assiduously to clean the mud from their homes and streets.

The 15-member team of visiting and local social workers and mental health personnel attended a church service at a local church in the community of Colihaut. Their church attendance served a dual purpose. It opened mental health week and church attendees talked about experiences post-Erika. One story focused on a family's heroic escape from the flood waters and losing their home and possessions. However, neighbours and church members helped each other by providing food, shelter, clothing and comfort. The team observed that there was a difference in the way survivors fared post-disaster in the two communities. In Colihaut there was a community spirit that spoke to 'we-ness' with residents helping each other to reconstruct their lives post-disaster. However, in Coulibistre, residents were reconstructing their lives with limited informal social support as they awaited assistance from government officials. In both communities, many of the traumatised survivors voiced that they had developed a fear of rain. The team observed the devastation of property and listened to survivors as they recalled how they had lost loved ones, their homes, schools and businesses. Some survivors were farmers or worked in agriculture and felt displaced, having lost their crops, livestock and entire livelihoods.

Survivors also spoke of landslides, rivers that had overflowed their banks, resulting in tremendous flooding. The team also observed the ways in which the rivers had created new pathways and how giant-sized boulders from the mountains had been deposited downstream among remaining houses and structures. Some survivors expressed feelings of guilt because they had been praying for rain but instead floods came suddenly during the drought.

The Government of Dominica was actively spearheading the clean-up and rescue efforts and, according to residents, this provided some relief. The major problem that survivors in both communities highlighted during the tour was the lack of 'piped' running water and repairs to homes. Bottled water was insufficient, so they also used muddy water from nearby rivers for personal and household use. They boiled water for cooking to avoid contamination. Usage of muddy water was risky because while some residents bathed in the water upstream, others were using the same water for household purposes downstream. Given these observations and other data collected by the mental health team that toured the affected communities, it is clear that apart from psychosocial counselling, social work intervention using an environmental approach would have been most appropriate in assisting residents to rebuild their lives. This approach post-disaster must entail ensuring environmental justice for residents (Dominelli, 2012), through the preparation of displaced residents for relocation, counselling of residents grieving over their losses, advocacy for improved housing and safer location of communities, adequate supplies of clean drinking on a daily basis for all residents, the cleaning up of the streams and rivers that flowed through the villages, and the proper reconstruction of roads and bridges.

Spirituality, resilience, coping and mental health

The importance of coping and maintaining good mental and physical health post-disaster to facilitate recovery must be emphasised. Many people in the Caribbean use spirituality to cope with adversity, build resilience and provide comfort. One of the churches in Roseau, the capital, organised a National Day of Prayer to reach out to disaster survivors. Members of the team attended this service. The visiting team also organised a visit to a guest house where male survivors were being housed and held a focus group with five young men from Petite Savanne, the community which had been declared an unsafe area by government. Its survivors had been removed from temporary shelters (schools) to live in guest houses in safer locations.

Building rapport and trust with the men was difficult, despite the team's warm and engaging presence, because team members were strangers. However, once rapport was established, the men shared their stories and spoke to the following:

- The sudden nature of the disaster. This caught them unprepared and they could save only their own lives.
- Loss of life of family members and friends. One survivor had just returned from a relative's funeral. The body had been recently discovered. He had lost eight family members and witnessed his parents' house being swept away with his parents inside. Their bodies were never found. He was physically hurt in the disaster and was still in shock.
- Their inability to or feelings of helplessness in being able to rescue relatives who had died resulted in feelings of extreme guilt. Separation of family members who were housed at different locations around the island post-disaster added to their pain and distress.
- Loss of livelihoods distressed the men who were farmers. Possible dangers prevented them from returning to their farms, but they felt idle and wanted to work. They reported feeling inadequate because they were unable to provide for themselves and family members. They felt ashamed to receive 'handouts' of food, personal items, toiletries, washing supplies and clean clothing. Their extreme feelings about the disaster revolved around being displaced and lacking control over their lives, producing an overall sense of helplessness and anomie among these young men. Some were withdrawn and others hurt, and angry about their

plight. These men, like other survivors, were in need of comfort, good mental health support and interventions to help them cope. Feelings of shock, uncertainty and fear prevailed among them. The sight, sounds, smells and experiences during the disaster remained vivid and they expressed fears about rain. The assessment of the counsellors was that the disaster undermined the men's basic assumptions and beliefs about life and had created anxiety and helplessness among them. The intervention by the team aimed to reduce their feelings of helplessness and bring their irrational thoughts back to a state of equilibrium with cognitive reality.

'Social work interventions in disaster have focused on the variety of ways that such events affect individuals, families, organizations and communities' (Pyles, 2007: 321). In post-disaster situations, individuals generally grieve for the loss of loved ones and property and relive the experience. The men from Petite Savanne suffered traumatic stress due to the disaster and multiple losses. Their social and cultural identity was fractured. Their sense of safety, shaken belief in each other and trust in God deepened their feelings of loss and grief. Some appeared depressed, anxious, fearful and guilty. Others were angry and expressed hostility towards the government for what they felt was an inadequate response by the formal agencies. The disaster had suddenly plunged them into poverty with implications for their survival (Pyles, 2007) and mental well-being.

The delayed effects of Erika and slow recovery were evident in Dominica. The local mental health team expressed concern about comments circulated by the media that the island was undergoing recovery. They felt that the public needed to be educated about the signs of post-traumatic stress and signs of recovery post-disaster. At the time of the interventions by the team, survivors were still in the 'honeymoon stage' where they were receiving some support from both formal and informal sources. After this stage, survivors could either experience disillusionment or come to grips with the reality that loved ones had died and that disruptions to their lives could be permanent. Ongoing psychological support was recommended by the counselling team to ensure that residents impacted by the disaster received help in overcoming adjustment problems and to aid their recovery.

Self-evaluation: lessons that might be useful for others

Useful lessons learned

From the perspective of GSW the joint team learned that:

- To house families together post-disaster is good social work practice. People are social beings who need to maintain interpersonal relationships and interaction with others. The men in the focus group did not have the daily support of family members and friends, and this added to their distress.
- The team of counsellors from UWI spent only a short time with survivors many of whom needed ongoing psychosocial interventions from trained counsellors to meet their long-term human service needs and assist with recovery. It is difficult for transient professionals, few in number, to be part of survivors' long-term goals and advocate for social justice for vulnerable groups and communities post-disaster. They lack knowledge about the resource base of the local social welfare, housing and bereavement services to which survivors may be referred.

- Dominicans have the cultural practice 'Koudmen' of people helping each other. The country is rich with natural resources – oceans, rivers, dense forest, rich soils, flora, fauna and wildlife – and many residents engage in agriculture and tourism, thus depending on the stability of the natural environment for their livelihoods. However, the ecology and typology of the country add to the vulnerability of the people during natural disasters. Thus, from a GSW perspective, social workers intervening in Dominica should focus on:

> the interdependencies amongst people; the social organisation of relationships between people and the flora and fauna in their physical habitats; and the interactions between socio-economic and physical environmental crises and interpersonal behaviours that undermine the well-being of human beings . . . reform[ing] the socio-political and economic forces that have a deleterious impact upon the quality of life of the poor and marginalised populations, secure the policy changes and social transformation necessary for enhancing the well-being of people and the planet.
>
> *(Dominelli, 2012: 25)*

- When countries have few resources, the psychosocial needs of survivors suffer due to the lack of professionals to provide psychological first aid and ongoing assistance to them. Dominica has a poorly resourced social service system to enable effective responses in times of disaster. There are few trained social workers in Dominica. Hence, Caribbean countries with larger numbers of trained social workers should create a team of social workers trained in culturally appropriate disaster management to respond to countries requiring post-disaster assistance. Shahar (1993) as cited in Javadian (2007: 343) notes that, 'individual social workers need to strengthen their knowledge of the impact of disasters on the victims' and a community's capacity to respond during the post-disaster period'. Stronger links between the universities in the region and Small Island Developing States (SIDS) of the Caribbean are, therefore, underscored.
- Although the people of Dominica had previously experienced natural disasters, the loss of lives from Erika will remain forever etched in the minds of persons who suffered multiple losses. 'Ironically, a country can never prepare enough for a disaster, particularly a natural disaster since it is often difficult to gauge, beforehand, the magnitude of destruction that may result' (Rock and Corbin, 2007: 383–384).

Furthermore, many characteristics of poor countries which increase vulnerabilities among their citizens in times of disaster are present in Dominica. These include the social dimensions of 'sub-standard housing, the precarious locations of the homes of poor people on flood plains and unstable hillsides, and poor response of badly managed bureaucracies to disaster relief efforts' (Ehrenreich, 2001: 6).

Theory and practice innovations

Some practice innovations

Dewane (2011) states that social workers have a repertoire of skills necessary for intervention in natural disasters. These skills include critical analysis, knowledge of community mobilisation strategies, and an understanding of relationship-building and conflict resolution. Lovell and Johnson (1994: 200–203) also note that that 'social work has a philosophy of equality, and a history of surmounting diversity to create common bonds'. Thus, 'the profession is well-positioned to bridge the gap between the natural and social environments'. When intervening following natural disasters, the use of social work approaches such as GSW which consider the natural environment and life spaces of survivors can have positive impact. Joseph (2017) agrees that the use of current social work community models can be adjusted to promote sustainable development. This entails building relations with communities, helping individuals to deepen their understanding of sustainable development, and assisting them to develop and work towards goals and objectives that lead towards improved economic, social and environmental outcomes.

Muldoon (2006) states that as the social work profession continues to work towards the equal and ethical treatment of all people, the fate of the natural environment is becoming increasingly significant. Dewane (2011) believes that the social work profession although governed by the 'person-in-environment' principle has long neglected the 'environment-in-person'. He emphasises that the environment includes not only the social and economic but also the natural world. Dewane (2011) asserts that social work purports to use an ecological and systems approach to assist people with their problems. Yet, that ecology rarely takes into account the unhealthy and depleted natural world. In her view, the exclusion of the environment is no longer acceptable because it is the prime determinant of life. Hence, the deteriorating natural world must become part of social workers' concern as advocated by green social workers (Dominelli, 2012).

Theory and practice innovations: the green social work approach

Older theoretical approaches such as ecological systems theory (Bronfenbrenner, 1995) and the Life Model of social work practice (Gitterman and Germain, 2008) complement the GSW approach (Dominelli, 2012). These theories are also relevant to practice with populations affected by natural disasters.

Ecological systems theory

Bronfenbrenner's (1995) ecological systems theory considers the microsystem which is concerned with the needs of individuals in their life space. It also considers the mesosystem, which serves as the interactive mechanism between components in the microsystem and the exosystem and which exposes the crises that clients experience in the wider social setting. The exosystem extends into the community and includes state or regional entities, while the macrosystem includes the national government; its agencies; national charitable, religious and benevolent organisations; the transportation system; and the culture of the people. The final system, the chronosystem, refers to the patterning of environmental events and transactions over the life span as well as social and historical circumstances that influence the individual, family, peers, co-workers and others. As the theory moves along a continuum from the microsystem to the chronosystem it involves transactions between and among individuals, groups and communities.

The Life Model

Dewane (2011) suggests that social workers revisit the Life Model by Gitterman and Germain (2008) which is a theoretical approach that incorporates the natural world by looking at the 'problems-in-living' and putting them in an all-inclusive environmental context. The Life Model recognises three areas of life space, namely, life transitions or crises, environmental pressures and maladaptive interpersonal relationships. Environmental pressure is seen as lack of resources for social and physical environments. This definition includes dwindling natural resources and unsustainable living conditions. Dewane (2011) believes that this model is a useful lens for assessing the life transitions of individuals that constitute a crisis, and environmental pressures such as lack of resources, like pipe-borne water, clean water for personal consumption, disposal of waste and other factors that impinge on the daily living of persons. Dewane (2011) also suggests that social workers could use the Life Model as their overarching approach to practice with other specific theories such as the ecological systems theories. She emphasises that social work's reliance on 'systems' thinking implies that change in one system can have a ripple effect in the others, and, therefore, the use of the Life Model as a meta-theory can impel social workers consistently to work to improve the natural world of clients/service users. Dewane (2011) further believes that the social work profession although favourable to the 'person-in-environment' principle has long neglected the 'environment-in-person' perspective – the environment referring not only to the social and economic conditions, but also to the natural world. Thus, GSW becomes a natural fit for work with clients/service users, particularly post-disaster, because this approach seeks to 'reform the socio-economic and political forces that have a deleterious impact upon the quality of life of poor and marginalised populations, secure policy changes and social transformations necessary for enhancing the well-being of people and the planet today' (Dominelli, 2012: 25).

Social workers in the Caribbean can use the GSW approach to help people and communities to function better in their life space before a disaster strikes and post-disaster. Social workers together with environmentalists and social planners must consider the impact of the environment on the lives of residents, pre- and post-disaster, and plan accordingly (Dominelli, 2012). As social workers intervene on a daily basis with communities they need to focus on the interplay between residents' lives and the natural and (hu)man-made environments (Dominelli, 2012). Shahar (1993) as cited in Javadian (2007: 343) notes that, 'individual social workers need to strengthen their knowledge of the impact of disasters on the victims' and a community's 'capacity to respond during the post-disaster period'. Residents in farming communities must be helped to understand how their practices impact their lives and livelihoods, as well as encouraged to advocate for conditions and technologies that will support their well-being. Green social work upholds social and environmental justice (Dominelli, 2012) and can assist the profession's continuing work towards the equal and ethical treatment of all people (Muldoon, 2006).

Conclusion

At a time of concern about global warming and climate changes and their impact upon humans and the natural environment, GSW has emerged as an approach that provides a holistic perspective for social work intervention (Dominelli, 2012). To understand more about the impact of climate change and disasters upon individuals and communities and the natural environment, research must be conducted on the coping strategies and experiences of persons affected by disasters such as Erika and most recently hurricanes Harvey, Irma and Maria which also severely affected the Caribbean. This should include research on the survival of vulnerable groups affected by disasters. Within the Caribbean, all departments of social work within the University of the West Indies should pool resources and collaborate with the UWI Centre for Resource Management and Environmental Studies (CERMES) and the Caribbean Disaster Emergency Management Agency (CDEMA). This will foster interdisciplinary and inter-organisational links for research on the weather, climate change, sustainable development and various environmental concerns in a region that is prone to disasters. Findings can inform interventions to mitigate future calamities (Dominelli, 2012).

Interventions using a GSW approach can be used effectively for working with clients before and after disasters such as Erika. Interventions must encompass knowledge, techniques and skills that social workers can use in their efforts not only to enhance the quality of living for clients but also to promote a 'fit' between clients and the natural world in which they live.

References

Bronfenbrenner, U. (1995). The bioecological model from a life course perspective: Reflections of a participant observer. In P. Moen; G. H. Elder, Jr, and K. Luscher (eds.), *Examining lives in context: Perspectives on the ecology of human development*. Washington, DC: American Psychological Association, pp. 599–618.

Caribbean 360. (2015). *Hundreds in shelters in storm-hit Dominica*. http://www.caribbean360.com/news/hundreds-in-shelters-in-dominica-as-a-result-of-damage-to-homes-in-tropical-storm-erika [Accessed 24 October, 2016].

CIA (2016). *The world factbook, Central America and the Caribbean: Dominica*. Available on www.cia.gov/library/publications/the-world-factbook/geos/do.html [Accessed 22 April 2017].

Crask, P. (2016). Become a Dominica traveller: It's worth the journey. *Dominica Traveller*, Issue 1: 4.

Dewane (2011). Environmentalism and social work: The ultimate social justice issue. *Social Work Today*, 11(5): 20.

Dictionary.com. (2017). *The definition of fight-or-flight response*. Available on www.dictionary.com/browse/fight-or-flight-response [Accessed 5 January 2017].

Dominelli, L. (2012). *Green social work: from environmental crises to environmental justice*. Cambridge: Polity Press.

Dominica News Online. (2015). *Petite Savanne, Dubique residents to be permanently relocated*. Available on http://dominicanewsonline.com/news/homepage/news/general/petite-savanne-dubique-residents-to-be-permanently-relocated/ [Accessed 24 October, 2017].

Ehrenreich, J. H. (2001). *Coping with disasters. A guidebook to psychosocial intervention*, Revised edn. Old Westbury, NY: Center for Psychology and Society State University of New York.

Gabriel, J. C. (2015). What shall become of our Koudmen tradition? *Dominica NewsOnline*, 6 September. Available on http://dominicanewsonline.com/news/homepage/features/commentary/what-shall-become-of-our-koudmen-tradition/ [Accessed 25 July 2017].

Gitterman, A., and Germain, C. B. (2008). *The life model of social work practice*. 3rd ed. New York: Columbia University Press, pp. 72.

Government of the Commonwealth of Dominica (2015). *Rapid damage and impact assessment: Tropical Storm Erika – 27 August*. A report by the Government of the Commonwealth of Dominica, 25 September 2015. Available on https://info.undp.org/docs/pdc/Documents/BRB/Commonwealth%20of%20Dominica%20-%20Rapid%20Damage%20and%20Needs%20Assessment%20Final%20Report%20-Oct5.pdf [Accessed 25 July 2017].

James, C. (2015). Erika's massive cost mounting. *The Sun*, 7 September, 19(43): 1.

James, R. and Gilliland, B. (2013). *Crisis intervention strategies*. Belmont, CA: Brooks/Cole.

Javadian, R. (2007). Social work responses to earthquake disasters: A social work intervention in Bam Iran. *International Social Work*, 50(3): 334–346.

Joseph, D. (2017). Social work models for climate adaptation: A case for small islands in the Caribbean. *Regional Environment Change* (Special Issue) 17(4): 1117–1126.

Lovell, M. and Johnson, D. (1994). The environmental crisis and direct social work practice. In M. Hoff and J. McNutt (Eds.), *The global environmental crisis: Implications for social welfare and social work*. Aldershot, England: Ashgate Publishers, pp. 199–218.

Muldoon, A. (2006). Environmental efforts: The next challenge for social work. *Critical Social Work* [online] 7(2). Available on http://www1.uwindsor.ca/criticalsocialwork/environmental-efforts-the-next-challenge-for-social-work [Accessed 5 January 2017].

Pash, R. and Penny, A. (2016). *National Hurricane Centre tropical cyclone report: Tropical Storm Erika*. (AL052015)

Pyles, L. (2007). Community organizing for post-disaster social development: Locating social work. *International Social Work*, 50(3): 321–333.

Raphael, S. (2015). Tropical Storm Erika destroys Jungle Bay Resort. *The Sun*, 7 September, 19(43): 3.

Rock, L. F. and Corbin, C. A. (2007). Social work students' and practitioners 'views on the need for training Caribbean social workers in disaster management. *International Social Work*, 50(3): 291–294.

Shahar, I. B. (1993). Disaster preparation and the functioning of a hospital social work department during the Gulf War. *Journal of Social Work in Health Care*, 18(3/4): 147–159.

The Commonwealth (2017). *Dominica*. Available at http://thecommonwealth.org/our-member-countries/dominica [Accessed 22 April 2017].

The Sun (2015a). Pettite Savanne evacuees: Words cannot describe the pain. Available on http://sundominica.com/articles/petite-savanne-evacuees-words-cannot-describe-the--2651/ [Accessed 24 October 2017].

The Sun (2015b). Can't go home: After Erika the people of Pettite Savanne find a home at the Dominica Grammar School. Available on http://sundominica.com/articles/cant-go-home-2649/ [Accessed 24 October 2017].

The Sun (2015c). Tropical Storm erika has taught Dominica another lesson in disaster risk management. Available on http://sundominica.com/articles/tropical-storm-erika-has-taught-dominica-another-l-2650/ [Accessed 24 October 2017].

Part III
Green agricultural practices

13
Developing green social work in a participatory small watershed management programme in China's tourism city of Lijiang

Tak Chuen Luk

Introduction

Lijiang City in Southwestern China was struck by a serious earthquake in 1996. Its reconstruction strategy involved tourism and in 1997 it gained UNESCO World Heritage Status (UNESCO, 1997). The rapid development of the tourism sector occurred at the expense of the Naxi and Yi – poor indigenous communities living along the Lashi Lake watershed. Water supply to Lijiang's tourism development had been secured by limiting these communities' access to the lake, land and forest. These restrictions triggered a vicious cycle of overfishing, de-forestation and landslides, causing further immiserisation. In 2000, the Green Watershed programme adopted the Participatory Small Watershed Management Programme (PWM) and collaborated with local government to break this vicious cycle. The PWM struggled to deal with stakeholder tensions involving government, communities and individuals pursuing ecological preservation and ecological justice. The PWM in China's Lashi Lake Green Watershed received the UNDP's 2015 Equator Prize in recognition of outstanding local achievement in promoting resilient, sustainable development for people, nature and resilient communities (UNESCO, 2015).

The PWM is a natural resources management programme typically found in development work to address ecological justice through participatory and gradually equitable decision-making over access to or redistribution of natural resources among communities living along a watershed. The PWM model puts together a systematic framework and toolbox useful in analysing and dealing with ecological injustice along the watershed. Addressing all forms of social and environmental injustice is at the heart of green social work (Dominelli, 2012).

As a social worker turned development action researcher, I echoed the ecological approaches of Besthorn (2012), Dominelli (2012) and Gray (2013) that social work should integrate the ecological environment as an important component of social development in social work (Hugman, 2016). As a co-manager of the PWM, I observed ample opportunities for synergy between social work and development work. I present my professional and intellectual journey in blending social work and development work and analyse the predicament of the Lashi Lake watershed communities in serving the development of tourism in Lijiang City in this chapter. I examine the intervention strategies of the Green Watershed in PWM and bottlenecks encountered and reformulate the PWM's implications for practice research as developmental social work turns towards green social work.

Background

Lijiang's historical reputation dates from the 12th century when it was an important tea distribution nexus in the ancient tea horse trail between Inland China and Tibet. Moreover, the beautiful indigenous Naxi cottages and community were embedded in a wisely designed water system that effectively supplied clean water and disposed of dirty water. Moreover, the integrated ecological system of the old town, Lashi Lake and Yulong (Snow Dragon) Mountain constitute the majestic landscape full of indigenous Naxi legends and imaginings that lure millions of tourists to pay tribute.

The application for World Heritage Site Status was part of the Lijiang Municipal Government's grand development plan for exploiting the exotic Naxi indigenous culture, ethnic settlements and architecture. The plan had been progressing slowly but speeded up after the serious 1996 Mw 7 earthquake. The central government supported Lijiang's World Heritage Status Application to initiate large-scale tourist post-earthquake reconstruction. The enormous scale of Lijiang as a tourist destination had serious repercussions for Lashi Lake and the riverside landscape of Lijiang Old Town. Expanding and replicating Lijiang's river town model to other towns and villages required the enlargement and securing of Lijiang's water supply, primarily through Lashi Lake.

The rural communities around the watershed of Lashi Lake have been affected to various degrees. The Naxi tribe used to live by the lake and are considered the indigenous people, having lived there thousands of years. The Yi people living uphill are deemed migratory groups from the large Liangshan region, the ancestral home of China's Yi people a thousand kilometres away.

Shifting social work development discourses

The textbook social work models of North America and Britain had been influential in shaping social work development discourses in Asia and other parts of the world. During my social work studies in the early 1980s, I was intrigued by the professional de-colonialisation argument (Midgley, 1981) which contained a critical reformulation of the disciplinary and institutional foundations of social work. Following the emerging quest for indigenisation and Sinification of social sciences in Taiwan, Hong Kong and China, I became more committed in developing alternatives to mainstream social work models from North America and Britain.

In the 1990s, I co-founded the Zigen Foundation in Hong Kong to work with poverty-stricken Miao ethnic communities in mountainous Guizhou. This involved collaborators trained in educational and development studies. Collaboration across these professions proved difficult. Unlike green social work, their change models relied heavily on technical transfers that paid scant attention to individual growth, group dynamics and community development. Deeper engagement with local service users was considered unnecessary and too expensive, viewing their training in capacity-building as enough.

The 'poverty' of Miao people in Guizhou was typified as 'poverty amid affluence' by mainstream development policymakers who argued that the Miao tribe was poor because they lacked 'market' consciousness or knowledge for exploiting the rich natural resources from the mountain for cash. They ignored the victimisation of Miao people through ecological destruction caused by over-logging following the rapid socialist industrialisation and economic expansion of the 1980s' economic reforms and open-door policies. Indigenous tribes were victimised again and again as central government, aware of the ecological problems, developed these resources and imposed severe protection measures over the ecological legacy that the Miao had inherited from their ancestors. This developmental mobilisation resulted in social and ecological injustices including the unfair redistribution of entitlements and rights of access to natural and cultural resources (Luk, 2005). These issues raised concerns beyond social work interventions. When Oxfam Hong Kong decided to set up a research and development centre in Beijing in 2005, I quit my university teaching job and became the director of the centre. As a development action researcher, I retained my social work identity within the development community in China.

Before I joined Oxfam, I first encountered the predicament of the Lashi Lake and Green Watershed's PWM when I attended the Gender and Development (GAD) Annual Conference in Lijiang in 2002. The Green Watershed, an environmental NGO of Yunnan Province, reported on the damages of Lijiang's tourism development to the communities around Lake Lashi, and therefore, the coping strategies of PWM in alleviating the plight of indigenous Naxi communities to compensate for their loss of living when arable lands were submerged into the lake. In 2003, I met Green Watershed and the PWM again in the Hydropower Summit, organised by UNDP in Beijing. From a PWM perspective, they organised dam-affected victims from various dam building projects of Yunnan to speak for their rights following involuntary displacement through the hydropower projects. Adopting PWM perspectives, the Green Watershed had been running impressive community-based development programmes and rights-based advocacy campaigns with affected people and communities across various issues of watershed development.

It came to my knowledge that Green Watershed's PWM programme had been supported by Oxfam America after I joined Oxfam Hong Kong in 2006. After a restructuring of Oxfam programmes within China, Oxfam Hong Kong took over the strategic collaboration with Green Watershed and I became the manager to collaborate with Green Watershed in the scaling-up of the PWM programme.

The predicament of small watershed management in Lashi Lake, Lijiang

Lijiang's development as a tourism city intensified the urban–rural bias in the redistribution of rights in natural resource management and further immiserised indigenous Naxi people living by the lake, initiating economic hardship and resistance. Lashi Lake was originally a seasonal wetland that became a lake during the rainy season. A sink hole in the lake turned it into a fertile wetland which enabled Naxi communities to grow rice, raise other cash crops and cows during the dry season. This seasonality governed the rhythms of Naxi family life and their livelihoods of fishing and cultivating crops. This changed dramatically when the sink hole was blocked and Lashi Lake dammed to form a reservoir that increased water supplies for the huge Lijiang tourist development. As water levels rose, the wetland was permanently submerged and even lakeside lands were flooded, thus severely undermining agricultural income for most of the Naxi households living by the lake. To compensate for this loss, Naxi peasants intensified their fishing in the lake, adopting many illegal and unsustainable practices. Overfishing brought the fish stock in Lashi Lake to the brink of extinction. Previously, the Lashi Lake wetlands had attracted many migratory birds, and the local government was concerned about overfishing that jeopardised the food chain of the wetland, especially for migratory birds. Consequently, it, adopted a harsh seasonal fishing ban without taking into account its impact on Naxi communities.

Rising water levels also intensified mudslides in communities close to lake. These were the outcomes of the mid- and upstream ecological degradation of the Lashi Watershed following the surge in economic development and reservoir project. This affected Yi communities living upstream in the upper part of the rugged mountain landscape where the temperature is cold, agricultural income is low and poverty is widespread. The older Yi people recalled that the mountain had been covered in thick forest during the 1980s. Rapid urbanisation within socialist China's economic reforms drove the huge demand for wood. Older people reminisced about the ability to amass considerable sums of money by cutting down the forest and selling wood to local merchants downhill around Lashi Lake and Lijiang City.

Along with their Miao counterparts, the strict ecological protection measures gave a heavy blow to the Yi community living upstream. Although extensive logging was halted, illegal logging and logging downhill with support from corrupt officials remained common practices that enabled the Yi community to recover part of their living expenses. The predicament of the Naxi and Yi communities downstream and upstream of the Lashi Watershed involved coping with complex ecological injustices including urban–rural inequality and inter-ethnic group inequalities.

The participatory small watershed management programme: a coping strategy for environmental degradation

Dr Xiao Gang Yu, founder of the Green Watershed when observing the predicament of Lashi Lake, thought about the PWM when studying at the Asia Institute of Management in Thailand. PWM seemed like a governance model capable of coping with the vicious cycle of ecological injustice in natural resource management, economic losses, rivalry over natural resources, ecological and community degradation, ecological inequality and community fragmentation. Receiving support from Oxfam America in 2000, he started the Lashi Lake participatory small watershed management programme in collaboration with the Lashi township government. Township officials were initially positive towards the collaboration. They believed Naxi community grievances over economic losses would be satisfied if the programme introduced alternative income-generation activities.

The PWM organised downstream and upstream communities into mini-watershed groups or committees. Representatives from each group or committee were invited to join the Lashi Lake Watershed Management Committee that consisted mainly of officials from the relevant township government departments. Each committee could provide a platform for officials and representatives of the mini-watershed groups to come together to deliberate issues raised by upstream and downstream communities along the watershed, such as overfishing, disaster prevention, cash crops, poverty alleviation and ecological protection.

A mini-watershed group was organised downstream in Xihu village, on the west side of Lashi Lake. The Green Watershed and Xihu village used participatory rural assessments (PRAs) to devise three projects. One was to build a dam along the river bank to prevent mudslides from damaging arable land and houses. The second aimed to promote agro-forestry along the river bank to prevent soil erosion and grow fruit trees. The third encouraged households to use bio-gas digesters which could reduce logs to firewood and provide organic fertilizers for fruit trees. Older people were organised into a singing and dancing troupe to publicise environmental protection in their community performances.

To address the problem of overfishing and illegal fishing that endangered fishing stock in Lashi Lake, the Green Watershed also developed a fishery association with agreement from the township government. Halting illegal fishing would enable fishing stock to return to normal levels and would be in the interest of fishing communities and their environments. Hence, the fishery association was tasked to collaborate with the government, and monitor and report illegal fishing practices to the fishing administration.

Green Watershed conducted a PRA exercise in Yangyu Chang (potato field), the upstream community inhabited by the Yi tribe to formulate poverty reduction projects. Many poor families could not afford to send their children to boarding school downhill, which left many children illiterate. Green Watershed obtained bursaries from Project Hope to enable some children to complete primary school and secondary school, as well as to graduate from college. Yi women who had been denied the opportunity to attend school requested a literacy project to help them learn to read and write Han Chinese. This learning could help them to buy and sell in the local market or seek employment downhill.

The third problem concerned food shortages for upstream mountainous communities located in rugged landscapes and cold climates where poor growing conditions for ordinary plant species lowered food production. The Green Watershed worked with the Agricultural Bureau to introduce high-yield potato species to the Yi community. A micro-credit programme was developed to deal with the issue of cash shortages. Villagers were able to get recurrent cash allocations to send their children to school, buy drugs for health problems and buy agricultural inputs for income-generation activities. Technical support was provided for villagers to raise chicken, cows and goats.

When the honeymoon ends: the limitations of development work

From a multi-stakeholders' management perspective, development projects follow a cycle of ups and downs in interactions between government and communities. By 2003, the PWM of the Green Watershed in Lashi Lake ran into difficulties. The immediate cause was triggered by the Green Watershed's seemingly active role in organising Naxi villagers to petition against the second phase of the enlargement of Lashi Lake. The township government cast Green Watershed as a trouble-maker. During a research interview conducted in 2010, Dr Yu explained that he might have exercised poor judgment in endorsing the villagers' position when asked to assist in a petition to be presented to the county government. Those who signed the petition wanted to express their discontent over the tiny compensation offered and economic difficulties they would encounter if more land were to be submerged. When the time for the rally arrived, villagers withdrew, leaving Green Watershed to be identified as the petition organiser. Furthermore, Green Watershed joined a nationwide environmental campaign against hydropower in advocating for the rights of involuntarily displaced people across southwestern China and along the Mekong River. The involvement of the Green Watershed in those highly sensitive campaigns put it under stringent surveillance by the security authorities. The local authorities even threatened to expel Green Watershed from Lashi Lake. The antagonistic attitude of local government turned the activists of the mini-watershed group away from the projects and activities of the Green Watershed.

Moreover, collaboration with local authorities had turned fishing communities against the Fishery Association and Green Watershed. The monitoring and reporting of illegal fishing practices had angered fisherman as well as heightened distrust and hostility towards the community workers and activist. Activists of the Fishery Association complained of being mocked by fellow villagers for betraying their communities and sometimes even their fishing gears were damaged or stolen as acts of revenge.

When Oxfam Hong Kong assumed co-management of the PWM in 2006, the programme almost became paralyzed. The antagonistic relationship with the township government persisted, although the government officials had stopped threatening to expel Green Watershed, having suspended the collaboration agreement and ignored Green Watershed's presence. Green Watershed began to realise that their organising approach was elite-biased and when elites were withdrawn from the programme, Green Watershed was unable to solicit support from ordinary villagers.

As in other developmental approaches, Dr Yu, the organisers of Green Watershed and the PWM could provide conceptual and institutional rhetorical devices; however development workers lacked the tactics and skills to implement the participatory watershed management model. They were not equipped to work with individuals, groups and communities, and to cope with being at the centre of a storm.

Developmental social work: the interface of environmental work and social work

As a development practitioner trained in social work and sociology, I adopted the development workers as potential or quasi-social workers. Development work and social work share similar values around social justice, ecological justice, and empowerment of individuals, groups and community (Dominelli, 2012). Social work has an urban tradition bias developed in liberal, democratic capitalist societies, and has limited working models addressing ecological issues in developing societies within semi-capitalist, authoritarian political contexts. For social work, PWM provides a heuristic conceptual and institutional model for NGOs to work with rural communities along the small watershed to deliberate and negotiate collaboration, benefits and risk sharing. A lot of adjustment is necessary for deliberative consultation mechanisms to accommodate authoritarian contexts, and intervention strategies that cope with income generation, ecological preservation, community organising and community building for sustainable development.

Besides providing an institutional design for resource management, PWM provided few tactics and skills for development workers to employ. Common skills are limited to a rigid routinized participatory methodology in visualisation, facilitation and decision-making processes within the community. In many cases, PWM developed mini-watershed groups and watershed management committees, but did not take seriously community mobilisation and organisation. The formation of groups and committees could easily mask nuanced dynamics and interactions among individuals, groups, community and the environment, which requires subtle tactics and skill sets that social workers could provide.

Such contexts could ensure development work and social work supplement each other. The synergy occurred during the organising of the Rural Community Work Learning Network which I collaborated on with an action researcher with a social work background. The learning network pulled together organisers from conventional development NGOs including the Green Watershed, leaders of peasant cooperatives and social work action researchers (Yang and Luk, 2013). Development work provides conceptual and institutional frameworks and strategies for community workers to formulate needs-based to rights-based approaches to work on meso- and macro-development issues ranging from technical training, income generation, community enterprises, cooperatives, gender equality, social inclusion, natural resource management through strategies affecting service delivery, capacity-building, and policy advocacy domestically or transnationally.

Social work can contribute to development work by providing more subtle intervention strategies and skills in working with activists, community groups and entire communities. My observations of the Rural Community Work Learning Network revealed that community workers or quasi-social workers had to learn the arts of switching from imposing organisation missions to addressing the interface with everyday lives; transforming income-generating activities to group organising and community-building strategies; working with authoritarian leadership and its transformation; dealing with jealousy, competition, rivalry, conflict resolution, sharing interests between groups and the community. In sum, social work has to blend meeting pressing needs, community organising and strategic interests in gender equity, community development, ecological protection and the like (Luk, 2012).

Using these general principles of developmental social work, I worked with the Green Watershed to assess the state of community organising, capacity-building of organisers and relationship with the township government. We came up with a two-year PWM strategy plan. To remedy the relationship with local government, Yu devised a strategy to re-shape collaboration with local government. He entered competition to 'renowned' institutions and environmental awards for PWM. The Lashi PWM got a Development Marketplace Project from the World Bank to develop the Water User Association. Furthermore, PWM got the Environmental Award from the SEE Foundation, China's largest environmental protection association formed by famous entrepreneurs, and another environmental award from Ford Motors. The grants and awards from national and multi-lateral organisations strengthened the legitimacy of Green Watershed. Furthermore, Yu encouraged local officials to participate in a good governance workshop offered by the School of Public Management in China's prestigious Tsinghua University, usually regarded as the MIT of China. These efforts stabilised a working relationship with local government.

The PWM in Lashi Lake was reformulated to substantiate the participatory watershed management mechanism and improve joint ownership of the programme with the local township government by undertaking joint strategic planning. This would enable Green Watershed to understand better local government goals and plans. This incorporated the interests of local government, and emphasised better formulation of coping strategies.

The PWM shared the values and empowering strategies of Asset Based Community Development (ABCD). It emphasised the utilisation of the community's ecological, cultural and social assets in developing a virtuous cycle of income generation, livelihood improvement, community cohesion, protection of environmental resources and sustainable development. Capacity-building initiatives supported community organisers in identifying community assets and organising strategies, and coping with the dilemmas of mobilisation and interest-based conflicts.

A critical dilemma for environmental NGOs working with grassroots communities is the practical, opportunistic and conservative attitudes which eschew empowering environmental approaches. Developing empathetic understanding is a critical principle and skill for development workers. Instead of simply convincing community activists to follow the principles of PWM, workers were encouraged to develop empathetic understanding of their situations in the community, government and ecology. Empathetic understanding could help workers to develop various strategies that aligned the interests of individuals, groups and communities with ecological preservation. Building capacity among activists would enable Green Watershed to facilitate informed and strategic decision-making in communities. Local community conservatism is usually linked to a lack of ownership, poorly imagined possibilities, inadequate decision-making, strategies and competency, and finally, control of the external environment. If the community could understand alternative possibilities, local activists could devise indigenous ways of imagining and doing things.

Strategies were also formulated to broaden and deepen community engagement in various mini-watershed groups using community and group work approaches to enable development workers to formulate diverse strategies for mobilising communities and develop potential activists beyond elite models. This strategy could also solicit broader community support and organisation for future work.

The final strategy concerned community group sustainability in PWM. Since the mini-watershed groups were developed largely through external support, many such groups ceased when external support was withdrawn. Green Watershed formulated strategies to increase ownership of these organisations, develop resources through direct contact with foundations, and generate self-sustaining income-based activities. Community-based peasant associations and cooperatives were proposed as potential organising modes for community workers and activists to consider.

Through these strategies, PWM assisted in restructuring individual community organisations. For example, a solid organisation and leadership in Xihu facilitated the broadening of community engagement and encouraged more fellow villagers to participate in agricultural training, fruit cultivation and organising fruit growers cooperatives. The community also explored organic farming methods to reduce agricultural pollution to Lashi Lake and increase income by selling higher-priced organic fruits. Finally, alternative organisational forms were explored to transform the mini-watershed groups into local community initiatives, such as a peasant association with a cooperative at the core, simultaneously promoting organic farming, ecological protection and participation in watershed management issues.

The Fishery Association was to reduce conflicts of interest by aligning with the fishing community. To avoid antagonism and direct confrontation in monitoring illegal fishing practices, Green Watershed worked with the Fishery Association to develop bird watching tours and to seek public funding and social donations to increase fishing stocks in Lashi Lake. This objective was achieved as fishing stocks rose gradually, restoring the public image of the Fishery Association and proving that the previous polemical campaign was necessary and appropriate. Eventually, the Fishery Association also explored how to develop a fishing cooperative that would sell authentic Lashi fish in the burgeoning tourism market.

Eco-tourism in the upstream Yi community incorporated community engagement and ownership. Green Watershed broadened the community activist base and created platforms for villagers to participate in community-based eco-tourism. Green Watershed workers and activists from the Yi community were supported in visiting other community tourism models, so that they could differentiate tourism models, make informed decisions and learn various tactics and skills for benefit sharing and sustainable development in their community.

In 2009, a local Naxi businessman threatened the Yi community with a large-scale eco-tourism project. He won political and financial support from the local government by framing the project as an ecological resettlement programme which was win/win for Yi communities living in poverty and ecological degradation. The project proposed to resettle the Yi community from the high altitude and rugged mountain to warm, fertile land by Lashi Lake. Those promises would be hard to realise as arable land by the lakeside was already occupied and the developer would be unlikely to spend large sums to procure these. Since the local boss had strong political support from the local government, the Yi villagers lacked confidence in withstanding pressure from the local developer.

The viability of community-led eco-tourism required that Green Watershed and community leaders urgently demonstrated to the Yi community that it was an alternative to the 'faked' ecological resettlement. Community-led eco-tourism had to be geared up to boost the morale of the villagers and ensure community cohesion in standing together to withstand the pressure. To deepen community engagement and benefit sharing in community tourism, various groups were mobilised to capitalise on their interest and abilities. Young people were trained as trail guides; they designed ecological trails with the help of older people so that local knowledge of the legends, history, landscape, plants and way of life could be incorporated as cultural learning for tourists. The embroidery skills of Yi women were used to teach others to prepare Yi souvenirs for tourists; they were also eager to learn cooking skills to serve the tourists. Some young people were also trained to promote tours in the inns and hotels of Lijiang City. A capacity-building forum was organised to provide various best practices in dealing with the dilemmas of tourism development, benefit sharing and cultural preservation.

Discussion

The Green Watershed's PWM in Lashi Lake exposed the ecological injustice inherent in development projects and NGO endeavours to empower local communities to cope with the vicious cycle of ecological injustice and immiserisation, predating ecological resources and leading to further immiserisation and ecological degradation. At the meso-level, PWM, like other natural resource management models, has elaborated frameworks and participatory tools for analysing the ecological injustice embedded along river courses and watersheds. It also provided the institutional framework for building the platform for deliberation, bargaining, collaboration, benefits and risk sharing along the watershed to promote an equitable and fair natural resource management system.

The reformulation of Green Watershed's PWM through developmental social work reveals how social work, particularly green social work as espoused by Dominelli (2012), can complement the participatory watershed management model. Development work and green social work share common goals in promoting social justice, as well as adopt similar rights-based and empowerment approaches. Development work also has a number of conceptual, analytical and working approaches for community workers to utilise. Working approaches include those from needs-based to rights-based approaches to work on meso- and macro-development issues including technical training, income generation, community enterprises, cooperatives, gender equality, social inclusion, natural resource management through strategies for service delivery, capacity-building, and policy advocacy domestically and transnationally.

As the bottlenecks of the Lashi Lake case unfolded, the PWM provided a working direction and guidance. However, it could not address the practical concerns and dilemmas of development workers dealing with individuals, groups and communities in subtle social, economic and political realities, and conflictual situations. The pilot project substantiating the PWM through the social work lens was intended to complement sustainable environmentally based development work by facilitating development workers to develop more subtle intervention strategies and skills in working with activists, community groups and communities. When it does so, it becomes green developmental social work.

During the co-management of PWM in Lashi Lake, the green developmental social work approach has generated more in-depth understanding of the dynamics of local state–community–group–individual–environment interaction in watershed management, and highlighted the need for further development in community intervention strategies. This includes skill sets in integrating group work, community work and casework. Reflecting upon my co-management experience of PWM, the reformulated intervention strategies include the following:

1   Development workers have to acquire the arts of transformation to address economic needs, organise groups and community building, and move from problem-based to strength-based approaches. The experiences of the Xihu mini-watershed group demonstrated that communities and local governments facing ecological problems have high expectations that external interventions will address practical problems in poverty reduction and minor infrastructures. Quick wins can become platforms to secure engagement from the community and local government, and provide the momentum for the potential transformation of

community strategies to cope with more subtle and complicated institutional and structural issues where ecological injustice is embedded.

2. In addressing issues of sustainable development, development workers should avoid a direct confrontation with the majority of the community. The tortuous journey of the Fishery Association demonstrated that development workers should not directly impose their organisational mission and strategies, but patiently observe and analyse the subtle community dynamics in managing ecological resources and identify the appropriate issues and moments to intervene. Building social capital is fundamental before launching direct campaigns against predatory environmental practices. Once the relationship with the community is broken, it takes years to repair. More strategic manoeuvres should be devised to understand the dynamics of ecological degradation and to devise wise strategies to create solidarity rather than fragmentation in pursuing sustainable development.

3. Group work and community work approaches are instrumental in substantiating group and community organising strategies in development work. The PWM, like other development projects, relies on a few elites acting as agents that represent the community (Mohan and Stokke, 2000). Many development projects focusing on community as a whole fail to identify and address cleavages within the community. Group work and community work from a green social work perspective can help development workers facilitate better democratic leadership, active participation in community groups, and broader community participation, as well as secure the rights of minorities in inclusive and sustainable development (Dominelli, 2012).

4. Amid the economic hardship brought forth by ecological degradation and immiserisation, social work should play a role to help individuals and families in difficulties by linking social or public resources, strengthening family and social support. Moreover, community activists are always enmeshed in tensions and conflicts involving community divisions and the government. In most cases the blows were fierce when their families withdrew support. Social workers should be able to provide personal counselling to activists to enhance their resilience in coping with these challenges.

5. Green Watershed's PWM has employed a number of working approaches including needs-based and rights-based approaches working on meso- and macro-development issues ranging from technical training, minor infrastructure construction, income generation, community enterprises, cooperatives, gender equality, social inclusion, natural resource management through strategies in service delivery, capacity-building, and policy advocacy domestically or transnationally. These approaches can enrich the toolbox from which social workers select options. Social workers can further substantiate these approaches and tools by integrating group and community organising skills.

6. Developmental social work in small watershed management programmes reflects the many projects that are involved in the distribution or redistribution of interest, entitlements, access to natural resources or compensatory measures. These issues could intensify active and passive rivalry within community groups and the community. Although the programme attempted to emphasise the values and norms of equity and benefit sharing, there is limited practice research that documents the methodology and skills used by development work and social work to demonstrate alternatives.

7. This case indicates that natural resources management issues often occur in areas where indigenous communities reside – an issue also highlighted by green social work which critiques industrial neoliberal capitalist development (Dominelli, 2012). Development work has to develop indigenous knowledge-based approaches that emphasise the importance of indigenous knowledge, methodology and data collection, as well as use the findings

in ecological protection and community organising. Social work has already developed strategy and skills in cultural competency to facilitate the sensitivity of social workers to the ethnicity of service users (Dominelli, 1988; Xiang and Luk, 2013). Indigenous knowledge approaches and cultural competency can complement each other in developing green developmental social work perspectives and skill sets to work with indigenous communities.

8   The predicament of Green Watershed's PWM in confronting authoritarian government, in most developing countries, may be the norm rather than the exception. In developing countries, the state usually takes advantage of ambiguous property rights regarding natural resources in indigenous regions by arbitrarily blocking access to or selling natural resources to other parties (Martinez-Alier, 2014). Participation within authoritarian government structures seems full of tensions and contradictions, which natural resource management programmes have to address. Ingenious strategies have to be developed to find ways to optimise affected peoples' rights and contributions to green social work.

Conclusion

The PWM revealed that social work and development work complement each other on multi-dimensional levels within their working models to increase the resilience of communities in coping with ecological degradation and injustice, and can promote green social work. Our reformulation of PWM through a green developmental social work perspective generated many strategical, tactical and skill issues for development and social workers to develop further.

My own experience ended in 2010 and I was unable to oversee how the developmental social work strategies in the PWM were implemented or modified, or advise additional capacity development for development workers coping with practical challenges on the ground. The programme has subsequently suffered from worker turnover, gradual withdrawal of Oxfam funding, and the inertia of communities and local government.

In 2015 being awarded the Equator Prize by UNESCO (2015) boosted the work of Green Watershed and the communities it encompassed. This enabled the programme to enhance resilience in indigenous communities when addressing climate change, amid the immiserisation and ecological injustices that resulted from the boost to tourism development that emerged when Lijiang City gained World Heritage Site Status in 1997.

For the past two years, the Chinese government has advocated that social work strengthens its role in rural poverty eradication (*China Daily*, 2016). In China, rural poverty is ecology-related and has resulted from poor natural resource management. The analysis and reflection from the developmental social work approach of PWM should provide a direction for practice research among green social workers and researchers dealing with social development issues of environmental justice.

References

Besthorn, F. H. (2012). Deep ecology's contribution to social work: A ten-year retrospective. *International Journal of Social Welfare*, 21(3): 248–259.
China Daily (2016). *China needs 1 million more social workers by 2020*. Electronic document, www.chinadaily.com.cn/china/2016-03/15/content_23884692.htm [Accessed 29 October 2016].
Dominelli, L. (1988). *Anti-Racist Social Work*. First Edition London: BASW-Macmillan. Second, Third and Fourth Editions published by Palgrave-Macmillan 1997, 2008, 2017 respectively.
Dominelli, L. (2012). *Green Social Work*. Cambridge: Polity Press.
Gray, M. (2013). *Environmental Social Work*. London: Routledge.
Hugman, R. (2016). *Social Development in Social Work*. London: Routledge.

Luk, T. (2005). Tourism under mobilizational developmentalism. *Visual Anthropology*, 18: 257–289.

Luk, T. (2012). The Lessons of Rural Community Work: the organizers' perspectives'. In Yang, J. and Luk, T. (eds.) *The Organising Methodology of Local Rural Community Organisations*. Beijing: The Social Press, pp.57–75. (In Chinese)

Martinez-Alier, J. (2014). The environmentalism of the poor. *Geoforum*, 54: 239–241.

Midgley, J. (1981). *Professional imperialism*. London: Heinemann.

Mohan, G. and Stokke, K. (2000). Participatory development and empowerment: The dangers of localism. *Third World Quarterly*, 21: 247–268.

UNESCO (1997). *World heritage list: The Old Town of Lijiang*. Electronic document, http://whc.unesco.org/en/list/811 [Accessed 28 October 2016].

UNESCO (2015). *Equator initiative: A partnership for resilient communities*. Electronic document, Available on www.equatorinitiative.org/index.php?option=com_winners&view=winner_detail&id=225&Itemid=683&lang=fr [Accessed 28 October 2016].

Xiang, R. and Luk, T. (2014). Ethnic social work in China. *Blue Paper of Social Work*, 2013: 120–135. (In Chinese)

Yang, J. and Luk, T. (2013). *The organising methodology of local rural community organisations*. Beijing: The Social Press. (In Chinese)

14
Reflections on a Tribal Kitchen Project
A case study about green social work in Taiwan

Ying-Hao Huang

Introduction

The Atayal tribes along the Ta-An River bank in Heping Township, Taichung County were near the epicentre of the 21 September 1999 (921) earthquake that hit Taiwan, suffering heavy casualties and severe damage. For example, in the tribal community of San-chia-Kan, 43 of 50 houses collapsed and six were partially damaged. Getting the community back to normal would require huge amounts of hard work. The situation had deteriorated prior to the earthquake through modernisation including interference by political power-holders, the election system, and the mainstream Western Christian culture that assailed the tribal area. These caused the tribe to lose their traditional heritage, culture and self-identity. Without internal support in restarting their lives after the earthquake, the tribes were relocated for safety reasons. Therefore, the 921 earthquake highlighted not only problems concerning emergency relief and rebuilding needs of the tribal villages, but also issues of economic disadvantage, organisational chaos, cultural disintegration, and the poor and uneven distribution of welfare resources. The earthquake brought social workers into the villages and opened a new page of community social work for Taiwan's indigenous people.

Compassion International Taiwan, a non-profit humanitarian organisation founded in Taiwan in 1995, helped needy children in Vietnam and indigenous communities in Taiwan. Following the 921 Earthquake, it sent social workers into tribal villages in March 2000 to provide welfare services and conduct a survey of social needs. From July 2000, Compassion International received subsidies from the Taichung County government and set up the 'Da-an River Work Station'. This work station, now called the Taiwan Indigenous Dmavun Development Association (TIDDA), enabled social workers to work with tribal villagers. Compassion International had changed its name to the Zhi-Shan Foundation Taiwan in 2007 (www.zhi-shan.org).

This chapter reflects upon what was learned about community social work and green social work in tribal areas. In it, I introduce the development of TIDDA and examine its work, achievements and influence. I consider social workers' reflections upon their experiences including those of green social work. I collect data through in-depth interviews and documentary analysis to raise new discussions on possible future trends for green social work education and multiculturalism in Taiwan.

Case study of the Taiwan Indigenous Dmavun Development Association (TIDDA)

Da'an River work station started with three full-time social workers; one was the author. None of us were local residents or indigenous people. One crucial goal was to empower local residents/indigenous people by thinking locally and reflecting deeply on their work, with the intention of ensuring that local residents/indigenous people would one day assume control. Currently, TIDDA has eight full-time staff and 15 part-time workers, and only two are not originally related to the local communities/tribes.

The original organisation of TIDDA followed a well-structured hierarchy. As head of the work station, and social worker supervisor, I held power by having the final say on everything. I was highly praised/respected for my professional background and license. However, TIDDA's hierarchy did not facilitate an environment that empowered people and encouraged bottom-up participation. Nor was it conducive to embedding practice in the indigenous culture. Following its organisational expansion, TIDDA has shifted to a more flexible and flat structure. Now, I am its general-secretary.

Brief history

(A) Post-disaster period

The Work Station expanded over 4.5 years by providing social welfare services, continued education and community development. The Work Station faced considerable criticism from the public sector. For example, the 2000 government/external appraisal indicated that its services were not cost-effective and asked that Compassion International be removed from the government's list of subsidised organisations. In responding to this, Compassion International workers and local residents began to think of other alternatives to secure the future of the tribal village.

The anticipated end to governmental grants would restrict Compassion International's capacity to maintain all its services. To achieve this, the tribe and local residents had to play more active roles in their retention. Hence, Compassion International supported the formation of the Taiwan Indigenous Dmavun Development Association (TIDDA) in 2006, with a mainly local membership. Once established, TIDDA assumed control of the tribe's sustainable development initiatives. TIDDA's mission coalesced around running a community interests company which would benefit local residents by supporting community enterprises covering diverse small businesses including traditional gourmet foods, handicrafts, guided tours and a café.

Before becoming responsible for the businesses, TIDDA surveyed the community to understand the unique characteristics of the village and build a consensus around issues of concern. From the survey, TIDDA found 'Gaga' – a traditional Atayal value which had been forgotten under the processes of industrialisation and modernisation. 'Gaga' means sharing everything within tribal villages. TIDDA wondered whether 'Gaga' could transcend the market economy's domination of the village and revive the community if they combined efforts.

TIDDA used the idea of 'Gaga' to work on The Tribal Kitchen Project with underprivileged families, hoping that food sharing would restore old sharing traditions and create a possible sustainable way of life for the future. Reaching a consensual process proved difficult. As indigenous people were unfamiliar with using administrative skills, the Compassion International social worker formed a programme to apply for grants. As a trained professional and a non-indigenous person, the social worker had difficulties to comprehend the idea of 'nonprofit' and 'sharing' as utilised locally and expressed by the tribe through its traditional value of "Gaga". The tribe retained this value. To indigenous people, the long-term impact of capitalism meant that the purpose of running a business was to make profits, so they questioned why they worked so hard for a non-profit business. Nor did they understand how people could earn a living by helping others. Eventually, the social worker convinced them of the value of helping on a non-profit basis.

(B) The beginning stage

The Tribal Kitchen Project included a set of initiatives drawing upon the core value of 'Community-based Mutual Care' to reach out and create a welfare network which began by serving meals for older people living alone, and ensuring job safety among kitchen staff. To retain staff and give them a bearable/liveable life, the project team (worker and village residents) started to think about linking their skills with the work of the kitchen. Providing ingredients for the kitchen looked promising, so they began to work the field. Farming proved to be hard work and required skills that social workers lacked. For example, they did not understand which seeds were most suitable for the land. And, their working styles and attitudes differed from the residents' given their different ethnic cultures. Also, 'balancing the books' made the farming business harder. Small-scale farming often meant a labour-intensive workforce, high costs and limited products. To solve the problem, the team held various meetings and discussions and then decided to recruit external sponsorship. By donating a small amount of money each year (NT$6000 per unit per year), sponsors were entitled to a share of the crops twice a year and were invited to visit the site to witness the project's development. This farming venture initiated new arguments around working status and payment. Doing desk work was regarded of higher status than labouring. People involved in the Kitchen were unhappy about that. Moreover, other staff were not convinced that social workers' labour deserved higher pay. In their culture, helping people is what 'Gaga' taught and needed to be done. So, no one should be paid for doing it. This, along with the negative bureaucratic impact on internal participation necessitated the transformation of the organisation.

Having secured the Kitchen's existence, it moved into caring about young people by providing scholarships and after-class activities for them. These opportunities became available to all households in the communities. These measures sparked another wave of acute internal discussions. The traditional 'Gaga' values guiding them did not easily translate into sharing practice, and not everyone from the village engaged with the Project's work. Fortunately, the core nonprofit values and working patterns laid down by social workers had begun to facilitate the settlement of arguments and ensure that the whole village benefitted.

(C) The transition stage

In 2008, after eight years of working with the village, Compassion International pulled out its full-time workers, but promised to cover part of TIDDA's staff costs. TIDDA had prepared for this since its formation, but it was still a big step to take. Despite having established the joint decision-making working pattern, not having a full-time TIDDA worker as team leader created some insecurity.

TIDDA has three divisions:

1 techniques and resources which includes setting up all institutional and technical systems;
2 welfare services which covers community care, cultural revitalisation, mutual aid and co-operatives; and

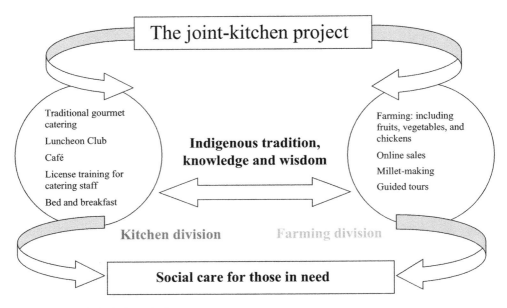

Figure 14.1 Tribal Kitchen Project

3 social enterprise development which covers the integrated tourism industry, which uses the Kitchen as the centre linking village farming businesses, traditional arts and crafts, action-learning and the guided tour.

The residents expect income generated from these activities to provide welfare services based on needs, and that the culturally embedded institutional systems would enable all activities to run smoothly. Moreover, the whole development process aims to help all residents enjoy a liveable life, instead of a bearable one, and keep decision-making powers concerning public affairs in their own hands. Figure 14.1 describes the activities of the Tribal Kitchen Project.

Literature review

A. Indigenous social work in Taiwan

Working with indigenous groups is not new to social work. However, a social worker entering an indigenous village soon after Taiwan's huge 921 natural disaster was. Finding publications of direct relevance was difficult because most were published after the earthquake. Indigenous-related research focused mainly on medical care or health. Those in social work-related fields were limited, often from a social change or social problems perspective, and unhelpful in developing solutions or explanations. In 2000, the Council for Aboriginal Affairs began a study called 'Building a Working System of Social Work for Indigenous People in Rural Areas: A clan-based integration model'. The ensuing report highlighted five principles for social workers working with indigenous people:

1 create tribe/community-based services;
2 replace the concept of welfare relief with self;

3   use teamwork to provide services via integrative resources;
4   empower and enable indigenous people; and
5   form partnerships between government and indigenous groups.

Apart from studies commissioned by the Council for Aboriginal Affairs, few scholars explored professional social work practice in and around indigenous areas, such as Ming-Chen Lee's (2003) book, *Cultural Welfare Rights*.

B. Social work practice in social (community) enterprise setting

Although social work is a profession aimed at dealing with poverty and social problems, social workers in Taiwan have rarely initiated economic projects. An increasing amount of overseas literature covers both social work and social enterprise subjects. Ferguson (2013) discusses the social enterprise approach to interventions and its outcomes for homeless young people with mental ill health in the Individual Placement and Support (IPS) project. In North America, Warner and Mandiberg (2006) published research on social businesses created to provide services and employ disabled people.

Neoliberal governments have shifted responsibility for social services to NGOs or social enterprises. However, Eikenberry and Kluver (2004) argues that democracy and citizenship in civil society will be damaged by this marketisation of social services. More and more NGOs have transformed themselves into social enterprises, raising the question of whether these will yield the marketisation of social work. For community organisers, running a business and providing a service places them in competition with other local businesses. Delgado (1996) found that small businesses, like grocery stores in low-income communities, played significant roles in providing assistance and emotional support to residents. Social workers may have ethical dilemmas if they invest money in community businesses. Amin (2009) claims the expectations of the social economy are unrealistic, and return the problems of socially disadvantaged people to the informal economy.

Thus, existing studies mainly consider practical or operational issues. I wonder how and why a programme that meets people's needs should/could be defined by social work professionals. Some include cultural differences in the service delivery process. Others emphasise the trends towards marketisation. However, very few writers discuss how social workers can engage indigenous people from a multi-cultural and green social work perspective, and what such an experience would mean for them.

C. Green social work

Radical views of ecosystems argue that the root causes of environmental problems are the current economic, political and social structures with industrialism as the dominant factor destroying the physical environment, necessitating transformation of economic developments and consumption patterns. Dominelli's (2012) book, *Green Social Work*, attempts to establish a new paradigm of social work. She argues that the global crisis comes from industrial capitalism and challenges neoliberal discourses, emphasising that the market is not the only choice and distribution mechanism. Given the global economic crisis and environmental catastrophes, social work can assist in bringing about change. Dominelli (2011; 2012) questioned the over-reliance of social progress on urbanisation and consumption as an industrial development model. She encourages social workers to work with local communities to coproduce alternative models of

Lessons learned from TIDDA

(A) Whose needs and who says so?

The core post-disaster service of TIDDA was providing social care for elders, a provision unappreciated by the public sector and a social work professional for not being cost effective. They thought that TIDDA served far too few service users and that their cost was too high. TIDDA argued that three perspectives required consideration before the final verdict could be reached. First, there were different attitudes towards who needed help. For the public sector, the household means-test and other welfare measurement mechanisms were methods to determine who would qualify for services. Scientific techniques were deemed the best mechanisms for deciding entitlement to services. For indigenous Atayal people, a person's reputation (being nice to people, working hard and so on) within the community, not poverty or disadvantage, defined someone as deserving help. This rendered meaningless the assessment indicators utilised by external experts and caused extensive disputes within the tribe, making service delivery almost impossible. Second, external service intervention eliminated existing tribal care services based in their life domains and cooperative caring systems. Bringing external professional caring services to the tribe not only broke ties to their cooperative caring system, but also deprived indigenous people of family- and relative-based help in meeting their needs. This shift to bureaucratic services also made them more expensive and less cost-effective. Third, tribal disadvantage would not be overturned if dependent on external resources. The public sector's focus on financial assistance to purchase welfare services undermined caring. To obtain services, people had to wait for a caseworker to approve their request and become completely reliant on external help. This placed indigenous people in passive positions and offered them little opportunity to assume decision-making powers and work on their own futures.

Three academic-trained non-indigenous social workers lacking local connections began working with the Ayatal community. They noticed that case-by-case service delivery was not working for local residents. They reflected upon it by immersing themselves fully into community life and looking for the best way of working with them. To fit into the community, these social workers proposed two projects: (1) collaborative housing construction whereby they regarded rebuilding houses for earthquake victims as a welfare measure, and engaged in housing planning and organising task forces and teams; and (2) forming a vegetable farm in which workers lived close to the local lifestyle and orchestrated community organisation and farming businesses. These two projects did not fully achieve their objectives, but TIDDA opened up an alternative way to do community work. These two projects failed due to strong criticism from the public sector and social work profession. Housing issues including housing planning and housing policy, regarded as important elements of social welfare and social policy globally, received little attention in Taiwanese social work. To make matters worse, house building belonged to another profession, engineering. Consequently, social workers who worked on building houses and vegetable farming in Taiwan were regarded as unprofessional. Public sector workers and social work experts called on them to work harder on personal social services and increase the number of cases they carried.

Despite this opposition these social workers refused to stop doing this work. Knowing that green social work requires trans-disciplinarity over a narrow self-limiting professionalism, they stood by their reflections. Learning from their experiences, they fought back by: (1) putting aside the government's domination of the project evaluation process. Although the performance of TIDDA was at the bottom of the appraisal list for two years, the team remained defiant. Workers continued to believe in themselves and remained self-reliant. They never stopped reflecting upon their work and continued doing it; (2) breaking down myths about prioritising personal services. The social workers trusted what they had seen, done and learned from the front line, rather than listen to advice the public sector and social work professionals gave about shifting their priorities back to personal services; and (3) fought for self-identity as social workers, despite doubts at points when 'experts' refused to accept their work as social work. Firm in believing that social workers get close to client/service user's needs, they worked to bridge the gap between resources and needs. Seeing emergent local needs around housing rebuilding and economic revival after the earthquake, they knew what they did was right and was something that social workers have a duty to fulfil.

(B) What is community work? – a social work perspective

Community work is a major method in social work training, but the general public does not understand this. After the earthquake, many trained professionals were involved in post-disaster work, including architects and local historians. What was social work's unique contribution to community development? People from different disciplines constantly asked this question.

From March 2002, TIDDA became an experimental model implementing two contracting-out projects for the Council on Cultural Affairs, and the only ones led by a social work professional. The two projects began to organise local groups and empower local residents. Through various meetings and activities, local residents had in-depth reflection on their traditions, culture, gender relations and power distribution. Through these, they produced their own plan of post-disaster construction and planning alongside a vision of the tribe's future. This unique characteristic of working with people ensured the importance of the social work profession in community development and raised the profile of important local needs.

Resources coming with the contracting-out projects helped TIDDA remain close to local needs, but also impacted negatively on community development processes. The government lauded the spirit of community autonomy without supporting its realisation. Having contracts with the government meant TIDDA had to follow public sector rules. For example, TIDDA had to meet the government's verification system requirements and participate in achievement exhibitions. For TIDDA, these activities were very time-consuming and took energy away from other work. What made matters worse, the government's requirements contained restrictions that raised tensions between local groups. From this experience, the workers realised that community work was not simply about channelling resources into communities to work with local residents on their issues, but also to engage local residents in maintaining self-autonomy by ensuring that introducing external resources into community did not break local integrity. Hence, social workers must know when and how to be with residents when saying 'no' to external support. This message had been ignored by academics. In Taiwan, academic training asked social workers to be neutral and build bridges to bring as many resources as possible into communities. It hardly talked about taking sides or turning down external help or make community social workers aware of this possibility.

Green social work's principles of recognising the economic and political power that create poor and marginalised populations enabled TIDA social workers to accept community initiatives that improved employment. Its role of translation, passing relevant information onto the community and service users accompanied by cultural understanding, awareness of and respect for diversity enabled TIDDA to deal with environmental issues on the Ayatal people's terms.

(C) What participation meant: to whom and to/for what?

The social workers used green social work perspectives to encourage the public to participate in local organisations and engage in community development. On the basis of their experience, however, these practitioners were most troubled about issues of internal participation and power-sharing. Two major internal problems of participation caught their attention. One was the top-down bureaucratic hierarchy; the other was the differentiation of social-economic status between 'blue collar' farming staff and 'white collar' office workers.

The social workers had tried to get everyone involved and affirmed one's right to self-expression. All participants had to take turns in chairing regular administration meetings and were encouraged to speak out for themselves. However, the original organisation was well-structured hierarchically. Social workers were not only regarded as trained professionals with higher paid jobs, but also as holding power over human resources management. Emphasising participation in administration and managerial issues was unusual. Solving this problem required changing the existing structures and payment system. This was hard to do immediately because TIDDA was dependent on Compassion International to subsidise the salaries of social workers and had its own system and requirements regarding the subsidisation of organisations. What TIDDA had to do was to lose a small sum from its human resources management system and move towards a more flexible, flat hierarchy.

In the beginning, TIDDA staff was like all other residents who farm for a living. Later, they dealt with desk work and enjoyed more job security. Once the Tribal Kitchen Project and farming division were established, tension over the socio-economic status of farming and administrative staff flared and affected the operation of TIDDA. To reduce this tension, the social workers established a new mechanism to bridge the gap between needs and resources and helped the two sides to communicate with each other. By job rotation and job enlargement, the workers gradually pulled people together and facilitated their mobility.

(D) Working with indigenous people: starting from where? Doing what? Deepening the roots of sustainable development

In tribal society, having land is a basic and essential element to secure people's living. Within the land, indigenous people could meet their needs by sharing and exchanging goods and services. The market economy caused the collapse of traditional sharing and exchange systems. Goods and military materials had to be traded in cash, the modern currency. People began to lose their capacities for self-support and self-sufficiency. TIDDA's original purpose was to help tribal villages to rebuild their lives through the post-disaster period. However, rebuilding a life was not just about survival along the way. The real goal of rebuilding tribal society should take every aspect of life into account, including culture and tradition, as advocated by green social workers. Therefore, social workers made the best use of a community survey and embedded traditional 'Gaga' values into its Tribal Kitchen Project.

The core concepts of the Tribal Kitchen Project are: (1) co-caring systems after the earthquake. Caring addressed the needs of considerable numbers of 'left-behind children' and older people living alone. Young people's employment in construction resulted in many residents losing family support and only a few had an extra-hand to help others. Social workers had anticipated that collective actions of caring and food sharing could recreate a safety net for the tribe's disadvantaged groups; (2) tribal currency is different from the cash-driven market economy. The social workers initiated discussions among indigenous people and developed a list of exchange mechanisms including the tribal currency. For example, residents could exchange their labour for a meal. By re-installing this unique traditional currency system, the tribe hoped to regain its trading power and stabilise its economic security; and (3) community business interests could have a sustainable future if the tribe had not depended on external help or resources. The tribe had to balance the pressures of competing within the modern economy with its sharing traditions. TIDDA made the Kitchen the centre of community life linked to village farming businesses, traditional arts and crafts making, acting, learning and the guided tour. The integrated tourism industry was expected to maintain the tribe's future self-sufficiency. TIDDA also promoted the idea of cooperative farming within mainstream society and obtained extra support from the general public to ensure that the co-working system became sustainable.

For a long time, many people treated helping indigenous people to retain their traditions as taking them back to their past. This is a fallacious myth. Basing indigenous people's lives today on their traditions could safeguard their future. Indigenous people have the right to create their new way of life guided by past traditions. Farming is a high-cost, labour-intensive industry. To reduce the threat of the mass-produced market-relations and natural disasters, small farmers need greater collective actions to protect themselves. Avoiding external sponsorship reduces the uncertainty caused by the tribe's environment or situation, and facilitates reviving tradition in a modern form. The threats of competing with a market economy are unavoidable. The tribe needs to keep people in the community. Facilitating the most suitable economic system to continue is critical to enabling young indigenous people to remain in the village. Currently, nearly 200 external sponsors help tribal farming businesses by donating a small financial sum yearly (NT$6000 units/year) in exchange for a share of the crops twice a year. They are also invited to visit the site to witness its entire development.

Looking back at the development of TIDDA, the primary goal was to solve the basic crisis created by the earthquake and make life bearable for the tribe. Then, it developed many innovative measures which became embedded in tribal traditions and culture to create a liveable future. Ferreira (2010) argues that eco-spiritual social work emphasises the importance of spirituality in social work. The rational and personal orientation of traditional social work models are not suitable for non-Western cultures, including indigenous social work in Taiwan. Social workers need to take care of the environment and spirituality, cultivate environmental awareness and spiritual sensitivity. Green social work emphasises the idea of spirituality, emphasising the relationship between people and living entities and the physical environment, nature's gifts through biological and material environments require care for current and future generations (Dominelli, 2012). Key to ensuring elements that this could take place was having social workers with a strong sense of multi-cultural awareness and the ability to reflect upon what they had learned in the field, respect tribal culture and learn to think like indigenous people did. Learning from indigenous people, these practitioners were able to contribute their professional skills to working with residents to initiate progress towards a sustainable future.

When indigenous people enter the global capitalist economic system, the economic development of tribal communities becomes fragile as external forces assume control. The issue is not only to let tribal community strive economically, but to sustain the autonomy of tribal communities and eliminate the fundamental problem of economic subordination. If social work is about social reform, then economic autonomy, free from the constraints of corporations and government, is of crucial importance. The possibilities of social reform or progressive social work in Taiwan have been significantly restrained due to the dual repression of professionalism and neoliberalism. In light of that, it becomes critical how indigenous people, who are often economically marginalised due to neoliberalism and globalisation, can form a progressive resistance structure within tribal communities. Indigenous economic solidarity may be one promising route that green social workers can explore.

The Da-an River Work Station began as a social work station to develop tribal industry. Upon realising the exploitive nature of capitalist markets, it adjusted its goals to work towards economic solidarity wherein the emphasis becomes to live better on tribal lands. This chapter begins with the experience at the cooperative Kitchen at the Da-an River tribal community of the Atayal people in Taiwan to examine the reality of social work in indigenous communities. It focuses on the processes and challenges that social workers in tribal communities face in developing tribal industries and economic solidarity from a green social work perspective in Taiwan.

Conclusion

The case of the Tribal Kitchen shows that green social workers continue to inherit the principles of social work in not assuming the role of leaders and direct actors, but acting as educators, organisers, advocates, co-ordinators and resource mobilisers. Green social work emphasises work practices that include individual, group, community work alongside the social aspects of interventions and working at all levels (micro, meso and macro) complement each other. There are several conclusions regarding the practices of green social work in one indigenous region of Taiwan. First, social workers should understand Atayal culture and tribal points of view. The core cultural concept in the Atayal area is the spirit of the ancestors – the traditional norm of 'Gaga' which social workers should learn and apply in the traditional Atyal system of mutual assistance and sharing. Second, this case study analyses the experiences of social workers in the Atayal tribe area and recognises that social work professionals should adjust their responses to the cultural differences of indigenous people through cross-cultural experiences. Third, to achieve a dynamic model of mutual-subjectivity with indigenous tribes, alongside the provision of traditional welfare services, indigenous social work should concentrate more on the land ethic and move towards green social work and economic solidarity in livelihoods.

The Han ethnic group regarded itself as more superior, a viewpoint that allowed them to believe they could 'improve' the life of the tribe, a view shared by Taiwan's trained experts. They brought great ideas and enthusiasm to the tribe, but forget to listen to what people really wanted. The transformation of Taiwan's political and economic environment emerged alongside multicultural awareness and mutual respect among different ethnic groups. The new generation of social workers is trained with greater cultural awareness and is more convinced about the power of empowerment and participation. After the 921 earthquake, when workers went to help the tribe, they brought this faith with them, and turned a new page for social work practice.

The Da-an River Work Station began as a social work station that developed tribal industries. Upon realising the exploitive nature of capitalist markets, it adjusted its goal to work towards economic solidarity with an emphasis on living better on tribal lands. Community work did not separate itself from TIDDA's staff and farmers, by distancing itself through professional planning and professionalism. It co-existed within the unique culture and heritage of the tribal community. For indigenous people, this meant returning to their roots – the land on which they stood and take these lands into account when planning service measures. Community work is not only about working with people, but also with organisations. People involved in community work need the courage to say 'no' to external help and resources if necessary, and listen to each other to permit many participative possibilities. By doing so, community work can continue to meet community needs and find and demonstrate the best ways of addressing these. TIDDA's experience suggests that social work professionals and trained social workers should go back to their original spirit. Listen carefully to what people say, make their autonomy central to their relationship with them and respect their power over decision-making. Become aware of all potential differences before intervening in a situation. Social workers cannot live people's lives for them, but they can live with them. To live with the community and be accepted by its members, social workers have to follow the local culture. In considering indigenous social work, understanding the impact of globalised capital is essential. Practices in tribal industry can assist reflections upon the concepts and action strategies encompassed by traditional social work. Incorporating greenism into the discussion of social issues (Dominelli, 2012), and creating a holistic rethinking of social work to encompass environmental ecosystems, social humanities and cultural differences, are deep reflections about green social work in indigenous issues.

References

Amin, A. (2009). Extraordinarily ordinary: Working in the social economy. *Social Enterprise Journal*, 5(1): 30–49.

Delgado, M. (1996). Puerto Rican food establishments as social service organizations: Results of an asset assessment. *Journal of Community Practice*, 3(2): 57-78.

Dominelli, L. (2011). Climate change: Social workers' roles and contributions to policy debates and interventions. *International Journal of Social Welfare*, 20(4): 430–438.

Dominelli, L. (2012). *Green social work: From environmental crises to environmental justice*. Cambridge: Polity Press.

Eikenberry, A. M. and Kluver, J. D. (2004). The marketization of the non-profit sector: Civil society at risk? *Public Administration Review*, 64(2): 132–140.

Ferguson, K. M. (2013). Using the Social Enterprise Intervention(SEI) and Individual Placement and Support (IPS) models to improve employment and clinical outcomes of homeless youth with mental illness. *Social Work in Mental Health*, 11(5): 473–495.

Ferreira, S. B. (2010). Eco-spiritual social work as a precondition for social development. *Ethics and Social Welfare*, 4(1): 3–23.

Lee, M. C. (2003). *Cultural welfare rights*. Taipei, Taiwan: Songhuai Publishing Co. (In Chinese)

Warner, R. and Mandiberg, J. (2006). An update on affirmative businesses or social firms for people with mental illness. *PS*, 57(10): 1488–1492.

15
Community gardening
The nexus for community, social work and university collaboration

Robin Sakina Mama

Introduction

Collaborations between universities and the neighborhoods or communities they are located within are no longer novel enterprises. Over the years, institutions of higher education in the US, Canada and England, especially those located in or near cities, have been very active with their communities. This trend has also included universities outside of cities for a variety of reasons. Increasingly, colleges and universities have not been able to ignore the communities they inhabit, especially those communities that have felt economic downturns or have experienced blight, gentrification or other social issues. Projects that help to strengthen the relationship between institutions of higher education and their neighbors are beneficial to both parties (Fisher et al., 2004). The end result is that universities and communities have been involved together in research projects, the creation of field internships and service-learning opportunities, as well as curriculum development and other projects (Fisher et al., 2004, Siemens, 2012; Ostrander and Chapin-Hogue, 2011).

This chapter will examine community collaboration through a community garden developed at Monmouth University, a small, private liberal-arts university located in a suburban area of New Jersey in the US. Its growth, successes and the lessons learned along the way will also be discussed. Community gardens are developed for a variety of reasons. However, their link to food insecurity and green social work cannot be overlooked.

The context

Food insecurity is a social problem that exists in many communities around the world (Bhawra et al., 2015; Roncarolo et al., 2016). Definitions for food insecurity vary. But briefly stated, it is 'limited or uncertain availability of nutritionally adequate and safe foods or limited or uncertain ability to acquire acceptable foods in socially acceptable ways (e.g. without resorting to emergency food supplies, scavenging, stealing or other coping strategies)' (Taylor and Loopstra, 2016, p 3).

In the United States (US), this translates into 48.1 million Americans, including 32.8 million adults and 15.3 million children who were food insecure in 2014 (www.feedingamerica.org). In

New Jersey, this means that 11.8 percent of the state's population is food insecure, with Monmouth County specifically having a 9.3 percent food insecurity rate (www.feedingamerica.org). Globally, this translates into 925 million people who will not have sufficient food to eat (www.globalgiving.org/sdg/no-hunger). The majority of the people who are food insecure globally are in the developing regions of the world (FAO, IFAD and WFP, 2015).

One would think that income is one of the triggers for food insecurity, and research has shown that, for children, food insecurity drops as a family's income increases (Gundersen and Ziliak, 2014). Income, however is only part of the puzzle with food insecurity. Several other themes emerge when examining the research that has been done on food insecurity. According to Gundersen and Ziliak (2014), these include:

- The mental and physical health of the adult caregiver – families where an adult caregiver (especially single-parented families) fare worse when depression, substance abuse and a low education level are factored in.
- Marital status of the head of household – living with a single parent, or a single parent in an extended household can lead to greater risk of food insecurity than in married couple families.
- Child care arrangements – spending time in child care that is provided by people other than one's parents have an implication for food insecurity for children.
- Certain populations are more vulnerable to food insecurity – these would include immigrant families and households where one parent is incarcerated.

Fighting hunger and its causes was one of the Millennium Development Goals of the United Nations (UN) and it is also now goal number 2 of the Sustainable Development Goals – to end hunger, achieve food security and improved nutrition and promote sustainable agriculture (www.un.org/sustainabledevelopment/sustainable-development-goals).

In high-income countries, when public assistance cannot meet the pressing needs of clients/service users, emergency food services are often developed. Food banks, for example, have played a role in helping to diminish food insecurity especially in a short-term, crisis situation. However, as a long-term solution to food insecurity, food banks are not able to improve overall food security outcomes. In a systematic review of the research on the role of food banks in addressing hunger and food insecurity, Bazerghi and colleagues (2016) found that food banks often have several limitations when trying to address food security outcomes. These limitations are sometimes beyond the control of the food bank, depending on how it has been established and how it is able to link with other donations and resources. Generally, in this review the authors found that most food bank clients have a deficiency in their diets in the consumption of fresh vegetables and fruits, milk, meat and other meat alternatives. The food provided to food banks tends to be limited in range and also limited in cultural content for the clients/service users they serve. This research also revealed that the number of people using food banks continues to increase, but that the donations to food banks are not keeping pace with this demand. Food bank staff also described an inadequacy in resources that the food banks need beyond donated food, such has additional space for storage, additional refrigeration and not enough funds to purchase supplies that clients/service users also need, such as toiletries (Bazerghi et al., 2016).

Another small response to food insecurity in local areas is the development of community gardens. Community gardens historically have been utilised in times of economic distress. Cities in America began utilising community gardens in the 1890s to assist families who were experiencing unemployment. These subsistence gardens were also popular during the First World

War, to augment the food supply domestically, and were turned into 'Victory Gardens' during the Second World War (Lawson, 2005: 2). Draper and Freedman (2010) suggest that, since 2009, community gardens can be termed 'recession gardens', which are used to 'help decrease individual and family food bills and provide for more self-sufficiency' (460). Community gardens tend to be found more commonly in cities and suburban areas outside of cities rather than in rural areas were farming is a mainstay livelihood.

Currently, community gardens have included a variety of functions other than supplementing family groceries:

> Community gardens often start by the want to improve food access but may become a focal point for community organizing around the promotion of neighborhood revitalization, community pride, and increasing a sense of community ownership.
>
> *(Lanier et al., 2015: 493)*

Some community gardens today often have multiple agendas, which can include education, social needs, as well as economic concerns (Lawson, 2005; Lanier et al., 2015). Roncarolo et al. (2016) see community gardens as an alternative intervention which often focus on empowerment, the development of skills and the support for better nutrition to assist in the reduction of food insecurity. These gardens are developed in a number of ways, under various auspices, with multiple sources of funding and with varied ways of functioning. Whatever the focus, community gardens as an intervention usually do not 'pursue the objective of impacting the economic factors at the root of food insecurity, nor the broader systemic factors that shape food production and distribution' (Roncarolo et al., 2016: 3).

The community garden at Monmouth University

During the spring semester of 2009, a group of academics, staff and administrators, who were members of the then-Center for Human and Community Wellness, were meeting to discuss possible projects for the Center to engage in. At some point in the conversation, the group discussed community gardening. One of the local neighborhoods, Long Branch, had previously established a community garden, which was sponsored by the municipality. However, it had recently closed and it seemed at the time that there was a need to establish another community garden based on what members of the group were hearing about the increase in soup kitchens and food pantries in the area.

While the university is partially surrounded by a fairly wealthy community one mile from the Atlantic Ocean, the other surrounding towns that encompass the campus community are not as well off. Census data from 2010 illustrates the disparities in income and poverty rates, based on the US poverty guidelines (US Poverty Guidelines, 2015) as follows:

Table 15.1 US Poverty Data

Town	Population (2010)	% < 18	% > 65	White	Black	Hispanic	% below poverty	Median household income
Asbury Park	16,116	23.8	10.3	36.5	51.3	25.5	29.4	$33,527
Eatontown	12,709	20.7	14.0	71.3	12.4	12.4	9.1	$60,188

Town	Population (2010)	% < 18	% > 65	White	Black	Hispanic	% below poverty	Median household income
Long Branch	30,719	21.7	11.3	65.3	14.2	28.1	14.5	$52,792
West Long Branch	8,097	19.6	13.6	94.5	2.2	5.0	8.2	$96,369
Tinton Falls	17,892	19.0	25.6	82.5	9.3	6.2	4.1	$78,894

It was suggested by Robin Sakina Mama, the Dean of the School of Social Work, that the group look to establish a community garden somewhere on the Monmouth University campus. She also felt that social work might be able to provide an MSW intern to get this venture started (with office space and supervision). As the School has a concentration in International and Community Development, this would be an excellent community development opportunity for the right student. The School of Social Work has a focus on human rights and social justice, and this project was congruent with the School's overall values.

The Center's Steering Committee agreed with this idea in the early spring of 2009, and work began with the Office of Field and Professional Education in social work to identify an incoming MSW student who might take this venture on as an internship experience. Fortunately, a student was identified. He was a young man who had completed his undergraduate degree in physics, but who had been deeply involved in environmental organising during his college years. He eagerly accepted the challenge, since it would be his responsibility to build this garden 'from the ground up'. Work to build this garden began in the fall (autumn) of 2009.

Community gardens vary – by definition, scope and purpose. One definition, by Ferris, Norman and Sempik (2001: 560) distinguishes between a private garden and community garden in 'terms of ownership, access, and degree of democratic control'. The American Community Gardening Association considers community gardens as 'any piece of land gardened by a group of people' (cited in Aftandilian and Dart, 2013: 56). In the UK, community gardening denotes a garden owned publicly that includes public access and follows democratic rules, whereas 'allotment' gardens are those which are tended by members who each have a plot of land. Some of the larger gardens allow for community participation in an open space but also provide facilities for education and training (Firth, et al., 2011). Some community gardens focus only on individual garden plot cultivation while others have a more collective purpose to the community they are located in. Some gardens are small, located on abandoned plots of land (if in an urban center), while others can be quite large, taking on multiple purposes and serving larger groups of people (Firth, et al., 2011).

The locus of control for community gardens varies as well. Generally speaking, there are usually three ways in which community gardens are sponsored: by municipalities, non-profit organisations or universities. Depending on how the garden is established (and by whom), its general purpose will also vary. In an extensive review of the literature on community gardening, Draper and Freedman (2010) discovered that the overall purposes of community gardens in the US tended to cluster into several areas:

- Health benefits – promoting both individual and community health;
- Food security – promoting food security in a community;

- Economic development – a more entrepreneurial approach to community gardening, where the community sells the produce it harvests;
- Youth education, development and employment – using gardens to serve as alternative forms of enjoyment and training for young people;
- Preservation of open space – preserving valued space in a community in addition to safe places for community members to gather;
- Crime prevention – this was sometimes seen as an unintended consequence of the establishment of a community garden;
- Neighborhood beautification – especially true in urban areas where gardens are established on vacant or abandoned property;
- Cultural preservation and expression – ethnic community gardens that have been established are seen as a mechanism to preserve as well as promote a culture;
- Relationship building – depending on the roles established in community gardens for members, the garden and the work surrounding its maintenance can be the impetus for the establishment of individual and group relationships in a community; and
- Community organising and empowerment – since community gardens are a gathering place, they can also be utilised as a place for people to join together to work on other community initiatives (Draper and Freedman, 2010: 480–485).

The first element in establishing the Monmouth University Community Garden was to find a piece of land that would accommodate a good-sized garden that was not already in use at the University. The garden intern worked with the vice-president for Facilities Management to identify three potential spaces for the garden, and the site that was chosen was the best of the three. It was located on a corner lot, with plenty of sun and access to street parking for people who were going to come to the garden. This lot was in an area on the north side of the campus across the street from resident dormitories, and next to a tennis court that included a restroom and electrical outlets if needed. The space measures approximately 90 feet by 90 feet square. It is also interesting to note that this parcel of land was once contested by the University's neighbors when a plan had been submitted to the town to build a dormitory on this property about 10 years ago. The neighbors won their lawsuit against the University, and the land remained vacant until the community garden was proposed for this site.

A number of elements were taken into consideration regarding the scope, purpose and functioning of the garden before the first shovel went into the ground. The Center for Human and Community Wellness Committee believed that the garden should allow for both individual plots that could be 'rented' for the growing season (April–October) along with community plots where the harvest would be donated to local agencies supporting food-insecure families. In a study that reviewed 15 community gardens that had been established in Illinois through the McLean County Wellness Coalition, the authors found that 53 percent of these gardens donated their produce to local service agencies, while 47 percent used the food in their own organisation (Lanier et al., 2015).

There was also the belief that the garden should help to promote good relationships between the university and its neighbors as well as foster new relationships between the gardeners themselves. It was also intended that the garden could be a place for student learning and volunteering. With all these ideas in mind, the Monmouth University Community Garden began to take shape in the fall semester of 2009.

Once the site was confirmed, the MSW intern began to work with several Monmouth County Master Gardeners to work out the logistics of the garden: planning the size and configuration of the plots (both individual and community), deciding whether to plant 'in ground' or use raised beds, what plants to begin with and other matters. The garden at Texas Christian University has utilised support from their county health department (Aftandilian and Dart, 2013), and demonstrated that others can be brought in to help in various ways. The Monmouth garden has received a great deal of both in-kind and financial support from the County Master Gardeners who have donated time, resources and knowledge to the garden. An additional support to the garden has come from the Home Depot Corporation. For the first two years of its existence, Home Depot provided a $2,000 HD gift card to the garden to purchase supplies, from dirt and manure to tools. When Home Depot supports a project like the garden, the local employees also supply 'sweat equity', and since 2011 has provided a crew on opening day to help till the soil, replenish dirt and manure to the beds, and to plant donated plants in the community side of the garden.

Deciding how to run the community garden was the next issue that required thought. An application was developed for community members who wanted a plot in the garden, and meetings and newspaper notices bought the first group of gardeners into the garden. However, after the first growing season in summer of 2010, there was a realisation that more structure was needed in terms of the weekly management and maintenance of the garden and so a Steering Committee was established. It comprised mostly of gardeners (four to five) who were renting plots along with the dean of the School of Social Work (since social work was housing and partially funding the garden) along with a professor of biology whose specialty was in plants. Stakeholders are important to all community gardens and depending on the purpose of the community garden, who these are will vary. However, the literature is quite clear that multiple stakeholders need to be involved to secure a garden's success (Scoggins, 2010; Henderson and Hartsfield, 2009; Firth et. al, 2011; Twiss et.al 2003). Siemens (2012) has also stated that the meaning of the partnership must also be clear and communicated effectively to all those involved in a university–community project.

The Steering Committee began to meet monthly in 2010 and worked on rules for the garden, how to establish harvesting days, where to donate and deliver harvest to community agencies, along with a host of other issues. The Steering Committee continues to exist and has had new members join the Committee over the years since its establishment. It is still predominantly comprised of gardeners who have been gardening in the community garden for some time and who have a great interest in seeing the garden flourish.

Since the community garden's inception in 2009, the Monmouth University Community Garden has enjoyed several accomplishments:

- Over 60 community residents or Monmouth University employees have been gardening annually. Gardeners tend to be local and reside in the surrounding communities next to the University. A number of the gardeners find the community garden an excellent place to grow their own vegetables or flowers, largely due to the resources that the garden is able to provide. It is fenced in, has a water supply, has its own tools for gardeners to share, along with the expertise that is shared with the gardeners by the Master Gardeners.
- Over 300 students have been involved in working in the garden, mainly through the 'Big Event', a volunteerism day at the University and in hosting other Monmouth University classes when the students go to the garden to learn.
- A Freshman Seminar class was called 'Playing in the Dirt' was developed. It involves faculty from social work and science and has the students learning about food insecurity, the biology of plants, and nutrition along with physically working in the School of Science greenhouse and the community garden. This class has run during the spring semester for four years and counting.

- Four local social service agencies and a girl scout troop have plots in the garden.
- The garden has begun to annually provide summer 'Lectures in the Garden', which are open to the general public and have focused on a variety of topics, including 'How to put your garden to bed', 'Good bugs, bad bugs', 'Composting' and 'The Beatles and Strawberry Fields Forever'.
- A Community Garden Conference was held for four days in August 2015, which brought in participants from several states to present and share information on four topic areas: health and gardening, community and sustainability, urban gardening and poverty, gardening and education.
- Donations from the community plots are provided on a rotating basis to 10 local agencies, including several food kitchens and soup pantries, a senior citizen center, and an organisation that works with and houses HIV-positive adults.
- Since the first growing season in 2010, the garden has donated over 14,000 pounds of fresh, organic produce to the 10 local agencies involved in the project.

These accomplishments have benefited a number of people and organisations. There is a direct link from the garden to the School of Social Work, as it allows the School to live its vision that revolves around human rights and social justice. Students have benefited from the garden as a tool for their learning. Gardeners have benefited from the ability to have fresh food themselves as well as participating in something tangible that allows them to give back to their community, and the University has also benefited from the ability to collaborate with the community on a 'green' initiative. All of these aspects are crucial to community development as taught in the social work curriculum and as promoted in the green social work model.

In terms of food security, there has been no research to establish the impact of the garden except through anecdotal evidence from the agencies to which the community harvest has been donated. During the summer months, when harvest donations occur, the influx of fresh vegetables to the food banks and soup kitchens in the local Monmouth area have been a welcome addition and have provided additional nutrition to clients/service users. Most food banks do not have access to fresh fruits and vegetables and so the diets of those using their services are lacking in certain nutrients.

Lessons learned

The building of a 'social community' in the community garden is a very important aspect of any gardening endeavor (McIlvaine-Newsad and Porter, 2013: 73). No matter how a community garden is established, it is necessary to tend to the relationships among and between all who are involved from the very beginning. Establishing a structure for how the garden will operate along with developing a communication strategy are necessary components of helping to build these relationships. The importance of clear communication in university–community collaborations is emphasised in the work of Siemens (2012) and Ostrander and Chapin-Hogue (2011).

The establishment of the Steering Committee greatly helped to provide structure and the beginning of communication patterns. The Steering Committee has only a secretary position in its formal structure (rather than the full complement of chair, treasurer and others). This was done so that the Committee was assured of one person being responsible for meeting minutes, emails to gardeners, as well as correspondence on behalf of the garden (thank you notes, for example). A website for the garden was developed and several Steering Committee members were organised to be able to access the website to make changes to it and to communicate with gardeners via this mechanism.

There have been fluctuations in overall communication with the gardeners from year to year, and it has been found that in those years where communication was more regular (on a weekly or bi-weekly basis as was needed), were those that the garden tended to have fewer difficulties. During the years where communication was not as regular, the garden tended to have some issues – for example, gardeners would not come out to help tend the community plots, some were leaving their plots to become overrun with weeds, and the main harvesting and delivery of community vegetables was being left to a handful of people.

Firth et al. (2011) speak to the concept of social capital as a central theme of how strong social networks and positive relationships can be developed: 'Social capital is viewed as the connections among individuals or social networks and the norms of reciprocity and trustworthiness that arise from those connections'(Firth et al., 2011: 558). In a case study of two community gardens in Nottingham, England, the authors look to identify three types of social capital: bonding, bridging and linking. These are all related to the interconnections between people from those connections that are very strong, like family ties (bonding), to connections that are more distant, like work colleagues or acquaintances (bridging) to those connections between people who are not very alike (linking). All three are needed to help build a strong community and there must be balance between all three types for the greatest participation among community members (Firth et al., 2011: 558).

The Steering Committee realised that positive relationships needed to be developed among all who were participating in the garden, and so in addition to communication, a number of activities have been developed in the garden to assist with this, like community weeding days or clean-up days where all the gardeners are invited to come out and help as a group. The lectures in the garden during the summer months have also provided educational opportunities for the gardeners, as did the community garden conference. Having students come to the garden to volunteer has also provided another means for gardeners to 'give back' to the University community and help teach another generation of young people to become interested in gardening, sustainability and the benefit of interacting with people one might not be as inclined to establish a relationship with.

Finding a stable source of funding for the community garden has been an ongoing issue. The 'rent' that annual gardeners pay for the growing season is $30 (up from the $25 the garden started with). This brings in a modest amount of money that can be put towards supplies that are needed in the garden, but it does not cover everything. After the first growing season, water irrigation lines needed to be installed in the garden with their connection to a water meter (from the township) was required. Monthly water bills are paid by the School of Social Work from a community garden account. However, the annual rental fees do not cover the year-round water bills. Water is shut off during the winter months, although the meter charge is for the entire year. Donations to the garden have come from local banks, individuals and local gardening clubs. However, these are not large enough to sustain the garden over time. Funding the garden remains a yearly priority for the dean.

Stakeholder support for a community garden is absolutely necessary. Scoggins (2010) makes a point of illustrating the various stakeholders that university gardens must work with, including faculty, students and administration. The community garden at Monmouth University has benefited from strong support from all three groups, especially our Facilities and Police Departments. The vice-president for Facilities at Monmouth University was involved in helping to choose the site for the community garden from the very beginning. As she saw the garden develop and the number of local community residents becoming involved rise, she continued to support this endeavor. There is a member of the facilities crew whose responsibilities include the community garden – for weed whacking, mowing grass and disposing of garbage or recycled material. Other members of the Facilities Department are responsible for the water turn-on or shut-off and have assisted in storing large pieces of machinery for the garden (e.g. the mulcher/chipper). In turn, the community garden has become part of the 'greening efforts' of the university, and three years ago, was actually placed on the university map.

The campus Police Department has also supported the garden. There are regular 'rounds' of the campus that also include the garden. The police also know that garden members all have orange baseball caps (a gift from one of the gardeners) so that they are identifiable. Campus police have actually stopped to question people in the garden without a baseball cap, and have also responded to one or two emergency calls when a gardener has been overcome by heat.

To thank these stakeholders, Steering Committee members make vegetable baskets each summer for the Facilities and Police Departments, the president of the University and the provost.

Questions for the future

The impact of the community garden on our community–university relationship (the town/gown phenomenon) has definitely been positive. The University has not conducted formal research on this topic, so this is an area to investigate for the future. However, the University does know that the garden has received positive feedback from the community – from members involved in the garden to those who come to garden events; or even those who pass the garden on their daily walk or run. Each year brings new gardeners who want to join the garden, and in the spring of 2015, we expanded the garden by another 10 feet outwards to accommodate several new individual plots.

Similarly, our impact on food security in our local area is another subject for research. The Steering Committee receives 'thank you notes' from the agencies that they donate to, and the community garden conference featured a panel presentation from representatives of three of the organisations that garden harvest has been donated too. All spoke of the benefits of being connected to our community garden, including the ability to provide fresh, organic food to their clients/service users, the ability to teach them about proper nutrition and the basic notion that the garden helped to provide more food to their clients/service users that was so necessary for their survival.

Those of us involved in the garden also need to examine how the garden has been of benefit to the gardeners and community in other ways – like eating habits, nutrition, health benefits. Additionally, there has not been an investigation into whether participation in the garden has been a conduit for other community organising efforts among the gardeners. Now that the community garden is fairly stable in terms of its operation and management, it is time to truly assess its influence in this local community.

References

Aftandilian, D. and Dart, L. (2013). Using garden-based service-learning to work toward food justice, better educate students, and strengthen campus-community ties. *Journal of Community Engagement and Scholarship*, 6: 55–69.
Bazerghi, C., McKay, F., Dunn, M. (2016). The role of food banks in addressing food insecurity: A systematic review. *Journal of Community Health*, 41: 732–740.
Bhawra, J., Cooke, M. J., Hanning, R., Wilk, P. and Gonneville, S. (2015). Community perspectives on food insecurity and obesity: Focus groups with caregivers of metis and Off-reserve first nations. *International Journal for Equity in Health*, 14: 96.

Draper, C. and Freedman, D. (2010). Review and analysis of the benefits, purposes, and motivations associated with community gardening in the United States. *Journal of Community Practice*, 18: 458–492.

FAO, IFAD and WFP. (2015). *The State of Food Insecurity in the World 2015. Meeting the 2015 international hunger targets: Taking stock of uneven progress*. Rome: FAO.

Ferris, J., Norman, C. and Sempik, J. (2001). People, land and sustainability: Community gardens and the social dimension of sustainable development. *Social Policy and Administration*, 35: 559–568.

Firth, C., Maye, D. and Pearson, D. (2011). Developing 'community' in community gardens. *Local Environment*, 16: 555–568.

Fisher, R., Fabricant, M. and Simmons, L. (2004). Understanding contemporary university-community connections: Context, practice and challenges. In Soska T., and Butterfield, A. (Eds.), *University-community partnerships: Universities in civic engagement*, pp. 13–34.

Gundersen, C. and Ziliak, J. P. (2014). Childhood food insecurity in the U.S.: Trends, causes and policy options. *The Future of Children*, Princeton-Brookings.

Henderson, B. R. and Hartsfield, K. (2009). Is getting into the community garden business a good way to engage citizens in local government? *National Civic Review*, 98(4): 12–17. doi: 10.1002/ncr271

Lanier, J., Schumacher, J. and Calvert, K. (2015). Cultivating community collaboration and community health through community gardens. *Journal of Community Practice*, 23: 492–507.

Lawson, L. (2005). *City bountiful: A century of community gardening in America*. Berkeley: University of California Press.

McIlvaine-Newsad, H. and Porter, R. (2013). How does your garden grow? Environmental justice aspects of community gardens. *Journal of Ecological Anthropology*, 16: 69–75.

Ostrander, N. and Chapin-Hogue, S. (2011). Learning from our mistakes: An autopsy of an unsuccessful university-community collaboration. *Social Work Education*, 30: 454–464.

Roncarolo, F., Bisset, S. and Potvin, L. (2016). Short-term effects of traditional and alternative community interventions to address food insecurity. *PloS ONE*, 11(3): e0150250, doi:10.137/journal.pone.0150250

Scoggins, H. L. (2010). University garden stakeholders: Student, industry, and community connections. *HorTechnology*, 20: 528–529.

Siemens, L. (2012). The impact of a community-university collaboration: Opening the "black box". *Canadian Journal of Nonprofit and Social Economy Research*, 3: 5–25.

Taylor, A. and Loopstra, R. (2016). Too poor to Eat: Food insecurity in the UK. *Food Security Briefing*. Available on http://Foodfoundation.org.uk.

Twiss, J., Dickinson, J., Duna, S., Kleinman, T., Paulsen, H. and Rilveria, L. (2003). Community gardens: Lessons learned from California healthy cities and communities. *American Journal of Public Health*, 93: 1435–1438.

U.S. Poverty Guidelines. (2015). Available on https://aspe.hhs.gov/2015-poverty-guidelines. [Accessed 5 January 2017].

Websites

Food security:
www.feedingamerica.org [Accessed 8 December 2016].
www.feedingamerica.org [Accessed 8 December 2016].
www.globalgiving.org/sdg/no-hunger [Accessed 8 December 2016].
Sustainable Development Goals:
www.un.org/sustainabledevelopment/sustainable-development-goals [Accessed 8 December 2016].

Part IV
Food (in)security

16
Food insecurity
Where social injustice meets environmental exploitation

Cheryl Molle

Introduction

Social justice refers to the equitable distribution of wealth, resources, and opportunity to promote the welfare of society, and is based on the premise that freedom and equality are fundamental human rights. An ideology valuing racial, gender, and economic equality; the fair treatment of vulnerable and oppressed populations; and the elimination of intolerance and discrimination, social justice is appealing to a variety of progressive socio-political movements. It is a key theme in the civil rights, women's rights, and LGBTQIA rights movements, as well as those linked to anti-war, animal rights, and environmental protection causes. Social justice is also a core principle of the social work profession (International Federation of Social Workers [IFSW], 2012). The social work profession aims to 'promote social change, problem-solving in human relationships and the empowerment and liberation of people to enhance well-being' (IFSW, 2012). Internationally, 'principles of human rights and social justice are fundamental to social work' (IFSW, 2012). To achieve human rights and social justice, and to 'intervene at the points where people interact with their environments' (IFSW, 2012), the social work profession must advocate for environmental justice.

Environmental justice refers to protecting the natural environment via the creation of laws and policies to prevent or reduce human practices that exploit the environment alongside the implementation of ecologically sustainable procedures. Similarly, green social work seeks 'reform of the socio-political and economic forces that have a deleterious impact upon the quality of life of poor and marginalised populations, to secure the policy changes and social transformations necessary for enhancing the well-being of people and the planet today and in the future' (Dominelli, 2012: 25). Advocates of green social work recognise that 'the logical consequence of the exploitation of natural resources is the exploitation of people' and that intervention is necessary (Dewane, 2011: 20). Because environmental exploitation directly affects entire communities, the social work profession has grown increasingly concerned with environmental issues such as deforestation, air and water pollution, and the use of toxic chemicals and pesticides (NASW, 2008). Despite the social work profession's shift toward observing environmental justice as an international social justice issue, evidenced by the incorporation of environmental justice into the International Federation of Social Workers' Core Mandates (IFSW, 2012) and the emergence of ecological social work literature, certain environmental justice issues require more of the profession's global attention, particularly food insecurity.

Food insecurity is an issue at the intersection of social and environmental justice, occurring where social injustice meets environmental exploitation. Globally, safe and nutritious foods are distributed unequally, even in societies with adequate or plentiful food resources, which places substantial obstacles in the path of vulnerable and oppressed communities as they attempt to procure nutritious, wholesome food. Food insecurity is a state in which individuals, households, and communities lack 'sufficient, safe, nutritious food to maintain a healthy and active life' (Food and Agriculture Organization of the United Nations [FAO], 1996, World Food Summit Plan of Action section, para. 1). Food insecurity rarely occurs in cases of social injustice that are not accompanied by environmental exploitation, nor does it tend to occur in cases of environmental exploitation that are not accompanied by social injustice. Green social work must, therefore, address food insecurity as an international socio-environmental issue.

To understand food insecurity as a global green social work issue, the recognition of food insecurity as an intersectional issue, occurring where social injustice meets environmental exploitation, must first be established. Developing this understanding requires examining the interrelated causes of food insecurity, including policy, environmental, and social factors; analysing the characteristics of food insecurity in a society with bountiful food resources to examine its social and environmental causes; and considering the role of green social work to intervene in and prevent cases of food insecurity through current direct-practice interventions and emerging community and policy practice interventions. To effectively intervene in situations of food insecurity, green social workers must constantly develop their knowledge and understanding of not only the complex factors contributing to food insecurity but also the communities affected by it.

Causes of food insecurity

Intersecting policy, environmental, and social factors contribute to food insecurity and hunger. According to the Food and Agricultural Organization of the United Nations (UN), 'Poverty … conflict, terrorism, corruption, and environmental degradation' each contribute to food insecurity (FAO, 1996, Rome Declaration on World Food Insecurity section, para. 5). Current economic policies allow the food industry to degrade the environment and exploit workers. Environmental degradation then decreases food production and reduces the availability of healthy food. Limited food production and the reduced availability of healthy food then raise the cost of food, and working-class individuals and families encounter difficulty obtaining nutritious food.

Policy factors

Neoliberalism – economic theories and policies favouring free-market capitalism – has caused significant harm to the environment and the suppression of wages, which has resulted in the limited production and availability of healthy food and increased poverty, the two primary causes of food insecurity (Robinson, 2004; Turje, 2012; Deepak, 2014). Neoliberal philosophy has guided economic policy since the 1980s, resulting in free trade, privatisation of the public sector, deregulation, and reductions in government spending. By privatising the instruments of food production (including land, water, and seeds) and through the expansion of agencies like the World Trade Organization, these policies have resulted in injurious food production practices that contribute to rapid ecological deterioration (Turje, 2012). With little to no government regulation and even less input from the public, a few select industrialised farms now produce a significant portion of all available food, and are able to do so using toxic herbicides and pesticides that deplete soil and are harmful to ingest (Tansey, 2002; Turje, 2012; Besthorn, 2013). In addition to harming the environment and the quality of available food, these policies are also credited with weakening the power of workers' unions, cutting funds for social services, and lowering wages (Robinson, 2004; Deepak, 2014). Although extremely beneficial to the food industry, the natural environment and working-class communities have suffered from these policies for more than three decades. Understanding the impact of neoliberalism is critical to green social workers engaging in policy practice.

Environmental factors

Environmental issues contributing to food insecurity include climate change, soil depletion, water shortages, and the use of toxic chemicals in pesticides and herbicides in the agricultural sector. Climate change, soil depletion, and water shortage are each associated with higher food production costs, resulting in sharp increases in the price of food products, which many low-income persons cannot afford (Deepak, 2014). Greenhouse gas emissions have caused global average temperatures to rise and resulted in extreme weather, seasonal shifts, and changed patterns of precipitation, thus impacting food production (Deepak, 2014). The global food cost increases in 2008, 2010, and 2012 are a result of the effects of climate change on food production systems, and further price increases are expected as climate change continues to impact crop and livestock production, and ultimately the availability of food (Deepak, 2014). Ploughing, overgrazing, and the use of fertilizers and pesticides have caused rapid soil erosion and the loss of approximately 40 percent of agricultural land globally (Paul and Wahlberg, 2008). Water shortages resulting from heavy pumping and dam-based irrigation have made it extremely difficult to farm the agricultural land that remains, as food production requires ample fresh water (Paul and Wahlberg, 2008). Environmental exploitation by humans has made it increasingly difficult to produce enough food, thus raising the cost of food for all (Paul and Wahlberg, 2008). Furthermore, the use of toxic chemical products such as pesticides and herbicides, a common practice in the agricultural sector, renders much of the food that is produced, and particularly food which costs less, to be unhealthy (Besthorn, 2013). Resisting destructive food production practices, green social work practitioners in community settings, including many in Europe and the United States (US), are often directly involved in the development of community gardens and organic farming.

Social factors

Income inequality and modern-day segregation are the dominant social contributors to food insecurity. Poverty is one of the leading causes of food insecurity. In developed and underdeveloped nations alike, the wealthy enjoy relatively stable access to food while the impoverished have minimal purchasing power and are significantly more likely to experience chronic hunger (Rosen and Shapouri, 2001). Modern segregation has contributed to food insecurity in the US since the 1950s, when affluent and predominantly Caucasian families fled to the suburbs from urban areas, and brought their resources, including food markets, with them (Bell et al., 2013). Today, barriers to accessing food resources are common in urban areas, resulting in food deserts in which supermarkets tend to be too far from low-income urban neighborhoods for residents to walk or take public transportation to (Freeman, 2007). When grocery markets offering healthy food options are located in or near low-income urban communities, prices are often inflated in comparison to suburban markets (Kaufman et al., 1997). However, insufficient purchasing power prevents low-income families from acquiring the high-priced, healthy food products that nearby food markets may offer. Green social workers should be cognisant of the social factors contributing to food insecurity, connect food-insecure individuals and families to food assistance services, work with affected communities to expose unjust food distribution procedures, and advocate for the equal distribution of food.

An intersectional analysis: food insecurity in the US

Food insecurity is generally associated with the developing world, due largely to depictions of developing nations as impoverished, overpopulated, and lacking in resources. This misconception, that food insecurity exists almost exclusively in developing nations, may impede progress toward understanding food insecurity as a human rights issue stemming from continued environmental exploitation and the systemic oppression of vulnerable social classes. Although many developing countries are indeed struggling with high rates of hunger and malnutrition (FAO, 1996), food insecurity also occurs in wealthier nations. Examining food insecurity among low-income and minority populations in a prosperous and powerful nation, the US, highlights the policy, environmental, and social factors associated with food insecurity and facilitates a deeper understanding of food insecurity as an intersectional social justice issue. Food insecurity's presence in a wealthy nation with plentiful food resources exposes the phenomenon as a socio-environmental injustice rather than a consequence of extreme poverty in developing countries, as it is commonly portrayed.

Approximately 10.7 million households in the US are experiencing low levels of food security and an additional 6.8 million households are experiencing what is considered very low levels of food security (Coleman-Jensen and Gregory, 2015). The majority of households experiencing low or very low food security in the US have been identified as African American and Latino households living below the poverty line (Ashiabi, 2005; Coleman-Jensen and Gregory, 2015). Furthermore, single mothers and their children are at greater risk of food insecurity than single fathers and their children (Garasky et al., 2014). Each of these groups – the low-income, ethnic and racial minorities, women, and children – is considered vulnerable, and each population has its own historical experiences of social, political, and economic hardship. Ethnic and racial minorities, specifically African Americans and Latinos, are more likely to be in poverty than other ethnic groups, and women, specifically lone mothers, are more likely to be in poverty than men (Macias, 2008; Brisson, 2012). Poverty is also associated with anxiety, depression, suicide, physical illness, crime, domestic violence, and substance use, alongside premature death at disproportionate rates among the same populations at risk of experiencing food insecurity (Robinson, 2004). The relationship between food insecurity and 'deeper structures of inequality . . . along lines of race, gender, and socio-economic status' is, therefore, indisputable (Macias, 2008: 1089).

Historically vulnerable and oppressed populations in the US are at a substantially greater risk of living in adverse environmental conditions and, in comparison to more privileged groups, are far more likely to experience waste dumping, pollution, and deforestation in their communities (Dewane, 2011). These careless and dangerous practices pose not only ecological risks but also severe physical health risks, and occur most frequently in communities of colour, embodying environmental racism (Bullard, 1993). Environmental racism may be understood as the 'targeting of minority communities or the exclusion of minority groups from public and private boards, commissions, and regulatory bodies' and the development and implementation 'of any policy, practice, or regulation that negatively affects the environment of low-income and/or racially homogeneous communities disproportionately in comparison to Caucasian or affluent communities' (Dewane, 2011: 22). Both race and class are linked to environmental inequity, with low-income communities of colour being most likely to live in contaminated areas (Bullard, 1993). As a result, the land on which these communities live may lack the natural resources necessary for food production or be too badly polluted to farm, particularly in urban areas. Therefore, the same populations targeted by environmental racism are also most likely to experience food insecurity.

Food insecurity is associated with a plethora of adverse physical and mental health conditions, obstacles to social and occupational development, and barriers to upward socioeconomic mobility. Food insecurity leads to medical conditions such as malnutrition, obesity, cardiovascular disease, type 2 diabetes, metabolic syndrome, infant mortality, several types of cancer, an increased likelihood of hospitalisation, and higher rates of infectious disease (Breaux et al., 2007; Offer et al., 2010; Gundersen et al., 2011; Besthorn, 2013). It is also linked to mental illness, placing persons experiencing food insecurity at a greater risk of developing anxiety and depressive disorders than their food secure counterparts (Ashiabi and O'Neal, 2007). Prolonged interruption to children's nutrition could result in lasting damage to their cognitive and socioemotional maturation (Breaux et al., 2007). Children and adolescents experiencing food insecurity are likely to have difficulty forging and enriching interpersonal relationships, developing language and motor skills, paying attention, and performing well in school (Breaux et al., 2007). The negative effects of food insecurity on physical and mental health may contribute to low socio-economic status by limiting food-insecure individuals' ability to complete a post-secondary education or work full-time. Such barriers to upward socioeconomic mobility are likely to perpetuate poverty in low-income communities and thus increase the likelihood that subsequent generations will experience food insecurity (Breaux et al., 2007).

The role of green social work

Food insecurity contributes to negative outcomes in the areas of physical and mental health and social and economic development among traditionally vulnerable and oppressed populations, including low-income individuals and families, people of colour, women, and children. Social workers are responsible for preventing the exploitation of persons and communities, empowering vulnerable and oppressed populations, meeting basic human needs, and advocating for the well-being of society and individuals. These responsibilities represent the unique values and ethics of the social work community. International ethical principles in social work practice relate specifically to food inequality, observing the issue as a global injustice and illustrating the need for social workers to intervene at the points where people engage with the environment, compelling social workers around the globe to critically analyse the effects of neoliberalism on international social welfare and the global food system, and to promote economic and environmental sustainability (Hayward et al., 2015).

Ethical responsibilities to clients, the profession, society, and the environment require social workers to address the intersecting policy, environmental, and social issues contributing to food insecurity. The social work profession and green social workers, in particular, must first work toward understanding the complex ways in which neoliberal economic policies, income inequality, modern-day segregation, climate change, and harmful agricultural practices have created the global food insecurity crisis. Green social workers are obligated to not only recognise food insecurity as a social and environmental injustice but also to intervene and should seek to resolve the social and environmental injustices and the policies, or lack thereof, contributing to food insecurity. The role of social work in responding to food insecurity is to continue current direct practice interventions with individuals and families and increase the profession's involvement in emerging community and policy practice interventions.

Current direct practice interventions

Social workers in case management and similar direct service roles frequently intervene in situations of food insecurity by conducting a food insecurity and hunger assessment with low-income clients. Two questionnaires commonly used to assess food insecurity include the comprehensive Food Security Questionnaire, used in the US, and the more concise Household Food Insecurity Access Scale, used worldwide by the United States Agency for International Development (USAID). These questionnaires and similar assessment measures may be adapted for use in other nations and by other global hunger relief agencies. The ability to categorise food insecurity by level of severity can help direct practice social workers determine appropriate, personalised interventions for food-insecure clients.

The Food Security Questionnaire, developed by the Food Security Research Team of the Food and Consumer Service in the 1990s and used by the United States Bureau of the Census to derive data on national food insecurity, is one example of an assessment tool that may be used to determine whether a client is experiencing food insecurity or hunger (Klein, 1996). The comprehensive Food Security Questionnaire contains 58 questions regarding clients' grocery shopping patterns and expenditures, participation in food assistance programmes, the amount of food eaten in their households, reasons why household members may not have enough to eat, and perceptions of their food circumstances (Klein, 1996). The questionnaire also asks clients how they cope with having less food, if they skip meals or do not eat for an entire day, and if they go hungry because they cannot afford food, and allows them to submit a report of their household food supply (Klein, 1996). Using this measure, social workers can group clients into four distinct classifications of food insecurity and hunger: (1) 'experience no hunger or food insecurity', (2) 'food insecurity without hunger', (3) 'food insecurity with evidence of adult hunger', and (4) 'food insecurity with evidence of child hunger and severe adult hunger' (Klein, 1996: 36).

A more concise food insecurity assessment tool, the Household Food Insecurity Access Scale (HFIAS) used by USAID is an 18-question survey that focuses primarily on clients' perceptions of their food circumstances. It solicits descriptions of their uncertainty or anxiety regarding their food situation, resources, or supply; perceptions that their household's quality and quantity of food is insufficient; instances of reduced food intake for adults and children; consequences of reduced food intake for adults and children; and feelings of shame related to socially unacceptable means of food acquisition (Coates et al., 2007). This brief food insecurity questionnaire asks whether respondents worry that their household does not have enough food and whether household members' food preferences could not be met. The succinct HFIAS survey is presumably easy to use in fast-paced social service settings, and allows social workers to group clients into four different categories of food insecurity: (1) 'food secure', (2) 'mildly food insecure', (3) 'moderately food insecure', and (4) 'severely food insecure' (Coates et al., 2007: 20).

Social workers in direct service roles intervene in situations of food insecurity by facilitating clients' access to hunger relief and nutrition assistance programmes. Social workers around the globe refer food-insecure clients to a variety of food assistance programmes. Food assistance programmes for individuals and families commonly include food voucher and cash assistance programmes, through which clients are given funds that they may use to purchase food. As of early 2016, cash assistance, food vouchers, and electronic funds transfers made up more than 25 per cent all food assistance provided by the United Nations' World Food Programme (World Food Programme, 2016). Food-insecure persons are also generally eligible to receive assistance from food banks, which are charitable organisations that distribute food to individuals experiencing hunger, and are often located in low-income urban areas (Kim, 2015). Though food voucher programmes and food banks tend to serve both adults and children, hunger relief programmes specifically for children experiencing food insecurity are fairly common. Nutrition assistance programmes for children may operate within charitable organisations or within a larger social welfare system. In many nations, like South Korea, hundreds of thousands of children are eligible to receive government-funded meal aid services (Kim, 2015). Social workers in direct service roles are generally knowledgeable of nutrition assistance programmes and corresponding eligibility requirements and restrictions, and work to connect food-insecure clients with the programmes that are best suited to address their specific needs.

Emerging community and policy practice interventions

Although a considerable majority of today's social workers hold direct service roles, the profession was founded on the macro-level values of social justice and human rights activism. Social work's highly political origins may be partially responsible for the profession's emerging involvement in community and policy practice, more commonly known as macro-social work or macro-practice. Returning to social work's roots in social and political advocacy is quickly becoming one of the profession's favoured responses to food insecurity and a myriad of related social and environmental justice issues, particularly among green social workers. Social workers around the globe are beginning to engage in community and policy practice by working to empower entire communities and to ensure that the profession's values are upheld in public policy. Much like their predecessors, modern social workers, and specifically those with a focus on green social work, are advocating for radical social and environmental change through community organising, community building, and policy advocacy, and must continue to do so in order to alleviate food insecurity.

Recognising the magnitude of food insecurity, social workers engage in community organising and community building and work directly with communities to combat food insecurity. A growing area of community organising and community building in social work practice is the food sovereignty movement (Turje, 2012). The term food sovereignty refers to nutritional and culturally appropriate food produced using environmentally friendly and sustainable methods, and power over one's own food and agricultural systems as a human right (Declaration of Nyeleni, 2007, in Deepak, 2014). In community organising and community-building roles, macro-level social workers ensure that the community itself is the most important focus by encouraging affected persons to assume responsibility for building their community (Hyde and Walter, 2012), a skill required of green social workers. Similarly, the food sovereignty movement prioritises local production, distribution, and consumption of food and the rights of consumers to control their food intake and nutrition, and seeks to encourage social relationships, established around food, that are free from inequality and oppression (Declaration of Nyeleni, 2007, in Deepak, 2014). To resist industrialised farming methods and the use of toxic chemicals in food production, the food sovereignty movement involves consumers, regardless of their background, in local agricultural projects such as community gardens (Purifoy, 2012; Deepak, 2014), much like green social workers throughout Europe and the US. These projects include community gardening programmes and other alternative food initiatives such as food cooperatives, which are organisations emphasising consumer decision-making in food production methods and the support of local farmers' markets (Turje, 2012).

Policy advocacy is an equally important function of macro-level social work practice and green social work. Macro-level social workers honour the profession's values by demonstrating an awareness of the impact of policy on practice, advocating for social justice to protect the vulnerable and oppressed, and acting to eliminate the exploitation of persons and the environment. Macro-level social workers are beginning to challenge the policies contributing to food insecurity and are working to develop just social and environmental legislation. Green social workers engaging in policy advocacy around these issues generally have knowledge of and practice with lobbying. Successful lobbying campaigns in the not-for-profit sector often follow a linear process similar to the following: (1) identifying the issue, (2) conducting research on the issue, (3) creating a fact sheet to highlight research findings on the issue, (4) developing a slogan or framework to brand the issue, (5) listing possible supporters and opponents of the cause, (6) building a coalition of stakeholders and supporters, (7) developing educational materials, (8) launching a media campaign to raise awareness about a cause, (9) approaching policymakers and elected officials, and (10) monitoring the progress of people or organisations pledged to advance the cause (Libby, 2012, p. 103). Green social workers engaging in legislative advocacy to alleviate food insecurity may use this model and similar methods to advocate for policy change or new legislation aimed at addressing any of the social, environmental, or policy determinants of food insecurity, ranging from income inequality to climate change to the privatisation of agriculture.

Lessons for effective interventions

Prior to engaging in food insecurity interventions at any level of practice, social workers should conduct a self-evaluation to critically examine both their knowledge of food insecurity and their level of cultural competence, and to acquire relevant knowledge and skills in these areas to ensure effective interventions. For many social workers, self-evaluation is an ongoing process through which continued learning and growth occur. The food justice pedagogical framework (Hayward et al., 2015) and the liberation education model (Freire, 1998) are useful tools for facilitating continued learning and growth and developing a deeper understanding of food insecurity. Together, these tools can help green social workers develop effective food insecurity interventions.

Direct service, community-based, and policy-related interventions require green social workers to develop a general knowledge of food insecurity. It is unlikely that social workers at any level of practice will be able to intervene effectively in situations of food insecurity without an understanding of the complex factors contributing to it. An important step toward increasing knowledge of food insecurity is to insert the food justice pedagogical framework into social work practice (Hayward et al., 2015). The food justice pedagogical framework asserts that the food system is connected to both the social and natural environment and that social and ecological injustices often result in food insecurity (Hayward et al., 2015). Service learning is a useful strategy for incorporating the food justice pedagogical framework into social work practice, and allows professional learners to connect their experience with social work concepts (Hayward et al., 2015). This educational method provides social workers with the opportunity to observe food insecurity, and thus enhances their knowledge and allows them to draw connections, based on their experiences, to the values and ethical standards of the profession. In direct service, community, and policy settings alike, considering the food justice pedagogical framework in social work practice is a useful way for social workers to begin examining intersecting social and environmental issues and exploring green social work interventions.

To honour the profession's values in direct service and community and policy practice, green social workers should be culturally competent, embrace social diversity, and promote social welfare. Without these essential qualities, social workers will experience little success in their efforts to address food insecurity. Social workers should have a basic understanding of a community's culture, recognise that individuals they are working with or advocating for have likely experienced oppression and discrimination, and begin considering cultural conventions and strengths that may be used as assets to the affected community. This can be accomplished by employing the key principles and strategies of the liberation education model, which aims to understand and fight oppression by encouraging dialogue about a community's struggles, critically analysing the social and historical foundations of those struggles, and conceiving and implementing collective action methods for change (Freire, 1998). In community organising and community building, in particular, it is extremely important that social workers collaborate with affected community members, view themselves as guides rather than experts, and allow the community to make decisions regarding which actions it will take to alleviate food insecurity.

Conclusion

At the intersection of social and environmental justice, occurring where social injustice meets environmental exploitation, food insecurity requires more of the international social work profession's attention. Because food insecurity disproportionately impacts traditionally vulnerable populations and is associated with negative physical, mental, and socioeconomic outcomes, the profession is bound by its values and ethical standards to address food insecurity. Historically rooted in advocating for social justice and human rights, and more recently observing environmental justice as a social justice issue, the social work profession must begin to address food insecurity at all levels of social work practice, but particularly in the emerging areas of community and policy practice. First and foremost, the profession must work toward understanding how neoliberal economic policies, income inequality, climate change, and deleterious agricultural practices have contributed to worldwide food insecurity.

Green social workers must be cognisant of food insecurity at all times, across practice specialties, and in micro-, mezzo-, and macro-settings alike. The role of green social work in responding to food insecurity is multifaceted and involves ensuring the continued utilisation of current direct practice interventions such as food insecurity questionnaires and food assistance programmes, as well as participation in emerging macro-level social work interventions including community organising, community building, and policy advocacy alongside affected populations. Green social workers can effectively intervene in cases of food insecurity if they are willing to conduct honest self-evaluations of their knowledge and cultural competency, participate in continuing education, and, more importantly, if the global profession is willing to fully incorporate green social work theory and macro-level interventions into generalist social work practice.

References

Ashiabi, G. S. and O'Neal, K. K. (2007). Food insecurity and adjustment problems in a national sample of adolescents. *Journal of Children and Poverty*, 13(2): 111–132.
Ashiabi, G. S. (2005). Household food insecurity and children's school engagement. *Journal of Children and Poverty*, 11(1): 3–17.
Bell, J., Mora, G., Hagen, E., Rubin, V., and Karpyn, A. M. B. (2013). *Access to healthy food and why it matters: A review of the research*. Philadelphia, Pennsylvania: The Food Trust Policy Link.
Besthorn, F. H. (2013). Vertical farming: Social work and sustainable urban agriculture in an age of global food crises. *Australian Social Work*, 66(2): 187–203.

Breaux, J., Chilton, M. and Chyatte, M. (2007). The negative effects of poverty and food insecurity on child development. *Indian Journal of Medical Research*, 126(4): 262–272.

Brisson, D. (2012). Neighborhood social cohesion and food insecurity: A longitudinal study. *Journal of the Society for Social Work and Research*, 3(4): 268–269.

Bullard, R. D. (1993). *Confronting environmental racism: Voices from the Grassroots*. Boston, MA: South End Press.

Coates, J., Swindale, A. and Bilinsky, P. (2007). *Household food insecurity access scale (HFIAS) for measurement of household food access: Indicator guide* (v. 3). Washington, DC: Food and Nutrition Technical Assistance Project, Academy for Educational Development.

Coleman-Jensen, A. and Gregory, C. U.S. Department of Agriculture, Economic Research Service. (2015). *Food security in the U.S.: Key statistics and graphs*. Available on http://1.usa.gov/1rSxRbI [Accessed 8 April 2016].

Declaration of Nyeleni. (2007). *Declaration of the forum for food sovereignty*. Available on http://www.nyeleni.org/spip.php?article290 [Accessed 13 October 2017].

Deepak, A. C. (2014). A postcolonial feminist social work perspective on global food insecurity. *Journal of Women and Social Work*, 29(2): 153–164.

Dewane, C. (2011). Environmentalism: The ultimate social justice issue. *Social Work Today*, 11(5): 20–23.

Dominelli, L. (2012). *Green social work: From environmental crises to environmental justice*. Cambridge, UK: Polity.

Food and Agriculture Organization of the United Nations. (1996). *World food summit*: 13–17 November 1996, Rome, Italy.

Freeman, A. (2007). Fast food: Oppression through poor nutrition. *California Law Review*, 95(6): 2221–2260.

Freire, P. (1998). *Teachers as Cultural Workers: Letters to those who dare teach*. Boulder, CO: Westview Press.

Garasky, S., Miller, D. P., Nanda, N. and Nepomnyaschy, L. (2014). Non-resident fathers and child food insecurity: Evidence from longitudinal data. *Social Service Review*, March: 92–133.

Gundersen, C., Kreider, B. and Pepper, J. (2011). The economics of food insecurity in the United States. *Applied Economic Perspectives and Policy*, 33(3), 281–303.

Hayward, R. A., Himmelheber, S., Lee Kaiser, M. and Miller, S. (2015). Cultivators of change: Food justice in social work education. *Social Work Education*, 34(5): 544–557.

Hyde, C. and Walter, C. L. (2012). Community building practice: An expanded conceptual framework. In M. Minkler (Ed.), *Community organizing and community building for health and welfare* (3rd ed., pp. 78–90). New Brunswick, New Jersey: Rutgers University Press.

IFSW (International Federation of Social Workers). (2012). *Statement of ethical principles*. Available on http://ifsw.org/policies/statement-of-ethical-principles/ [Accessed 13 October 2017].

Kaufman, P. R., MacDonald, J. M., Lutz, S. M. and Smallwood, D. M. (1997). *Do the poor pay more for food? Item selection and price differences affect low-income household food costs*. Agricultural Economic Report, 759, 1–23. U.S. Department of Agriculture, Economic Research Service: Food and Rural Economics Division.

Kim, S. (2015). Exploring the endogenous governance model for alleviating food insecurity: Comparative analysis of food bank systems in Korea and the USA. *International Journal of Social Welfare*, 24: 145–158.

Klein, B. W. (1996). Food security and hunger measures: Promising future for state and local household surveys. *Family Economics and Nutrition Review*, 9(4): 31–37.

Libby, P. (2012). *The lobbying strategy handbook: 10 steps to advancing any cause effectively*. Thousand Oaks, California: Sage Publications.

Macias, T. (2008). Working toward a just, equitable, and local food system: The social impact of community-based agriculture. *Social Science Quarterly*, 89: 1086–1011.

National Association of Social Workers (NASW). (2008). *Environmental policy*. Available on www.socialworkers.org/da/da2008/finalvoting/documents/Environmentper cent20Policyper cent202ndper cent20round-Clean.pdf [Accessed 20 April 2016].

Offer, A., Pechey, R. J. and Ulijaszek, S. (2010). Obesity under affluence varies by welfare regimes: The effect of fast food, insecurity, and inequality. *Economics and Human Biology*, 8: 297–308.

Paul, J. A. and Wahlberg, K. (2008). A new era of world hunger? The global food crisis analysed. *FES Briefing Paper*, July, 1–12. Available on www.globalpolicy.org/images/pdfs/07paulwahlberg.pdf [Accessed 21 April 2016].

Purifoy, D. M. (2012). Food policy councils: Integrating food justice and environmental justice. *Duke Environmental Law and Policy Forum*, 24: 375–398.

Robinson, T. (2004). Hunger discipline and social parasites: The political economy of the living wage. *Urban Affairs Review*, 40(2): 246–268.

Rosen, S. and Shapouri, S. (2001). Issues in food security: Effects of income distribution on food security. *Agriculture Information Bulletin*, 765(2): 1–2.

Tansey, G. (2002). Patenting our food future: Intellectual property rights and the global food system. *Social Policy and Administration*, 36(6): 575–592.

Turje, M. (2012). Social workers, farmers and food commodification: Governmentality and neoliberalism in the alternative food movement. *Canadian Social Work Review*, 29(1): 121–138.

World Food Programme. (2016). *Food assistance: Cash-based and in-kind*. Available on www.wfp.org/cash-based-transfers [Accessed 20 December 2016].

17

The food security crisis and CSA movement in China

Green social work practice in Yunnan Province

Hok Bun Ku and Hairong Yan

Introduction

There is an old Chinese saying that 'food is the first necessity of the people, and food security comes first!' However, today in China, food as the basic necessity is no longer safe (Zhang, 2011; Yan et al., 2016). In recent years, the mass media exposed many food scandals. To local Chinese people, food safety has become a major concern (Liu and Ma, 2016). Recently, food security has been listed as the first major issue to be tackled by the Chinese government at the Chinese Communist Party (CCP)'s Economic Work Conference, the Central Rural Work Conference as well as in the published *No. 1 Central Document* (Ghose, 2014). At the CCP Economic Work Conference which was held 10–13 December 2013, ensuring effective food security was listed as the top of six major tasks. The CCP has come up with a slogan to illustrate its goals – *'guwu jiben ziji, kouliang juedui anquan'* ('grain self-sufficiency, absolute security of food rations') (*China Daily*, 2013). What happened to Chinese food security? What caused this problem and how have Chinese people responded to this food security crisis?

Since 2006, collaborating with a local social work organisation in China, author Hok Bun Ku has had the opportunity to participate in rural community development using participatory action research (PAR) in Chinese villages in Yunnan Province. During this period, the research team began to understand how the market economy and the industrialisation of agriculture influenced China's agricultural development and caused the food security crisis. In facing this situation, the research team organised a movement of Community Supporting Agriculture (CSA) in Yunnan. Social workers worked together with local community residents in the villages to form production cooperatives and encourage them to return to organic farming. In the city, social workers developed consumer networks to support producer cooperatives. For both authors, CSA is one of many kinds of green social work practices responding to environmental and agricultural crises (Dominelli and Ku, 2017). The idea of green social work has been developed by Lena Dominelli. She explicates the links between the social, economic and environmental dimensions of sustainability. She explores the concept of 'green social work' to address poverty and other forms of structural inequalities in the context of global environmental and socio-economic crises (Dominelli, 2012). In this chapter, the authors argue that local producers and consumers are not passively waiting for government policy changes, but, organised by green social workers, are actively searching for alternatives to achieve self-sufficiency and food security through a new initiative, the rural–urban alliance.

Food security crisis in China

Food security issues in China relate to food self-sufficiency and safety

Although the CCP media stated that 'China's grain output has risen for the 10th consecutive year' and 'China can achieve grain self-sufficiency' (*The Economic Times*, 2013), the situation on the ground is not so optimistic. The director of the Crop Cultivation Department, Zeng Yande, said that although grain production has risen for the 10th straight year, tight food supplies will persist with the increase in grain demand, which is now at 100 million tons per year due to expansion in animal husbandry. In 2011, the State Council Development Research Centre had predicted that Chinese grain imports would increase to 22.24 million tons by 2020, up by 416 million tons since 1997. China's total grain imports reached over 70 million tons in 2012. *Finance* magazine pointed out that based on imports of cotton, oil and grain in 2010, the number of China's agricultural imports is equal to the use of 700 million *mu*'s (1 *mu* is equal to 0.1647 acre) of foreign cultivated land, or the whole land mass of Heilongjiang Province. In October 2010, the *China Food Science and Technology* magazine reported that not only have CCP central granaries been virtually emptied, the state-owned granaries and the privately owned granaries in the northeast, which is a major grain production region, are also nearly empty (NTD TV, 2014). In the article titled 'China's Largest Catastrophe Cannot be Avoided', academician Yuan Longping (2014) said a food crisis cannot be avoided and a social crisis could erupt at any time. His article revealed that China's grain self-sufficiency rate is only 80 per cent and China imports more than 80 per cent of its edible oil. In 2012, the US Department of Agriculture said that drought would cause a decline in US corn and soybean production (*Science Daily*, 2014). This will impact China heavily because imports of this type were more than 6 million tons in 2011.

By using soybean production as an example, Chen et al. (2016) discovered that China is experiencing a food crisis around self-sufficiency and safety. China is the place where the soybean was domesticated and emanated from (Wang and Li, 2000). Until the mid-1990s, China was not only self-sufficient in soybean, but also a net exporter (Wang, 2013). However, in 2000, China surpassed Europe as the biggest soy importer on the global market. Its imports, over 70 million tons in 2014, accounted for 57.7 per cent of global soybean trade and about 80 per cent of China's soybean consumption (BBC, 2015). In 2012, China imported 44, 41, 10 and 5 per cent respectively from the US, Brazil, Argentina and other soy-producing countries (China Soybean Industry Association [CSIA], 2014: 49). Soybean has become a key crop implicated in the changing political-economic relations between China, the US and South America (Oliveira and Schneider, 2014). Soybeans, not aircraft, are now the US' top export to China (*Global Post*, 2014). As the US was already a major producer and exporter of soybeans before 2000, China's growing imports are in tandem with South America's fast expansion in soy production since the mid-1990s. In Brazil, soybean export serves as an instrument to balance the country's booming imports from China. China surpassed the US in becoming Brazil's largest trade partner in 2009 (Oliveira, 2015: 17). Some observers in China, aware of the dominant role played by US-based transnational corporations in the global soy complex, perceive the situation to be that 'South

America produces soybeans, China buys soybeans, and the US sells soybeans' (Zhou, 2014; Guo, 2012).

Importing soybean is not only an issue of food self-sufficiency, but also a question of food safety because the massive import of soybean is genetically modified (GM) and patented by Monsanto and a few other transnational companies. The massive import of GM soybeans, in the context of China's entry into the WTO (World Trade Organization) and the growing presence of global agribusiness in China, has challenged the long-held principle of self-sufficiency and food safety. It has opened up heated debates about food security, consumer rights and inequality, scientific authority, the relationship between corporate interests and science, food as commodity or public good, the paradigm of development, socialism and capitalism, issues highlighted by green social work.

China's food safety problem is no longer news for the public. In 2008, the Chinese mass media exposed the scandal of poisoned milk powder after 16 infants in Gansu Province were diagnosed with kidney stones. The babies were fed infant formula produced by the Shijiazhuang-based Sanlu Group. The scandal involved milk and infant formula along with other food materials and components being adulterated with melamine. China reported an estimated 300,000 victims in total. Six infants died from kidney stones and other kidney damage with an estimated 54,000 babies being hospitalised. In a separate incident four years earlier, watered-down milk had resulted in 13 infant deaths from malnutrition. The issue raised concerns about food safety and political corruption in China, and damaged the reputation of China's food exports. At least 11 countries stopped all imports of Chinese dairy products. Not only poisoned milk powder, other food scandals (e.g. clenbuterol), lean meat powder, and fake eggs are reported by mass media from time to time and such occurrences have become a social fact of Chinese society.

Social economy, food production and green social work practice in China

The social economy provides us a new framework to rethink economic development and think about alternatives to capitalism, as recommended by green social work (Dominelli, 2012). The concept of the 'social economy' is an option which has a clear vision 'to put the economy at the service of human beings, rather than putting human beings at the service of the economy' (Neamtan, 2010: 241), and emphasises social justice, democracy and collectivism. The social economy highlights links to the well-being of different economic subjects (e.g. producers, consumers), inhabitants of a local community, and humankind; for example, impacts on cultural or environmental commons. It enables practitioners to understand the structural factors causing environmental disasters and their significant social consequences. It also gives local NGOs insight into searching for emancipatory alternatives which can inform their practical strategies for social transformation. In contrast with the market economy, the principles of the social economy should be people centred, community based, cooperative and democratic, as well as uphold a vision of a pluralistic society in which production is not for consumption but for servicing the needs of people (Wright 2006) and the flora and fauna of planet earth (Dominelli 2012).

Unsustainable development in China

Currently, China is at the crossroads of its second revolution. Confronted by the social issues and ingrained social contradictions engendered by the development of the market economy in the past 30 years, the 12th five-year plan of the Chinese government proposes to maintain the rapid development of the economy, while strengthening social development. Emphasising the needs of the people, focusing on the co-ordination of sustainable development, and protecting and improving people's livelihood are proposed as measures to promote social equality and justice. However, the chasm engendered by rapid industrialisation and urbanisation through large-scale migration within China has, for a long time, made more than 250 million migrant labourers, rural to urban migrant workers with 'quasi-complete' statuses and identities. Consequently, these migrant workers are left with precarious working and living rights, and their well-being and dignity become a distant dream. How to resolve the migrant labour and *sannong* problem (i.e. 'three rural problems' of peasants, villages and agriculture) is now a focal point in the process of social development (Pun and Ku, 2011).

Rapid urbanisation became Chinese government's strategy to remedy the chasm between the rural and urban areas. The principal goal of this urbanisation was to gradually transform the rural migrant population into urban citizens, and thoroughly transfer the right to land and its management to the market. In other words, urbanisation will soon be brought into full throttle to complement the process of industrialisation. The curse which has been cast on to the migrant population will disappear in a blink of an eye, as they are granted liberating urban citizen status through urbanisation. To one author, this way of transforming a village into a city has become an effortless feat (Pun and Ku, 2011).

How can farmers live fulfilling, dignified and self-sufficient lives when land is rapidly encroached upon by capital? As China's agricultural reality suggests, the identity and spatial transformation that has accompanied the changes brought about by industrial and real estate capital cannot solve the *sannong* problem. On the contrary, the means of production for farmers' livelihoods may be lost and the basic protections of farmers further degraded (Ku, 2003, 2011).

Behind the expansion of industrial parks is the bitter life of migrant workers and peasants. Rural reconstruction and urbanisation, in the name of 'city and countryside integration', continue the miracle of transnational capital dominance. But this process has brought about the process of proletarianisation of farmers and migrant workers in China. Not only do they lose their community lives and connections to wider society, they are also placed in incredibly difficult living conditions. It is impossible for rural migrant workers to ensure employment and secure other forms of social security under such circumstances (Pun and Lu, 2010).

The process of urbanisation also renders people who depend on the land homeless and dispossessed. Furthermore, older farmers, stripped of their means of production and subsistence, do not have the opportunity to sell their labour power, since factories and other relocated manufacturing corporations refuse to hire them due to their age. The impenetrable alliance between industrial and real estate capital facilitates further land enclosures rather than truly unifying villages and cities. A mode of industrialisation that is not driven from the needs of rural communities or initiated by the farmers themselves can neither solve the *sannong* problem nor the predicaments of migrant workers. Instead, it further dismantles rural society, creating mass dislocation among farmers.

Capitalist development is not people centred and environment friendly, but instead relies on corporations and capital maximising profits as their sole goal, and ultimately creates disjunctions among other forms of local socio-economic development. Thus, this mode of production hampers social development and cannot resolve the deeply embedded contradictions of contemporary Chinese society. Worse, this market-driven development model has caused environmental crises in China.

The food-security crisis of China caused by unsustainable development has diminished China's farmland through a large number of land acquisitions, ecological restorations, agricultural structural adjustments, natural disasters, pollution and other issues. A significant amount of farmland was requisitioned and overexploited. There are increasingly fewer farmers. Many heavily polluting enterprises relocate to rural areas from big cities and discharge large amounts of industrial wastewater without treatment. This industrial waste threatens the safety of the drinking water, enters the food chain via irrigation, greatly reduces grain production and continuously reduces self-sufficiency rates. The food problem will not be solved if soil and water pollution are not eliminated. To end soil and water pollution, the state environmental supervision and inspection departments have to inspect polluting enterprises. However, the CCP's environmental protection department has not done anything regarding this during the past decade. By the end of 2013, an investigation by the Ministry of Land and Resource showed that about 3.33 million hectares of agricultural land are unusable due to heavy pollution (Duggan, 2014).

Participatory action research in a Chinese village

In 2001, Hok Bun Ku began a cross-disciplinary participatory action research project involving an anthropologist, agricultural specialist, natural scientist and social workers in a Zhuang ethnic minority village named Pingzhai which is located in the northeastern region of Yunnan Province in southwest China. Pingzhai has a 300-year history and is currently an administrative village, which comprises eight natural villages and covers an area of approximately 23 square kilometres. Its residents belong primarily to the Zhuang minority group and include some Han people from China's majority ethnic group. There is only one tractor-ploughed road connecting it to the outside world. According to the census carried out in 2000, the entire village contains 347 households comprised of both Zhuang and Han groups, and a population of 1469. Pingzhai was officially classified by the Chinese government as a 'poor' village because the villagers were unable to support themselves in meeting basic needs for food and clothing.

The project team's chosen method was participatory action research (PAR), which has been used by community workers to strengthen and support the capacity of communities to grow and change (Zuber-Skerritt, 1996; McTaggart, 1996). The primary goal of PAR is to create a more just society through transformative social change (Small, 1995; Park, 1993; Vickers, 2005; Reason and Hilary, 2008), and is consistent with the participatory coproduction approaches of green social work (Dominelli, 2012). Research is no longer seen solely as a means of creating knowledge; it is also a process of education, a development of consciousness, and a call to action (Small, 1995; Park, 1993, 1999; Reason and Hilary, 2008). The fundamental principles of PAR are: 1) participation wherein peasant/poor/marginalised people who are often regarded as 'knowers' and their knowledge and experiences respected; 2) researchers temper their own 'expert' status, while not dismissing their own specialist skills and do not presume to have a superior perspective; 3) the agency of participants is recognised and encouraged as integral to them and researchers; and 4) participants enter into a reciprocal relationship in the research process (Kesby, 2000: 424).

Guided by the action research method, the research team initiated by Hok Bun Ku used different skills at different stages to implement action and record the processes of engagement. To learn about the needs and assets of the community, the team employed participant observation, in-depth interviews, and asset mapping methods. Focus groups were used mainly to facilitate group discussions, explore ideas, and find strategies for action. When implementing community activities, participant observation and informal feedback were recorded as field notes. Sometimes public meetings were held to encourage participants to articulate and share their sentiments. In-depth interviews were also conducted with local officials, community leaders and selected representatives of various age groups (children, young people, adults and senior citizens). All members of the research team were required to keep notes and record their reflections in journals. Women from the community were also recruited and trained to help with data collection. One characteristic of action research is that data collection and analysis cannot be separated. The research team analysed data on an ongoing basis and had group discussions with the women's group at each stage to plan and consider actions. The data presented in the following section are based primarily on our field notes and journals.

In the first stage of action research – identifying problems, undertaking needs assessments, and employing the oral history method – the research team found that in villagers' life stories, many households in the village regularly suffered food shortages of four to six months yearly. The research team also discovered that many villagers, especially those living in mountainous areas where the soil is poor, had to pay exorbitant rates of interest on money borrowed to buy food. Additionally, many children in Pingzhai village were also denied educational opportunities because they could not afford to pay school fees. Without the green social work perspective developed by Lena Dominelli (2012), social work practitioners would have easily adopted the conventional view that the local government had attempted to combat poverty. For example, local officials had encouraged farmers to grow high-tech crops, engage in agricultural development in winter and make structural adjustments. However, the commercialisation of agriculture and its integration into the global capitalist market made these farmers more vulnerable, getting themselves deeper into financial hardship alongside losing their ethnic and cultural identities (Ku, 2011; Ku and Ip, 2011).

The project's research team also discovered that the mainstream agriculture development in the village was unsustainable in three respects: a) economic dependence; b) environmental degradation; and c) cultural loss:

a) *Economic dependence.* When farmers shift to producing commodity crop, they depend on the market to get high-yielding seeds, chemical fertilizers and pesticides that increase their production costs, especially when the market price of these production inputs rise every year. The monopoly of big capital, fluctuations of market price and exploitation by middle-men also make farmers' livelihoods unsustainable – high production costs versus low market prices for food crops.
b) *Environmental degradation.* The heavy use of chemical fertilizers, pesticides, weeding liquids and genetically modified seeds cause water and soil pollution which threaten food safety and people's health. Also, mass mono-crop production affects biodiversity.
c) *Cultural losses.* Culturally, farmers lose their traditional skills and confidence through the modernisation of agriculture. In this village, the most drastic change came from the local government's 'green revolution' initiatives. Driven by good intentions and conceptualised as a strategy to assist local farmers to generate more income and reduce poverty, the local government strongly encouraged villagers to switch from growing rice to growing ginger because ginger was able to fetch a much higher market price. Consequently, virgin forests were cleared for producing ginger, causing much ecological damage. Worse, the ginger market collapsed during the following year as there was an oversupply nationally. Prices dropped dramatically to a level where farmers could not even recoup production costs, let alone generate sufficient income to pay for food and basic daily expenses. In short, they were let down by the promises of the new market economy; made to feel that their traditional values and life skills were irrelevant; and having lost confidence in controlling their livelihoods in agricultural production, they also lost their self-esteem and cultural identity (Ku, 2011; Ku and Ip, 2011).

Food production and green social work practice

Green social work practice goes beyond the logic of capitalism and emphasises social justice, democracy and collectivism. It connects social work practice to fighting for environmental justice (Dominelli, 2012). When the team read Dominelli's work on green social work in 2012, we suddenly found our alternative rural social work practice which started in 2007 in China and echoed the emphasis in green social work of challenging capitalist models of industrialisation that treat the earth as a means to be exploited primarily to meet neoliberal industrialisation's end of producing profits for the few (Dominelli, 2012). These insights led to our green social work practice of encouraging villagers to return to organic farming, producing arts and crafts, using local resources for urban green consumption while simultaneously helping local people in generating additional income, preserving and revitalising their cultural pride and identity, protecting soil and seeds, fostering community participation, strengthening community life and cohesion, and buffering the corrosive forces of globalisation.

The predicament faced by the villagers first came to social workers' attention in 2002, but no project related to economic development or income generation was launched then. In 2006, inspired by the idea of social economy, the research team set up six essential objectives for the project: to search for alternative ways of development; reclaim food sovereignty; promote organic farming and green consumption; protect traditional peasant agriculture and rural environment; promote the idea of Community Supporting Agriculture (CSA); increase producers' income with equal exchange via fair trade; and promote cooperation between peasants and consumers to resist monopoly capital and exploitation.

For achieving these objectives in this rural setting, the social workers first had to foster community participation. The social workers organised villagers' group meetings to enable them to understand the importance and value (economic and cultural) of organic farming and traditional agricultural skills. After many years of planting hybrid rice with chemical fertilizers and pesticides, the villagers no longer believed in the feasibility of planting traditional rice. As transformation of the villagers' consciousness was critical for this project, the research team invited an agricultural scientist to train the villagers and convinced them to do the experiments. At the beginning, only three households were willing to try. Because they had already lost their traditional seeds, social workers and villagers went to remote mountain villages to search for traditional rice seed. Finally, 12 kinds of old seed were found and the old villagers certified that *xiangmi, hongyou, babao, hongmi* and *heinuomi* were the traditional seeds of Pingzhai village. In 2007, these three households used one *mu* of farmland to experiment with organic rice planting. They adopted their traditional way of farming including seeding, irrigating and ploughing the field, and harvesting. These villagers totally replaced the chemical fertilizers and pesticides with farmyard manure and natural pesticides which were made by using different types of herbs. The young villagers interviewed old farmers and learned the local knowledge of preventing and controlling insect pests of rice. Together, they produced natural pesticides by using herbal medicine and other natural materials. They also tried different ecological forms of production, like raising ducks in paddy fields because ducks could kill insect pests and weeds, and their dung provided manure for the paddy field.

After several years of returning to organic farming, the research team found that soil fertility level was greatly enhanced by the long-term addition of local farmyard manure. Evidence of returned fertility to the land was that the four-leafed grass was growing in fields again. The old villagers explained that only fertile fields grew four-leafed grass which had disappeared after using a lot of chemical fertilizers and pesticides. Its reappearance meant organic farming practices had restored land fertility.

To help producers promote organic rice at fair prices in urban areas, the research team went to the city to connect them with consumers whose consciousness of food security was high. Collaborating with a local university, the project team met members of the property management company and house-owner committee in a middle-class housing estate in Kunming city. Natural scientists from a local NGO were invited to give public health talks on the harm caused by food pesticide residues. As Chinese consumers paid more and more attention to food safety, these talks raised consumers' consciousness of green consumption. After the rice harvest, the next important step was to promote the idea of fair trade and connect rural villages with urban communities to rebuild cooperative relationships between producers and consumers. To promote mutual understanding and create a fair-trade relationship, social workers organised exchange meetings between urban consumers and villagers. The urban residents came to taste the organic rice and set the price together with the farmers. Following the principle of fair trade, the price needed to be fair to the producers (Zhang, Yeung and Ku, 2008). At the beginning when consumers found the price was triple that of the market price of non-organic rice, they showed their disagreement. It was a normal consumer reaction because they had never before participated in the price-setting process. They had no idea about the unfair practices of mainstream markets. The authors concluded that fair trade is important for this initiative because it changes the unfair practice of the mainstream market economy. It rebuilt cooperative relationships between producers and consumers. Social workers invited village representatives, introduced labour-intensive processes of rice production and explained how consumers could calculate the price to include their actual labour input in production. This promoted mutual understanding between producers and consumers. After listening to the villagers' explanations, some older urban residents empathised with the villagers and claimed that the price was fair because they had participated in the movement of 'up to mountain, down to village' (*shangshan xiaxiang*) during Mao's period and knew the rural situation well. They knew the practice of planting rice, supported the price set and convinced other urban consumers to follow this path. The process revealed a transparent and democratic practice within the social economy.

The experiment's first year was very successful and all the organic rice was sold out within one month. This strongly motivated other villager households to participate in organic farming. In July 2009, the production cooperative was formally registered. Fourteen households joined the cooperative. In 2014, the cooperative had expanded to 50 households and the total area of production reached 150 *mu*.

For sustaining the consumer network, social workers invited urban residents to participate in a harvest festival organised by the rural cooperative and visit the land that produced the rice they consumed. Urban residents' purchases not only supported the agriculture development, but also benefitted from safe food. The urban residents had become friends of the villagers and accidentally became the quality controllers of rice production as they frequently visited the village. This provided the basis for a rural–urban alliance that protected the interests of both groups – income generation and retaining traditional agricultural skills for the villagers, and food security for the urban residents.

Conclusion

In the authors' view, no matter whether in China or the world, economic development must return to society and gradually shift away from a market-driven development to a people-centred and environment-friendly development. Instead of allowing capital to intrude freely into rural society, commodifying farmland and subsequently dispossessing agricultural producers/rural residents from their means of production and livelihoods, a pluralistic green economic model, which takes into account the realities of rural areas and builds upon the foundations of rural society alongside the food needs of urban residents, must be promoted and implemented in the process of rural development. This case demonstrates the possibility of green social work in responding to agricultural crisis and food safety. In contrast with the market economy, green social workers promote the social economy which is people-centred, community-based, cooperative, and democratic, as well as being defined by harmony between people and the environment, and providing a societal system in which production is not for commodified consumption but for servicing the needs of the people (Dominelli, 2012).

This case also demonstrates that green social work practice includes macro-critiques of the structural causes of environmental crises and micro-interventions in responding to these crises. The social economy is an important social theory that can guide green social work practice. It helps to understand that the problem of market-driven development lies in its inevitable domination by capital, commodification of people and land, and the destruction of society and the environment (Dominelli, 2012). It also envisions an alternative economic development which embeds the economy within sustainable social relations. It is pluralistic, bottom-up, democratic, non-monopolistic, and truly prioritises the developmental needs of communities and individuals while respecting the environment. Cooperatives of producers and consumers, social enterprises, fair trade, a community economy, and a collective economy are all concrete examples of the social economy in practice because it intervenes to protect the environment and enhance people's well-being by integrating people and their socio-cultural, economic and physical environments within an egalitarian framework that addresses prevailing structural inequalities and unequal distribution of power and resources (Wright, 2006).

The model of rural–urban alliance constructed through ongoing experimentation and participatory action research in a Yunnan village proves it is an effective model of green social work which connects producer and consumer through the CSA and fair-trade network to tackle the crisis in food security. This case has implications for government policy and sustainable agricultural development. After 30 years of the planned economy and another 30 years of the market economy, China is facing the huge simultaneous pressures of developing economically and socially. The rural–urban alliance and CSA could be a new route for China's sustainable development which will change the pathway of forms of economic development that cause inequality and undermine people's livelihoods, and provide for the holistic, resilient, sustainable future green social workers advocate.

Acknowledgement

The research was funded by Hong Kong Research and Grants Council (Project No. B-Q39N). Acknowledgement is also given to Li and Fung Foundation's financial support for our social economy research in mainland China.

References

BBC. (2015). *Five ways China's economic crisis will affect Africa*, August 27. Available on www.bbc.com/news/world-africa-34060934 [Accessed 28 January 2016].

China Daily. (2013). *2013 China central economic work conference*, December 16. Available on www.chinadaily.com.cn/bizchina/2013-12/13/content_17173591.htm

China Soybean Industry Association. (CSIA) (2014). *Dadou chanye jiance yujing baogao [The report of Soybean Industry]*. Beijing: China Soybean Industry Association.

Global Post. (2014). *Good news: US export to China soar, setting a new record*, January 21. Available on www.globalpost.com/dispatch/news/regions/asia-pacific/china/140120/good-news-us-exports-chinasoar-setting-new-record [Accessed 13 May 2015].

Dominelli, L. (2012). *Green social work: From environmental crises to environmental justice*. Cambridge: Polity Press.

Dominelli, L. and Ku, H. B. (2017). Green social work and its implication for China's social development. *China Journal of Social Work*, 10(1): 3–22.

Duggan, J. (2014). China could lose millions of hectares of farmland to pollution. *The Guardian*, January 23. Available on www.theguardian.com/environment/2014/jan/23/china-lose-millions-hectares-farmland-pollution [Accessed 12 November 2014].

Ghose, B. (2014). Food security and food self-sufficiency in China: from past to 2050. *Food and Energy Security*. Available on http://onlinelibrary.wiley.com/doi/10.1002/fes3.48/full [Accessed 26 Nov 2016].

Guo, Y. (2012). Guochan dadou chanyelian chu zai bengkui de bianyuan' [Domestic soybean industry is on the brink of collapse]. *Zhongguo shangbao (China Business Newspaper)*, July 4. Available on www.caas.cn/nykjxx/fxyc/64560.shtml [Accessed 12 November 2014].

Kesby, M. (2000). Participatory diagramming: Deploying qualitative methods through an action research epistemology. *Area*, 32(4): 423–435.

Ku, H. B. (2003). *Moral politics in a South Chinese village: Responsibility, reciprocity and resistance*. Lanham, MD: Rowman and Littlefield Publishers.

Ku, H. B. (2011). 'Happiness being like a blooming flower': An action research of rural social work in an ethnic minority community of Yunnan Province, PRC. *Action Research Journal*, 9(4): 344–369.

Ku, H. B. and Ip, D. (2011). Designing development: A case study of community economy in Pingzhai, Yunnan Province, in PRC. *China Journal of Social Work*, 4(3): 235–254.

Liu, P. and Ma, L. (2016). Food scandals, media exposure, and citizens' safety concerns: A multilevel analysis across Chinese cities. *Food Policy*, 63: 102–111.

McTaggart, R. (1996). Issues for Participatory action researchers. In O. Zuber-Skerritt (Ed.), *New directions in action research* (pp. 243–256). London: The Falmer Press.

Neamtan, N. (2010). The solidarity economy, state organization and political power. E. Kawano, T. N. Mastersonand and J. Teller-Elsberg (Eds.). *Solidarity economy I: Building alternatives for people and planet*. Amherst, MA: Center for Popular Economics.

NTD TV (2014). *Food security crisis is imminent*, January 22. Available on www.ntdtv.com/xtr/b5/2014/01/22/atext1048521.html [Accessed 13 May 2015].

Oliveira, de L. T. Gustavo. (2015). The geopolitics of Brazilian soybeans. *The Journal of Peasant Studies*, 43(2): 1–25.

Oliveira, de L. T. Gustavo and Schneider, M. (2014). *The politics of flexing soybeans in China and Brazil*. Transnational Institute (TNI), Think Piece Series on Flex Crops and Commodities, No. 3.

Park, P. (1993). What is participatory research? A theoretical and methodological perspective. In P. Park, M. Brydon-Miller, B. Hall et al. (ed.), *Voices of Change: Participatory research in the United States and Canada* (pp. 1–20). Westport, CT: Bergin B Garvey.

Park, P. (1999). People, knowledge, and change in participatory research. *Management Learning*, 30(2): 141–157.

Pun, N. and Ku, H. B. (2011). China at the crossroads: Social economy as the new way of development. *China Journal of Social Work*, 4(3): 197–201.

Pun, N. and Lu, H. (2010). Unfinished proletarianization: Self, anger and class action of the second generation of peasant-workers in reform China. *Modern China*, 36(5): 493–519.

Reason, P. and Hilary, B. (2008). *The Sage handbook of action research: Participative inquiry and practice*. London: Sage.

Science Daily. (2012). USDA: *Ongoing drought causes significant crop yield declines*. August 10. Available on www.sciencedaily.com/releases/2012/08/120810140603.htm [Accessed 10 May 2014].

Small, S. A. (1995). Action-oriented research: Models and methods. *Journal of Marriage and Family*, 57(4): 941–955.

The Economic Times. (2013). China's grain output rises for 10th consecutive year, November 29. Available on http://economictimes.indiatimes.com/news/international/business/chinas-grain-output-rises-for-10th-consecutive-year/articleshow/26587012.cms. [Accessed 13 May 2015].

Vickers, M. (2005). Action research to improve the human condition: An insider-outsider and a multi-methodology design for actionable knowledge outcomes. *International Journal of Action Research*, 1(2): 190–218.

Wang, S. (2013). Dadou de gushi: ziben ruhe weiji renlei anquan [The story of Soybeans: How capital endangers human security]. *Kaifang Shidai [Open Times]*, 3: 87–108.

Wang, K. and Li, F. (2000). Woguo yesheng dadou (G. soja) zhongzhi ziyuan jiqi zhongzhi chuangxin liyong [The germplasm resources of China's wild Soybean G. Soja and their developing utilization]. *Zhongguo Nongye Keji Daobao [Journal of China's Agricultural Science and Technology]*, 2(6): 69–72.

Wright, E. O. (2006). Compass points: Towards a socialist alternative. *New Left Review*, 41: 93–124, September–October.

Yan, H., Chen, Y., Ku, H. B. (2016). China's Soybean crisis: The logic of modernization and its discontents. *The Journal of Peasant Studies*, 43(2): 373–395.

Yuan, L. (2014). Zhongguo zuidade yi wufabi' [China's biggest disaster cannot be avoided], *Tianya Luntan (Tianya Forum)*. Availble on http://bbs.tianya.cn/post-free-4051916-1.shtml [Accessed 12 November 2014].

Zhang, J. (2011). China's success in increasing per capita food production. *Journal of Experimental Botany*, 62(11): 3707–3711.

Zhang, H., Yeung, S. C. and Ku, H. B. (2008). Strength perspective in rural social work: A practical model of capacity and assets building in rural China. *Sociological Studies*, 6: 174–193.

Zhou, L. (2014). Nongqi he xiaonong de jingzheng: zai tan dadou weiji' [Competition between agribusiness and small peasants: Further discussion of soybean crisis], *Jingji Daokan (Economic Herald)*, 12. Available on www.shiwuzq.com/food/rights/producer/2015/0126/1277.html [Accessed 12 November 2014].

Zuber-Skerritt, O. (1996). Emancipatory Action Research for Organizational Change and Management Development. In O. Zuber-Skerritt (Ed.), *New directions in action research*. London: The Falmer Press, pp. 83–105.

Part V
(Hu)man-made disasters

18
Environmental issues and controversies in Latin America
A challenge for social work

Nilsa Burgos Ortiz

Introduction

The complexities of the debates around environmental issues are well known around the world, and Latin America is not an exception. In grassroots world conferences and global organisations such as the United Nations (UN) and its associated agencies, discussions about disasters have led to declarations and treaties. The Stockholm and Rio Declarations are the results of the first and second global environmental conferences. These are, respectively, the United Nations Conference on the Human Environment in Stockholm, 5–16 June 1972, and the United Nations Conference on Environment and Development (UNCED) in Rio de Janeiro, 3–14 June 1992 (Handl, 2012). Adopted 20 years apart, they represent major milestones in the evolution of international environmental law, bracketing what has been called the modern era of international environmental law (Handl, 2012). This author considers that the most important provisions of both declarations related to the prevention of environmental harm. The other major World Conference was held in Johannesburg on Sustainable Development, where the commitment to sustainable development and to build a humane, equitable and caring global society, cognisant of the need for human dignity for all was reaffirmed (United Nations, 2002). The UN celebrated another conference on sustainable development, Rio + 20, at Rio de Janeiro, Brazil on June 2012. The document resulted from the conference contained clear and practical measures for implementing sustainable development for 20 years (United Nations, 2012).

One of the most significant decisions in a recent forum of Latin American and Caribbean ministers of the environment was the *Initiative for Sustainable Development: Moving together Towards a Sustainable Future* (Oficina Regional para América Latina y el Caribe, 2016). The Latin American and Caribbean region also follows a strategy for the promotion of public participation in sectors; the sharing of responsibility between governments and civilian society; access to different levels of government; access to information, political process and the justice system; transparency; and respect for the contributions of the public (Comisión Económica para América Latina y el Caribe, 2016a). Sustainable development must take into consideration regional disaster risk reduction. For Narváez et al. (2009), this involves actions and measures in an organised way that society applies to avoid or impede the construction of the risk for disaster, and for the reduction or control in case that it is already there. These authors added that it also means the ability to respond in an event of danger, to recuperate when it has occurred and to work for the reconstruction of the affected areas (Narváez, et al., 2009). In other words, the disaster risk reduction is an integral strategy of sustainable development.

The analysis of environmental issues involves multiple social, economic and political factors. Some of the controversies are related to the economic interests of big companies versus the safety and health of people, especially the poorest. Evidently the greater the profits obtained by these companies, the more influence they exert on governments to be on their side. On the other hand, sustainable development emphasises economic development in harmony with the protection of the environment.

In the present chapter, I will refer to environmental disasters and the struggles of people to defend their families, land and homes in Latin America. Specific recent examples will be given of disasters and other environmental issues in the region. The Latin American mass media reported that defence of the land by Lenca, one of the indigenous groups from the Honduras, has led to the assassination of hundreds of environmental activists. The earthquake in Ecuador had terrible effects for people, especially poor people. Hurricane 'Otto' devastated areas of Costa Rica, Nicaragua and Panamá. The profession of social work should approach these situations from a perspective of human rights and social justice. All individuals have the right to live in a safe environment. Although in Latin America the concept of green social work is not generally used, the environmental community work is consistent with Dominelli's definition of green social work, particularly to the interactions between socio-economic and physical environmental crisis (Dominelli, 2012, n.d.).

Participatory action research, an important strategy in green social work, has been used in the region in order to understand environmental issues and look for alternatives to confront the problems. Social workers should accompany community groups in their decisions to defend their environmental and other rights. The participation of social work organisations in the formulation and evaluation of social policies must be a priority of green social workers. Some traditional social work techniques such as education and prevention may be used with the participation of the people affected by environmental problem to co-devise solutions they feel they can own, as advocated by green social work (Dominelli, 2012).

This project considered here started in 2005 as a research project of two professors (Araya Jarquín y Cerdas Guntanis, 2008). The University of Costa Rica requires 300 hours of community work from all students (Portal de Vicerrectoría de Acción Social, n.d.). The University Community Work Project in seven communities at Cachi involves students and professors of different university departments (including social work), representatives of the community and government institutions (Universidad de Costa Rica, Escuela de Trabajo Social, 2013). The students learn about strategies for the reduction of disaster risk and actively participate in the community decisions (Universidad de Costa Rica, Escuela de Trabajo Social, 2013). This model, like green social work, may be applied in social work supervised practice in community environmental work.

Social movements

Contemporary theoretical social work perspectives view social movements as a central concept for social action (De Garza Talavera, 2011). In Latin America, many of the social movements have been related to resistance to neoliberal reforms, questioning institutional policies influenced by growing participatory ideologies, the utilisation of non-institutional forms of political participation and politicisation of issues traditionally considered moral or economic topics (De Garza Talavera, 2011). In many instances, social movements have occurred spontaneously in a crisis or as a response to a reality of oppression or injustice. The intention to privatise or reform public services has been a main reason for the rise of some social movements. That was the case of the proposed reform of the Costa Rican Electricity Institute (ICE, in Spanish), a state institution that controlled the telephone and electricity services. According to Menjivar Ochoa (2012), the presence of a variety of social actors with a common objective, the non-hierarchical coordination, and the diversity of decision-making centres, were ingredients that strengthened citizen participation during the period.

Important social movements may be described at the beginning of the 1990s. Amin and Houtart (2009) considered the opposition to the North American Free Trade Agreement (NAFTA) signed by the United States (US), Canada and Mexico with the intention of generalising its provisions to the whole American Continent to be a big step in the formation of social movements. These authors understood that this agreement was a threat of the integration and subordination of the continent to the US economy (Amin and Houtart, 2009). More than 50,000 persons protested against this free trade deal (ALCA, in Spanish) during the closing of the World Social Forum (WSF) celebrated in Porto Alegre, Brazil in 2002. The WSF is the largest gathering of civil society to find solutions for problems that started in 2001 in Brazil and brought together in each of its events tens of thousands of participants in more than a thousand activities; for example, workshops, conferences, and artistic performances on various themes including the social, solidarity, economy, environment, human rights, and democratisation (World Social Forum, 2016).

Another social movement present in Latin America is the peace movement. The mass media in Colombia reported for many years the killings of people, innocent peasants defending their cultivated lands in the rural areas. Wars constitute a menace for environmental safety (Dominelli, 2012). Widespread concern about these environmental effects began during the Vietnam War when the US military sprayed 79 million litres of herbicides and defoliants over about one-seventh of the land area of southern Vietnam (Worldwatch Institute, 2017). The United Nations Environment Programme (2009), in several studies, has found that armed conflict causes significant harm and leads to environmental risks that can threaten people's health, livelihoods and safety. The peace movement, prominent in Colombia, organised in 1997. It has promoted the permanence of communities, strengthened collective participation and the defence of rights, coordinated humanitarian help for the victims, among other objectives (Movimiento por la Paz, n.d.). Finally, a peace agreement was signed in Cuba by representatives of the Colombian government and the guerrilla armed forces.

The women's movement is another social movement in Latin America. The movement comprised women of diverse characteristics and backgrounds including feminists, indigenous peoples, black minority peoples, ethnic groups, lesbians, women with disabilities. The goals of their struggles varied from political, economic, human rights, justice, environmental issues and initiatives against violence. The movement of the mothers and grandmothers of Plaza de Mayo, a very important square in Buenos Aires, Argentina where all kinds of protests are celebrated, was related to the disappearance of sons, daughters and grandchildren caused by the dictatorship in Argentina. Their denunciation of all kinds of violence against women united women of different characteristics. The feminists were the first ones to make public intimate partnership violence which had originally been considered a private matter. Women organised marches and rallies, as well as used all kinds of mass media (newspapers, electronic networks, newsletters, TV, radio) to obtain justice and the approval of laws to protect women. The majority of Latin American countries have at least one law against intimate partnership violence. This movement also has joined forces for specific struggles related to the environment.

The participation of women in environmental social movements focus their struggles on the defence of water, land and air, mainly to safeguard these common goods from the deleterious effects of the productive model that exploits the environment. It aims to stop the State or force the State to formulate or make laws for the protection of the environment. Examples of those environmental movements are: Latin America Network of Women Defenders of Social and Environmental Rights (Red Latinoamericana de Mujeres Defensoras de Derechos Sociales y Ambientales), Censat Agua Viva in Colombia (an organisation that defends water, land, climate justice, food sovereignty) and ACKnowl-EJ (Academic-Activist Co-Production of Knowledge for Environmental Justice). Those organisations want to make visible the role of Latin American women in the defence of their territories and resistance strategies (Red Latinoamericana de Mujeres Defensoras de los Derechos Sociales y Ambientales, 2017).

Silva (2010) affirmed that environmental movements in Latin America, especially in Brazil, wanted the State to approve policies for a healthy habitat and encourage ecologically sustainable practices (Silva, 2010). Pollution of the water, soil and air; the increasing deterioration of the quality of life; the uncontrolled exploitation of natural resources; and ecological disasters have made ecology a main concern of non-governmental organisations and popular movements, including indigenous movements and women's movements. In Brazil, the ideology of sustainable development gained prominence in the proposals of various sectors of society that mobilised around the challenge of making compatible economic development and sustainable environment (Silva, 2010). Poor people are victims of the waste of natural resources in the search to satisfy their immediate needs, and since they are more numerous, they use more intensively the natural resources (Silva, 2010). In Costa Rica the environmental social movement established the Green Ecological Party (Partido Verde Ecologista Costa Rica). Its purpose is to attain respect for environmental laws and the protection of all ecological wealth. Nevertheless, the Green Ecological Party does not have representation in the Legislative Assembly of the Costa Rican government.

Illustrative environmental cases

The newspapers of Latin America are full of stories of abuse of power against people, especially poor people, who defend their small portion of land or their access to water. One of these stories started in 2013 when the people of Río Blanco in western Honduras awoke to a group of armed security guards blocking their access to the nearby river, where the indigenous Lenca people have lived for generations. The security forces belonged to a Honduran energy company that had received a concession to build a dam on the river (Fendt, 2016). Berta Cáceres, a Lenca defender of the environment and the rights of the indigenous people and recipient of several awards including the Goldman Environmental Award and Champion of the Earth, fought against the construction of a dam in the riverbed. The United Nations Environmental Programme in Panama included in a newsletter that Berta's assassination was one among more than 100 environmental activists killed after a 2009 coup in Honduras (Programa de las Naciones Unidas para el Medioambiente, 2016). This murder, in particular, has drawn heavy media attention, spurring protests in Honduras, and was denounced in Latin America. For instance, the Latin American Association of Education and Research in Social Work (ALAEITS in Spanish), the IFSW of the Latin American Region and a Committee of Social Work Associations in Latin America and the Caribbean (COLACATS in Spanish) produced a joint statement against the murders of environmental activists in Honduras. The Latin international human rights organisations and activists in Honduras are pressuring the government to allow an independent investigation into this murder (Fendt, 2016). The year 2015 was the worst on record for the killing of environmentalists who defended the land and people struggling to protect their land, forests and rivers through peaceful actions, against mounting odds (*Global Witness*, 2016). From 2010–2015, these killings rose to 207 in Brazil, 109 in Honduras, 105 in Colombia and 50 in Peru (*Global Witness*, 2016). Furthermore, according to the findings of *Global Witness*, the criminalisation of land defenders is extremely common in Latin America, especially in Central America. *Global Witness* (2017) reported that widespread corruption allowing business and political elites to impose mining, hydropower and other industries on rural communities with impunity means dissent can be silenced violently without consequence.

Natural disasters like earthquakes are another type of environmental disaster. The earthquake that happened in Ecuador in April 2016 caused 655 deaths, injured 12,492 people and left a lot of people missing (*Earthquake Report*, 2016). The solidarity of people from non-damaged provinces in Ecuador, countries in South America and international help from the UN and the International Federation of the Red Cross and Red Crescent Societies (IFRC) were crucial in addressing the aftermath of the earthquake. Help given was massive, including workers of different occupations and professions; donations covered money, food, clothes, medicines and water. Authorities had set up various shelters in six provinces to accommodate people who had lost their houses or had houses with structural damage (Earthquake Report, 2016). The main fiscal implications of this natural disaster consist of changes to budget items and the establishment of legally binding solidarity contributions (Comisión Económica para América Latina y el Caribe, 2016b). For green social workers, these actions constitute a demonstration of the interactions between socio-economic and physical environmental crisis.

The results of research about natural disasters conducted in Latin America by the Economic Commission for Latin America and the Caribbean (CEPAL, in Spanish) found that the damage to goods and services cease to be provided during a period of time that begins almost immediately after the disaster and can extend into the rehabilitation and reconstruction phases (CEPAL, 2002). Disasters also have major indirect effects which cause 'intangible' damage or benefits. Damage might include human suffering, insecurity, effects on national security, and many other factors which have an impact on well-being and the quality of life. Some benefits are feelings of pride at the way in which authorities have dealt with the consequences of the disasters, solidarity and altruistic involvement (CEPAL, 2002). The majority of disaster victims in developing countries, where poverty and population pressures force growing numbers of people to live in harm's way – on floodplains, in earthquake-prone zones and on unstable hillsides – make them vulnerable to the consequences of and damage caused by disasters (CEPAL, 2002).

Hurricanes and storms constitute natural disasters, most common in Central America and the Caribbean. Unlike earthquakes, these phenomena give some time for preparation. Responses depend on the agencies in charge; on the analysis of weather; and the economic, social, political, physical and psychological levels of vulnerability among people. Poverty, housing conditions, health conditions, community organisation, government agencies' responses and preparation of people are some of the factors to be taken into consideration in the analysis of the effects from a passing hurricane or storm. This natural disaster may bring strong winds and a lot of rain that may end in floods. Bradshaw (2004) explained that a gendered approach is very important because women are invisible in emergency and reconstruction situations due to their exclusion from relief and assistance projects. The failure to take into account the range of activities that women undertake, or their triple roles – reproductive work, productive work, and community work – translates into an absence of recognition of women beyond their role as mothers and housewives (Bradshaw, 2004). Different newspapers reported that Hurricane Otto had claimed several lives, injured dozens and damaged property in Costa Rica, Nicaragua and Panamá. Videos of the ravaged regions showed flooding and mud-covered houses, many of which had lost their roofs. Nearly 1,200 houses were damaged and dams, bridges and roads were also destroyed (Hurricane Otto, 2016).

After Hurricane Mitch, which affected Central America, especially Honduras, in 1998, a disaster risk reduction management initiative was started by the State with a vision that its development would undertake actions that could help to reduce the impacts of disasters (Elvir and Kawas, 2011). Researchers in the Honduran Autonomous University found the focus of this risk reduction management strategy was in mitigation measures, not in prevention. However, important information was gathered about the country not having the capacity to provide needed responses to moderate and high levels of disaster risk reduction management (Elvir and Kawas, 2011). In Ecuador, there is a law that established a national system that explains the objectives of risk reduction management (Cajas Albán, 2010). But laws are meaningless without the involvement of well-informed people and the institutions in charge capable of making available these resources to communities.

Pollution is another environmental problem observed in the Latin American region. A specific example, in Puerto Rico, is in the municipality of Peñuelas, in the southern coast of the island where protests are building over the disposal of toxic coal ash in landfills. In the struggle over coal ash disposal, poor communities are being forced to sacrifice their health and the health of their environment to support the island's energy-intensive economy and lifestyle. The company established in Puerto Rico is a subsidiary of the Advançion Energy Storage (AES) Corporation, a Fortune 200 global power company in the US (AES home page, n.d.). According to their home page, the company supports a sustainable social, economic and environmental future. However, the company is doing the opposite on this island. The executives of the company expressed in a TV interview that coal ash is not dangerous to the environment or to the health of people, and that the company obtained all the permissions. However, Physicians for Social Responsibility (n.d.) concluded that coal ash is dangerously toxic and poses a threat to human health. Furthermore, the organisation Earth Justice (n.d.) expressed the view that coal ash is filled with toxic levels of multiple pollutants such as arsenic, mercury and lead.

Puerto Rico is a territory of the US, with limited political or economic influence that made the population vulnerable to exploitation by corporations like AES. Nevertheless, people in Peñuelas recognise that landfilling coal ash threatens the resources that they depend upon. Small-scale protests began in 2014, but opposition has grown since. Last December, the demonstration drew an estimated 1,000 people from the town and different parts of the island. All Puerto Rican mass media reported that protesters have been routinely harassed by police and arrested.

Implications for green social work

Social workers should examine the issues of the environment from their complexities. The profession should be in position to learn from the good results of other countries in confronting and preventing disasters. It is important to point out that the concept of green social work defined by Dominelli (2012) is coherent with some of the environmental work done by social workers in Latin America. For instance, Silva (2010) states that social work should be integrated to an environmental culture in the institutions or organisations where it is present. In particular, social work should participate in an environmental education that incorporates sustainable development and environmental protection. The social work curriculum must include topics on environmental protection, natural disasters and forms of confronting the disaster's consequences. The experience of the University of Costa Rica included not only content, but also visits to one of the areas affected by Hurricane Otto (Personal communication with a professor of University of Costa Rica, San Ramón Campus in December 2016).

The profession of social work has demonstrated the important role of prevention in many areas. Environmental protection is one of these. Education and prevention are fundamental to confronting environmental problems and for the reduction or management of disaster risk. Two social work professors at the University of Costa Rica had a project on disaster risk reduction. They worked with diverse actors in a poor community using a human rights perspective (Araya Jarquín y Cerdas Guntanis, 2008). The project had important results in understanding the vulnerable areas of the community and the elaboration of a map with the different risks zones such as faults, water sources and levels of the land. The participants also learned to recognise their own abilities and capacity of negotiation, to demand human rights, and fulfil citizenship rights and duties (Araya Jarquín y Cerdas Guntanis, 2008).

Access to environmental information, complete and clear, is essential to everybody. Social workers have the responsibility to obtain the correct information about natural disasters from experts and translate them for community use (Dominelli, 2012). Prevention in the environment may comprise constituting alliances with different community actors for joint work, teamwork and the organisation of social networks to defend the environment. Some Social Work Codes of Ethics make reference to the environment. For instance, the code of Chile promotes the environmental sustainability (Colegio de Trabajadores Sociales de Chile, 2014). Another example is the code of Colombia that establishes social workers respect for the legal dispositions that guarantee the preservation of the environment, territorial identity and the prevention of the effects of disasters (Consejo Nacional de Trabajo Social, 2002). Other countries should include in their codes the commitment to the protection of the environment, sustainable development, and the mitigation and prevention of disasters, including climate change.

Social workers might be activists in denouncing any harm to the environment, including the problem of garbage and pollution. A representation of this activism is the participation of Puerto Rican social workers in demonstrations against the disposal of toxic coal ash. Activism is not the only form of participation. Our profession as a collective has the capacity to collaborate in the formulation of social policies in the areas of health and environment, particularly around needs identified by communities that will help in the protection of natural resources and the environment. For specific proposed laws, lobbying might be required in coordination with other professionals and community groups. When conflict arises, mediation may be an appropriate technique. The United Nations Environmental Programme (2015: 11) defines mediation 'as a non-adversarial and collaborative process through which an impartial third party helps parties in a dispute reach a resolution through interest-based negotiations'. In cases requiring sophisticated knowledge, social workers might facilitate the identification of mediators.

Research is one of the tools that social workers are able to perform as academics and professionals providing direct services. An example is the elaboration of a questionnaire by Ecuadorian social workers for the purpose of exploring the most important needs after the earthquake (Personal communication with a social worker of Esmeralda, January 2017). In communities, it is advisable to engage in the collection of experiences during recuperation from disasters and in successful prevention measures. Participatory action research is a strategy used by social workers in understanding environmental issues and in looking for solutions, as advised in green social work. An example is a Colombian social worker in her environmental work. Izasa (2016) reported an environmental agenda for peace in which several organisations worked collectively towards the management of biodiversity, natural ecosystems and cultural patrimony.

As professionals committed to justice, autonomy, democracy and the defence of human rights, social workers are against the violence of the State and big companies. The knowledge of the means for citizen participation is relevant in the defence of the right to live in a healthy environment. Latin American social workers' organisations support the struggles of indigenous people to defend their land, access to water, natural resources and the integrity of their communities. As social workers, we should accompany people in their confrontation of social inequalities that are noticeable within neoliberal policies and globalisation. Social workers should also work for the protection and preservation of the environment facing the economic interests of international and multinational enterprises. As Berta Cáceres said in her acceptance speech at the 2015 Goldman Prize Ceremony, 'mother earth, where basic rights are systematically violated demands that we take action' (Goldman Environmental Prize, 2015). Green social workers concur.

References

AES Home Page (n.d.). Available at www.aes.com [Accessed 30 January 2017].
Amin, S., and Houtart, F. (2009). América Latina. In Elisabete Borgianni and Carlos Montaño (Orgs.), *Coyuntura actual, Latinoamericana y Mundial: Tendencias y movimientos* (p. 354–378). Brasil: Cortes Editora.
Araya Jarquín, M. and Cerdas Guntanis, L. (2008). *Serie Atlantea 4 Política Social y Trabajo Social, Comunidades y políticas sociales, entre la academia y la práctica cotidiana* (N. M. Burgos Ortiz y J. B. Nazario, Eds.). San Juan: Proyecto Atlantea, Universidad de Puerto Rico.
Bradshaw, S. (2004). *Socio-economic impacts of natural disasters: A gender analysis.* Chile: CEPAL.
Cajas Albán, M. L. (2010). *La incorporación de la gestión de riesgos como una Política de desarrollo en el quehacer institucional público, el caso del Ecuador.* Quito: CLACSO Sede Ecuador.
Colegio de Trabajadores Sociales de Chile (2014). *Código de Ética.* Santiago de Chile: Autor.
Consejo Nacional de Trabajo Social (2002). *Código de Ética Profesional de los Trabajadores Sociales en Colombia.* Colombia: Grupo Editorial Ibañez.
Comisión Económica para América Latina y el Caribe (CEPAL) (2016a). *Sociedad, derechos y medio ambiente.* Chile, Autor.
Comisión Económica para América Latina y el Caribe (CEPAL) (2016b) *Estudio económico de América Latina y el Caribe.* Chile: Autor.
De Garza Talavera, R. (2011). Las teorias de los movimientos sociales y el enfoque multidimensional. *Estudios Politicos* (Mexico). Available on www.scielo.org.mxIn [Accessed 21 January 2017].
Dominelli, L. (2012). *Green social work.* Cambridge: Polity Press.
Dominelli, L. (n.d.). *Green social work and environmental justice in an environmentally degraded, unjust world.* Available on www.ulapland.fi/loader.aspx7id=738c09c1-fa9b-4475 [Accessed 28 May 2017].
Earth Justice (n.d.). *The coal ash problem.* Available on earthjustice.org/features/the-coal-ash-problem [Accessed 28 May 2017].
Earthquake Report (2016). Available on earthquake-report.com [Accessed 25 January 2017].
Economic Commission for Latina America and the Caribbean (2002). *Manual for estimating the socioeconomic effects of natural disasters.* Available on www.cepal.org/publications [Accessed 27 January 2017].
Elvir, O. and Kawas, N. (2011). *Ruta de la gestión para la reducción del riesgo de desastres en Honduras.* Honduras: Universidad Nacional Autónoma de Honduras.
Fendt, L. (2016). In Latin America, environmentalists are an endangered species. *Latin American Perspectives.* Political Report #1173. Available on lap@ucr.edu [Accessed 26 January 2017].
Global Witness (2016). *On dangerous ground,* June 20. Available on www.globalwitness.org [Accessed 26 January 2017].
Global Witness (2017). *Exposing corruption and environmental abuse,* April 7. Available on www.globalwitness.org [Accessed 21 May 2017].
Goldman Environmental Prize (2015). *Berta Cáceres acceptance speech.* Available on www.youtube.com [Accessed 29 May 2017].
Handl, G. (2012). *Declaration of the United Nations Conference on the Human Environment (Stockholm Declaration), 1972 and the Rio Declaration on Environment and Development, 1992.* United Nations. Available at www.un.org/law/avl [Accessed 23 January 2017].
Hurricane Otto (2016, November). *Costa Rica and Nicaragua evacuate a storm grows.* Available on https://theguardian.com [Accessed 25 January 2017].

Izasa, M. (2016). *Informe final de investigación – Apropiación social del conocimiento territorial y ambiental en la vereda Mundo Nuevo, Pereira, Risaralda, para la construcción colectiva de una agenda ambiental de paz*. Colombia: Universidad Libre seccional Pereira, Facultad de Derecho Programa de Trabajo Social CISJ.

Menjivar Ochoa, M. (2012). El referéndum de las calles. Lucha social y reforma del instituto costarricense de electricidad. *Revista Electrónica de Historia*, 13(2). Available on www.scielo.sa.cr [Accessed 25 January 2017].

Movimiento por la Paz (n.d.). Available on www.mdpl.org.nuestro-trabajo/cooperación/colombia [Accessed 25 January 2017].

Narváez, L., Lavell, A. and Pérez Ortega, G. (2009). *La gestión de riesgo de riesgo de desastre: Un enfoque basado en procesos*. Perú: Secretaria General de la Comunidad Andina.

Oficina Regional para América Latina y el Caribe (2016). *XX Foro de Ministros del Medio Ambiente*. Cartagena, Colombia: Programa de las Naciones Unidas Para el Medio Ambiente.

Silva, M. Das G. (2010). *Questao ambiental e desenvolvimiento sustentavel*. Brasil: Cortes Editora.

Partido Verde Ecologista Costa Rica. Available on partidoverdeecologista.cr.yolasite.com [Accessed 24 January 2017].

Physicians for social responsibility (n.d.). *Coal Ash: Hazardous to Human Health*. Available on www.psr.org/assets/pdfs/coal-ash-hazardous-to-human-health.pdf [Accessed 25 May 2017].

Portal de Vicerrectoría de Acción Social (n.d.). *El trabajo comunal universitario*. Available on https://accion-social.ucr.ac.cr/trabajo comunal universitario [Accessed 23 July 2017].

Programa de las Naciones Unidas para el Medioambiente (2016). *Medioambiente por el desarrollo*. Panamá: UNEP – Oficina Regional para América Latina y el Caribe.

Red Latinoamericana de Mujeres Defensoras de los Derechos Sociales y Ambientales (2017). *Mujeres Latinoamericanas tejiendo territorios*. Available on movimientom4.org/mujeres-Latinoamericanas-tejiendo territories [Accessed 26 May 2017].

United Nations (2002). *Johannesburg Declaration on Sustainable Development*. Available at www.un.org [Accessed 23 January 2017].

United Nations (2012). *United Nations Conference on Sustainable Development, Rio +20*. Available at https://sustainabledevelopment.un.org/rio20 [Accessed 14 May 2017].

United Nations Environmental Programme (2009). *Protecting the environment during armed conflict*. Available at www.un.org/zh/events/environmentconflictday/pdfs [Accessed 25 May 2017].

United Nations Environmental Programme (2015). *A guide for mediation practitioners*. Available at www.unep.org [Accessed 23 January 2017].

Universidad de Costa Rica, Escuela de Trabajo Social (2013). *Hoy en nuestra unidad académica*. Available on http://www.ts.ucr.ac.cr/index.Php/2013-05-30-20-41-54/udets/2-uncategorized/192

World Social Forum (2016). *What is a social forum?* Available at https://fsm2016.org [Accessed 23 May 2017].

Worldwatch Institute (2017). *War and the environment*. Available on www.worldwatch.org/node/5520 [Accessed 25 May 2017].

Climate change-driven disasters section

19
Green social work requires a green politics

Carolyn Noble

Introduction

This article explores the more critical 'discontents' of capitalism and global neoliberalism (Stiglitz, 2002) by highlighting the ecological damages, natural disasters and social problems that have resulted from its rapid growth with less and less government sanctions and political and social control to check its domination and impact. Neoliberalism relies almost exclusively on unfettered economic growth from extracting the Earth's limited natural and non-renewable resources to fuel energy and manufacturing products for mass consumption while squirreling millions of dollars for a select few individuals and corporations in charge and/or owners of manufacturing sites and resource extraction projects (Giroux 2001, 2015; Klein, 2015). I do this to develop further the emerging green social work discourse by strengthening its political voice in addressing current environmental and socio-political impacts. I argue that social workers need to re-focus their practice on grassroots activism, alternative economic models and sustain criticism of capitalism to redress its massive industrial consumerism to protect human and non-human species and show a clear platform for action. Green social work has undertaken this challenge, but this is only the beginning.

The capitalist question: the impact of economic neoliberalism

The cry from UK Prime Minister Margaret Thatcher in the 1980s was that 'there is no alternative' (TINA) to the neoliberal vision of a free economy and minimalist government intervention into private and public activities of the nation-state has become the common-sense economic activity of modern times (Roelvink, 2016). Although the growth of neo-economic politics and its implementation across the Western world has been uneven, most if not all Western countries have embraced a free market monetarism and minimalist government approach to managing their economies and citizens' fortunes, and the remaining developing countries are encouraged to join the club. The impact on social work and human services more generally has been dramatic. The privatisation of public services and goods and widespread increase in surveillance, accountability, risk aversion and fiscal restraint policies of the new public management (NPM) has created a crisis in confidence in professional knowledge and practice to act independently and creatively with people accessing services and social care (Dominelli, 2012; Noble et al., 2016). NPM and privatisation have resulted in government-supported services and their funding being cut, while private providers taking up the slack have flourished. Advocates and commentators supportive of neoliberal policies criticise the welfare state as costly, supporting an unwieldly bureaucracy which is largely ineffective because it interferes with the natural order based on self-interest, merit, competition, efficiency and profit (Ozanne and Rose, 2013). These advocates of neoliberal policies argue that the welfare state produces passive, dependent citizens who lack the incentive to work and require a large bureaucracy to support their non-productive labour, creates a cycle of dependency among the poorer classes while failing to eliminate poverty and inequality (Mullaly, 2007; Jamrozik, 2009; Dominelli, 2009). Interference in economic activity by nation-states is regarded as impeding free market action and hindering the inevitable economic growth needed to increase productivity, profit and living standards. Corporations, these proponents posit, should determine economic policies and markets for consumption and delivery (Jamrozik, 2009). These, not the government, are best placed to manage the costs and profits for future growth and make decisions about prices, fees and market production. Distribution should be left to market demand and unregulated competition within this market. Utilities such as electricity, transport, health services, energy, banking, postal services, prisons, education and communications among others should be delivered by this 'apolitical' market of independent (privately owned) suppliers, motivated to provide a competitive low price and value for their product (Mullaly, 2007; Gray and Webb, 2013). This political-economic activity gives corporations a great deal of power and influence over nation-states, communities and individuals while simultaneously reducing governmental interventions and societal control over their enterprises and retaining profits in private hands while government coffers are depleted (Jamrozik, 2009). The domination of the neo-economic agenda makes the pursuit of social justice and human rights-informed social work practice an almost daunting task (Ife, 2010).

Leonard (1997: 113) foreshadowed this in 1997 when he wrote:

> the old ideas which ruled the modern welfare state – universality, full employment, increasing equality – are proclaimed to be a hindrance to survival. They are castigated as ideas which have outlived their usefulness; they are no longer appropriate to the conditions of a global economy.

Much of the world's global economy is linked to the resource extraction industries of mainly non-renewable resources such as gas, coal, oil and uranium mining and to a lesser extent renewable resources (if not over extracted) such as ocean fishing, rainforest harvesting and logging of old growth forests. Limiting global capital's exploitation of the Earth's renewable and non-renewable resources is a huge task given the world's embeddedness in neoliberal discourses of profit-seeking and investing heavily in unlimited economic growth activities because corporations have much to lose if a 'no growth' path is followed. The challenge is to convince the world's citizens that: the remaining non-renewable resources should be left in the ground, eco-friendly alternatives are developed in all resource extraction industries and money for socio-economic development is invested in sustainable energy and product production to ensure a healthy future for us all (Dominelli, 2012; Ibrahim, 2012; Giroux, 2015; Brand, 2014; Klein, 2015).

How did we get here?

The global domination by capital and pervasiveness of neoliberalism was accomplished by a series of economic and social policy and workplace compromises (Jamrozik, 2009). Australia was one key Western government to experiment with a tripartite agreement (known as The Accord) in the 1980s between previous adversaries, the government, the unions and industry to guarantee productivity, economic growth, technological investment, production efficiencies, product standardisation and a stable workforce (Marston and McDonald, 2014). Initially, it was assumed that the nation-state's concern for people's welfare could coexist with these economic arrangements and that, despite the rise of neoliberalism, the state would still continue to ensure that measures of social protection for the most vulnerable, mainly women, children, elders, unemployed people, disabled people, sick people, asylum seekers and new immigrants would be a priority. On this premise, most human service organisations and agencies went along with these reforms and enacted many economic, social and political compromises that fostered the new public management ethos (Dominelli, 2004; Gray and Webb, 2013; Ozanne and Rose, 2013).

What was not factored into this arrangement was the stagnation of capital growth that faced the world in the late 1980s after a period of relative prosperity. In response, capital undertook to reorganise itself by investing in technological change, automation, downsizing, mergers with smaller competitors, acceleration of capital turnover and outsourcing labour costs off-shore, along with their profits, administration and headquarters. Pressure was placed on nation-states to reduce labour and environmental regulations and maximise tax benefits to free up market competition. These changes averted a short-term economic crisis but at a cost. Most nation-states lost their role as key players in directing their country's economy. This was now in the hands of large multinational global corporations that, paradoxically, created the serious fiscal issues (deficits) that nation-states now faced. While nation-states lost their economic hold, these global corporations' profits had risen dramatically (Jamrozik, 2009).

Many states have never recovered financially from the 2007–2008 crisis and cost-cutting exercises became one way of addressing deficits, current and future. For human service agencies these developments heralded the gradual demise of the welfare state's social contract with its citizens and the dominance of the enterprise culture in delivering social welfare services and programmes. A change of ideology towards more punitive approaches to individual and social problems and privatisation of services and resources occurred across the sector without much resistance from the human service workforce and professional associations (Dominelli, 2004; Gray and Webb, 2013). Market-based capitalism was pitted in opposition to social investment and its inevitability as a modern economic activity. Welfare gradually became a business enterprise with business rules, logos, plans and a company ethos at the centre of organisational culture (Ozanne and Rose, 2013) and individuals became consumers of services from which they had little control in determining. This ethos was gradually accepted across most Western countries, changing the face of welfare significantly.

What environmental and social challenges are linked to neoliberalism?

On one level, there is no limit to economic growth until we reach the actual depletion of all natural resources fuelling it. But, the question is whether society wishes to stop this unchecked growth before its end is reached to protect the species and the Earth from current and future disasters. McKibben (2007: 184) argues that it is physically impossible for the whole world to live the same current high-energy lifestyles of the Western countries. '[W]e'd need extra planets, several of them' to sustain current levels of economic growth. Bob Brown (2004) says that the ecological footprint from 1900s to present day is 150 per cent larger than the planet's ability to regenerate. The world's population has tripled in the last 60 years. These issues are placing a huge burden on the Earth's ability to feed and support this growth.

The challenge seems to be 'save the planet and ditch capitalism or save capitalism and ditch the planet' (Ibrahim 2012: 310). It appears that the decision to protect capitalism has been the preferred response as evidenced by most Western governments' neoliberal responses following the 2007 financial crisis (Harvey, 2005) and, since 1997, the decades-long failure of the UN Conferences on Climate Change to establish binding commitments to reduce greenhouse gases (CO_2) in the atmosphere (Dominelli, 2012; Alston, 2013; Ibrahim, 2012). Jettisoning capitalism will put large segments of the economy out of business and fundamentally change the way of life, significantly reducing current standards of living in Western societies (Urry, 2010). However, extracting and converting natural resources such as rivers, forests, oceans, fertile lands into a material utility for the abstract financial concept of money and profit has left huge environmental disasters across the world in its wake (Featherstone, 2013; Klein, 2015).

The increasing incidences of major disasters such as earthquakes, floods, droughts, bush fires, global warming, rising sea levels, mass migration and human pollution add to the looming potential of large-scale ecological catastrophes. Human activities such as sonic mining, overfishing, land and forest clearing, and crop burning have resulted in increasing levels of air, water and soil pollution; 40 to 50 per cent loss of bio-diversity; ocean warming; and the build-up of greenhouse gases (Garnaut, 2008; Dominelli, 2009; Klein, 2015; Dimdam, 2013). The massive extraction of non-renewable resources creates waste products which are stored or buried on what was pristine land or emptied into what were uncontaminated water reserves, thus adding further to ongoing ecological damage (see Alberta tar-sand mining or the palm oil industry's destruction of rainforests in South East Asia). Man-made industrial 'accidents' such as nuclear exposure, deforestation, mud and tailing landslides, and toxic waste spills – for example, Three Mile Island's nuclear meltdown (USA, 1979); Union Carbide's gas leak in Bhopal, India 1984; the Exxon Valdez oil spill in Alaska in 1989; the Jilin chemical plant explosion in China, 2005; and the 2011 Fukushima Daiichi nuclear disaster in Japan are further examples of damages to the already expanding list.

This catalogue of environmental changes and resulting damages paints a grim future for environmental sustainability and places the Earth's ecosystem under huge threats for current and future generations (Garnaut, 2008; Dimdam, 2013; Klein, 2015). Not jettisoning capitalism means almost certain environmental disaster for the Earth and its people this century (Brand, 2014; Giroux, 2015; Klein, 2015). Brand (2014) and Giroux (2015) link the acceleration of global capital to the 'western global juggernaut' and rampant consumerism and wastefulness linked to this activity as the biggest obstacle to any real societal and economic change. Overcoming this obstacle requires acceptance that natural things have intrinsic value and ecological wholes, such as species (human and non-human), communities and ecosystems, not just their individual constituents, have certain moral responsibilities (Singer, 2011). This position challenges the traditional notion of social-work-in-the-environment to re-position itself within and of the environment, an important consideration for green social work to explore.

Only concentrating on the environmental losses and crises associated with climate change ignores the very real problem of capitalism and its uneven distribution of wealth and growth and the uneven impacts of climate change on people's well-being as well as the social structures of democracy (Dominelli, 2012; Giroux, 2015). Democracy is undermined by corporations operating outside the nation-state's control and free trade treaties giving more power to global corporations at the expense of national trade, manufacturing and environmental protection. The pursuit of 'profit no matter what the costs' makes poverty and inequality the first casualties, despite promises of the trickle-down effect (Keller, 2015).

The divide between rich people and poor people makes poor people more vulnerable to natural disasters like flooding, drought and fires, as well as exposed to pollutants and other environmental hazards and industrial accidents. Cutting corners to maximise profits can result in toxic waste pollution, unsafe working practices, increased work hours, social isolation and time poverty (Dominelli, 2012, 2013; McKinnon and Alston, 2016). To isolate the impact of CO_2 and all the other environmental disasters from the unequal social, political and environmental relations from which neoliberalism depends is to obscure the deep politics that informs not only the inaction and, in some cases, the denial of climate change politics but is the root cause of such environmental impacts. Coates (2005) argues that the pressures to exploit the Earth for profit are the same pressures that result in social injustice. For social workers, extreme economic inequality is primarily a violation of social justice with devastating impact on social works' clientele (Dominelli, 2013). In Australia, a rich country, the wealthiest 20 per cent have 70 times more assets than the poorest 20 per cent (Oxfam Australia, 2016). Even the IMF admits that, in recent decades, nearly one-fifth of the world population has economically regressed. A fact not to be missed here is that the richest 0.1 per cent continue to commandeer profits and riches as their fortunes are linked to industries that create much of the damaging climate changes and environmental vandalism (Oxfam, 2015).

Global and national responses

If the growing complexities of socio-environmental dilemmas are the most pressing challenge facing the 21st century (Rudd, 2007), then the question is what are the responses so far? Kythreotis (2012) argues (and what is most evident) is that current responses to climate change are a paradox. On the one hand, society acknowledges there is a problem while on the other hand, society continues to feed its growth fetish and deny the science of climate change and its damaging impact on both the social fabric and the environment. While Australia is a signature to both the Kyoto (1997) and more recently the Paris Agreement (2015) where world leaders revisited their commitment to addressing climate change by agreeing to keep CO_2 emissions at below 2°C pre-industrial levels, current national policies and actions undermine this commitment by continuing to support a politics which prefers to protect coal, oil, gas and uranium mining as the primary economic sources to power and fuel the country's growth to maintain the high standard of living many Australians enjoy. It is easier to have neoliberal business as usual rather than look to the environmental concerns and looming social problems linked to climate change.

Since the current neoconservative (Neo-con) Liberal National Coalition federal government came back into power in 2013 the Climate Change Commission has been abolished, the Council of Australian Governments (COAG) Environment Ministers' Forum has been disbanded and the carbon pricing legislation was repealed in 2014 (Appleby et al., 2015). Many other initiatives such as COAG's National Strategy for Disaster Resilience, established in 2011, was placed on hold and severe funding cuts were directed towards reducing Commonwealth Scientific and Industrial Research Organisation's (CSIRO) current and future climate change research activities. And, its initiatives have been curtailed and all public information of their activities and facts and figures about the severity of the problem have been deleted from their website (Appleby et al., 2015).

Ibrahim (2012) argues that even if governments try and address climate change the internal logic of the capitalist system and the lobbying and influence of global corporations trading in non-renewable resources and desire to protect their huge profits will defeat them every time. As this reality sinks in, there is a gradual awareness that a new way of thinking about economics and politics is needed especially as environmental destruction linked to capitalism continues to damage the Earth and impoverish the many (Dominelli, 2009). Foregrounding the contested character of neoliberalism is necessary for shaping economic and political green alternatives. As

Che Guevara (1965: 2) aptly said, 'Living in a capitalist system is a contest among wolves. One can win only at the cost of the failure of others'. There are many challenges. As corporations operate outside nation-states, citizens are deprived of political power and effective decision-making, and just as disturbingly, a low capacity for local organising and what Gray and Coates (2011) and others call environmental illnesses, sensitivities and loss of personal and societal resilience (Dominelli, 2012; Jones et al., 2012). While the immediate impact of climate change is experienced by workers, poor people, women, indigenous peoples, older peoples, minority race groups and inevitably everyone will be affected as the limit to growth, the overuse of non-renewable resources and environmental degradation is a global problem which has important policy and practice implications for social work (Mullaly, 2007; Dominelli, 2012).

What's the next step?

> Never doubt that a small group of thoughtful committed citizens can change the world. Indeed, it is the only thing that ever has.
>
> Margaret Mead (n.d.)

Having defined the issues, identified the problem and suggested the causes, the question is: What next for social work? Is the dominant neoliberal order fracturing enough for progressive social work practice incursions to take hold (Gray and Webb, 2013)? Does social work have the required courage to become more overtly political? Does it have community support to surrender the battle for full professional recognition, registration, and ideological and professional autonomy, as well as the social care framework to work politically to imagine a better future in which resources are shared; equality, social justice and human rights are paramount; and the Earth's finite bounty is protected (Dominelli, 2009, 2012; Ife, 2010; Gray and Webb, 2013)? Although the ecological debate is not new, social work has been slow to act (Dominelli, 2011). Social work's emancipatory politics has, according to Mullaly (2007) and Gray and Webb (2013) (among others), always been contaminated and immobilised by its ongoing role in maintaining social control, human order and the safety of vulnerable people through its legislated social care policies and responsibilities. However, the recent concerns of social work professional associations are far removed from the very real environmental and social issues raised in this chapter. All is not lost, though, as a significant response has emerged as innovative and progressive scholars have begun to identify a need for a green or ecologically informed social work practice (Dominelli, 2012, 2013; Besthorn, 2011; MacKinnon and Alston, 2016). A green social work response, it is argued, needs to re-link with progressive politics and re-imagine a new world beyond capitalism and its neoliberal economic rationality, politics and practices, and its promotion of austerity, managerialism, punitive welfare cuts, self-interest and boundless consumerism in the interest of maintaining global profits for the few (Dominelli, 2012; Noble, 2016).

Green social work

Despite international efforts from natural and social scientists, environmentalists, philosophers and political scientists about the imminent human, social and environmental impact of (hu)man-made climate change and the resultant destruction of natural resources that are likely to follow, social work has continued to promote its social work-in-environment approach by paying scant attention to the looming ecological disasters in the natural world. However, it is heartening to see that social work is now developing a green response to climate change and taking the scale

Green politics

of environmental disasters seriously (Dominelli, 2012; Gray, Coates and Hetherington, 2013; Alston, 2013; McKinnon and Alston, 2016; Noble, 2016). For Dominelli (2013: 247), the aim of green social work is to:

> work for the reform of the socio-political and economic forces that have a deleterious impact upon the quality of life for poor and marginalized populations, secure the policy changes and social transformation necessary for enhancing the well-being of people and the planet today and into the future and advance the duty of care for others and the right to be cared by others. . . . Its interventions are holistic and tackle structural forms of oppression, environmental degradation and injustice to empower people.

Gray et al. (2013: 6–10) list many aspects for an environmentally conscious social work practice such as: respect for ecological limits; sustainable practices including the real cost of consummative products and foods; globally just practices linked to political philosophies and environmental social movements that advocate for reduction in growth at all cost; direct challenges to unfettered consumerism and exploitation of the world's natural resources; and more sustainable environmental practices. The myth of unending economic growth needs challenging and its link to using up the natural resources quicker than it can regenerate needs constant reminding. Dominelli's (2012, 2013) environmentally just social work practice demands a re-thinking of neoliberalism's push for growth and disposable consumerism and use of non-renewable sources of energy to fuel this growth as major factors in environmental degradation and subsequent physical, social, cultural and health problems. McKinnon and Alston (2016: 7) argue for a professional response committed to ecological social work, to social and environmental justice, and a new consciousness of the 'indivisible links between the two', while Noble (2016) argues that green social work is the next frontier for social action for progressive social workers.

An ecologically focused social work practice needs to include the non-human with the human in its radar of concern and action. It needs to develop a real connection with the Earth and people's relationship and interdependence with its health and prosperity. It requires social workers to recognise relevant environmental issues in all practice situations and to advocate for environmental awareness and improvements, locally, nationally and internationally (Dominelli, 2012; McKinnon and Alston, 2016). It also requires an ontological shift to recognise the inherent value of the environment for its own sake. It means that social work practice, values and ethics, policy and research need to place environmental ecosystems above economic and social goals as the only long-term and sustainable solution to current pressing environmental issues. It challenges social work's historical anthropocentric position with a new, eco-centric view of social work, as we all need reminding that we are not separate from the Earth but of the Earth (Klein, 2015). This presents a new challenge for social work to move beyond seeing the individual and the social systems in which s/he lives as the primary concern with an overarching view of environmentally just practices at all levels of intervention (Dominelli, 2012; McKinnon and Alston, 2016). It demands that social work returns to its radical political roots, a space eroded by the new management practices of neoliberalist economics and anti-welfare rhetoric (Dominelli, 2004; Lavalette, 2011; Gray and Webb, 2013). As Lavalette (2011: 204) says, social workers are here 'to make the social [and the ecological] work, not the markets work'.

The politics of collective action: green politics

Gray and Webb (2013) ask whether there are any exemplars and attempts to build a politics of action focusing on new kinds of economic reality for a changed future that social workers can link up with. Finding examples requires social workers to look at the collective activism aimed against these failed neoliberal policies as potential sites for international solidarity: beginning with the Anti-IMF riots of the 1980s, and followed by Occupy Wall Street, Democracy Now!, The Other 99 Percent, World Social Forum (WSF), Films for Action, Truthout, GetUp, WikiLeaks, Architects and Engineers for 9/11 Truth, Counterpunch, Adbusters and more targeted resistances such as the Arab Spring, Black Lives Matter, anti-war and peace movements, Free West Papua campaign, and many other forms of local and global resistance to wage exploitation, modern slavery, austerity measures, poverty, inequality, unfair trade policies and gender justice. Destroy the Joint and Women for Justice provide current examples of international solidarity and neoliberal resistance. Harvey (2005: 179–180) posits that post-modern social movements have rightly become the main focus of anti-globalisation struggles and that:

> [w]ith the core of the political problem so clearly recognised, it should be possible to build outwards into a broader politics of creative destruction mobilized against the dominant regime of neoliberal imperialism foisted upon the world by the hegemonic capitalist powers.

More potent examples of sites of resistance are coming from indigenous colleagues and communities. In particular, indigenous activism to save traditional lands and protect the environment through indigenous sovereignty. Indigenous people's protests currently include the: Oglala Lakota Sioux tribe in North Dakota (US) objecting to the gas pipeline; Caribou and Beaver Lake Cree First Nation's (Canada) opposition to Alberta tar-sand mining; Lenca-Honduras (Central America) indigenous peoples' opposition to government grabbing their traditional lands; and Australia's Wangan and Jagalingou peoples' opposition to the Adani coal extraction in the Galilee basin. Indigenous land-based activism focuses on indigenous peoples fighting to protect their land, culture and cosmo-vision from capitalist exploitation and destruction, and represent some of the most robust current acts to prevent ecological crises that social workers must support. The Tangata Whenua Social Workers Association of Aotearoa New Zealand support for the North Dakota Sioux (US) stand against the Bakken pipeline being built across their traditional lands is an example of cross-nations support. Klein (2015) and Muller (2014) see indigenous communities still practicing and defending their cultural lands as the last frontier of defence for Earth.

Many non-indigenous peoples including green social work activists also see the inherent value of relating to the land in ways that are not purely extractive and support indigenous colleagues in their efforts (Dominelli, 2012). Other examples include eco-feminism which sees the repression of women by patriarchy and the offensive against nature by capitalism as interconnected (Sulleh, 2009). Deep ecology, along with green and indigenous social work, argues for a reconnection of human beings with nature and seeing all life forms as interconnected and in a delicate balance (Dominelli, 2004; McKibben, 2007; Besthorn, 2011). Each approach suggests an environmental practice that is more sustainable and life-affirming. A healthy environment is essential to human and the planet's well-being (Dominelli, 2012). A return to indigenous communities and their traditional way of life, women's connection with nature, and a spiritual connection with the land once resisted as essentialist and apolitical, or patronised and/or marginalised by the dominant Western economic system and ideologies, are now more likely to be looked upon as exemplars of sustainable livelihoods (McKibben, 2007; Klein, 2015; Baard, 2015).

While green social work explores its place in environmental politics, a hybrid activism has been developed in the citizenry outside professional social work discourses as a sustainable and equitable way of fighting neoliberalism's individualistic mentality and widespread economic inequality. This hybrid citizen activism is gaining momentum. For example, citizens are creating and protecting green spaces (e.g. community gardens, parks, play areas and sporting grounds); recreating a sense of the commons both environmental (e.g. open-source ecology, open-source seed initiatives, common housing, community land trusts) and digital (e.g. free and open software, wikis, open-source hardware). They are using social media such as Facebook and other social media activities (e.g. Getup to undertake activist work such as protecting old growth forests, anti-coal seam gas extraction, and anti-mining and dam construction). Local action is also evident as citizens become involved in building ecological health and environmental justice movements to help transition to sustainable societies and link with other local citizens working for social recovery after natural disasters including social recovery activities following the 2008 Wenchuan and 2015 Nepal earthquakes by national and international networks (Roelvink, 2016). By building alliances with these communities of practice, strengthening networks with citizen groups already working to resist the 'business as usual growth society' and learning from their successes and failures, social workers can further guide their green activism to support a healthy environment.

Further examples of alternative livelihoods can be seen in the growth of *localism* and re-emergence of *cooperatives* and *social economies*. Localism represents an attempt to foster a local democracy and local ownership of the economy such as 'buy local' campaigns, setting up alternative media outlets, and introducing local currencies, urban agriculture, local organic farms, local transportation, local ownership of electricity designed to give local people greater sovereignty over their future and take direct action against the global juggernaut (Brand, 2014). Cooperatives and social economies promote people over profit, solidarity over individualism, democratic member control, cooperation and concern for community (Brand, 2014), as well as occupy the third space between the public and the private. An excellent example of a successful contemporary co-operative is small town in Marinaleda in the Andalusian region of Spain. It calls itself a social-democratic and co-operative municipality and its 30-year history represents a successful attempt to struggle against capitalism, neoliberalism and TINA by showing that small communities can survive, thrive even, with no desire for profits. This small municipality boasts full employment, affordable housing, provision of community services, and low crime without interference from a centralised power (Hancox, 2014).

These multiple or hybrid movements are the tip of the iceberg as many resistances go unreported, ignored or actively suppressed by a conservative press. Moreover, activism is inhibited and activists gaoled as the people most affected by the economic policies and environmental destruction look to protect themselves and build new institutions for social justice and a new positive green economic paradigm (Serres, 2016).

Conclusion

My argument is that unless social workers who work with the most vulnerable people know how social, political, cultural and economic structures inform power relations and join the dots to capitalism and its destructive practices and environmental disasters, then a green response will be inadequate for the challenges ahead. Social workers know that the Earth's absorptive capacity is limited and that severe climate change is already evident due to past inaction, with more disasters to follow. Many vulnerable people and communities suffer at the uneven hand of capitalism and the environmental disasters linked to its economic activity. Scientific advances and technological tools for developing alternative energy sources are currently being developed, but many are a long way off for large-scale use in the transition to sustainability (Lysack, 2011). Sooner or later, everyone will be caught up in the environmental impact from climate change regardless of wealth or poverty, gender, and indigeneity.

Green social workers need to embrace a politics that garnishes the collective will of the people to work towards changes in consumption, turn away from the need for unending growth and introduce sustainable green technologies, local community greening and alternative economic models as a way of linking green social work with a green politics. Replacing capitalism and neoliberal economics, embracing the many economic hybrid economic models, joining collective activism, and linking up with indigenous land and cultural protection complete the political arc.

References

Alston, M. (2013). Environmental social work: Accounting for gender in climate disasters,' *Australian Social Work*, 66(2): 218–233.

Appleby, K. Bell, K. and Boetto, H. (2015). Climate change adaptation: Community action, disadvantaged groups and practice implication for social work,' *Australian Social Work*, doi:10.1080/0312407x.2015.108855

Baard, P. (2015). Managing climate change: A view from deep Ecology,' *Ethics and Environment*, 20(1): 23–45.

Besthorn, F. H. (2011). Deep ecology's contributions to social work: A ten-year retrospective. *International Journal of Social Welfare*, 21: 248–259.

Brand, R. (2014). *Revolution*. London, UK: Cornerstone.

Brown, B. (2004). *Memo for a Saner world*. Australia: Penguin Books.

Coates, J. (2005). Environmental crisis: Implication for social work. *Journal of Progressive Human Services*, 16(1): 25–49.

Che Guevara. (1965). *Socialism and man in Cuba*. www.marxists.org/archive/guevara/1965/03/man-socialism.htm [Accessed 4 May 2016].

Dimdam E. (2013). *Man-made disasters*. http://list25.com/25-biggest-man-made-environmental-disasters-in-history/ [Accessed 5 May 2016].

Dominelli, L. (2004). *Social work: Theory and practice for a changing profession*. Cambridge: Polity Press.

Dominelli, L. (2009). *Introducing social work*. Cambridge: Polity Press.

Dominelli, L. (2011). Climate change: Social workers' contributions to policy and practice debates. *International Journal of Social Welfare*, 20(4): 430–439. doi: 10.1111/j.1468-2397.2011.00795.x

Dominelli, L. (2012). *Green social work: From environmental crises to environmental justice*, Polity Press, London.

Dominelli, L. (2013). Environmental justice at the heart of social work practice: Greening the pprofession. *International Journal of Social Welfare*, 22: 431–439.

Featherston, D. (2013). *The contested politics of climate change and the crisis of neo-liberalism*. http://uk.oneworld.net/article/view/166581/1/7467

Garnaut, R. (2008). *The Garnaut climate change review: Final report*. Cambridge, UK: Cambridge University Press.

Giroux, H. (2001). *The mouse that roared: Disney and the end of innocence*. Oxford, UK: Rowman and Littlefield.

Giroux, H. (2015). *Against the terror of neo-liberalism: Politics beyond the age of greed*. New York: Routledge.

Gray, M. and Coates, J. (2011). Environmental ethics for social work: Social work's responsibility to the non-human world. *International Journal of Social Welfare*, 21: 239–247.

Gray, M. Coates, J. and Hetherington, T. (Eds.) (2013). *Environmental social work*. London and New York: Routledge.

Gray, M. and Webb, S. (Eds.) (2013). *The new politics of social work*. Basingstoke, UK: Palgrave Macmillan.

Hancox, D. (2014). *The village against the world*, London, Verso.

Harvey, D. (2005). *A brief history of neo-liberalism*, OUP, Oxford, UK.

Ibrahim, F. (2012) *Capitalism versus the planet earth: An irreconcilable conflict*. London: Muswell Press.

Ibrahim, F. (2012). *Capitalism versus the planet earth: An irreconcilable conflict*. Muswell Press, London, UK

Ife, J. (2010). *Human rights and social work: Towards a rights-based practice*, Port Melbourne: Cambridge University Press.

Jamrozik, A. (2009). *Social policy in the post-welfare state: Australian society in a changing world*, 3rd ed. Frenchs Forest, NSW: Pearsons Education Australia.

Jones, P., Miles, D., Francis, A., and Rajeev, S.P. (2012). Working towards eco-justice: Reflections on an International, cross-institutional social work collaboration. *Asian Journal of Research in Social Sciences and Humanities*, 2(6): 146–158.

Keller, J. (2015). *The IMF confirms that 'trickle down' economics, is, indeed a joke*. Available on https://psmag.com/the-imf-confirms-that-trickle-down-economics-is-indeed-a-joke-207d7ca469b#.ub9f18sch [Accessed 30 September 2016].

Klein, N. (2015). *This Changes Everything*. Harmondsworth: Penguin.

Kyoto Protocol-United Nations framework convention on climate change. (1997). Available on http://unfccc.int/kyoto_protocol/items/2830.php [Accessed 18 September 2016].

Kythreotis, A.P. (2012). Progress in global climate change politics: Reasserting national state territoriality in 'post-political' world, *Progress in Human Geography*, 36(4): 457–474.

Lavalette, M. (Ed.) (2011). *Radical social work today*. Bristol: The Polity Press.

Leonard, P. (1997). *Postmodern welfare: Reconstructing an emancipatory project*. London: Sage.

Lysack, M. (2011). Building capacity for environmental engagement and leadership: An ecosocial work perspective. *International Journal of Social Welfare*, 21: 260–269.

Marston, G. and McDonald, C. (2014). *The Australian welfare state: Who benefits now?* South Yarra, Melbourne: Palgrave Macmillan.

McKibben, B. (2007). *Deep ecology*. New York: Times Books.

McKinnon, J. and Alston, M. (Eds.) (2016). *Ecological social work: Towards sustainability*. London: Palgrave Macmillan.

Mullaly, B. (2007). *The new structural social work*, 3rd ed. Toronto: Oxford University Press.

Muller, L. (2014). *A theory for indigenous health and human service work: Connecting indigenous knowledge and practice*. Crows Nest, Australia: Allen and Unwin.

Noble, C. (2016). Green social work: The next frontier for action. *Social Alternatives (special issue)*, 34, 2: 14–19.

Noble, C., Gray, M. and Johnston, L. (2016). *Critical supervision for the human services: A social model to promote learning and value-based practice*. London: Jessica Kingsley Publisher.

Oxfam. (2015). *Wealth: having it all and wanting more*. Available on www.oxfam.org.au/wp-content/uploads/2014/06/ib-wealth-having-all-wanting-more-190115-embargo-en.pdf [Accessed 30 June 2016].

Oxfam Australia. (2016). *An economy for the 1percent: Wealth and Income Statistics for Australia*. Available on http://australianpolitics.com/2007/08/06/rudd-says-climate-change-is-great-moral-challenge.html [Accessed 30 March 2016].

Ozanne, E. and Rose, D. (2013). *The organisational context of human service practice*. South Yarra, Victoria, Australia: Palgrave Macmillan.

Peck, J. and Tickwell, D. (2002). Neoliberalising Space, *Antipode*, 34(3): 380–404.

Roelvink, G. (2016). *Building dignified worlds: Geographies of collective action*. Minneapolis, USA: University of Minnesota Press.

Rudd, K. (2007). *The greatest moral challenge of our generation*. Available on http://australianpolitics.com/2007/08/06/rudd-says-climate-change-is-great-moral-challenge.html [Accessed 5 June 2016].

Serres, D. (n.d.). *The comprehensive activist guide to dismantling neoliberalism*. Available on http://organizingchange.org/guide-to-dismantling-neoliberalism/ [Accessed 4 July 2016].

Singer, P. (2011). *Practical ethics*. Cambridge: Cambridge University Press.

Stiglitz, J. (2002). *Globalization and its discontents*. London: W.W. Norton.

Sulleh, A. (2009). *Eco-sufficiency and global justice: Women write political ecology*. New York: Pluto Books.

Urry, J. (2010). Consuming the planet to excess, *Theory, Culture and Society*, 27(2–3): 191–212.

20
Green social work within integrated coastal zone management
Mauritius and Barbados

Komalsingh Rambaree and Letnie F. Rock

Introduction

Mauritius and Barbados have demographic, socio-economic, and cultural differences, but share similar sustainable development challenges as Small Island Developing States (SIDS). Both countries are physically small, have a narrow resource base, high susceptibility to natural hazards, low economic resilience, and limited human and technological capacity for mitigating and adapting to the effects of climate change (Nurse and Sem, 2000). Both countries are very dependent on tourism, coastal resources, and international trade. There has been a growing concern in both Mauritius and Barbados regarding the negative impacts of climate change and environmental pollution on agriculture, water, fisheries, erosion of beaches, degradation of reef systems and bleaching of corals, loss of wetlands and depletion of biodiversity. Both countries have been at the forefront of development programmes and strategies for SIDS which produced initiatives such as *The 1994 Barbados Programme of Action* and *The 2005 Mauritius Strategy of Implementation*.

SIDS produce less than 1 per cent of global greenhouse gases, yet are highly vulnerable to the impacts of climate change (Steiner, 2014). In SIDS there is a growing concern about environmental injustice, environmental sustainability and climate change. Such a context should compel community-based social workers in Mauritius and Barbados to adopt a green social work (GSW) approach to ensure that the people they serve have sustainable livelihoods. GSW is defined by Dominelli (2012: 25) as:

> A form of holistic professional social work practice that focuses on: the interdependencies among people; the social organization of relationships between people and the flora and fauna in their physical habitats; and the interaction between socio-economic and physical environmental crises and interpersonal behaviour that undermine the well-being of human beings and Planet Earth.

This chapter discusses the activities and roles of community-based social workers who work with diverse stakeholders in Mauritius within Integrated Coastal Zone Management (ICZM).

It also considers the need for similar activities and roles to be performed by social workers in Barbados to ensure that people in vulnerable coastal communities are able to sustain their livelihoods. Coastal zones consist of several stakeholder groups ranging from wealthy hoteliers to chronically poor artisanal fishers and micro-business owners who earn their livelihoods through a range of activities. Management for sustainable outcomes in the coastal zones extends across different sectors, organisations and ownership boundaries, and encompasses different stakeholders' needs, interests and concerns (Rockloff and Lockie, 2004). ICZM requires social workers to play an active role within coastal communities through the promotion of sustainable livelihoods and development, as well as capacity-building for resilience with regards to the effects of climate change, natural disasters and environmental degradation.

In this chapter, the Sustainable Livelihoods Approach (SLA) (as shown in Figure 20.1) is used to answer the following questions in a comparative manner for Mauritius and Barbados:

1. What are the strategies, methods, and techniques being used by social workers in: (a) assessments of vulnerability and livelihoods; (b) inventions for transforming structures and processes; (c) promoting livelihood strategies; and (d) accounting for and reporting livelihood outcomes achievement from their interventions?
2. What are the main challenges for social workers working within ICZM for: (a) a multidisciplinary and multi-sectoral collaborative approach; and (b) participation of marginalised, disenfranchised, and vulnerable individuals and groups?
3. What lessons for GSW can be drawn from the two case studies?

The context: Mauritius and Barbados

Mauritius is 2,040 square kilometres in size and has an Exclusive Economic Zone that extends over an area of 1.9 million square kilometres and a population of 1.2 million. It is world famous as a tropical holiday destination, with 1.2 million tourists visiting the country yearly. Tourism and the finance, service, and textile sectors are important pillars of the Mauritian economy, while sugar production – the traditional pillar of the island's economy – is declining in relative importance (BTI, 2016). Since gaining independence from Great Britain in 1968, Mauritius has made remarkable socio-economic progress by diversifying its economy and developing its welfare system. Since the early 1980s, the island has had an average annual economic growth of around 4 per cent, while successive governments have made continuous efforts to consolidate the welfare state, providing free healthcare, free education at all levels, and a basic old age pension at universal level (Rambaree, 2011a, b; 2013).

Mauritius is promoting sustainable development through various socio-economic incentives. A major focus within sustainable development initiatives has been coastal zone management. The government of Mauritius and several international organisations like the Indian Ocean Commission, European Commission, and World Bank, are operating within the ICZM framework in Mauritius. ICZM is based on the recognition that coastal zone management is a complex, dynamic, and interconnected field of physical, biological, human socio-economic, and political systems and processes. Community well-being and community participation as part of stakeholders' engagement within ICZM has been defined as a key component and strategy for achieving success with sustainable development processes (McFadden, 2008; Rambaree, 2011b).

Barbados, a small country located in the Atlantic Ocean north of the equator in the archipelago of Caribbean islands, has a land mass of 430 square kilometres and coastline of 97 kilometres, and is much smaller than Mauritius. Barbados attained political independence from Britain in 1966, two years before Mauritius. It has a population of approximately 285,154 (World

Population Review, 2016), and 'face[s] an ageing population and a growth rate of almost zero' (Government of Barbados, 2013: 3). Like Mauritius, it is among the most densely populated countries in the world.

Barbados boasts a literacy rate of 99.7 per cent compared to Mauritius's 89.2 per cent (UNDP, 2016). It has a universal healthcare system and free education from preschool to tertiary level. The Gross Domestic Product (GDP) of Barbados was worth US$4.45 billion in 2015 (Trading Economics, 2016), and its GDP per capita is approximately US$25,100 (CIA, 2016). The main natural resources of Barbados are coral reefs, fish, petroleum, and natural gas. Its main industries include tourism, fisheries, by-products of natural gas and petroleum, by-products of sugar particularly rum, agriculture, and light textile manufacturing. The country 'is experiencing a loss of competitiveness in the manufacturing and agricultural sectors' (Government of Barbados, 2013: 3). Barbados is highly dependent on tourism; 1 million tourists visit the island annually (Barbados Statistical Service, 2015). Tourists are attracted to the island's climate, coral reefs, beaches, and marine life. The socio-economic development of Barbados is particularly vulnerable to the impact of regional and global environmental changes and climate change. Like Mauritius and other countries in the Caribbean, Barbados is a SIDS with a fragile economy and inimitable vulnerabilities.

Barbados, a member of the Caribbean Community (CARICOM), worked towards attaining the Millennium Development Goals (MDGs). In 2015, the government adopted the UN 2030 Agenda for Sustainable Development (CARICOM, 2016), and has signed but not yet ratified several international agreements to address environmental and climate change-related issues that continue to assail the island. These international agreements include biodiversity, climate change, desertification, endangered species, hazardous wastes, marine dumping, ozone layer protection, ship pollution, and wetlands (CIA, 2016). Government adopted a Coastal Zone Management Unit (CZMU) created in 1996 and 1998 Coastal Zone Management Act (Government of Barbados, 1998). Barbados has a cooperative approach to coastal zone management and environmental protection and government has realised that effective ICZM helps Barbados's social and economic development.

Social work in Mauritius and Barbados

The ramifications of climate change and environmental degradation impact individuals, families, and communities (Erickson 2012; Besthorn and Besthorn, 2012), and work negatively against people's livelihoods and sustainable development. The multiple effects of climate on societies globally is creating new career paths for social workers in disaster management and environmental management, matters discussed by Dominelli (2012); Besthorn and Besthorn (2012); McKinnon (2012); and Erickson (2012). Besthorn and Besthorn (2012: 58) note that 'for a growing number of social workers in developed countries, the recognition began to emerge that the natural environment shares a complex and evolutionary link to personal and social development'. The *Global Agenda on Social Work and Social Development*, devised by the International Association of Schools of Social Work (IASSW), International Federation of Social Workers (IFSW), and International Council on Social Welfare (ICSW) has environmental sustainability as one of four pillars requiring action from social workers (IASSW, IFSW and ICSW, 2012).

The government in Mauritius employs most professional social workers in occupational positions like 'social security officer', 'community development officer', 'regional development officer', 'youth officer', and 'family welfare officer'. Almost all professional social workers are trained in social work to at least Bachelor level. Non-governmental organisations (NGOs) are another major employer of professional social workers. Some professional social workers with university qualifications in social work are employed by international organisations based in Mauritius, including the Red Cross, United Nations (UN) organisations, and the European Commission Decentralised Cooperation Programme. A small number of social workers are employed by private companies where they operate within Corporate Social Responsibility mandates.

Social workers in Barbados are trained mainly as generalist practitioners. Ring and Carmichael (2015) who conducted a workforce study on social work in Barbados found that most social workers hold a Bachelor's degree in social work, with casework as the main form of practice. A small number engage in group work and community work. Ring and Carmichael (2015: 26) note that:

> direct casework practice is the main form of social work activity, which . . . suggests that social workers perform their duties within a remedial model of service delivery where the focus is on individual pathology and treatment of social problems.

The majority of social workers in Barbados are employed in the government sector with a small number in local NGOs and the private sector (Ring and Carmichael, 2015). The agencies and organisations in which they work include, among others, the Welfare Department, the Probation Department, the Government Industrial Schools, the prison, Youth Service, the Child Care Board (child welfare agency), the National Council on Substance Abuse, the National Assistance Board which provides services to older people, the Disability Unit, the Community Development Department, and various local charities. There are also trained social workers who work in the fields of nursing, law enforcement and teaching.

In Barbados, social workers employed by the Community Development Department (CDD) engage in community development initiatives and capacity-building programmes within communities that focus on self-help initiatives and other traditional areas of community work. However, community-based social workers in Barbados need to give greater attention to the 'asset-based' approach in working with communities to enable the development of community strengths, and the promotion of social sustainability and social development. Despite the growing impact of climate change-related issues such as beach erosion, prolonged droughts, depleted coral reefs, periodic flooding, and land slippage on communities and their residents, social workers are not employed by the Ministry of the Environment, the Water Resources and Drainage Department (under which CZMU sits) or the Department of Emergency Management (DEM).

The DEM coordinates the national response to disasters. Providentially, 'social workers employed by the Government Welfare Department and the CDD are members of the planning and response teams' (Rock and Corbin, 2007: 385) of DEM. Additionally, 'all social workers employed by the Government of Barbados are charged with responding to the physical, social and mental health needs of persons affected by the trauma of disasters' (Rock and Corbin, 2007: 385). Thus, they have clearly defined roles to play in situations of natural disaster through their involvement with DEM. However, social workers in Barbados are not adept in responding to the socio-economic issues that arise in the everyday interplay between the natural environment and people. This infers that social workers need to be trained to think and respond to social, economic, and environmental changes – macro-issues that impact negatively upon sustainable development, environmental justice, and livelihoods of people in particularly vulnerable communities.

The sustainable livelihoods approach: applicability to green social work

Since its conceptualisation in the 1990s, the Sustainable Livelihoods Approach (SLA) shown in Figure 20.1 has been a popular model used to identify important assets in livelihoods, their trends over time and space as well as the nature and impacts of shocks and environmental, economic and social stresses upon these assets (Morse et al., 2009). A livelihood consists of the capabilities, assets (material and social resources), and activities required to earn a living (Chambers and Conway, 1991). For a livelihood to be sustainable it has to cope with and recover from stresses and shocks and maintain or enhance its capabilities and assets both now and in the future, while not undermining the natural resource base (Carney, 1998). The SLA can be regarded as a genuinely transdisciplinary model that offers a fresh vision of a holistic and/or integrative approach with the capacity to analyse and understand the complexity related to sustainable development (Knutsson, 2006).

Social work is defined as 'a practice-based profession and an academic discipline that promotes social change and development, social cohesion, and the empowerment and liberation of people' (IFSW, 2016: 1). Promoting social changes towards development is explicitly expressed in the global definition of social work. Thus, it becomes the role, responsibility, and moral obligation of social workers to ensure that social changes within our society are in line with sustainable development. In this sense, Dominelli (2012: 7) presents GSW for 'holistic understandings about various environments and their impacts upon people's behaviour'. GSW provides social workers with a sound understanding about environmental injustices which are considered oppressive, and obliges social workers to intervene for the cause of social justice and human rights (Dominelli 2012; Rambaree 2013; Rambaree and Ahmadi, 2017). For Dominelli (2012), the mission of GSW is to protect the environment and enhance people's well-being by addressing prevailing structural inequalities and the unequal distribution of power and resources, as well as by promoting harmonious relationships among humans, plants, and animals within the socio-cultural, economic, and physical environment. The main aim of GSW is particularly centred towards protecting and promoting the livelihoods of vulnerable and marginalised populations (Ibid).

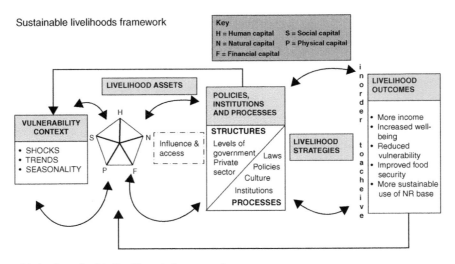

Figure 20.1 Sustainable livelihoods framework
Source: DFID (1999), page 1. Used with permission

SLA could be considered a suitable framework for GSW. Similarly, Hugman (2016) argues that GSW is based on the recognition that ecology is part of the development of livelihoods. SLA can facilitate green social workers to see livelihoods in a dynamic, historical context by allowing practitioners, researchers, and policymakers to understand the complexities involved in working for sustainable livelihoods. In particular, GSW discourses highlight the complexities and interdependence between ecology and social issues within the context of a heightened concern for the global energy crisis and climate change challenges, prevailing structural inequalities, and unequal distribution of power and resources of interest to social workers (Dominelli, 2012). GSW is a holistic approach. SLA's strength is that it belongs to the group of holistic approaches that seek to capture the enormous complexities of development problems (van Dillen, 2002). The SLA, therefore, can support social workers in stimulating their thinking and mapping the complexities surrounding their practice towards sustainable development.

In the original SLA framework, the neglect of power relations was an important flaw, and a subsequent generation of livelihood studies managed to integrate the analysis of power relations in a meaningful way by focusing more attention on influences, institutions, structures, and processes (De Haan, 2012). For Dominelli (2012), GSW is based upon the insights of radical and anti-oppressive social work that challenges structural inequalities and unequal distribution of power with the aim of promoting harmonious relationships and sustainable livelihoods. The way ecosystem services and resources and other livelihood opportunities are distributed locally is often influenced by informal structures of social dominance and power within society (Krantz, 2001). The SLA can support social workers in identifying the complexities of power dynamics and suggest ways and means to direct power towards the emancipation of people who are trapped or pushed towards marginalisation, exclusion and poverty, and who are victims of environmental injustices. Social workers have a major concern in tackling environmental injustices through a better understanding of societal power structures and processes. In this endeavour, the SLA can be used as an interdependent framework to guide social workers to attain some of the aims of GSW.

Assessment of vulnerability and livelihoods

Mauritius has an extremely rich coastal zone consisting of near-shore wetlands and mangroves, lagoon coral, fringing coral reef, and all their associated marine life (Ministry of Environment, 2007). However, marine scientists are warning that coastal zones in Mauritius are undergoing enormous ecological pressure as a result of rapid growth in land- and sea-based activities alongside the effect of climate change (Rambaree, 2013).

Coastal areas of Mauritius have a history of inequalities. By the time of independence in 1968, most prime land (over 70 per cent of the beach front) was occupied by Franco-Mauritians (2 per cent of the population), 'extremely wealthy sugar barons' who had established an elite lifestyle in Mauritius (Salverda, 2010, 2013; Salverda and Hay, 2014). In 2007, when the European Union decided to end the special sugar trading status accorded to former colonies, the then-Mauritian government introduced the Integrated Resort Scheme (IRS) (which became the Property Development Scheme [PDS]), whereby sugar estate owners could convert acres of their agricultural land mostly in coastal areas into luxury villas to be sold to foreign buyers with Mauritian citizenship being granted to the buyers (Rambaree, 2013). The IRS enables large-scale landowners to construct exclusive resorts with a variety of high-quality amenities, such as marinas, golf courses, restaurants, shops, water sports centres, and wellness centres, thereby occupying large surface land areas and beaches (Sharpley and Naidoo, 2010).

Local people from the coastal communities are becoming increasingly worried about 'Mauritius being sold to foreigners' and their representatives are anxious about the increasing number of gated communities that are blocking access to the beach for local people (Rambaree, 2013). Side-by-side with the gated communities in the coastal areas of Mauritius, people are living in chronic poverty and become squatters of state-owned land. Social workers have a big challenge in countering the dualisation of the coastal communities in Mauritius. There is a map on Google Earth which provides an example of dual communities in Mauritius. Click on the following URL to access it. It requires Google Chrome to download; instructions for a free download are available through this URL.

https://earth.app.goo.gl/?apn=com.google.earth&ibi=com.google.b612&isi=293622097&ius=googleearth&link=https%3a%2f%2fearth.google.com%2fweb%2f%40-20.27039599,57.77344752,44.39843483a,7404.12157048d,35y,0h,0t,0r

The fishing community of Mauritius regularly voice their concerns regarding their disrupted livelihoods in coastal zones. Almost all Mauritian coastal villages have a vibrant history of traditional artisanal fishing. However, most fishers come from a marginalised socio-economic background, living in chronic poverty, with more than 77 per cent having no formal education (Sobhee et al., 2008). The fishers' families often consist of individuals who are in low-paid and highly unstable jobs. Fishers report high concern for socio-economic issues such as lack of education, unemployment of their children, poverty, and environmental degradation (Rambaree, 2011a). In particular, fishers are very concerned about the degradation of the marine ecology, due to the rising number of resorts and ocean-based activities in the coastal zones.

Furthermore, Rambaree (2013: 267), among others, found that the owners of micro-businesses located on Mauritian coasts received only residual benefits from the tourism industry and medium-scale industries such as restaurants and shops, and were not able to compete with the multinational groups that provide all-inclusive services. Additionally, the livelihoods of small-scale vegetable planters from the east coast of Mauritius are threatened as they are constantly being blamed for over-fertilising the soil which is said to be leading to the bulk accumulation of algae at the Belle Mare/Palmar beaches (Ministry of Environment, 2007) and negatively impacting the tourism sector.

Barbados has similar coastal zone and environmental-related issues such as the building of marinas and hotels on the beaches leading to beach erosion when the tide surges, and the docking of giant ships and cruise liners and resultant pollutants which have been depleting marine life. Across the island there is an increase in new housing developments built on agricultural lands which compromise the ecology of the island. Other problems include sewage disposal, prolonged drought, extreme flooding and soil erosion during the rainy season, land slippage, and the illegal dumping of refuse, all of which directly or indirectly impact the lives of people and communities. Professional social workers in Barbados have not been engaged in the assessment of the vulnerabilities of people in affected communities so that they can be provided with the information required to help preserve community resources and empower residents. They appear to be comfortable operating under the premise that 'their expertise is in matters social, and therefore natural environmental factors are not germane to . . . social work's professional interests' (McKinnon, 2012: 266). They must be made aware that social and environmental justice issues are of grave importance and that using an environmental lens would provide them with insights about the impact of natural and environmental hazards and climate change on the socio-economic development of the country and the well-being of the clients/service users that they serve (Dominelli, 2012). It would also help enlighten them about the value of an authentic and holistic eco-systemic approach to their interventions.

Interventions for transforming structures and processes

Social workers have a critical role to play in assessing risk and vulnerability and transforming structures and processes that would enable communities to be proactive instead of being reactive in mitigating disaster, environmental hazards, and injustices. Erickson (2012: 184) states that, 'despite our long-held principle of eco-systemic practice, social work has been slow to consider the natural environment as part of our practice'. Social workers do not pay enough attention to how climate change and the degradation of the environment is impacting the people they serve. Erickson (2012: 184) notes that, 'social work has almost completely disregarded the integration of issues of the natural environment into . . . existing models that include the human environment'. To this end, they have not been able to impact the structures and processes that are trying to promote environmental sustainability (Dominelli, 2012). Possible explanations for disregarding environmental problems could be the profession's training orientation and social workers' view that such issues are the purview of other disciplines, as they are already overwhelmed 'with a plethora of "real life" problems of the . . . most vulnerable people' (Besthorn and Besthorn, 2012: 56).

Social workers in Mauritius need to adopt a political agenda to intervene in conflicts between various stakeholders and secure social justice for vulnerable groups (Rambaree, 2017). For too long, political elites (predominantly Indo-Mauritians) have worked together in areas of common interest with the economic elites (predominantly Franco-Mauritians) on a win/win basis (Rambaree, 2013, 2017; Salverda, 2013) to the exclusion of poor people. With globalisation and the rapid growth of neo-liberalism, Mauritius is vulnerable to conflicts between different stakeholders from coastal communities. Such conflicts necessitate social workers' interventions as mediators to protect the livelihoods of vulnerable groups such as the planters and the fishers. Dominelli (2013: 436) notes that, 'resolving these conflicts often involves multi-stakeholder partnerships composed of internal and external actors working alongside each other'.

Promoting livelihood strategies and livelihood outcomes

In Mauritius and Barbados, social workers need to focus more attention on environmental justice through redistribution of ecosystem services, which are vital in promoting and protecting the livelihoods of people. Ecosystem services are the benefits people obtain from the ecosystem, which is a dynamic complex of plant, animal, and micro-organism communities and non-living environment, interacting as a functional unit together with human beings (Alcamo et al., 2003). Scientific discourses have established that ecosystems provide sufficient ecosystem services to humans supporting their basic needs for survival, mental health, and well-being (Sandifer et al., 2015). In particular, coastal resources are an asset within ecosystem services, made up of living organisms and non-living materials that can be used to support livelihoods for economic gain (Rambaree, 2013). In Mauritius, the vast majority of the poor people live in the coastal areas and, the marine ecosystem is an important source of livelihoods and well-being.

Challenges for social workers

Collaborative approach

A large number of professional social workers in Mauritius are involved in multidisciplinary and multi-sectoral collaborative approaches through environmental projects related to ICZM.

The governmental organisation that has the overall responsibility for coordinating the ICZM projects in Mauritius is the Ministry of Environment, Sustainable Development, and Disaster and Beach Management. The UN through the *Supporting Integrated and Comprehensive Approaches to Climate Change Adaptation in Africa* project and the European Union through the *Regional Programme for the Sustainable Management of the Coastal Zones of the Indian Ocean Countries* work in close collaboration with social workers from various governmental and non-governmental organisations. In a study of organisations involved in ICZM projects in Mauritius, Rambaree and Cheetamun (2009) found that eight out of 35 organisations had employed workers with social sciences backgrounds. Mauritian social workers operate in multidisciplinary teams to contribute towards environmental projects through activities such as education and campaigns with various population groups, community-based environmental enhancement projects, social needs and impact assessment, disaster intervention, and policy formulation and implementation.

The biopsychosocial functioning of the individual is dependent not only on the social environment but also the natural environment. Social workers have to make the paradigm shift to include the natural environment as a field of expertise. This shift has not yet resonated with the social work community in Barbados and social workers are losing opportunities to engage with experts in other disciplines on issues of climate change and the environment that impact their clients/service users. They may have 'difficulty in integrating a comprehensive understanding of the natural environment and its influence on individual and collective development as well as issues of social and economic justice' (Besthorn and Besthorn, 2012: 57). However, given the unprecedented occurrences of natural and manmade disasters the time has come for all sectors of society and academic disciplines to examine the issues around climate change, environmental degradation, and environmental injustice and to work together to find solutions that would secure the livelihoods of vulnerable groups (Dominelli, 2012).

Participatory approach

Social workers operate in partnership with marginalised, disenfranchised, and vulnerable people whose stories spur them into action. Social workers must engage with residents of local communities and empower those who are disenfranchised due to environmental injustice. This involves hearing their stories, engaging in advocacy for squatters, persons facing environmental hazards such as land or beach erosion and who need to be relocated, and poor persons whose livelihoods are in further jeopardy due to development projects such as hotel construction on the beach front. Generally, social workers employed by governments do not intervene in these matters when government is involved in one way or another, for fear of losing their jobs. However, it behooves them to act through their local professional association to petition government to intervene on behalf of the disadvantaged.

In both Mauritius and Barbados, social workers are required to work towards fairness and social justice by challenging inequalities, marginalisation, and oppression. In this sense, a GSW approach is required to identify strategies that give voice to marginalised and oppressed people, and assist them to express their needs, rights, and concerns in having a fair share in ecosystem services (Rambaree, 2013). For instance, using the SLA, social workers can identify, analyse, and highlight complexities and their power dynamics to suggest how power may be utilised for the emancipation of those people who are trapped or pushed towards vulnerabilities, marginalisation, exclusion, and poverty. Enhancing the capabilities of marginalised and vulnerable groups for emancipation is what makes social work a transformative practice (Rambaree, 2017). In such endeavours, social workers need to work for and with marginalised, disenfranchised, and vulnerable individuals and groups. GSW is based on participatory principles in decision-making processes for achieving the goals of sustainable development. As Dominelli (2013: 435) argues:

> Meeting development needs, particularly those linked to raising people out of poverty, can cause extensive environmental degradation if the development is not planned sustainably and if poor people are not involved in multi-stakeholder partnerships to find solutions alongside experts.

Lessons from the case studies and conclusion

The case studies from Mauritius and Barbados indicate how two countries with similar environmental challenges can undertake social work interventions in the field of ICZM. Social workers in these countries have to consider seriously the impact of the natural environment and climate change on the biopsychosocial functioning of humans, to meet the goals of sustainable development effectively. They must become advocates for marine, coastal and environmental conservation in securing the well-being of those vulnerable groups that depend on these resources for their socio-economic well-being. Social workers in Barbados have missed opportunities for multidisciplinary and multi-sectoral collaborations that could *transform structures to meet the needs of clients/service users* affected by environmental problems by focusing mainly on casework approaches to practice. Environmental sustainability, social sustainability, and people's livelihoods are linked together and require structural changes as highlighted in GSW.

The Mauritian case study calls for a more radical approach to social work: GSW, which is founded on a radical philosophy of fighting against injustices and working for the rights of marginalised and vulnerable populations. Protecting the livelihoods of people is central to GSW. Engaging in GSW requires social workers to have a good understanding of the societal agencies, structures, and processes that impact upon the livelihoods of people. In this endeavour, social workers can utilise the SLA to intervene for the well-being of society and our planet.

The authors conclude that the GSW model presented by Dominelli (2012) has successfully managed to awaken the social work profession to take a more active role in affirming environmental justice and environmental rights as crucial components in promoting the well-being of humans and all living beings on planet Earth. GSW provides social workers with guidelines for critical reasoning and thinking from a more radical and anti-oppressive perspective. Such perspectives are much needed in contemporary societies, where neo-liberal forces have anchored their exploitative power in various social structures. GSW is essentially targeted at empowering marginalised and vulnerable groups and individuals. Moreover, GSW has opened avenues for the social work profession to play influential roles within multidisciplinary collaborations that meet the goals of sustainable development. Hence, social workers from all around the world, including Mauritius and Barbados, can benefit from GSW's ideologies, values, and guidance in promoting the central identity of social work as a liberating and emancipatory profession.

References

Alcamo, J., Ash, N. J., Butler, C. D., Callicot, J. B., Capistrano, D., Carpenter, S. R. (2003). *Ecosystems and human well-being: A framework for assessment.* Washington, DC: Island Press.

Barbados Statistical Service (2015). *Annual report of tourist arrivals 2015/2014.* Available from www.bhta.org/images/Stats/2015/2015Report.pdf [Accessed 12 December 2016].

Besthorn, M. A., and Besthorn, F. H. (2012). Environment and sustainability. In K. Lyons, T. Hokenstad, M. Pawar, N. Heugler, and N. Hall (Eds.), *The Sage handbook of international social work*. London, UK: Sage, pp. 56–69.

BTI (2016). *Mauritius Country Report*. Available on www.btiproject.org/fileadmin/files/BTI/Downloads/Reports/2016/pdf/BTI_2016_Mauritius.pdf [Accessed 12 May 2016].

Caribbean Community [CARICOM]. (2016). *CARICOM has made great strides in HIV/AIDS reduction but challenges remain, Prime Minister Harris tells the United Nations*. Press release 09 June 2016. Available on www.caricom.org/media-center/communications/news-from-the-community/caricom-has-made-great-stridesn-in-hiv-aids-re duction-but-challenges-remain-prime-minister-harris-tells-the-united-nations [Accessed 30 October 2016].

Carney, D. (1998). *Sustainable rural livelihoods: What contribution can we make?* Papers presented at DfID Natural Resources Advisers' Conference, July 1998.

Chambers, R. and Conway, G. (1991). *Sustainable rural livelihoods: Practical concepts for the 21st century*. Available on www.smallstock.info/reference/IDS/dp296.pdf [Accessed 18 September 2016].

CIA (2016). *The world factbook: Barbados*. Available on www.cia.gov/library/publications/the-world-factbook/geos/bb.html [Accessed 16 September 2016].

De Haan, L. (2012). The livelihood approach: a critical exploration. *Erkunde*, 66(4): 345–357.

DFID (1999). *Sustainable livelihoods guidance sheets*. Available from www.eldis.org/vfile/upload/1/document/0901/section2.pdf [Accessed 12 May 2016].

Dominelli, L. (2012). *Green social work: From environmental crises to environmental justice*. Malden, MA: Polity Press.

Dominelli, L. (2013). Environmental justice at the heart of social work practice: Greening the profession. *International Journal of Social Welfare*, 22(4): 431–439.

Erickson, C. L. (2012). Environmental degradation and preservation. In L. M. Healy and R. J. Link (Eds.), *The handbook of international social work: Human rights, development and the global profession*. New York: Oxford, pp. 184–189.

Government of Barbados (1998). *Coastal Zone Management Act 1998, CAP 394. Laws of Barbados*. Available on http://faolex.fao.org/docs/pdf/bar18058.pdf [Accessed 15 September 2016].

Government of Barbados (2013). *Barbados National Assessment Report*. For The Third International Conference on Small Island Developing States, September 1–4, 2014, Apia, Samoa. Available on https://sustainabledevelopment.un.org/content/documents/1054241Barbados_National_Assessment_Report_2014August%20edition-2.pdf [Accessed 27 December 2016].

Hugman, R. (2016). *Social development in social work: Principles and practices*. London: Routledge.

IFSW (2016). *Global Definition of Social Work*. Available from http://ifsw.org/getinvolved/global-definition-of-social-work/ [Accessed 21 May 2016].

IASSW/IFSW/ICSW (2012). *The Global Agenda on Social Work and Social Development*. Available from: http://cdn.ifsw.org/assets/globalagenda2012.pdf [Accessed 12 June 2016].

Knutsson, P. (2006). The sustainable livelihoods approach: A framework for knowledge integration assessment. *Human Ecology Review*, 13(1): 90–99.

Krantz, L. (2001). *The sustainable livelihood approach to poverty reduction. An introduction. Swedish International Development Cooperation Agency*. Available from www.sida.se/contentassets/bd474c-210163447c9a7963d77c64148a/the-sustainable-livelihood-approach-to-poverty-reduction_2656.pdf [Accessed 17 October, 2016].

McFadden, L. (2008). Exploring the challenges of integrated coastal zone management and reflecting on contributions to 'integration' from geographical thought. *Geographical Journal*, 174(3): 299–314.

McKinnon, J. (2012). Social work and changing environments. In K. Lyons, T. Hokenstad, M. Pawar, N. Heugler, and N. Hall (Eds.), *The Sage handbook of international social work*. London, UK: Sage, pp. 265–278.

Ministry of Environment (2007). *National status report on the marine and coastal environment in Republic of Mauritius*. Available on www.unep.org/NairobiConvention/docs/Draft%20NAtional%20Report%20Mauritius%20oct%202007.pdf [Accessed 12 May 2016].

Morse, S., McNamara, N. and Acholo, M. (2009). *Sustainable livelihood approach: A critical analysis of theory and practice*. London, UK: University of Reading.

Nurse, L. A. and Sem, G. (2000). Small island states and climate change: Impacts, adaptation and vulnerability. In J. J. McCarthy, O. F. Canziani, N. A. Leary, D. J. Dokken, K. S. White (Eds.), *Contribution of working group II to the third assessment report*. Cambridge: Cambridge University Press, pp. 843–876.

Rambaree, K. (2017). Environmental activism and justice: A case-study of People's Cooperative Renewable Energy (PCRE) in Mauritius. In A-L. Matthies and K. Nährí (Eds.). *Eco-social transition in social work*. London: Routledge, pp. 121–136.

Rambaree, K. (2013). Social work and sustainable development: Local voices from Mauritius. *Australian Social Work*, 66(2): 261–276.

Rambaree, K. (2011a). Social Work in Rural Communities: A Case study of Empowerment Interventions for the Eradication of Absolute Poverty in Southeast Rural Coastal Villages of Mauritius in L. Ginsberg (Ed.), *Social work in rural communities*, 5th ed. Virginia, USA: Council of Social Work Education, pp. 39–67.

Rambaree, K. (2011b). Community participation within integrated coastal zone management in Western Indian Ocean Countries: A factor analysis of perceived benefits and barriers. *Journal of Environmental Research and Development*, 6(1): 147–154.

Rambaree, K. and Ahmadi, F. (2017). Eco-social work for sustainable development: Implications for social work education practice and research. In A. Fagerstrom and G. M. Cunningham (Eds.), *A sustainable life for all*. Gävle: University of Gävle Press.

Rambaree, K. and Cheetamun, A. (2009). *ICZM Training Needs and Demands*. Quatre Bornes, Mauritius: ReCoMaP Consultancy Report, authorised by the Indian Ocean Commission.

Ring, K. A. and Carmichael, S. (2015). Barbados social work workforce study. *Caribbean Journal of Social Work*, 11(1): 9–53.

Rock, L. F. and Corbin, C. A. (2007). Social work students' and practitioners' views on the need for training Caribbean social workers in disaster management. *International Social Work*, 50(3): 291–294.

Rockloff, S. F. and Lockie, S. (2004). Participatory tools for coastal zone management: Use of stakeholder analysis and social mapping in Australia. *Journal of Coastal Conservation*, 10(1/2): 81–92.

Salverda, T. (2013). Balancing (re)distribution: Franco-Mauritians landownership in the maintenance of an elite position. *Journal of Contemporary African Studies*, 31(3): 503–521.

Salverda, T. and Hay, I. (2014). Change, anxiety and exclusion in the post-colonial reconfiguration of Franco-Mauritian elite geographies. *The Geographical Journal*, 180(3): 236–245.

Salverda, T. S. (2010). *Sugar, Sea and Power*. Vrije: Universiteit Amsterdam.

Sandifer, P. A., Sutton-Grier, A. E. and Ward. B. P. (2015). Exploring connections among nature, biodiversity, ecosystem services, and human health and well-being: Opportunities to enhance health and biodiversity conservation. *Ecosystem Services*, 12(1): 1–15.

Sharpley, R. and Naidoo, P. (2010). Tourism and poverty reduction: The case of Mauritius, *Tourism and Hospitality Planning & Development*, 7(2): 145–162.

Sobhee, S. K., Jankee, K. and Rambaree, K. (2008). *Socio-economic study of the fishing community in Mauritius and Rodrigues*. Food and Agriculture Organisation (FAO). Report, 2008.

Steiner, H. (2014). *Reflections. Our Planet*, September 2014. Available on https://sustainabledevelopment.un.org/content/documents/1693UNEP.pdf [Accessed: 19 July 2016].

Trading Economics (2016). *Barbados GDP*. Available on www.tradingeconomics.com/barbados/gdp [Accessed 27 December 2016].

UNDP (2016). *About Barbados*. Available on www.bb.undp.org/content/barbados/en/home/countryinfo/barbados.html [Accessed 29 December 2016].

van Dillen, S. (2002). Book review: Rural livelihoods and diversity in developing countries. *Journal of Development Economics*, 70(1): 248–252.

World Population Review (2016). *Barbados population 2016*. Available on http://worldpopulationreview.com/countries/barbados-population/ [Accessed 27 December 2016].

21
Social protection options for women farmers in the face of climate change
A case study of women farmers and agriculture in Goromonzi, Zimbabwe

Mildred T. Mushunje and Vishanthie Sewpaul

Introduction

Climate change is an increasing global threat (Food and Agriculture Organisation of the United Nations (FAO), 2012; World Bank, 2008; Winkler, 2010). It is contributing to catastrophic environmental crises such as drought, veld fires, and extreme temperatures, hurricanes, floods and other social challenges such as forced migrations, poverty, loss of property and of lives, and public health concerns (Enarson and Fordham 2001, Giddens, 2009, Winkler, 2010), all of which have particular salience for the profession of social work (Dominelli, 2012). Its adverse effects are a major drawback to the global development trajectory (Giddens, 2009). As Robin and Norton (2010: 1) argued, 'climate change is arguably the most profound challenge facing the international community in the 21st century'. In a seminal text on *Green Social Work*, Dominelli (2012) cogently discussed the relationship between social work and environmental issues, and highlights the impacts of ecological crises, engendered largely by neoliberal capitalism, on the lives of the most vulnerable, particularly in the Global South.

Climate change is also contributing to civil unrest and conflicts emanating from poverty, food insecurity and conflicts over land. Christian Aid (2007: 2) noted that climate change 'destabilizes whole regions where increasingly desperate populations compete for dwindling food and water'. It can be argued that Africa has been disproportionally affected by climate change compared to many other regions of the world. The Intergovernmental Panel on Climate Change asserted that:

> Africa is one of the most vulnerable continents to climate variability and change because of multiple stresses and low adaptive capacity. Some adaptation to current climate variability is taking place; however, this may be insufficient for future changes in climate.
>
> *(2007: 14)*

The Panel argues that by 2020 between 75 million and 250 million people are projected to be exposed to increased water stress due to climate change and this will inadvertently affect livelihoods and exacerbate water-related problems. Climate change has also significantly contributed to the decline in agricultural production, which ultimately leads to increasing food insecurity, reliance on food aid, reduced income, and increased poverty. Women, according to Agarwal (2000), are disproportionally affected by climate change as they have to increase manual labour and find alternatives to food supply while they are still expected to fulfil other gender roles such as caring for the children and domestic chores. Women have been assigned tasks that are a reflection of an extension of their reproductive roles, which seriously disadvantage them. Acker (1989: 238) remarks, 'society including class structure, the state and the political economies cannot be understood without a consideration of gender. Gender is implicated in the fundamental constitution of all social life'. Gender involves inequalities in the sexual division of labour, the separation of public and private spheres, the overvaluation of production and undervaluation of social reproduction, and consequent devaluation of women's paid and unpaid caring work (Agarwal, 2012). As the Least Developed Countries Expert Group (2002: 3) observed:

> Climate change will have different impacts on men and women and in most cases the adverse effects of climate change disproportionately affect women. For example, with increasing drought it is women who have to walk longer distances to collect water.

The Intergovernmental Panel on Climate Change (2007: 17) explained that 'a person's vulnerability to climate change depends in part on gender roles and relations; rural women in developing countries are one of the most vulnerable'. Paradoxically, this gendered nature of climate change is underrepresented in climate change literature and also in the emerging social work field of green social work (Dominelli, 2012). As Robin and Norton (2010: 2) observed, 'current discussions on climate change pay scant attention to the significant ways in which climate change impacts and adaptation practices are gendered'.

Women's role in agriculture and implications of climate change on rural women's livelihoods and food security in Zimbabwe

Zimbabwe's economy is reliant on agricultural production. The nation was once regarded as the bread basket of the region (Mutasa, 2008). Brown et al. (2012: 5) noted that agriculture accounted for approximately 15–18 per cent of Zimbabwe's Gross Domestic Product and for approximately 60 per cent of the raw materials required by the manufacturing industry. It also contributes 40 per cent of total export earnings. Policies such as the highly contested Fast Track Land Reform Programme, a populist land redistribution programme, was retrogressive, chaotically implemented and led to poor agricultural production (Chagutah, 2010). Prior to this controversial land reform programme, commercial farmers contributed significantly to food production (Matondi, 2012). Today, subsistence farming is the major contributor to food security. Other than the 'chaotic' land and agricultural policies implemented by the ZANU-PF led government, climate change has equally adversely affected agricultural production as evidenced by reduced rainfall, increased temperatures and continued droughts (Brown et al., 2012).

Impacts of climate change have also resulted in the El Niño effect where the country experienced less rainfall required for maize for the 2015/2016 season compared to the last two seasons (Government of Zimbabwe, Jan 2016). Chagutah (2010: 6) noted that, 'the reliance of the vast majority of Zimbabweans on rain-fed agriculture and the sensitivity of major sectors of the economy to the climate makes Zimbabwe particularly susceptible to climate change'.

In rural Zimbabwe women are the main producers of food (Chagutah, 2010) and contribute to household and national food security. Their agriculture-based livelihoods include animal husbandry, herbal and nutritional gardens and, in some instances, large-scale commercial farming. The Zimbabwe National Statistical Agency (ZIMSTATS) (2013) recorded that over 50 per cent of women were involved in agriculture in rural Zimbabwe and approximately 35 per cent of rural households were headed by women. This high representation of women in agriculture is not unique to Zimbabwe but a phenomenon across the world. The United Nations Food and Agricultural Organisation (FAO) (2012) highlighted that among all the women who lived in rural areas across the world, 61 per cent of them were farmers and they provided 70 per cent of the labour. Women in Sub-Saharan Africa spent at least 49 per cent of their time on agricultural activities and 25 per cent on domestic activities, working 16 to 18 hours a day (ibid).

Women's role in agriculture has long been established, but their contribution to agriculture is hampered by prevailing structural gender inequalities and poverty (Mushunje, 2013), and a number of factors including lack of access to productive resources (Meizen-Dick and Quisimbing, 2012). This vulnerability is further exacerbated by the impacts of climate change. In Zimbabwe, gender inequality is deep seated and men's domination cuts across almost all social spheres such as education, religion, law, economy and politics. Mushunje (2013: 5) noted that 'in Zimbabwe, 70 per cent of farmers are women, making agriculture a women-dominated industry but they do not own the means of production. Their access to land is impaired through male power and control'.

The FAO *State of Food and Agriculture 2010–2011* report emphasised the need to close the gender gap in access to agricultural resources, education, extension, financial services and labour markets; to invest in labour-saving and productivity-enhancing technologies and infrastructure to free women's time for more productive activities; and to facilitate women's participation in flexible, efficient and fair rural labour markets (Meinzen-Dick and Quisumbing, 2012). By investing in women, the gains accrue to the entire household as women tend to be concerned about translating their benefits to their households (World Bank, 2008). There is agreement that gender inequalities and lack of attention to gender in agricultural development contribute to lower productivity, lost income and higher levels of poverty alongside under-nutrition (World Bank, 2008). Climate change is affecting rural women's livelihoods in profound ways and has changed the rural agricultural landscape. Males are migrating to urban areas and crossing the borders in a bid to find alternate sources of livelihoods (FAO, 2011). Thus, women are taking on multiple functions in addition to their traditional reproductive caring roles. Brown et al. (2012: 34) conducted a study in Shurungwi District, a rural area in the middle of Zimbabwe, to assess the impact of climate change on women-led livelihoods. The study concluded that there has been disruption and a drastic reduction in production due to drought and high temperatures. They noted:

> Women in some areas of Shurugwi reported a shift in livelihood strategies to commercial beer brewing, which led to higher alcoholism and an increase in domestic violence and abuse against women. In other cases, the impacts of drought and extreme weather resulted in women travelling long distances to fetch water.
>
> *(2012: 34)*

Expressing how gender inequality increases women's vulnerability to climate change, the United Nations Development Programme (2007) argued:

> Gender inequalities intersect with climate risks and vulnerabilities. Women's historic disadvantages – their limited access to resources, restricted rights, and a muted voice in shaping

decisions – make them highly vulnerable to climate change. The nature of that vulnerability varies widely cautioning against generalisation. But climate change is likely to magnify existing patterns of gender disadvantage.

Research methodology

Rationale for the study

Despite women being one of the most disadvantaged groups by climate, their voices are under-represented in the climate change adaption, mitigation and reduction discourses (FAO, 2011). This is worse with women in rural areas whose contributions to policy issues are rarely considered. This is a huge missed opportunity and gap, as women have profound experience in developing coping mechanisms to ensure household food security and they also have a rich wealth of indigenous knowledge. Their knowledge and experiences are crucial in the development of sustainable and gender-sensitive climate change policies.

We undertook a study in Goromonzi to understand the extent to which climate change has impacted on households, especially with regards to women's interface with agriculture. The area examined is depicted in Figures 21.1 and 21.2.

Research objectives

The research objectives were:

- to understand the impacts of climate change on rural women; and
- to explore sustainable social protection options for rural women in the face of climate change.

Guiding questions

The following questions guided the discussions:

1. What do women and men understand to be climate change?
2. How has this affected their livelihoods?
3. What social protection measures are in existence for households?

Data Collection

Data were collected using the qualitative method, underscored by an ethno-methodological approach. This was targeted at deriving in-depth responses from the respondents, replies that go beyond the quantitative aspects but also tell a story as to how the household has been impacted by climate change. Home visits, in-depth interviews and observation were the primary sources of data. The interviews were tape recorded and transcribed verbatim, and analysed thematically. Interviews were held in the home settings of the respondents, allowing for a natural environment that allowed them to express themselves in a candid manner. The research was informed by critical theory, which provides criticisms and alternatives to mainstream social theory, and it is particularly concerned with how social criteria such as race, class and gender intersect to influence access to power and resources (Dominelli, 2002; Sewpaul, 2013). It is motivated by the need for emancipation of the oppressed (Freire, 1973), the unlearning and undoing of privilege (Pease, 2010), and the provision of alternatives to oppressed people by informing and educating them on available possibilities (Sabia and Wallulis, 1983). The underlying assumptions of this research were:

- Women farmers are being negatively affected as a result of climate change.
- Women's roles in households are changing as a result of climate change.
- Climate change has resulted in food insecurity in households.
- Food insecurity is a result of structural inequalities and needs to be addressed at the structural levels before households that are food insecure can become self-sufficient.

Sampling

There is a total of 25 wards in Goromonzi district with the smallest ward having 258 people and the largest having 30,123 people. The average household size is four. Ward 11 was targeted as this was an area we had prior experience and knowledge of. The district was also chosen because it is readily accessible in terms of road networks and even the political climate. A total of 15 females were identified. A deliberate effort was made to have a mixed group of married and widowed women. The respondents were identified through collaboration with an NGO that is known to us, the Cluster Agriculture Development Services, which is the NGO that has worked consistently in Goromonzi.

Figure 21.1 Map of Goromonzi

Source: Maps developed by Kudzai Kariri using vector data from the Department of Surveyor General and Central Statistics office.

Social protection for women farmers

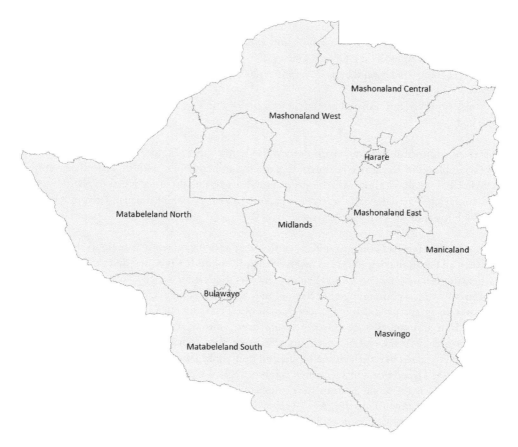

Figure 21.2 Map of Zimbabwe showing the location of Goromonzi in Mashonaland East Province

Source: Maps developed by Kudzai Kariri using vector data from the Department of Surveyor General and Central Statistics office.

Presentation of findings

The ages of the participants ranged from 30–63 years of age; the average age was 50 years old. Levels of education ranged mostly from Grade 7 to Form 4. Ten women had completed primary school, three had finished secondary school and two had tertiary education. The women noted that the opportunities for them to attend school were limited during their time and they felt to some extent this was still the case, though the situation has slightly improved as households were now aware of the importance of education. Five of these were widowed and thus heads of households.

All the respondents were subsistence farmers and understood climate change to be the changing patterns of the rainfall seasons. They had always assumed that agriculture would give them sufficient food throughout the years. Those who had excess in past years would barter this for items like sugar and clothing. Over the last couple of years they had noted that the rains were at times late and the winters also very cold. This was attributed to the phenomena which they had now come to understand as climate change. All the single women attested to the fact that they felt more vulnerable with regards to their sources of livelihoods as they did not have husbands who could work in the urban areas or migrate to other places to look for alternate sources of livelihoods. They now also engaged in activities such as petty trading and bartering. One widow said, 'for us widows, it's particularly harder'.

This was, however, not a shared sentiment as some of the married women had a different view. One said:

> Even if our husbands can work outside the home, there are no jobs out there. We are all scrambling for the scarce resources that are found here. Now, with this rain that is unpredictable, we don't know whether to plant, what to plant and even when to plant. It's quite confusing. The elders also seem to be confused as they would normally give direction in such instances.

All the participants had come to the conclusion that agriculture was a 'gamble' as they called it, and they all began making efforts to diversify their livelihoods. One such diversification was the participation in income savings and lending schemes to generate money. These are comprised of a group of women coming together to pool money which is then lent out to the group members over an agreed period, usually, over one month. This is then paid back with interest, which is agreed on and ranges from 10–20 per cent over a month. The interest is where the group makes its money. At the end of a cycle (usually a year) the money is shared out to members, and they purchase items like agricultural inputs and household utensils.

There was a sense that climate change was more than a weather condition. The older women felt that the changes in the patterns were associated with the changing lifestyles and the ancestors were not happy about this. A 55-year-old widowed woman said, 'it's the gods turning against us for not following our traditions. We no longer follow our cultures of giving sacrifices to the dead. Since I came here some 20 years ago, I don't remember any time we have sat as a community to call on the gods to give us rain'.

With regards to social support to mitigate the impacts of climate change, all the respondents reported that they had benefitted in the past from the Presidential scheme. Under the Presidential scheme, government acquired inputs comprised maize, wheat and cotton worth US$200 million to benefit 1.6 million households in 2014. Most farmers were able to register through the influence of the local committees which had been set up to administer the programmes. The coverage was meant to be universal. However, not all households have benefitted. Participants noted the cumbersome process which they had to endure to register for the allocation. This included registering with the local chief/community leader then being vetted for consideration. It seemed to be easier for those who knew the committee members to have better access to such programmes. All the women indicated that they did not cope well when there was insufficient food for the household. Women testified that they would rather go hungry and feed their children than for them to share the little they had and allow the children to suffer. Their hope was that when the children grew up, they would have better livelihood options and provide care and protection for their parents. A widowed respondent said:

> you know, we never really had hand-outs before. But now, we appreciate anything that comes and the Presidential scheme is one among many. It is my prayer that my children see the struggles that I am enduring so they can to go school and support me when they start working and also when I reach old age.

The participants also explained that there used to be programmes like the Chief's Granary which provided food for vulnerable members of the community. This, however, was not as vibrant or reliable because community members have become individualistic and inward looking. One woman said, 'I would really like to contribute to the Chief's Granary but you can only give what you have. I don't even have enough food for my household for the season so I cannot even start to think of other community members'. The individualism was, therefore, an indication of the economic hardships that the women were facing.

Other current social protection mechanisms were provided by NGOs in the form of agricultural inputs. This was a challenge as there were no irrigation facilities which meant that with the unpredictability of the rainfall due to climate changes, the households could still be vulnerable to food insecurity even if they had inputs.

Intersection between social protection and women farmers

Social protection has evolved significantly over time from the more welfare-based interventions to what Sabates-Wheeler and Devereux (2007) refer to as being transformative. In the varied discussions on social protection in agriculture, Devereux (2012) argues that there does not have to be a conflict between the provision of social protection and agricultural enterprises. According to FAO (2016), social protection and agriculture are complementary and mutually reinforce each other in reducing hunger and poverty. In the face of climate change, social protection is key to maintaining positive human development indicators as these tend to decline during external shocks such as those induced by climate change. FAO, through its Protection to Production (PtoP) (FAO, 2016) Programme has generated evidence that shows that agricultural interventions can promote growth in smallholder productivity by addressing structural constraints that limit poor households' access to land and water resources, inputs, financial services, advisory services and markets. Additionally, social protection can provide liquidity and certainty for poor smallholders, allowing them to invest in agriculture, re-allocate their labour to on-farm activities, invest in human capital development, increase participation in social networks (which constitute an important source of informal risk management) and better manage risks, thereby allowing them to engage in more profitable livelihood and agricultural activities. Devereux (2009) argues social protection can be defined as being protective (i.e. providing relief from deprivation). It can also be preventative (i.e. averting deprivation) and be promotive by enhancing household capacity to access inputs. The transformative aspect that accrues to the households is important. The provision of social protection has the catalytic effect of improving social indicators such as health, food and nutrition security and education levels. This has wider impacts at national levels and stimulates local economic growth.

Social protection can be categorised through informal and formal systems. Informal social security needs to be enhanced by combining with other formal support systems. Evidence suggests that the two can co-exist. For instance, the remittance of pension funds may result in a re-direction of flows within the family network, which eventually proves to be welfare-enhancing for the entire network.

Social protection should be targeted at women farmers who are likely to be left out of the national schemes because of the informality of their work. Much of Zimbabwe's social protection schemes are centred on formal sector employment. The Zimbabwe government has set up a compulsory national social security pension scheme which is provided for by the National Social Security Authority (NSSA). NSSA is a corporate body which was established by an Act of Parliament in 1989 to administer social security schemes in the country. Women farmers are largely excluded from formal social protection systems. Yet, social protection has the potential to mitigate against the impacts of climate change on rural women's livelihood. The following social protection options are suggested:

Social protection options

Informal systems

Locally based social protection provisions

The legacy of colonialism impacted on the locals with regards to social protection options. The colonial government never put in place a system for black people to benefit from social protection. The understanding was that the black people were in the urban areas only to work and would go back to the rural home on retirement. Consequently, black people created mechanisms to cope with retirement and economic hardships. Thus, communities came up with ingenious coping mechanisms and these are quite evident in Goromonzi and they need to be strengthened.

Zunde raMambo

Access to food at household level depends on own production, the availability of income to purchase food and the availability of both formal and informal sources of food transfers. This production or ability to purchase food is made possible by utilising the livelihood assets essential to their livelihood strategies: human, natural, financial, social and physical capital (Jayne et al., 2002). Zunde raMambo or the 'Chief's Granary' is a pre-colonial practice to promote food security, particularly among vulnerable members of society. The system was suppressed during colonial rule by corroding the authority of traditional chiefs. The primary aim of the Zunde was to ensure that a community had food reserves which could be used in times of food shortage (Mararike, 2001; Olivier et al., 2008). It also embodied the traditional values that promote togetherness and a sense of belonging (Mararike, 2001). And, it was meant to provide social protection against drought and famine, and thus mitigated the impact of food insecurity in the community (Mushunje, 2006).

The Zunde raMambo has been affected in a number of ways by developments in Zimbabwe. For instance, the land reform programme resettled people by bringing people from different areas onto a communal area such as the case in Goromonzi. This meant that people with different values were brought together under a chief whom they had to select. This had the potential to cause conflicts and misunderstandings. Given the efficacy of the Zunde raMambo in previous times, it is prudent for communities to revitalise this and adapt the concept to community needs. Communities have to brace against climate change and one effective way forward is as Kaseke and Dhemba (2007) observed: the concept of Zunde raMambo has always been seen as a manifestation of community responsibility. According to Kaseke and Dhemba (2007: 91) participants to the Zunde raMambo Project did not consider themselves as volunteers, but rather as beneficiaries of the programme. These two authors further explain, 'fulfilment comes from being able to solve community problems especially those of orphaned children, widows and the elderly [sic], particularly with respect to food security'.

Income from internal savings and lending schemes (ISALs) and income rotating schemes

Internal savings and lending schemes (ISALs) are not simply an end in themselves; rather they are a means to strengthen community processes so that people can mobilise money to achieve their multiple and diverse needs. According to a ZIMSTATs report, a total of 53 per cent households were members of agricultural extension groups while 28 per cent were ISAL members. Pooling money has evidently assisted households to acquire inputs.

Rotating schemes popularly known as 'maRound' should also be strengthened. In this model, members contribute $2 per week and they advance one member of the group the money. At the end of the week, the members contribute again and give the funds to another group member until all the members have benefitted. They impose few transaction costs on members which is important for women, thereby fostering reciprocity that can be called upon in times of difficulties and emergencies (Kurmalineva, 2003).

Formal systems

Provision of inputs and irrigation facilities

Support with inputs is key to addressing food insecurity and this should include the instalment of irrigation water. This would mitigate against unpredictable rainfall patterns and reduce women's time spent on fetching water to water gardens.

Targeted national social and cash transfers for women

Women can be supported with cash and/or social transfers. These can influence the productive dimension of beneficiary households. Participants in this study indicated that they lacked access to finance and other productive resources such as inputs. An injection of cash into their households would help them to meet other needs and free the household members to engage in productive work. Currently, the household members have to sell their labour to other households at the expense of their agricultural fields. Research data, across several countries, show the direct impact of cash transfers in alleviating poverty (Mushunje and Mafico, 2010).

Devereux (2009) argued that governments should implement permanent national social transfer programmes that are integrated into agricultural and broader development policies. This would require a strong shift on the part of funding partners from the small-scale pilot projects to nationwide initiatives. We concur strongly with this and argue that there have been enough pilot projects which have generated sufficient evidence for interventions. We cannot continue in the piloting mode when families are very obviously deeply affected by climate change.

Short-term food aid

In the short term, households can also be supported with food aid. This is an intervention that is usually provided in the short term beyond which it is usually integrated with other programmes such as Zunde raMambo and other livelihoods and social protection programmes. We take note of Devereux's (2009) proposal that food that goes towards food aid should be grown locally. Farmers should therefore be supported with inputs and capital assets such as irrigation schemes. Contrary to some beliefs that food aid could increase dependency, a review of food aid by Barrett and Maxwell (2005) concluded that it rarely induces dependency, because food transfers are too small and unpredictable to affect beneficiary behaviour. The researchers' discussions with participants showed that they were rational beings and they did not think it made sense for them to sit back and expect to be fed. They were in a precarious position, but not out of choice. They actually preferred to work and be self-sufficient.

Conclusion

Women in this study were acutely aware of the consequences of climate change and how this affected their livelihoods as rural small-scale farmers. Livelihood options had been diversified to include income savings and lending schemes to generate income for petty business trades and migratory work. Although the women diversified in order to provide for household food security, there needs to be in place social protection initiatives tailor made to suit the specific needs of women.

With regards to the assumptions, we can conclude that climate change is a contributor towards changes in women farmers' livelihoods. Though outward migration of men used to happen even without climate change, it was usually to the urban areas and always with the understanding that this was for a specific period. The men would return to be in time to participate in the cropping season. Currently, the men are gone for long stretches and they are migrating beyond the borders of Zimbabwe. Climate change is not the only cause of food insecurity. There needs to be in place social protection mechanisms that can support women and households to access food. This could be through programmes such as public works. The challenges were therefore structural in that local and national government systems were not providing sufficient alternatives for women to participate.

As social workers engage with people who suffer the consequences of ecological crises and climate change, they are ideally suited to highlight the interconnections between social, economic and environmental issues and to lobby and advocate with and/on behalf of those most affected (Dominelli, 2012). Social workers can strive towards integrated socio-economic and environmental development by supporting the goals of the Global Agenda (IFSW, IASSW, ICSW, 2012) that is committed to the International Labour Organisation's (ILO) Decent Work Agenda and the United Nations Social Protection Floor Initiative.

The World Bank Group and the ILO joined forces in June 2015 to support the launch of universal social security, which is a key mechanism to ensure the fulfilment of socio-economic rights, arguing that:

> Social protection systems that are well-designed and implemented can powerfully shape countries, enhance human capital and productivity, eradicate poverty, reduce inequalities and contribute to building social peace. They are an essential part of National Development Strategies to achieve inclusive growth and sustainable development with equitable social outcomes.

This calls for redistributive and regulatory roles of states that social workers must support, rather than laissez-faire capitalist states that transfer responsibilities of health, education and well-being to private providers, and to individuals, families and local communities, often in the disguise of choice, empowerment, self-reliance, and community care (Sewpaul, 2016). We conclude by citing Dominelli who asserted that:

> The aim of green social work is to work for the reform of the socio-political and economic forces that have a deleterious impact upon the quality of life of poor and marginalised populations and secure the policy changes and social transformations necessary for enhancing the well-being of people and the planet today and in the future.

(2012: 25)

References

Acker J. (1989). The problem with patriarchy. *Sociology* 23 (2) : 235–240.

Agarwal, B. (2000). Conceptualizing environmental collective action: Why gender matters. *Cambridge Journal of Economics*, 24: 283–310.

Agarwal, B. (2012). *Food security, productivity and gender inequality.* IEG Working Paper No. 320. Institute of Economic Growth University Enclave. India: University of Delhi Delhi 110007.

Barrett, C. and Maxwell, D. (2005). *Food aid after fifty years: Recasting its role.* London: Routledge.

Brown, D., Chanakira, R., Chatiza, K., Dhliwayo, M., Dodman, D., Masiiwa, M., Davison, D., Mugabe, P. and Zvigadza, S. (2012). *Climate change impacts, vulnerability and adaptation in Zimbabwe*, Climate Change Working paper number 3. Available online http://pubs.iied.org/pdfs/10034IIED.pdf [Accessed 15 September 2016].

Chagutah T. (2010). *Climate change vulnerability and preparedness in Southern Africa: Zimbabwe Country Report.* Cape Town: Heinrich Boell Stiftung.

Christian Aid. (2007). Human tide: The real migration crisis. *Christian Aid.* www.christianaid.org.uk/Images/human_tide3__tcm15-23335.pdf [Accessed 15 November 2016].

Devereux, S. (2009). *Social protection for agricultural growth in Africa.* FAC Working Paper No. SP06, January 2009.

Devereux, S. (2012). Social Protection for Enhanced Food Security in Sub-Saharan Africa, WP 2012-010: February 2012, United Nations Development Programme. Regional Bureau for Africa. Available on http://www.undp.org/content/dam/rba/docs/Working%20Papers/Social%20Protection%20Food%20Security.pdf [Accessed 5 November 2017].

Dominelli, L. (2002). *Anti-oppressive social work theory and practice.* Basingstoke: Palgrave Macmillan.

Dominelli, L. (2012). *Green social work.* Cambridge: Polity Press.

Enarson, E. and Fordham, M. (2001). From women's needs to women's rights in disasters. *Environmental Hazards*, 12(3): 133–136.

FAO (Food and Agriculture Organisation of the United Nations) (2011). *Women in agriculture. Closing the gender gap for development. The State of food and agriculture 2010–2011.* Rome: FAO.

FAO (Food and Agriculture Organisation of the United Nations) (2012). *Gender equality policy.* Rome: FAO.

FAO (Food and Agriculture Organisation of the United Nations) (2013). *Climate change a further challenge for gender equity, how men and women farmers are differently affected.* Available online www.fao.org/newsroom/en/news/2008/1000809/index.html [Accessed 13 August 2016].

FAO (Food and Agriculture Organisation of the United Nations) (2016). *Social protection for rural poverty reduction, Rural Transformations.* Technical Papers Series #1. Rome: FAO.

Freire, P. (1973). *Education for critical consciousness.* New York: Seabury Press.

Giddens, A. (2009). *The politics of climate change.* Cambridge: Polity Press.

Government of Zimbabwe (2016). Unpublished weekly updates on rainfall situation. January.

Inter-governmental Panel on Climate Change (IPCC) (2007). Summary for Policymakers. In *Climate change 2007: Impacts, adaptation and vulnerability.* Contribution of Working Group II to the Fourth Assessment Report of the Intergovernmental Panel on Climate Change (M. L. Parry, O. F. Canziani, J. P. Palutikof, P. J. van der Linden and C. E. Hanson, Eds.). Cambridge: Cambridge University Press. E_8Mar.pdf [Accessed 5 November 2017].

Jayne, T., Govereh, J., Mwanaumo, A., Nyoro, J. and Chapoto, A. (2002). False promise or false premise? The experience of food and input market reform in Eastern and Southern Africa. *World Development*, 30 (11): 1967–1985.

Kaseke, E. and Dhemba, J. (2007). Community mobilisation, volunteerism and the fight against HIV/AIDS in Zimbabwe. The Social Work Practitioner-Researcher, *Journal of Social Development in Africa – A special issue*, 50(1): 85–99.

Kurmalineva, R. (2003). *Microfinance and the vulnerable communities.* London: Routledge. Least Developed Countries Expert Group. *Annotated guidelines for the preparation of national adaptation programmes of action* (2002). New York: United Nations Framework Convention on Climate Change.

Least Developed Countries Expert Group (2002). *United Nations Framework Convention on Climate Change: Annotated guidelines for the preparation of national adaptation programmes of action.* Available on http://unfccc.int/resource/docs/publications/annguid_e.pdf [Accessed 5 November 2017].

Mararike, C. (2001). Revival of indigenous food security strategies at the village level: the human factor implications. In *Review of Human Factor Studies* 6(2): 93–104.

Matondi, P. B. (2012). *Zimbabwe's fast track land reform programme.* London: ZED Books.

Mushunje, M.T. (2006). Child Protection in Zimbabwe: Past, Present and Future. *Journal of Social Development in Africa.* 21(1): 12-34.

Mushunje, M.T. (2013). Paper presented at Southern African Social Protection Experts Network (SASPEN), *Social Protection for those working informally.* International Conference 16–17 September 2013, Johannesburg. Available online on www.saspen.org/conferences/informal2013/Paper_Mushunje_FES-SASPEN-16SEP2013-INT-CONF-SP4IE.pdf [Accessed 20 September 2016].

Mushunje, M. T. and Mafico, M. (2010). Social protection for orphans and vulnerable children in Zimbabwe: The case of cash transfers. *International Social Work,* 53(2): 261–275.

Mutasa C. (2008). *Evidence of climate change in Zimbabwe.* Paper presented at the Climate Change Awareness and Dialogue Workshop for Mashonaland Central and Mashonaland West Provinces Held at Caribbea Bay Hotel, Kariba, Zimbabwe, 29–30 September.

Olivier, M.P., Kaseke, E. and Mpedi, L.G. (2008). *Paper prepared for presentation at the International Conference on Social Security organised by the National Department of Social Department, South Africa,* 10–14 March 2008, Cape Town.

Pease, B. (2010). *Undoing privilege: Unearned advantage in a divided world.* London: Zed Books.

Meizen-Dick, R. and Quisumbing, A. (2012). *Women in agriculture: Closing the gender gap.* IFPRI Global Policy Report, Washington, DC: IFPRI. Available on www.ifpri.org/ gfpr/2012/women-agriculture

Robin, M. and Norton, A. (Eds.) (2010). *Social dimensions of climate change: Equity and vulnerability in a warming world.* Washington, DC: The World Bank.

Sabia, D. and Wallulis, J. (eds.) (1983). *Changing social science. Critical theory and other critical perspectives.* Albany: State University of New York Press.

Sabates-Wheeler, R. and Devereux, S. (2007). Transformative social protection: The currency of social justice. In A. Barrientos and D. Hulme (Eds.), *Social protection for the poor and poorest. Risk, needs and rights.* London: Palgrave Macmillan.

Sewpaul, V. (2013). Inscribed in our blood: Confronting and challenging the ideology of sexism and racism. *Affilia: The Journal of Women and Social Work,* 28(2): 116–25.

Sewpaul, V. (2016). The west and the rest divide: Culture, human rights and social work. *Journal of Human Rights and Social Work.* 1(1): 30–39. doi:10.1007/s41134-016-0003-2.

United Nations Development Programme (2007). *Human Development Report 2007/2008 – fighting climate change: Human solidarity in a divided world.* New York: United Nations Development Programme.

Winkler, H. (2010). *Taking action on climate change, long term mitigation scenarios for South Africa.* Cape Town: UCT Press.

World Bank (2008). *Development and climate change: A strategic framework for the world bank group.* Washington, DC: World Bank.

Zimbabwe National Statistical Agency (ZIMSTATS) (2013). *Facts and Figures 2013.* Harare: ZIMSTATS. Available on http://www.zimstat.co.zw/sites/default/files/img/publications/Other/Facts_2013.pdf [Accessed 5 November 2017].

22
Climate justice, capabilities and sustainable livelihoods
Insights from an action research project

*Sunil D. Santha, Sowmya Balasubramaniam,
Anup Shenai, Asha Banu Soletti, Sharvan Verma,
Jaydip Solanki and Rupali Gaikawad*

Introduction

Climate variability and extreme hazard events can severely affect the life and livelihoods of many marginalised and vulnerable groups. Livelihood comprises the capabilities, assets (stores, claims and access) and activities required for a means of living (Chambers and Conway, 1992). Extreme changes in their natural environment not only restrict the vulnerable groups' access to basic livelihood resources, but it also reduces their capabilities to function as individuals and communities. Green social workers shaping local level responses to climate change should aim at developing both vulnerability reduction and just adaptation strategies. This chapter demonstrates that such initiatives are possible by enhancing the capabilities of tribal communities through action research.

This chapter is based on insights drawn from the action research project carried out with a tribal community in the Thane district of Maharashtra, India. The chapter's primary aim is to describe the process of action research that enabled the key stakeholders in designing and implementing local adaptation strategies to climate variability, resource scarcity and livelihood uncertainties. The various sections of the chapter are arranged as follows. To begin with, the vulnerability of tribal communities is analysed in its political economy context. This lays down the context of the action research project. A discussion of the study's theoretical framework and methodology follows. Subsequently, the various steps and trajectories that evolved in the action research project are considered. Some of the visible outcomes are also presented in continuation to the discussion of the action research process. This is followed by a discussion of key insights gained by the research process.

The context of action research

This chapter is based on an action research project initiated by a team (referred to as 'project team' from now on) of seven social workers at the School of Social Work, Tata Institute of Social

Sciences in Mumbi, India. The project team consisted of two faculty members and five students who were committed to both green social work and action research. The setting of this action research project is a tribal hamlet named Jambulpada in Aghai village of the Thane district in Maharashtra. Surrounded by mountains, forests and agrarian dry lands, the hamlet consists of 35 households with a population of 511 people. The Warli tribes are the main inhabitants of the hamlet, while a few households belong to the Mahadeo Kolis tribe.

Vulnerability, from a political economy perspective, refers to people's lack of access to resources, lack of representation in decision-making structures and lack of effective agency to influence governance decisions in their favour, which reduces their ability to anticipate, respond or recover from socio-economic, political and environmental changes. Vulnerability of individuals, households, groups or community includes their ability to anticipate, cope with, resist and recover from, or adapt to any shocks or external stress placed on their livelihoods and well-being (Wisner et al., 2004; Kelly and Adger, 2000). Our primary understanding revealed that the people of Jambulpada have been historically marginalised in terms of socio-economic, political and related structural inequities. This has resulted in the progression of their vulnerabilities in terms of unemployment, migration of men to cities in search of better work opportunities, insecure land tenure, lack of access to education, healthcare and other public infrastructures.

Out of the 35 households, only around 12 households possess legal ownership of land. The rest do not have any valid land deeds with them. Most of these households are involved in seasonal agriculture, mainly in the cultivation of a local variety of paddy crops. Their agriculture is sustenance-oriented and mainly meant for household-level consumption. Surplus paddy is sold to the local market in Aghai. Their sustenance is also dependent on minor forest produce such as procurement and sale of mohua flowers and some kind of sweetener gums collected from the forests. However, their local trading systems are highly exploitative because outsiders often cheat them by bartering their produce with low-priced goods or by paying less than the market price.

Participative interactions with community members revealed that their vulnerability contexts have worsened with climate variability in the last decade. Climate variability according to the local people's construction of their reality could be associated with their reference to erratic monsoons, sporadic rainfall, drought, water scarcity for both farming and household consumption, high atmospheric temperature or the heat, sleeplessness and fatigue, damage to crops or low yield and so on. For instance, their farm-based activities are dependent on the monsoon rains. Severe drought conditions over a decade have drastically reduced their farm-based outputs. Post-monsoon, farming is not practiced due to severe water shortage. This has subsequently resulted in large-scale migration of men from the households to the nearest urban centres such as Shahpur or Mumbra to work as daily wage labourers or construction workers. The migration of men from the village to the cities has resulted in increased women's burdens in the households in terms of accessing basic livelihood resources and single-handedly managing the day-to-day domestic chores. As drinking water availability has also become very scarce, women are forced to procure water from water bodies that are far away from their homes.

Theoretical framework

The larger approach that guided the project team in this action research is green social work (Dominelli, 2012). A key dimension of green social work is that it entails vulnerability reduction and the promotion of social and environmental justice through the designing and strengthening of institutions, values and practices facilitating just adaptation. Green social work aims at reforming the socio-political and economic forces that contribute to the vulnerabilities of marginalised populations (Dominelli, 2012). It aims at securing 'policy changes and social transformations necessary for enhancing the well-being of people and the planet today and in the future and advancing the duty to care for others and the right to be cared for by others' (Dominelli, 2012: 25).

This chapter advocates climate justice as a crucial component of green social work practices. Green social work focuses on how responses to environmental crisis must both challenge and address poverty, structural inequalities, socio-economic disparities including limited access to natural resources (Dominelli, 2012). Social and environmental justice, including climate justice are inherent elements of green social work. Climate justice entails the fair distribution of goods, recognising cultural differences and removing procedural obstacles that prevent marginalised groups from participating meaningfully in decisions that affect their property, well-being and risk (Shi et al., 2016). Such a perspective emphasises that 'those whose lives and livelihoods are most vulnerable to the consequences of climate change and who have contributed the least to its causes should receive preferential support' (Mearns and Norton, 2010: 10). Adaptation to climate change has often been regarded as involving both distributive and procedural theories of justice (Paavola and Adger, 2002; 2006; Comim, 2008) which are also consequences of a lack of cultural recognition or procedural inclusion. Bulkeley et al. (2014) have argued that recognising vulnerable and marginalised groups and including these groups in decision-making procedures creates social and political space for them to share their concerns and priorities in climate change adaptation. Providing these groups with the resources to act ensures that the most vulnerable are able to adapt effectively to the impacts of climate change, resource scarcity and livelihood uncertainties.

Green social work as a form of practice is rooted in the improved well-being of people and their environment (Dominelli, 2013). In this regard, the action research project also gathered insights from the capabilities approach (Sen, 1999; Nussbaum, 2000), which has the potential to recognise the vulnerabilities and basic needs of marginalised communities in the context of climate change and its impact (Schlosberg, 2012a). Here, one needs to emphasise that the green social work approach encourages such multidisciplinary understanding of capabilities, vulnerability and climate justice, which is crucial to deliver just adaptation strategies. Capabilities refers to 'the conditions or states of enablement that make it possible for people to achieve things; capabilities are people's real opportunities to achieve outcomes they value' (Nussbaum, 2000: 70–80). Capabilities refer to what people are actually able to do and to be (ibid). The extended forms of the capability approach also recognise environmental factors as a meta-capability that could enable human functioning and flourishing (Holland, 2008; Schlosberg, 2012a). Like green social work, it acknowledges human dependence on the environment and provides for those ecological support systems that make their functioning and flourishing possible (Schlosberg, 2012a). Climate variability and extreme hazard events affect the capabilities of vulnerable communities in terms of their health and ability to earn a living, social networks, housing, and access to crucial livelihood assets (Dryzek et al., 2011). Through action research, the project team aimed to rebuild certain sets of capabilities, which would strengthen other capabilities. It also seemed to the authors that this would facilitate the restoration of ecological justice without displacing cultural and participatory forms of justice (Figueroa, 2011 in Dryzek, 2011).

The role of green social workers has been envisaged as to address structural inequalities and in promoting ecologically just practices and institutions (Dominelli, 2012). Such perspectives inspired the action research processes and enabled both the social workers and the community involved in the project to co-design the interventions. Embedded in green social work values, the key to climate justice is protecting these vulnerable tribal communities through recognition and democratic participation, and what it takes for them to function normally even during events of extreme shocks and uncertainties (Schlosberg, 2012b). Vulnerable groups require better socio-ecological security systems, and social workers can facilitate these processes between the community, their natural environment and other relevant stakeholders such as the state government and Corporate Social Responsibility (CSR) organisations.

Green social work in India is yet to become a subject of importance. This chapter is thus an attempt to demonstrate that green social work as part of the wider social work profession has an important role to play in vulnerability reduction, climate change adaptation and challenging social inequities. Dominelli (2011) envisaged that social workers could play a mediating role in helping people understand environmental issues and mobilise people to protect their futures. Social workers with their expertise in action research processes could work together with vulnerable communities and the system to facilitate, design and implement adaptive social protection strategies. This chapter demonstrates that green social workers can promote climate justice by helping people mobilise and organise activities that restore or protect their natural environment. In addition, it is also an opportunity to provide insights on how green social work practices could facilitate the co-production of knowledge and facilitate partnerships between local communities and experts (Dominelli, 2013).

The action research process

Action research could be defined as 'a term used to describe a family of related investigative approaches that integrate theory and action, with the goal of addressing important organisational, community and social issues together with those who experience them' (Coghlan and Brydon-Miller, 2014: xxv). As social workers, we felt that action research could create democratic spaces for a deeper engagement between the practitioners and the community (Reason, 2006). The social workers' critical practice was influenced by enquiring about several points: a) whose knowledge counts in climate change adaptation, b) how are different types of knowledge represented in these processes, and c) whose knowledge is reproduced and maintained in ways that lead to the present inequalities? These queries are also inherent to the values that green social work is embedded within. Our guiding principle was that all the processes that emerged would be designed and shaped in a participatory and collaborative manner with the community (i.e. coproduced). The broader action research processes that were carried out were briefly as follows.

Phase 1 – Situational Analysis: In this phase, a socio-historical analysis of the hamlet was carried out through key informant interviews, oral histories and in-depth group discussions. It has to be understood that in this phase, community participation was minimal and was largely initiated by the project team. The team members stayed in the hamlet itself to build trust with the villagers. The historical analysis of the village contexts revealed that this community was neither recognised nor its needs represented adequately in any forms of governance. A crucial challenge during this phase was to initiate and sustain trust-based relationships with the community, nurture local leadership and collaborative decision-making processes. The participatory techniques that we adopted in the following phases helped us to overcome these challenges.

Phase 2 – Vulnerability Analysis: Our next set of processes was to collaboratively gather data on the vulnerability contexts of tribal households. The tribal households in Jambulpada are vulnerable due to specific relations of exploitation, unequal bargaining and discrimination within the political economy of their day-to-day livelihood struggles. The initial phase of the project was thus guided by queries and observation of how the vulnerability contexts of tribal households are embedded within the wider political economy of their day-to-day livelihood struggles. The intent was to identify, discuss and deliberate on some of the significant factors influencing ecological and livelihood uncertainties in the community. Various participatory research techniques such as community profiling, transect walk, risk mapping, oral histories and focused group interviews aided us to analyse social and ecological vulnerability in the village. The idea was to strengthen a shared meaning of their own historicity, identities, past experiences, success stories and failures in collective action.

During this phase, there were issues of positionality still hindering the reinforcement of mutual trust and commitment. We were (are) still identified as 'outsiders' who are engaging with the community (insiders) on a specific temporal and spatial plane with a certain set of professional goals and expertise (which the community necessarily may not have). Moreover, in the day-to-day discourses and memories of community life, we were similar to those officials from the government departments who used to deliver a lot of unmet promises to them. Nevertheless, the methods of practice and our fieldwork skills as social workers enabled us to overcome these challenges to a large extent. In the words of a female colleague of ours:

> At one stage, it was very difficult for us to proceed further with community organisation and planning. Only some men used to participate in our discussions. The women in these households were rather shy and unwilling to engage with us. However, we felt that without the participation of women in our processes the whole notion of just adaptation is skewed and void! I had no other option. To motivate them to participate in the processes, I had to become one among them. I went and lived with them. I learned to wear sarees like they wear . . . that was a turning point. Almost all women came forward to teach me how to wear a saree . . . and after some time they began to sit in all our meetings and discussions.

Phase 3 – Need Analysis and Planning: By this time, the project team had already succeeded in establishing a sense of being-ness with the community. To understand the different needs and aspirations of the community, we began to engage with diverse impact groups including men, women and young people in the hamlet. Convergent interviews, group discussions and household-level surveys were employed during these occasions. These sessions were also aimed at a systematic deliberation of needs, awareness generation and determining immediate intervention strategies.

Phase 4 – Resources, Stakeholders and Institutional Mapping: During this phase, the project team focused on the prioritisation of needs identified by the community. Our immediate steps were to identify key stakeholders and collaborate with significant institutions to mobilise appropriate resources. This was also a moment for us to reflect on the diverse values, interests, knowledge and power of partnering stakeholders. For instance, the project team realised that while the community members maintained a kind of dependency relationship with state authorities, they had yet to develop a sense of trust with the Corporate Social Responsibility (CSR) organisation that was willing to provide them assistance in ecological restoration.

Phase 5 – Prioritisation of Adaptation Strategies: The community organisation and planning processes helped us to evolve three major adaptation streams: a) watershed management; b) social enterprise development; and c) adaptive social protection. Watershed management refers to the adoption of land and water conservation practices, water harvesting in ponds and recharging of groundwater for increasing water resources potential within the natural boundaries of a drainage area to meet the basic needs of people in a sustainable manner (Singh, 2000). The approach also stresses on crop diversification, use of improved variety of seeds, integrated nutrient management and integrated pest management practices. Social enterprises are small-scale businesses created in the community to further a social purpose such as livelihood enhancement in a financially sustainable manner. Adaptive social protection refers to a series of measures which build resilience among the poorest people and most vulnerable to climate change by combining elements of social protection, disaster risk reduction and climate change adaptation in programmes and projects (Arnall et al., 2010). Each of these interventions had their own action–reflection processes embedded in them. These are described in the sections a) watershed management, b) social enterprise development and c) adaptive social protection respectively.

a) Watershed management

To begin with, the project team and the villagers participated in analysing the factors contributing to water scarcity in the village. Participatory techniques such as a transect walk, seasonal analysis, livelihood matrix and resource mapping were supplemented through group discussions and observations. Our next attempt was to strengthen the engagement of diverse stakeholders towards watershed management. We organised group meetings and stakeholder mapping exercises were conducted at the community level to identify key stakeholders within the village to plan and implement the watershed project. We also interacted with professionals from a CSR organisation who had earlier attempted to work with these tribes in addressing the issue of water scarcity. Throughout these processes, we also focused on a strengths-based approach to enhance actors' capabilities. For instance, the project team facilitated the re-designing of their intervention plan with a prime emphasis on community interests and local knowledge systems. Several meetings and group discussions were held between the project team, community members and CSR organisation. In due course, both the community and the CSR organisation were ready to put aside their differences and pursue their mission of addressing water scarcity. While community members were identified as the planners, implementers and those doing impact assessments, the role of the CSR organisation was outlined in terms of funding, capacity-building, technology provision and evaluation. Community awareness and confidence in constructing water-harvesting structures were also enhanced through the screening of relevant documentaries and follow-up discussions.

Our next step was to initiate participatory resource mapping and micro-level planning to implement watershed management. The community representatives and water conservation experts from the CSR organisation deliberated further on the prioritisation and planning of water conservation strategies including the construction of storage tanks, check dams and recharging aquifers. Training programmes were also conducted by the CSR organisation in ecological restoration and watershed management techniques and System of Rice Intensification (SRI) procedures. Training was also conducted on accounting and book-keeping procedures. The project team was able to pool various forms of expertise across different government and private organisations to support capacity-building processes in this regard. It took extra precautions to maintain community interests and increase participation levels in these programmes gradually.

Almost five months after the commencement of these community organisation and planning processes, community members began to construct water-harvesting structures as per the plan. This was immediately followed by the distribution of the initial wages to the community members who participated in the construction work. The initiation of watershed management works provided immediate income-earning opportunities to people in the hamlet without their having to migrate to the cities in search of work. Thus, migration of men from the households was reduced to some extent through employment opportunities generated in the village. Our preliminary estimates indicate that at least one male member in each household did not migrate this year during the summer months, as they were able to find employment in their village.

Tangible results in terms of increased water storage were also visible with the onset of monsoons after a couple of months. According to the community, after the post-monsoon evaluation of these water-harvesting structures, water availability during summer months would have been extended by another two to three weeks. This observation gains significance as the water required for their subsistence homestead agriculture would be met during this time. Both the community and CSR organisation were happy with their achievements. In the words of a tribal woman who was an active participant in these processes:

> We are so happy to see that our efforts have begun to show some results. With the pre-monsoon showers, now there is water near our fields . . . some water conservation and storage has happened. This water will remain for two or three more weeks, which is sufficient to initiate our farming . . . then the monsoon rains will begin.

Seeing the interest of the tribal people, the CSR organisation also reciprocated its commitment to build the capacities of the communities for a continuous period of five years. In the words of an official representing the CSR organisation:

> We were apprehensive in the beginning whether the present project will take off in Jambulpada. The people were resistant to our efforts. We also did not have sufficient trust to engage with them. However, the consistent presence of social workers and continuous engagement of the community through participatory processes has enabled us to stabilise the project in this hamlet.

The project team has now initiated necessary steps to establish the Village Development Committee so as to sustain these initiatives over time. The community is presently engaged in discussion with the Gram Panchayat, Forest Department and the CSR organisation on a viable institutional structure and is in the process of evolving bylaws that outline the norms, roles and responsibilities of each actor. These institutions need to evolve as key providers of climate justice at the local level and the discussions on our experiences in watershed management demonstrate that green social work has an important role in facilitating the evolution of appropriate resilient institutions.

b) Social enterprise development

At the time of our first visit to the village, women were exploring alternate means of enhancing their livelihoods, so that they would become able to generate supplementary income to meet essential needs. Earlier efforts by the state government departments, banks or CSR organisations to organise women or other community members into collective enterprises did not succeed due to diverse factors like the difficulties officials encountered in maintaining access to the village, top-down approaches in programme design and failure to regularly motivate and follow up the activities of the group. Nevertheless, some women in the community felt that there should be adequate mechanisms towards livelihood enhancement along with ecological restoration initiatives. However, they were skeptical, as previous attempts by government departments had resulted only in the formation of now defunct self-help groups.

Several motivation and ideation sessions were held with the women who were interested in forming a collective enterprise. Individual and group sessions were carried out to build the confidence of women who had volunteered to organise and start a collective initiative. Documentaries on successful self-help groups were shown to the group and participatory deliberations were nurtured. The willingness of the women to engage with group activities was very important. Several interactive sessions were conducted to identify the strengths and skill sets that members had as a group. Local knowledge supplemented by easily available resources was identified as a key factor in starting and sustaining the collective enterprise. Subsequently, the group decided to initiate a food processing business, with *papads* and *fryums* as the key products. (*Papads* are a thin, crisp and circle shaped food that is made out of rice and peeled black gram flour; *fryums* are cereal-based ready-to-fry pellets). The other products included chutneys made from local herbs.

The older women in the group carried out a few demonstration sessions on *papad* making. The group then began the handmade production of *papads* and *fryums*. It was decided that to begin with each member would produce *papads* from their homes. The first set of products was shared among the households in the hamlet for their own consumption. In the second phase of production, product samples were given to city-based retailers for trying out with prospective customers. As this was a pilot phase, the project team accepted the responsibility of marketing this produce. In the third phase of production, the group earned a profit of 1000 rupees and also earned the confidence of few reliable customers. Though, the profit amount does not guarantee any form of sustainability, it delighted the heart of the group members as it was their first visible income.

The group has been registered as a self-help group and opened a bank account. We are also in the process of strengthening links with the state government's women's self-help group promotion body. Currently, the project team is in the process of building the capacities of the group to make *papad* and *fryums* that suit customer demands. Considerable skill and technical improvisation are still required in terms of packaging and marketing. The product output in terms of quantity has been very low and needs to be enhanced through the provision of appropriate technology such as rollers and dryers. The group needs to be motivated to pool resources collectively to buy *papad*-making equipment, to maintain the quality of production and consistently meet customer demands. There is also a need for proper market research and analysis to establish the enterprise, which the self-help group and the project team will address in the near future.

c) Adaptive social protection

Drawing insights from community processes that have been initiated towards watershed management and social enterprise development, the project team began to work towards strengthening adaptive social protection through the convergence of various social protection schemes (Mupedziswa and Ntseane, 2013). In this regard, the project team conducted a household-level survey to find out who are excluded from state-sponsored social protection programmes such as pensions, scholarships or welfare funds, and the reasons behind their exclusion. In this process, the community identified different groups such as older people, widows, lactating mothers, disabled people and youth struggling to access their entitlements and benefits due to either lack of information or inability to access these institutional provisions. Separate meetings were held with young people in the hamlet to understand their specific needs and the challenges they faced while trying to access social welfare provisions. Meetings were also held with diverse government department officials to gather information on different schemes and assess their relevance to the people in Jambulpada. The project team is presently working with concerned government authorities and the community in ensuring that all vulnerable households gain access to the benefits of relevant public social welfare schemes. Responding to differentiated vulnerabilities is a task green social workers undertake with the community groups concerned.

Conclusion

The project team's action research interface as social workers with the tribal community in Jambulpada commenced around three years ago. It is too early to describe precisely the impacts and sustainability of these processes. However, team members were able to qualify certain developments for both livelihood adaptation and capabilities. The whole action research could be analytically reflected through the McNiff model (1988) of action research, which takes the following steps: a) beginning with identifying an area of practice to be investigated, b) imagining a solution, c) implementing the solution, d) evaluating the solution and e) changing the practice in the light of solution (Figure 22.1). However, in all these processes there could be iterations that could spin-off from the main research suggesting that the outcome of the investigation may not be its original focus (McNiff, 1988). Though watershed management was our initial and primary focus, co-designing and empathising with the needs of the community, the project team also began to work on social enterprise development and embedding the processes towards adaptive social protection.

Our efforts have begun to address certain sets of capabilities, mainly working towards creating spaces for democratic participation and freedom. In this case, the environmental context served as the meta-capability to begin the processes of strengthening other capabilities including community imagination, decision-making experiences, emotions, applied knowledge and strengthening social capital. Social workers have an important role in identifying diverse elements of social capital and strengthening them at different levels, namely, social support, social participation and community bonds (Norris et al., 2008).

For livelihood adaptation, the project team were able to address either certain sets of maladaptive strategies or strengthen certain positive adaptation strategies. For instance, members of the community were happy to find work within the village rather than migrate to town and cities. The project team were able to address outmigration to some extent, and for a short period. With the continuation of the watershed management works and entrepreneurship development at the local level, this trend could be sustained. Harvesting water, recharging aquifers and storing water for future use has been one of the visible impacts. Also, the purpose of water harvesting has become a key discourse in the villagers' day-to-day life. People have begun to come together with a purpose, be it in the form of Village Development Committee, self-help groups or youth

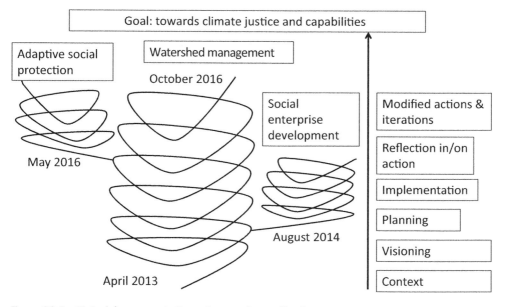

Figure 22.1 Pictorial representation of our action–reflection process

associations. Community members are demonstrating their potential to address diverse livelihood uncertainties, and at the same time negotiate with other dominant actors. An important adaptation strategy poorer households use to deal with environmental and livelihood uncertainties has been livelihood diversification (Agrawal, 2010). This action research project has also begun to spread out different forms of livelihood strategies such as sustenance-based farming and forestry, wage labour generated from watershed management activities, food processing and sales, kitchen gardening and so on. And, it simultaneously nurtured community-private partnerships in addressing ecological and livelihood insecurity.

This chapter has also demonstrated how certain theoretical concepts defining the values and boundaries of green social work could be transformed into local practical action. This transformation from theoretical (and classroom contexts) to the real world is an important goal of sustainability-focused education including social work education (Jones, 2013; Brundiers and Wiek, 2011). Action research as a research orientation enables green social workers to address structural inequities arising out of unequal power relations as well as shape interventions that are self-critical of unsustainable forms of development (Dominelli, 2013; Philip and Reisch, 2015). It also promotes grassroots movement fostering the values and principles of sustainable development. Through action research, green social workers can critically interface with the forces shaping the social contexts and its natural environment. This chapter also demonstrates that green social workers, with their expertise in micro-practice, are capable of working with marginalised communities to enhance their skill and agency, and facilitate just adaptation to risks and uncertainties. It also contains the explicit demonstration of the commitment of green social workers in valuing local knowledge systems and co-designing actionable solutions in partnership with relevant actors towards achieving social and environmental justice.

References

Agrawal, A. (2010). Local Institutions and adaptation to climate change. In R. Mearns, and A. Norton (Eds.), *Social dimensions of climate change: equity and vulnerability in a warming world. New Frontiers of Social Policy*, World Bank, p. 173-197, Available on https://openknowledge.worldbank.org/handle/10986/2689 License: CC BY 3.0 IGO [Accessed 5 November 2017].

Arnall, A., Oswald, K., Davies, M., Mitchell, T., and Coirolo, C. (2010). *Adaptive social protection: mapping the evidence and policy context in the agriculture sector in South Asia*. IDS Working Paper 345, Brighton: IDS.

Brundiers, K. and Wiek, A. (2011). Educating students in real-world sustainability research: Vision and implementation. *Innovative Higher Education*, 36, p. 107–124.

Bulkeley, H., Edwards, G. and Fuller, S. (2014). Contesting climate justice in the city: Examining politics and practice in urban climate change experiments. *Global Environmental Change*, 25: 31–40.

Chambers, R. and Conway, G. (1992). *Sustainable rural livelihoods: Practical concepts for the 21st century*. IDS Discussion Paper 296. Institute of Development Studies, University of Sussex, Brighton.

Coghlan, D. and Brydon-Miller, M (eds.) (2014). *The Sage encyclopedia of action research*. New Delhi: Sage.

Comim, F. (2008). Climate injustice and development: A capability perspective. *Development*, 51: 344–349.

Dominelli, L. (2011). Climate change: Social workers' roles and contributions to policy debates and interventions. *International Journal of Social Welfare*, 20: 430–438.

Dominelli, L. (2012). *Green social work*. Cambridge: Polity Press.

Dominelli, L. (2013). Environmental justice at the heart of social work practice: Greening the profession. *International Journal of Social Welfare*, 22(4): 431–439.

Dryzek, J. S., Norgaard, R. B. and Schlosberg, D. (Eds.) (2011). *The Oxford handbook of climate change and society*. New York: Oxford University Press.

Figueroa, R. M. (2011). Indigenous peoples and cultural losses. In J. S. Dryzek, R. B. Norgaard, and D. Schlosberg (Eds.), *The Oxford handbook of climate change and society*. New York: Oxford University Press, pp. 191–202.

Holland, B. (2008). Justice and the environment in Nussbaum's 'capabilities approach': why sustainable ecological capacity is a meta-capability, *Political Research Quarterly*, 61(2): 319–332.

Jones, P. (2013). Transforming the curriculum: Social work education and ecological consciousness. In M. Gray, J. Coates, and T. Hetherington (Eds.), *Environmental social work*. London: Routledge, pp. 213–230.

Kelly, P. M. and Adger, W. N. (2000). Theory and practice in assessing vulnerability to climate change and facilitating adaptation. *Climatic Change*, 47: 325–352.

McNiff, J. (1988). *Action research: Principles and practice*. London, Routledge.

Mearns, R. and Norton, A. (2010). Social dimensions of climate change: Equity and vulnerability in a warming world. *World Bank*. Available on https://openknowledge.worldbank.org/handle/10986/2689 License: CC BY 3.0 IGO [Accessed 5 November 2017].

Mupedziswa, R. and Ntseane, D. (2013). The contribution of non-formal social protection to social development in Botswana, *Development Southern Africa*, 30(1): 84–97.

Norris, F. H., Stevens, S. P., Pfefferbaum, B., Wyche, K. F. and Pfefferbaum, R. L. (2008). Community resilience as a metaphor, theory, set of capacities, and strategies for disaster readiness. *American Journal of Community Psychology*, 41: 127–150.

Nussbaum, M. C. (2000). *Women and human development: The capabilities approach*. Cambridge, New York: Cambridge University Press.

Paavola, J. and Adger, W. (2002). *Justice and adaptation to climate change*. Working Paper 23. Norwich: Tyndall Centre for Climate Change Research.

Paavola, J. and Adger, W. N. (2006). Fair adaptation to climate change. *Ecological Economics*, 56: 594–609.

Philip, D. and Reisch, M. (2015). Rethinking social work's interpretation of 'Environmental Justice': From local to global. *Social Work Education*, 34(5): 471–483.

Reason, P. (2006). Choice and quality in action research. *Journal of Management Inquiry*, 15(2): 187–203.

Schlosberg, D. (2012a). 'Climate justice and capabilities: a framework for adaptation policy', *Ethics and International Affairs* 26(4): 445–461.

Schlosberg, D. (2012b). Justice, ecological integrity and climate change, in A. Thompson and J. Bendik-Keymer (Eds.), *Ethical adaptation to climate change: Human virtues of the future*. Cambridge, MA: MIT Press, pp. 165–184.

Sen, A. (1999). *Development as freedom*. New York: Oxford University Press.

Shi, L., Chu, E., Anguelovski, I., Aylett, A., Debats, J., Goh, K., Schenk, T., Seto, K., Dodman, D., Roberts, D., Roberts, J. and VanDeveer, S. (2016). Roadmap towards justice in urban climate adaptation research. *Nature Climate Change*, 6: 131–137. doi: 10.1038/nclimate2841.

Singh, R. V. (Ed.) (2000). *Watershed planning and management*. Rajasthan, India: Yash Publishing House.

Wisner, B., Blaikie, P., Cannon, T. and Davis, I. (2004). *At risk: Natural hazards, people's vulnerability, and disasters*. London: Routledge.

Part VI
Extreme weather events

23
The 2015 Chennai Floods
Green social work, an emerging model for practice in India

Miriam Samuel, Prince Annadurai and Sowndarya Sankarakrishnan

Introduction

The deluge in Chennai in the month of November and December in 2015 has brought severe devastation to the city and necessitated the social work profession to reconsider its roles and responses by evolving appropriate models like the community-based disaster preparedness model. This model can be emulated with similar situations elsewhere, which was proved to be successful in other countries (Hossain 2012). Social work has a significant and responsible role to play in such disasters. According to NASW Code of Ethics, 'Social workers should provide appropriate professional services in public emergencies to the greatest extent possible' (NASW, 1999). Though volunteers did an incredible job during the relief work, there was lack of coordination among government, NGOs and volunteers. To overcome this problem, a model for practice needs to be developed. The authors undertook a research study to examine the role of social workers in disasters to supplement those existing in the Community Based Disaster Preparedness and Response Model. Additionally, there is need for sustainable development with proper urban planning to manage disasters. The link between green social work and disaster relief work is brought out in this chapter.

The 2015 Chennai Floods in Tamil Nadu

Chennai is located in the coastal plain of South India, which receives moderate rains through North-East Monsoons. A sudden and unusual outbreak of rainfall in the months of November and December 2015 resulted in severe flooding with a death toll of 347 people (*Correspondent*, 2015). Rapid urbanisation, migration, climate change, lack of urban planning, and lack of disaster preparedness accounts for some of this outcome. Heavy and torrential rainfall began on 8 November 2015 and lasted for a week. The second set of rains started at the end of November and lasted until first week of December. Chennai received 1,049 mm of rainfall during this period, the highest recorded since November 1918. The breach of Chembarambakkam Lake on 2 December 2015 resulted in the flooding of the Adyar River, placing a 4-kilometre radius of land around the river completely under water. No warning was given to the people (Janardhanan, 2015).

Urbanisation resulted in migration leading to overcrowding and rapid uncontrolled development. Chennai was originally a city with several lakes. Due to climate change and global warming, these lakes eventually dried up. The Chennai Metropolitan Authority Report stated that the 1.5 Lakh (a lakh is 100,000) illegal structures that have been constructed have destroyed 300 water bodies in Chennai over a period of time (Jayaraman, 2016). This raises crucial issues for consideration. Chennai's geographical structure is being destroyed and this affects the ecosystem which in turn results in such calamities. The need for green social work arose at that moment.

Disaster and its dimensions

The IFRC (2014) defines the term disaster as 'a serious disruption of the functioning of a community or society'. Disasters involve 'widespread human, material, economic or environmental impacts, which exceed the ability of the affected community or society to cope using its own resources'. Disasters pose major threats to society. Any society is encompassed in different units which overlap in different sectors such as social, political, economic and cultural (Lindell, 2011). Society can be viewed through different systems. The systems theory states that any change in one system affects the other systems. Disaster is a likely crisis that can happen to any individual and affects the individual's entire system. In the context of the recent deluge, the impact was seen in significant ways in all sectors. Chennai is also a city of many cultures. People from different parts of the country have migrated there for many years for various reasons. This implies that cultural practices pertain not to the few, but to the many. This also impacts upon social, economic and political structures. This particular disaster has impacted all these structures.

The social impacts were seen to more positive after the flood hit Chennai. People were able to positively value family relationships. Neighbours were no longer strangers, and this flood united more of them. People helped each other by providing food, shelter and clothing (Stalin, 2016). There were huge numbers of volunteers who were a mixture of trained social workers and individuals who assisted these professionals, acted as bridges to connect needs and resources. The social support was boundless, and there were many organisations like the World Vision and Action Aid, which worked on humanitarian basis. The social life of the people was affected because many were stuck in water-logged places. People were not able to go out of their houses and were left stranded. This drastically affected workers in the unorganised sector, many of whom were either homeless or slum dwellers that depended on daily or weekly wages.

The severity of the impact depended upon the economic status of the people. Unlike many disasters, this disaster-affected people of all classes. However, different classes face different problems. Higher class people took refuge in luxury hotels and had their basic needs met. Their material losses did not affect them to the same extent as the middle and lower classes. Those most affected by material losses were middle-class people because most of the household properties were bought in EMI (Equated Monthly Instalment) and they lacked the option of claiming from insurance (Stalin, 2016). This group, however, had most of their basic needs met through the reserves held in their houses. The lower-class groups facing the worst scenario regarding the fulfilment of their basic needs were homeless people and slum dwellers. Material loss had a significant impact, but most of them were resilient to the economic stresses because they had few material possessions. Economic losses in the city reached $0.755 billion (*The New Indian Express*, 2016), placing more pressure on the government to meet these losses, and affected the local economy as a whole.

The government took no prior measures to prepare for the disaster. Lack of urban planning combined with the illegal destruction of lakes by corporate industries was major reasons for the severity of the impact. Alongside these social, economic and political dimensions, is the ecological dimension that forms the basis of society. The ecology of the city has been destroyed rapidly in the past two decades. Illegal construction of buildings, destruction of water bodies, rapid urbanisation processes, poor urban planning, and improper maintenance of the water bodies by not cleaning and deepening them has severely damaged the ecological structure. Because of this, when the torrential rains came the natural flow of waterways and storage of water bodies have been clogged. This resulted in flooding and many buildings in low-lying areas became submerged under water, making the impact even worse. This implies the need for taking an ecological perspective into account to prevent disasters and reduce their impacts in the long run before considering development projects.

Practice interventions used by social workers during floods

The disaster history in India has required the government to develop constantly the intervention method through which bad practices and poor work are identified for improvement. To understand these practice interventions, it is essential to understand the importance of India's disaster intervention strategies.

Review of disaster intervention in India

India, a peninsular country with unique geo-climatic and socio-economic conditions, is constantly facing disasters both natural and (hu)man-made. It is highly vulnerable to disasters like floods, droughts, cyclones, earthquakes, landslides and avalanches. Out of the total land surface, almost 58.6 per cent is prone to earthquakes, over 40 million hectares are prone to floods, 5700 km of the 7516 km-long coastline is prone to cyclone and tsunamis, and hilly areas are prone to landslides and avalanches (National Institute of Disaster Management, 2012). India ranks 11th among the most hazardous countries and 60th among the most disaster vulnerable countries in the world.

The National Institute of Disaster Management 2012 has given India the following national profile:

1   India is one of the 10 most disaster-prone countries in the world. Environmental degradation, urbanisation, industrialisation, population growth, geo-climatic conditions are some of the factors associated with this.
2   The natural geological setting of the country is the primary basic reason for its increased vulnerability making the region susceptible to earthquakes, landslides and water erosion.
3   The Himalayan plains are more prone to earthquakes, avalanches and landslides due to its tectonic features. Also many major rivers flow from the Himalaya and large amount of sediments result in river siltation which causes floods. Floods in Uttar Pradesh and Bihar are the examples of this type of disaster.
4   Monsoons play a major role in bringing rains to the country. If these worsen, drought results. The major drought areas are in the western part of the country including Rajasthan, Gujarat and some parts of Maharashtra.
5   The extreme weather conditions, huge quantities of ice and snow stored in the glaciers are other natural factors which make the country prone to various forms of disasters.
6   Along with the natural factors, human-induced activities such as deforestation, demographic pressure, rapid urbanisation, usage of genetically modified crops and faulty agricultural practices there are among many disasters that are happening. Global warming is a recent phenomenon which has considerable impact on the climatic conditions which leads to many disasters.

The Chennai Floods calamity, 2015 was a good example for the combination of both natural and (hu)man-made disasters.

History of interventions

Disaster management in India is developing rapidly. Based on the Report of Ministry of Home Affairs (2011), the following history of intervention has been deduced. Disaster management has evolved from:

- Activity based set-ups to proactive institutionalised structures.
- Singe Institutional (government agencies) domain to multi-stakeholder setup.
- Relief-based approach versus a multi-dimensional, pro-active holistic approach for reducing risk.

Disaster management in India can be divided into two phases: the British Administrative Phase and Post-Independence Phase.

British Administrative Phase

The institutional structure began during the British period with the series of famines that occurred during the years 1900, 1905, 1907 and 1943, and the Bihar-Nepal earthquake of 1937. During the British period, Relief Departments were set up and relief works following a reactive approach were carried out.

Post-Independence Phase

Post-Independence, the relief commissioners in each state managed the disasters. These functioned under the central relief commissioner. Their major role was to distribute relief materials and money in the affected areas. The five-year plans addressed flood disasters under the Irrigation, Command Area Development and Flood Control programmes. With the emergence of institutional arrangements, a permanent institution began in the late 1990s. The Disaster Management Cell was set-up under the Ministry of Home Affairs, following the declaration of 1990s as the International Decade for Natural Disaster Reduction (IDNDR) by the UN General Assembly.

Disaster Management shifted to the Ministry of Home Affairs in 2002 under the Cabinet Secretariat's Notification No. DOC.CD-108/2002 dated 27/02/2002. The Indian government formed a hierarchical structure to deal with disasters during this period. Although history had shown that measures taken in earlier years were important, the turning point in the disaster management practices came only after the Indian Ocean Tsunami hit Southern India in 2004. The *Disaster Management Act, 2005* (23 December 2005), No. 53 of 2005, was passed by the Indian government and became significant after the tsunami.

Research on social work and disasters

Not much literature is available on social work and disaster in India although social work institutions responded robustly during a massive earthquake in Bhuj, Gujarat on 26 January 2001, the tsunami on 26 December 2004, and more recently the earthquake on 25 April 2015 in Nepal. Much of this work is inadequately documented, but social workers performed incredible relief work. Chou's (2003) research on disasters states that social work functions in disaster aid can be summarised as follows:

1   Support for individuals and families.
2   Link individual's needs and resources and help the clients to access resources.
3   Prevent severe physical and mental problems.
4   Prevent individuals, families, groups, organisations, communities from breaking down.
5   Intervene to change micro- and macro-systems to improve clients'/service users' well-being.

Furthermore, social workers are an important part of disaster recovery plans, including at the micro-, mezzo-, and macro-levels, such as organising a community's recovery, searching out benefit programmes, writing grants and advocating for government programmes (Sundet and Mermelstein 1996; Dodds and Nuehring 1996; Cooke 1993; Dufka 1988). Mohammad Reza Iravani and Kazem Ghojavand (2005), referring to their work on the 2003 earthquake in Iran, point out that

> social workers need to know how to deal with crisis interventions including information and resource integration, volunteer organization, distribution of materials, food and monetary compensation distribution, death and funeral management, needs survey, vulnerable people identification and discovery, housing arrangements

and so on. However, the difficulties that social workers have include lack of procedural and system integration, leadership uncertainty, 'their instructions, the ambiguity of policies and rules, chaotic rescue bases, their own uncertain roles, limited concentration of aid services due to mishandling, overlapping of resources, and inflexibility of related legislations'. A study done by the Department of Social Work, Madras Christian College (2015) on the flood relief work shared similar concerns. Based on the disaster relief work in Nepal, Dominelli (2017) says that developing transdisciplinary approaches that link the sciences (physical and social) to community expertise in the coproduction of solutions that enhance prevention, preparation and resilience are indispensable in disaster work.

A research study, 'The Role of Social Workers in Disaster Management', was conducted in relation to the Chennai Floods. It was a student-driven research along with faculty supervisors in the Department of Social Work, MCC. It focused on finding out social workers' opinions about the standard of existing disaster management strategies in Chennai and what the roles of social workers were. The specific objectives were to:

- understand the impact of knowledge, skills, and attitudes gained through the practice of social work in the field of disaster management; and
- study the level of understanding of the various phases of disaster management by social workers to assess the various roles played by professional social workers in case of floods and to ascertain the link between social work education and practice.

Methodology

The research study used mixed methods (i.e. both qualitative and quantitative). The qualitative data was conducted with the professional social workers in the field of disaster management. The inclusive criteria were: the social workers should have been in the field for more than five years and should have contributed to the 2015 Chennai Floods. A total of four professional social workers were interviewed who took part in the relief work. Discussions were stimulated through in-depth interviews on the impact of the catastrophic event in the lives of the people and what interventions could be made by social workers. The respondents were able to draw inferences from the previous catastrophes and were able to analyse the disaster management system in India, specifically Tamil Nadu. The researchers developed an interview guide to elicit information on disaster management and personal experience in it. The in-depth interviews helped the researchers gain specific concepts and focus on developing models to respond to similar disasters. The respondents were gathered using purposive sampling technique. Each interview was recorded and transcribed later. The researcher and her faculty supervisors reviewed and analysed the transcripts to highlight themes.

For the quantitative study, an online questionnaire was used as tool of data collection. By using a snowball sampling method, data was collected from 35 respondents who worked as volunteers during the flood relief. The criteria for inclusion were that the respondents should have completed a Master's in Social Work and worked in the relief phase for a minimum of 10 days. The questions were framed so as to derive the important roles of social workers in such disasters. The awareness of social workers of the various phases of disaster management was also analysed. This helped the researcher to understand the impact of social work education on the social workers in responding to disasters. Later, the quantitative and qualitative data were interpreted using the convergence model of triangulation and the results were generated.

Major findings

Analysis of the quantitative data showed that a majority of (54.3 per cent) of the social workers felt that the public's level of understanding of the risks of natural disaster was moderate and 45.7 per cent of social workers felt the government's understanding for the same was low. This was alarming as government's intervention is extremely important in any disaster.

On understanding the importance of various factors of disaster management, the following results were highlighted: 80 per cent of the respondents stated that the warning system was the most important technological factor. Chennai which is on the coastal area needs more preparedness in terms of warning and that was also felt by the respondents of this research study. A vast majority of the respondents stated that imparting literacy, strict legal measures to monitor the city's infrastructure and development projects by the state, stringent environmental preservation and protection measures by the state and civil societies are important components of disaster management.

Half of the respondents felt said they strongly agreed that there is a link between the social work profession and disaster management which in turn projects the need for the inclusion of disaster management as a subject in the social work education. Chou (2003) quoting Taiwan's 1999 earthquake pointed out that most Taiwanese social workers participating in the emergency response had limited training in disaster aid. Disaster aid was not included in the social work curriculum at the college level. This means that society and professional educators in Taiwan have not realised social work roles and functions during disasters. Dominelli (2010) played a key role in devising IASSW's policies on disasters and climate change based on her research and practice linked to disaster relief work in various countries. In our research, interestingly 54 per cent of the respondents preferred an integrated approach for disaster management against the existing response-centric one which is part of social work intervention in India.

On addressing the preparedness phase, it was found that 85 per cent of respondents felt that the government should focus on proper planning well ahead of a disaster occurring. This includes preparation at the local level. Almost two-thirds of respondents (66 per cent) felt that empowering the local government would increase the pace of process in bringing the community back to the normal life. Also, 63 per cent of the respondents preferred risk reduction as a strategy in disaster management process against effective response which is practiced by the Indian government-in-large.

This study also revealed there is a need for social workers' involvement in disaster management, to enhance the process of effective intervention and response and for them to receive training in this area during their programme of studies. The social work education programme in India does not focus on disaster management. This makes social workers less effective during times of disaster. The qualitative data also highlighted the need for social work students to receive disaster simulation training. The respondents were more concerned with the seriousness of environmental degradation made impact of the disaster more severe. The evidence from the Chennai Floods revealed that illegal constructions destroyed natural water bodies. This resulted in people facing more trauma when compared to others not so affected. Untreated solid waste dumped on the banks of the Coovam and Adayar rivers mixed with the flood water made it more polluted. When carefully examining marginalised communities (mostly those living on low-lying areas, succumbed easily to the floods), the study showed that they were the ones affected most. Slums located on the banks of rivers and water bodies were worst affected. Their houses were completely immersed and made them homeless. Critically analysing this issue, the root cause of this problem was the government's carelessness in approving the construction of buildings that destroyed water bodies and catchment areas, which is both a violation of human rights and environmental justice. This research found that there is a need for green social work which focuses on environmental justice. People should be made aware of the destruction caused by environmental degradation and this can be achieved by empowering communities.

Discussion on disasters

The Chennai Floods is a combination of both natural and (hu)man-made disasters. It is natural because rain is natural, but the amount is affected by human factors embedded in drastic climate changes. It is an exacerbated (hu)man-made disaster because the necessary preventive measures were not taken and the apathy shown by government and politicians. Mitigation work which includes preparing the community by creating awareness and mapping hazardous areas were not done properly by the state disaster management authorities and often neglected. In a news article, a water resource management expert expressed the view that Chennai reached this mess due to lack of proper planning and poor maintenance of the water bodies (*The New Indian Express*, 2016).

The respondents of this research considered that the government did not involve professional social workers in the disaster team during the intervention process which was initiated to rehabilitate the affected community after the Chennai Floods. Involving them would have enriched the relief process. More specifically, their intervention could have been made from the people's point of view, a bottom-up approach as an ingredient of green social work. Social work associations in India are either dysfunctional or not focusing on disaster relief and rehabilitation, which led to lack of combined and coordinated relief work. This study also found that government projects that are created to enhance disaster management did not employ social workers. Rather, officials with more experience from the field were preferred. These officials focus on completing project targets (e.g. just distributing the relief grant from the government) rather than providing any effective interventions.

The capacity-building program which is supposed to educate and prepare people for disasters did not have the expected result as most people were unaware of the disaster and preventive measures proposed for it. The scientific mapping of the hazardous zones along the river banks and other water bodies was not undertaken. Also, slum dwellers along the water bodies were unaware of the severity of the disaster. The encroachments on these areas did not gain the attention of the government and early intervention was not made to rehabilitate these communities into safer zones. An analysis by the Union Ministry of Earth Sciences has revealed that floods in the city were caused by poor drainage systems and could have been avoided if the government had taken enough mitigation measures (Venugopal, 2016).

Surprisingly, during the response phase of Chennai Floods, numerous volunteers and NGOs stepped in to do relief work. But there was no organised distribution of collected relief materials, which again resulted in insufficient relief work. Also, most of the relief materials did not reach people on time and perishable materials became spoilt. There were many political issues that were observed in distributing the relief materials which was due to rivalry among Chennai's political parties (Jayaraman, 2016). Most of the relief materials were forcefully distributed by the dominant political parties in the affected areas, reaching their voting constituencies first. The local politicians predominantly decided the places and persons for the distribution of relief materials. Without their support, many NGOs were not able to enter into the affected communities. This relief was not streamlined and created many more complex problems. The demand for the basic food materials exceeded supply and the government could not provide for the entire population. This resulted in price hikes of almost all foodstuffs making these items unaffordable by many people. Also, most of the ATMs were not working and people could not access money. This worsened their situation. Although some people had their basic needs met, psychological support was not made widely available. The resilience shown by the marginalised communities was highly significant. Social workers should conduct further research on this.

Based on all these observations, the major inference from the research was the need for creating a streamlined process of disaster management which is specific to the type of disaster. The government focused more on the traditional practice of concentrating on the response and recovery phase rather than the preparatory one. This creates a need for developing more capacity-building programmes and training of people living in hazardous zones. Urban planning needs to be taken into detailed consideration because good planning can reduce the effects of a disaster considerably. The creation of a common association of social workers in India could potentially lobby for the recognition of social workers' centrality to disaster risk reduction, mitigation, adaptation and resilience-building strategies. By creating a common forum, social workers can plan interventions on a larger scale which can make the process more effective.

The Chennai disaster and green social work

The effect of the flood was felt mainly on land along the river beds and near the lakes. A close observation of the populations living in these areas would reveal that the majority belong to lower economic groups and are mostly slum dwellers. As per the 2011 census, 29 per cent of Chennai's population resides in slums and most of these are near the lakes and rivers. Slums are increasing with rapid urbanisation. Despite the government's rehabilitation efforts, slums continue to persist. Green social work is to support difficult causes and advocate for marginalised and disenfranchised groups. An important element within the lives of marginalised peoples is achieving a balance between livelihoods, the centralisation of jobs in cities, and environmental degradation. In *Green Social Work*, the growth of megacities, often associated with slums as the living habitat for poor peoples, is termed *hyper-urbanisation*. Given the popularity of ever-larger cities globally, this issue has to be addressed because the infrastructures in cities – water, sanitation, power supplies, transportation, housing, schools, and health facilities are being stretched beyond their limits (Schumacher, 1973; Dominelli, 2012). Meanwhile, the physical environment becomes more and more stressed to meet the needs of ever increasing numbers of people (Parry et al., 1979; Dominelli, 1997). The maps that can be accessed through the following URL show the devastation made to Chennai city over two decades (Madhavan, 2016).

The first picture shows Chennai's image in the year 1982 and the second picture in the year 2012. The traditional rainwater harvesting system has been destroyed because of the construction of buildings over ponds and lakes. The natural water storage bodies have been vastly destroyed due to uncontrolled urbanisation, which affected the city's ecological structures.

This also leads to injustice in the society because marginalised people suffer most due to their lower socio-economic position. Social justice for marginalised groups remains a big challenge during any disaster. Social workers are responsible for upholding the value of social justice (AASW, 2010). Green social work can respond to this social injustice because:

> Green social work is a form of holistic professional social work practice that focuses on the: interdependencies amongst people; the social organization of relationships between people and the flora and fauna in their physical habitats; and the interactions between socio-economic and physical environmental crises and interpersonal behaviours that undermine the well-being of human beings and planet earth. It proposes to address these issues by arguing for a profound transformation in how people conceptualise the social basis of their society, their relationships with each other, living things and the inanimate world.
>
> *(Dominelli, 2012: 25)*

Social workers have a major responsibility in looking into social and ecological structures in communities and provide interventions which are sustainable. The introduction of green social work practice theories in social work education is imperative in responding to disasters, an important lesson learned from this study.

Theory and practice innovations

Community Based Disaster Preparedness (CBDP) theory involves local communities in the disaster reduction process. Those that adopted disaster interventions that were driven by top-down approaches planned externally (whether nationally within the country or overseas), were less likely to succeed. Thus, encouraging bottom-up or grassroots approaches provided appropriate countermeasures. Hierarchal relations are also a key challenge for social workers to address in their responses to tragic events (Dominelli, 2012). A study by Said et al. (2011) following the 2004 tsunami outlines the effectiveness of the CBDP approach which enhances the resilience of communities and their disaster preparedness while considering the culture of each community. Thus, CBDP is people oriented, focuses on community members, and encourages the community to learn from their experiences. These lessons could result in the formation of new legislation and theories for practice, including preventive measures at all levels – individual, local, societal and national – as advocated by green social workers.

The CBDP approach needs community participation which is crucial for any intervention. Hossain (2012) suggests that Community Based Disaster Management (CBDM) is effective for working in communities with disasters. The roles of social workers, especially those of community mobiliser, advocate, networker, liaison worker and enabler (Dominelli, 2011) are important in facilitating community participation by creating disaster awareness among the people particularly those in rural areas. Social workers can explain their duties and responsibilities and motivate them to participate as a community to demand their needs and rights. They can develop programmes that minimise damage and better prepare the community for calamitous events and empower people to build social capital and mobilise for emergencies. Social workers raise funds for the community alongside its residents. They also assess the disaster situation and assist the most vulnerable populations.

This study revealed that not all people in flood affected areas have been helped. Marginalised people, especially the Dalits, tribal peoples, widows, disabled people and older people were not prioritised by government agencies and local politicians in the relief work. The gender bias against women, identified by Enarson and Morrow (1998) during Hurricane Andrew in the US, remains a grave concern and was prominent in the 2004 Indian Ocean Tsunami in many organisations (Pittaway et al., 2007; Dominelli, 2012). Women were at greater risk through all stages of the disaster, and often excluded from receiving aid or making decisions about disaster risk reduction and interventions. Thus, social workers can facilitate disaster intervention processes by identifying vulnerable people and linking them to relief work and resources.

Conclusion

Disasters are inevitable and disaster responses evoke new strategies. Social workers intervening in disaster fields play a crucial role in responding to its effects and promoting ecological security in a professional way through locality-specific, culturally relevant green social work. Each community is unique and their social dynamics differ. For example, coastal communities will have different knowledge about floods compared to those on the mainland. Local cultures and practices should be valued and disaster responses should be drawn out of these. This will ensure that people participate in devising their own strategies and methods for disaster preparation.

The Chennai Floods indicate the crucial roles social workers play. An approach that combines both CBDM and CBDP can be appropriate for disaster situations. Coastal communities and those along water bodies can be given capacity-building training that highlight community-based disaster factors including culture, resilience and geo-politics. In doing this, community participation will ensure that disaster interventions will be effective and sustainable. Hence, a new indigenous method can be developed based on 'Community Based Participation and Disaster Management' approaches. Green social work prioritises holistic practice, the interdependencies between people and the physical environment, and connections among people because these are essential to linking social and environmental justice together (Dominelli, 2012).

Chief Seattle (1786–1866), a prominent Native American tribal leader, pursued a path of accommodation without white settlers. Seattle, in Washington State in the US, was named after him. A widely publicised speech arguing in favour of ecological responsibility and respect for Native Americans' land rights had been attributed to him. He said:

> Humankind has not woven the web of life. We are but one thread within it. Whatever we do to the web, we do to ourselves. All things are bound together. All things connect.

This interconnectedness of and interdependencies between people, animals, plants and the physical environment lies at the heart of green social work (Dominelli, 2012) and has much to offer in mitigating risk to those living in flood-prone geographies.

References

ASSW (Australian Association of Social Workers) (2010). *Code of Ethics*. Canberra: Australian Association of Social Workers.

Chou, Y. C. (2003). Social workers involvement in Taiwan's 1999 earthquake disaster aid: Implications for social work education. *The International Online-Only Journal*, 1: 1–22. Social Work and Society. www.socwork.de/SW-earthquaketaiwan(Chou2003).pdf [24 October 2005].

Cooke, M. (1993). The Newcastle Lord Mayor's Newcastle earthquake appeal: Empowerment via radical social casework. *Australian Social Work*, 1: 47–56.

Correspondent, S. (2015). Death toll in floods mounts to 347. *The Hindu*. Available on www.thehindu.com/news/national/tamil-nadu/death-toll-in-floods-mounts-to-347/article7973293.ece [Accessed 21 September 2016].

Department of Social Work, Madras Christian College (2015). *Report on the flood relief work*. (unpublished report)

Dodds, S. and Nuehring, E. (1996). A primer for social work research on disaster, *Journal of Social Service Research*, 1: 27–56.

Dominelli, L. (1997). *Sociology for Social Work*. London: Macmillan.

Dominelli, L. (2010). *Climate Change Policy for IASSW, ICSW, and IFSW*. Presentation at Metropole Professional University Climate Change Conference, 9 December 2009. Copenhagen: IASSW Board Minutes, January 2010.

Dominelli, L. (2011). Climate change: Social Workers' roles and contributions to policy debates and interventions, *International Journal of Social Welfare*, 20(4): 430–439.

Dominelli, L. (2012). *Green social work: From environmental crises to environmental justice*. Cambridge: Polity Press.

Dominelli, L. (2017). Green social work and the uptake by the Nepal School of Social Work: Building resilience in disaster stricken communities, in Bracken, L., Ruszczyk, H., Robinson, T. (Eds.) *Evolving Narratives of Hazard and Risk: The Gorkha Earthquake, Nepal 2015*. London: Palgrave-Macmillan.

Dufka, C. L. (1988). The Mexico City earthquake disaster. *Social Casework*, 3: 162–170.

Enarson, E. and Morrow, B. (1998). *The gendered terrain of disaster: Through women's eyes*. Miami: Florida International University.

Hossain, M. A. (2012). Community participation in disaster management: Role of social work to enhance participation. *Sociology*, 159: 171.

IFRC (2014). *About Disaster Management*. Retrieved from International Fedration of Red Cross and Red Crescent Society on http://www.ifrc.org/en/what-we-do/disaster-management/about-disaster-management/ [Accessed 5 November 2017].

Iravani, M. R. and Ghojavand, K. (2005). *Social work skills in working with survivors of Earthquake: A social work intervention*. Iran: Islamic Azad University.

Janardhanan, A. (2015). *Chennai floods: The day city went under, who did what – and who did not*. The Indian Express. Available on http://indianexpress.com/article/india/india-news-india/chennai-floods-the-day-city-went-under-who-did-what-and-who-did-not/ [Accessed 8 July 2016].

Jayaraman, N. (2016). *Why is India's Chennai flooded? – BBC News*. BBC News. Available on www.bbc.com/news/world-asia-india-34992004 [Accessed 12 July 2016].

Lindell, M. (2011). *Disaster studies*. Sage Publication. Available on www.sagepub.net/isa/resources/pdf/disaster%20studies.pdf [Accessed 17 August 2016].

Madhavan, D. (2016). These satellite images spanning 30 long years show how chennai brought these floods upon itself. *indiatimes.com*. Available on www.indiatimes.com/news/india/destruction-of-lakes-rivers-and-flood-plains-satellite-images-show-how-chennai-brought-upon-the-floods-on-itself-248050.html [Accessed 24 July 2016].

NASW (1999). *Code of Ethics of the National Association for Social Workers*. Washington, DC. NASW Press.

NIDM (2012). *India Disaster Report 2011*. Available on http://nidm.gov.in/PDF/pubs/India%20Disaster%20Report%202011.pdf [Accessed 14 August 2016].

Parry, N., Rustin, M., and Satyamurti, C. (Eds.) (1979). *Social work, welfare, and the state*. London: Edward Arnold.

Pittaway, E., Bartolomei, L. and Rees, S. (2007). Gendered dimensions of the 2004 Tsunami and a potential social work response in post-disaster situations. *International Social Work*, 50(3): 307–319.

Said, M A., Ahmadun, F. L. R., Rodzi, M. A. and Abas, F. (2011). Community preparedness for tsunami disaster: A case study. *Disaster Prevention and Management: An International Journal*, 20(3): 266–280.

Schumacher, E. F. (1973). *Small is beautiful: Economics as if people mattered*. London: Blond and Briggs. Available on http://www.daastol.com/books/Schumacher%20(1973)%20Small%20is%20Beautiful.pdf [Accessed 5 November 2017].

Sundet, P. and Mermelstein, J. (1996). Predictors of rural community survival after natural disaster: Implications for social work practice. *Journal of Social Service Research*, 1: 57–70.

Stalin, J. (2016). *How People Of Chennai Are Coming Together To Help Flood-Affected*. NDTV.com. Available on www.ndtv.com/chennai-news/how-people-of-chennai-are-coming-together-to-help-flood-affected-1253094 [Accessed 14 August 2016].

Stalin, J. (2016). *In Chennai Floods, Middle Class Among The Hardest Hit*. NDTV.com. Available on www.ndtv.com/chennai-news/in-chennai-floods-middle-class-among-the-hardest-hit-1253988 https://en.wikipedia.org/wiki/Chief_Seattle [Accessed 8 May 2017].

The New Indian Express (2016). Chennai Floods in November Washed Away Over Rs.14,000 crore. Retrieved 13 August 2016. Available on www.newindianexpress.com/business/news/Chennai-Floods-in-November-Washed-Away-Over-Rs-14000-crore/2016/03/31/article3355588.ece

Venugopal, V. (2016). *Severe flooding in Chennai could have been avoided*. [online] The Economic Times. Available at: https://economictimes.indiatimes.com/news/politics-and-nation/severe-flooding-in-chennai-could-have-been-avoided-centre/articleshow/50815738.cms [Accessed 5 November 2017].

24
Mitigating the impact of drought in Namibia
Implications for social work practice, education and policy

Peggie Chiwara and Antoinette Lombard

Introduction

The International Association of Schools of Social Work (IASSW) (2016) argues that sustainable development is rooted in healthy and inclusive societies, based on the principles of social, economic and environmental justice, while recognising the need to protect the environment and its resources for future generations. In the 2015/2016 agricultural season, all of Southern Africa, including Namibia, suffered a devastating drought, following one of the strongest El Niño events in the last 50 years (World Food Programme, 2016a). Drought as an effect of climate change threatens food and nutritional security and is accompanied by ecological degradation, loss of animal and plant life, and livelihoods (IASSW, 2016). Drought is considered a serious threat to sustainable development in Africa because of its far-reaching adverse impact on people's health, economic activity and environment (United Nations Economic and Social Council, 2007). Disasters (e.g. drought) are 'increasingly important in social work theory and practice as they grow in both frequency and the number of people affected' (Dominelli and Ioakimidis, 2015: 1).

For Namibia, the 2015/2016 drought was the worst in 80 years, according to the Namibia Red Cross Society (NRCS, 2016). Although Namibia is the driest country in Southern Africa (World Bank, 2009), social work practice there has not yet made an adequate connection between social work and environmental issues, relying instead on an exclusively social interpretation of the person-in-environment principle (Coates and Gray, 2012).

This chapter aims to extend the focus of social work in Namibia to include ecological justice and environmental sustainability (Dominelli, 2012; Gray et al., 2013). It will show that social policy needs to pay attention to drought crises (Alston, 2011) and broaden the currently limited discussion on the implications of climate change to include its implications for social work practice, education and research (Dominelli, 2012; IASSW, 2016; Moth and Morton, 2011). The chapter draws on the green social work model (Dominelli, 2012) for insights into the roles social workers can play in drought mitigation within a framework that advocates and works for the reform of those socio-political and economic forces that have a deleterious impact on the quality of life of poor communities. The chapter outlines the research method and literature used, followed by an overview of drought in Namibia, including its social, economic and environmental impacts on human well-being. Drought mitigation in Namibia is considered and followed by a look at Namibian social work practice. Then, the possibilities of practising green social work in Namibia are discussed. Finally, the conclusion reflects on the findings of the study and the way forward.

Research method

The empirical research for this chapter was guided by the questions: How is the impact of drought in Namibia mitigated? What is social work's role in this mitigation? The study was conducted in seven of Namibia's 14 administrative regions, namely Omusati, Ohangwena, Oshikoto, Oshana, Kavango West, Kavango East and Kunene. These regions are some of the country's most populous rural regions. In the 2015/2016 drought, 50 percent of households in urgent need of drought relief were in these regions (Haidula, 2016).

The qualitative study adopted a collective case study design (Stake, 2005), sourced from multiple case sites (Harling, 2012). The 51 participants in the study included 19 household participants, 12 social workers, 11 school principals, seven student social workers and two drought relief coordinators, all selected through purposive and key informant sampling methods (Delport and Strydom, 2011). One-on-one interviews guided by a semi-structured interview schedule were used to collect research data. Interviews were conducted face-to-face or telephonically. Participants could also submit detailed responses via electronic mail. Data were analysed using a thematic qualitative data analysis process (Creswell, 2014). Themes generated from this process were integrated with the literature and supported by the direct voices of research participants across the respective regions. Regions are indicated as pseudo alphabet letters to protect participants' identities. The University of Pretoria granted the study ethical clearance.

The context of drought in Namibia

Since 2008, Namibia has experienced increasing drought, sometimes concurrent with (flash) floods, with a deleterious impact on rural livelihoods and food security (Office of the Prime Minister [OPM], 2016). This situation is familiar to the study's participants:

> The most unforgettable challenge is lack of rainfall. If it doesn't rain then drought is an obvious outcome. If it rains again, it becomes even worse, especially when it turns into floods because our houses and possessions are washed away.
>
> *(Household participant-1E)*

Namibia was still recovering from the 2013 disastrous drought (NRCS, 2013) when the 2015/2016 one struck. Article 26(1) of the *Constitution of the Republic of Namibia* provides for the president to declare a national disaster if a disaster threatens the nation (Republic of Namibia, 1990), and did so in 2013. As an arid country, Namibian policy is not to declare drought a national disaster too frequently to avoid the serious financial implications for the government (Republic of Namibia, 1997). Sadly, little was learnt from the 2013 experience, and little was done to strengthen Namibia's capacity to prepare holistically for future droughts. Hence, the unprecedented impact of the 2015/2016 drought on Namibia's population of around 2 million (National Statistics Agency, 2011) forced the country to declare another national disaster (World

Food Programme, 2016b). The impact was worst on rural households. Almost a third of the population (729,134) were classified as food insecure by the second quarter of 2016. Of these, 595,839 people are barely managing to stay alive and are considered to be living below human survival thresholds (OPM, 2016).

The International Strategy for Disaster Reduction (2003: 1) argues that 'drought by itself does not trigger an emergency. Whether it becomes an emergency depends on its impact on local people. And that, in turn, depends upon their vulnerability to such a shock'. Similarly, 'if hazards today are disrupting more lives and livelihoods than in the past, this is often not driven by the intensity of the hazard but rather by socio-economic causes of human vulnerability' (Fara, 2001: 60). Such arguments necessitate examination of the macro-socio-economic, political, and cultural contexts that contribute to vulnerability to drought in Namibia.

According to the Food and Agricultural Organisation (FAO, 2016), Namibia is an economically thriving upper middle-income country, but its Gini coefficient of 0.597 makes Namibia one of the most unequal countries in the world (World Bank, 2016). This inequality is evident in the agricultural sector, where only 10 percent of the population own 44 percent of the agricultural land and 60 percent of the population is relegated to unproductive subsistence agriculture in communal land that accounts for 41 percent of the total agricultural land (FAO, 2016). Life in rural Namibia is hard. It is enmeshed with poverty, unemployment, limited income-generating opportunities, isolation from markets, high HIV/AIDS incidence and poor agricultural production (FAO, 2016; International Fund for Agricultural Development, 2014). These factors perpetuate the vulnerability of marginalised groups and exacerbate the effects of natural disasters such as drought. Responses to drought crises must therefore challenge and address existing poverty and structural inequalities (Dominelli, 2012), as discussed in the section on the social, economic and environmental impact of drought on human well-being.

Social, economic and environmental impact of drought on human well-being

Rural communities in Namibia depend on fragile subsistence crop and livestock farming in areas with low and variable rainfall, and inherently poor, degraded and unproductive soil (FAO, 2016). One household participant (2E) said that nothing:

> makes things better. We get water from far, we have no fertile soil or manure and there is not enough rainfall.

Land degradation in communal areas is accelerated by a lack of incentives for sustainable land management practices in the absence of exclusive land tenure rights (Fara, 2001). Given such pre-existing challenges, drought affects communal farmers in several ways – the social impact of drought relates to people's health, safety and access to basic necessities; its economic impact relates to loss of income and livelihoods, and environmentally, it destroys habitats and significantly reduces food and water supplies (National Drought Mitigation Centre, 2016). Communal farmers already live on the margins of survival, with few resources to fall back on in times of crises (Desai, 2007):

> Even before the drought, these people were already vulnerable and now with the drought they were not able to harvest ... they sell these assets to get food, so their asset base is eroded.
> *(Drought relief coordinator-2)*

The study's findings show that droughts place many rural households at risk of starvation. These households do not have the financial muscle to purchase food from shops, and if they cannot farm, they cannot eat:

> We have had people in the office who have not eaten for the past two to three days ... they don't even know where their next meal is going to come from.
>
> *(Student social worker-5C)*

> People are despondent because they haven't had meals in three to four days.
>
> *(Drought relief coordinator-2)*

Drought-induced food shortages have dire consequences on school performance and attendance:

> [It] is really taxing on the lives of these children. ... We are experiencing drop-outs because of hunger.
>
> *(Principal-2D)*

> This issue of drought, hunger and poverty ... is affecting our learners negatively. They cannot cope with school.
>
> *(Principal-11C)*

When unprecedented food insecurity levels are worsened by drought, some learners either adapt to hunger or adopt risky survival strategies:

> You can even see with their hunger ... running around in the school premises. But honestly speaking they are running on empty stomachs.
>
> *(Principal-10B)*

> Drought really affects these learners ... they are being preyed on in exchange for food. ... They will do anything just to get food ... and when I say anything, even being exploited, sexually.
>
> *(Principal-2D)*

> The girls now, due to the impact of the drought are getting into early marriage. ... They also ... exchange sex for benefits.
>
> *(Social worker-8F)*

Remote rural communities in Namibia lack access to safe drinking water, and source water from unprotected wells and earth dams which run dry during drought (Kapolo, 2014):

> We used to survive on getting water from wells but they have all dried up and the government has stopped digging any further.
>
> *(Household participant-1E)*

> We are sharing [borehole] water with the community, sometimes we spend three to four days without water. We end up sending the learners home because we do not have water at school.
>
> *(Principal-7F)*

Apart from securing food and some form of income through farming, rural communities in the study regions mostly lack alternative livelihoods – one household participant (1G) said:

> Neither in my household nor in our community do we have any projects to do [for income]. We really need to combat this situation.

Moreover, the 2015/2016 drought reduced agricultural labour employment opportunities by almost 80 percent (NRCS, 2016):

> Most women plough in the fields to feed their families, they also help others to harvest, then they get a little bit [of income] but when there is drought, there are no jobs, there is no way to make money because no one wants their assistance.
>
> *(Student social worker-4B)*

Those most vulnerable and, therefore, most affected by climatic events tend to have limited livelihood options (Alston, 2011), leading communities to despair and sometimes to over-indulgence in alcohol:

> In one village . . . this man was saying, 'I feel so hopeless that I have started entertaining ideas of suicide. I don't know what to do, I can't provide for my family. I am so depressed and feel terribly inadequate as a parent. . . . I am a cattle herder, I don't have anything left, most of my cattle died . . . what can I do?'
>
> *(Drought relief coordinator-2)*

> When there is rain, you find that the people are in the fields but now that there is no rain, there is nothing to do, they spend most of their time . . . at the bar.
>
> *(Social worker-6C)*

It is a vicious cycle: the inherent fragility of poor people's livelihoods makes them unable to cope with stresses such as droughts or influence their environment to reduce those stresses, making them increasingly vulnerable (Department for International Development, 1999). With no alternative livelihood options during drought periods, and livestock dying, many men, and young people of both sexes, migrate to urban areas to find work:

> We are hit by drought here. Our children tried to work on the fields but now they are being pushed to migrate to towns to seek for employment because of harsh drought.
>
> *(Household participant-1E)*

The Republic of Namibia (1997) stresses the importance of diversifying livelihoods in addition to rain-fed agriculture:

> If you are . . . a subsistence farmer, who depends on rain-fed agriculture and that is your only livelihood. . . . You have to look at it and say, how do I move away from this so that I can have another source, whether it is income or food? If you have diversified livelihoods . . . even if you cannot have food in your garden . . . you can at least have access to an income which can give you access to the market.
>
> *(Drought relief coordinator-2)*

To ensure sustainable livelihoods in rural areas, it is essential to mitigate the socio-economic and environmental impact of drought.

Drought mitigation in Namibia

Drought mitigation is a multi-sectoral, multidisciplinary effort. It

> comprises any structural or physical measures (. . . appropriate crops, dams, engineering projects) and non-structural measures (. . . policies, awareness, knowledge development, public commitment, legal frameworks, and operating practices) that are undertaken to limit the adverse impacts of drought.
>
> *(Tadesse, 2016: 16)*

Namibia has always implemented practical measures to mitigate the impact of drought on communities, adopting a drought policy in 1997, seven years after independence. The drought policy, currently under review, sought to shift from 'an exclusive focus on emergency drought programmes to a broader, longer-term perspective' (Republic of Namibia, 1997: 4). Nevertheless, as Haraseb pointed out in an interview with Schlechter (2016a), Namibia has maintained an exclusive emergency focus regarding drought. This has not changed much in the 15 years since Fara's (2001: 58) research identified government's action as reactive, 'attempting to limit the socio-economic impact of drought, rather than . . . an on-going proactive strategy'.

In August 2016, recognising that most African countries intervene reactively to drought, rather than enhance the preparedness and adaptive capacity of communities most vulnerable to climate change, Namibia hosted the first African Drought Conference (Republic of Namibia, 2016). One author, Chiwara, attended this historic conference, and observed the absence of delegates from the social welfare sector. The conference was dominated by environmentalists, meteorologists and representatives from the agricultural sector.

The 2015/2016 drought prompted the Namibian government to set up a year-long emergency drought relief programme, officially ending 31 March 2016, but the unrelenting drought resulted in extending the programme by three months from May 2016 (Schlechter, 2016b). In Namibian drought crises, food security is equated to short-term food relief interventions to prevent widespread malnutrition and loss of life, rather than long-term strategies to protect the livelihoods of those at risk (Fara, 2001). Dominelli (2012) argues that such programmes fail to address specific environmental issues and calls for active citizenship and empowering processes to assist those affected in rebuilding their lives and environments. Under the drought relief food assistance programme, households receive a 12.5 kilogram bag of maize flour, two tins of fish and a bottle of cooking oil, at irregular intervals every two to three months (*New Era Newspaper*, 2016). This is manifestly inadequate:

> We really suffer . . . the government spends two months without providing us with maize meal for drought relief. The government gives us one bag of maize meal and we are eight, so it doesn't last long. There are times when we go to bed on empty stomachs.
>
> *(Household participant-1E)*

> We only eat in the evening because if you eat in the afternoon and evening then the [drought relief] food won't last.
>
> *(Household participant-2C)*

Although most rural households need drought food aid, only households with 'children aged five years and under, pregnant and lactating mothers, people over 60 years of age, mentally and physically handicapped persons, and persons certified as malnourished by hospital or clinic staff' (Republic of Namibia, 1997: 14) receive assistance. Hence, 'food distribution programmes during drought have been inefficient, poorly targeted, and of limited impact in ensuring household food security' (Republic of Namibia, 1997: 11):

> This drought relief is really small. You will see how they [the community] are quarrelling for food and this unfair distribution of drought relief.
>
> *(Principal-10B)*

Besides food assistance, the government and NRCS assist with drilling new boreholes and rehabilitating old ones (Schlechter, 2016b; Thomas, 2016). Funding limitations from June 2016 meant that NRCS could only operate four of the planned 12 soup kitchens in selected drought-stricken localities (Thomas, 2016).

The problems that emerge during drought in Namibia are not only caused directly by the natural disaster, but also by failure to address social and economic disparities (Giorgis, in Fara, 2001). In addition to undertaking immediate relief operations, it is essential to plan and implement effective rehabilitative measures to sustain people's lives (James, 2007) – disasters cannot be met in isolation, without tackling poverty to ensure that people are food secure even in times of drought (Kapolo, 2014). This then raises the question of where social work in Namibia fits into a sustainable response to drought. Dominelli (2012) notes that climate change and disaster interventions require the social work profession to develop new theories and practices that enhance social workers' capacities to intervene in such situations.

Social work practice in Namibia

In Namibia, social work is a statutorily regulated profession. The country's only social work training institution is at the University of Namibia (UNAM). In 2012, UNAM introduced a module in disaster management in its undergraduate social work curriculum. This is a promising move regarding future social workers' capacities in integrated social, economic and environmental interventions. However, without a social policy framework to guide the provision of social welfare services (Chiwara, 2015), social workers in Namibia operate mostly at the micro-level; casework is their preferred method of practice (Ananias and Lightfoot, 2012) and borne out by this study:

> We are more into therapy . . . even though we did community work [at university], we are not deeply into it . . . practice . . . and this idea of counselling and crisis intervention just here and there does not prepare the community for any eventuality like drought.
>
> *(Social worker-6C)*

> That's why other professions . . . are looking down on us. . . . Basically, we are not doing much . . . we do counselling [although] . . . we are capacitated to do much more than [counselling].
>
> *(Student social worker-5C)*

This micro-level practice suggests that social workers have not engaged in enough macro-level practice to have a voice in policy efforts to mitigate vulnerability arising from environmental crises:

> I haven't had a platform where we specifically had social workers being represented and articulating their role . . . [and] contributions to the [drought] response.
>
> *(Drought relief coordinator-2)*

> For a fact we are not part ... of the implementation and all the [drought] plans.... We only see the impact but we ... don't really have substantial [input].
>
> *(Social worker-6C)*

These remarks suggest that social workers in general do not engage in sustainable targeted poverty, hunger, unemployment, inequality and livelihood options. This puts already vulnerable people at even more risk when drought strikes.

The first step towards enabling social work practitioners and educators to facilitate sustainable social development outcomes, including the prevention and mitigation of and response to disasters is to acknowledge their role in socio-economic development. In pursuit of social justice, which Isbister (2001: 4) refers to as 'the bedrock social virtue' and as a right, social workers should prioritise addressing poverty. From a structural perspective, Dominelli (2012: 3) explains that poverty is 'a constant, on-going disaster in its own right and not simply an additional factor to be considered in determining individual vulnerability to disasters'. A 'structural notion of poverty to social justice' creates a pathway for social workers to develop socio-economic models that do justice to 'low-income people who cannot overcome poverty or participate in market-based solutions to social problems, including climate change' (Dominelli, 2012: 3), as in Namibia.

In the context of climate change, where the impact of natural disasters is aggravated by poverty and widespread food and water shortages exacerbated, social work should become more proactive and resilient to deal with these problems. Rural communities may starve even in an economically prospering nation, because they are excluded from economic development. Without comprehensive and targeted interventions that address structural issues of poverty and inequality (Midgley, 2014), poor people have very little chance of recovering after a drought crisis; they are already marginalised and excluded. Moreover, the well-being of future generations is compromised when children drop out of school due to hunger, or adopt risky coping mechanisms that may hinder their childhood development and transition into adulthood. From this perspective, social workers cannot afford to apply only individual therapeutic social work methods that do not have a significant impact on poverty and environmental issues.

The effects of drought in Namibia on the people, animals and land emphasise the relevance of adopting the green social work model to pursue social, economic and environmental justice. The research findings indicate that there is not yet a best practice model in Namibia to share regarding social work's involvement in drought and disaster management in general, but there is considerable scope for adopting a green social work model in the country. Dominelli defines 'green' social work as:

> that part of practice that intervenes to protect the environment and enhance people's well-being by integrating the interdependencies between people and their socio-cultural, economic and physical environments, and among peoples within an egalitarian framework that addresses prevailing structural inequalities and unequal distribution of power and resources.
>
> *(2012: 8)*

Towards green social work in Namibia

Adopting a green social work model in Namibia opens up space for new paradigms of production and consumption by 'advocating for changes; research that demonstrates the suffering of poor and marginalised people; promoting robust resilience in communities; and developing alternative models of production and consumption' (Dominelli, 2012: 198). Green social workers and other actors can work in collaborative partnerships with the people affected to build resilience and coproduce models of sustainable socio-economic development.

Research and assessment of vulnerabilities

The assessment of vulnerabilities is an important step towards evidence-based drought mitigation. This study has provided a comprehensive overview from various stakeholders' experiences of and perspectives on the current impact of drought, and areas of vulnerability. New paradigms of production and consumption (Dominelli, 2012) should be prioritised in Namibia. With heightened environmental crises, there is an urgent imperative for social work in Namibia to 'encourage and facilitate research into the social work role in relation to disasters and environmental challenges' (Global Agenda, 2012: 4). One participant aptly commented:

> Continued research should be used to influence policies ... to address the [drought] phenomenon in a better and more informed manner.
>
> *(Social worker-5A)*

Social workers can help communities by documenting their cases and bringing research evidence to the table (as this study has done) to influence policy and development. Multi-sectoral community initiatives that mobilise community involvement, backed up by empirical research, can be harnessed in environmental justice arguments that advocate for poor people's rights. Green social work can empower communities 'in power struggles with more powerful others if they have access to the skills and expertise needed to make their case and insist that they also have rights, including that of being heard' (Dominelli, 2012: 41).

Advocating for change

The main aim of advocacy practice is the 'pursuit of social justice' (Hoefer, 2012: 2). It aligns with green social work in its holistic view of seeing the connection between individuals, larger numbers of people and the environment because government policies 'impose costs, monetary or otherwise, or deny services to people in need' (Hoefer, 2012: 1). The findings reported in this chapter reveal the absence of social workers from advocacy practice:

> At this stage I don't know if social workers are advocating and lobbying for the rights of the people affected by drought.
>
> *(Student social worker-3C)*

> Without anyone advocating on their behalf, communities tend to despair. It's difficult to go through this drought without any help from the government. If there's no help we might just die.
>
> *(Household participant-1F)*

Social workers may be aware of their role in advocacy, but they are not acting upon it:

> We need to advocate for these people ... in order for the government to avail certain resources ... we can do much better if we advocate for them. We can ... influence policymakers in coming up with policies to help people who are affected by drought.
>
> *(Social worker-11G)*

These comments expose the need for advocacy work as suggested by Dominelli (2012). Social workers need to lobby for the government to implement policies on rural employment and access to social and economic development (Republic of Namibia, 1997) to tackle poverty and inequality. Because Namibia is characterised by skewed land distribution patterns that consign unfertile farming areas to subsistence farmers, social workers could advocate for 'a more equitable distribution of the Earth's material resources within their existing mandate and advocate for its realisation' (Dominelli, 2012: 31). In view of green social work's criticism of 'the unequal distribution of goods, services and natural resources and seek[ing] to rectify these … green social work, like other progressive forms of social work, becomes explicitly political' (Dominelli, 2012: 25). In Namibia, the impact of drought cannot be effectively mitigated by targeting selected households with food assistance to sustain them for a short while, until the drought ends. Social workers in Namibia should function as change agents who influence policy changes designed to build capacity in drought-prone communities, and bring about coordinated stakeholder actions and community engagement, and the political will to address the long-term needs of communities affected by drought. Psychosocial support is an important component of social work, but in itself it is not a comprehensive response to social, economic and environmental injustices; it also does not address the macro-issues of poverty, lack of resources or opportunities for sustainable livelihoods. Nor does it build resilience to respond to future disasters. Therefore, there is urgent need for advocacy and green social work practices that create strategies that build resilient communities.

Promoting resilience in communities

Social work interventions to mitigate the effects of drought should empower and build poor people's resilience (Tadesse, 2016). This case study demonstrates that without interventions to strengthen their resilience, individuals may resort to negative coping measures, including alcoholism, and contemplating suicide. People suffering the impact of drought cannot be left alone, in the hope that they will bounce back by themselves:

> We have not seen any councillor or advisor from the government … It could be easier if we had somebody to lead us, because you can't gather people when you have nothing to tell them. In that case we could discuss ways of moving forward such as digging wells or mini dams to store water or make gardens to plant crops.
>
> *(Household participant-1E)*

Developing alternative models of production and consumption

People in rural Namibia rely on the Earth for their survival and can only value themselves in relation to their natural environment. Without this environment, their agency, livelihood and future are at stake. This realisation is central to social workers' advocacy role in influencing policy and holding government accountable for sustainable green strategies. Subsistence communities can be supported in transitioning to alternate and sustainable sources of livelihood, such as village-based eco-tourism, where communities can showcase their culture, rural lifestyle and natural environment to gain income (Kiper, 2013). Such initiatives can help to strengthen interdependencies between people and their ecosystem(s), and may provide incentives for subsistence farmers in Namibia to care effectively for their natural environment. This may ultimately reduce the urge to migrate to urban areas in times of drought, and communities may gain sustainable alternative livelihoods. Namibia has excellent case studies on 'sustainable community development practice ... that includes protecting the environment by caring for it when meeting human needs' (Dominelli, 2012: 41). One of these is the Sustainably Harvested Devil's Claw Project (Cole and Du Plessis, 2001). Devil's Claw is an indigenous natural product that thrives in Namibia's semi-arid climate and has medicinal uses. It is internationally sought after. Government regulations coupled with sustainable harvesting of this plant has demonstrably improved livelihoods and the food security of the subsistence farmers involved (National Botanical Research Institute, 2016).

Partnerships

A holistic approach such as green social work focusing on social relationships that bring experts together (Dominelli, 2012) is required to mitigate the impact of drought. The study sought the views of a wide array of stakeholders, who all highlighted the lack of partnerships to mitigate the effects of drought in Namibia and the absence of social workers in drought mitigation:

> The only programme that I am aware of is the one provided by the government, where they provide drought relief food. . . . I am not aware of any other programmes that are directly assisting [with the drought].
>
> *(Student social worker-6C)*

> We are thankful for that one bag of maize-meal [from the government]. Although it is not enough, we do not have other organisations to help us.
>
> *(Household participant-2 E)*

Partnerships are indispensable in drought mitigation because they facilitate thinking differently about people's relationships between themselves and their environments – social, economic, emotional, spiritual and physical (Dominelli, 2012).

Social work education

Until 2012, social work education in Namibia focused mainly on capacitating social work practitioners to respond to psychosocial issues:

> I think more training on drought, sustainable livelihoods . . . social workers need to be enlightened and trained in this area because it's an area that we lack so much as professionals. I think if there could be more training . . . we would be able to do more work out there, to help people cope with such [drought] events.
>
> *(Social worker-4B)*

UNAM's incorporation of disaster management in its social work curriculum may be a first step towards moulding change agents with an integrated social, economic and environmental justice focus. Student social work field placements should afford students mentorship and opportunities to put into practice integrated social, economic and environmental development strategies:

> Theory alone is easy but being exposed to the issue directly is another thing . . . with your theory alone with no direct practice, you might fail in your duties because out there is the true reality.
>
> *(Student social worker-3C)*

> I did not have an opportunity to apply my skills in disaster management. . . . I haven't seen the social worker at my placement engaged in addressing problems related to drought.
>
> *(Student social worker-2G)*

Conclusion

The link between people and their environment and its impact on their social and economic development has been demonstrated in the case of Namibia. It is evident that social workers, in partnership with other stakeholders, may play a role in mitigating the impact of drought. Training in green social work and disaster management can be a radical departure from teaching social work students only how to deal with the psychosocial aspects of disaster, and can become a tool to empower future social workers to become social change agents who actively promote social, economic and environment justice. Such training should include a policy dimension, introducing all policies relevant to the environment and socio-economic development, along with skills to influence and develop policy. If they adopt the green social work model, social workers can mitigate the socio-economic and environmental impact of drought in Namibia.

References

Alston, M. (2011). *Advanced practice or social work advancing?* Retrieved 06/12/2016 from www.aasw.asn.au/document/item/3366

Ananias, J. and Lightfoot, E. (2012). Promoting social development: Building a professional social work association in Namibia. *Journal of Community Practice*, 20(1–2): 196–210. doi:10.1080/10705422.2012.644227

Chiwara, P. (2015). *Social work's contribution in promoting social and economic equality: A Namibian case study.* (Master's thesis). Retrieved 06/10/2016 from http://repository.up.ac.za/handle/2263/48945 [Accessed 5 November 2017].

Coates, J. and Gray, M. (2012). The environment and social work: An overview and introduction. *International Journal of Social Welfare*, 21: 230–238. doi:10.1111/j.1468-2397.2011.00851.x

Cole, D. and Du Plessis, P. (2001). *Namibian devil's claw.* Available on www.the-eis.com/data/literature/CRIAA%20Devils%20Claw%20Case%20Study.pdf [Accessed 13 November 2016].

Creswell, J. W. (2014). *Research design: Qualitative, quantitative, and mixed methods approaches.* (4th ed.). Los Angeles, CA: Sage.

Delport, C. S. L., and Strydom, H. (2011). Sampling and pilot study in qualitative research. In A. S. de Vos., H. Strydom., C. B. Fouché., and C. S. L. Delport (Eds.), *Research at grassroots for the social sciences and the human services professions.* (4th ed.). Pretoria: Van Schaik, pp. 390–396.

Department for International Development. (1999). *Sustainable livelihoods guidance sheets.* Available on www.eldis.org/vfile/upload/1/document/0901/section2.pdf [Accessed 5 November 2017].

Desai, A. S. (2007). Disaster and social work responses. In L. Dominelli (Ed.), *Revitalising communities in a globalising world. An empirical approach to ordinary hermeneutics.* Aldershot: Ashgate, pp. 291–314.

Dominelli, L. (2012). *Green social work: From environmental crises to environmental justice.* Cambridge: Polity Press.

Dominelli, L., and Ioakimidis, V. (2015). Editorial: Social work on the frontline in addressing disasters, social problems and marginalization. *International Social Work*, 58(1): 3–6. doi: 10.1177/0020872814561402

Fara, K. (2001). How natural are "natural disasters"? Vulnerability to drought of communal farmers in southern Namibia. *Risk Management*, 3(3): 47–63. Available on www.jstor.org/stable/3867913

Food and Agricultural Organisation (FAO). (2016). *Namibia at a glance.* Available on www.fao.org/namibia/fao-in-namibia/namibia-at-a-glance/en/ [Accessed 15 June 2016].

Global Agenda for Social Work and Social Development Commitment to Action. (2012). Available on http://cdn.ifsw.org/assets/globalagenda2012.pdf [Accessed 5 November 2017].

Gray, M., Coates, J., and Hetherington, T. (2013). Conclusion. In M. Gray., J. Coates, and T. Hetherington (Eds.), *Environmental social work*. New York, NY: Routledge, pp. 299–318.

Haidula, T. (2016). *Reports Paints Grim Drought Picture*. Retrieved 14/07/2016 from www.namibian.com.na/Report-paints-grim-drought-picture/42626/152848/archive-read/Report-paints-grim-drought-picture

Harling, K. (2012). *An Overview of Case Study*. Retrieved 19/06/2016 from www.farm foundation.org/news/articlefiles/1028-1_harling.pdf

Hoefer, R. (2012). *Advocacy practice for social justice* (4th ed.). Chicago, IL: Lyceum.

International Fund for Agricultural Development. (2014). *Rural poverty in Namibia*. Available on www.ruralpovertyportal.org/ar/country/home/tags/namibia [Accessed 10 June 2016].

International Association of Schools of Social Work (IASSW). (2016). *Theme 3: Promoting environmental and community sustainability*. Available on www.iassw-aiets.org/wp-content/uploads/2015/10/IASSW-Theme-3-Statement-24-August-2016.pdf [Accessed 25 May 2016].

International Strategy for Disaster Reduction (2003). *Drought Living with Risk: An integrated approach to reducing societal vulnerability to drought*. Available on www.unccd.int/Lists/SiteDocumentLibrary/Regions/Asia/meetings/regional/TPN5_7_2003/ annex3.pdf [Accessed 02 July 2016].

Isbister, J. (2001). *Capitalism and justice. Envisioning social and economic fairness*. Bloomfield, IN: Kumarian Press.

James, L. (2007). International aid in disasters: A critique. In L. Dominelli (Ed.), *Revitalising communities in a globalising world. An empirical approach to ordinary hermeneutics*. Aldershot: Ashgate, pp. 281–293.

Kapolo, I. N. (2014). *Drought conditions and management strategies in Namibia*. Retrieved 19/07/2016 from www.droughtmanagement.info/literature/UNW-DPC_NDMP_Country_Report_Namibia_2014.pdf

Kiper, T. (2013). Role of ecotourism in sustainable development. In M. Özyavuz (Ed.), *Advances in Landscape Architecture*. Retrieved 13/11/2016 from http://dx.doi.org/10.5772/55749

Midgley, J. (2014). *Social development: Theory and practice*. London: Sage.

Moth, R. and Morton, D. (2011). *Social Work and Climate Change: A call to action*. Retrieved 10/06/2016 from www.socialworkfuture.org/articles-resources/uk-articles/101-social-work-and-climate-change-a-call-to-action-rich-moth-a-dan-morton

Namibia Red Cross Society (NRCS) (2013). *Emergency appeal Namibia: Drought*. Available on ww.ifrc.org/docs/Appeals/13/MDRNA008ea.pdf [Accessed 12 June 2016].

Namibia Red Cross Society (NRCS) (2016). *The Formation of NRCS*. Available on www.redcross.org.na/aboutus.php?id=15&title=Who%20we%20are [Accessed 04 June 2016].

National Botanical Research Institute (2016). *Devil's Claw*. Available on www.nbri.org.na/sections/economic-botany/INP/sectors/Devils-claw [Accessed 13 November 2016].

National Drought Mitigation Centre (2016). *Types of Drought Impacts*. Available on http://drought.unl.edu/DroughtforKids/HowDoesDroughtAffectOurLives/typesofdroughtimpacts.aspx [Accessed 13 June 2016].

National Statistics Agency (2011). *Population and housing census indicators*. Windhoek: National Statistics Agency.

New Era Newspaper (2016). *Drought relief, what relief?* Available on https://weekend.newera.com.na/2016/10/31/drought-relief-what-relief/ [Accessed 31 October 2016].

Office of the Prime Minister (OPM) (2016). *Namibia rural food security and livelihood vulnerability assessment report: Forecast for 2016/2017 consumption year*. Windhoek: OPM.

Republic of Namibia (1990). *Constitution of the Republic of Namibia. Government Gazette*. (No. 2).

Republic of Namibia (1997). *National drought policy and strategy*. Available on www.the-eis.com/data/literature/National%20Drought%20Policy%20and%20Strategy%201997.pdf [Accessed 16 August 2016].

Republic of Namibia (2016). *African drought conference event programme*. Available on www.unccd.int/Documents/Call%20for%20abstracts%20final%20ADC.pdf [Accessed 16 August 2016].

Schlechter, D. (2016a). *New Drought Policy in the Making – Haraseb. New Era Newspaper*. Available on www.newera.com.na/2016/04/05/drought-policy-making-haraseb/ [Accessed 11 April 2016].

Schlechter, D. (2016b). *Cabinet Approves N$90 million for Drought Relief.* Retrieved 31/05/2016 from www.newera.com.na/2016/05/31/cabinet-approves-n90-million-drought-relief/

Stake, R. E. (2005). Qualitative case studies. In N. K. Denzin and Y. S. Lincoln (Eds.), *The Sage Handbook of Qualitative Research.* (3rd edn.). Thousand Oaks, CA: Sage.

Tadesse, T. (2016). *Strategic Framework for Drought Management and Enhancing Resilience in Africa.* Retrieved 24/08/2016 from www.unccd.int/Lists/SiteDocumentLibrary/Publications/02_White_paper_second_draft.pdf

Thomas, M. (2016). Red Cross funding for drought relief hard to find. *The Namibian Newspaper.* Available on Awww.namibian.com.na/Red-Cross-funding-for-drought-relief-hard-to-find/41402/read [Accessed 06 June 2016].

United Nations Economic and Social Council (2007). *Africa review report on drought and desertification.* Available on www.un.org/esa/sustdev/csd/csd16/ rim/eca_bg3.pdf [Accessed 10 June 2016].

World Bank (2009). *Namibia Country Brief.* Availble on www.openknowledge. worldbank.org/handle/10986/2630 [Accessed 11 June 2016].

World Bank (2016). *Namibia Overview.* Available on www.worldbank.org/en/ country/namibia/overview [Accessed 23 July 2016].

World Food Programme (2016a). Famine Early Warning Systems Network, European Commission's Joint Research Centre and Food and Agriculture Organization. *El Niño set to have a devastating impact on southern Africa's harvests and food security.* Available on www.wfp.org/news/news-release/el-nino-set-have-devastating-impact-Southern-Africa's-harvests-and-food-security [Accessed 09 June 2016].

World Food Programme (2016b). *Drought emergency declared in Namibia: More than 560,000 people in need.* Available on www.un.org.na/index_htm_files/Drought%20Emergency%20Declared%20in%20Namibi1.pdf [Accessed 1 June 2016].

Part VII
Disaster-driven migration

25
Understanding poverty through the experiences of women who are forced migrants

Considerations for a social work response

Mehmoona Moosa-Mitha, Feinula Bhanji and Fariyal Ross-Sheriff

Introduction

Poverty, as Dominelli argues, is a 'constant, on-going disaster in its own right and not simply an additional factor to be considered in determining individual vulnerability to disasters' (2012: 3). This structural definition of poverty points to an important feature of disasters as systemic, holistic and interconnected to other forms of deprivations. A focus on understanding poverty through the lived experiences of forced migrants reminds us that it is impossible to isolate economic poverty from other forms of deprivation for women in disasters, nor are these a result of local events solely; but also transnational in nature.

Poverty, like other forms of disaster is socio-political in nature, as Hyndman suggests: 'Disasters, whether natural or man-made, are profoundly discriminatory. Wherever they hit, pre-existing structures and social conditions determine that some members of the community will be less affected, while others will pay a higher price' (Oxfam International 2005, cited in Hyndman, 2008: 101). The effects of disasters are unevenly distributed, based on an intersectionality of identity factors including gender, class, relations of power and nationalism (Hyndman, 2008, Seager, 2006). Acknowledging the socio-political nature of disasters is important in poverty alleviation interventions and practices since social structures and political systems maintain and exacerbate poverty for particular sectors of population, hindering their capacity to overcome these (Dominelli, 2012).

This chapter considers two narratives of poverty through two case studies of the lived experiences of two families told by women forced migrants. Case studies enable researchers to collect rich, in-depth data that can be used to identify issues and concepts of the subjects under study. Although case study data is not generalisable, they are useful for hypothesis testing in future research. Knowledge gained through analyses of case study data can be invaluable for social work researchers and practitioners. These case studies are indicative of the life experiences of large numbers of refugee women with whom the authors have worked over two decades.

We undertake a transnational feminist analysis that examines the lived realities of women and their interconnections to wider socio-political systems. The case studies enable us to derive a definition of poverty that is holistic, gendered/cultured, structurally embedded in power relationships and transnational in nature. This contributes to a broader understanding of women's experiences of poverty, traumatic experiences of disasters, strengths and resilience and the implications for poverty alleviation strategies.

Experiences of women refugees

Refugee women bear a disproportionate share of emotional and mental distress during all stages of displacement, which include: (1) pre-uprooting in the homeland; (2) uprooting when refugees depart their country of origin; (3) transition in either refugee camps or countries of first asylum; (4) resettlement in first countries of asylum, second countries or repatriation, and (5) integration to the new society for resettled refugees or repatriation to the country of origin (Ross-Sheriff et al., 2012). During these stages, women refugees are exposed to experiences of sexual exploitation, assault, torture, threats of personal violence and violence to their family members, and related atrocities. Forced migration correlates with living in economic poverty in countries of settlement for the first few years (Goździak and Long, 2005). The stories of refugee women's journey to relative safety are simultaneously narratives of resilience and survival (Rehn and Sirleaf, 2002; Amnesty International, 2004, 2005; Goździak and Long, 2005; Jansen, 2006).

Case study I: Somali refugee woman

Sharifa is a 28-year-old Somali woman who fled Somalia with her husband, Mohammed, their 11-year-old daughter, Ayesha, and two younger sons, Bashir and Caadil. They lived in Kismayo, a southern Somali border town that was controlled by rival militant groups. The soldiers from the rival groups in Somalia had been clashing violently for months. Sharifa's family and neighbours feared for their lives, and knew that eventually they would have to flee their home, even while hoping that the war would end. When the heavily armed Al-Shabaab took control of Kismayo, Sharifa and her husband, Mohammed, decided to leave with their family because they feared what they saw. Marginalised Bajuni clan members were targeted by Al-Shabaab to enact violence or to 'buy' children from poor households as recruits to building their military base. Young girls were recruited for domestic support and forced into marriage or served as sexual slaves for Al-Shabaab warriors. Sharifa and her husband feared for their children's lives. They mapped their escape overnight, and for safety joined another group of Somalis from the same village who were fleeing on foot to the nearby Kenyan border, towards Dadaab, one of the largest refugee camps.

They were overcome with mixed emotions, fear and relief, as they crossed the border into Kenya. Having crossed the border, they heard guns being fired into the air. People in the group tried to escape by running in different directions and got detached from one another. Sharifa held onto Ayesha for dear life, but got separated from her husband and sons. Sharifa and Ayesha were captured by four Kenyan police officers, who proceeded to beat and kick them while yelling at them. While Sharifa pleaded for mercy for her daughter's life, the officers gang-raped both mother and daughter.

Sharifa was in a lot of pain and had difficulty getting up, but the sight of Ayesha on the ground gave her strength to pick her up as she lay unconscious. Concerns about her daughter and the hope of finding her husband and sons kept Sharifa going. They finally reached Dadaab, already overcrowded with over 250,000 people taking refuge. Some lived in tents, and others in mud huts or shelters made from sticks and canvas. Sharifa received help in setting up a temporary home and arranged for blankets and food rations. Once settled, Sharifa knew that her priority should be medical treatment for Ayesha. However, she feared that revealing the rape would result in being ostracised from the community who would deem Ayesha unmarriageable. She would also be blamed by her husband for being raped. She asked Ayesha not to say a word of what the soldiers did to them both. The camp social worker noted the reluctance on Sharifa's part to be examined by a physician and recommended a female physician.

The social worker, Hadiya, also helped them search for their family. After three weeks, the family was reunited. Camp life involved managing her children, protecting them from getting into trouble, or being abused, working hard to get enough wood to cook their daily food, feeding the family and surviving. Sharifa had nightmares and feared being raped again by police. The emotional turmoil was unbearable for Sharifa as she watched Ayesha's anger and aggression towards her brothers escalate. Although Sharifa was depressed and sometimes experienced hopelessness, she was glad that they had a place to live and she kept a watchful eye on her family, especially Ayesha.

Sharifa was concerned that Mohammed was struggling to find a stable livelihood and missing Kismayo and the life they once enjoyed there. She knew many Kenyans did not like Somali refugees. This made it difficult for Mohammed to get a job in the camp or outside it. After six months of daily struggle to manage one daily meal for her family, Sharifa convinced her husband that he should sell the gold bangles that she had received as gifts for her wedding, to buy a cart, fruits and vegetables to sell in the camp market started by refugees. She continued to worry about her son and daughter, but wanted them to go to the camp school. However, afraid of someone molesting her daughter, she did not let Ayesha attend the camp school or let her out of her sight.

After months of living in the camp, Sharifa started attending a women's group where women shared experiences and supported each other. Hadiya had organised this because she knew that culturally, Somali women confide and protect each other. Sharifa found comfort in listening to other women's stories and heard about their experiences of rape and assault by the police. Though several women had reported these crimes to camp officials, their complaints had not been heard. For Sharifa, hearing other women's stories, the support they provided and strategies they developed for their children's safety was comforting. The women's major concerns were education, good health, and safety of their children. Sharifa wanted to bring Ayesha to the group. However, Ayesha had become withdrawn and did not want to leave 'home'.

Sharifa then turned her attention to their future, and began discussing this with Mohammed. Camp life was not good for their children and Sharifa was aware of the precariousness of their existence due to the negative attitudes that Kenyans held towards them. She also feared being sent back to Somalia. In her discussions with other women, Sharifa had learned that Somali families were settling in the Eastleigh area of Nairobi, capital of Kenya, where they would be near a *masjid* (mosque) and get support from other Somalis. She discussed plans to save funds and explore options of travel to Nairobi with her husband. However, she was fearful of being caught by the police during their escape from the refugee camp. With support from Hadiya, the family started application processes for refugee status in the US and Canada.

Over time, Sharifa began to trust Hadiya more and asked her for help with Ayesha's emotional outbursts. The social worker spent more time with Ayesha and recognised her depression, anger, aggression and withdrawal from daily life as symptoms of rape and post-traumatic stress disorder (PTSD). She worked closely with Ayesha to support her to work through these issues.

Sharifa began to recite poetry/song (known as *vave*) with the children during the evening hours. The *vave* was sung yearly during tree-planting season, expressing the socio-political and religious attitudes and perspectives of the Banjunis. This was an artistic expression that preserved the memory of the oppression they had suffered and beseeched God for help. Sharifa did not give up her silent prayer or this evening ritual, as it helped Mohammed, the children and her.

Within three years, Sharifa and Mohammed had saved enough money to get a small plot of land outside the camp where Sharifa could plant potatoes and cassava for their own consumption and sell at the local market. Five years later, Sharifa contacted her cousin Jamila who encouraged her to travel to Nairobi where their children could attend school near a *masjid* that supported refugee families. Inspired by opportunities to improve the quality of her children's lives, Sharifa convinced Mohammed to travel to Nairobi.

Life as self-settled refugees in Nairobi was very challenging. Mohammed struggled to find a job; Sharifa worked hard to get their sons in schools. She attended a training program for women to learn embroidery skills. Sharifa constantly worried about her daughter Ayesha's future. She was then a teenager. Her hope for resettlement in the US or Canada had dwindled and she prayed daily for peace in Somalia so that they could return home.

Case study II: Afghan refugee woman

Saba and her husband Mirza had made the decision to stay in their village in Baghlan Province with their five children throughout the Afghan civil war. They took comfort in knowing that Northern Alliance soldiers would protect them. Early one morning, Taliban forces entered their village, ransacked the homes of several villagers and shot some of the adult males to establish their presence and power, and defeat the Northern Alliance soldiers. They shot Mirza and their eldest son in the presence of Saba and her children, despite her desperate pleas to spare their lives.

Traumatised but fearing for the life of her remaining children, Saba was convinced by her brother to flee with him and his family to Pakistan. The extended family of 10, Saba and her four young children, Saba's brother with his wife and their three children, travelled by night, fully aware that if captured they would experience worse violence than what they had experienced in the village. Finally, after eight days they reached a camp in Pakistan operated by the United Nations High Commission for Refugees (UNHCR) where they received refuge. They thanked Allah for His mercy and for protecting them on their journey.

During the first year in the camp, Saba's older son, Sohrab, reacted to the violence he had witnessed by becoming extremely vigilant of his mother and would not let her out of his sight. The youngest daughter, two-year-old Hila, cried and demanded her mother's attention all the time. Support and comfort from her sister-in-law and protection from her brother enabled Saba to survive the perils and stresses of the camp. A UNHCR social worker, Anna, who befriended Saba while her children attended the camp school, listened to Saba as she recalled her year at the camp. Saba cried as she vividly recollected the time when a camp official sexually assaulted her while she made her way to a nearby toilet. Saba could not disclose this to anyone, fearing the stigma and community ostracisation that she would experience and because victim-blaming would hold her responsible for the assault.

Anna, noting Saba's feelings of hopelessness and depression, wanted to assist her in imagining a future for herself and her children, knowing that culturally Afghans place great emphasis on their children's future with the hope that their children will care for them in old age. So, Anna helped Saba focus on the next chapter of her life. She asked Saba what her hopes were for their future. Saba's greatest desire was for her and her children to apply for refugee status in the US. She told Anna that she wanted a good education for her children, a place of safety and peace for herself and her children, especially her daughters, and to live without the constant fear of violence.

Anna helped Saba to seek sponsorship from the Lutheran Family Services (one of many faith-based American refugee agencies, e.g., Catholic Charities and Jewish Community Services) for resettlement as refugees in the United States (US) under a special category. The sponsorship was granted and Saba prayed many times a day, thanking Allah for this blessing. However, it would be difficult to leave her brother and his family. They had been a great source of strength for them.

The Lutheran Family Services sent Allison, a social worker, to meet Saba and her four children at Baltimore airport and assist them with housing, food, and access to healthcare. Allison also supported their social settlement needs, including encouraging Saba to negotiate appropriate school places for her older children, Sohrab, Laila and Malook and become an active advocate for her children at the school. Allison also helped Saba attend English language classes, anticipating that she would get a job when her youngest daughter, Hila, entered kindergarten.

Most nights during the first year in Baltimore, Saba cried herself to sleep, feeling afraid and lonely without her brother's support. She continued to have nightmares about her husband and eldest son. Being socially isolated by culture, language and shyness, Saba did not make new friends. There was hardly anyone to whom she could turn, but found comfort in prayer.

After a few months, Saba began to trust Allison and shared her nightmares over the murder of her husband and eldest son, her constant fear following the sexual assault at the camp and her worries about her children growing up in a new environment. Allison also learned that Saba found comfort in prayers. Allison had to decide which of the three concerns to focus upon: the pre-flight experience of seeing her husband and son killed, the camp experiences of stress and assault, or the current stresses of loneliness and feelings of inadequacy in bringing up four children. Allison wondered how she could build on Saba's one source of support, her faith.

Allison introduced Saba to Fatima, a Muslim Community Caseworker at a local *masjid* who mobilised volunteers to transport the family to and from the *masjid*. Saba began attending a women's group organised by Fatima, where she met and spoke with women from various parts of Afghanistan. They had had similar life experiences before coming to the US and subsequently.

Two years after settling in the US, Saba began to earn an income. Allison and Fatima discovered that Saba was a good cook, and they encouraged and assisted her to begin catering Afghan food from her home. Fatima helped Saba negotiate with a few local ethnic grocery stores to provide supplies at a discount; and recruited customers from the *masjid* to order Saba's food when they entertained.

Allison and Fatima continued to monitor the family's progress for five years and noted that Saba gradually began to feel hopeful. She continued to worry about her siblings and their families, who by this time had repatriated but found their village homes destroyed and land ownership disputed.

The women who were part of the Afghan refugee network at the *masjid*, helped Saba discover her extended family members who lived in Annandale, Virginia. Mina, her cousin, was excited to meet Saba and family after being separated for so many years. Mina and her family owned a restaurant and hired Saba until she

> found a job to her liking. Saba discussed the possibility of moving with her children, and they agreed to move to be near family. Saba enjoyed the positive social influence of extended families, and was an asset to the restaurant business.

Transnational feminist analysis of poverty

Transnational feminists are particularly interested in the complex interconnections between life experiences of poverty for women within specific contexts and its relationship to wider social and political systems. They define poverty as a social phenomenon that cuts across the local/global divide and across nation-state boundaries in the context of emergent global capitalism (Grewal, 2005; Mohanty, 2006; Mohanty, 2013). Transnational feminists also challenge narrow definitions of poverty that are income-based to promote a broader understanding of poverty that is multi-dimensional and grounded in women's lived realities (Jaggar, 2009, 2013b). Transnational feminists undertake intersectional analyses that examine experiences of poverty according to race, gender, nationalism, class and other divisions. They also examine women's resistance and resilience in the face of poverty. They emphasise poverty's socio-political nature, making it both a public issue and a private experience (Moosa-Mitha and Ross-Sheriff, 2010; Moosa-Mitha, 2016).

Analysis of the case studies

Five themes relevant to defining poverty emerged from the transnational feminist analysis of the case studies: (a) holistic understanding of poverty; (b) women's vulnerability to violence that exacerbates poverty; (c) marginalised power relations as a form of poverty; (d) women's unpaid care work as poverty; and (e) transnational nature of poverty.

Defining poverty holistically

The debate on defining poverty has a long history. Townsend (2010) when exploring the meaning of poverty in the 1960s argued against the prevailing income-based definitions of poverty on three grounds: (a) poverty was a relative concept and understanding it through a universal, single indicator simply did not do justice to its complexity. He pointed out that people's definition of necessities differed according to their class and culture as it did in comparison to other countries; (b) any universal standard sociologists adopted to define poverty was arbitrary rather than based on objective fact. The subjective nature of poverty, Townsend (2010) contended, would make it impossible for one standard to capture the multiple ways in which people living in poverty would themselves define deprivation; and (c) poverty was not a static, but a dynamic concept that changed and responded to the web of relationships within people's lives. Standards. on the other hand, were static.

In the 50 years since Townsend first argued against a universal, economically based, standard definition of poverty, not much has changed in how it is defined. The normative definition of absolute poverty is that of the World Bank Organization (WBO) which measures poverty using the universal standard of the 'International Poverty Line' (IPL) which is measured at earnings of $1.90 a day (World Bank Organization, 2015).

There are vigorous debates and critiques of IPL as the standard way of assessing poverty. A number of attempts have sought to introduce more multi-dimensional definitions of poverty that are not entirely income-based or universal. Survanien (cited by Anand et al., 2010) has suggested garnering information on the national level of the cost of goods and services specific to each country. Others have attempted a definition of poverty that assesses 'distress and degradation', or non-economic measure such as well-being and longevity (Anand et al., 2010). Hunt (2010) argues for a broader definition of poverty giving the example of Indigenous peoples who consider themselves poor as a result of the loss of relationships with kin. Yet, the IPL continues to dominate governments', non-governmental organisations' and social services' definitions of poverty.

The case studies of these two migrant women reveal the paucity of an income-based notion of poverty. In both cases, forced migration temporarily suspended their ability to participate in the formal economy. As forced migrants living in refugee camps they remained largely outside the formal economic system. Income-based definitions of poverty have no way of articulating the particular circumstances of refugees living in refugee camps. They cannot be assumed to earn an income. Moreover, the women themselves articulated their own definition of a quality of life that was not entirely income-based when they spoke of the importance of housing, education, peace and safety as primary considerations when seeking alternative refuge. This, however, does not mean that income is not important to a sense of well-being, as is clearly evident in both case studies. Rather, a singular notion of poverty that is entirely income-based does not reflect the multi-dimensional nature of poverty. Moreover, Jaggar (2013b) argues that among its other flaws the IPL has a gender bias as it does not take into consideration other forms of poverty that women are particularly vulnerable to. We consider this in our subsequent discussion.

Women's vulnerability to violence

One of the salient features of the case studies presented is the sexual violence that the women experienced and the fear of sexual violence that marked these women's lives. Sexualised violence leaves a deep and traumatic effect on the lives of women. The case studies highlight sexual violence as a barrier to education and other social services for fear of exposing oneself to further violence, impeding efforts at income elevation and impacting upon mental health.

Experiences of violence more generally is a fact of forced migrant women's lives. Saba witnessed the murder of her husband and son prompting their move to Pakistan and forced migration. Sharifa's family lived with the spectre of violence hanging over them due to the resentment at their presence that some Kenyans expressed in violent forms. Raising the income level of these two families would not result in a better quality of life on this count. Ignoring the gendered nature of violence and the degree to which it impoverishes the lives of women overlooks a significant aspect of what constitutes a poor quality of life.

Unequal power relationships

Poverty is a structural issue that exists within unequal power relationships where one group of people maintains a dominant status over another economically, politically and socially. Inability to affect change against dominant systems is a common experience for people living in poverty as demonstrated by the case studies. While both women in the case studies showed incredible resilience and agency in changing their life conditions, their ability to do so was constrained by the power dynamics in the refugee camps. These were gendered, racialised and nationalist. For example, in spite of the strength they displayed in fighting for the survival of their families, they did not have the power to seek redress for the sexualised violence they experienced. Their marginalisation was particularly apparent given that their rights of protection as refugees were violated by the police officers and camp guards who were entrusted with the task of safeguarding them. Furthermore, patriarchal cultural traditions in both cases barred them from seeking justice due to victim-blaming where the women would be held responsible for the sexualised violence that they had endured. Jaggar (2013b) speaks to broadening the definition of poverty so that it takes into account women's experiences of marginality in relation to exercising power within systems and structures that dominate them.

Gendered dimensions of unpaid care work

Labour is a gendered concept where care work, overwhelmingly undertaken by women, is either unpaid or undervalued monetarily both locally and globally (Pyle, 2006). The work of social reproduction involved in looking after the needs of the family is simply not counted as 'labour' unlike the 'productive' work performed by working in the marketplace (Jaggar, 2013). It is striking how much 'work' both women put into primary care, taking responsibility for providing emotional support to their children, particularly their daughters, attempting to protect them from further sexualised violence. The women were actively involved in ensuring that their families not only survived but also thrived by experiencing a greater sense of belonging in the refugee camps, utilising economic, affective and cultural resources, such as continuing the tradition of the *vave*, to make this happen. In both case studies, the women take the initiative to plan long-term to get the family out of the refugee camp. For refugee women who are in a precarious labour market, not receiving material rewards for the indispensable care work that they undertake produces even greater economic poverty.

Poverty as transnational

Government and non-governmental inter/national agencies such as the WBO, assume a state-centred approach to defining poverty. The narratives of forced migrants reveal the transnational nature of poverty in several ways. Refugee camps themselves occupy a transnational, liminal space within nation-states, existing at the margins of society that are usually maintained by international organisations like the Red Cross and the UNHCR (Amnesty, 2005). Due to lack of funding, these refugee camps are often unable to provide for adequate shelter, food, clothing and schools for children. Nation-state based assessments of poverty do not take into account a vast number of people living in refugee camps and detentions centres.

The transnational status of forced migrants as a result of their movement from one nation-state to another results in poverty due to loss of income because their education, credentials and skills are often downgraded by receiving societies (Ross-Sheriff et al., 2012). It can take up to five years for forced migrants to reintegrate fully into receiving societies (Goździak and Long, 2005).

Global capitalism is a transnational phenomenon, which due to deregulation of markets across nation-states has substantially increased the gap between rich people and poor people (Grewal, 2005). This has caused economic hardship resulting in forced migration with people seeking economic stability in other countries. This renders them vulnerable to harsh treatment by receiving countries, resulting from commonly held anti-immigrant sentiments reflected by the richer countries in the global North (Rygiel, 2011). Globalisation and the increased movement of people forced to migrate has triggered a rise in nationalist rhetoric and sentiments as can be seen in the rise in racist violence, closing of borders and anti-immigration policies not just in countries in the global North but more widely (Mohanty, 2013). Sharifa's family was forced to migrate due to a nationalist civil war in their country and was met with further violence in the refugee camp. This made it harder for these two families to immigrate to more stable societies, whether Kenya or the US. Living as a minority in conditions of nationalist extremism is a facet of poverty that undercuts local/global boundaries (Rygiel, 2011). In a world where refugees account for 65 million people globally and rising (Edwards, 2016), this oversight in policy and scholarship is striking.

Implications for social work practice

Transnational feminist analyses of poverty based on the lived realities of the two families offer important lessons for social work practitioners that we discuss next, according to the five themes identified earlier. Understanding poverty in holistic terms (Samuels and Ross-Sheriff, 2008) requires social workers to work in multi-faceted ways with families rather than simply targeting income generation, as the examples of Hadiya and Anna demonstrate. These social workers understood that the cultural, psychological, social and economic deprivations were all a part of what it meant to experience poverty. It required them to prioritise different aspects of intervention depending on what the families presented. At the same time, they also worked on income asset formation. This is exemplified by the way in which Anna worked with Saba to identify and encourage her talent in cooking to generate income. Given the barriers to income generation, this constitutes an important area of intervention (Eltaiba, 2014). Simultaneously, Anna intervened to address the educational, health, mental health, safe housing, and culturally satisfying relationship needs of the family.

Gender and cultural sensitivity is an important aspect of social work practice with families living in poverty, particularly forced migrants. Given that poverty is a gendered phenomenon, it is important that social workers practise in a gender-sensitive manner. Gender sensitivity is not divorced from culturally sensitive practice, as is evidenced in these case studies. Both women lived in patriarchal cultures that made it impossible for them to disclose sexual violence without being blamed for it. Eltaiba (2014) also identifies the importance of gender sensitivity when working with women refugees experiencing poverty. All three social workers in the case studies showed their capabilities in working in nuanced, gendered and culturally sensitive ways. For example, Alison working with Saba in Baltimore made good use of culture and faith-based resources to address Saba's needs. Green social workers develop locality-specific, culturally relevant forms of practice to empower those they work with (Dominelli, 2012).

The marginalised status of forced migrants requires that social workers use the powers that they have as professionals to engender structural changes (Dominelli, 2012). For example, Hadiya and Anna both recognised the sexual assault that the women had experienced and while they helped the women individually to heal, they did not attempt to address structural changes by getting the officials at the refugee camps to address this injustice. It is possible that their doing this would not have been tolerated by the officials. However, social workers should view it as part of their mandate to challenge oppressive systems within which they work on behalf of their clients/service users, as encouraged by green social work (Dominelli, 2012). The case studies also reveal the effectiveness of working within a strengths-based model of practice. All three social workers identified, acknowledged and valued the sources of resiliency in these two women. For example, Anna understood that faith and culture were important sources of Saba's strength and used these effectively to enhance Saba's quality of life.

Social work practice with families experiencing poverty is intensive, long-term work. As both case studies show, it took these families over five years before they acquired some sense of hope and belonging in the countries in which they had settled. Government settlement programmes in most countries do not take a long-term view and offer short-term settlement services for refugees. These overlook the complexity of their needs.

Transnational social work practice entails understanding the transnational lives of forced migrants. This means taking into consideration the different effects of the journey/ies undertaken on each member of the family. These families may have close relatives who live in refugee camps or countries from which they have fled. Concern about their welfare and whereabouts will also affect them. Social workers should be sensitive to the anxiety, survival guilt, and divided sense of belonging that many forced migrants experience. Like Alison, they should seek ways of forging connections between the families they serve and other community and family networks that are available in the same country and occupy a similar transnational status.

Conclusion

Jaggar (2013) has argued that conceptual analyses of poverty overlook the voices and lived experiences of people living in poverty. We have analysed the definition of poverty based on the narratives of women who are forced migrants to address this gap. This located our alternative understanding of poverty within the specific contexts of the lives of two families who became forced migrants. Transnational feminist analyses enabled us to examine and make connections between the lived realities of two women's families living in poverty and their wider sociopolitical systems. We conclude that an alternative definition of poverty is holistic, gendered, intersectional, political and transnational.

At the end, we consider the implications of our conceptual analysis for social work practices and recommend a set of practices that are congruent with transnational feminist insights into poverty. Transnational feminists focus on the uneven effects of poverty because a disaster leaves some people more devastated in its aftermath than others. Green social workers' holistic orientation provides a useful model for working with forced migrant women.

References

Amnesty International (2004). *Lives blown apart: Crimes against women in times of conflict.* (Online). Available on www.amnesty.org/en/documents/ACT77/075/2004/en/ [Accessed 10 February 2017].
Amnesty International (2005). *Amnesty International Report 2005: The state of the world's human rights.* (Online). Available on www.amnesty.org/en/documents/pol10/0001/2005/en [Accessed 10 February 2017].
Anand, S., Segal, P., and Stiglitz, J. (2010). *Debates on the measurement of global poverty.* London: Oxford University Press.
Dominelli, L. (2012). *Green social work: From environmental crises to environmental justice.* Cambridge: Polity Press.
Edwards, A. (2016). *Global forced displacement hits record high.* (Online: The UN Refugee Agency). Available on www.unhcr.org/en-us/news/latest/2016/6/5763b65a4/global-forced-displacement-hits-record-high.html [Accessed 03 February 2017].
Eltaiba, N. (2014). Counselling with Muslim refugees: Building rapport. *Journal of Social Work Practice*, 28(4): 397–403.
Goździak, E. M. and Long, K. C. (2005). *Suffering and Resiliency of Refugee Women: An Annotated Bibliography, 1980–2005.* Washington, DC: Institute for the Study of International Migration.
Grewal, I. (2005). *Transnational America: Feminisms, Diasporas, Neoliberalisms.* Durham: Duke University Press.
Hunt, J. (2010). Assessing poverty, gender and well-being in Northern Indigenous Communities. In S. Chant (Ed.), *The International Handbook of Gender and Poverty: Concepts, Research, Policy.* Cheltenhan: Edward Elgar Publishing.

Hyndman, J. (2008). Feminism, conflict and disasters in post-tsunami Sri Lanka. *Gender, Technology and Development*, 12(1): 101–121.

Jaggar, A. M. (2009). Transnational cycles of gendered vulnerability: A prologue to a theory of global/gender justice. *Philosophical Topics*, 37(2): 33–52.

Jaggar, A. M. (2013a). Does poverty wear a woman's face? Some moral dimensions of a transnational feminist research project. *Hypatia*, 28(2): 240–256.

Jaggar, A. M. (2013b). We fight for roses too: Time-use and global gender justice. *Journal of Global Ethics*, 9(2): 115–129.

Jansen, G. G. (2006). Gender and war: The effects of armed conflict on women's health and mental health. *Affilia*, 21(2): 134–145.

Mohanty, C. T. (2006). US empire and the project of women's studies: Stories of citizenship, complicity and dissent. *Gender, Place and Culture*, 13(1): 7–20.

Mohanty, C. T. (2013). Transnational feminist crossings: On neoliberalism and radical critique. *Signs: Journal of Women in Culture and Society*, 38(4): 967–991.

Moosa-Mitha, M. (2016). Geography of care: Syrian refugees and the welfare state. *Affilia*, 31(3): 281–84.

Moosa-Mitha, M. and Ross-Sheriff, F. (2010). Transnational social work and lessons learned from transnational feminism. *Affilia*, 25(2): 105–109.

Pyle, J. L. (2006). Globalization and the increase in transnational care work: The flip side *Globalizations*, 3(3): 297–315.

Rehn, E., and Sirleaf, E. J. (2002). *Progress of the World's Women: Executive Summary*. New York: UN Development Fund for Women.

Ross-Sheriff, F., Foy, R., Kaiser, E. and Gomes, M. (2012). Refugee women: Mental health and well-being. In U. Segal and D. Elliot (Eds.), *Refugees worldwide*. Santa Barbara: Praeger, pp. 109–132.

Rygiel, K. (2011). Governing mobility and rights to movement post 9/11: Managing irregular and refugee migration through detention. *Review of Constitutional Studies*, 16: 211–221.

Samuels, G. M., and Ross-Sheriff, F. (2008). Identity, Oppression, and Power: Feminisms and Intersectionality Theory. *Affilia*, 23(1): 5–9.

Seager, J. (2006). Noticing gender (or not) in disasters. *Geoforum*, 1(37): 2–3.

Townsend, P. (2010). The meaning of poverty. *British Journal of Sociology*, 1(61): 85–102.

World Bank Organization (2015). *FAQs: Global poverty line update*. Available on www.worldbank.org/en/topic/poverty/brief/global-poverty-line-faq [Accessed 28 March 2017].

26
Positioning Social Workers Without Borders within green social work
Ethical considerations for social work as social justice work

Lauren Wroe, Bridget Ng'andu, Matthew Doyle and Lynn King

Introduction

'Green social work' is a new theoretical concern for the social work profession and specifically for social work with people crossing borders. Social work, while addressing environmental factors, whether in the family, housing or poverty, that form the backdrop to service users' lives, pays little attention to the natural environment (Dominelli, 2012). However, the theoretical bridge between environmental degradation, and mass movement of people is well-forged in the social and environmental sciences (Gemenne, 2011; Bettini et al., 2016; UNICEF, 2017; Gemenne and Blocher, 2017; Climate and Migration Coalition, 2017).

This chapter, written by four authors, each of whom contributes a specific part to it, will focus on the social and the environmental dimension of Dominelli's (2012) *Green Social Work*. It starts by problematising the link between environmental justice and the global mass movement of people to introduce the work and goals of Social Workers Without Borders (SWWB), a grassroots organisation of social workers formed for the purpose of advancing social justice in respect of refugees, migrants and those left vulnerable by borders. It then explores our organisations' experience of practicing a new model of working – social justice work across borders, before considering the challenges posed when applying traditional social work models to new, unchartered terrains.

Environmental justice, an issue for refugees and asylum seekers

First, the authors consider why environmental issues and/or refugees and asylum seekers are a concern for social workers? It is apparent there are huge safeguarding issues presented by the political (lack of) response to refugees. Increasing numbers of women, families and separated children have crossed borders to Europe recently (UNHCR, 2014). This presents a host of additional safeguarding issues for first responders across the European Union (EU) migration route. The Women Refugee Commission highlighted this concern, stating that protection risks for women and girls are present at every stage of the EU migration route and that opportunities to mitigate potential risks are missed (Women Refugee Commission, 2016). Having arrived in Europe, the mass exclusion of people and their families from welfare, health and work requires a trans-nationalist, person-centred and social justice social work approach to ensure that people's needs are met and they fulfil their goal of finding safety.

Second, environmental degradation as well as political instability and poverty, and positive factors such as health, work prospects and family ties are factors in why people choose, or are forced to move. UNICEF's Report (2017) claims 'climate-related events' are increasingly behind the forced 'up-rooting' of children. It notes that one in 45 children around the world have been forced to leave their homes in search of safety in their own or in other countries. Climate change and environmental justice, alongside social justice are issues for social workers to consider when working with displaced populations, including children.

Climate-related events can be a precursor to forced migration and can alert social workers to safeguarding issues. This requires social workers to scrutinise and understand discourses of climate migration and their assumptions. The term climate refugee, and the causality implied by this naming, first featured in environmental and academic literature in the 1980s (Gemenne, 2011) and has not gone unchallenged. One problematic narrative concerning green issues and displacements of people is: environmental damage, with an increasing focus on climate change, displaces, and will increasingly displace, populations of people who will be forced to migrate to find new, habitable environments. This migration will typically happen from South to North and is pathologised as impacting negatively on those fleeing, and the environmental stability of the receiving communities (Bettini, 2013; Bettini et al., 2016). Such migration causes political, environmental and financial instability, and population growth in receiving countries. The poverty, instability and conflict brought about by mass migration can cause further environmental damage.

This understanding is problematic for a profession whose values are embedded in notions of internationalism and social justice (IFSW, 2012). The narrative draws on a reductionist logic that does not address or challenge the structural causes of climate change or forced migration. A current example of this foreshortened understanding of these issues is the continued political conflict in Syria. Syria is one of the most complex wars in modern history and accounts for a large proportion of refugees entering Europe since 2011 (UNHCR, 2015). Before the civil uprising, which political scientists and historians thought highly improbable for Syria (Quinn and Roche, 2014), the country was plagued by severe drought lasting from 2006 to 2011 and led over 1 million farmers to flee rural areas for cities such as Daraa. This climatic event fuelled the desperation and unrest regarding the Assad regime which ultimately sparked the rebellions from which the current conflict grew (Quinn and Roche, 2014). The drought was not a purely environmental or climatic issue. Poor governance under Assad coupled with irresponsible, government-led agricultural policies for stimulating production, have been identified as key factors predicting the drought (Kelley et al., 2014). Globalised capitalism, that intensifies competition and embeds poverty into communities, undermines poor populations' capacity to respond to environmental crises and may directly contribute to them (Dominelli, 2012; Global Justice Now 'This is Not a Migrant Crisis' Briefing, 2016). Most families crossing the borders to the EU in March 2016 were Syrian. They could be labelled climate or political refugees, or both.

Social workers, as advocates, know that ordinary Syrians (and other people crossing borders) are not to blame for the violence inflicted on the natural environment or in the countries that they are fleeing from or to. Over the past year, migrants and refugees have been scapegoated by politicians, far-right groups and mass media not only for further environmental crises (e.g. subsequent droughts in receiving Syrian cities), but also for bringing violence, disorder and unrest to Europe. To understand environmental concerns and 'climate refugees' from a social justice perspective, social workers have to examine the structural sources of environmental and human exploitation. For green social workers, this includes a concern with the built infrastructures within which people, regardless of their status live. Social justice considerations turn the lens towards the political and economic regimes that facilitate climate-related events and forced migration. This reframing of the debate undermines and de-politicised narratives that peddle security solutions that further limit the movement of people and their freedoms, such as restrictive migration policies, population management, or humanitarian solutions that rely on alarmist rhetoric concerning 'waves' of helpless victims that erase refugees' political histories and stories (Nyers, 2006; Wroe, 2012, Bettini, 2013; Bettini et al.,, 2016).

Green social work is a straightforward issue for Social Work Without Borders (SWWB). As social workers committed to environmental and social justice, alongside the rights and dignity of migrants and refugees, we have to unpick and challenge dominant political narratives that attempt to solve the problem *of refugees*, rather than those that force people to *become refugees*. This perspective produced Social Workers Without Borders (SWWB). Working in the camps in France and Greece in March 2016, Social Workers Without Borders proposed that the 'refugee crisis' was not one of people crossing borders, but of the political responses to refugees. At World Social Work Day in Manchester, March 2016, SWWB proposed that the 'refugee crisis' was a safeguarding crisis because nation-states and those responsible for meeting the needs of vulnerable adults and children had failed to safeguard new arrivals from further harm and risk.

Social work without borders and transnational support

SWWB was formed in March 2016 to: offer direct, skilled interventions to promote the rights and dignity of children and adults in refugee camps; educate social workers on the specific needs and stories of people crossing borders; campaign for adequate political and professional responses to migrants and asylum seekers; and ensure that people are protected from further risk or harm and had their needs met. As an organisation, SWWB promotes transnationalism in social work practice and advocates for the just treatment of those who cross borders, through choice or force. This requires a re-politicising of our understanding of refugees and social work.

For the first year, SWWB focused on developing a model of social work practice that embodied these values. Prior to the destruction of the Calais refugee camp in France, it had a weekly presence there. At first it worked alongside NGOs and volunteers offering direct work sessions and art classes with children and young people. As the situation escalated to the 'demolition' of the camp, SWWB conducted Best Interest Assessments with separated children seeking asylum in the UK. Thus, SWWB is practicing a form of state social work outside the state, and in direct opposition to it. The campaigning element of SWWB's work had focused on the legislation that underpinned safe passage options for these children and young people. The Dubs Amendment to the Immigration Act 2016, which allowed a legal route to the UK for asylum-seeking children in Europe, was scrapped in February 2017, and asylum applications put forward on behalf of these young people were largely refused. SWWB raised funds to re-assess these children which, at the time of writing, will form the basis of a High Court legal challenge to the Home Office of their refusal of these applications. We are developing a model of social work in and against the state (Mitchell et al., 1979) in both literal and ideological terms.

Additionally, SWWB delivered training and workshops to social workers and students based on our experiences of working in the camps and stories that young people have shared with us. This narrative approach brings to the fore the personal and political aspects of people's histories, informing an understanding of refugees as ordinary people in extraordinary circumstances (Wroe, 2012) and allows social workers, to consider the care and support needs of people crossing borders from a person-centred perspective. Social work without borders consists not only of people crossing borders, or practicing social work outside the state, but is also an activity of everyday social work. Social work without borders is practised by ensuring that assessments and care plans reflect need, regardless of age, nationality or immigration status, and are not resource led or over-ruled by immigration policy. Social workers are not immigration officers.

Practising social work across borders

The next part of this chapter explores the experiences of social workers practicing this model of social work in Calais over the past year. Then, it considers the crucial issue of burnout in volunteers specifically engaged in social work across borders, addressing social and environmental injustice in unfamiliar and transient terrains.

Social work as a profession has been involved in disaster relief for a very long time. Social workers have intervened in the microenvironments of people to improve their health status, residential living environment, workplace conditions, and social and psychological functioning (Zakour, 1996a). Its involvement dates to the 19th century and was closely related to the Settlement Movement which began at Toynbee Hall in East London, in the 1880s. Toynbee Hall aimed to improve the impoverished conditions of those living in East London, through volunteerism. This model grew in other parts of the UK and later in America, promoting social change and community action (see Gilchrist and Jeffs (2001) on Settlement Movements in the UK). These responses are similar to those currently seen across Europe in support of asylum seekers and refugees arriving from war and poverty torn countries in Africa, Syria and Afghanistan.

British social workers' responses to the plight of migrants in Calais seemed slow. Camps began emerging around Calais for those seeking asylum in the UK in 1999. We note that numbers of people, including women and children, slept on the streets of Calais and surrounding towns, leading to the opening of the Sangatte in 1999. The Sangatte Centre aimed to support 600 people, but numbers rose to 2000, with people living in squalid conditions. Sangatte was closed in 2002 and replaced by various camps of which the 'Jungle' was the latest iteration. When closed in 2016, over 7000 people lived there. The French government moved asylum seekers from the 'Jungle' to government centres to process them (Calais Migrant Solidarity, 2016).

The migrant situation became a crisis in 2014/2015, when unprecedented numbers of people crossed into Europe. Many died enroute. Turkey, Greece and Italy were the primary receiving nations for new arrivals. This coincided with the rapid expansion of grassroots and NGO-led responses to asylum seekers in Europe. In Calais, predominantly French and British non-governmental organisations raised the profile of the activism and volunteering that had been occurring for the previous decade. Grassroots organisations of volunteers such as the Refugee Youth Service, Women's and Children's Service, and Jungle Books Kids Cafe filled the gaps left by the absence of UNHCR and government provisions. The Social Work Action Network (SWAN) in 2016 had taken aid to Calais to demonstrate social work solidarity and collect narratives of refugees and successfully raised the profile of the camp and its inhabitants within the UK social work profession.

SWWB's involvement in March 2016 was the first British attempt at developing a co-ordinated social work response to the plight of young people in the camp with a consistent presence.

The need to challenge the government's (lack of) response to this disaster was becoming increasingly urgent. Throughout 2016, as governments hesitated in responding to the disaster unfolding in Europe, social workers including the authors, began to step 'into the vacuum', supporting migrants and refugees at a time when political opinion was strongly against immigration. The role of social workers was beginning to receive attention in the media, not only in the UK, but in Germany, Austria and Greece, where increasing numbers of people were arriving. Attention was placed on the role of social work support for the unaccompanied children in different camps across Europe (Hardy, 2016).

For UK social workers, the emphasis was on the children and young people living in the Calais camp. SWWB sought to involve social workers in the UK to participate actively in its volunteer scheme, and experience the day-to-day lives of these children and young people to inform its interventions and stand up for justice and human rights. Social workers provided their time by travelling to Calais and volunteering their services in the camp. The authors went equipped with safeguarding knowledge and skills, direct work, and undertaking Best Interest Assessments (BIA) with young people, but needed to adopt a more flexible approach to social work practice, especially the entrenched form of managerialism prevailing in the UK (Banks, 2014; Payne, 2014). One of SWWB's members, Lauren Wroe, described this as 'lay social work', unhampered by the bureaucracy that restricts practice in the UK (Hardy, 2016). SWWB provided the necessary flexible social work approach that challenged the dominant political rhetoric against refugees and migrants.

Questions about the safety of vulnerable children were being asked, highlighting the need for a clear response from social work. Fagerholm and Verheul (2016), in the *Taskforce Children on the Move*, reported on the high risks that children experienced trying to cross different borders to get to their destinations. This concern was shared by social workers volunteering in the Calais Camp. A flexible approach was required when undertaking Best Interest Assessments (BIA) with young people. Initially, SWWB adapted the British Department of Health's Assessment Framework for Children and Families, and as the work grew, the tool was adjusted to incorporate articles within the United Nations Declaration on Human Rights. This was to ensure that its practice demonstrated an international approach (Dominelli, 2010; Cox and Power, 2013). In all, 62 assessments were completed, identifying the needs of children and young people, and the urgency of moving them to a place of safety.

The opportunity to meet young people and hear their stories was both emotionally challenging and humbling. The opportunity to share the lived experience of children in the camp with practitioners in the UK, many of whom work in Local Authorities that will have received children from Calais, further enhanced understanding of the desperation they were facing and how the profession should respond to their needs. The direct work not only assessed the needs and best interests of children and young people, but also brought humanity to these interactions, with art, smiles and without judgement. This allowed young people to be children, if only for a moment.

For many social workers and students, both internationally and in the UK, defining what social work is and practitioners' role within the profession will be subjective, and reflective of each individual's own personal and professional experiences of social work practice. The questions 'What is social work?' and 'What do social workers do?' are important to reflect upon as they re-centre each individual's own understanding of what is expected from oneself as student and social worker, and what society expects from the social work profession as a whole.

The definition of social work jointly owned by the International Association of Schools of Social Work and the International Federation of Social Work considers the profession's primary role to be to promote social justice, uphold human rights and enhance the well-being and agency of individuals (IFSW, 2012). This overarching definition of social work serves as a scaffold for the development of more specific definitions and models of practice such as green social work considered in this book. At a fundamental level, social work has a strong connection to the advancement and safeguarding of adults' and children's rights (Reichert, 2011).

A key objective of this ethics-based social work is to uphold human and children's rights, alongside the responsibility to safeguard children from harm (Dominelli, 2009), and challenge oppression (Mullaly, 2010). Motivated by these principles, the authors joined a number of other UK-based social workers and social work students to respond to the developing humanitarian crisis unfolding within Calais and the wider European region. For many, like us, the evocative media coverage of vulnerable children in Calais trapped in a vacuum perpetuated by social stigma, intolerance, and political apathy could not be ignored. The lack of resources, safe passage options and political co-ordination to meet the most basic needs of people in Calais presented real concerns for the welfare and safety of children in the camp. Alongside our colleagues, we felt that there was an increasing need for social workers to work directly with children and young people in the camp, to promote social justice, and safeguard the rights and autonomy of the children there.

By responding to the developing disaster on Britain's doorstep, the authors came across new challenges and dilemmas that defied our practice as social work students and professionals. For example, conducting child-focused assessments within chaotic and unknown settings required us to familiarise ourselves with the people and places in the camp and to spend time with children and young people, creating art and chatting, as part of our assessment work. We also had to develop an awareness of the evolving risks to children, from fire hazards to people traffickers, and advocate for their right to legal representation.

Working within the complex environment of the camp was also fraught with dynamic and fluid obstacles. Trying to establish and develop trust and partnership with multiple voluntary and statutory organisations with varying organisational cultures, approaches and agendas was particularly challenging. This was closely tied to the need to develop a relevant model of working, and role for social workers that was communicable across professional, cultural and language barriers in a space where traditional UK methods of safeguarding children were not being enacted. The children in Calais came from a myriad of communities with individual faiths, cultures and heritages, and many had witnessed traumatic events and were processing emotions incomprehensible to most individuals from the UK.

Despite these challenges, SWWB could implement successfully, a model of social work that responded to these complex needs in a flexible and creative manner. This work was particularly rewarding when it contributed to the successful reunification of several young people with family members in the UK. This reflective approach enabled the authors to work together to find creative solutions. An example of this was the creative use of social media and mobile applications such as WhatsApp, Facebook and Google Translate. Usually no-go areas for social workers, these systems were used to assist volunteers to reflect and share experiences, disseminate best practice knowledge, coordinate assessments, and respond to those in crisis by communicating with multiple communities and individuals irrespective of geographical location. This has been particularly useful for our ongoing communication with vulnerable children.

Reflective practice in the camp also involved the development of self-awareness. This also covered Western cultural influences and societal privilege (Welbourne, 2012). Such awareness enabled SWWB members to become accountable for their worldviews and acknowledge the impact that Western organisational social work perspectives had on their practice. By recognising Western influences and narratives within core social work knowledge and models, social work assessments for child refugees are less likely to be culturally relative (Metcalfe, 1992 cited in Healy 2007) and reflect the wishes and interests of the child. For example, considering the resilience that young people had developed along their journeys and the responsibilities young people may have had at home, could facilitate resistance to paternalistic models of child social care.

Volunteering in Calais

Volunteering in Calais was not only an exercise of reflective social work but also of applying social work theory to practice. From child development theory (Meggitt, 2012) and radical social work (Turbett, 2014) to systems theory (Stein, 1974) as students and long-qualified professionals, we (authors) worked together to share and access new and traditional social work knowledge. In summary, the work that SWWB is carrying out in Calais presents crucial learning points not just for us personally, but for social workers' responses to future international crises. We encourage those within the profession across the globe to reflect on what their role and commitment is as qualified or aspiring social workers to children and adults irrespective of culture, 'race' or border.

There has been a surge in volunteers across the world responding to disaster situations, and a terminology has been created which defines them as 'spontaneous volunteers' (SVs), 'convergent' or 'unaffiliated' volunteers. These are volunteers who have arrived to assist during emergencies and in disaster situations (Whittaker et al., 2015). Harris et al. (2016) explored the involvement and management of such volunteers in relation to the winter floods in England. They studied the paradoxical relationship between the SVs and official responders (ORs). SVs offer additional support, but this includes an element of risk, as many volunteers will be untrained, unaffiliated to any organisation, and be unaware of established processes. Therefore, tensions may arise. While ORs can benefit from the resource gap that the SVs fill, they may need to surmount their fears and manage the positive risks that SVs can offer, such as the innovative and spontaneity, however, tempered by a lack of tried-and-tested interventions.

In the Calais refugee camp, there was an absence of ORs. The French authorities were largely unrepresented in the camp and the main charitable organisations were neither overtly apparent nor vocal. This meant that 'spontaneous volunteers' had to coordinate the response to the refugees, including women, children and unaccompanied children, in surroundings fraught with environmental danger, internal risks from traffickers and child abusers, and the external risks associated with the aggressive behaviour of the police and sections of the local community.

The wider context of the refugee 'crisis' (or the lack of an ethical response) reflects a polarisation of opinion throughout Europe. Public sympathy for refugees, aligned with many people's experiences of economic strain and concerns for a coherent social and cultural environment, creates uncomfortable dissonance in many people's minds. People may not want to see refugees subject to the appalling circumstances revealed by TV and social media. However, their fears for their own socioeconomic conditions, and those of their children, also need to be addressed. To resolve these contradictory views, and the uncomfortable feelings they induce, the dominant political narrative in Europe has provided a convenient escape route. This narrative blames refugees for the economic strains and community conflict, labels refugees as the perpetrators of their own victimisation (King and Grant, 2016). Against this backdrop, and the lack of action from governments and mainstream charities, 'spontaneous volunteers' from across the globe have stepped into the breach. This has often exposed them to criticism and even hostility from large sections of society in their own countries, which, as relayed to the authors in our dialogue with volunteers, can include their families and friends.

Evidence-informed practice (EIP) encompasses research, expertise of the professional, and the experiences of those involved in practice interventions (Nevo and Slonim-Nevo 2011). Using the parameters of EIP, the authors describe experiences of volunteerism, burnout and professionalism in the Calais refugee camp using relevant research, our professional observations and experiences of other volunteers in the camp.

Self-care, an issue of concern

The phenomenon of volunteer burnout, often incorporated into studies pertaining to secondary traumatic stress and/or vicarious trauma, has been recognised as a hazard within the helping professions for many years and is well documented in the literature (Figley, 1995; Jenkins and Baird, 2002). Both secondary trauma and vicarious trauma can arise as a result of a single event exposure or an accumulation of exposure to the distress and anguish of others (Conrad and Kellar-Guenther, 2006; Bride, 2007). SWWB's work in Calais throughout 2016 revealed that the effects of burnout are prevalent among the volunteering community, and that these effects appear to manifest themselves within the emotional responses and behaviours of the volunteers. Numerous studies exist regarding vicarious stress, secondary stress, burnout and compassion fatigue in the professional sector, but there appears to be limited studies on volunteering within current refugee crises. Understanding and supporting vicarious trauma in volunteers working in this field will have an impact on the future practice of social work in supporting refugees, as the volunteering community is a pivotal factor in establishing and overseeing existing support structures. In lieu of this research, the authors reflect on our experience of burnout in the Calais camp alongside the barriers imposed by the professional/volunteer dichotomy and how social justice informed social work can overcome this problem. Social justice is also a cornerstone of green social work.

When SWWB started to recruit social work volunteer activists to offer direct support to refugees in the Calais camp, it expected to be able to integrate with existing established organisations there. However, the authors discovered that there were many barriers to our involvement, including suspicion, hostility, territorialism, lack of communication and engagement, all arising from many in the established volunteering community. Many of the 'spontaneous volunteers' had grouped together to establish small, voluntary NGOs. SWWB's offers of support, ranging from one-to-one reflective support for volunteers, training, and respite support, were often ignored or met with no response. After a period spent scratching our head and nursing professional egos, the authors managed to develop a relationship with several organisations in the camp by joining in with existing activities. This simple approach had been overlooked given the authors' pre-determined ideas of what 'social work' looks like. SWWB began to offer regular 'hands-on' support and solidarity which allowed SWWB to understand that the volunteer's responses were often due to the effects of the sustained trauma they were experiencing and lack of support from established organisations and government.

According to the American Counselling Association (2017), burnout is defined as having the following symptoms which can include: (1) behavioural: sleep disturbance, nightmares, appetite change, hypervigilance, jumpiness, losing things and negative coping strategies; (2) cognitive symptoms: minimising vicarious trauma, i.e. not practicing self-care, keeping going, working harder, lowered self-esteem and increased self-doubt, trouble concentrating, confusion/disorientation and repetitive images of the trauma.

The authors posed the following questions to several refugee support organisations operational in Calais:

1   Is there a problem with volunteer burnout?
2   Is there support available?
3   What support would be beneficial?

SWWB received responses from two organisations, both stating that burnout is a problem. Respondent 1 stated that symptoms generally appear around the second week, fourth week and fourth month period while Respondent 2 stated that 'burnout' appears as a rapid turnaround in volunteers, volunteers leave without giving much notice and additionally it manifests as inability to sleep, mood swings, tearfulness, even breakdown of relationships. Respondent 1 stated that there is counselling available for them on return to the UK, while Respondent 2 said that there was no support. Both Respondents stated that additional support could be provided and included ground support counselling and pre-volunteer information packs.

Conclusion

In conclusion, a social justice model of social work, operating in the unknown terrain of the Calais refugee camp required the crossing of geographical borders, especially those imposed by immigration controls, alongside those imposed by the 'professional-volunteer' dichotomy and rigid forms of practice that are not responsive to need and changing socio-political landscapes. To support and work with refugees, and all those displaced by borders, poverty or environmental crises, the authors had to challenge the negative and damaging political narrative which dehumanises volunteers as well as those they attempt to support. Social workers, along with established charities and NGOs, must work together to respond to the rise in xenophobia, hate crime and racism and promote the dignity and rights of refugees and migrants, and those who stand shoulder to shoulder in supporting them. This support should encompass an understanding of vicarious trauma and burnout, alongside strategies which can prevent and ameliorate its effects and a flexible professionalism that is open to working in non-traditional ways.

During times of massive geopolitical and ecological change, social workers need to develop a transnational approach embedded in social justice (Dominelli, 2012). In doing this, practitioners will need to continue to explore a model of green social work practice, focusing on interlocking social and environmental justice, the beginnings of which we developed in the Calais camp. This will liberate professionals from the managerialist forms of social work that is imposed to promote a neoliberal agenda within the welfare state in the UK and elsewhere. SWWB proposes a more radical version of social work practice (Turbett, 2014) that is led by need and does not blame structural inequality or scarcity on those most brutalised by various political systems. A social justice model of social work, which can serve the interests of substantial numbers of 'disenfranchised and marginalized people' (Dominelli, 1996) is achieved by working alongside them to effect both personal and societal change as advocated by green social work.

References

American Counselling Association (2017). Fact-sheet 9. Available on www.counseling.org/docs/trauma-disaster/fact-sheet-9 - -vicarious-trauma.pdf [Accessed 21 April 2017].

Banks, S. (2014). Ethics in Iain Ferguson and Michael Lavalette (Eds.), *Critical and Radical Debates in Social Work*. Bristol: Policy Press.

Bettini, G. (2013). Climate barbarians at the gate? A critique of apocalyptic narratives on 'climate refugees'. *Geoforum*, 63–72.

Bettini, G, Nash, S. L. and Gioli, G. (2016). *One step forward, two steps back? The fading contours of (in)justice in competing discourses on climate migration.* Available at [Online] http://onlinelibrary.wiley.com/doi/10.1111/geoj.12192/full [Accessed 11 April 2017].

Bride, B.E. (2007). PhD, LCSW; Prevalence of secondary traumatic stress among social workers. *Social Work*, 52(1): 63–70.

Calais Migrant Solidarity (2016). *Introduction to Calais*. Available on https://calaismigrantsolidarity.wordpress.com/introduction-to-calais/ [Accessed 10 April 2017].

Climate and Migration Coalition (2016). *Fixing climate-linked displacement: are the climate talks enough?* Available on http://climatemigration.org.uk/project/fixing-climate-linked-displacement-climate-talks-enough/ [Accessed 11 April 2017].

Conrad, D. and Kellar-Guenther, Y. (2006). Compassion fatigue, burnout, and compassion satisfaction among Colorado child protection workers. *Child Abuse and Neglect*, 30(10): 1071–1080.

Cox, D. and Pawar, M. (2013). *International Social Work*, 2nd Edition, London: Sage Publications

Dominelli, L. (1996). Deprofessionalizing social work: Anti-oppressive practice, competencies and post-modernism. *British Journal of Social Work*, 26: 153–175.

Dominelli, L. (2009). *Introducing Social Work*. 1st ed. Cambridge: Polity Press.

Dominelli, L. (2010). *Social Work in a Globalizing World*, Cambridge: Polity Press.

Dominelli, L. (2012). *Green Social Work*. Cambridge: Polity Press.

Fagerholm, K. and Verheul, R. (2016). *Call for the EU and European Countries to implement a child rights perspective in the reception of Migrating children*, ENOC Taskforce Children on the Move, Amsterdam/Stockholm

Figley, C. R. (Ed.) (1995). *Compassion fatigue: Coping with secondary traumatic stress disorder in those who treat the traumatized*. New York: Brunner/Mazel.

Gemenne, F. (2011). *How they became the face of climate change. Research policy interactions in the birth of 'environmental migration' concept*. Available at [Online] www.environmentalmigration.iom.int/how-they-became-human-face-climate-change-research-and-policy-interactions-birth-%E2%80%98environmental [Accessed 11 April 2017].

Gemenne, F. and Blocher, J. (2016). *Migration, environment and climate change*. Working Paper Series. No. 1/2016. Available on [Online] http://environmentalmigration.iom.int/migration-environment-and-climate-change-working-paper-series-no-12016 [Accessed 11 April 2017].

Gilchrist, R. and Jeffs, T. (Eds.) (2001). *Settlements Social Change and Community Action: Good Neighbours*. London and Philadelphia: Jessica Kingsley Publishers.

Global Justice Now (2016). *This is Not a Migrant Crisis. Why free movement is vital in the battle for global justice*. Available on www.globaljustice.org.uk/sites/default/files/files/resources/migrant_briefing_web_2016.pdf [Accessed 11 April 2017].

Hardy, R. (2016). The role of social work in the refugee crisis. *The Guardian*. Available on www.theguardian.com/social-care-network/2016/mar/15/social-work-refugee-crisis [Accessed 10 April 2017].

Harris, M., Shaw. D., Scully. J., Smith. C. M. and Hieke, G. (2017). The involvement/exclusion paradox of spontaneous volunteering: New lessons and theory from winter flood episodes in England. *Non-Profit and Voluntary Sector Quarterly*, 46(2): 352–371. doi:10.1177/0899764016654222

Healy, L.M. (2007). Universalism and cultural relativism in social work ethics. *International Social Work*, 50: 11–26.

International Federation of Social Workers (2012). *Code of ethics*. Available on www.ifsw.org [Accessed 21 April 2017].

Jenkins, S. R. and Baird, S. (2002). Secondary traumatic stress and vicarious trauma: A validational study. *Journal of Traumatic Stress*, 15: 423–432. doi:10.1023/A:1020193526843

Kelley, P. C., Mohtadi, S., Cane, M. A., Seager, R. and Kushnir, Y. (2014). *Climate Change in the Fertile Crescent and Implications of the Recent Syrian Drought*. Available at [Online] www.hidropolitikakademi.org/wp-content/uploads/2016/04/Climate-change-in-the-Fertile-Crescent-and-implications-of-the-recent-Syrian-drough.pdf [Accessed 21 April 2017].

King, L. and Grant, K. (2016). Meet the social workers supporting refugees in Calais', *Community Care*. Available at [Online] www.communitycare.co.uk/2016/08/24/meet-social-workers-supporting-refugees-calais/ [Accessed 21 April 2017].

Meggitt, C. (2012). *Understand Child Development*. 1st Edition. London: Hodder Education.

Mitchell, J., Mackenzie, D., Holloway, J., Cockburn, C., Polanshek, K., Murray, N., McInnes, N and Mcdonald, J. (1979). *In and Against the State*. Available at [Online] https://libcom.org/library/against-state-1979 [Accessed 11 April 2017].

Mullaly, R. and Mullaly, R. (2010). *Challenging Oppression and Confronting Privilege.* 1st Edition. Don Mills, Ont.: Oxford University Press.

Nevo, I. and Slonim-Nevo, V. (2011). The myth of evidence-based practice: Towards evidence-informed practice. *British Journal of Social Work,* 41(6): 1176–1197.

Nyers, P. (2006). *Rethinking Refugees: Beyond States of Emergency.* London: Routledge.

Payne, M. (2014). *Social Work Theory,* 4th Edition, Basingstoke: Palgrave/Macmillan.

Quinn, A. and Roche, J. (2014). *Syria's Climate Conflict.* Available at [Online] http://yearsoflivingdangerously.tumblr.com/post/86898140738/this-comic-was-produced-in-partnership-by-years-of [Accessed 11 April 2017].

Reichert, E. (2011). *Social Work and Human Rights.* 1st Edition, New York: Columbia University Press.

Stein, I. (1974). *Systems Theory, Science, and Social Work,* 1st Edition, New Jersey: The Scarecrow Press.

Turbett, C. (2014). *Doing Radical Social Work,* Basingstoke: Palgrave and Macmillan.

UNHCR (2014). *World at War. UNHCR Global Trends. Forced Displacement in 2014.* Available at [Online] www.unhcr.org/556725e69.pdf [Accessed 11 April 2017].

UNHCR (2015). *Seven Factors Behind the Movement of Syrian Refugees to Europe.* Available at [Online]www.unhcr.org/uk/news/briefing/2015/9/560523f26/seven-factors-behind-movement-syrian-refugees-europe.html?query=syrian%20refugees%20europe [Accessed 11 April 2017].

UNICEF (2017). *No Place to Call Home: Protecting children's rights when the changing climate forces them to flee.* Available at [Online] www.unicef.org.uk/publications/no-place-to-call-home/ [Accessed 11 April 2017].

Welbourne, P. (2012). *Social Work with Children and Families.* 1st edn. New York: Routledge.

Whittaker, J., McLennan, B., and Handner, J. (2015). A review of informal volunteerism in emergencies and disasters: Definition, opportunities and challenges. *International Journal of Disaster Risk Reduction,* 13: 358–368.

Women Refugee Commission (2016). *No safety for refugee women on the European route: Report from the Balkans.* Available on www.womensrefugeecommission.org/gbv/resources/1265-balkans-2016 [Accessed 11 April 2017].

Wroe, L. (2012). *A Study of Asylum Seeker/Refugee Advocacy: Paradoxes of Helping in a Climate of Hostility.* Available on www.escholar.manchester.ac.uk/uk-ac-man-scw:190074 [Accessed 11 April 2017].

Zakour, M. J. (1996). Disaster research in social work. *Journal of Social Service Research,* 22(1/2): 7–25.

Part VIII
Health disasters

27
Intersectionality in health pandemics

Susan A. Taylor

Introduction

The multiple and diverse environmental challenges of the 21st century require new ways of thinking across all disciplines, including social work. What is becoming unequivocal is that 'global warming and climate change will have wide-ranging effects on the environment, socio-economic, and other related sectors including health' (Singh and Purohit, 2014: 112). The nuances of these effects are and will increasingly take the form of extreme weather events including heat waves, droughts, ocean acidification, species extinctions, and erratic rainfall patterns leading to water shortages in some areas, and flooding in others (Haines et al., 2006; Bowen and Friel, 2012; Hens and Stoyanov, 2014; Anderko et al., 2014; Hoy et al., 2014; McMichael et al., 2006). Additionally, alongside these changes in the physical environment is the projected rise in zoonotic and vector-borne illnesses (Ebi et al., 2006; Sachan and Singh, 2010; Goodman, 2013), the majority having no pharmaceutical interventions available.

Ebi et al. (2014: 1318) provide a broad parameter of questions that begin to engage with these environmental challenges:

> What are the current environmental stresses and issues that form the backdrop for potential additional impacts of climate variability and change? How might climate variability and change exacerbate or ameliorate existing problems? What coping options exist that can build resilience to current environmental stresses and also possibly lessen the impacts of climate change? And finally, what are the priority research and information needs (near and long-term) that can better prepare . . . policymakers and the public to reach informed decisions related to climate variability and change?

Such questions require a larger scope of investigation, transdisciplinary in nature, reviewing existing theories and frameworks in natural and social sciences for points of intersection, and increasingly investigating 'the whole' as well as the nuances of the parts (Krieger, 2008, 2012). This chapter follows Krieger's lead and is anchored in a strong belief in transdisciplinary research and practice, informed by theories and models that encompass epidemiological (e.g. 'One Health') and socio-epidemiological models of social, physical, and environmental determinants of health to provide critical points of knowledge necessary for social work in the 21st century. This perspective supports Dominelli's (2012) green social work lens with its emphasis on interdependency and interrelatedness in investigation of environmental matters.

Five stories worth telling: images, narrative, and thinking outside the box

Environmental investigations, whether involving the natural or social sciences, need to broaden in scope. Five stories told through videographic narratives highlight out-of-the box thinking, and suggest where transdisciplinary perspectives could be effective. These five stories uniquely emphasise the intersection of environment, species, socio-economic, socio-political and/or inter- and cross-species health.

The first video investigates the intersection of poverty, economic development, and environmental health. University of California, Berkeley student Khalid Kadir produced the video based upon a book by Timothy Mitchell (2002). Mitchell's book, *The Rule of Experts: Egypt, Technopolitics and Modernity*, describes the Egyptian malaria epidemic of 1942, the narrow problem definition (the mosquito), and expert technical interventions that exacerbated the environmental degradation of the region (see www.youtube.com/watch?v=8jqEj8XUPlk). The video highlights the dangers of single-discipline experts looking only downstream at a specific problem, and using only their expertise rather than integrating multidisciplinary upstream approaches investigating possible environmental and socio-political dimensions.

The second and third videos involve animals with specific instinctual characteristics used to work alongside humans for the betterment of all species. The first of these two videos highlights the humane use of rats in Mozambique to detect landmines (see *Bomb sniffing rats saving lives in Mozambique* at https://youtu.be/H1O_vtfX1sY), the results of which have enhanced the lives of all species inhabiting the area. The second is the use of gaggles of ducks for pest control in the South African wine industry (video, *The Quack Squad*, at https://youtu.be/H6Ehoxu9QY8), rather than using toxic pesticides to contaminate the land. These short segments emphasise cross-species collaboration producing positive outcomes for humans, animals, and the fauna and flora of geographic regions.

The fourth video emphasises the work of a young veterinarian in Uganda specialising in mountain gorillas. Although her primary concern is the mountain gorillas, her research and practice expanded to include protecting humans against zoonotic disease, specifically the spread of Bovine tuberculosis through infected cow's milk; the Ebola virus through eating infected bush meat; Marburg hemorrhagic fever from exposure to bat reservoirs; and among her own patients, protecting the gorillas from scabies and tuberculosis from human reservoirs (see www.pbs.org/frontlineworld/stories/uganda901/). Her work shows the complexities that face healthcare providers at the artificial intersection of species divides.

The fifth video highlights the nuances of the worldwide AIDS pandemic – one that has all but been forgotten in some Western countries. The four-hour series, *The Age of Aids* (www.pbs.org/wgbh/pages/frontline/aids/) traces the roots of the global AIDS pandemic: the zoonotic origins; epidemiological investigations conducted by research centres in the United States (US), Belgium, and France; global socio-political and socio-economic disruptions; healthcare concerns; sociological biases (e.g. race, gender, sexual orientation, ethnicity, occupation [sex workers]); overlapping disease transmission reservoirs (IV drug use); and health practices (unprotected sex) that contribute to the evolution of the disease. Most sobering about the series is the realisation that the AIDS pandemic is not unique in the unfolding of zoonotic and vector-borne illnesses, as the recent Zika virus exemplifies. The video series provides a road map for future environmental and health challenges anticipated from microbial vector acceleration due to climate change.

A transdisciplinary approach for environmental challenges

The enormous complexity of climate change and expected effects on the social, physical and biological environments (Hens and Stoyanov, 2014), necessitate research and intervention collaborations of disciplines in natural and social sciences, alongside other related and non-related fields. Such collaboration provides an interlocking weave so as to better understand the multiple dimensions of environmental degradation, multi-species health, and disproportionate environmental justice concerns. Dominelli (2012) highlights the importance of crossing disciplinary and professional boundaries in green social work to emphasise this point. Expanding traditional disciplinary boundaries allows for a taxonomy of environmental concerns to be expanded at the nexus of a new scientific paradigm. Green social work is a current example, and can be further developed and redesigned through its coproduction processes and transdisciplinary perspective (Dominelli, 2012).

Transdisciplinary research and practice is often associated with medical and primary health research and practice (Benessh et al., 2015; Lobb and Colditz, 2013) as well as disaster social work (Dominelli, 2012, 2017). This framework has facilitated the investigation of environmental health, negative environmental exposure, and environmental justice (Dominelli, 2012; Betz et al., 2014). The strategy encompasses broad input, and has also enabled the involvement of indigenous voices and religious/spiritual leaders who embrace animism within their spiritual and cultural heritage (Darlington, 2007; Harvey, 2006; van Schalkwyk, 2011; Wallace, 2012; Dominelli, 2012). Evidenced by the tree-ordination ceremony involving the ordaining of trees as 'Buddhist monks', actual Buddhist monks designate trees as sacred in ritual and role, thus preventing the mass deforestation of northern Thailand through logging. Conservation acts supported by animism have allowed Thailand to reforest its depleted ecosystem (Darlington, 1998). Green and mainstream social workers can learn from such examples.

What is transdisciplinary research? The Washington University School of Medicine describes this as 'team science', where 'scientists contribute their unique expertise but work entirely outside their own discipline ... striving to understand the complexities of the whole project, rather than one part'. Dominelli (2017) utilises this approach in green social work, adding that the team includes community residents in developing a common theoretical framework, concepts, values, objectives, and processes for proceeding to solve problems. Transdisciplinary investigations 'transcend their own disciplines to inform one another's work, capture complexity, and create new intellectual spaces' (www.obesity-cancer.wustl.edu/en/About/What-Is-Transdisciplinary-Research). The Harvard School of Public Health defines transdisciplinary research as 'efforts conducted by investigators from different disciplines working jointly to create new conceptual, theoretical, methodological, and translational innovations that integrate and move beyond discipline-specific approaches to address a common problem' (www.hsph.harvard.edu/trec/about-us/definitions).

Green social work interrogates its methodology through critical, reflexive approaches to research, practice and education (Dominelli, 2017) and asks questions like: How is transdisciplinary collaboration different from multidisciplinary, and interdisciplinary approaches? Although subtle, the differences are profoundly important in setting the tone and direction for collaborative investigation and practice. Multidisciplinary research involves 'researchers from a variety of disciplines work(ing) together at some point during a project, but having separate questions, separate conclusions, and disseminating in different journals' Interdisciplinary research is described as 'researchers interact(ing) with the goal of transferring knowledge from one discipline to another ... allowing researchers to inform each other's work and compare individual findings' (www.obesity-cancer.wustl.edu/en/About/What-Is-Transdisciplinary-Research). Given the complexities of environmental concerns, moving towards broader research and practice approaches is beneficial, and may yield the greatest success in conservation, adaptation, and mitigation when responding to environmental crises. Meanwhile, multidisciplinary strategies are invested in asking larger questions and seeking holistic answers. These should be explored and viewed as informing key features in the development of a 'toolkit' that targets collaborative possibilities and key interventions. Such a toolkit would involve multiple disciplinary theories, best practices, various datasets, as well as the narratives of those most directly affected.

Unique risks for clinical health professionals and social workers

Like clinical health professions such as public health, medicine, and veterinary services, social work is at the interface of the first responder and health exposure in all manner of environmental disasters such as hurricanes and floods, the emerging health risks through zoonosis and vector-borne diseases like AIDS, Ebola, and Zika, as well as alongside 'man-made' environmental emergencies including oil spills, fracking, water and air pollution, and toxic chemical releases. Multidisciplinary, interdisciplinary, and transdisciplinary efforts directed towards reducing environmental exposure and assessing risk and impact, should include the multidimensionality of the socio-political and biophysical determinants, and emerging environmental determinants of health across all species and locations.

While limited by an 'interdisciplinary' lens, Addy et al. (2015) instance inter-professional training that involves social work, nursing, pharmacy, public health, and medicine. This mandated curriculum endeavour is now required in public health programmes in the US. Such programmes would likely be applauded by Pocket (2014) and Fish and Karban (2014) who argue that social work should include the broad concept of 'health' at the centre of its curricula. Green social work includes the planet's health alongside that of all living things – people, plants, and animals (Dominelli, 2012). Gorin (2002) and Moniz (2010) would also agree with these authors for arguing that social work is uniquely positioned to collaborate with public health, as social work operates in the upstream, midstream, and downstream dimensions of health assessment and interventions, while emphasising the macro-, mezzo-, and micro-dimensions of social issues.

Getting our bearings: investigating the environment through a public health lens

Any public health taxonomy includes levels of investigation across social and physical determinants of health. A broad public health taxonomy has categories and sub-categories within a framework of upstream, midstream, and downstream domains including government policies and programmes, categories of communicable, non-communicable disease, and injury elements that provide a theoretical perspective on particular issues (Knickman and Kovner, 2015). Significant indicators in the overall health of individuals, families, neighbourhoods, and communities are considered foundational for designing appropriate interventions.

In the public health model, upstream elements involve 'preventing ill health, protecting populations from health threats, and improving and promoting health' (Goodman, 2013: 50). Attention to social and health indicators at the upstream level are expansive and can transform societies (Brownson et al., 2010; McKinlay, 1998; Padilla et al., 2016). In Europe and the US, 20th-century life expectancy improved drastically as a result of upstream factors. Frieden (2010: 590) notes that these included 'universal availability of clean water, rapid declines in infectious disease, broad economic growth, rising living standards, and improved nutritional status'.

Figure 27.1 visually represents the Canadian Integrative Model of Population Health and Promotion. It combines domains of *health determinants*, *levels of action*, and *comprehensive action*

Intersectionality in health pandemics

strategies that add texture to the contexts of potential points of intervention and impact. The intersectional points in the three domains provide the most significant aspects in upstream, midstream, and downstream determinants to benefit overall human health.

Added in Figure 27.1 is the Canadian 'domain of social determinants', showing downstream determinants. While specific to how Canada conceptualises health/social determinants, it represents potential baseline determinants in other international (e.g. the World Health Organization) and national categorisations of social factors (e.g. United States Center for Disease Control's Healthy People 2020 initiative; Baum and Fisher, 2010; Brownson et al., 2010; Bunyavanich, and Walkup, 2001; English et al., 2009).

The intersection of 'climate change' and 'environment' could interface with health determinants in physical environments, biology, and genetics. This approach leaves open the weaving of environmental variables into research and practice investigating the impacts of various environmental health concerns (Bell and Edwards, 2015; Daley et al., 2015; Houghton, and English, 2014; Samarasundera et al., 2014).

Typical traditional uses of such models include social epidemiological research and practice involving social inequities, social relationships, social capital, and work stress (von dem Knesebeck, 2015). Merzel's and D'Afflitti's (2003) work in community-based AIDS health promotion exemplifies this. Expansion of analysis into the physical environments and biological and genetics determinants, allows for research and practice models to investigate areas like disproportionate exposures to health risks in rural environments, especially in subsistence hunting and fishing activities (Gotchfeld and Burger, 2011) as well as the provision of health promotion and care to migrant farm-worker families in high environmental exposure environments where there is excessive use of agricultural pesticides (Connor et al., 2010). Also, an analysis of upstream issues that create lethal downstream health outcomes is illustrated by the legacy of lead-tainted drinking water in Flint Michigan (Greenberg, 2016; Rosner, 2016).

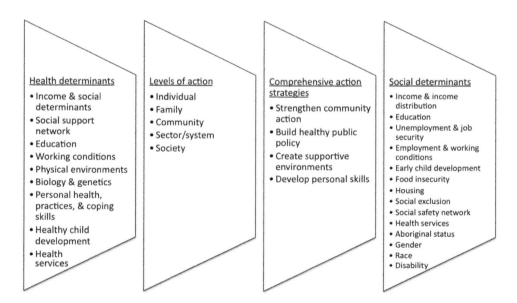

Figure 27.1 Canadian integrative model of population health and promotion

Source: adapted from the Public Health Agency of Canada (available at www.phac-aspc.gc.ca)

Investigating through a social epidemiological lens, health vulnerability, interventions, and assessment frameworks must deal with the very real impacts of climate change. Numerous scholars (Ebi et al., 2006; McMichael et al., 2006; Walker, 2009; Hens and Stoyanov, 2014; Hoy et al., 2014) have contributed to designing models for investigating particular environmental issues. Regarding climate change, Bowen and Friel (2012: 10) 'outline the relevance of climate change adaptation to global health, highlight the importance of linking social determinants of health and sustainable development agendas with climate change adaptation measures, and investigate global health and climate change activities'. Additionally, these authors describe financial mechanisms for adaptation in developing countries. For example, Haines et al. (2006) investigate climate change and human health from three perspectives: current associations between climate change and infectious diseases that are vector-borne; the effect of recent changes in climate including heat waves, flooding, droughts; the evidence base for projecting future impacts of climate change on health including investigating changes in disability adjusted life years (DALYs); and climate scenarios relative to climate-based baselines. Nilsson et al. (2012) also provide research that explores the nuances of how public health fits into overall global climate change agendas related to human health.

A One Health lens for environmental health

The One Health lens is a developing model that investigates environmental and health determinants at intersections with medicine, veterinary science, and public health. The definition of such collaboration put forth by the One Health Commission states, 'One Health is the collaborative effort of multiple health science professions, together with their related disciplines and institutions – working locally, nationally, and globally – to attain optimal health for people, domestic animals, wildlife, plants, and our environment' (www.onehealthinitiative.com). Evidence suggests that this model's transdisciplinary perspective, not only informs, but could include social work as a collaborative partner. Figure 27.2 suggests how this might occur in practice.

Figure 27.2 identifies three broad areas (animals, aquaculture, and vegetation) of microbial infection and resistance for both animal and humans. Animal, aquaculture, and vegetation are not exclusive categories. Rather, these provide broad visual points of intersection where zoonotic threats, generally referred to as 'zoonotic disease' can occur. Sachan and Singh (2010: 520) define zoonotic disease as 'those that can be passed between vertebrate animals and humans'. Scholars (Degeling et al., 2015; Travis et al., 2014) note that these types of diseases encompass 75 percent of new emerging diseases. They will be most expansive in the coming years, and possibly the most devastating. Types of zoonotic diseases include: AIDS, Ebola, SARS (severe respiratory syndrome), Avian influenza (AI/H5N1), West Nile virus, dengue fever, Rift Valley fever, swine flu, Japanese encephalitis (JE), rabies, leptospirosis, Zika, to name a few. A recent example of cross-species infectious threats was SARS which 'moved from a natural reservoir, probably bats, to civet cats in animal markets in Guangdong province, China and then carried by infected humans to hospitals in Toronto, Canada' (Fisman and Laupland, 2010: 111).

The many elements of a One Health model are represented in Figure 27.3.

Figure 27.3 adapts research conceptualised through a 'One Health' lens by Zinsstag et al. (2011). The health determinants in this model range from 'health and well-being in human and animals to systems of biology of humans, domesticated animals, and wildlife across scales from populations to molecules' (Zinsstag et al., 2011: 153). Additionally, interactions between health determinants and social, cultural, economic, and political elements are included alongside those that investigate the importance of ecosystem health as a whole including soil and vegetation. Zinsstag et al. (2011) provide single subject scholars and those involved in transdisciplinary

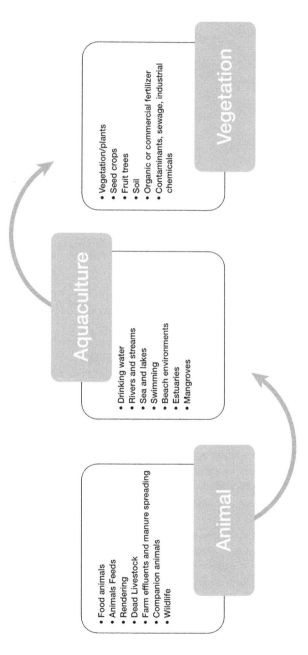

Figure 27.2 Flow chart of microbial reservoirs in human and animal interfaces

Source: adapted from the Canadian Integrated Programme for Antimicrobial Resistance Surveillance (CIPARS) (available at www.phac-aspc.gc.ca/cipars-picra/index-eng.php)

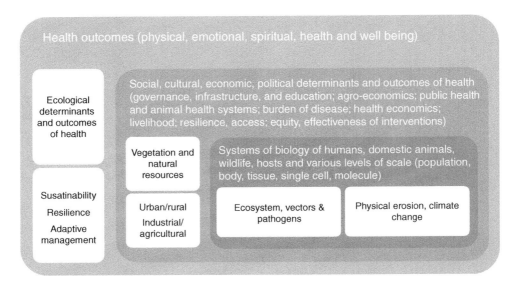

Figure 27.3 Intersections of human and animal health through a 'One Health' lens

Source: adapted from Zinsstag, J., Schelling, E., Waltner-Toews, and Tanner, M. (2011). From 'one medicine' to 'one health' and approaches to health and well-being. *Preventive Veterinary Medicine, 101*: 148–156.

projects, a framework that is rich in detail and depth of diverse variables for complex environmental research and practice.

To link the visual narratives in Figures 27.1, 27.2, and 27.3, this chapter ends with a brief discussion of the impact of oceans on all environmental exposures. This content area is important, as with a few exceptions, the majority of world's countries are maritime nations. This underscores the importance of understanding ocean environments and their mutuality for all manner of life.

Scholars have described the various nuances of ocean impact. Topics of exploration include: seafood safety (Marques et al., 2010); sustainability of fishing communities (Clay and Olson, 2008); health of sentinel animals who share the food web with humans (Bossart, 2006; Lafferty, 2015; Fossi and Panti, 2016); agreeing ocean health priorities and regulations in Europe (Fleming et al., 2014); and increases in harmful algal blooms due to ocean cycles and microbial contamination (Moore et al., 2008). Other authors have investigated sustainable governance of oceans including: overfishing; water contamination; oil spills; disruption in coastal ecosystems; integrated watershed management (Costanza et al., 1999); the oceans' contributions to human health centres in the US (Laws et al., 2008); susceptible populations; media pathways for adverse health outcomes in ocean environments; the microbial effects of flooding (Kite-Powell et al., 2008); and non-point sources of contamination in ocean environments, direct pathogen detection; sentinel species and habitat; non-enteric diseases from water or aerosol transmissions; and zoonotic and emerging diseases (Fleming et al., 2006; Stewart et al., 2008). These investigations only scratch the surface of research still to be done.

Fleming et al. (2015) in their expansive *Oceans and Human Health Challenges Report*, identify critical factors for ocean health including: climate change, extreme weather, harmful algal blooms, microbes, antibiotic resistance, anthropogenic chemicals, sustainable fisheries, aquaculture, coastal communities, sustainable marine biotechnology, sentinel species, biodiversity, and the significance of views encompassed by One Health. Green social workers should be involved in these discussions to make their own unique contributions to identifying and resolving issues with their feet embedded in community consciousness-raising and problem-solving (Dominelli, 2012).

Missed opportunities for practice and research in ocean environments

In the US, the Ocean and Human Health Initiative (OHHI), launched in 2004, encouraged the integration of public health and ocean research. In the US, centres for oceans and human health were funded by the federal government in five locations: the University of Washington, University of Hawaii, the University of Miami, University of California-San Diego, and the Woods Hole Oceanographic Institution in Massachusetts. These university-based centres have targeted geographies that include ocean environments in the 95,000 miles of coastline comprising the continental US, and the larger Pacific Ocean Basin including the Arctic Sea. Three of the four university-based centres have Schools or Departments of Social Work within their university-wide systems. So far, however, as noted in their research annals, no publication, conference report, or list of interprofessional actors, has included social work personnel in their interdisciplinary investigations. This gap is one that green social workers have been advised to address (Dominelli, 2011).

Taylor (2013) highlights that in 2009, the Social Science Workgroup of NOAA (National Oceanic and Atmospheric Administration) argued for social scientists' involvement in interdisciplinary research on ocean environments. The location of the OHHI Centers and Sea Grant programmes housed at 35 universities including many with social work programmes, offer social workers possibilities for engaging in environmental research and practice across all levels of social work practice. As oceanographer Sylvia Earle claims:

> even if you have never had the chance to see or touch the ocean, the ocean touches you with every breath you take, every drop of water you drink, every bite you consume ... drives climate and weather, regulates temperature ... holds 97 percent of the Earth's water ... embraces 95 percent of the biosphere.
>
> *(2010: 11)*

Green social workers would do well to investigate this subject area.

Conclusion

Locating oneself in environmental research and practice is not easy, as it requires practitioners and researchers to venture away from familiar arenas of social work and seek collaborative thinkers from other disciplines to investigate larger phenomena. A 'One Health' model is but one framework that can provide a common place to begin to discuss transdisciplinary concerns across health and social dimensions. This chapter argues for social workers to think more broadly as green social workers, acquire knowledge traditionally not taught in social work curricula, and become involved in transdisciplinary research and practice locally, nationally, and globally. It will take knowledge and skills from various professional and community stakeholders to meet the environmental challenges of this century.

Acknowledgements

To Joanne Handley, Lee Jackrel, and Frances Gulland for their enthusiastic and long-standing commitment to ocean environments.

References

Addy, C. L., Browne, T., Blake, E. W. and Bailey, J. (2015, Supp.1). Enhancing interprofessional education: Integrating public health and social work perspectives. *American Journal of Public Health*, 105: s106–s108.

Anderko, L., Davies-Cole, J. and Strunk, A. (2014). Identifying populations at risk: Interdisciplinary environmental climate change tracking. *Public Health Nursing*, 31(6): 484–491.

Baum, F. and Fisher, M. (2010, September). Health equity and sustainability: Extending the work of the Commission on the Social Determinants of Health. *Clinical Public Health*, 20(3): 311–322.

Bell, S. M. and Edwards, S. W. (2015, November). Identification and prioritization of relationships between environmental stressors and adverse health impacts. *Environmental Health Perspectives*, 123(11): 1193–1195.

Benessh, E. C., Lamb, L. E., Connors, S. K., Farmer, G. W., Fuh, K. C., Hunleth, J. and Gehlert, S. J. (2015). A case study approach to train early stage investigators in transdisciplinary research. *Transdisciplinary Journal of Engineering and Science*, 6: 13–22.

Betz, L., Kunze, I., Parameswaran, P., Suma, T. R. and Padmanabhan, M. (2014). The social-ecological web: A bridging concept for transdisciplinary research. *Current Science*, 107(4): 572–579.

Bossart, G. D. (2006, June). Marine mammals as sentinel species for oceans and human health. *Oceanography*, 19(2): 134–137.

Bowen, K. J. and Friel, S. (2012). Climate change adaptation: Where does global health fit in the agenda? *Globalization and Health*, 8:10 doi: 10.1186/1744-8603-8-10

Brownson, R. C., Seiler, R., Eyler, A. A. (2010). Measuring the impact of public health policy. *Preventing Chronic Disease*, 7(4): A77. Available on http:www.cdc.gov/ped/issues/2010/jul/09_0249.htm [Accessed 15 August 2016].

Bunyavanich, S. and Walkup, R. B. (2001). U.S. health leaders shift toward a new paradigm of global health. *American Journal of Public Health*, 91(10): 1556–1558.

Clay, P. M. and Olson, J. (2008). Defining 'fishing communities': Vulnerability and the Magnuson-Stevens Fishery Conservation Act. *Human Ecology Review*, 15(2): 143–160.

Connor, A., Layne, L. and Thomisee, K. (2010). Providing care for migrant farm worker families in their unique sociocultural context and environment. *Journal of Transcultural Nursing*, 21(2): 159–166.

Costanza, R., Andrade, F., Antunes, P., va den Belt, M., Boesch, D. Boersma, D . . .Young, M. (1999). Ecological economics and sustainable governance of oceans. *Ecological Economics*, 31: 171–187.

Daley, K., Castleden, H., Jamieson, R., Furgal, C. and Ell, L. (2015). Water systems, sanitation, and public health risks in remote communities: Inuit resident perspectives from the Canadian Arctic. *Social Science and Medicine*, 135: 124–132.

Darlington, S. M. (1998). The ordination of a tree: The Buddhist ecology movement in Thailand. *Ethnology*, 37(1): 1–15.

Darlington, S. M. (2007). The good Buddha and the fierce spirits: Protecting the northern Thai forest. *Contemporary Buddhism*, 8(2): 169–185.

Degeling, C., Johnson, J., Kerridge, I., Wilson, A., Ward, M., Stewart, C. and Gilbert, G. (2015). Implementing a one health approach to emerging infectious disease: Reflections on socio-political, ethical, and legal dimensions. *BMC Public Health*, 15: 1307–1317.

Dominelli, L. (2011). Climate change: Social workers' contributions to policy and practice debates. *International Journal of Social Welfare*, 20(4): 430–439.

Dominelli, L. (2012). *Green Social Work: From Environmental Crises to Environmental Justice*. Cambridge: Polity Press.

Dominelli, L. (2017). Green social work and the uptake by the Nepal School of Social Work: Building resilience in disaster stricken communities. In L. Bracken, T. Robinson, and H. Ruszczyk (Eds.), *Risk and resilience in disasters*. London: Palgrave-Macmillan.

Earle, S. A. (2010). *The world is blue: How our fate and the ocean's are one*. Washington, DC: National Geographic.

Ebi, K. L., Mils, D. M., Smith, J. B. and Grambsch, A. (2014). Climate change and human health impacts in the United States: An update on the results of the U.S. national assessment. *Environmental Health Perspectives*, 114(3): 1318–1324.

Ebi, K. L., Kovats, S. and Menne, B. (2006). An approach for assessing human vulnerability and public health interventions to adapt to climate change. *Environmental Health Perspectives*, *114*(12): 1930–1934.

English, P. B., Sinclair, A. H., Ross, Z., Anderson, H., Boothe, V., Davis, C . . . Simms, E. (2009, November). Environmental health indicators of climate change for the United States: Findings from State Environment Health indicator collaborative. *Environmental Health Perspectives*, 117(11): 1673–1681.

Fish, J. and Karban, K. (2014). Health inequalities at the heart of the Social Work curriculum. *Social Work Education*, 33(1): 15–30.

Fisman, D. N. and Laupland, K. B. (2010, Autumn). The "One health" paradigm: Time for infectious diseases clinicians to take note. *Canadian Journal of Infectious Disease and Medical Microbiology*, 21(3): 111–114.

Frieden, T. R. (2010). A framework for public health action: The health impact pyramid. *American Journal of Public Health*, 100(4): 590–595.

Fleming, L. E., Broad, K., Clement, A., Dewailly, E., Elmir, S., Knap, A., . . . Walsh, P. (2006). Oceans and human health: Emerging public health risks in the marine environment. *Marine Pollution Bulletin*, *53*(10–12): 545–560.

Fleming, L. E., McDonough, N., Austen, M., Mee, L., Moore, M., Hess, P., Smalley, A. (2014). Oceans and human health: A rising tide of challenges and opportunities in Europe. *Marine Environmental Research*, 99: 16–19.

Fleming, L., Depledge, M., McDonough, N., White, M., Paul, S., Austen, M., . . . Stegeman, J. (2015). The oceans and human health. In *Environmental Science: Oxford Research Encyclopedias* (1–25). Oxford Research Encyclopedia, USA: Oxford University Press.

Fossi, M. C. and Panti, C. (2016). Sentinel species of marine ecosystems. In *Environmental Science: Oxford Research Encyclopedias* (1–25). Oxford Research Encyclopedia, USA: Oxford University Press.

Goodman, B. (2013). Role of the nurse in addressing the health effects of climate change. *Nursing Standard*, *27*(35): 49–56.

Gorin, S. H. (2002). The crisis in public health revisited: Implications for social work. *Health and Social Work*, 27(1): 56–60.

Gotchfeld, M. and Burger, J. (2011). Disproportionate exposures in environmental justice and other populations: The importance of outliers. *American Journal of Public Health* (Supp. 1): s53–s63.

Greenberg, M. R. (2016). Delivering fresh water: Critical infrastructure, environmental justice, and Flint, Michigan. *American Journal of Public Health*, 106(8): 1358–1360.

Haines, A., Kovats, R. S., Campbell-Lendrum, D. and Corvalan, C. (2006). Climate change and human health: Impacts, vulnerability, and mitigation. *Lancet*, 367: 2101–2109.

Harvey, G. (2006). Animals, animists, and academics. *Zygon*, *41*(1): 9–16.

Hens, L. and Stoyanov, S. (2014). Education for climate changes, environmental health, and environmental justice. *Journal of Chemical Technology and Metallurgy*, 49(2): 194–208.

Houghton, A. and English, P. B. (2014). An approach to developing local climate change environmental public health indicators, vulnerability assessments, and projections of future impacts. *Journal of Environmental and Public Health*. Volume 2014, Article ID 132057, 7 pages. Available on http://dx.doi.org/10.1155/2014/132057 [Accessed 20 March 2016].

Hoy, D., Roth, A., Lepers, C., Durham, J., Bell, J., Durand, A. and Souares, Y. (2014). Adapting to the health impacts of climate change in a sustainable manner. *Globalization and Health*, *10*(82): 1–5. http://dx.doi.org/10.1186/s12992-014-0082-8 [Accessed 20 March 2016].

Kite-Powell, H. L., Fleming, L. E., Backer, L. C., Faistman, E. M., Hoaland, P., Tsuchiya, A., Younglove, L. R. and Gast, R. J. (2008). *Linking the oceans to public health: current efforts and future directions*. Supp. 2.

Knickman, J. R. and Kovner, A. R. (Eds.) (2015). *Health Care Delivery in the United States*. New York: Springer Publishing.

Krieger, N. (2008). Proximal, distal, and the politics of causation: What's level got to do with it? *American Journal of Public Health*, 98(2): 221–230.

Krieger, N., Dorling, D. and McCarthy, G. (2012). Mapping injustice, visualizing equity: why theory, metaphors and images matter in tackling inequalities, *Public Health*, 126(3): 256–258.

Lafferty, K. D. (2015). Sea otter health: Challenging a pet hypothesis. *International Journal for Parasitology: Parasites and Wildlife*, 4: 291–294.

Lobb, R. and Colditz, G. A. (2013). Implementation science and its application to population health. *Annual Review of Public Health*, 34: 235–251.

Laws, E. A., Fleming, L. E. and Stegeman, J. J. (2008, November 7). Centers for oceans and human health: Contributions to an emerging discipline. *Environmental Health*, 7 SI (Suppl 2).

Marques, A., Nunes, M., Moore, S. and Strom, M. (2010). Climate change and seafood safety: Human health implications. *Food Research International*, 43: 1766–1779.

McKinlay, J. B. (1998, July–August). Paradigmatic obstacles to improving the health of populations-implications for health policy. *Salud Publica de Mexico*, 40(4): 369–379.

McMichael, A. J., Woodruff, R. E. and Hales, S. (2006). Climate change and human health: Present and future risks. *Lancet*, 367: 859–869.

Merzel, C. and D'Afflitti, J. (2003). Reconsidering community-based health promotion: Promise, performance, and potential. *American Journal of Public Health*, 93(4): 557–574.

Mitchell, T. (2002). *Rule of experts: Egypt, techno-politics, modernity*. Berkeley, CA.: University of California Press.

Moniz, C. (2010). Social work and the social determinants of health perspective: A good fit. *Health and Social Work*, 35(4): 310–313.

Moore, S. K., Trainer, V. L., Matua, N. J., Parker, M. S., Laws, E. A., Backer, L. C. and Fleming, L. E. (2008). Impacts of climate variability and future climate change on harmful algal blooms and human health. *Environmental Health* (Suppl 2). 7: S4.

Nilsson, M., Evengard, B., Sauerborn, R. and Byass, P. (2012). Connecting the global climate change and public health agendas. *PLos Medicine*, 9(6): e1001227.

Padilla, C. M., Kihal-Talantikit, Perez, S., and Deguen, S. (2016). Use of geographic indicators of healthcare, environment, and socioeconomic factors to characterize environmental health disparities. *Environmental Health*, 15: 79. doi: 10.1186/s12940-016-0163-7

Pocket, R. (2014). Health in all places' as a curriculum strategy in social work education. *Social Work Education*, 33(6): 731–743.

Rosner, D. (2016). Flint Michigan: A century of environmental injustice. *American Journal of Public Health*, 106(2): 200–201.

Sachan, N. and Singh, V. P. (2010). Effect of climate changes on the prevalence of zoonotic diseases. *Veterinary World*, 3(11): 519–522.

Samarasundera, E., Hansell, A. Leibovici, D., Horwell, C. J., Anand, S. and Oppenheimer, C. (2014). Geological hazards: From early warning systems to public health toolkits. *Health and Place*, 30: 116–119, September.

Singh, A. and Purohit, B. M. (2014). Public health impacts of global warming and climate change. *Peace Review: A Journal of Social Justice*, 26: 112–120.

Stewart, J. R., Gast, R. J., Fujioka, R. S., Solo-Gabriele, H. M., Meschke, S., Amaral-Zettler, L. A. and Holland, A. F. (2008). The coastal environmental and human health: Microbial indicators, pathogens, sentinels, and reservoirs. *Environmental Health*, 7: S3 (Suppl 2).

Taylor, S. A. (2013). Social science research in ocean environments: A social worker's experience. In M. Gray, J. Coates and T. Hetherington (Eds.). *Environmental Social Work*. New York: Routledge, pp. 88–101.

Travis, D. A., Sriramarao, P., Cardona, C., Steer, C. J., Kennedy, S., Sreevatsan, S. and Murtaugh, M. P. (2014). One medicine one science: A framework for exploring challenges at the intersection of animals, humans, and the environment. *Annals of the New York Academy of Sciences*, 133: 26–44.

van Schalkwyk, A. (2011). Sacredness and sustainability: Searching for a practical eco-spirituality. *Religion and Theology*, 18: 77–02.

von dem Knesebeck, O. (2015). Concepts of social epidemiology in health services research. *BMC Health Services Research*, 12: 357–360.

Walker, R. (2009). Climate change and primary health care intervention framework. *Australian Journal of Primary Care*, 15: 276–284.

Wallace, M. I. (2012). Christian animism, green spirit theology, and global crisis today. *Journal of Reformed Theology*, 6, 216–233.

Zinsstag, J., Schelling, E., Waltner-Toews, D. and Tanner, M. (2011). From 'one medicine' to 'one health' and approaches to health and well-being. *Preventive Veterinary Medicine*, 101: 148–156.

28
The arrival of chikungunya on the Caribbean island of Curaçao
The important role of social workers

Odette van Brummen-Girigori and Auronette Girigori

Introduction

Chikungunya is an alphavirus member of the Togaviridae family (Robinson, 1955), first described in 1952 when an outbreak was observed in southern Tanzania (Pialoux et al., 2007). The term chikungunya is derived from an African Makonde word 'kungunyala' which means 'that which bends up', following the stooped posture adopted as a result of the arthritic symptoms of the disease (Mohan et al., 2010). The virus is transmitted by the aedine mosquito species, which also transmit Zika and Dengue viruses; the main disease vectors are *Aedes aegypti* and *Aedes albopictus* (Pialoux et al., 2007; Schuffenecker et al., 2006; Tsetsarkin et al., 2007). The virus is transmitted to humans through bites from female aedine mosquitoes infected with the chikungunya virus. These mosquitoes may bite at any time, but they are most active outdoors in the early morning (dawn) or late afternoon (dusk) (Chow et al., 2015). Mosquitoes inside the home are active both night and day.

Chikungunya infections generally cause fever, headache, myalgia, maculopapular rashes, acute joint swelling, persistent arthritis, and even life-threatening neurological or cardiovascular complications (Lee et al., 2012; Pellot et al., 2012). Additionally, days of acute illness can be followed by weeks, months, and even years of disabling joint pain, loss of mobility, fatigue, decreased dexterity, and an inability to perform daily tasks (Caglioti et al., 2013; Thirberville et al., 2013). Moreover, some patients report additional complaints involving the eyes, heart, and nervous system. Chikungunya virus infections rarely seriously impact overall health, but they may contribute towards death, usually among elderly people with weak immune systems (Chow et al., 2015). The pathogenesis of chikungunya is not well understood, and there is no vaccine or specific antiviral treatment (Abdelnabi et al., 2015; Weaver et al., 2012). Therefore, treatment focuses on alleviating its symptoms (De Lamballerie et al., 2008; WHO, 2016).

In recent years, the chikungunya virus has caused outbreaks over a large geographical area. Between 2004 and 2011, approximately 6 million cases of chikungunya infection have been reported in countries across Africa, Asia, and Europe (e.g. Thirberville et al., 2013; Suhrbier et al., 2012). The first cases of chikungunya in the Caribbean were reported on the island of St. Martin (Cassadou et al., 2014) in 2013. Six months later it reached Curaçao. Specifically, the Analytical Diagnostic Centre (ADC) reported the first suspected cases of chikungunya to the Public

Health Office in Curaçao in May 2014. Between August 2014 and the beginning of 2015, other inhabitants of Curaçao succumbing to this virus were surprised by its symptoms, as this had not previously been common on their Island. According to the Public Health Office of Curaçao, approximately 20,000 inhabitants of Curaçao succumbed to the chikungunya virus, covering over 10 per cent of the population.

Due to this massive outbreak, the States of Curaçao requested that the *Algemene Rekenkamer Curaçao* (ARC) (Curaçao's Audit Office) investigate to what extent the chikungunya virus was addressed by the Ministry of Health, the Environment, and Nature between 2012 and January 2015. This investigation sought insights into the measures taken by the Ministry to prevent the spread of the disease and confront the outbreak. Furthermore, this investigation made recommendations regarding the procedures, skills, and quantity of staff required to respond adequately to similar virus outbreaks in the future (ARC, 2016). Several studies on chikungunya virus infection have been conducted in various other countries, including Thailand (Rudnick and Hammon, 1962), India (Myers et al., 1965), La Reunion (Schuffenecker et al., 2006; Charrel et al., 2007; Geradin et al., 2008), Italy (Rezza et al., 2007), France (Granadam et al., 2011; Gould et al., 2010), China (Wu et al., 2012), and the Caribbean Sea Islands (Leparc-Goffart et al., 2014), but only a few in Curaçao (e.g. Anfasa et al., 2017). Recently, Anfasa and colleagues (2017) published the first report about the emergence of chikungunya in Curaçao. Their phylogenetic analysis showed that the chikungunya outbreak was caused by an Asian genotype. Additionally, they found an association between hyperferritinaemia with chronic chikungunya.

However, no study has been conducted from a social work perspective to assess the experiences and living environments of the inhabitants of Curaçao who succumbed to the chikungunya virus. This study fills this gap and clarifies how green social workers can contribute to eliminating the future spread of chikungunya and related viruses. Green social work (Dominelli, 2012a) has been introducing new issues in debates about the environment including making disaster interventions key elements in the repertoire of knowledge, skills, capacity-building, and curriculum formulation of social workers. Social workers can intervene and enhance people's well-being because they can have an important voice and play a key role in environmental issues, whether these are caused by climate change, industrial accidents, or human conflict (Dominelli, 2013b).

The aim of green social work is defined as

> work[ing] for the reform of socio-political and economic forces that have a deleterious impact upon the quality of life or poor marginalized populations and secure the policy changes and social transformation necessary for enhancing the well-being of people and the planet today and in the future.
>
> *(Dominelli, 2012: 25)*

It is essential that green social work continues to develop in Curaçao so as to encourage its inhabitants and all stakeholders to engage in developing culturally relevant and locality-specific health activities to safeguard the environment and avoid further major outbreaks of diseases occurring. Green social workers in Curaçao, will have to provide sustainable alternatives through collaborative participation and action (see Dominelli, 2014). Examining environmental issues from a green social work perspective is crucial in exploring possible community initiatives that social workers can promote to enhance people's quality of life without damaging the environment. Our study adds to the literature by examining how Curaçao's inhabitants coped with the chikungunya virus infection, and what steps they took to deal with their symptoms and complaints. Finally, this study assessed the population's opinion regarding the possible reasons for the chikungunya outbreak and suggests how green social workers can contribute to preventing future outbreaks here.

The study investigated the following research questions:

1   How did the chikungunya virus manifest among those who became infected?
2   What steps did the inhabitants of Curaçao take to alleviate their symptoms after becoming infected with chikungunya virus?
3   What constituted the living environments of people who succumbed to chikungunya virus?
4   According to its inhabitants, what were the reasons for the massive outbreak of the chikungunya virus in Curaçao?

Methodological considerations

Participants

The final sample consisted of 240 participants; 10 respondents who did not return completed survey questionnaires were removed. Women in the sample were slightly older than men. The sample included 61.6 per cent women with a mean age of 36.65 years ($SD = 18.40$) and 38.4 per cent men with a mean age of 33.39 years ($SD = 17.42$). All participants lived in Curaçao during the study period (January to March 2015). The sample consisted of respondents born in Curaçao (84.8 per cent), and those born in other countries including Holland (5.7 per cent), the Dominican Republic (2.4 per cent), Colombia (1.4 per cent), and surrounding islands such as Bonaire, Aruba, St. Kitts, and St. Martin. Among the respondents, 21.9 per cent indicated they had no education or a low educational level, 53.8 per cent attained a medium educational level, and 24.3 per cent a high educational level. Also, 35.3 per cent of respondents revealed they had no income, 32.1 per cent indicated low income, 29.4 per cent had middle incomes and 3.2 per cent claimed a high income.

Methodology

This study was approved by the Ethical Committee for Social Sciences at the University of Curaçao, Dr Moises da Costa Gomez. The data collection took place in several neighbourhoods of Curaçao during the early months of 2015. The sampling was purposive (Bryman, 2013). Respondents were asked to participate voluntarily in this study if they had succumbed to the chikungunya virus. Informed consent was obtained from each participant before they were asked to complete the questionnaire and their willingness to continue was checked out throughout the interview. A hard copy of the survey questionnaire was distributed to each participant. At the end of the interview, participants were asked to indicate whether they would be interested in participating in future chikungunya research. The survey questionnaire was offered in Papiamentu and English and required approximately 15 minutes to complete. Papiamentu is the native language of Aruba, Bonaire, and Curaçao. It is a Creole language in part derived from African languages, with considerable influence from Spanish and Portuguese, alongside some influence from Amerindian, English, French, and Dutch. Papiamentu is the language most commonly spoken in Curaçao, followed by Dutch, Spanish, and English. The collected data were entered into IBM SPSS Statistics for Windows and analyzed by the principal researcher, Odette van Brummen-Girigori. Data were stored in a locked closet at the Research Centre of the University of Curaçao, under Dr Moises da Costa Gomez. Participant anonymity and confidentiality were ensured by the principal researcher.

Survey questionnaire

Hard copies of the survey questionnaires were distributed. Each survey questionnaire consisted of four sections: demography, disease symptoms, post-infection actions, and living environment. The demographic section included questions about participants' age, place of birth, educational and income levels. In the second section, the respondents indicated which symptoms they had experienced and for how long (in days). A total of 16 symptoms were provided. These included walking difficulties, complications when standing, sleepiness, weakness, fever, and headache. Additionally, a category for other symptoms and space to describe them was provided. In the third section, respondents were requested to indicate what steps they took after becoming infected by the chikungunya virus, including visiting a doctor and having their blood tested, which products they used to combat their symptoms including whether they had used natural products to treat their symptoms. In the fourth section, the living environment (e.g. environment in which they lived, including their yard/gardens and homes) and possible reasons for the chikungunya outbreak were assessed.

The respondents were asked to indicate on a scale from 1 (completely disagree) to 5 (completely agree) the extent to which they were in (dis)agreement with certain statements. Examples of statements regarding their living environments included: 'In general, the street where I live was clean', 'People dumped old stuff/garbage in my neighbourhood', 'In my street, there were places where water collected and (possibly) created a good environment for mosquitoes', 'I had drums and cans in my garden where the mosquitoes could lay eggs', 'I had garbage on a regular basis in my backyard', and 'I had enough insecticide to kill mosquitoes'.

Examples of statements regarding the possible sources of the chikungunya outbreak included, 'A lot of people got chikungunya because water pooled in particular places due to trash on the streets, providing breeding grounds for mosquitoes', 'People that throw garbage on the streets or in public areas must be penalized', 'The government must do more to protect people; e.g., clean up the streets and insist people clean up their yards', and 'The government did not sufficiently prepare the residents for chikungunya'.

Results

The first research question asked how the chikungunya virus symptoms manifested among those who had become infected. The results showed that respondents had experienced chikungunya-associated symptoms for an average of 11.31 days (range: 2–90 days) and were extremely ill for an average of 7.21 days (range: 1–30 days). However, working people returned to work after an average of 3.93 days (range: 1–35 days). More than half of the respondents (52.1 per cent) claimed to have had a relapse after they thought they had recovered. Over two-thirds of them (67.5 per cent) did not know where (location-wise) they had been bitten by the infected mosquito (vector). Remarkably, 36.4 per cent of respondents indicated that not everyone in their household had become infected. This is an interesting finding which merits further investigation. It suggests that in some cases the victims were not bitten by the vector at home.

As shown in Table 28.1, the respondents reported having experienced muscle and joint pain, walking difficulties, problems when standing, weakness, fever, drowsiness, headache, rash, flu symptoms, diarrhoea, swollen glands, peeling skin, vomiting, and other symptoms.

Table 28.1 Reported complaints due to the chikungunya virus

Complaints	Prevalence	M_days	SD	Minimum	Maximum
1 Muscle pain and joint problems	90.7%	9.42	14.09	1	90
2 Walking difficulties	90.5%	6.55	10.15	1	90
3 Standing difficulties	87.2%	7.45	13.02	1	90
4 Weakness	86.2%	5.58	4.43	1	30
5 Fever	77.7%	3.44	2.15	1	14
6 Drowsiness	76.4%	5.84	8.00	1	60
7 Headache	76.3%	4.17	2.44	1	14
8 Rash	52.3%	3.95	3.83	1	28
9 Influenza-like symptoms	41.8%	5.50	4.82	1	30
10 Diarrhoea	40.5%	3.82	3.17	1	14
11 Swollen glands	38.6%	4.28	3.03	1	21
12 Skin peeling	31.9%	8.94	14.13	1	60
13 Vomiting	31.4%	3.38	3.65	0	21
14 Other complaints: accelerated heart rate, palpitations, dizziness, itching, and chills	21.2%	8.38	6.55	1	21
15 Vision problems	20.8%	7.23	14.61	1	60

Note: M_days = mean number of days

Differences in chikungunya symptoms among diverse groups. As illustrated in Table 28.2, respondents who had a relapse after the first round of chikungunya had walking difficulties, problems when standing, sleepiness, weakness, and muscle pains/joint problems for significantly longer periods of time than those who did not have a relapse. In addition, a t-test analysis showed that respondents with a history of Dengue Fever reported experiencing weakness for significantly longer periods of time than those without a history of Dengue Fever. Finally, no significant differences were observed between male and female respondents regarding the symptoms of chikungunya ($p > 0.05$).

Complaints after chikungunya infection. At the time of the survey, many respondents still had several complaints associated with the chikungunya virus infection, including joint pain, walking difficulties, problems when standing, weakness, swollen glands, and vision problems (Table 28.3).

Table 28.2 Mean values of participants who had a relapse after the first manifestation of the chikungunya virus infection and those with a history of dengue fever

Status		No		Yes		Comparison		95%	CI
	Complaints	M	SD	M	SD	t	d	LL	UL
Relapse	Walking	4.32	5.16	9.24	13.62	−2.86*	−.48	−.82	−.14
	Standing	3.74	3.85	11.91	18.12	−3.68*	−.64	−.98	−.29
	Weakness	4.76	4.21	6.53	4.51	−2.21*	−.41	−.77	−.04
	Drowsiness	3.89	3.22	8.53	11.63	−2.98*	−.58	−.96	−.19
	Joint pain	4.76	4.21	6.53	4.51	−2.02*	−.41	−.78	−.04
Past Dengue fever	Weakness	5.15	4.23	7.24	15.03	−2.11*	−.15	−.59	.29

Note: d = Cohen's d (Effect size of between-group differences); 95% CI = 95% confidence interval of Cohen's d; LL = lower limit; UL = upper limit; * $p < 0.05$ (two-tailed)

Table 28.3 Chikungunya-associated symptoms

Complaints	Prevalence
1 Muscle pain and joint problems	67.2%
2 Walking problems	12.2%
3 Standing problems	6.9%
4 Weakness	2.3%
5 Swollen glands	2.3%
6 Vision problems	0.9%

The second research question asked what steps the inhabitants of Curaçao had taken after becoming infected with the chikungunya virus. The results showed that 36.4 per cent of respondents had visited a doctor and that 31.7 per cent had their blood tested. The majority of those who visited a doctor received a prescription for anti-inflammatory drugs (e.g. Aspirin or Dolo-neurobion). In this study, 12.5 per cent of respondents indicated that they had used a pharmaceutical product. In contrast, 31.3 per cent of respondents indicated that they had used natural products including papaya leaves, mango leaves, lemongrass, and oregano to treat the symptoms. Chi-square analysis showed that those who used natural products instead of pharmaceutical products reported less muscle pain (χ^2 (1, N = 100) = 4.81, p = 0.02), fever (χ^2 (1, N = 101) = 3.91, p = 0.04), and influenza-like symptoms (χ^2 (1, N = 99) = 3.85, p = 0.04). The t-test analysis showed that those who used natural products only reported significantly fewer days of fever (t (50) = 2.99, M^{pharma} = 4.88, SD = 3.56; $M^{natural}$ = 2.85, SD = 115, p = 0.00). However, those who used pharmaceutical products reported fewer walking difficulties (χ^2 (1, N = 98) = 3.45, p = 0.05) and a shorter duration for these symptoms than those using natural products (t (50) = −2.31, M^{pharma} = 3.33, SD = 1.71; $M^{natural}$ = 7.12, SD = 7.34, p = 0.02). These findings merit further investigation by medical experts.

The third research question assessed the living environment of people infected by the chikungunya virus. The results showed that only 42.5 per cent of respondents could fully state that their neighbourhood was clean; while 53.4 per cent thought that their own street was clean. Moreover, 24.4 per cent of respondents admitted that they had containers and barrels in their garden which could become potential breeding places for the vector. Additionally, 17.1 per cent of respondents regularly had bulky waste in their garden that was not cleaned up. Almost one in three (31.8 per cent) reported waste being dumped in their streets, and 37.0 per cent reported pooling in their streets, creating possible breeding grounds for mosquitoes. Also, 36.3 per cent of respondents indicated that they had enough insecticide at home at the time they were infected by the chikungunya virus. Moreover, 38.6 per cent of respondents had an electric fly swatter, 40.2 per cent a mosquito swatter, 16 per cent had a 'mosquito trap', and 33.3 per cent regularly applied a substance to their bodies (e.g. repellent) to protect themselves against mosquito bites before leaving home.

The fourth research question asked the inhabitants of Curaçao to identify the possible reasons for the chikungunya virus outbreak. The majority of respondents (60.4 per cent) believed that many in Curaçao had become infected due to multiple sites containing dumped bulky waste, which may have created breeding grounds for mosquitoes. Furthermore, 79.5 per cent of them believed that there were many individuals who polluted the environment without penalty. For example, 29.1 per cent of the respondents indicated that they did their best to protect themselves, but were unsuccessful because their neighbours did not clean up their yards to remove potential mosquito breeding sites. Nevertheless, 82.5 per cent of respondents felt that the government should take measures to force individuals who do not keep their streets and/or garden clean to do so, and when necessary, government should impose hefty fines to protect non-polluters. Apart from that, 70.1 per cent of respondents believed that the government had not provided sufficient information in a timely manner to prepare them adequately for the arrival of the chikungunya virus. Finally, 81.3 per cent of respondents believed that the government should procure funds to conduct research on chikungunya and 81.1 per cent stated that the government should urgently cooperate with other international organisations to prevent Curaçao from facing future chikungunya epidemics. Zika, another disease spread by *Aedes aegypti*, may create havoc among the population of Curaçao unless urgent preventative measures are taken, because some people living in Curaçao succumbed to this virus during the last months of 2016. Removing potential mosquito breeding sites would be very useful in this regard. This was a lesson learned in Southern Europe after World War II when swamps were drained to eradicate the (Anopheles) mosquito that transmitted the malaria virus (Majori, 2012).

Discussion

The present study assessed the experiences, living environments, and opinions regarding the chikungunya outbreak among people who succumbed to the chikungunya virus in Curaçao. Our results showed that the manifestations of the infection were diverse: not everyone reported the same symptoms or duration. Significant differences were observed in the symptoms reported by the respondents who had had a relapse after the initial symptoms of chikungunya appeared and those with a history of Dengue Fever. The majority of respondents indicated they had experienced muscle pain, joint pain, walking difficulties, problems when standing, weakness, fever, drowsiness, and headaches. A lower proportion of them reported complaints such as accelerated heart rate, heart palpitations, dizziness, itching, and vision problems. In general, the symptoms reported in Curaçao were similar to those reported elsewhere (Rezza et al., 2007; Chattopadhyay et al., 2016; WHO, 2016).

Suspicion of chikungunya should be treated with prompt medical attention and correct diagnosis (e.g. CDC, 2014; Thirberville et al., 2013). However, only one-third of respondents visited a doctor, and only one-third had their blood tested. A significant number of respondents indicated that they had used natural products such as mango leaves, papaya leaves, oregano, and lemongrass to treat their symptoms. The results of the current study showed that the use of natural products appeared to be more effective in relieving certain symptoms compared to the use of pharmaceutical products. However, additional research is necessary to validate this observation. We did not ask the respondents when they started to use the natural or pharmaceutical products after experiencing the symptoms of chikungunya virus infection. In addition, we do not know if those who had more walking difficulties used the natural products immediately or after the walking difficulties appeared. In other words, we cannot exclude the possibility that the timing of the use of the pharmaceutical or natural products was a confounding variable. Thus, these findings merit further research by medical experts.

Furthermore, respondents who succumbed to the chikungunya virus returned to work after an average of four days, while the respondents reported experiencing chikungunya symptoms for an average of 11 days. This observation may be due to the rules and instructions of the Social Insurance Law on Curaçao (see Bonafasia, 2016). However, it is important to emphasise that expecting and demanding infected employees to return to work may increase the risk of spreading the virus in the workplace. Non-infected co-workers may be infected if a non-infected vector bites an infected co-worker at the workplace and consequently bites a non-infected co-worker. Therefore, developing a policy regarding the isolation of infected individuals during the transmission period instead of requiring their return to work too soon is necessary. The same is true for students who return to school while still sick.

In addition, the results of this study revealed that only around 40 per cent of the respondents could fully claim that their neighbourhood was clean. Several respondents admitted having containers and barrels in their garden that had not been removed. Furthermore, almost one in three respondents stated that bulky waste items had been dumped in their streets, even though there is evidence that *Aedes aegypti* lay their eggs, and their larvae and pupae develop in standing water, containers, rubbish, and tires that collect rainwater (e.g. Higa, 2011; pamphlet of Ministry of Health, the Environment, and Nature, 2016; Weaver and Reisen, 2010; WHO, 2016). Moreover, only approximately one-third of respondents indicated that they took sufficient protective measures, including the application of insect repellents (e.g. pamphlet of the Ministry of Health, the Environment and Nature (2016) and Nasci et al. (2013); clothing that covers as much skin as possible; sprayed insecticides; or used products recommended to reduce the chances of being bitten by mosquitoes (e.g. WHO, 2016).

Moreover, the majority of respondents indicated that they did not receive sufficient information from the government in a timely manner to prepare adequately for the arrival of chikungunya on the island. These findings are concordant with the conclusions in the report of the ARC (2016). For example, pamphlets with information regarding chikungunya were not distributed on time, and not every target group was reached; the pamphlets were initially only available in Papiamentu, the most commonly spoken language on the island. Furthermore, the general practitioners and other stakeholders in healthcare were not informed in a timely manner (not until April–May 2014).

Similarly, a significant number of respondents indicated that there were many people who polluted the environment without repercussion because hefty fines were not imposed by the government. Therefore, we may conclude that in general, not enough preventive measures were taken. Yet, a well-functioning public health infrastructure could have helped to prevent the massive outbreak of infection, especially because the chikungunya outbreak was vector and water-related (see also Bhatia and Narain, 2009). Therefore, the chikungunya epidemic on the island of Curaçao may also be an indicator of a weakness in the public health system and a failure to anticipate and respond adequately to the emerging epidemic. More specifically, the investigation conducted by the ARC (2016) confirmed that the Ministry of Health, the Environment, and Nature quantitatively and qualitatively did not have sufficient staff available before or during the outbreak of chikungunya. Furthermore, it was concluded that the Ministry of Health Environment and Nature had a lack of protection products and (technical) equipment for vector control in stock. Besides that, the mosquito control was only intensified by more human resources in December 2014 when the outbreak had been ongoing for a few months already.

Thus, there is a need to improve the efficacy and efficiency of the public health system in Curaçao in order to prevent emerging diseases (ARC, 2016). For this reason, the government should work more intensively on increasing public awareness to prevent Curaçao from being overtaken by Zika, Mayaro or similar viruses in the short term. For example, the government should take more active measures when inhabitants are found to be negligent in eliminating possible breeding places and actively enforce environmental laws (see the report of ARC (2015) entitled: *Randvoorwaarden Uitvoering Mileubeleid* (Preconditions for carrying out the Environment Policy). It is also important that the inhabitants of Curaçao realise that only a holistic approach, in which there is mutual cooperation among different stakeholders in mitigating risk factors and implementing control strategies, will protect them against the further expansion of chikungunya, Zika, Denque, Mayaro, or other viruses (see Bhatia and Narain, 2009; WHO, 2016).

Additionally, green social workers can play an important role in encouraging the inhabitants of Curaçao to engage in health activities to safeguard the environment and prevent a major disease outbreak in the future. This can be accomplished according to equitable and ethically sound principles (see also Dominelli, 2012, 2013a). Inspired by Dominelli's (2012a) green social work model, the authors suggest that social workers in Curaçao undertake the following tasks:

1   *Doing no harm to the physical environment* whereby social workers explain to the community the importance of *not* polluting the environment and *not* creating breeding grounds for mosquitos.
2   *Consciousness-raising* whereby social workers help the community of Curaçao adopt preventative measures, such as visiting schools, community centres, and homes for older people and disabled people, and coordinate with health professionals and government officials to produce an effective, holist intervention to: mitigate risk and provide effective responses; develop resilience; and prevent the further spread of disease. Furthermore, social workers can facilitate discussions across relevant disciplines, institutions, schools, and societies.
3   *Lobbying* for preventive measures taken at local level. For instance, social workers can help to inform public policy and practice on a regular basis. It is also desirable that more companies besides the health organisations (e.g. medical centres and doctor's surgeries or clinics) unify and contribute to preventing vector-related outbreaks. Large insurance companies on Curaçao did this by offering and distributing pamphlets. In other words, a multidisciplinary and multifaceted approach is necessary to generate the desired results.
4   *Mobilising communities* whereby social workers can stimulate residents/clients/service users during their daily practice to take preventive measures (including by referring to pamphlets from Ennia, 2016; the Ministry of Health, the Environment, and Nature, 2016; and the WHO, 2016) and reminding them of the difficulties faced by those affected by the chikungunya virus.
5   *Coproducing solutions*, whereby social worker researchers continue to investigate the underlying motives of those who pollute the environment and consequently design interventions aimed at behaviour modification. Besides that, research should be performed by medical experts to review the symptomatology of chikungunya and explore other unanswered questions. Specifically, future studies should investigate the ingredients present in papaya leaves, mango leaves, and other natural products that appeared to inhibit the symptoms of chikungunya virus infection. Social workers and social work researchers may also assist in these research tasks.
6   *Dialoguing* with social scientists, medical scientists, physical scientists, other professionals, and policymakers to change policies at local, national, and international levels. The community of Curaçao can also be reached through productive partnerships with the mass media and several non-governmental organisations which have a wider reach and greater credibility within the wider community of Curaçao.
7   *Developing curricula* by arranging lectures, because it is important that the community of Curaçao is well-informed in order to support public health interventions aimed at behaviour modification.

Conclusion

This chapter demonstrates that green social workers play critical roles in undertaking research that links human behaviour to environmental challenges that undermine well-being. It also highlights how they can engage local residents in behavioural change including cleaning up mosquito breeding grounds that are created through everyday routines like the inadequate disposal of garbage. This is a promising start for Curaçao, but greening the profession has further to go to become more confident in its capacity to be a significant player in this area and sit as equal professionals alongside the others sitting at the environmental mitigation table in the pursuit of social justice and healthy, resilient, sustainable communities.

Acknowledgements

We are grateful to our interviewers for their cooperation and dedication. We also thank the respondents for their participation in this study. Without their help, we could not have conducted this study.

We also thank Lena Dominelli for the encouragement and help she gave to this project. In particular, it was her explanation of the green social work perspective and its use in participatory action research at a conference in July 2013 that gave rise to this project and subsequently her internet-based support which continues. She encouraged the use of social work students in conducting holistic, community-based research to safeguard people's health, engage multiple stakeholders in health activities aimed at avoiding major outbreaks of disease. Green social work is continuing to develop in Curaçao.

References

Abdelnabi, R., Neyts, J. and Delang, L. (2015). Towards antivirals against Chikungunya virus. *Antiviral Research*, 121: 59–68. doi: 10.1016/j.antiviral.2015.06.017

Algemene Rekenkamer Curaçao (2015). *Randvoorwaarden uitvoering milieubeleid*. Registratienummer: 2014-0022. Available on www.scribd.com/document/288707240/2015-10-Xx-Algemene Rekenkamer [Accessed 25 November 2016].

Algemene Rekenkamer Curaçao (2016). *Chikungunya. Aanpak van de bestrijding*. Registratienummer: 2016-002. Available on www.scribd.com/ document/329704856/Rapport-Algemene-Rekenkamer-Curacao-Aanpak-Bestrijding-Chikungunya-Okt2016 [Accessed 14 November 2016].

Anfasa, F., Provacia, L., Geurts van Kessel, C., Wever, R., Gerstenbluth, I., Osterhaus, A. D. M. E. and Martina, B. E. E. (2017). Hyperferritinemia is a potential marker of chronic chikungunya. *Journal of Clinical Virology*, 86: 31–38. doi: 10.1016/j.jcv.2016.11.003

Bhatia, R. and Narain, J. P. (2009). Re-emerging chikungunya fever: some lessons from Asia. *Tropical Medicine and International Health*, 14(8): 940–946. doi: 10.1111/j.1365–3156.2009.02312.x.

Bonafasia, M. F. (2016). *Inleiding tot Sociale verzekeringsrecht op Curaçao*. Willemstad: Emergency Printing and Publishing n.v.

Bryman, A. (2013). *Social Research Methods*. New York: Oxford University Press Inc.

Caglioti, C., Lalle, E., Castilletti, C., Carletti, F., Capobianchi, M. R. and Bordi, L. (2013). Chikungunya virus infection. *New Microbiologica*, 36(3): 211–227.

Cassadou, S., Boucau, S., Petit-Sinturel, M., Huc, P., Leparc-Goffart, I. and Ledrans, M. (2014). Emergence of chikungunya fever on the French site of Saint Martin Island, October to December 2013. *Eurosurveillance*, 19.

Center for Disease Control and Prevention (CDC). (2014). *Chikungunya clinical evaluation and disease*. Available on www.cdc.gov/chikungunya/hc/clinicalevaluation.html [Accessed 12 June 2016].

Charrel, R. N., de Lamballerie, X. and Raoult, D. (2007). Chikunguya outbreaks. *The New England Journal of Medicine*, 356(8): 769–771.

Chattopadhyay, S., Mukherjee, R., Nandi, A. and Bhattacharya, N. (2016). Chikungunya virus infection in West Bengal India. *Indian Journal of Medical Microbiology*, 34(2): 213–215.

Chow, D. L., Miller, D., Seidel, J. A., Kane, R. T., Thornton, J. A. and Andrews, W. P. (2015). The role of deliberate practice in the development of highly effective psychotherapists. *Psychotherapy*, 5(3): 337–345.

De Lamballerie, X., Boisson, V., Reynier, J. C., Enault, S., Charrel, R. N., Flahault, A., Roques, P. and Le Grand, R. (2008). On chikungunya acute infection and chloroquine treatment. *Vector Borne Zoonotic Diseases*, 8(6): 837–839.

Dominelli, L. (2012). *Green Social Work*. Cambridge: Polity Press.

Dominelli, L. (2013a). Mind the gap. *Australian Social Work*, 66(2): 204–217. doi: 10.1080/0312407X.2012.708764.

Dominelli, L. (2013b). *Green social work*. Available on www.ulapland.fi/loader.aspx?id=738c09c1-fa9b-4475-af63-a506967870e1 [Accessed 5 December 2016].

Dominelli, L (2014). *Greening social work:* Available on www.academia.edu/10256999/GreeningSocial-Work [Accessed 15 June 2017].

Ennia (2016). *Don't Give Zika a Chance*. Willemstad. Available on https://www.facebook.com/enniaprevention/posts/? ref=page_internal [Accessed 21 November 2016].

Géradin, P., Guernier, V., Perrau, J., Fianu, A., Le Roux, K., Grivard, P., Michaualt, A., de Lamballerie, X., Flahault, A. and Favier, F. (2008). Estimating Chikunguya prevalence in La Reunion Island outbreak by serosurveys: two methods for two critical times of the epidemic. *BMC Infectious Diseases*, 8–19. doi: 10.1186/147-2334-8-99.

Gould, E. A., Gallian, P., de Lamballerie, X. and Charrel, R. N. (2010). First cases of autochthonous dengue fever and chikunguya fever in France: from bad dream to reality! *Clinical Microbiology Infection*, 16(12): 1702–1704.

Granadam, M., Caro, V., Plumet, S., Thilberge, J. M., Souares, Y., Failloux, A. B., Tolou, H. J., Budelot, M., Cosserat, D., Leparc-Goffart, I. and Desprès, P. (2011). Chikunguya virus, southeastern France. *Emerging Infectious Diseases*, 17(5): 910–913.

Higa, Y. (2011). Dengue vectors and their spatial distribution. *Tropical Medicine and Health*, 39(4): 17–27. doi: 10.2149/tmh.2011-S04.

Lee, V. J., Chow, A., Zheng, X., Carrasco, L. R., Cook, A. R., Lye, D. C., Ng, L. C. and Leo, Y. S. (2012). Simple clinical and laboratory predictors of Chikungunya versus dengue infections in adults. *Plos Neglected Tropical Diseases*. Retrieved from http://journals.plos.org/plosntds/article? id=10.1371/journal.pntd.0001786 [Accessed 12 June 2016].

Leparc-Goffart, I., Nougairede, A., Cassadou, S., Prat, C. and de Lamballerie, X. (2014). Chikungunya in the Americas. *The Lancet*, 383 (9916): 514. doi: 10.1016/S0140-6736(14)60185-9.

Majori, G. (2012). Short history of Malaria and its eradication in Italy and short note on the fight against the infection in the Mediterranean Basin. *Mediterranean Journal of Hematology and Infectious Diseases*, 4(1): e2012016. doi: 10.4084/MJHID.2012.016

Ministry of Health, the Environment and Nature (MHEN) (2016). *Mosquitoes and diseases*. Willemstad, Curaçao: MHEN.

Mohan, A., Kiran, D. H., Manohar, I. C. and Kumar, D. P. (2010). Epidemiology clinical manifestations, and diagnosis of chikungunya fever. *Indian Journal of Dermatology*, 55(1): 54–63.

Myers, R. M., Carey, D. E., Reuben, R., Jesudass, E. S., De Ranitz, C. and Jadhav, M. (1965). The 1964 epidemic of dengue-like fever in South India. *Indian Journal of Medical Research*, 52: 676–683.

Nasci, R. S., Zielinski-Gutierrez, E., Wirtz, R. A. and Brogdon, W. G. (2013). Chapter 2: Protection against mosquitoes, ticks, and other insects and arthropods. In *CDC Health Information for International Travellers 2014* (Yellow book). Available on www.cdc.gov/ travel/ yellowbook/2014/ chapter-2-the-pretravelconsulation/ protection-against-mosquitoes-thicks-and-other-insects-and arthropods [Accessed 20 November 2016].

Pellot, A. S., Allessandri, J. L., Robin, S., Samperiz, S., Attali, T., Brayer, C., Pasquet, M., Jaffar-Bandjee, M. C., Benhamou, L. S., Tiran-Rajaofera, I. and Ramful, D. (2012). Severe forms of chikungunya virus infection in a paediatric intensive care unit on Reunion Island. *Medicine Tropical*, 72: 88–93.

Pialoux, G., Gauzere, B. A., Jaureguiberry, S. and Strobel, M. (2007). Chikungunya, an epidemic arbovirosis. *The Lancet Infectious Diseases*, 7: 319–327.

Rezza, G., Nicoletti, L., Angelini, R., Romi, R., Finarelli, A. C., Panning, M., Cordioli, P., Fortuna, C., Boros, S., Magurano, F., Silvi, G., Angelini, P., Dottori, M., Ciufolini, M. G., Majori, G. C., Cassone, A. and CHIKV study group. (2007). Infection with chikungunya virus in Italy. *Lancet*, 370: 1840–1846.

Robinson, M. C. (1955). An epidemic of virus disease in Southern Providence, Tanganyika Territory, in 1952–53. I Clinical features. *Transaction of the Royal Society of Tropical Medicine and Hygiene*, 49(1): 28–32.

Rudnick, A. and Hammon, W. M. (1962). Entomological aspects of Thai haemorrhagic fever epidemics in Bangkok, the Philippines and Singapore, 1956–1961. *SEATO Medical Research Monograph*, 2: 24–29.

Schuffenecker, I., Iteman, I., Michault, A., Murri, S., Frangeul, L., Vaney, M., Lavenir, R., Pardigon, N,. Reynes, J., Pettinelli, F., Biscornet, L., Diancourt, L., Michel, S., Duquerroy, S., Guigon, G., Frenkiel, M., Bréhin, A., Cubito, N., Després, P., Kunst, F., Rey, F. A., Zeller, H. and Brisse, S. (2006). Genome micro-evolution of chikungunya viruses causing the Indian Ocean outbreak. *PloS Medicine, 3*: 263.

Suhrbier, A., Jaffar-Bandjee, M. C. and Gasque, P. (2012). Arthritogenic alphaviruses. *Nature Review Rheumatology*, 8: 420–429.

Thirberville, S. D., Moyen, N., Dupius-Maguiraga, L., Nougairede, A., Gould, E. A., Roques, P. and de Lamballerie, X. (2013). Chikungunya fever. *Antiviral Research, 99*(3): 345–370. doi: 10.1016/j.antiviral.2013.06.009 PMID: 23811281.

Tsetsarkin, K. A., Vanlandingham, D. L., McGee, C. E. and Higgs, S. (2007). A single mutation in Chikunguya virus affects vector specificity and epidemic potential. *PLoS Pathogens*, 3(12): 201.

Weaver, S. C., Osorio, J. E., Livengood, J. A., Chen, R. and Stinchcomb, D. T. (2012). Chikungunya virus and prospects for vaccine. *Expert Review Vaccines, 11*(9): 1087–1101. doi: 10.1586/erv.12.84.

Weaver, S. C. and Reisen, W. K. (2010). Present and future arboviral threats. *Antiviral Research, 85*(2): 328–345. doi: 10.1016/j.antiviral.2009.10.008.

World Health Organization (WHO) (2016). *Chikungunya*. Available on www.who.int/mediacentre/factsheets/fs327/en [Accessed 23 November 2016].

World Health Organization (2016). *Zika virus and complications*. Available on www.who.int/emergencies/zika-virus/en/ [Accessed 23 November 2016].

Wu, D., Wu, J., Zhang, Q., Zhong, H., Ke, C., Deng, X., Guan, D., Li, H., Zhang, Y., Zhou, H., He, J., Li, L. and Yang, X. (2012). Chikungunya outbreak in Guangdong Province, China 2010. *Emerging Infectious Diseases*, 18(3): 493–495.

29

The challenge of maintaining continuity in health and social care during extreme weather events

Cross-sectoral and transdisciplinary approaches

Sarah Curtis, Lena Dominelli, Katie J. Oven and Jonathan Wistow

Introduction

Global climate change presents the crucial and growing challenge of how to ensure continuity of health and social care to meet the specific needs of populations requiring access to services on an ongoing basis due to chronic ill health, disability or social disadvantage. We specifically consider extreme weather events producing conditions under which health and social care systems face special challenges in maintaining continuity of care. The discussion in this chapter draws especially on illustrations from England, an example of a country with a well-developed health and social care system and an ageing population, where governmental agencies and other partners, including academic researchers, are working together to address these issues.

In the first part of this chapter we set out the key elements of the complex health and social care system considered here. In the second part we introduce a transdisciplinary approach to address these challenges developed in a research project in England focused on *'Built Infrastructure for Older People's Care in Conditions of Climate Change'*, and highlight this topic as one for green social workers to engage with fully within a transdisciplinary framework.

The complex problem of older people's health and social care during extreme weather events

The issue considered here has a number of dimensions which include: demographic trends producing relatively rapid growth of older populations; growing complexity of health and social care systems and care needs; and increasing risk of extreme weather events, associated with climate change. We argue that strategies to enhance preparedness and resilience to extreme weather require enhanced collaboration and integration across professional sectors and diverse knowledge bases. We therefore focus on the arguments for transdisciplinary and cross-sectoral approaches, an approach central to green social workers (Dominelli, 2012).

The increasing demand for continuing care among older populations

Older people are a diverse group and should not be considered as universally 'vulnerable', since many of them are in relatively robust health and able to draw on considerable reserves of accumulated social and economic capital, and knowledge and skills acquired over a lifetime. However, a relatively large proportion of older people, especially those in the oldest age groups are especially likely to be impacted by extreme weather events in ways which affect their physical and mental health. This is partly because, compared with younger adults, older people are more likely to be physically and mentally frail, due to existing health problems that are exacerbated by extreme weather. Furthermore, a relatively large proportion of this age group needs to use health and social care services on an ongoing basis arising from chronic and sometimes quite complicated health problems, so they are among the groups that will be most severely affected if health and social care delivery is disrupted due to extreme weather.

This demographic group is growing as a proportion of the total population globally, which is why, for example, the *Sendai Framework for Disaster Risk Reduction* (United Nations, 2015:10) refers to 'demographic change' as a 'compounding factor' which is contributing to vulnerability to disasters. In Europe, a region where the 'demographic transition' is relatively advanced, 27 per cent of the population is expected to be aged 65 years or over by 2050 (WHO, 2012). The oldest age groups are expanding particularly rapidly. For example, in England, population projections suggest that the size of the population aged 85 years and over will have increased from 2.2 per cent to 4.6 per cent between 2008 and 2033 (Oven et al., 2012). In other world regions, while the population profile at present includes a smaller proportion in older groups, the demographic trends are generally shifting towards significant ageing. At the global scale, it is anticipated that there will be increasing demand for health and social care services for older people, and that a growing number of people will be dependent on continuous care. This makes it even more important to ensure that, looking ahead, the services required will be available.

Growing complexity of health and social services for service users requiring continuous care and support

In many countries internationally, health and social services for those needing regular and frequent access to care have developed into complex systems involving many different partners and a variety of different types of carers, infrastructures and resources. This is particularly evident in high-income countries that have been able to invest in health and social care over an extended period. Health and social care systems comprise crucial built, institutional and social infrastructures which are all necessary to ensure continuity of care. The World Health Organization (WHO) states that:

> A good health system delivers quality services to all people, when and where they need them. The exact configuration of services varies from country to country, but in all cases requires a robust financing mechanism; a well-trained and adequately paid workforce; reliable information on which to base decisions and policies; well-maintained facilities and logistics to deliver quality medicines and technologies.
>
> *(WHO, 2017)*

Thus, it is understood that health systems extend beyond the medical staff and equipment necessary to provide clinical treatment, social care and include a range of organisational and policy-making functions. Understanding this complexity is essential for adult social care workers adopting a green perspective. The IPCC (2014: 20) has argued that to strengthen health systems internationally 'a broad partnership of stakeholders can deliver a richer understanding' of the ways that systems will respond to change, 'what synergies can be harnessed and what negative emergent behaviour should be mitigated'. This is particularly relevant for development of 'green' (sustainable) health and social care systems that take action to prepare effectively to reduce disruption during extreme and potentially disruptive events. Research on green social work (Dominelli, 2012) can help to inform this agenda by demonstrating how social care can be made more responsive to social stressors arising from changing environmental conditions and pressures, and make societies more resilient. Green practices also place emphasis on adaptation and evolution in ways that help to mitigate the challenges faced due to environmental change.

Climate change and the growing challenges of maintaining continuity of care during extreme weather events

Assessments including the report published in 2014 by the Intergovernmental Panel on Climate Change Assessment (IPCC, 2014) have identified a range of risks associated with climate change that are likely to impact on human health over the 21st century. The main impacts are expected to be through exacerbation of existing health problems since, for example, those with a range of health problems including cardiovascular and respiratory illnesses are especially vulnerable to increasing risks of extreme heat and poor air quality. These are points for green social workers to consider when assessing vulnerability.

Globally there is also a growing risk of injury due to more frequent storms, floods and tidal surges, wildfires, and geophysical disasters such as landslides precipitated by changing meteorological conditions. There is also concern about increased vulnerability to vector-borne diseases, as environmental conditions become more suitable for some insects and animals carrying diseases, while infectious disease risks are likely to increase if extreme weather events damage infrastructures including water and sewerage systems. Mental, as well as physical, health is known to be impacted by extreme weather events such as major floods, due to the trauma and loss that is often experienced during the event and also post-traumatic stress and the long-term impacts of extreme events on families and livelihoods. Problems arising from disaster-related stress and trauma are also associated with the broader impacts of extreme weather associated with climate change, such as drought-induced water shortages and poor quality of water supply; challenges to agricultural production; and threats to economic systems and ecosystems that affect people's standards of living. As a consequence of periods of extreme weather, food shortages are expected to contribute to health problems due to inadequate nutrition in some regions of the world. These problems are related to social and economic vulnerabilities as well as physical hazards, and have implications for social care systems and medical care, because these risks are most elevated for the poorest populations that are already disadvantaged by relatively poor health and are likely to require social and welfare support.

There are particular pressures on both health and social care systems that arise from increased demand during extreme weather events. The challenge of meeting these exceptional demands for care is further heightened by the risks of disruption to the various infrastructures upon which these services depend, such as damage to built infrastructure and supply systems and lack of access to professional or informal care givers. The *Sendai Framework for Disaster Risk Reduction*

(United Nations, 2015: 12) emphasises that it is important to 'substantially reduce disaster damage to critical infrastructure and disruption of basic services, among them health . . . including through developing their resilience by 2030'.

In the UK, the latest national climate change risk assessment by the HM Government Committee on Climate Change (2017) has evaluated the risks for health and health systems posed by the impacts of climate change on health. Compared with many parts of the world, the UK has a relatively mild climate. However, this means that the national population and care systems are not well adapted to 'extreme' events that might seem less serious in other countries with a more variable climatic regime. For example, temperatures of 25–32°C trigger heat alerts in the UK health system, although these might seem more 'normal' summer temperatures in other countries. Although events such as extreme drought and hurricanes are not considered likely events in the UK, the Climate Change Risk Assessment (CCRA) indicates concern about the increasing risk of heat waves and flooding and recognises that very cold weather involving prolonged snow and ice will continue to occur (although cold weather events are projected to occur less often over the long term). It is acknowledged that planning for these events is made more difficult because the changing frequency of extreme weather events over the long term is more difficult to predict than trends in average climatic trends, so that there is a good deal of uncertainty involved (Oven et al., 2012). The CCRA indicates the need to improve nationwide measures to ensure that there is ongoing preparedness for such events in various sectors, including health and social care. As one of the priorities for future action it was noted that it will be necessary to ensure that guidelines and advice on preparedness issued by national agencies are appropriately applied at the local level.

Transdisciplinary and cross-sectoral planning: examples from applied research in England

Given the growing complexity of health and social services and the growing challenges presented by climate change, health and social care services are among those essential systems which have to adapt in order to be resilient to changing global conditions, and it has been argued that adaptation will require 'transformative' change (WHO, 2016). For example, it will be necessary to introduce new methods of working in order to become better adapted to environmental changes including extreme weather events (United Nations, 2015; WHO, 2017). Significant progress has been made in the National Health Service (NHS) for England through the development of a Sustainable Development Unit (SDU) (www.sduhealth.org.uk/) which emphasises the importance of learning from previous extreme events and the need to 'reset' systems to perform better under future conditions (Haines, 2012; Pencheon, 2013). Advice from the Sustainable Development Unit also recognises that a system as extensive and complex as the NHS is itself one of the *contributors* to environmental and climate change because its operations involve significant energy use, emission of various waste products and it occupies large areas of land. This means that, in addition to adapting to the 'external' impacts of climate change, 'internal' adjustments need to be made to ensure that 'green' practices will be introduced more extensively into routine activity of the health sector. Green social workers can also assist in the identification and implementation of such practices (Dominelli, 2012).

In addition to these reports from central government via the CCRA and SDU, the national government in England also issues other detailed guidance and recommendations for local agencies regarding actions to be taken to prepare for specific events such as heat waves, cold weather and floods, which are the types of extreme weather events most likely to occur in the

UK. These have been published by Public Health England (PHE) (PHE, 2015a, PHE, 2015b) and by the Department of Environment, Food and Rural Affairs (Defra) (Defra, 2014).

Thus, it is evident that a diverse array of national governmental agencies in England are involved in the development of extreme weather planning for the health sector, not all of which are directly positioned within the NHS. A considerable breadth of different sorts of professional and technical expertise are called into play, including not only fields of medical and social care, but also aspects of environmental science and management, epidemiology and engineering. The other countries that make up the United Kingdom (UK) also have similar planning mechanisms, although these are not discussed in detail in this chapter.

The system for extreme weather planning is further complicated by the need for vertical allocation of roles and responsibilities between national and local agencies. NHS England has published an *Emergency Preparedness, Resilience and Response Framework* (England, 2016) which sets out how responsibility for preparedness and response during emergencies, including extreme weather events, is distributed between national, regional and local agencies in the health and social care sector. Except in very extreme conditions affecting extensive areas of England, this responsibility rests at the more local level. It is, therefore, important that key actors at the local level are prepared and positioned to act during an emergency. Service coordination is an additional consideration in which green social workers have extensive expertise.

Local preparedness planning also involves engagement of a wide range of partners. In recent decades, England has moved towards a 'market model' for health and social care, through which local public sector commissioning groups are charged with the expenditure of government funds that are used to contract with a wider range of partners in the independent, as well as the state sectors, in order to provide services to the local population. In principle (though in practice this may be difficult to achieve) the commissioning process should take into account the extent to which service providers have in place measures that will make them resilient to extreme weather (Carr-West et al., 2011; Evans, 2011). The system of service commissioning at the local level involves partners in the NHS (administrative organisations), local government organisations (locally elected bodies) and adult social care service providers. Most recently, there have been moves towards greater devolution of responsibility for healthcare management through the establishment of Accountable Care Systems (ACS) involving locally devolved powers and responsibilities for both health and social care. This model for health and social care in England has some parallels with the Accountable Care Organization models used in the United States (US) (Shortell et al., 2014). The implementation of this model in England to date has been limited to the Greater Manchester region, where in 2016 a new administrative system was put in place giving local government greater autonomy over both health and social care provision. Plans for a further eight ACS schemes were also announced in 2017 (NHS England, 2017). The justification for these more devolved methods of health service management is that these should, in theory, encourage better coordination across different sectors to meet local needs more effectively, including more robust linkages between health and social care provision for clients with complex needs. At present, however, these systems are very new and it remains to be seen how effectively they will operate to ensure resilience to extreme weather.

From this brief summary, the picture emerges of a very complex and dynamic system of management for health and social care in England which implies that extreme weather planning requires both horizontal and vertical integration and coordination through various public and independent sector agencies. In the next part of this chapter we present one example of applied research which explored through local case studies what might be an effective, adaptable approach to address this situation.

An illustration from England of transdisciplinary working to address the complex issue of extreme weather resilience in health and social care

In this section we illustrate the potential of transdisciplinarity to address the complex issue of extreme weather resilience in health and social care. We consider this issue with reference to the case study of a research project carried out in England, designed to develop a transdisciplinary and cross-sectoral approach to planning for extreme weather events in the health and social care sector. This project, entitled *Built Infrastructure for Older People's Care in Conditions of Climate Change* (BIOPICCC) (www.dur.ac.uk/geography/research/researchprojects/biopiccc/) was funded by the Engineering and Physical Sciences Research Council UK under their *Adaptation and Resilience in the Context of Change network* (ARCC), and carried out between 2009 and 2012 in parts of England. The funding source reflects the fact that this was a transdisciplinary project engaging specialists in environmental science and engineering, as well as public health and the social sciences spanning the interface with health research including the sociology of health, health geography and green social work. The research team engaged with a range of policymakers and service providers working at the local level in two case study local authority areas with the aim of making health and social care for older people more resilient to extreme weather. BIOPICCC demonstrated the importance of cross-sectoral working and collaboration with local communities during extreme weather events. It also illustrated the scope for vertical as well as horizontal coordination and knowledge exchange since it has helped to inform national strategy making in the UK, including the 2013 *National Adaptation Programme* for the UK (Defra, 2013) and the *Climate Change Risk Assessment for 2017* (HM Government Committee on Climate Change, 2017).

Our overall approach was informed by, and contributed to, research on complex socioecological systems as they relate to human health, which are also reviewed elsewhere (Curtis and Riva, 2010a, Curtis and Riva, 2010b). In our research findings from the BIOPICCC project (Curtis et al., 2017) we identified evidence illustrating key attributes of complex networked systems. These include features such as: diversity of agents operating through linked networks; a degree of openness of different parts of the system, so that change in one part of the network influences the operation of other parts; and a tendency to develop in ways that are 'path-dependent' (influenced by previous experience). Complex systems like those providing health and social care are also 'emergent', being dynamic and subject to change that is difficult to predict, with capacity for self-organisation and interactive co-evolution of different parts of the system.

Given the diverse composition of our academic team we were able to demonstrate the value of a transdisciplinary approach to researching the interplay between environmental processes linked to extreme weather events, and the various (built, institutional and social) infrastructure systems upon which health and social care depend. For example, in the initial stages of the project we assessed local variability in hazard and vulnerability across England, in order to identify parts of the country where it might be especially relevant and useful to carry out case study research (Oven et al., 2012). We collated and mapped information at the scale of local authorities which are key administrative units for coordination and management of health and social care. The indicators we used included demographic projection data to map trends in the growth of the older population, in order to identify areas where large relative and absolute numbers of people in the oldest age groups were currently located, where these were expected to expand most rapidly in future, and also where there were concentrations of relatively disadvantaged and socially isolated groups who may be less resilient to extreme weather. We carried out modelling using the UK Climate Projections 2009 Weather Generator to generate estimates of projected trends in the likelihood of heat waves and cold weather events looking ahead to 2030–2050; and used the river and coastal flooding projections for the 2050s from the UK government's Foresight Flood and Coastal Defence Project (Environment Agency, 2004). In doing so, we deployed the knowledge of engineers and health geographers in the team to define the kinds of 'critical' extreme weather events that were likely to impact on health service infrastructures and on human health. We noted (Oven et al., 2012) that the areas likely to see the most rapid change in risk were not always those where the risks were currently greatest, and we considered that adaptation might be most challenging in places where weather-related risks were likely to be changing most quickly.

On the basis of this rapid nationwide risk assessment we identified a number of local authorities where we considered that issues of preparedness for extreme events in order to protect health and healthcare of older people were likely to be particularly pressing. We approached local NHS and government contacts in these areas to invite them to take part in our research and we were interested to find that there were more places volunteering to act as case studies than we were resourced to cover. This highlighted to us that for many local actors there was value in collaborating with an academic team which boosted their local resources for planning in this field. We maintained ongoing links with all those areas who had wanted to provide case studies, and we have subsequently followed up with them to explore how they could independently apply some of the learning from the two BIOPICCC case studies which were located in separate parts of the North and the South of England. The case study areas we selected were both in semi-rural areas served by small- to medium-sized towns, reflecting the significance of the issues in question for places outside the major cities in England. Extensions to the project also explored the relevance of our findings for older populations in London, giving us further insights into the experiences of ethnically diverse groups in major cities that were not the focus of the main BIOPICCC study.

The selection process for our case studies illustrated the geographical variability and complexity of the challenges we were aiming to assess. It was clear that, even within a relatively small country such as England, preparedness and resilience strategies would need to be adapted to quite different local conditions across the country. At the same time, there were clear parallels among some different localities in the types of problems they were likely to face, indicating that individual case studies chosen purposively to be representative of certain constellations of hazard and vulnerability might usefully help to inform strategy in other similar localities.

We therefore piloted our local research strategy with preparatory fieldwork in a third area in the North of England, which shared some of the attributes of our selected study areas. This helped us to identify the kinds of local partners with whom we would need to work and what kinds of issues might arise. We were also able to test aspects of our methodology before using them in our main case study. In this initial trial of our approach, we found that it was valuable to be able to engage with partners working in professional roles in various health and social care and other sectors, as well as with informants from the informal sector, many of whom were older people with complex health and social care needs. A key finding that re-emerged at various points in the research, was that informal networks were especially important as 'first responders', often taking critical action before the formal emergency services and health and social care agencies were able to reach the affected communities and intervene (Wistow et al., 2015). It was further noted that there were implications in terms of socially constructed and gendered roles of carers, who were predominantly women, reflecting other research which also emphasises the significance of women's roles in building resilience to the impacts of disasters (Dominelli, 2013; Drolet et al., 2015). Recognising the need to include in our research informants who might be physically or mentally infirm, we tested our approach with respect to the ethical and practical issues that arise when working with these groups. This was important to help us ensure that our ethical frameworks for further case study work were robust and that our methods were feasible.

In the core case studies conducted for this project, we first worked with local participants to build up a picture of the diverse groups of actors in the formal and informal sectors that had an important role to play in resilience planning. We then brought representatives of these different actors together in group discussions, and also conducted individual interviews with other informants, especially older people who were frail or housebound. Participants identified numerous examples where cross-sectoral action and knowledge sharing were essential to prepare in advance for extreme weather events. Participants also described several instances when communication across the system helped to maintain some continuity of essential services during extreme weather events (Curtis et al., 2017). Those involved needed to be able to exchange information about the nature and location of problems or possible solutions as they were occurring, and there were several examples of local collaboration to redeploy or draw upon local assets, such as staff working in care agencies who lived nearby, four-wheel drive vehicles for transport, or neighbourly assistance in order to cope with disrupted transport and supply networks.

At the same time, it was clear that (as is typical of complex systems) communication across the network was often partial and sometimes failed completely. For example, local residents were sometimes unaware of the provision made for them by formal sector services in organised rest centres in their locality (Curtis et al., 2017) or felt that informal networks were more important than formal services during extreme conditions (Wistow et al., 2015). There were occasions when different parts of the formal care system did not communicate effectively with each other about the resources that they could have potentially combined to ensure that medical and social care services were available in the areas worst effected by extreme weather (Curtis et al., 2017).

Consistent with the idea of 'path dependency' and contingency of complex systems, we were able to confirm that much valuable information could be collected from the accounts given by individuals based on their personal experiences of extreme weather. More recent experiences figured most prominently in these accounts so that, for example, problems of very cold weather that occurred during 2010, just before our fieldwork took place, figured much more prominently than issues associated with heat waves. We noted at this point, and throughout the BIOPICCC project, that it was more useful to engage with local actors on the basis of their own experiences and priorities (mainly related to very cold weather and flooding) than to impose an agenda based purely on scientific climate change risk assessments, which tended at the time to be focused strongly on heat waves, in light of climate change scenarios and scientific assessments of outcomes in southern England during the 2003 heat wave events. Indeed, while the question of 'climate change' was referred to, it was not one around which it was helpful to frame our enquiry, since it tended to divert the discussion into contentious and not very constructive debate about whether climate change was a real phenomenon.

Our experience in this project contributes to a significant body of research showing why it is more productive to empower participants to play an active role in shaping the agenda and the basis for planning for extreme weather than to construct an approach solely on the basis of predictions of risk from experts in the medical, environmental or engineering sciences. The fact that we were able to combine a range of disciplinary approaches in our study, including capacity in social sciences, helped us to explore how we might draw upon previous experience of different types of extreme weather to build a shared vision of what might help to enhance resilience, and how workable, locally adapted preparedness strategies might usefully draw on local lay knowledge. For example, the use of participatory mapping and diagramming helped us to capture local knowledge to identify the built infrastructure to which continuous access was most essential for local users (Figures 29.1 and 29.2). At the same time, scientific knowledge was important in our discussions. For instance, it provided the basis to combine and visualise information about the nature and spatial distribution of local risks and the architecture of important infrastructural networks (Holden et al., 2013), and it helped to identify which might be the most vulnerable parts of the built infrastructure in local areas and how they might be strengthened. Green social workers should ensure that they acquire the skills relevant for translating scientific expertise to lay audiences and local/indigenous knowledges to experts (Dominelli, 2012).

Some of the learning we produced has subsequently led us to work with PHE to produce guidance for local actors which distils previously separate sets of advice focused on different types of extreme weather, into generic basic principles which would be helpful in various extreme weather scenarios, including those associated with heat, cold or flooding. These PHE specific guidelines were only one of several illustrations from our work of the need for local, regional and national systems to be well-integrated and the challenges of producing national guidance which can be suitably adapted to varying local conditions. We found that national agencies were very open to findings from local studies, which enabled them to assess the local effectiveness of their current advice and guidance and how it might need to be altered or differently communicated. The work we undertook also helped to inform the work of the NHS Sustainable Development Unit (Sustainable Development Unit, 2014) and a toolkit produced

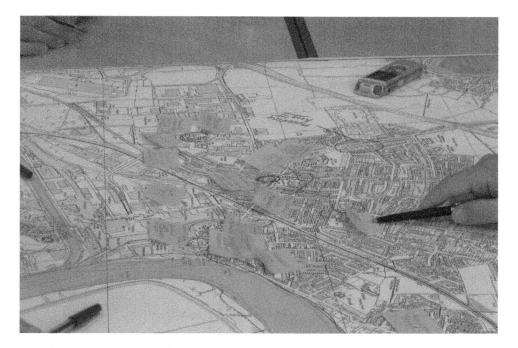

Figure 29.1 Service users and providers map the built infrastructure to identify vulnerability

During the consultation with service providers and service users a map of the local area was used to record local knowledge about the location of different parts of the complex care systems used by older people. This helped to identify parts of the service infrastructure that might be most vulnerable to effects of extreme weather.

Curtis et al.

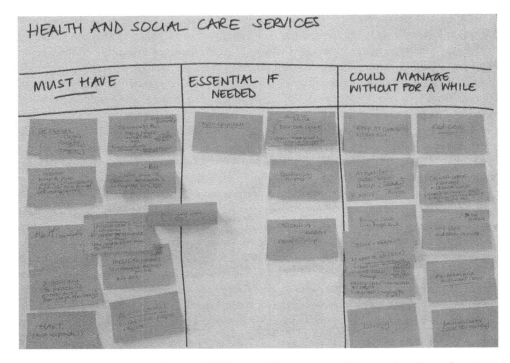

Figure 29.2 Prioritising service availability and impact according to duration of extreme weather event

Groups of participants in the discussion groups considered which parts of the local health and social care infrastructure were most essential for service users. The most essential parts of the system were often those to which older people needed continuous access. These should be prioritised in measures to improve resilience to extreme weather.

by the BIOPICCC project is referred to in the UK's National Adaptation Programme (Defra, 2013). Knowledge accumulated during this project contributed to the risk reviews conducted as part of the *Climate Change Risk Assessment* published in 2017 (HM Government Committee on Climate Change, 2017). We have discussed elsewhere (Curtis et al., 2017) how this cycle of vertical transmission of knowledge from the local 'grassroots' level to national government agencies, and back down to local level, in the form of revised national guidance informed by local experience, forms a crucial part of resilience planning.

Conclusions

The BIOPICCC approach seems relevant beyond the UK context and the wider literature suggests that similar strategies have been used elsewhere. The approach clearly reflects the 'green' principles that are at the core of this *Handbook*. The kind of approach we describe here, which enabled us to apply our understanding of complex health and social care systems in ways that help to make them more resilient to environmental risks, needs to be based on a transdisciplinary perspective. Risk assessment and planning for extreme events in these sectors has in the past tended to focus especially on scientific evidence which can be quantified and is amenable to systematic reviews using the kinds of methods that have been developed to inform evaluation and application of medical treatments. However, there is a growing realisation that qualitative research which captures local knowledge, especially when undertaken in combination with scientific knowledge, allows us to better understand how expertise and assets can be deployed more effectively during emergencies. A limitation of in-depth qualitative studies is their restricted applicability to the settings where they have been carried out. However, as more qualitative studies of this type are undertaken, there is increasing scope for quasi-systematic assessment of information from multiple studies (for example, using constant comparison techniques) drawing out the whole body of evidence that they represent. Green social workers constantly collect qualitative evidence in communities and more of this can be made available to other sciences. This will help researchers to identify elements which may be more widely and internationally applied to help inform local practice, as well as identifying aspects of local experience that are strongly contingent upon local conditions and which may not be transferrable to other situations. Green social work has a lot to contribute, in terms of methods and empirical evidence, to such work. This can help local communities acting in collaboration with other agencies working at regional, national and international scales to take effective steps to build preparedness for extreme weather.

References

Carr-West, J., Lucas, L. and Thraves, L. (2011). *Risk and Reward: Local Government and Risk in the New Public Realm*. Local Government Information Unit (LGiU), London. Available on www.lgiu.org.uk/wp-content/uploads/2012/04/Risk-and-Reward.pdf [Accessed 19 July 2017].

Curtis, S., Oven, K. J., Wistow, J., Dun, C. E. and Dominelli, L. (2017). Adaptation to extreme weather events in complex local health care systems: the example of older people's health and care services in England. *Environment and Planning C: Politics and Space*, in press.

Curtis, S. and Riva, M. (2010a). Progress report: Health geographies I: Complexity theory and human health. *Progress in Human Geography*, 34: 215–223.

Curtis, S. and Riva, M. (2010b). Progress report: Health geographies II: Complexity and health care systems and policy. *Progress in Human Geography*, 34: 513–520.

DEFRA (Department for Environment, Food and Rural Affairs) (2013). National Adaptation Programme. Available from https://www.gov.uk/government/publications/adapting-to-climate-change-national-adaptation-programme [Accessed 29 July 2017].

DEFRA (2014). *The national flood emergency framework for England*. Available on www.gov.uk/government/publications/the-national-flood-emergency-framework-for-england [Accessed 29 July 2017].

Dominelli, L. (2012). *Green Social Work*, Cambridge, UK: Polity Press.

Dominelli, L. (2013). Mind the gap: Built infrastructures, sustainable caring relations and resilient communities in extreme weather events. *Australian Social Work*, 66(2): 204–217. doi:http://dx.doil.org/10.1080/0312407X.2012.708764

Drolet, J., Dominelli, L., Alston, M., Ersing, R., Mathbor, G. and Wu, H. (2015). Women rebuilding lives post-disaster: Innovative community practices for building resilience and promoting sustainable development. *Gender and Development*, 23: 433–448.

England, N. (2016). *NHS England emergency preparedness, resilience and response framework*. Available on www.england.nhs.uk/wp-content/uploads/2015/11/eprr-framework.pdf [Accessed 29 July 2017].

Environment Agency (2004). *Foresight flood and coastal defence project*. Bristol, UK: Environment Agency.

Evans, S. (2011). *Climate change and sustainable public services. ICL-UK/British Society of Gerontology Think Piece*. March 2011. Available on file:///C:/Users/dgg3kjo/Downloads/pdf_pdf_166.pdf [Accessed 19 July 2017].

Haines, A. (2012). Sustainable policies to improve health and prevent climate change. *Social Science and Medicine*, 74: 680–683.

HM Government Committee on Climate Change (2017). *UK Climate Change Risk Assessment 2017*. London: HMSO. Available on www.gov.uk/government/uploads/system/uploads/attachment_data/file/584281/uk-climate-change-risk-assess-2017.pdf [Accessed 19 July 2017].

Holden, R., Val, D., Burkhard, R. and Knodwell, S. (2013). A network flow model for infrastructures at the local scale. *Safety Science*, 51–60.

IPCC (Intergovernmental Panel on Climate Change) (2014). *Climate change: 2014 synthesis report*. Available on www.ipcc.ch/pdf/assessment-report/ar5/syr/SYR_AR5_FINAL_full_wcover.pdf [Accessed 29 July 2017].

NHS England (2017). *Next Steps on the NHS Five-year Forward View*. London: NHS England.

Oven, K. J., Curtis, S. E., Reaney, S., Riva, M., Stewart, M. G., Ohlemuller, R., Dunn, C. E., Nodwell, S., Dominelli, L. and Holden, R. (2012). Climate change and health and social care: Defining future hazard, vulnerability and risk for infrastructure systems supporting older people's health care in England. *Applied Geography*, 33: 16–24.

Pencheon, D. (2013). Developing a sustainable health and care system: Lessons for research and policy. *Journal of Health Services Research and Policy*, 18: 193–194.

Public Health England (2015a). *Cold weather plan for England, 2013*. Available on www.gov.uk/government/collections/cold-weather-plan-for-england [Accessed 29 July 2017].

Public Health England (2015b). *Heatwave plan for England 2014*. Available on www.gov.uk/government/uploads/system/uploads/attachment_data/file/429384/Heatwave_Main_Plan_2015.pdf [Accessed 29 July 2017].

Shortell, S., Addicott, R., Walsh, N. and Ham, C. (2014). *Accountable Care Organizations in the United States and England: Testing, Evaluating and Learning What Works*. London: Kings Fund.

Sustainable Development Unit (2014). *Healthy, Sustainable and Resilient Communities*. London: Public Health England Sustainable Development Unit. Available on www.sduhealth.org.uk/areas-of-focus/community-resilience.aspx [Accessed 29 July 2017].

United Nations (2015). *Sendai framework for disaster risk reduction 2015–2030*. Available on www.preventionweb.net/files/43291_sendaiframeworkfordrren.pdf [Accessed 29 July 2017].

WHO (2012). *Strategy and action plan for healthy aging in Europe 2012–2050*. Available on www.euro.who.int/__data/assets/pdf_file/0008/175544/RC62wd10Rev1-Eng.pdf?ua=1 [Accessed 29 July 2017].

WHO (2016). *Reform of WHO's Work in Health Emergency Management*. Available from http://apps.who.int/gb/ebwha/pdf_files/WHA69/A69_30-en.pdf?ua=1&ua=1&ua=1 [Accessed 29 July 2017].

WHO (2017). *Health topics: Health systems*. Available on www.who.int/topics/health_systems/en/ [Accessed 29 July 2017].

Wistow, J., Dominelli, L., Oven, K. J., Dunn, C. E. and Curtis, S. (2015). The role of formal and informal networks in supporting older people's care during extreme weather events. *Policy and Politics*, 43: 119–135.

Part IX
Industrial and urban issues

30
Sowing the seeds
A green social work project in Sri Lanka

Yasmin Perera

Introduction

Sri Lanka's disaster scenarios include annual floods, droughts, the 2004 Tsunami and human-made disasters covering large garbage dumps, industrial effluents and polluted waterways. The Social Work Programme at the National Institute of Social Development (NISD) which is responsible for social work training has a Disaster Management Unit. While useful once disasters occur, it does not cover the country's serious environmental protection problems. In the 21st century, it is crucial that Sri Lanka's social work training incorporate environmental protection in the curriculum. This chapter explores a project on environmental protection that involved students from NISD and this author, their supervisor.

My concerns about environmental degradation in Sri Lanka resulting from perennial issues of waste disposal including plastic prompted me to support my neighbourhood in addressing these. I have not studied environmental social work, but rose to the challenge after some reading. Following various discussions between NISD and the local municipality, Dehiwala Mount Lavinia Municipality (DMM) agreed that four final year social work students that I supervised would undertake a six-month environmental social work project.

With limited literature, I had a steep learning curve. The project is indebted to Lena Dominelli who visited Sri Lanka after the tsunami, and understood the need to build capacity in Sri Lankan social work. Using her book, *Green Social Work*, as the foundation, I proposed a project with a two-fold agenda: demonstrating the integration of theory and practice in supervising students to foster the further development of social work in Sri Lanka; and introducing environmental social work to generate professional social work interest in and critical discussion of environmental degradation.

Serious environmental issues in Sri Lanka

Garbage disposal: plastic and polythene

For over a decade the media have highlighted the problems of garbage and plastic with headlines such as:

> The rot piles up as blame game continues among residents, local councils and recycling plants.
> *(News, 2016)*

> Drowning in waste: Garbage problems out of control, No land, no money, no options for solutions.
>
> *(Christopher, 2016)*

Hikkaduwa et al.'s claim that:

> the composition of solid waste in Sri Lanka is mainly polythene, plastic waste and shopping bags. An important issue in addressing this is the lack of appropriate waste separation mechanisms.
>
> *(2015: 2)*

They maintain that storing waste in polythene/polybags, a widespread practice, leads to degradation inside the bags which create issues including leachate and bad odour. Waste can be turned into resources, if separation is practiced at source. However, habits and mind-sets are hard to change. Until attitudes change, municipalities will need to contend with mixed waste.

To reduce the use of plastic shopping bags, some supermarkets offer discounts for using reusable bags. However, limited public awareness means very few people use these. Staff automatically put items into plastic bags. To achieve sustainable change, explaining the reasons for not using plastic to management, staff, and consumers, is essential.

The health hazards of using plastic have also been highlighted recently (Ismail, 2017). Dr Gunathilake, director of the National Poisons Information Centre, warns that food can be contaminated through the leaching effects of non-food grade plastic. Sri Lankan consumers are not informed of whether food grade plastic is used or not.

Coastal pollution

Nordrum (2015) estimates that, in 2010, Sri Lanka ranked fifth among countries polluting the oceans by dumping plastic and polythene into the sea and harming marine life. The Federation of Environmental Organizations Sri Lanka (2015), highlighted the seriousness of Sri Lanka's impact in this regard because the four top pollutants had populations of over 80 million, Sri Lanka's was only 20 million, making Sri Lanka the biggest pollutant per capita. This behaviour requires urgent intervention.

Carving a niche for a green social work project

Environmental goals of the Dehiwala Mount Lavinia Municipality

Dehiwala Mount Lavinia Municipality is the second largest in Sri Lanka. The students interviewed the Municipality's deputy commissioner, Mrs Balasooriya, to prioritise the Municipality's environmental goals. Mrs Balasooriya confirmed media reports that indicated that its environmental priority was garbage disposal. The lack of suitable disposal facilities resulted in their using a huge dump site at an adjoining Urban Council Area, Karadiyana, where appropriate standards were not followed. Various interested parties and local communities had instigated numerous court cases over its very serious problems to resolve these. The Waste Management Authority Western Province (WMAWP) was given control and standards are improving. There is a court order to create a composting area for separated biodegradable waste.

Although the Municipality distributed leaflets and garbage collectors informed residents to separate waste, many did not comply. Separating garbage was particularly problematic in high-rise buildings where non-complying individuals could not be identified. Penalties for non-compliance are due to be introduced.

A particular problem was residents using plastic bags for food waste separation. Without mechanized facilities, garbage collectors have to remove food waste from these bags for composting by hand, but often refuse because it is dirty work. Residents who comply complain that their efforts are wasted when garbage collectors mix all garbage together. Consequently, much biodegradable matter is not composted or contains plastic pieces, diminishing its quality, and the possible reduction in quantity is not achieved.

The deputy commissioner indicated that as dirty plastic bags could not be recycled, their disposal was difficult. Not separating these from recyclable non-biodegradable waste resulted in their being dumped in landfill sites. Thus, reducing the use of plastic bags would be environmentally beneficial. Furthermore, dengue fever is a serious health hazard in the area. Stagnant water in plastic bags provides a habitat for the dengue-bearing mosquito.

The Municipality's beaches suffer coastal pollution because canals bring in plastic bottles and other plastic pollutants. Littering is rife and not penalised. Clean-ups are not effective as there is nowhere to dispose of the rubbish as the Municipal garbage trucks cannot cross the railway line to pick it up. Without an alternative, people bury, burn or dump rubbish inappropriately. It was considered valuable to address this problem in this project.

The Central Environmental Authority

The Pilisaru National Solid Waste Management Project, managed by the Central Environmental Authority, comes under the purview of the Ministry of Mahaweli Development and Environment of Sri Lanka. The project director, Wimal Wimaladasa, was interviewed in March 2017. He stated that there are many plans afoot to address Sri Lanka's Solid Waste Management (SWM). Initiatives include: source segregation at generation; composting; fertilizer production; recycling of items such as plastics and polythene; minimising usage of thin polythene of less than 20 microns; incineration; sanitary landfills; and waste for energy projects. The Pilisaru Project also encourages recycling and reduced usage of plastics and polythene in communities, schools and other areas. Also, biodegradable paper bags are being manufactured and promoted as an alternative to plastic bags. He indicated that Pilisaru will work jointly with this project in relation to beach clearance as a part of their SWM objectives in the DMM.

Karadiyana garbage dump

Interviewees did not mention the impact of Karadiyana, the garbage dump used by Dehiwala Mount Lavinia Municipality, on local residents. Several newspapers did. It is alleged that 'Karadiyana, is the largest garbage dumping site in South Asia' (Sabry, 2016), and includes hospital waste and toilet sewage. This has poisoned water, preventing the use of 77 wells. Nearly 6,000 families living nearby face 400–500 metric tonnes of garbage being dumped there daily. Serious health issues prevail. One in three has had dengue fever and respiratory problems are common. Karadiyana is a human-made disaster.

Moreover, the National Environment Winning Movement (NEWM), claims that the garbage in the area contains highly toxic dioxins (Sabry, 2016), and contamination of the nearby Bolgoda Lake has caused many of the 21 indigenous fish species to become virtually extinct.

Social work and the physical environment

Today, awareness of the devastating impact of human behaviour on environmental degradation and sustainability of nature and humankind is growing rapidly. Social work which mainly focused on the social environment is redefining its scope. An increasing number of authors argue that social work has a crucial role in this changing world and needs to change its frameworks of practice to include the physical environment (Dominelli, 2011; Peeters, 2012; Gray et al., 2013).

To gain an appreciation of environmental theory in social work and develop a suitable theory-based framework of practice as a learning experience for students, various theoretical approaches were explored. Conservation social work argues that ecological social work's focus on persons-in-context is to be expanded to include the physical environment's interrelationships between humans and non-human animals. This includes 'thoughtful stewardship of natural resources, and advocacy and skills for environmental health and resilience' (University of Denver Graduate School of Social Work, n.d. page 1). Dewane (2011: 5) insists that 'if social workers know that context is a prime determinant for quality of life, the deteriorating natural world must become part of social workers' concern'. Dominelli (2012: 25), who invented green social work, promotes a very broad framework for practice. It incorporates socio-political and economic factors that contribute to inequalities in society and destruction of nature, and includes 'protecting the earth's flora and fauna' as a legitimate task for green social work.

Having considered the literature discussed in this section, a project to assist the DMM by working with the community to develop more effective garbage separation practices; reduce plastic usage; address garbage disposal problems; coastal and marine pollution; and ultimately protect the environment, was planned. The project rightly proclaimed itself a green social work project.

Dominelli (2012) and Scholberg (2013) refer to the concept of 'environmental justice' to explain the inequity in the distribution of environmental risks, with poorer communities facing more of these risks and the social injustice of this. This would apply to the garbage disposal methods used by municipalities wherein garbage dumps are situated in poorer areas like Karadiyana. Moreover, the communities there experience environmental risks in the form of health hazards, water contamination, and many ill effects of the environment including flies and odours, without having their voice heard. Sabry (2016), reported a resident as saying, 'We cannot even take our meals. As we start having our meals, our plates get covered with swarms of flies coming from the large dumpsite'. This is socially and environmentally unjust and unacceptable.

Scholberg (2013) and Dominelli (2012), maintain that the physical and 'natural' environment be considered an entity in its own right. Dominelli (2012: 25) sees environmental justice as including justice for the environment itself. An instance of this trend is the granting of 'legal personhood' for New Zealand's River Whanganui. Dominelli (n.d.: 1), argues that the theoretical and practice base of social work be widened 'to ensure that social and environmental justice are considered integral to any environmental … involvement by social workers'. Thus, extending the principles of environmental justice to the community and environment of Karadiyana, and pollution of the coast in the project would be very important.

Dominelli (2012: 194–195) suggests that social work practice incorporates 'a moral and ethical standpoint that is rooted in the 'spiritual notion of valuing relationships between people, other living entities and the physical realm', and promotes a duty of care and respect towards the world and all living things by working with communities in their 'everyday life practices'. In this case, garbage separation, reduction of plastic use and beach littering ought to be covered. To bring about some change where environmental injustice prevails, Dominelli (2012: 25) recommends community engagement in discussions that consider the interdependencies among diverse groups of people, the physical environment, and the 'deleterious impact' one group can have on another including the planet, and work to foster a social transformation of consciousness. Thus, discussions that highlight the importance of environmental justice for the people at Karadiyana, the poor beach communities, and the physical environments at Karadiyana – the coast, ocean and marine life – can now encompass the notion of a moral standpoint of a duty of care, and respect for the relationships between all things. These have produced strategies to promote the social transformations needed for sustainable change. Also, examining the prevailing unconscious anthropocentrism that underpins much of human behaviour around environmental justice was deemed important in changing social consciousness.

Other concepts that strengthen the arguments for a moral responsibility for the earth and could facilitate this social transformation include Mary's (cited in Duwane, 2011) idea of stewardship of the earth. Coates et al. (2006: 20) reference Berger's and Kelly's claim that humanity's 'task is to live in the knowledge of a connectedness to the earth, developing a compassionate awareness that . . . not only do other people and other species have a right to live, but a right to have a reasonable quality of life'. Coates' (2003) view that fostering a love of nature can transform values, can convince people to protect it because nature offers its own spiritual gifts to those accepting of it. The beach is loved by many, strengthening this and fostering a compassionate awareness about what is being destroyed will be very important in this project.

Most of these ideas are new for many Sri Lankans, especially the anthropocentrism and rights of the environment arguments. However, for Buddhists, the belief that all living things are sentient beings could facilitate the acceptance of such ideas.

The project

Target groups for intervention and implementation

The project is ongoing. It is targeting five sub-sections of the community in a small area of the DMM, to facilitate easier management, and enable the testing of the potential of different theoretical concepts to transform community consciousness. The project reached selected groups in the following locales:

- 16 apartment buildings;
- Four schools;
- Six religious institutions;
- Two independent supermarkets and three supermarket chains; and
- One beach community including restauranteurs and fisher folk.

Interventions, applied across the board to all targeted groups, aimed to:

- Evaluate current behaviour relating to garbage separation, plastic use and beach littering through observation and discussions.
- Promote the changes needed, particularly garbage separation, by outlining the municipalities' difficulties, the court orders, the penalties soon to be implemented, and damage to humans, animals, and the environment through use of plastic.
- Discuss strategies to reduce plastic, particularly shopping bags and promoting the 5-step strategy developed in the project:
    1. Always take a reusable bag or recycle bags when shopping.
    2. Select food not wrapped in plastic.

3   Avoid putting food in individual plastic bags when weighing.
4   Use reusable bags or request boxes at the checkout.
5   Have the reusable bags ready for next time.

- The project plans to take into account Dominelli's (2012: 194–195) argument that green social work incorporates the ethical and moral standpoints of environmental justice, social responsibility, duty of care for other beings and the planet during discussions that refer to Karadiyana and the destruction of the ocean, the beach and life forms therein with the various participating groups.
- Awareness programmes and workshops on the impact of plastic on the environment, animal life and human health.
- Exploring opportunities for recycling non-degradable material, including plastic, and making appropriate linkages between recyclers and community groups.
- Encouraging a spiritual transformation by fostering an appreciation of the interconnectedness with the earth, challenging the prevailing anthropocentrism, promoting a love of nature and stewardship, and evoking compassion and empathy for what is being destroyed. This will be done mainly in conjunction with religious organisations and incorporating religious teachings (insofar as they include these notions), reflections, rituals and prayer. As all religions consider supporting poor people, links with poor people at Karadiyana and the beach will be made.
- Highlighting the great impoverishment of the earth and its position as a 'victim' of human action.
- Highlighting that three months into the writing of this project on 14 April 2017 (Good Friday and Singhala/Tamil New Year's Day) the news in Sri Lanka focused on the disaster from the collapse of part of the biggest garbage dump by volume, Meethotamulla in Colombo (Karadiyana is the biggest by area). Methane build-up, a fire and heavy rain caused the dump to collapse, claiming at least 26 lives, damaging 145 houses, and displacing 645 persons (*News First*, 2017). Methane levels there remain dangerously high. All discussions that the project is having include the danger of a similar occurrence at Karadiyana. With the spotlight on Meethotamulla, people, receptive and empathic to the potential danger for Karadiyana, are willing to engage with recycling issues. This project also emphasises their moral and social responsibility to change behaviours.

Interventions in apartment buildings

Garbage separation was deemed most difficult to implement in apartment buildings, so 16 were selected for specific intervention. These were visited and their garbage areas observed. Students met security staff in all 16 buildings and the presidents of the Management Committees in five buildings. As the Committee members are usually unavailable during office hours, the students will contact them and the Committees of the other apartment buildings during weekends. All security staff knew of the need to separate garbage. This was done well in one apartment building; three separated garbage but placed it in plastic bags.

The second visit revealed improvements in three buildings with residents bringing food in buckets for emptying into the bins. Separation was more likely to happen where the Management Committee or security staff took an interest in it. One apartment building invited the students to a residents' meeting attended by 35 residents. Most were unaware of the extent of environmental damage wrought through plastic, became committed to reducing plastic bag usage, and were receptive to environmental justice issues.

> **A conversation of change**
>
> When a student was discussing garbage separation with a security staff member, a resident passing by commented, 'When are you going to stop all the separating business? It is such a nuisance for us'. The student explained the issues for the Municipality, the impact of the garbage on people at Karadiyana and environmental justice and social responsibility to this resident. He responded by saying, 'I had not thought about these things. You've convinced me to separate'.

Representatives from the apartment buildings will be invited to a meeting at the Municipality to discuss any unresolved garbage disposal and separation issues, create more awareness of the importance of reducing plastic and polythene usage, and provide feedback about changes that supermarkets (discussed later) may undertake, and their willingness to promote the '5 step guide to reducing plastic bag usage'. The social work students will undertake the roles of coordination and mediation between the Municipality and residents regarding complaints, facilitating exchanges of ideas to solve problems, and take educational roles in raising awareness.

Interventions with children and youth from schools and religious institutions: schools

Children were targeted on the basis of being more receptive to change and there being more opportunity to engage with them regularly through schools and religious groups to generate sustainable changes. Four schools were selected – two Singhala Schools and two Tamil Schools. Meetings with the principals of these indicated that they were aware of garbage separation and waste management and interested to comply, but found it difficult to get staff and students to cooperate. Four teachers interviewed from two of the schools were not very aware of the importance of waste separation and environmental damage from plastic. They became interested during the discussions and were willing to become involved in the project.

The social work students co-facilitated three awareness-raising programmes conducted by the CEA for students in three of the schools. As the CEA did not focus much on garbage separation or reduction of plastic use, they intend to have more awareness-raising programmes on these issues themselves. One school is planning an art project on the environment. Two first-year social work students were placed at two schools, two days per week for the first three months to assist with awareness-raising and engage with different concepts to explore social transformations. They will have access to students when teachers are absent.

Religious institutions and religious instruction programmes

One Muslim student met the head of the religious studies programme at one mosque and was able address 120 students at an assembly. Many were interested to become involved in the project. Two other mosques are also interested. The Imam of one will discuss this topic in the Jummah (Friday talk). The mosque will also sponsor an environmental leaflet and beach clean-up with their young people.

A Buddhist student met with the head monk of a Buddhist temple, who knew of the need to separate, but had a problem with the garbage not being collected regularly. Some people burnt their garbage along with plastic. Unaware of the danger of dioxin, the priest was interested to educate himself about it. This temple has a community with a women's group, a religious education programme and a group of parents to support this work. A residents' group in the neighbourhood might also participate. The student has met representatives of all these groups and all are interested in this project. Her first awareness programme was attended by 75 children and 25 parents. Future interventions in this community include plans to develop social responsibility in children via a beach walk, discussion of damage and beach clean-up by as many children as live along the beach. A fieldtrip to Karadiyana for members of the residents' group to gain an appreciation of the damage there, and awareness programmes for the women's group are also planned. This community presents many opportunities for community development on environmental issues.

I have written an article on this project for a Sunday paper to introduce green social work, and will undertake sessions at the Sunday School Programme in a Catholic church. The Pope's (2015) *Encyclical, the Laudato Si* has been a valuable resource for use among Christians as it contains the core notions espoused by green social work: environmental justice, ecological renewal, and transformation of consciousness. I wrote an article promoting this to the Catholic paper, and developed a PowerPoint presentation on this. A pastor of a local Methodist church based his entire Sunday sermon on this paper, and wanted the congregation to become involved in a beach clean-up.

Supermarkets

While working with the community groups to reduce the use of plastic shopping bags, this project also aims to work with supermarkets to consider ways of reducing the amount of plastic bags they give out to the community. The set-up at supermarkets is such that a number of plastic bags are used at the point of weighing because each item is placed in separate bags and the price tag seals it. The checkout is at another counter. Staff express concern that when consumers use unsealed reusable bags at the point of weighing, they could pick up more items on the way to the checkout. Strategies to change this set-up and find alternatives to the plastic bags will be needed to resolve these problems.

To date, a student has met with the managers of five supermarkets, three from outlets of the biggest chains, two independent supermarkets, and the Community Social Responsibility (CSR) unit of one chain. All except one were very interested in being involved in the project and many indicated that they had not thought of how their set-ups promoted the use of plastic bags. They were shown alternative cloth and net bags, which again they were interested in. With two of the chains further contact will be needed with their CSR units to explore possible changes to their policies. A manager from an independent supermarket indicated that methods of implementing changes at the point of weighing will be seriously considered. One manager did not think the habits of consumers could be changed.

After individual discussions to make contact and build rapport, the plan is for the DMM to invite representatives from the CSR units and branches of the supermarkets, the CEA and interested community members to a meeting to discuss strategies for reducing the use of plastic shopping bags. As a background, the topics identified to promote social transformation will be included. Also, the social responsibility of supermarkets for what they give out will be raised. The group will be invited to share ideas to deal with the issues. One suggestion developed by this project is for the supermarkets to explore the possibility of having video clips near the counters. These will show the plastic impact at Karadiyana and Meethotamulla dumpsites, the ensuing damage to the communities there, and danger to animal and marine life (the programmes to date indicated that the public is poorly informed about this damage), highlight Sri Lanka as the fifth highest ocean pollutant per capita with much of this coming from plastic, and outline the five steps to reduce plastic bag usage. If a video is not possible a request will be made to display some posters, preferably done by the school children. The social work students will undertake the social work roles of coordinating, consciousness-raising, mobilising, and promoting 'coproduction' of solutions (Dominelli, 2012).

The beach and ocean

The aim here is to find a sustainable strategy to address the issues of ocean pollution, degradation and beach littering, by fostering the social transformation inherent in the framework of the project and developing a sense of community and common ownership of a valuable resource for enjoyment, tourism and the fishing industry. The social work students have met with the Marine Conservation Department, the Coastal Guard and the Coastal Conservation Department to discuss strategies for managing the littering and pollution along the beach and ocean pollution from the canal. The main difficulty is access to the road to dispose of garbage.

Managers and staff of six beach restaurants have also been interviewed to discuss waste disposal and beach pollution. All managers were aware of the requirement to separate their waste, and except for one, were non-compliant due to a lack of knowledge about the importance of it, and lack of commitment on the part of staff. Almost all complained that the Municipal waste collection was irregular. Some dumped their garbage on the beach, buried it there or burned it. They were not aware of the toxic effects of burning plastic and were educated about this. Coastal Guard personnel undertook clean-ups but these were not consistent.

All those interviewed were interested in considering methods of preventing beach pollution and expressed a willingness to be involved in beach clean-ups if this could be coordinated. One mosque next to the beach has set a date for a clean-up. The plan is to coordinate a meeting between the DMM, the CEA, the Marine Conservation Department, the Coastal Conservation Department, Coastal Guard, restaurant staff, representatives from the mosque, beach dwellers, beach users, interested community people, and service clubs in the area to discuss strategies to keep the beach clean. It is intended to hold some awareness programmes for the beach community and Coastal Guard with the assistance of the Coastal Conservation Department. I have done such a programme for the Coastal Guard previously.

The finale for the project will be a big beach clean-up where all the groups that the project has worked with – apartment residents, school children, religious instruction participants, and the general community will be invited to participate. Awareness-raising activities of environmental damage and social responsibility discussions will be conducted, along with beach events and art displays by children to foster interest. The Coastal Conservation Department and the CEA have already agreed to support this. From these activities it is hoped that a group that will be interested in sustaining the beach environment and advocates for less pollution will emerge.

The Coastal Conservation Department and the Coastal Guard have requested a meeting with the DMM to consider avenues for preventing pollutants from the canals from flowing into the ocean, having bins located on the beach and getting garbage across the railway line for pick-up by the Municipal garbage vans. Taking on a coordinating role, the social work students plan to arrange a meeting to discuss getting these organisations and other stakeholders involved in developing solutions, and if necessary supporting them to advocate for solutions from the Municipality. Pilisaru's promise of support will be valuable here. Such participation would strengthen the community.

Common issues identified and interventions

Virtually all residents from the various groups complained that the garbage collection did not happen on a regular basis and that garbage collectors were often rude. The Municipality staff explained their difficulties in providing a regular service as the trucks were old, broke down often and the absenteeism rate among garbage collectors was high, with ill health often being the cause for this. Furthermore, the separation of garbage was a new initiative and Municipal staff continues to fine-tune the pick-up schedules. Adopting a mediating role, the students raised the concerns of the community with the DMM Municipal staff and explained to residents the issues of the Municipality with a request for understanding and patience. The issue will be resolved only when the Municipality has completed their schedules and addressed its logistical problems.

To address the complaint that garbage collectors were often rude, taking a supportive and encouraging role, the students held a meeting with the garbage collectors and their supervisors, to give empathy, recognition of their difficulties, appreciation of their valuable role, offer encouragement, and acknowledge their arduous jobs. Some garbage collectors were able to admit their rude behaviour and indicated this was often the result of their frustration with residents not separating the garbage appropriately, and creating more work for them. Using good 'active listening' skills and fostering good relationships is a role that social workers often take in community building and are inherent in green social work.

Evaluation of the project's progress and the capacity of green social work in Sri Lanka

The students have been successful in engaging interest in garbage separation by many sections of the community that they contacted and obtaining their participation. Some changes have been achieved in several apartment buildings and the networks needed for other interventions are underway. It is too early to comment on what changes the project will ultimately achieve and how sustainable these will be.

The social work students were very keen and worked hard within their capacities, to make good progress. Their feedback has been that they have never before had the supervision needed for environmental work, or been required to use a body of theory and link it to practice. They usually only practised with the skills they possessed naturally, the 'use of self'. In this project however, they are learning to articulate practice in specific detail rather than in general terms, and reflecting more deeply on using theory and identifying skills. Feedback from the field coordinator and students' faculty supervisor is similar to the students' in many ways. All comment that supervision has provided these students with a better capacity to integrate theory and practice. In my view, this is not necessarily due to any extraordinary skills that I possess, but a fundamental difference in standards between Australian and Sri Lankan social work education and practice. This demonstrates the dire need for capacity-building in Sri Lankan social work education and supervision to enable students to understand the more complex ideas and transformation of consciousness inherent in green social work.

Conclusion

With the numerous disasters, environmental degradation and environmental justice issues that Sri Lanka encounters, green social work practice would be very valuable for the country. Green social work requires an ability to think outside the box, analyse issues at the socio-political and economic levels, and have the capacity and confidence to articulate these, and advocate skilfully to ensure good results. These are areas to be developed within the NISD (National Institute of Social Development) social work curriculum.

A panel discussion celebrating International Social Work Day with Environmental Social Work and Sustainability indicated an interest among young social workers to engage in good practice around environmental issues. However, lack of expertise in the field and poor funding pose limitations. I suggest that this be considered a social justice issue because richer countries have resources to develop social workers' capacities more. Better pay and more opportunities for professional development means that Sri Lankan practitioners' abilities could be strengthened substantially. The global South with more environmental ills has fewer resources and capacity to address these. The support of organisations including the International Association of Schools of Social Work and International Federation of Social Workers and goodwill of skilled practitioners, particularly in green social work, would be enormously valuable for developing capacity in Sri Lanka. These issues are critical for the sustainability of earth itself, not just that country.

Finally, as an off-shoot of the project, the director of Pilisaru has approached NISD to do an environmental education programme for students and faculty. NISD plans to include an element of green social work in this. Following the disaster of Meetotamulla the Sri Lankan government proposes to ban plastic bags and other plastic products from September 2017.

References

Christopher, C. (2016). Drowning in waste: Garbage problems out of control, no land, no money, no options for solutions. *Sunday Times*, 16 January. Available on www.sundaytimes.lk/160619/news/drowning-in-waste-garbage-problems-out-of-control-197746.html [Accessed 23 March 2017].

Coates, J. (2003). *Ecology and Social Work: Towards a New Paradigm*. Halifax: Fernwood Books.

Coates, J., Gray, M. and Hetherington, H. (2006). An 'ecospiritual' perspective: Finally, a place for Indigenous approaches. *British Journal of Social Work*, 36: 381–399. Available at https://academic.oup.com/bjsw/article-abstract/36/3/381/1688811/An-Ecospiritual-Perspective-Finally-a-Place-for [Accessed 27 March 2017].

Dewane, C. (2011). Environmentalism and social work: The ultimate dsocial justice issue. *Social Work Today*, September/October, 11(5): 20. Available on https://sites.temple.edu/dewane/author/cdewane/ [Accessed 27 March 2017].

Dominelli, L. (n.d.) *Greening social work: Linking social and environmental justice in social work theory and practice*, University of Durham. Pdf provided by Dominelli.

Dominelli, L. (n.d). *Green social work and environmental justice in an environmentally degraded, unjust world*. Available at www.ulapland.fi/loader.aspx?id=738c09c1-fa9b-4475-af63-a506967870e1 [Accessed 27 March 2017].

Dominelli, L (2011). Climate change: Social workers' roles and contributions to policy debates and interventions. *International Journal of Social Welfare*, 20: 430–438.

Dominelli, L. (2012). *Green social work: From environmental crisis to environmental justice*, Cambridge, UK: Polity Press.

Federation of Environmental Organizations Sri Lanka (2015). *Sri Lanka vs The Ocean*, May 12. Available on http://feosl.org/?p=212 [Accessed 23 March 2017].

Gray, M., Coates, J. and Hetherington, T. (2013). Introduction: Overview of the last ten years and typology of ESW. In M. Gray, J. Coates, and T. Hetherington (Eds.), *Environmental Social Work*. London: Routledge, pp. 1–28.

Hikkaduwa, H. N., Gunawardana, K. W., Halwatura, R. U. and Youn, H. H. (2015). *Sustainable Approaches to the Municipal Solid Waste Management in Sri Lanka*. Paper presented at the 6th international conference on structural engineering and construction management, Kandy, Sri Lanka, 11th–13th December. Available on www.civil.mrt.ac.lk/conference/ICSECM_2015/book_3/book_3.pdf [Accessed 25 March 2017].

Ismail, I. (2017). Plastics detrimental to health and environment. *Daily Mirror*, 6 February.

News. (2016). The rot piles up as blame game continues among residents, local councils and recycling plants. *The Sunday Times*, 17 January. Available on www.sundaytimes.lk/160117/news/garbage-collection-and-recycling-in-the-dumps-178941.html [Accessed 22 March 2017].

News First (2017). Collapsing Meethotamulla garbage dump damages 145 houses, displaces 625 persons, 15 April.

Nordrum, A. (2015). *China, India, US Among World's Worst Marine Polluters: Country-By-Country Breakdown Of Plastics In Oceans*. IBT, 2 December. Available at www.ibtimes.com/china-india-us-among-worlds-worst-marine-polluters-country-country-breakdown-plastics-1813476 [Accessed 27 March 2017].

Peeters, J. (2012). The place of social work in sustainable development: Towards ecosocial practice. *International Journal of Social Welfare*, 21(3): 287–298.

Pope Francis. (2015). *Laudato Si. Encyclical letter on care for our common home*. Libreria Editrice Vaticana.

Sabry, H. (2016). Karadiyana: Largest garbage dumping site in South Asia. *Sunday Leader*, 17 January. Available on www.thesundayleader.lk/2016/01/17/karadiyana-largest-garbage-dumping-site-in-south-asia/ [Accessed 27 March 2017].

Scholberg, G. (2013). Theorising environmental justice: the expanding sphere of a discourse', *Environmental Politics*, 22(1): 37–55. Available at http://dx.doi.org/10.1080/09644016.2013.755387 [Accessed 25 March 2017].

University of Denver Graduate School of Social Work (n.d). *Global practice: Conservation social work*. Available on http://gsswblog.du.edu/globalpractice/about/conservation-social-work/ [Accessed 27 March 2017].

31
The ecological hazards of nuclear waste disposal

Tensions between aspirations for economic prosperity and community sustainability in a small Croatian municipality

Nino Žganec and Ana Opačić

Introduction

The Croatian small municipality of Dvor is located in south central Croatia. The war circumstances during the 1990s in the former Yugoslavia heavily affected this part of the country which was populated mostly by a Serbian population. The whole territory around Dvor was occupied by a Serb minority for almost five years until Croatian forces conducted a military operation after which majority of Serbian residents left. Some of them decided to return till the end of the 1990s. Since the mid-1990s, the municipality of Dvor as well as its surrounding area started their socio-economic recovery which is progressing very slowly. Nowadays the municipality has 5570 inhabitants that are distributed through 64 small settlements (villages). Croatia built the first and only nuclear power plant in the former Yugoslavia as a joint venture with the Republic of Slovenia. The nuclear power station began working in 1983. According to the agreement between Republic of Slovenia and Republic of Croatia, the nuclear waste was to be jointly considered once the containers surrounding the nuclear power plant became full. This meant that initially, the Republic of Croatia would have to find the way of how and where to store the nuclear waste. The first information about the possible location for disposing of the nuclear waste around the municipality of Dvor began to appear during the 1990s. But it was a bit later that the first studies on environmental impact were conducted. However, all the processes regarding the disposal of nuclear waste in this area were conducted far from the eyes of local citizens with only sporadic and partial information being given to the interested public. With the aim of finding out hidden and visible processes that occurred around this development in the municipality of Dvor, research was carried out among key stakeholders. The special interest in conducting this research was to consider the actual and potential interest and influence that social work as profession could have on the whole situation and what lessons could be learned for the future development of nuclear waste disposal processes.

Literature review

Since the beginning of its professional development, social work has had to address tensions about which dominant orientation and influences should be taken into account when human development is studied and how it could be improved. In both the everyday social work practice and people's lives in Croatia, individualism is growing as the dominant paradigm while collectivism is considered old, conservative and unpopular. The community as a romantic aspiration is a concept from earlier times and faces major difficulties in empowering the ideas of mutual responsibility, solidarity and understanding for others. Besides, Jani and Reisch (2011) note that the relationship between persons and the environment is viewed in a static, individually oriented manner that fails to recognise the differences that exist, among and within nations, based on cultural norms and political-economic realities. Although individualism is emphasised, the immediate victims of the (political) decisions are communities and community members. Poor communities that very often have neither capacity nor resources for their own defence come under particularly strong political pressure. The phenomenon of the unequal impact of environmental degradation upon poor people was elaborated by Bullard (2000), Pyles (2007), Dominelli (2012) and (2013a,b) and others. Bullard (1993–1994) introduced and defined the term 'environmental racism'. Dominelli (2013a,b) extensively elaborates the concept of 'environmental justice' that had been earlier introduced by Ungar (2002), but not linked to social justice as Dominelli has done.

With the introduction of the concept of green social work, Dominelli (2012) opened a new era in elaborating relationships between people and their environments inside the social work profession. As noted by Dominelli green social work:

> is a form of holistic professional social work practice that focuses on the: interdependencies amongst people, the social organisation of relationships between people and the flora and fauna in their physical habitats; and the interactions between socio-economic and physical environmental crises and interpersonal behaviours that undermine the well-being of human beings and planet Earth. It proposes to address these issues by arguing for a profound transformation in how people conceptualise the social basis of their society, their relationships with each other, living things and the inanimate world.
>
> *(2012: 25)*

Through several decades of elaborating upon the relationships between people and their environment – for example, Germain (1973); Grinnell (1973); Coates (2004); Mckinnon (2008); Bay (2010); and Alston (2013), to mention a few – most did not write so clearly about the concrete roles of the social workers in tackling environmental issues as did Dominelli (2012), Jarvis (2013) or Williams and Tedeschi (2013). In describing the green social worker's tasks, Dominelli (2012) mentions activities that are oriented towards protection of the human rights violations, engagement in the process of bettering health and social services provisions, and influencing the economic system that perpetuates inequalities. A clear idea in the concept of green social work is that of empowering social workers to tackle structural issues when dealing with such visible deterioration in the human environment as has been witnessed during the past few decades. A similar approach can be found in Grey et al. (2012) when they argue that social workers' interest in working with environmental issues opens a space for radicalising the profession. This gives social work the chance for revitalising its own roots and overcoming neoliberal influences. The 'Global Agenda for Social Work and Social Development', adopted by three global organisations – IFSW (International Federation of Social Workers), ICSW (International Council of

Social Welfare), and IASSW (International Association of Schools of Social Work) – recognises a collective commitment to promote social and economic equalities, human rights and dignity, social relationships, and environmental sustainability (*Global Agenda*, 2012).

The differences between natural and human-made influences and disasters in the environment should be clarified. But regardless of cause, 'disasters are conceptualized as having three phases: immediate relief, recovery and reconstruction' (Dominelli, 2015: 661). The social work profession faces major challenges around the consequences of the diverse impacts of climate change and different types of disasters increasingly caused by humans. The sustainability of the natural environment is insecure and provokes professional reactions requiring answers. First, social work should show appropriate professional curiosity, find theoretical and methodological approaches to tackle these issues, and actively include all stakeholders in the process. Social work educators, students, and practitioners together with service users and other citizens are challenged in their practice and their lives to consider complex, interrelated, and systemic problems that require new approaches and innovations. Relying on professional principles and values, and moving towards more just communities, contemporary social workers should find and offer new ways of opposing current destructive tendencies to create sustainable societies.

Case study of the Dvor municipality in Croatia

This chapter presents a case study of a small Croatian municipality, Dvor, which was developmentally underprivileged for a long time, and currently faces decisions about disposing of nuclear waste on its territory. Municipality Dvor has a very low development index (38.59 per cent of the Croatian average). In the early 1990s, it was exposed to war, and its population includes Serbian nationals that depict a minority ethnic group in Croatia. Ethnic relations have become very complex, and after the War, the majority of the Serb population left, while the Croatian population previously living in Bosnia and Herzegovina has settled in Dvor. The municipality is along the border with Bosnia and Herzegovina, isolated from the centres of power, facing strong demographic decline and holding a disadvantaged overall socio-political status (Miljenović, 2015). The general atmosphere in the community is nihilistic and not supportive of locally driven development (Miljenović, 2015). This is a result of a long period where Dvor, as an underdeveloped community, to a great extent relied on the central Yugoslavian government for funds. When the demographic structure changed after Croatia's Homeland War, it continued to be dependent of external support. Dvor municipality faces the same problems of the deconstructed communities typical of many other post-war communities in Croatia (Miljenović and Žganec, 2012). These are communities where the social fabric, including its social relations and economic background, has completely deteriorated. After 1995, these communities have had to deal with establishing new relations and finding new development perspectives.

In 2015, the central government imposed a project of developing a nuclear waste disposal unit in the former military complex in the area of Trgovska Gora located in Dvor municipality. This story, however, is much older. It goes back to the period of Yugoslavia, but has now become more intensified under the auspices of the European Union. Croatia had previously an obligation to take care of its own nuclear waste which had so far been stashed in Krško, a joint nuclear power station with Slovenia.

This example illustrates several key concepts in framing green social work: environmental justice, human rights violation, deterioration of the quality of life, and environmental tendencies towards degradation within the context of continuing economic inequalities. Furthermore, it was particularly important to recognise community processes in order to better understand community social capital.

The data presentation is organised to address: a) strategies that decision-makers use to deliver ecologically risky action in a community; b) community processes that are triggered by ecological issues; and c) human rights discourses and possibilities of structurally engaged social work practice. This research is based on multiple data sources – interviews with key stakeholders, activists, social workers and residents, media sources, and researchers' participatory observation. Interviews were conducted with 19 key informants that were somehow involved directly in the process: four out of eight representatives of the local municipality (LM), two out of three social workers (SW), three local activists heading two activist organisations (ACT), six representatives of the youth population (YOU) working within two local youth associations, and four local farmers (FA) as members of the municipal council composed of 15 members overall. The data were analysed using thematic analysis (Braun and Clarke, 2006).

Strategies to deliver a nuclear waste disposal project within a community

The first research topic was to cover strategies in delivering nuclear waste to the community. There is a strong sense of violated environmental justice and one cannot avoid thinking about this initiative in the context of perpetuating economic inequalities. The consequences of nuclear waste disposal on human health still are not visible. However, there is a sense that the distribution of environmental burdens among the local population is not just and that decision-making processes about this project are not transparent. Several sub-topics were included here: placing the burden onto a community already burdened by economic inequalities, prevailing negative attitudes, acknowledged multidimensional developmental risks (ecological, economic, political, and social), information strategies that reduced substantially citizens' resistance, and unclear ideas about how this issue will develop further.

Burdening a disadvantaged community

The community that has already suffered severe developmental issues now faces additional ecological burdens. The community is characterised by chronic economic deprivation accompanied by a general atmosphere of nihilism, lack of developmental prospects and a decreased population figures:

> Simply, I have a feeling that we have all stumbled down, that we have lost a faith that anything positive is possible. If they ignore you, if they don't respect what you have to say, if they don't respect your rights ... I don't know about you, but I have a feeling that other people decide on our destiny, our future.
>
> *(YOU, 4)*

Economic deprivation is recognised not solely as a result, but also a long-term process wherein local resources were neither recognised nor used properly. This is due to previously described conditions when the community was not supported to be autonomous and proactive in its past. In this context, the notion of developing nuclear waste disposal facilities was to a great extent received with a prevailingly negative attitude. This local community's resistance was explained through the multidimensional developmental risks that would occur if the nuclear disposal facility were to be established. People recognised risks not only in ecology, but also in the local economy, social relations and community stigmatisation. Risks were already evident during transportation because the traffic infrastructure was not adequate for this purpose. Several informants pointed out health risks having in mind that terrain for nuclear waste disposal is close to a residential area and water sources along the border with Bosnia and Herzegovina.

Some informants identified direct threats to the local economy by reducing the quality of agricultural products. However, the greatest threat was most often found in further *local community stigmatisation* that would also transfer to local agriculture:

> Because people's consciousness . . . no matter how much something can be good, he [*sic*] always has it in his head that it is bad, and runs far from it . . . so just thinking about local honey, [he] says NO, he leaves and turns away . . . regardless, it can be a thousand times OK, but this is it.
>
> (ACT, 2)

Some informants have concluded that this process will eventually lead towards total community deprivation and further depopulation.

Since previous opinions clearly demonstrate local community resistance and scepticism, an informant recognised that *leading figures have deliberately chosen information strategies that favour the lowest level of citizens' resistance*. However, these increased the local population's sense that the process is not transparent. These information strategies include a *lack of consistent information*. This would change from time to time; for example, changing the site of the terrain that would house the disposal unit, alongside the *lack of information or even hiding information*. Information on developing the nuclear waste disposal facility was hidden from its very beginning and some informants found about it accidentally. Some question whether the disposal unit for radioactive waste has already been built, but information about that is unavailable. Also, some information that was distributed was false, such as false population presentations displaying a worse education structure than it really was. Due to hidden or not widely distributed information, *online communication channels became the dominant form* for informing others (e.g. Facebook).

The most dominant information strategies *presented the situation as completely risk-free and promoted economic benefits as a key discourse*. From official information channels and experts that worked on the project, the only information that was sent demonstrated no risks for the community whatsoever. This was clearly suspicious:

> Absolutely, for them there is no risk . . . not for water, it doesn't matter that [it] is near the Una river, no, not a chance, or that the terrain is seismically active. Hold on, how did they manage to build all this without risk in such a short period of time?
>
> (LM, 2)

The second information strategy was *placing economic benefits as a central discourse*. External actors believed this would be attractive to an economically deprived population. There was a message that approximately 1.1 million Euros would be distributed for local level infrastructural benefits (e.g. roads, sanitation, and school facilities as compensation) or that children will be awarded by symbolic gifts (e.g. tablets or free holidays). This information strategy raised a lot of mistrust among local residents that will be explained in the section on community processes.

This topic was, and still is, very challenging not only for the local community, but also for the central government. All respondents pointed out that this is an old subject going way back to the period of the former Yugoslavia, and that there is no clarity about *what will happen in the future.* The talk about the project is currently less intense, without clear feedback about whether something is going on behind the scenes, or the topic has been set aside to a future time.

> If I could know that this will be over tomorrow, that this story will end . . . but it won't end, we are wasting our time. . . . This is just a short slack, we all know that is not over.
>
> *(ACT 5)*

Community processes in light of developing a nuclear waste disposal unit

In this thematic section, community processes are considered as a ground for developing community social capital. The central concept that appeared at all levels is *mistrust among community stakeholders*. This will be analysed as a separate issue. Another visible feature is the *appearance of community activism* and *dualism among the local population and local political structures*. These topics were the most prominent ones. Community processes were additionally strengthened as people *recognised the oppressed position of local community*. Community processes are strongly coloured *by intense emotional responses* that are somehow interwoven within the previous topics. In many ways, the issue of trust became central during the interviews with local informants.

Distrust of community structures

This seems to take place at almost all levels of functioning. Distrust is partially deriving from the current situation, but it also appears due to previous circumstances connected with the War at the beginning of the 1990s. Being faced with misused local resources and in conditions of severe material deprivation, local habitants accepted that every kind of economic benefit would not be fairly distributed, and that key local figures would agree on siting a nuclear waste disposal unit in their municipality to gain significant personal material rewards:

> As soon as someone mentions money, it's like the bone is thrown. And you know how it's like with people, they are poor and then they change. [The] majority of people are against this because they know that the money wouldn't reach them. But those that expect some benefits are mostly in higher political positions.
>
> *(YOU, 3)*

Mistrust prevented or at least made it difficult to talk about the issue openly and objectively since any kind of objective interest also had a significant chance of being interpreted as being in favour of a nuclear waste disposal unit. Thus, this topic eventually turned out to be a sort of local taboo. Clear distrust is also shown towards central state representatives, including its expert delegates. Local residents had no confidence that in this case, state politicians would show sufficient responsibility. They claim that if this is a good proposal, it would definitely not be offered to the Dvor municipality. According to local informants, many other infrastructural projects were previously conducted without an adequate level of professional analysis.

Mistrust is also demonstrated towards the local municipality resulting in deteriorating relations towards local politicians and a *dualism among local population and local political structures*. The local municipality decided to position itself as a mediator between the central state and local population, sending a message that this process in unavoidable and that the local community needs to be wise enough to secure the most out of this situation. They were also a messenger sending information from central state level to residents. This was interpreted as positive attitude for developing a nuclear waste disposal unit and local municipality representatives to claim that they were pushed between these two forces: the central government and the local population. This position is followed by continuous verbal conflicts and pressures on an everyday basis whereby local political structures are blamed for developing nuclear waste disposal sites:

> Who decided this? Few names? Why did you decide this? Why haven't you consulted with the people? We are all here only temporarily, this is not our ownership. We have borrowed this from our grandchildren.
>
> *(FA, 4)*

However, local politicians also claim that a certain level of this conflict was in favour of their political opponents since local elections have been announced for 2017. This is also in line with a continuously non-constructive political climate and culture of nurturing divisions among local residents.

An intense emotional response is found among local informants through not only the proposal to build a nuclear waste disposal unit, but also community processes marked with significant levels of mistrust. Informants reported feelings of fear, helplessness, hysteria, considered this disposal unit a new trauma among an already over-traumatised population, and demonstrated strong distress:

> I was 18 . . . when this news was announced, I couldn't sleep for nights because the idea that we have beautiful nature, and that everything could be destroyed. . . . I live in a village and nature is my life, and when someone destroys your life, you are not happy with this at all, and associations raise something even worse.
>
> *(YOU, 3)*

The closed local context and experiences make inhabitants highly sensitive about being blocked from participating in objective discussions about the issue. Some informants, deeply involved in this process, felt fatigued and eventually thought of giving up:

> People are still not aware, they would like to push this aside, and they long for clear decision and finishing the process, but don't want to participate in all this.
>
> *(LM, 1)*

Strong emotional engagement, dominant negative orientation and lack of trust among stakeholders eventually resulted in the *appearance of community activism*. There is no previous experience of community activism and this seems to be a recent pioneer example. At first, activism appeared outside the community in neighbouring municipality, and just recently on a local level. Activists are mostly acting in synergy even though the activist scene outside the community is led by a youth leader and within the community by female activists. Activism in the community appeared instantly through a group of people who had not acted together previously. Activists are using creative and symbolic techniques such as satire, movie production, performance, and provocation to get heard:

> We made a performance where I showed up in white and brought a box. Police came. They didn't know what was in the box, and I acted as if radioactive waste was inside. I wanted to say that you don't see radiation, you don't feel it.
>
> *(YOU, 5)*

Also, community activists are developing their power by creating a wider network of their allies particularly foreign experts, eco-activists, media, other politicians and other people from neighbouring communities. Due to problems being found in information-sharing processes, activists found their roles in sharing widely available and expert-based information to challenge the official one. Their approach is reactive waiting for the situation to develop further before providing adequate responses. In future, activists will include legal action. Activists are visible, but a significant proportion of the local population remains passive, in the belief that their action does not matter, and allowing outdoor activists to act on their behalf.

All these processes reveal that *local relations are complex*. First, local residents are united in holding prevailingly negative attitudes. On the level between residents and decision-makers, there are tensions and the general atmosphere is that this topic is taboo, resulting in a reluctance to even raise the subject for further discussion:

> I was all for hearing about this in silence, and then carefully ask about it. But, someone provoked hysteria on purpose and challenged us who were in a position and in a situation to make fast decisions.
>
> *(ACT, 8)*

Finally, this event emancipated the idea that community is facing an *oppressed position*. This can be also strongly connected to the lack of environmental justice and structural inequalities. Local informants believed that stigmatisation was not only a result, but also a source of the proposal to build nuclear waste disposal unit here. Dvor was one of proposed locations, but there were also several more that eventually were not chosen. Informants believe that other locations had strong lobbying agents with sufficient political power. Some of them suspected that choosing a deprived area with a mostly older and less-educated population would cause the least disruption. There is a strong belief that the community cannot manage its own development and that the state can easily find legal sources to impose its final decision. One example that demonstrates this opinion is that legal legislation is unclear about this issue. The local community has the authority to express its own opinions. However, according to local informants, the term *community* for them is vague and it can be literally anything – a certain village, municipality, several municipalities, or the county.

As this community shares a border with Bosnia and Herzegovina, holding a dialogue on this with Bosnia and Herzegovina cannot be avoided. This relation is currently ambivalent. Bosnian stakeholders could become 'natural allies', however, new sources of conflict have arisen, particularly at the political level. Relations between these countries have become fragile due to the history of war between them, but they can be turned into a mutually beneficial developmental resource through which to develop joint projects. The situation is now worse and the level of tensions has heightened. This can be seen in local Bosnian media that accuse the Croatian municipality for imposing hazardous nuclear waste in the area without consulting them in this matter.

Awakening human rights discourses and making space for social work

This point raises the concepts of human rights and quality of life as central to green social work. Although the topic of a nuclear waste disposal unit raised complex emotional, social, and economic responses, the discourse of human rights has not developed enough. Instead, it was replaced with a summation of the direct risks to the local economy. When asked, local informants had just become aware that human rights discourse is a potential platform for advocating for the local population's interests. Thus, this category is named *awakening human rights discourses*. This resulted in the recognition of the violation of the right to choose and the right to be informed. The right to a healthy environment, a key justification for green social work, was recognised to a lesser extent. Due to the violation of the right to be informed, several informants demonstrated anger and feelings of being undermined as indicated in the following exchange:

Interviewer: Do you feel if some of your rights have been violated?
Respondent: Of course they have. To begin with, let's start with this study. We say that we are near the water sources, they say 'No'. We say that we are in a flood-risk area, they say 'No'. We say that we are in a seismic active area – they say 'No, you are not.'

(FA, 6)

The right to choose and participate in decision-making processes is strongly violated according to these informants. This would entail not only a right to express personal opinions in public debates, but also clearly understood regulation of the formal local decision-making processes. For example, the local municipality has been unable to receive a clear response about whether it is entitled to hold local referendum and if so, what its legal strength would be.

When it comes to responsibility for protecting human rights, most informants acknowledge the responsibility of the local, regional and state politicians. This is a dominant point where the role of local people or other experts are considered unimportant. So far, social work has not been included in this process in any way. Thus, informants reflected on the topic *making space for social work*. They perceived social work as a profession that has roles in facilitating communication, informing citizens about the drawbacks and advantages of siting such a facility in their community, and protecting human rights. Social work is considered especially important in reaching vulnerable and isolated groups, and encouraging participation in decision-making processes. Social workers can implement such roles because they can access the most vulnerable populations, have an impact in the community, and are interested in community development. Building this new space has been burdened by poor cooperation among local institutions and the view that social workers engage mainly in social care:

In our municipality social workers resolve literally life threating issues for basic existence. Something in . . . raising consciousness, encouragement, protection of rights – no . . . it is possible that there are some experts with this capacity, but I don't see them in our surroundings.

(LM, 2)

The new role of critical social work in responding to ecologically hazardous circumstances

This case study could be illustrative for detecting concepts relevant to green social work and community processes in situations where community environments are threatened. They provide a starting point to think about the role of social workers in light of each topic in the research findings as indicated in Table 31.1.

Table 31.1 Green social work roles in community development

Topic	Suggested role of social worker
a) Issues of environmental justice and perpetuated economic inequalities	
• further burdening of disadvantaged communities • prevailing negative attitudes in the community	• advocacy efforts on a national level for balanced and just local development • mobilising community members to accomplish small successes that can raise feelings of self-confidence and strength • mobilising people to form alliances, taskforce groups, and local associations that can resist and provide productive ideas on community development
• acknowledged multidimensional developmental risks including health, ecology, production, area stigmatisation	• developing creative ways to incorporate community-based participatory action research in the development and planning processes, including impact studies and community health profiles (Dominelli, 2012)
• information strategies that discourage citizens' involvement: lack of consistent information, hiding information, false information, presenting a situation as completely risk-free, and emphasising economic benefits in key discourses	• using broad scale communication tools – local newspapers, electronic media, social media, public engagement – debates, round tables, and mini conferences to inform community members about current and future developments • nurturing transparent and competent information sharing
b) Community processes in the context of environmental threats	
• mistrust of community structures	• supporting people in organising and conducting information channels that provide proper information flows in both directions: top-down and bottom-up • facilitating joint actions that promote community trust
• appearance of community activism and creating ally networks	• empowering community members in sustaining local action groups that are based on local knowledge, experience, resources and needs
• dualism among local population and local political structures.	• facilitating and mediating solution-oriented discussions between stakeholders to develop viable alternatives to environmental projects that prioritise environmental sustainability over profits (Philip & Reisch, 2015)
• oppressed position of a local community: stigmatisation as a source of problem, the belief that a community cannot manage its development	• empowering and strengthening community leaders to influence political decision-making processes inside and outside of community
• intense emotional responses: fear, helplessness, strong distress, fatigue	• developing and supporting community self-help groups, establishing a community center with skilled professionals who can raise the quality of community mental health
• complex local relations – a population united through prevailing negative attitudes; raised tensions around decision-makers	• Integrating community members to community assets to maximise existing community potential. Helping community members in negotiating processes involving different parts of the community.

Conclusion

Potentially dangerous effects to communities often tend to be hidden from residents. Such processes usually develop mistrust and animosity among the main community stakeholders. The community's political structures for electing representatives to act in the interests of community members, as shown by the results of this research, do not act properly when they leave the community uninformed and confused about the realisation of its own future. Regardless of the fact that Croatia as a country has adopted all the main human rights conventions and related documents, practice and everyday life show how difficult it may be to transfer these principles and duties into practice. It seems that community members are very often left to act alone without any structured and organised support or needed resources. This challenges social work as a human rights-oriented and social justice-based profession. Although environmental influences on the lives of community members have become more intensively the subject of practice, research, and theoretical elaboration in social work, only recently has the existing state of the art shown that social work faces numerous possibilities that can offer useful solutions to such issues. As noted by Drolet et al. (2015), sustainability, environmental justice and green social work are of growing interest to social work students, faculty, and social workers at local and global levels. Social workers are challenged in their practice to consider complex, interrelated and systemic problems that require new approaches and innovations. Using multiple methods and techniques from the broad range of community development practices and research, alongside political, critical, and radical approaches to social problems, and connecting scientific expertise to appropriate local knowledges and citizen's skills in coproducing new solutions, social workers can play very significant roles in shaping the future of the world. Green social work provides them with a model for pursuing this ambition in Dvor – to address the issues raised by placing a nuclear waste disposal unit in its locality.

References

Alston, M. (2013). Environmental social work: Accounting for gender in climate disasters. *Australian Social Work* (special edition) 66: 218–233.

Bay, U. (2010). Social work and the environment: Understanding people and place. *Australian Social Work*, 63(3): 366–367.

Braun, V. and Clarke, V. (2006). Using thematic analysis in psychology. *Qualitative Research in Psychology*, 3(2): 77–101.

Bullard, R. D. (2000 [1990]). *Dumping in Dixie: Race, class, and environmental quality*, 3rd ed. Boulder, CO: Westview Press.

Bullard, R. D. (1993–1994). Environmental racism and invisible communities. *West Virginia Law Review*, 96: 1037–1050.

Coates, J. (2004). From ecology to spirituality and social justice. *Currents: New Scholarship in the Human Services*. Available on www.ucalgary.ca/currents/files/currents/v3n1_coates.pdf

Dominelli, L. (2012). *Green social work: From environmental crises to environmental justice*. Cambridge: Polity Press.

Dominelli, L. (2013a). Environmental justice at the heart of social work practice: Greening the profession. *International Journal of Social Welfare*, 22: 431–439.

Dominelli, L. (2013b). Mind the gap: Built infrastructures, sustainable caring relations and Resilient communities in extreme weather events. *Australian Social Work*, 66(2): 204–217.

Dominelli, L. (2014). Promoting environmental justice through green social work practice: A key challenge for practitioners and educators. *International Social Work*, 57: 338–345.

Dominelli, L. (2015). The opportunities and challenges of social work interventions in disaster situations; *International Social Work*, 58(5): 659–672.

Drolet, J., Wu, H., Taylor, M. and Dennehy, A. (2015). Social work and sustainable social development: Teaching and learning strategies for 'Green Social Work' curriculum. *Social Work Education*, 34(5): 528–543.

Germain, C. B. (1973). An ecological perspective in casework practice. *Social Casework*, 54(6): 323–330.

Global Agenda. (2012). *Global agenda for social work and social development*. Available on www.globalsocialagenda.org/

Gray, M., Coates, J. and Hetherington, T. (2012). *Environmental social work*. London: Routledge.

Grinnell, R. M. (1973). Environmental modification: Casework's concern or casework's neglect. *Social Service Review*, 47(2): 208–220.

Jani, J. S. and Reisch, M. (2011). Common human needs, uncommon solutions: Applying a critical framework to perspectives on human behavior. *Families in Society: The Journal of Contemporary Social Services*, 92: 13–20.

Jarvis, D. (2013). Environmental justice and social work: A call to expand the social work profession to include environmental justice. *Columbia Social Work Review*, 4: 36–45. Retrieved from http://cswr.columbia.edu/?article=environmental-justiceand-social-work-a-call-to-action-for-the-social-work-profession

Miljenović, A. (2015). *Conceptualization of Developmentally Sensitive Communities in Croatia: An Eclectic Approach*. Doctoral thesis.

Miljenović, A. and Žganec, N. (2012). Disintegration and possibilities for rebuilding of war-affected communities: The Vojnić Municipality case. *International Social Work*, 55(5): 645–661.

McKinnon, J. (2008). Exploring the nexus between social work and the environment. *Australian Social Work*, 61: 256–268.

Philip, D. and Reisch, M. (2015). Rethinking social work's interpretation of 'Environmental Justice': From local to global. *Social Work Education*, 34(5): 471–483.

Pyles, L. (2007). Community organizing for post-disaster development: Locating social work. *International Social Work* 50(3): 321–333.

Ungar, M. (2002). A deeper, more social ecological social work practice. *Social Services Review*, 76: 480–497.

Williams, J. H. and Tedeschi, P. (2013). Developing a research agenda that supports global practice', *Social Work Research*, 37(3): 165–167.

32
Integrating green social work and the US environmental justice movement
An introduction to community benefits agreements

Amy Krings and Hillary Thomas

Introduction

The attainment of environmental justice requires the *participation* of residents who are affected by land-use decisions, as well as the equitable *distribution* of environmental resources, including access to clean air, land, and water. Urban land-use decisions are a necessary, although under-examined, intervention point for green social workers in preventing or mitigating environmental injustice. This chapter suggests that community benefits agreements (CBAs) are a mechanism by which green social workers can ally with residents and community organisations to protect the health and well-being of people living in proximity to undesirable development.

In this chapter, the authors begin by defining environmental justice and examining the scope of environmental inequity in the United States (US). As with any social issue, the conditions that give rise to the problem must be understood in order to design and implement effective interventions. Therefore, the authors apply growth coalition theory to explain how the political economy shapes land use decisions that culminate in environmental injustices, incentivising the disproportionate placement of hazardous, undesirable facilities in neighbourhoods occupied by racial minorities and the poor. To prevent or mitigate harm from undesirable land uses (such as waste incinerators, hazardous industries, or heavy transportation facilities), the authors suggest that green social workers consider community benefits agreements (CBAs). In some cases, CBAs have enabled host communities in the United States to secure local accountability and investments in schools, housing, and green spaces in exchange for hosting new development. The chapter will conclude by discussing potential limitations associated with CBAs and suggests opportunities for green social workers to strengthen local influence and, ultimately, promote environmental justice.

Environmental injustice in the US

Scholars, policymakers, and environmental justice advocates have documented the widespread placement of what urban planners call 'locally undesirable land uses' or 'LULUs' within low-income communities of colour (Bryant, 1995; Bullard, 1993; Mohai and Bryant, 1992). Examples of LULUs include heavy industries, airports, interstates, waste facilities, and other land uses that contaminate the air, land, or water. The placement of LULUs matters because they can negatively affect the health of host community residents. For example, nearly all (94 per cent) of the 23,000 largest polluting facilities in the US release their waste on site into the air, water, or soil (Gee and Payne-Sturges, 2004). As a result, people who reside nearby are exposed to industrial pollutants and chemicals that, in some cases, can result in birth defects, miscarriages, cancers, breathing difficulties, and damage to the central nervous system (Rogge and Combs-Orme, 2003; Rainey and Johnson, 2009). Children, in particular, are vulnerable to chemical exposure as they grow and develop. These contaminated neighbourhoods have been described by environmental justice advocates as 'sacrifice zones' (Lerner, 2010) because, when LULUs are spatially concentrated, the health of the environment and its proximate residents may be sacrificed to drive profit. Residents of sacrifice zones may experience other social inequities including crumbling infrastructure, deteriorating housing, inadequate public transportation, unemployment, high poverty, and an overloaded healthcare system, all of which can exacerbate environmental health impacts (Bryant 1995; Bullard 1993; Srinivasan et al., 2003).

Low-income communities of colour are disproportionately burdened by other problems in addition to the nearby placement of LULUs. Environmental regulations and laws are not enforced as strongly within neighbourhoods that are predominately populated by the poor and racial minorities. Companies are also less likely to reduce the capacity of LULUs in neighbourhoods where racial minorities live so as to minimise impact (Been, 1994). When fines are levied against polluting industries, White communities see faster action, stiffer penalties, and stronger enforcement than communities where Blacks, Hispanics, and other racial minorities live (Lavelle and Coyle, 1992).

Environmental burdens are not experienced equally across populations. Instead, the most polluted urban communities in the US are disproportionately populated by people of colour, the poor, women, and children (Bullard, Mohai, Saha, and Wright, 2008). These burdens influence the magnitude of issues to which social workers respond, including health and mental health disparities, poverty, child safety, and the lack of access to housing. Environmental justice and its resulting health impacts are social justice issues in which social workers must intervene (Dominelli, 2012; 2013).

The resolution of these inequalities is a goal of green social work (Hoff and Rogge, 1996). Towards this end, green social workers are called to advance environmental justice which the United States Environmental Protection Agency (US EPA) defines as:

> The fair treatment and meaningful involvement of all people regardless of race, ethnicity, income, national origin or educational level with respect to the development, implementation, and enforcement of environmental laws, regulations and policies. Fair treatment means that no population, due to policy or economic disempowerment, is forced to bear a disproportionate burden of the negative human health or environmental impacts of pollution or other environmental consequences.
>
> *(US EPA, 1998: 2)*

To address what has been called 'environmental racism', a term that refers to racial inequalities within environmental policy-making processes such as the siting of polluting industries and waste disposal and the unequal enforcement of environmental regulations and laws (Chavis, 1993; McGurty, 1997), affected residents should be included in decision-making processes. They deserve to be protected from environmental impacts associated with LULUs or compensated to address these impacts. However, to design effective interventions that advance environmental justice, social workers must begin with an understanding of the root causes of environmental injustices. They need a theory to connect land-use decisions with human and environmental health disparities. In the next section, the authors will apply growth coalition theory to explain power dynamics within urban development decisions and we emphasise opportunities for residents, community-based organisations, and green social workers to secure the right of all people to live in a healthy environment.

Growth coalition theory and urban development

Urban political theorists suggest that, within a capitalist economy with private property, market competition, and economic inequality, the most important concern of cities and their governmental leaders is *growth*, which happens through development (Molotch, 1976). Yet, land-use decision-making processes are frequently ignored by social workers. As a result, social workers may miss important opportunities to influence policies and political decisions that benefit a small proportion of the population and burden others. We suggest that growth coalition theory not only helps to explain power dynamics within land-use decisions, but also can shed light on why environmental justices occur.

Growth coalition theory asserts that cities depend upon private investment for public revenues. Local government officials, who must compete with leaders of other cities to retain or attract capital, are therefore incentivised to create formal or informal 'pro-growth coalitions' with business leaders to prioritise policies that promote economic development (Stone, 1989; Molotch, 1976, Mollenkopf, 1989). Given these constraints, urban theorists conceptualise the city as a 'growth machine' in which governmental leaders enter formal or informal coalitions with business leaders to promote development. Consequently, these government–business pro-growth coalitions are reluctant to attach restrictions to development policies for fear that they will burden developers and scare off capital (Peterson, 1981). For example, leaders may offer incentives, such as limiting corporate taxes, resisting environmental or labour regulations, and providing businesses with the infrastructure and transportation facilities. In some cases, city leaders will even subsidise new developments with tax incentives in an effort to provide a good business climate. They are likely to resist policies in which citizens can disrupt or delay new development or in which businesses are required to pay higher taxes, additional labour costs, or investments in the surrounding community.

In contrast, residents and local stakeholders may oppose new development, particularly if it means that public spending goes towards private development as opposed to city services. Additionally, if the development is proposed for construction in proximity to their homes, residents may have fears relating to displacement (through eminent domain or gentrification) or attendant pollution, traffic, noise, and other nuisances. In short, residents want to have a 'good neighbour' rather than to have local land used for what they deem undesirable purposes (Salkin and Lavine, 2008). As a result, civic groups will sometimes organise to prevent the construction of a new facility or to influence project design and impacts.

Growth coalition theory predicts that the business sector will support land-use policies and decisions that allow for the commodification and privatisation of public goods to generate profits while residents will favour policies that preserve resources, such as land, for public use to support, service, and sustain community (Cain, 2014; Mollenkopf, 1989; Stoecker, 2010). These conflicting ideals centre on the Marxist theoretical distinction between exchange values or the commodification and production of goods and services for exchange with others and use values or the production of goods and services for one's own use. In general, the city leadership will align with the business sector to promote exchange values through economic development. However, in some cases, new developments will be contested so as to protect use values and the growth coalition is constrained by local resistance. In part, this is because city leaders are motivated to remain in power and they understand that to do so they need to maintain their legitimacy through the support of community members (O'Connor, 1979). Thus, they need consent from potential challengers such as neighbourhood organisations, community groups, organised labour, or environmentalists who may oppose new development. In some cases, particularly when the anti-development groups possess economic and political influence, city leaders will cater to citizen demands by opposing new development or requiring developers to engage with residents.

Given that developers and city leaders want new development, and also want to appease opposition to its construction, they are incentivised to select host communities that are perceived to have less capacity for resistance, perhaps due to lower levels of education, income, or limited political networks. These are systemic injustices that disproportionately affect racial and ethnic minorities (Hoff and Rogge, 1996; Logan and Molotch, 2007). Similarly, poor communities may be chosen to host LULUs because of their potential willingness to tolerate pollution-generating development in the hope of gaining associated jobs and civic improvements (Pellow, 2004; Austin and Schill, 1991). Critics have described these dynamics as 'economic blackmail', suggesting that economically depressed communities are so desperate that they have to choose between employment and public health (Kazis and Grossman, 1982). In the absence of universal and robust policies designed to protect low-income communities of colour from the construction of new LULUs or to address racial and economic inequality, it is probable that developers and members of the growth coalition will continue to build LULUs in the most vulnerable communities, ultimately producing and reproducing economic inequalities.

Disproportionate placement of LULUs in poorer communities of colour occurs across the globe as well (Dominelli, 2013). Scholars outside of the US have also critiqued the neoliberal assumption that unrestricted land-use policies benefit everyone. As an example, Romao (2016) evaluated the distribution of oil revenue within Brazilian municipalities and found that, despite growth in profits, income inequality grew while life expectancies in these locations remained lower than the national average. As a result, the local growth coalition which included the owners of private business and political elites reaped the fiscal benefits of the oil extraction, but failed to include the people most likely to be negatively affected by the associated environmental contamination. Furthermore, Piketty and Saez (2014) extensively examined the relationship between economic growth and collective wellbeing. Their analyses of the global market economy suggest that, although wealth grew at an average of 6–7 per cent per year from 1987 to 2013 for those in top income fractals, income inequality was also on the rise. Thus, evidence suggests that development projects enabled by free market economic policy and supported by strong growth coalitions may not inherently distribute benefits equitably and may in fact exacerbate socio-economic inequality (Storey and Hamilton, 2003). In sum, urban land development can produce winners and losers.

Community benefits agreements (CBAs)

In an attempt to pre-empt opposition to economic development, growth coalition members may suggest that development benefits all community members due to its associated job creation and tax revenue (Cain, 2014; Saito, 2012). However, as environmental justice advocates and the residents of sacrifice zones suggest, economic growth does not inherently benefit all people and, in some cases, passes along financial or health burdens, particularly to those living in proximity to a LULU. Perhaps New York City's master planner Robert Moses summarised this dynamic best when he justified the demolition of neighbourhoods to construct an interstate system by stating that 'you can't make an omelette without breaking some eggs' (Caro, 1974).

Community benefits agreements (CBAs) aim to mitigate harm associated with new development while sharing the benefits of anticipated positive outcomes with existing residents of the host community (Gross, 2008; Gross, LeRoy, and Janis-Aparicio, 2002; Salkin and Lavine, 2007). CBAs are legally binding agreements between a private developer and coalition of community-based organisations, such as environmentalists, neighbourhood groups, and labour unions in which the coalition agrees to support a development in return for local investments and decision-making authority (Parks and Warren, 2009). Under some conditions, CBAs can advance environmental justice by reducing power inequalities between pro-growth coalitions and local stakeholders. At their core, they rely upon the organising power and influence of the community for their emergence, implementation, and enforcement. CBAs attempt to shift power dynamics by building trust and promoting shared decision making between community members and developers, effectively advancing local self-determination.

It is unlikely that a developer will be initially willing to cut profits by investing in the surrounding community. Thus, community coalitions are more likely to compel a developer to negotiate with them when bargaining is perceived to be less costly than ignoring the community's concerns. Baxamusa (2008) traced CBA negotiations associated with the expansion of the Los Angeles Airport and a stadium in San Diego, California. He suggested that community coalitions are most influential when a new project requires some form of public participation and approval process, especially when projects use public funds. When local groups were mobilised and able to slow down or complicate the project approval process, they created uncertainty for the developer. To reduce the risk of having their project delayed or denied, developers will sometimes engage in CBA negotiations. Thus, cities that have a rigorous public approval process, combined with organised grassroots coalitions, are comparatively likely to secure CBAs as opposed to those with a strong growth coalition and limited civic engagement.

During CBA negotiation processes, community members pledge their support for the development in exchange for investments, such as funds for green space, affordable housing, or training for living wage jobs (Salkin and Lavine, 2007). Additionally, community members can negotiate for decision-making authority, including access to clear and timely information about the project's environmental or health impacts. This strategy aligns with green social work practice by amplifying the voices of residents and communities that often go unheard (Dominelli, 2012; Teixeira and Krings, 2015).

Given that CBAs are negotiated within highly contextualised environments rather than based upon standardised regulations, their strength, and thus their ability to reduce environmental health disparities, varies. In their evaluation of CBAs, Salkin and Lavine emphasised:

> It should not be assumed that [CBAs] are always ideal vehicles to promote social justice issues. Practical problems – from organizing coalitions of community groups to negotiating with legally and politically sophisticated developers – sometimes combine to make the process of negotiating a CBA an unwieldy exercise.
>
> *(2008: 293).*

Krings (2015) warns that, to effectively compel a developer to bargain with a host community and, ultimately, implement a CBA, grassroots power is required. Thus, while CBAs have been found to mitigate harm and promote the health of host communities that are confronted with LULUs, it should be noted that not all communities are powerful enough to secure them. In the following section, the authors will suggest that green social workers are ideally positioned to align with and support host communities as they pursue CBAs as a means to advance environmental justice at a local level.

Opportunities for green social work practice

Urban growth coalitions, including developers, are incentivised to place locally undesirable land uses (LULUs) in low-income communities of colour because land is comparatively affordable and residents are perceived to be less politically powerful than those in more affluent areas. These are the same neighbourhoods in which many social workers practice. Green social workers can 'think globally and act locally' to promote accountable development by assisting with the creation and implementation of meaningful community benefits agreements (CBAs) that allow communities identified for the placement of a LULU to influence subsequent decisions while securing investments that mitigate associated health and environmental impacts.

When a LULU is proposed for construction in a vulnerable community, green social workers can utilise skills relating to community organising, coalition building, research, and negotiation. They can support and collaborate with residents, community-based organisations, environmentalists, and organised labour. Social workers can use their clinical, observational, and assessment skills to assist in documenting concerns expressed by community members in order to help prioritise their concerns (Teixeira and Krings, 2015).

Green social workers can support residents and environmental justice advocates when they call for transparency and accountability from developers. This may involve utilising economic or political pressure to encourage developers to provide meaningful local investments that protect residents' health and the surrounding environment. They can raise critical questions to ensure that participation processes and development decisions are locally relevant, culturally appropriate, and environmentally sustainable, as advocated by the green social work model (Dominelli, 2012). They can help translate scientific jargon into accessible language to facilitate community innovation and ingenuity or to inform individuals and families about physical and psychosocial risks associated with pollution and contamination (Dominelli, 2012).

Green social workers can also apply skills and knowledge relating to policy practice to change socio-political and economic systems of oppression that cause harm to oppressed groups and give rise to environmental and racial inequalities (Teixeira and Krings, 2015). To do this effectively, green social workers should be aware of the policies and processes that facilitate or have potential to interrupt the creation of sacrifice zones. At the organisational level, green social workers may develop programmes that facilitate the participation of young people in projects that emphasise leadership development and civic engagement skills so that they are able to effectively engage with policymakers and people charged with monitoring and regulating polluting facilities.

Green social workers can challenge growth coalitions to advance alternative visions of development that include paradigms of sustainability and equity. They can challenge ideas about the deserving and undeserving poor in order to transform the belief that sacrifice zones are places where 'disposable waste' is dumped among 'disposable people' to generate 'disposable income' for others (Martin-Brown and Ofosu-Amaah, 1992). They can use their creativity and imagination to challenge neoliberal assumptions about the merits of unregulated development while emphasising care for vulnerable people and the environment (Dominelli, 2012).

Implications for social work education

Green social workers, who often practice in the same communities that are contaminated by locally undesirable land uses, possess knowledge and skills that can be applied at micro, mezzo, and macro levels to advance environmental justice. However, we want to conclude by reminding social worker educators and students that many environmental justice advocates have been organising to promote inclusive decision-making and equitable access to environmental resources for years. Therefore, social workers must not only bring assets to community partnerships, but they must also learn from residents' wisdom and practice knowledge as suggested by the green social work model. In addition to learning from residents and activists, social workers can align themselves with urban planners, public health officials, and economists to better understand and influence urban development patterns.

In this chapter, we have demonstrated that hazardous and contaminating facilities are disproportionately placed within neighbourhoods where residents are poor and racial minorities. These land-use patterns contribute to health and mental health disparities. Thus, it is imperative that social work educators include content on urban politics and the mechanisms that shape economic development so that social workers can use this knowledge to inform community interventions that effectively prevent environmental injustice. Social work curricula should include content about the individual and community health impacts of living in proximity to hazardous facilities so that green social work can be cultivated across micro-, mezzo- and macro-levels of practice.

Additionally, the authors suggest that social work scholars should evaluate CBAs to determine to what extent, and how, community organising efforts can effectively challenge urban growth coalitions. Are there similar interventions available outside of the US and, if so, how does the local political-economic context influence land-use decisions? This question has grown in relevance given that a chief economist of the World Bank has recommended the migration of 'dirty industries' to less developed countries (Liu, 1997).

Finally, we suggest that CBAs provide an important case example for students to consider ethical and strategic dilemmas found within community interventions. For example, CBAs offer a means to mitigate harm and share benefits associated with new development in some cases. However, not all communities are powerful enough to secure these advantages. Additionally, in her political ethnographic study of a CBA campaign in Detroit, Michigan, Krings (2015) found that the decision to pursue a CBA was made, in part, because residents and organisers did not believe that they held sufficient political power to prevent the construction of a LULU. Thus, CBAs do not always represent a community's true preference but may instead represent a 'second-best' option when a proposed development cannot be stopped. Thus, green social workers should be aware of strategies to cancel infrastructure projects including highways (Gotham, 1999; Gregory, 1999), airports (Flores et al., 2013), heavy industries (Almeida and Stearns, 1998; Checker, 2005; Pulido, 1996), and waste facilities (Pellow, 2004; Sze, 2007).

Conclusion

The advancement of environmental justice which requires local participation in decision-making as well as an equitable distribution of environmental resource is central to the practice of green social work. This chapter has demonstrated that, although land-use decisions influence environmental and human health, social workers can do more to ensure that the benefits and costs of land development are distributed evenly. The chapter has built upon Dominelli's (2012) contention that, within a market economy in which stakeholders struggle for access to valuable natural resources, those who are least able to mobilise resources will most likely bear the brunt of environmental harm. The authors suggest that growth coalition theory can help to explain some of the root causes of environmental inequalities and that, without protective mechanisms such as community benefits agreements, it is probable that developers will continue to disproportionately place locally undesirable land uses in communities populated by low-income people of colour. Social workers, who often practice within these 'sacrifice zones' and whose mission includes the advancement of social justice, have an opportunity to join community-based coalitions with residents, community organisations, environmentalists, and organised labour to promote sustainable, equitable, and healthy development practices in accordance with green social work principles.

References

Almeida, P. and Stearns, L. (1998). Political opportunities and local grassroots environmental movements: The case of Minamata. *Social Problems*, 45, 37–60.

Austin, R. and Schill, M. (1991). Black, Brown, poor and (and) poisoned: Minority grassroots environmentalism and the Quest for eco-justice. *Kansas Journal of Law and Public Policy*, 1: 69–82.

Baxamusa, M. H. (2008). Empowering communities through deliberation: The model of community benefits agreements. *Journal of Planning Education and Research*, 27(3): 261–276.

Been, V. (1994). Locally undesirable land uses in minority neighbourhoods: Disproportionate siting or market dynamics? *The Yale Law Journal*, 103(6): 1383–1422.

Bryant, B. (Ed.) (1995). *Environmental justice: Issues, policies, and solutions*. Washington, DC: Island Press.

Bullard, R. D. (1993). *Confronting environmental racism: Voices from the grassroots*. Cambridge, MA: South End Press.

Bullard, R. D., Mohai, P., Saha, R. and Wright, B. (2008). Toxic wastes and race at twenty: why race still matters after all of these years. *Environmental Law*, 38, 371–411.

Cain, C. (2014). Negotiating with the growth machine: Community benefits agreements and value-conscious growth. *Sociological Forum*, 29(4): 937–958.

Caro, R. (1974). *The power-broker: Robert Moses and the fall of New York*. New York: Vintage Publishing.

Chavis, B. (1993). Foreword. In R. Bullard (Ed.), *Confronting environmental racism: Voices from the grassroots*. Boston: South End Press, pp. 3–5.

Checker, M. (2005). *Polluted promises: Environmental racism and the search for justice in a Southern Town*: New York: New York University Press.

Dominelli, L. (2012). *Green social work: From environmental crises to environmental justice*. Cambridge: Polity Press.

Dominelli, L. (2013). Environmental justice at the heart of social work practice: Greening the profession. *International Journal of Social Welfare*, 22: 431–429.

Flores Dewey, O. and Davis, D. E. (2013). Planning, politics, and urban mega-projects in developmental context: Lessons from Mexico City's airport controversy. *Journal of Urban Affairs*, 35(5): 531–551. doi:10.1111/juaf.12012

Gee, G. and Payne-Sturges, D. C. (2004). Environmental health disparities: A framework integrating psychosocial and environmental concepts. *Environmental Health Perspectives*, 112(17): 1646–1653.

Gotham, K. F. (1999). Political opportunity, community identity, and the emergence of a local anti-expressway movement. *Social Problems*, 46: 332.

Gregory, S. (1999). *Black corona: Race and the politics of place in an urban community*. Princeton, NJ: Princeton University Press.

Gross, J. (2008). Community benefits agreements: Definitions, values, and legal enforceability. *Journal of Affordable Housing and Community Development*, 17(3): 58.

Gross, J., LeRoy, G., and Janis-Aparicio, M. (2002). *Community benefits agreements: making development projects accountable*. Washington, DC: Good Jobs First and the California Public Subsidies Project.

Hoff, M. and Rogge, M. E. (1996). Everything that rises must converge: Developing a social work response to environmental injustice. *Journal of Progressive Human Services*, 7(1): 41–57.

Kazis, R. and Grossman, R. L. (1982). *Fear at Work: Job Blackmail, Labour and the Environment*. Pilgrim Press.

Krings, A. E. (2015). *Building bridges where there is nothing left to burn: The campaign for environmental justice in a Southwest Detroit border community*. (Unpublished doctoral dissertation.) Ann Arbor, Michigan: The University of Michigan,.

Lavelle, M. and Coyle, M. (1992). Unequal protection: The racial divide in environmental law. *National Law Journal*, 15(3): S1–S12.

Lerner, S. (2010). *Sacrifice zones: The front lines of toxic Chemical Exposure in the United States*. Cambridge, MA: MIT Press.

Logan, J. R., and Molotch, H. L. (2007). *Urban fortunes: The political economy of place*. Oakland: University of California Press.

Liu, F. (1997). Dynamics and causation of environmental equity, locally unwanted land uses, and neighbourhood changes. *Environmental Management*, 21(5): 643–656.

Martin-Brown, J. and Ofosu-Amaah, W. (1992). *Proceedings of the global assembly of women and the environment "Partners in Life"*. Washington, DC: United Nations Environmental Programme and WorldWIDE Network, Inc.

McGurty, E. M. (1997. From NIMBY to the civil rights: The origins of the environmental justice movement. *Environmental History*, 2(3): 301–323.

Mohai, P., and Bryant, B. (1992). Environmental injustice: Weighing race and class as factors in the distribution of environmental hazards. *University of Colorado Law Review*, 63(1): 921–932.

Mollenkopf, J. (1989). Who (or what) runs cities, and how? *Sociological Forum*, 4(1): 119–137.

Molotch, H. (1976). The city as a growth machine: Toward a political economy of place. *American Journal of Sociology*, 82(2): 309–332.

O'Connor, J. (1979). *The fiscal crisis of the state*. Piscataway, New Jersey: Transaction Publishers.

Parks, V. and Warren, D. (2009). The politics and practice of economic justice: Community benefits agreements as tactic of the new accountable development movement. *Journal of Community Practice*, 17(1-2): 88–106.

Pellow, D. N. (2004). *Garbage Wars: The struggle for environmental justice in Chicago*. Cambridge, MA: MIT Press.

Peterson, P. E. (1981). *City limits*. Chicago, IL: University of Chicago Press.

Piketty, T. and Saez, E. (2014). Inequality in the long run. *Science*, 344(1686): 1913–1998.

Pulido, L. (1996). *Environmentalism and economic justice: Two Chicano struggles in the Southwest*. Tucson, AZ: University of Arizona Press.

Rainey, S. and Johnson, G. (2009). Grassroots activism: An exploration of women of colour's role in the environmental justice movement. *Race, Gender, and Class*, 16(3-4): 144–173.

Rogge, M. and Combs-Orme, T. (2003). Protecting children from chemical exposure: Social work and U.S. social welfare policy. *Social Work*, 48(4): 439–450.

Romao, F. L. (2016). Pre-salt oil, royalties, and sovereign and social funds in Brazil: Challenges and social control. *International Social Work*, 59(1): 5–17.

Saito, L. T. (2012). How low-income residents can benefit from urban development: The LA live community benefits agreement. *City and Community*, 11(2): 129–150.

Salkin, P. and Lavine, A. (2007). Negotiating for social justice and the promise of community benefits agreements: Case studies of current and developing agreements. *Journal of Affordable Housing and Community Development Law*, 17(1-2): 113–144.

Salkin, P. and Lavine, A. (2008). Understanding community benefits agreements: Equitable development, social justice and other considerations for developers, municipalities and community organizations. *UCLA Journal of Environmental Law and Policy*, 26(2): 291–331.

Srinivasan, S., O'Fallon, L. R. and Dearry, A. (2003). Creating healthy communities, healthy homes, healthy people: Initiating a research agenda on the built environment and public health. *American Journal of Public Health*, 93(9): 1446–1450.

Stoecker, R. (2010). *Defending community: The struggle for alternative redevelopment in Cedar-Riverside*. Philadelphia, Pennsylvania: Temple University Press.

Stone, C. N. (1989). *Regime politics: Governing Atlanta, 1946–1988*. Lawrence, Kansas: University Press of Kansas.

Storey, K., and Hamilton, L. C. (2003). *Planning for the impacts of megaprojects*. New York: Springer.

Sze, J. (2007). *Noxious New York: The racial politics of urban health and environmental justice*. Cambridge, MA: MIT Press.

Teixeira, S, and Krings, A. (2015). Sustainable social work: An environmental justice framework for social work education. *Social Work Education: The International Journal*, 34(5): 513–527.

U.S. Environmental Protection Agency (EPA) (1998). Guidance for Incorporating Environmental Justice in EPA's NEPA Compliance Analysis. Retrieved from https://www.epa.gov/risk/guidelines-ecological-risk-assessment [Accessed 5 November 2017].

Part X
Practicing green social work

33
Historical trends in calls to action
Climate change, pro-environmental behaviours and green social work

Erin Kennedy

Introduction

Social works' relationship with the environment and the role of social workers in addressing environmental issues under climate change are usually neglected in mainstream practice. I begin this chapter by discussing the importance of social work as a field of research and practice that needs to actively carve out a position of expertise and engagement with emerging environmental issues at the micro-, meso- and macro-levels of society and government. I consider the profession's past, taking a historical account of social work's relationship with the environment and the roles that social work has held in addressing environmental concerns by referring to one of its founders in the US, Jane Addams, and her work as 'Garbage Inspector' at Hull House. I then map and discuss three main environmental frameworks that have emerged within social work: ecological, eco-social and green social work. I identify three parallel themes that run through social work in addressing environmental issues: a technical approach, philosophical idealism and political economy. In considering the role of social work in engaging with environmental issues I discuss the need to understand political economy as an example of what is currently missing in social work research, education and practice. I conclude this chapter with a discussion on how social work can ensure its relevance to the future.

As a social work researcher I am engaged at the local community level because I have observed an untapped source of knowledge, understanding and interaction with one's social network, physical and natural environments that are necessary in the transformation towards sustainability. As a social worker who is engaged with environmental issues I actively work in research and practice to develop the framework of green social work and to identify the role of social workers in addressing environmental issues such as climate change. One key role that social workers need to fill, both in practice and research is to act as the bridge between the community (i.e. local residents) and the local or upper levels of government, special interest groups and outside sources of knowledge, technology, influence and power. As the bridge, between often disparate groups, social work research and practice need to work across disciplines and collaborate with members who are working within environmental research, technology innovation, policy implementation, social welfare and economic development. The emerging field of green social work requires social workers to be the links and advocates that connect the interest and needs of the population with the many bodies of power that influence development. Within my research on environmental issues, I encounter two main questions from social workers and academics in other fields of research:

How does your research relate to social work?
What is the role of social work in addressing environmental issues?

These questions present the opportunity and interested audience for social work to claim its role as an expert and contributor to global and local level discussions on environmental issues. In order for social work to maintain relevance as a practice and area of research, it is time for social work to stretch its 'traditional' boundaries and become an important contributor to interdisciplinary collaborations that address environmental issues such as climate change.

Climate change and social work

Social work has arrived late to discussions on today's environmental crises (Dominelli, 2011) and is slow, sometimes even resistant, to becoming engaged in actions to address environmental issues such as climate change. Climate change is a global problem that brings to light structural weaknesses within the political, social and economic systems and emphasises inequalities in income, class and access to resources. Populations that live within disparate circumstances – those living in or on the border of poverty, humanitarian crisis, conflict, limits in food security, access to clean water, and who live in regions that are vulnerable to the environmental changes brought on by climate change – are more at risk of suffering environmental inequalities and environmental injustice. The people who are most vulnerable to climate change are the populations that social work, both in practice and research, work with most closely. 'The human impacts of environmental challenges fall most heavily on those to whom social workers are most accountable' (Kemp, 2011: 1205). Social work's involvement in environmental issues is time-sensitive for two main reasons: dragging its feet, and losing future relevance. Kemp (2011: 1205) suggests that 'while social work drags its feet, its constituents face increasingly devastating environmental realities'. The longer social workers take to become an active voice within discussions surrounding environmental issues, the numbers experiencing the impact of environmental disasters increase, alongside a disaster's magnitude and long-term impact on human lives. Lena Dominelli (2012) takes up these concerns in her book, *Green Social Work: From Environmental Crises to Environmental Justice*. Dominelli (2012) points out that if social work remains on the periphery of discussions surrounding issues such as climate change and their long-term human impact, then opportunities for prevention will be missed. Discussing the need for social workers' voices to be heard in the media, at higher levels of government and within policy development and implementation, Dominelli (2012: 2) states that the voice of social workers 'is absent from many of the decision-making structures formulating policy for preventing large-scale devastation in the future, and addressing needs during calamitous events and afterwards'. The second time-sensitive issue is that social work needs to be aware of is its future relevance. It is absolutely necessary for social work to add its expertise and carve out its role within discussions on climate change and environmental issues. Social workers' expertise needs to develop beyond the micro- or local level – often working with the 'aftermath of environmental disaster' (Dominelli, 2012: 2), and extend into the meso- and macro-levels of social policy and global environmental discussions and international agreements. As Dominelli (2012: 3) states, 'practice has to engage with both local and global contexts to develop those that are locality-specific and culturally-relevant and that engage with global interdependencies within and between countries'. Social work is at a risk of losing its voice and relevance as a practice and body of research within today's emerging social issues:

> social work has a vested interest in attending to environmental issues as an integral part of its daily remit if it is to retain its currency in contemporary societies, emphasise its relevance to the social issues that peoples have to resolve in the twenty-first century and widen its scope if it is to prevent the haemorrhaging of its activities to related professions including health, geography, psychology and psychiatry.
>
> *(Dominelli, 2012: 3)*

If social work does not carve out its importance within climate change and environmental crises research and policy, then the access and contact it has with human well-being can be easily lost to other professions. This would be a disservice to the populations social workers serve. Kemp (2011: 1205–1206) sees this as an ethical concern claiming that,

> when the profession remains on the margins of environmental efforts, it both neglects its ethical responsibilities to vulnerable populations and loses vital opportunities to participate in shaping contemporary responses to environmental challenges, particularly around interconnections between environmental and social issues.

Maintaining relevance is not a new concern for social work. Meyer (1989: 151–152) expressed similar concerns when she examined the maturing of social work as a profession, stating:

> Social Workers, wanting to salvage social services and themselves, are all trying to find ways to do that. . . . There is no doubt that there will always be a system of social services, and some kind of personnel to staff it. The concern is about whether or not professional social workers will remain at the core of social services.

Social work needs to move beyond insular traditions dominated by national agendas and closed off towards emerging global social processes. Social workers have to engage with policy-making, operate within multiple societal structural levels, actively engage and support populations in transformations towards sustainability in the face of climate change. To understand more clearly social work's present-day role in addressing environmental issues, I reflect on the work of a social work environmental pioneer, Jane Addams.

Social work environmental pioneer: Jane Addams

Engagement with the environment to take care of the environment and understand the interconnected relationship between the environment, health and development of human life and populations, has a long history within the profession. Jane Addams (1860–1935) challenged urban and industrial development practices that left many wards in Chicago living in squalid slum conditions. Following a trip to Toynbee Hall, the showpiece of such work within the Settlement Movement in London, Addams founded Hull House in Chicago in 1889. Addams (1961) worked to address housing issues, and social inequalities that developed from unregulated and corrupt city planning and infrastructure practices that took advantage of poor people and placed poor and lower- to middle-class people at risk of disease and death due to poor working conditions, industrial pollution, overcrowded housing, poor sanitation and inadequate waste removal. Addams identified a high mortality rate in Hull House ward due to excessive garbage that attracted insects, vermin and other animals that spread disease to its residents (Addams, 1961:188). In response to the high death rate and environmental contaminants surrounding Hull House and other wards in Chicago, Addams (1961) took action. She followed the garbage collection process, and noted that the system was ineffective, incomplete and corrupt. Addams (1961) acknowledged the extreme filth and squalor of the houses and surrounding neighbourhoods and assumed the role of Garbage Inspector. She enrolled women from Hull House to observe and enforce proper waste management by neighbours and garbage collectors. Addams (1961) engaged children in the collection of recyclable items including tin cans that had monetary value if deposited for recycling. Addams (1961) engaged the community of the ward – she operated on multiple societal levels, including the residents, landlords, garbage collectors, the ward alderman and mayor – in the process of creating cleanliness in the ward and improving residents' health and well-being. This process held people accountable to fulfil their roles in the maintenance of the ward. Addams (1961: 190) wrote about the experience of the garbage inspection and noted the importance of enforcing an equality of justice:

> even-handed justice to all citizens irrespective of 'pull,' the dividing of responsibility between landlord and tenant, and the readiness to enforce obedience to law from both, was, perhaps, one of the most valuable demonstrations which could have been made.

From this experience, Addams demonstrated that the process of identifying an issue at ground level and developing actions and interventions from experienced knowledge was more valuable in initiating change than discussions with civic officers in faraway offices: 'Such daily living on the part of the office holder is of infinitely more value than many talks on civics for, after all, we credit most easily that which we see' (Addams, 1961: 190). The outcomes of Addams's (1961) garbage inspection interventions were improved sanitation and cleanliness that reduced mortality rates within the ward. Besides the improved quality of health, an increased sense of community developed from participation in the garbage inspection project:

> The careful inspection, combined with other causes, brought about a great improvement in the cleanliness and comfort of the neighborhood and one happy day, when the death rate of our ward was found to have dropped from third to seventh in a list of city wards and was reported to our Women's Club, the applause which followed recorded the genuine sense of participation in the result, and a public spirit which had 'made good'.
> *(Addams, 1961: 190)*

Jane Addams' work demonstrates the role of social work in identifying and addressing environmental issues and the importance of fostering the interconnected relationship that exists between people, communities and their environments. Addams worked at the micro-, meso- and macro-levels of society to bring about sustained change, and more importantly, developed connections and opportunities for knowledge sharing and intervention among different societal levels. By engaging with the women of the Hull House ward, Addams was able to educate and demonstrate how to demand that individual rights and justice be afforded to all individuals and enforced. Addams expanded on the previous knowledge of sanitation and cleanliness, and identified the importance of caring for one's home alongside that of the environment that exists past one's doorstep. It is important to note that there is a gender critique to be made regarding Addams's work. The underlying theme of 'cleanliness is next to godliness' identifies the responsibility of caring for the home – home economics – to be a woman's role as outlined and re-enforced by society – consider here Mary Douglas's work on Purity and Danger and the gendered understanding of cleanliness (Douglas, 1966). The woman's role of 'cleaning up the mess', regardless of who is responsible for making the mess, extended beyond the home to impact the positions available to women in the public health sector. Although Addams did challenge power structures, she also contributed to the discourses on the gender-based roles for women.

Jane Addams's lasting impact within social work today is the practice to 'educate and mobilise local communities in finding their own solutions to problems' (Dominelli, 2012: 22) a practice that is regarded as 'empowering and anti-oppressive' (Dominelli, 2012: 22). Although, protection of the environment for the sake of sustainability and environmental justice may not have been at the forefront of her discussions and interventions, the importance of interacting with and caring for the surrounding environment was evident in Addams's work. From her, social work can capture examples of what it means to 'do' social work through action, intervention and research.

This is just one example from the work of a pioneer social worker that was at the forefront of environmental awareness and activism. However, this illustrates social work's historical roots in addressing environmental issues and working to develop a more sustainable relationship between local communities, governing bodies and the natural environment. I will leave Addams and move on to explore the more recent trajectories of social work's engagement with environmental issues.

During the 1990s, some social workers were developing conceptual frameworks to identify social work's relationship with the environment and the role of social work in responding to environmental changes. Kemp (2011) provided a summary of these efforts and identified three conceptual camps that engage with environmental issues from different points of departure: ecological, eco-social and 'beyond'. Lena Dominelli's (2012) *Green Social Work* is introduced with regards to Kemp's (2011) 'beyond' concept. These environmental frameworks are paralleled by three main themes that run through social work and environment: a technical approach, philosophical idealism and political economy. These themes will be brought into the discussions on the individual frameworks.

Ecological framework

The ecological framework focuses on 'developing person-environment frameworks for direct practice' (Kemp, 2011: 1201). Practice includes work with 'individuals, families, groups, and neighborhoods' (Kemp et al., 1997: xii). Urie Bronfenbrenner (1979) contributed to the development of the ecological framework with his research on human development, wherein he analysed the social ecology of the family. Bronfenbrenner (1979) conceived the ecological environment as a 'set of nested structures, each inside the next, like a set of Russian dolls. At the innermost level is the immediate setting containing the developing person. This can be the home, the classroom, or as often happens for research purposes – the laboratory or the testing room' (Bronfenbrenner, 1979: 3). Bronfenbrenner (1979) was interested in the development of the person in connection to the environment and the evolving relationship between different levels. Focused on the analysis of the social ecology of the family, Bronfenbrenner (1979) viewed the social support networks, welfare system, access to childcare, parent's work schedules and level of safety of the neighbourhood as interrelated pieces that interacted with each other to create the ecological environment that impacted upon a child's development. This is a scientific and technocratic way of making sense of the world from the level of human behaviour to the larger scale social systems.

The person-environment framework develops a client's environmental competence through active participation in engaging and assessing the environment and developing an awareness of the surrounding environment. This includes recognising the symbiotic relationship between the client/service user and the environment and then broadening this identified relationship with the environment to move from the local and familiar experience to 'distal and foreign' conceptual experiences (Kemp et al., 1997: 3).

The person-environment framework creates a connection between the individual's concerns, resources, capabilities, and shared or collective actions (Kemp et al., 1997: 3). The overall goal of the person-environment framework is to assist the development of 'an informed client able to act effectively in the many contexts of his or her life' (Kemp et al., 1997: 3). This involves being aware of one's surroundings, resources and networks that may be called upon in times of need, but that also have to be cultivated for the benefit of the individual, the local and global community alongside the environment that supports life. Intervention within the ecological framework is *environmental intervention*, defined as 'both action in the environment and the process of transforming individual and collective perspectives through critical analysis of the impact of environmental conditions' (Kemp et al., 1997: xi). The concepts of place – physical, spatial, social, time – and *life course* (see Gitterman and Germain, 2008) are identified as key points for intervention (Saleebey, 2004; Kemp, 2010, 2011). The main critique of the person-environment framework as social work practice is that despite the intention to focus on both the person and environment, the lens remains focused on the person. As Kemp et al. (1997:21) stated:

> there has been a persistent tendency to elevate person-centered knowledge and interventions . . . environmental practice languishes on the margins of direct practice, routinely invoked but accorded relatively little meaningful attention. This lack of balance has been troublesome at least since the 1920's, when social casework adopted psychodynamic theory as its primary knowledge base.

The adoption of this technical approach as a method to understand the relationships between the individual and social systems limits social work's ability as a practice and profession to stretch beyond its traditional boundaries and adopt roles that respond to environmental issues. Referencing remarks by social work theorist Carol Meyer (1989), Kemp (1997) reiterates Meyer's (1989) sentiments, 'the vexed issue of environmental practices is the 'historical gnat' of the American social profession' (Kemp, 1997: 21).

If considering the ecological framework's point of intervention within society, it appears that this framework operates at the micro/personal/local level with the goal of extrapolating the knowledge and experiential gains out towards the macro-level or 'bigger picture' understanding, experience and lived connection. In reality, within the field of social work this has proven to be difficult. The intervention focus remains on the person and the natural environment is not considered an equal part of the relationship.

Eco-social framework

The eco-social framework opposes the ecological model for its failure to see humans as a part of nature rather than above nature:

> The innate tendencies of nature, when seen as a foundation for human behaviour, can be translated into values which act as both a sense of vision and guidance for humanity. Such an ecocentric world view places the human community within nature, unlike modernity, which operates as if humans are outside and above nature.
>
> *(Coates, 2003: 78)*

Within the ecological framework the natural environment, if considered at all, is limited to the 'social' aspect of the environment. The eco-social framework, which Coates (2003) details in his book, *Ecology and Social Work: Toward a New Paradigm*, makes the necessary connection between nature and human life and the importance of the interconnectedness of this relationship. Drawing from Coates (2003:2) the eco-social framework is described as 'holistic', focused on a 'mutually enriching and sustainable human/Earth relationship' (Kemp, 2011: 1201). The main theme of the eco-social framework is philosophical idealism – it focuses on thinking, spirituality and our relationships with nature and with each other. The eco-social framework emphasises the 'spiritual connection of people with the Earth, the fundamental interdependence of living and physical systems, and the values of indigenous ecological knowledges' (Kemp, 2011: 1201). Focused on human attitudes, key concepts include values, respect, communication and action. These concepts and the spiritual connection between humans and nature are values shared with green social work and will be explored later in this chapter.

The eco-social model calls into question unbridled ambition for development – consumption and the convenience of the 'modern life', at the expense of the environment. The modern life runs on the unsustainable economic model most societies run on – one that does not consider the use of natural resources as a cost, only as a free and unlimited resource to be exploited.

The eco-social framework places the focus (possibly onus) on the individual as the source of change. Individual change, such as incorporating responsibility into daily life habits, may take on the form of some of the following examples: becoming an informed consumer; questioning the consumption of 'stuff' as a source of identity and value; using purchasing power as a communication tool; buying locally; and avoiding products that use harmful chemicals.

Networks or communities of people who share the same values support change at the individual level, thereby creating opportunities for larger endemic change. The role of social workers is to identify the inherent structural inequalities that hinder individual change (Coates 2003). The main critique of the eco-social framework is that it overlooks the structures (social, political, cultural, technological) that lock individuals and entire nations into high carbon-emission lifestyles. For example, there is resistance from large energy corporations to shift to renewable energy sources. Maintaining 'business as usual', although catastrophic for the earth and human population, brings monetary profits to a small population who are not willing to cede this short-term gain for the long-term survival and well-being of the human population.

Another example is to shift to using public transportation or commuting more by bicycle. If this responsibility is borne only by the individual, then people are locked into the limited alternatives available to them. The quality of the public transportation, access to safe bicycle paths that do not force cyclists to ride alongside busy and dangerous roadways impact an individual's ability to make a pro-environmental behaviour change. Inequalities in access to job opportunities within close proximity of where an individual lives impact an individual's quality of life and his/her carbon footprint. If jobs are not available in areas of affordable housing, then placing the responsibility on the individual to make changes towards a more sustainable lifestyle is ineffective. The responsibility is shifted away from governments and industries towards the individual, without addressing the larger systemic practices that must change to allow individuals to choose feasible alternatives.

Culture, values and identity can also limit an individual's capability to change. For instance, the choice to reduce meat consumption is an option that is often met with contention and hostility in some countries or populations. As I discovered while conducting field research, in urban China, vegetarianism, is for many, an inconceivable solution to the reduction of carbon emissions and presses against the burgeoning concepts that indicate success, wealth and development.

As one Chinese student interviewee stated, 'No vegetarian! That's just a stupid lifestyle' (World Café participant, 23 November 2014).

The eco-social framework overlooks the practicality and accessibility of some of these individual changes. This brings up the issue of social injustices and inequalities that are not accounted for within the eco-social framework. People are busy, they have kids to raise, mortgages to pay, multiple jobs, and responsibilities – life is hectic. To implement changes at the individual level requires large-scale lifestyle shifts towards a degrowth model, something that is not equally accessible or possible for everyone. Trying to change at the individual level when social, political, economic, cultural and technological structures do not facilitate change can cause feelings of anguish and the desire to look for an exit from the conversation or call to action. Unsupported requests for individual change often result in disengagement. The individual person may have the feeling that their singular action, regardless of whether it is 'good or bad' for the environment, does not have any impact at the end of the day. It is necessary for social work to understand the structure in which implementations are introduced. If you do not understand the social, political, economic, cultural and technological structures then implementations will fail – people will feel defeated and give up.

. . . and beyond

Kemp (2011) introduces concepts that move beyond the ecological and eco-social frameworks, stating that future frameworks need to focus on the right to a healthy environment. Within this third wave of environmental social work, attention is given to 'global ecological threats, with a particular emphasis on environmental justice, or the disproportional impact of environmental hazards and degradation on the health and well-being of people of colour and poor' (Kemp, 2011: 1201–1202). The concept green social work, developed by Dominelli (2012), works with the elements of the ecological and eco-social frameworks and adds to them the realities of social injustices and environmental injustices that are tightly intertwined with today's environmental crises. In the book *Green Social Work*, Dominelli (2012) identifies the need for social work to participate in the discussions on climate change at all levels and urges social workers to become active participants in the co-production of solutions. Dominelli's (2012) definition of green social work calls upon the profession to take responsibility and action in developing theories and practices that work with the multidimensional, local and global realities of today. The framework captures the interrelated workings of the social, political, economic and environmental. She highlights the importance of both practice and education to be not only interdisciplinary but to operate within transdisciplinarity, where disciplines develop common frameworks and coproduce solutions with residents (Dominelli, 2012). The framework gives social workers permission to move forward with confidence into the realm of environmental crises, to advocate for action and intervention and to embed this work in 'education and practice' (Dominelli, 2012: 25). Green social work turns the abstraction of climate change into a real complex problem for social workers to be engaged with and committed to. Keeping up with real problems is in line with Meyer (1989: 158), who advocated against complicity within social work, and to maintain its relevance by continuing to do more: 'today the real world from which we draw [the] context of practice is so complex . . . and so public . . . we know more, and responsibly, we see more. Thus, we feel obliged to do more'. Green social work asks social workers to operate at the local community level, within the daily lives of people, and build networks that connect the local to the national and global levels so that social workers' voices and advocacies of the people and their environment can have a pathway to travel to the ears of upper levels of government and policymakers.

Green social work involves:

> social workers working closely with people in their communities through everyday life practices to: respect all living things alongside their socio-cultural and physical environments; embed economic activities, including those aimed at alleviating poverty, in the 'social'; and promote social justice and environmental justice.
>
> *(Dominelli, 2012: 18)*

Dominelli (2012: 18) describes *how* social workers are to fulfil this responsibility:

> This will require social workers to engage in action at the local, national, regional and international levels and to use the organisations that they have formed to advocate for changes that favour the equal distribution of power and social resources, and protection of the Earth's physical bounty, including its flora and fauna.

By including the environment as an entity in its own right, Dominelli (2012) illustrates the interdependent relationship between humans and nature. In doing so, Dominelli (2012) has brought nature and the environment to the discussion table as entities to be considered with equal value when policies are being created, social programmes are being developed, and when interventions are being implemented.

The role of social work in engaging with environmental issues: what is missing?

Social work practice and research has struggled to locate itself among the theoretical philosophies that are used to address environmental issues. Efforts to understand what is going on and what actions should be taken up by social work in response to environmental issues has produced the ecological framework, the eco-social framework and now green social work. Among the discussed frameworks, green social work calls for action from multiple societal levels to apply the necessary pressure and to develop relationships with institutions that hold power in order to move from the theoretical to effective practice.

Social work can endure criticism from other fields of research. Social works' adaptability makes it difficult to pin down the theoretical lineages to which social work adheres. This topic is often discussed within academia where there are courses and conferences titled: *What is social work theory?* A common critique for social work that extends into the discussion of addressing environmental issues is a lack of theoretical specificity and inability to develop:

> mid-level theoretical frameworks that identify the mechanisms or pathways connecting environmental factors and human outcomes and can thus inform the design and implementation of environmental interventions.
>
> *(Kemp, 2011: 1202)*

One area that needs to be strengthened in social work research, education and practice is a working understanding of political economy. This requires delving into socio, political and economic understandings of capitalism and examining existing biases. Political economy connects our environmental crises to the structural frameworks that support the continued expansion of modern and post-modern capitalism. Coates (2003) is cognisant of these concepts; however a deeper examination is required. Harvey (1996) takes a contemporary umbrella view of major philosophies and modernises them to fit with current realities, for example, materialism, culture and class. It is important for social work research, education and practice to be comfortable working with concepts such as political economy – it 'firmly ties our environmental crises to the machinations of modern and post-modern capitalist expansion and the logic and power relations within the social, political and cultural framework within which we are currently living' (Dominelli, 2012; Tester, 2017). This broader knowledge is necessary in order for social work to effectively engage with environmental issues.

Discussion

If social work wants to salvage itself as a profession and field of research, then social work needs to adapt to the realities of the contemporary world – beginning with the causes and impacts of climate change (Dominelli, 2011). Social workers' ability to be flexible and adaptable is both a strength and weakness. It is a strength because adaptation keeps social work relevant. With a strong connection to society, social work has the ability to 'see the world as it is' (Meyer, 1989: 159) and develop interventions based on knowledge. Social workers have opportunities to listen and observe reality without moulding a reality to suit their comforts:

> reality will send out its own messages to us, to not distort what we see so as to suit our personal treatment interests, to search for the knowledge that will help us to manage our work and to develop the flexibility to suit intervention to case problems, even when both are new to us.
>
> *(Meyer 1989: 159)*

As a weakness, social work's flexibility and adaptability can cause resistance within the field. Continuously pushing both the profession and research forward to keep step with changing realities, and because the field of social work is so broad, there can be tensions when deciding whose reality should be pursued.

The purpose of social work is to develop a comprehensive understanding of a phenomenon or trend and form knowledge-based interventions. The strength of social work is that it is both academic and field-based. Social work maintains a close connection with the realities of the communities. It works with and is sensitive to a spectrum of changes that occur from the micro- to macro-levels. When practitioners work in the 'field', social work makes the 'abstractions real' (Meyer, 1989: 154). A strength of social work is the ability to stay engaged, have a strong knowledge-base rooted in experience and theoretical frameworks, while simultaneously adapting to constant change. This is difficult to do, whether as an individual practitioner or a researcher in the field. Taking experiences from the micro-level of society and translating observations and interventions up the hierarchal ladder to macro-level bodies of government and vice versa is challenging. My perception of social work is that it is the bridge that connects the realities of different populations with sources of power that can support and facilitate sustainable interventions. To be an effective connection the bridge needs to be informed in socio, political and economic understandings of capitalism with knowledge of the local, national and international implications. Environmental issues, such as the causes and impacts of climate change, are realities social work needs to inform and be informed about. Social work has to be active in developing awareness and sustainable interventions towards the impacts of climate change, and widen its role from crises intervention and disaster relief to prevention (Dominelli, 2012). Prevention means identifying emerging local level issues, maintaining active lines of communication and networks where information can be relayed to bodies of power that can assist in prevention and a shift towards sustainable transformation, a key goal for green social work.

References

Addams, J. (1961). *Twenty Years at Hull-House.* New York: New American Library, a division of Penguin Group (USA), Inc.
Bronfenbrenner, U. (1979). *The ecology of human development: Experiments by Nature and Design.* Cambridge, MA: Harvard University Press.
Coates, J. (2003). *Ecology and social work: Toward a new paradigm.* Blackpoint, Nova Scotia: Fernwood Publishing.
Dominelli, L. (2011). Climate change: Social workers' roles and contributions to policy debates and interventions. *International Journal of Social Welfare,* 20: 430–438.
Dominelli, L. (2012). *Green social work: From environmental crises to environmental justice.* Cambridge, UK: Polity Press.
Douglas, M. (1966). *Purity and danger: An analysis of the concepts of pollution and Taboo.* London: Routledge & Kegan Paul (Recent publication London: Routledge, 2002).
Gitterman, A. and Germain, C. N. (2008). *The life model of social work practice,* 3rd ed. New York: Columbia University Press.
Harvey, D. (1996). *Justice, nature and the geography of difference.* Cambridge, MA: Blackwell Publishers Inc.
Kemp, S. P. (2010). Place matters: Toward a rejuvenated theory of environment for social work practice. In W. Borden (Ed.), *Reshaping theory in contemporary social work: Toward a critical pluralism in clinical practice.* Chicago: University of Chicago Press, pp. 114–145.
Kemp, S. P. (2011). Recentring environment in social work practice: Necessity, opportunity, challenge. *British Journal of Social Work,* 41: 1198–1210.
Kemp, S. P., Whittaker, J. K., and Tracy, E. M. (1997). *Person-Environment Practice: The Social Ecology of Interpersonal Helping.* New York: Aldine de Gruyter.
Meyer, C. H. (1989). Practice in context: The maturing of a profession. *Journal of Teaching in Social Work,* 3(1): 151–160.
Saleebey, D. (2004). 'The power of place': Another look at the environment, *Families in Society,* 85(1): 7–16.
Tester, F. (2017). *Supervision correspondence.* [email].
World Café participant, 23 November 2014. From collected research notes.

34
Community resistance and resilience following an environmental disaster in Aotearoa/New Zealand

Heather Hamerton, Sonya Hunt, Kelly Smith and Rebecca J. Sargisson

Introduction

New Zealanders have a genuine pride in their natural environment. Tourism New Zealand brands our country as '100 per cent pure' with a focus on the purity of nature. Perhaps partly due to the 100 per cent pure image, the residents of the Bay of Plenty were horrified when the container ship MV Rena ran aground on Astrolabe Reef 12 nautical miles off the coast of the Bay of Plenty in October 2011. Dismay and anger was expressed that this accident could have happened at all as the reef is clearly marked on marine charts, and second because media reported that the vessel had previously failed maintenance checks and not carried out required maintenance between surveys (Donnell and Warmington, 2011). Media accounts also noted that the ship's cargo included containers with hazardous material (Backhouse, 2011). Within days, a large crack appeared in the hull and oil began to leak from the vessel, with a trail of oil visible and oiled seabirds being rescued from the sea. A day later, oil was haemorrhaging into the sea amid fears of a major environmental disaster. Five days after the ship grounded, coastal communities woke to 'black tides' as oil washed up on the beaches.

Maritime New Zealand, the government agency mandated to respond to oil spills, ordered people to stay away from beaches because of danger of oil toxicity and risk of spreading contamination. However, their advisories went unheeded and people flocked to the beaches to remove the oil. The vehemence and anger expressed at public meetings demonstrated that those charged with cleaning up the oil needed to quickly respond with a plan for local citizens to contribute. As an interviewee responsible for organising the response to the unfolding disaster stated:

> People there said to me 'right we need you to sit down and listen to us because we're not prepared to [stay off the beach] and we want you to listen really hard ... because this is a community who wants to be involved here'. And so I listened and then the next two weeks was about ... just continually lobbying people about the importance of listening to their community, measuring up the risks associated with it, and mitigating those risks.
>
> *(Key informant)*

As a result of mounting public pressure, a volunteer clean-up programme was organised by the Incident Command Centre (ICC) set up to respond to the oil spill. Over the next few weeks, 7,950 people registered to volunteer; over the course of the clean-up these volunteers collectively contributed 19,725 hours of beach cleaning (Fraser, de Monchy, and Murray, 2012). Local people were trained as team leaders and clean-up stations were set up along the coast. Several Māori groups organised their own clean-ups, initially operating independently, later gaining more support from authorities.

The value of action for communities has been previously documented (Verity, 2007; Winkworth et al., 2009). Negative impacts of a disaster are exacerbated by authorities failing to deal with communities in a helpful way (Picou, 2011). Communities and citizens will react responsibly, constructively and pro-socially to a disaster rather than with shock and panic (Helsloot and Ruitenberg, 2004) and their resilience can be enhanced if engaged in mitigation (Norris et al., 2008).

The context

The reef on which the Rena grounded is near the city of Tauranga, New Zealand's largest port. Approximately 115,000 people live in Tauranga; 17 per cent are Māori (indigenous peoples) (Tauranga City Council, 2016). Many people live along the coastal strip. A recent report on socioeconomic deprivation in New Zealand (Atkinson, Salmond, and Crampton, 2014) shows that the coast affected by the oil spill contains huge variability, with two (largely indigenous) communities in the 'most deprived' category (see Figure 34.1). Although many wealthy people live along this coast, surrounding suburbs score highly on the deprivation index.

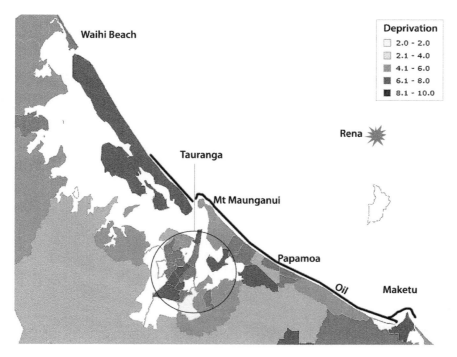

Figure 34.1 Tauranga City and Western Bay of Plenty showing deprivation scores
Source: adapted with permission from Atkinson et al. (2014)

The Bay of Plenty coast contains many kilometres of beautiful beaches and waterways which are a major tourist attraction. During summer, international and domestic tourists flock to the coast, with more than 80 international cruise ships calling at the port of Tauranga (www.port-tauranga.co.nz/). The Rena oil spill occurred in October, which is springtime in New Zealand; tourism operators were concerned that the disaster would keep tourists away over summer, resulting in loss of revenue (Tapaleao, 2011).

Many fishers who operate out of Tauranga Harbour were concerned about their potential loss of livelihood (Fletcher, 2011). For Māori, not being able to fish or collect seafood was devastating. Māori living in the hinterland were also affected, as this coastline is their 'foodbasket' (Environment Bay of Plenty, 2009; Waitangi Tribunal, 1989).

Our research

An important role for social workers and other social scientists when disasters occur is social research (Coates and Gray, 2012; Dominelli, 2012, 2013). Following the Rena grounding a group of social work and psychology academics and students researched the experiences of clean-up volunteers. Our research was supported by the regional council, sanctioned through the university ethics approval process and financially supported by the University of Waikato and Bay of Plenty Polytechnic. Council provided access to resources and circulated our survey in official communications. As authors, our location in Tauranga meant that we could respond quickly, which was important since crisis volunteer groups tend to be transitory and spontaneous (Voorhees, 2008). Green social work advocates for localism and devolution in the promotion of volunteerism, supporting formation of partnerships with local communities (Dominelli, 2012, 2015).

Our research was conducted in two phases. The first phase was an online survey circulated to the volunteer database to gather information about people's thoughts and feelings about the oil spill, their motivations to volunteer and their volunteering experience (Sargisson, Hunt, Hanlen, Smith and Hamerton, 2012). The second phase involved qualitative interviews with 39 volunteers and nine people who had been involved in organising the volunteer effort (Hamerton et al., 2015). For the interviews, we used a stratified random sampling method to ensure equal numbers of Māori and non-Māori participants.

People were interviewed individually or in small focus groups, and asked about their volunteering experiences, the need for support and suggestions for improvement. We asked volunteers about the impact of the oil spill on their lives and communities, and their motives for volunteering. We probed for information about their levels of hope or optimism prior to and after volunteering (Hamerton et al., 2015). Organisers were asked about their roles, their experiences of working with volunteers, stressors of the role, support received and suggestions for potential improvements (Hunt et al., 2014).

The research was designed with a critical theoretical base to illuminate people's experiences from a socio-cultural and political perspective. In the interviews, we probed for political, cultural, spiritual and critical views (Gray et al., 2009); and analysed the findings within a framework of environmental justice and equity (Miller, Hayward, and Shaw, 2012).

Research findings

Participating in the clean-up had a positive effect on those who volunteered. They described feelings of satisfaction, pride in what the community achieved together and a lessening of anger and helplessness (Sargisson et al., 2012). However, they found the work physically taxing, and the size of the problem at times seemed overwhelming. Overall, participants reported a positive experience; in addition to their own increased sense of hope and optimism, the volunteers successfully cleaned oil from many kilometres of sandy beaches and rocky shorelines. By January, 2012 most of the clean-up was over and beaches restored to their original state (Lockwood et al., 2016).

Participants talked about their emotional responses to the oil. One person described, 'a big cloud of sadness, anger and a feeling of helplessness'. Another person said, 'the thought of the beaches being contaminated was pretty devastating. We use it a lot for our socialising, our spiritual well-being, our fitness. The main reason we live in Tauranga is the sea' (Hamerton et al., 2015: 261).

Many people reported they had volunteered out of a sense of obligation or duty. One person noted, 'we have a responsibility to look after our natural resources, we are the guardians for the future generations' (Hunt et al., 2014: 38). This latter statement echoes the Brundtland Report's (1987) definition of sustainable development which underpins New Zealand's approach to resource management. Green social work similarly emphasises the importance of meeting current needs, while safeguarding future generations' needs, not only for people, but for all living things and planet earth (Dominelli, 2012).

Indigenous response in Maketū

Several different Māori communities live on the Bay of Plenty coast. Our research included a particular focus on the community of Maketū, as our survey results demonstrated that volunteers from Maketū were much more likely to have attended multiple clean-up events than volunteers in other locations (Sargisson et al., 2012). Maketū, located approximately 35 km east of the city of Tauranga, has a population of just over 1,000 people of which 67 per cent are Māori (Statistics New Zealand, 2013). This community has the highest possible deprivation index rating (Atkinson et al., 2014). However, the Maketū community is heterogeneous; alongside many people with low incomes are other, more wealthy residents. Regardless, it was the indigenous group in this community who were in the strongest position to lead the response to the Rena disaster. Although the clean-up group was led by Māori, non-Māori also participated and research participants reported that an unexpected outcome was enhanced community relationships between these groups.

Mathbor (2010) reported that communities have invisible assets which may not be readily apparent to outside responders. Māori communities have pre-existing structural strengths (Durie, 1998a). Marae (community buildings and grounds) are the focal point of Māori communities, located in the heart of their tribal lands. Marae complexes include a carved meeting house, dining hall and kitchen, toilet and shower facilities. Extended family groups can be very quickly mobilised to respond to emergencies, and their cultural values provide guides for behaviour (Proctor, 2010). Indigenous communities have considerable environmental knowledge and wisdom gathered and maintained over generations (Becker et al., 2008; Mercer et al., 2010). However, their strengths and capabilities for responding after disasters are often overlooked by decision-makers (Busby, 2010; Hudson and Hughes, 2007).

In the Māori world, the notion of whakapapa (loosely translated as genealogy) highlights the relatedness of people to all living things (Harmsworth and Awatere, 2013). When one part of the ecosystem experiences a shock, the entire system is put out of balance. Through ancestral ties to the natural world, Māori carry responsibilities to 'sustain and maintain the well-being of people, communities and natural resources' (Harmsworth and Awatere, 2013: 275). The view of earth as a sacred living thing is of primary importance to many indigenous peoples (Gray et al., 2007; Gray et al., 2008), including Māori (Walsh-Tapiata, 2004). This worldview is often in conflict with capitalist, global, neoliberal agendas based on individualism and consumerism (Tester, 2013), and often overlooked in Western social science (Briskman, 2008; Gray et al., 2008). However, green social work privileges deep ecology, reminding us of the fundamental holistic relationship between people and the natural world (Dominelli, 2013).

When oil began to reach the shore, Maketū was badly affected. Following a public meeting at the local fire station, a small group of Māori residents decided to begin to clean up the oil themselves rather than waiting for authorities to get organised (Smith et al., 2016). They sent one of their leaders to be trained in oil spill clean-up; she then trained about 450 volunteers who returned day after day to clean up the oil. The clean-up leaders were all members of the local Māori community who were quickly able to get support from elders to run the clean-up from their marae which was situated on the shore of the estuary.

Emotions were still raw, and participants talked about how devastated they were by the oil washing up on their beaches, and their concern about how the oil would affect their fishing:

> I think the first thing was that the food source was going to be affected . . . one of the major concerns for our local people, the fisher people. . . . It was quite a painful time too, because all you could do was stand and wait and see what more damage the oil was going to do to our environment.
>
> *(Focus group participant) (K. Smith et al., 2016: 5)*

Initially Maketū received no outside assistance, and relied on local residents and businesses for support:

> Our first help came from private people, local Kai (food) came from our locals. Baking, every day somebody would drop in baking.
>
> *(Focus group participant)*

> Some came down and brought sandwiches and cakes . . . others came down and worked in the kitchen. Everyone contributed in their own way. If they couldn't get on to the beach and contribute in that way, they found some other way of contributing.
>
> *(Focus group participant) (K. Smith et al., 2016: 3)*

Through our research, we found that over the four months of clean-up at Maketū, leadership roles emerged according to the people's different skills. Each evening one group member wrote a brief news flash that was circulated via email outlining highlights of the day and clean-up times for the next day. Others organised the clean-up itself, making sure that protective clothing was available and the decontamination unit was operating. Another group cooked food to feed the volunteers after they returned from the beaches, while others led small groups of volunteers down to the beaches to clean up oil.

The ICC in Tauranga supported Maketū, supplying protective clothing and equipment, and sent international oil-spill clean-up experts to Maketū. However, these experts were not well-received when they did not respect the knowledge of the locals. Clean-up leaders commented:

> We had several different people from different parts of the world come and try and say, 'you're doing things wrong, don't use this, you don't have permission to use that material'

and we just had to work out what's the safest option for us and most efficient to clean up the oil.

(Focus group participant)

They sent out their special shoreline coastal teams . . . they do the assessment and tell you how much oil there is . . . we asked them right from day one, 'take one of us with you to show you where we think you should look, the natural collection points. You don't know our beach, where the collection is, and please listen or give us some credit that we know where the oil will be'.

(Focus group participant) (K. Smith et al., 2016: 7)

The Maketū community's response demonstrated both resilience and responsiveness to the unfolding disaster. Furthermore, their local knowledge was valuable in predicting the path of the oil and which parts of the beach were mostly likely to be affected. Using their knowledge of currents and wind patterns, local Māori accurately predicted where the oil would wash ashore. Other writers have also noted the value of local and traditional environmental knowledge acquired through continual observation of, and interaction with, the environment (Becker et al., 2008; Colten et al., 2012; Mercer et al., 2010).

The actions of Māori in Maketū were a clear example of a small community asserting their sovereignty and their right to make decisions about their beaches. Participants told us it was important to follow their cultural and spiritual protocols in order to sustain the mauri (life-force) of the area and restore the balance disturbed by the oil spill. They discussed their responsibility as kaitiaki (guardians) of the natural environment to ensure its protection for future generations, noting that the oil spill was a breach of the covenant that binds people to the environment.

Resilience has been defined as the ability of human communities to return to equilibrium following a stress or shock, although resilience also includes the ability to adapt to changing circumstances (Dominelli, 2012; Norris et al., 2008). One aspect of Māori resilience noted by writers in Aotearoa/New Zealand is that of resistance. Mason Durie (2005) notes that resilience is an important aspect of Māori endurance in the face of colonisation and continued attempts to undermine Māori sovereignty. Since colonisation, Māori have resisted attempts to rob them of their land and treasures (Bargh, 2007; L.T. Smith, 1999); resistance occurs 'through everyday practices in which people reshape experience and actively participate in power relationships' (Proctor, 2010: 29). Resistance can be defined broadly to include both overt activism and everyday cultural practice and is an exercising of indigenous power' (Bargh, 2007).

Proctor (2010) has noted that both resilience and resistance characterise Māori people's striving to respond to threats within the natural environment. Their resilience, she claims, lies in their rich cultural heritage and strong social structures that make them well placed to respond in emergency situations, such as arose with the Rena oil spill. Their resistance, as noted by Bargh (2007) and Smith (1999), lies in their exercising sovereignty and taking leadership when disasters occur. The Maketū example fits well with green social work concerns to ensure that indigenous voices and values related to the natural environment are front and centre of social work theory and practice. It also provides additional evidence of the importance of fostering resilience within communities, and of recognising indigenous communities' knowledge, strengths and capabilities.

Lessons

Our research demonstrated that local citizens were well placed to respond when the Rena oil spill occurred, for two main reasons. First, their close proximity to the disaster location meant that they could act quickly, without waiting for the wheels of bureaucracy to grind into action. Second, local communities were those most affected, and therefore the most motivated to respond. The social and physical structures characteristic of Māori communities placed them in a particularly strong position as responders. The facilities available at marae, made them a suitable base for clean-up operations. Additionally, the ability of Māori to draw on extended family ensured they had enough people to take on all the various roles required. Māori values that emphasised the strong whakapapa links to the natural world, in this case to the sea and coastline, placed on them an additional obligation to be active in caring for their coastline.

Participants' stories highlighted the importance of environmental justice and the unequal impact on communities of environmental degradation. For example, a Waitangi Tribunal Report (1989) articulates the significance of kaimoana (seafood) for cultural activities for Māori of the area, including those living further inland. Much has been written about the unequal effects of disasters on different groups, noting that indigenous groups are particularly vulnerable and in need of specific protection (Besthorn, 2013; Bizzarri, 2012; Mercer et al., 2007). However, this assumption may be based on a failure to acknowledge both the deep environmental knowledge held by indigenous groups that has helped them to endure in specific locations over centuries (Mercer et al., 2010) and the contested and complex nature of vulnerability and resilience (Ellemor, 2004; Norris et al., 2008). The Maketū example shows how, despite their vulnerability, an indigenous community mobilised resources quickly, used their local knowledge to predict the path of the oil and resisted authorities' attempts to take control of clean-up operations. From this example, we believe that indigenous communities in Aotearoa/New Zealand have much to offer in disaster response and mitigation. Because of their long histories of resisting colonisation they are also skilled at resisting bureaucracy and asserting their sovereign right to make decisions that affect their resources and environment.

In addition, we noted a link between action and resilience. As people took action to clean up the oil, their resilience and hope for the future were similarly restored. We concluded that vulnerability and resilience are not fixed or static factors, but complex and multidimensional notions that change over time as a function of the interplay between people and their environment, as discussed in green social work (Dominelli, 2012). Māori communities, with their long history of struggle and resistance to colonisation, may be seen in many ways as vulnerable, but are also capable of drawing on cultural strengths that constitute their resilience.

In our view, the greatest lesson for green social work is to affirm the importance of recognising indigenous peoples' enduring relationships with the natural world and their deep knowledge about living sustainably within it. Authorities also came to recognise the value of working alongside communities, acknowledging the deep connection between well-being and the environment, and the healing effects of being involved in the clean-up.

Implications for social work practice

Social work academics have argued that the curriculum needs greater emphasis on strengthening students' understanding of the links between human society and the natural environment (Dominelli, 2012; Hayward et al., 2013). As well as employing students as research assistants, we incorporated our research findings into the curriculum. They became a vehicle for integrating issues of environmental sustainability and citizen action including empowerment, social capital formation, and resilience-building (Dominelli, 2012; Peeters, 2012; Thornley, Ball et al., 2015), enhancing global citizenship and eco-literacy in our students, through alerting them to the importance for social workers and psychologists to get involved in local issues (Adamson, 2014; Boetto and Bell, 2015; Hunt, et al., 2014; McKinnon, 2008).

Social work as a profession, alongside other professions, is increasingly engaging with environmental issues as part of an effort to respond effectively to the physical environment and recognise human interconnectedness to the planet and environment (Coates and Gray, 2012; Dominelli, 2012). This engagement expands the focus of social workers from considering the person only in the social environment and introduces concepts such as deep ecological social work which extends the focus of the discipline to include the natural environment (Besthorn, 2012). Opposition to further intervention to halt and reverse environmental degradation appears to be linked to Western notions of the individual as somehow separate from the natural world that lead to competitive exploitation of natural resources (Coates and Gray, 2012), consumerism, wastefulness and global neoliberalism (Urry, 2010; Dominelli, 2012). The 'separation of humans from nature through modernisation, industrialisation and urbanisation' (Gray et al., 2013: 4), demonstrates the inadequacy of Western knowledge systems in addressing environmental issues (Coates and Gray, 2012).

In Aotearoa/New Zealand, social work has a strong bicultural focus and concepts of indigeneity, alongside a holistic worldview including spirituality, create space for environmental issues to be considered within social work practice. Social work students learn about holistic models of well-being, such as Te Whare Tapa Whā (the four-sided house), a Māori model of health which defines well-being as having four dimensions: the body/physical; the mind and emotions; social and family; and spiritual (Durie, 1998b). Connections to the natural environment are part of the spiritual dimension. In this holistic view, if one aspect is unhealthy or in a state of dis-ease, then the person's well-being as a whole is compromised, echoing the tenets of green social work (Dominelli, 2012).

Our research participants clearly demonstrated an understanding of the interconnectedness of the physical environment and people's social and personal well-being, also emphasised in green social work. By utilising a narrative approach, we were able to learn how participants positioned themselves within their natural environment, when a part of that environment was under threat. We learned that an environmental disaster, such as the Rena oil spill, has a profound effect on both individual and community well-being. The health of people was clearly linked to the health of the environment. This notion is well-captured in the Māori proverb 'Toitū te whenua, toitū te tangata' ('When the land flourishes, the people prosper'). All of our participants reported adverse effects from the oil spill. Māori participants in particular clearly articulated this connection. Conversely, participating in the clean-up had a positive effect on individual and community well-being.

Conclusion

Our research contributes to the challenge facing social work educationalists and practitioners to increasingly and collaboratively develop a consciousness on environmental and ecological scholarship and green social work practice (Dominelli, 2012; Gray et al., 2013; Schmitz et al., 2013). Through conducting research on a disaster in our own 'back yard', we were able to demonstrate the value of engaging local citizens in disaster response, thus affirming a tenet of green social work. The oil spill clean-up gave people an opportunity to channel their grief and anger into action, resulting in both a greater sense of individual self-efficacy and satisfaction and also a successful environmental outcome.

References

Adamson, C. (2014). A social work lens for a disaster-informed curriculum. *Advances in Social Work and Welfare Education*, *16*(2): 7–22.

Atkinson, J., Salmond, C. and Crampton, P. (2014). *NZDep2013 Index of Deprivation*. Dunedin: University of Otago.

Backhouse, M. (2011). Stricken ship to remain overnight. *New Zealand Herald*, Auckland, 5 October 2011. www.nzherald.co.nz/shipping/news/article.cfm?c_id=&objectid=10756799 [Accessed 27 July 2017)].

Bargh, M. (2007). *Resistance: An indigenous response to neoliberalism*. Wellington, NZ: Huia.

Becker, J., Johnston, D., Lazrus, H., Crawford, G. and Nelson, D. (2008). Use of traditional knowledge in emergency management for tsunami hazard. *Disaster Prevention and Management: An International Journal*, 17(4): 488–502. doi:10.1108/09653560810901737

Besthorn, F. H. (2012). Deep ecology's contributions to social work: A ten-year retrospective. *International Journal of Social Welfare*, 21(3): 248–259. doi:10.1111/j.1468–2397.2011.00850.x

Besthorn, F. H. (2013). Radical equalitarian ecological justice: A social work call to action. In M. Gray, J. Coates and T. Hetherington (Eds.), *Environmental social work*. Oxford: Routledge, pp. 31–45.

Bizzarri, M. (2012). Protection of vulnerable groups in natural and man-made disasters. In A. de Guttry, M. Gestri, and G. Venturini (Eds.), *International disaster response law*. The Hague, Netherlands: T. M. C. Asser Press, pp. 381–414.

Boetto, H. and Bell, K. (2015). Environmental sustainability in social work education: An online initiative to encourage global citizenship. *International Social Work*, 58(3): 448–462. doi: 10.1177/0020872815570073

Briskman, L. (2008). Decolonizing social work in Australia: Prospect or illusion. In M. Gray, J. Coates and M. Yellowbird (Eds.), *Indigenous social work around the world: Towards culturally relevant education and practice*. Aldershot, UK: Ashgate, pp. 83–93.

Brundtland, G. H. (1987). *Our common future: Report of the world commission on environment and development*. New York, NY: Oxford University Press.

Busby, E. (2010). *The response to and recovery from the 2004 Eastern Bay of Plenty flood event* (Unpublished MPhil thesis). Massey University, Palmerston North, New Zealand.

Coates, J. and Gray, M. (2012). The environment and social work: An overview and introduction. *International Journal of Social Welfare*, 21(3): 230–238. doi:10.1111/j.1468–2397.2011.00851.x

Colten, C. E., Hay, J. and Giancarlo, A. (2012). Community resilience and oil spills in coastal Louisiana. *Ecology and Society*, 17(3): 5. doi:http://dx.doi.org/10.5751/ES-05047-170305

Dominelli, L. (2012). *Green social work: From environmental crises to environmental justice*. Cambridge, UK: Polity Press.

Dominelli, L. (2013). Social work education for disaster relief work. In M. Gray, J. Coates and T. Hetherington (Eds.), *Environmental social work*. Oxon, UK: Routledge, pp. 280–297.

Dominelli, L. (2015). The opportunities and challenges of social work interventions in disaster situations. *International Social Work*, 58(5): 659–672. doi:10.1177/0020872815598353

Donnell, H. and Warmington, A. (2011). Oil spill: Defence Force deployed. *New Zealand Herald*. Auckland, 10 October 2011. www.nzherald.co.nz/nz/news/article.cfm?c_id=1&objectid=10758052 [Accessed 18 October 2011].

Durie, M. (2005). *Ngā tai matatū: Tides of Māori endurance*. Melbourne, Australia: Oxford University Press.

Durie, M. (1998a). *Te mana te kawanatanga: The politics of Māori self-determination* (2nd ed.). Auckland, New Zealand: Oxford University Press.

Durie, M. (1998b). *Whaiora: Māori health development*, 2nd ed. Auckland, New Zealand: Oxford University Press.

Ellemor, H. (2005). Reconsidering emergency management and indigenous communities in Australia. *Environmental Hazards*, 6(1): 1–7. doi:10.1016/j.hazards.2004.08.001

Environment Bay of Plenty. (2009). *Kaituna River and Ōngātoro/Maketū Estuary Strategy*. Whakatane: Environment Bay of Plenty.

Fletcher, H. (2011). Rena disaster threatens fishing industry. *New Zealand Herald*, Auckland, 14 October 2011. www.nzherald.co.nz/business/news/article.cfm?c_id=3&objectid=10758866 [Accessed 18 October 2011].

Fraser, B., de Monchy, P. and Murray, W. (2012). *The Rena Volunteer Programme* Unpublished report to Bay of Plenty Regional Council. Whakatane: Bay of Plenty Regional Council.

Gray, M., Coates, J. and Hetherington, T. (2007). Hearing indigenous voices in mainstream social work. *Families in Society*, 88(1): 55–66. doi:10.1606/1044-3894.3592

Gray, M., Coates, J., and Hetherington, T. (2013). Introduction: Overview of the last ten years and typology of ESW. In M. Gray, J. Coates, and T. Hetherington (Eds.), *Environmental social work*. Oxon, UK: Routledge, pp. 1–28.

Gray, M., Coates, J. and Yellow Bird, M. (2008). Introduction. In M. Gray, J. Coates and M. Yellowbird (Eds.), *Indigenous social work around the world: Towards culturally relevant education and practice*. Aldershot, UK: Ashgate, pp. 1–10.

Gray, M., Plath, D. and Webb, S. (2009). *Evidence-based social work: A critical stance*. Abingdon, England: Routledge.

Hamerton, H., Sargisson, R. J., Smith, K. and Hunt, S. (2015). How volunteering reduced the impact of the Rena oil spill: Community responses to an environmental disaster. *International Journal of Mass Emergencies and Disasters*, 33(2): 253–273.

Harmsworth, G. and Awatere, S. (2013). Indigenous Māori knowledge and perspectives of ecosystems. In J. R. Dymond (Ed.), *Ecosystem Services in New Zealand: Conditions and Trends*. Lincoln, New Zealand: Manaaki Whenua Press, pp. 274–286.

Hayward, R. A., Miller, S. E. and Shaw, T. V. (2013). Social work education on the environment in contemporary curricula in the USA. In M. Gray, J. Coates, and T. Hetherington (Eds.), *Environmental social work*. Oxon, UK: Routledge, pp. 246–259.

Helsloot, I. and Ruitenberg, A. (2004). Citizen response to disasters: A survey of literature and some practical implications. *Journal of Contingencies and Crisis Management*, 12(3): 98–111.

Hudson, J. and Hughes, E. (2007). The role of marae and Māori communities in post-disaster recovery: A case study. GNS Science Report 2007/15, 51pp. Available on http://disasters.massey.ac.nz/pubs/GNS/SR%202007-015%20Role%20of%20marae%20and%20Maori%20in%20post%20disaster%20recovery.pdf

Hunt, S., Smith, K., Hamerton, H. and Sargisson, R. J. (2014). An incident command centre in action: Response to the Rena oil spill in New Zealand. *Journal of Contingencies and Crisis Management*, 22(1): 63–66. doi:10.1111/1468–5973.12036

Hunt, S., Sargisson, R. J., Hamerton, H., and Smith, K. (2014). Integrating research on the impact of volunteering following the Rena oil spill into the University of Waikato Social Work teaching curriculum. *Advances in Social Work and Welfare Education*, 16(2): 36–45.

Lockwood, S., Weaver, C. K., Munshi, D. and Simpson, M. (2016). The self-organising of youth volunteers during the Rena oil spill in New Zealand. *New Zealand Journal of Marine and Freshwater Research*, 50(1): 28–41. doi:10.1080/00288330.2015.1063515

Mathbor, G., M. (2010). Surviving disaster: The role of invisible assets in communities. In D. F. Gillespie and K. Danso (Eds.), *Disaster concepts and issues: a guide for social work education and practice*. Alexandria, VA: Council on Social Work Education, pp. 145–162.

McKinnon, J. (2008). Exploring the nexus between social work and the environment. *Australian Social Work*, 61(3): 256–268. doi: 10.1080/03124070802178275

Mercer, J., Dominey-Howes, D., Kelman, I. and Lloyd, K. (2007). The potential for combining indigenous and western knowledge in reducing vulnerability to environmental hazards in small island developing states. *Environmental Hazards*, 7(4): 245–256.

Mercer, J., Kelman, I., Taranis, L. and Suchet-Pearson, S. (2010). Framework for integrating indigenous and scientific knowledge for disaster risk reduction. *Disasters*, 34(1): 214–239. doi:10.1111/j.0361-3666.2009.01126.x

Miller, S. E., Hayward, R. A. and Shaw, T. V. (2012). Environmental shifts for social work: A principles approach. *International Journal of Social Welfare*, 21(3): 270–277. doi:10.1111/j.1468–2397.2011.00848.x

Norris, F. H., Stevens, S. P., Pfefferbaum, B., Wyche, K. F. and Pfefferbaum, R. L. (2008). Community resilience as a metaphor, theory, set of capacities, and strategy for disaster readiness. *American Journal of Community Psychology*, 41: 127–150. doi:10.1007/s10464-007-9156-6

Peeters, J. (2012). The place of social work in sustainable development: Towards ecosocial practice. *International Journal of Social Welfare*, 21(3): 287–298. doi:10.1111/j.1468-2397.2011.00856.x

Picou, J. S. (2011). The BP catastrophe and sociological practice: Mitigating community impacts through peer-listener training. *Journal of Applied Social Science* 5(2): 1–12.

Proctor, E.-M. (2010). *Toi tu te whenua, toi tu te tangata: A Holistic Māori Approach to Flood Management in Pawarenga* (Unpublished Masters thesis). University of Waikato, Hamilton, New Zealand.

Sargisson, R. J., Hunt, S., Hanlen, P., Smith, K. and Hamerton, H. (2012). Volunteering: A community response to the Rena oil spill in New Zealand. *Journal of Contingencies and Crisis Management*, 20: 208–218. doi:10.1111/1468-5973.12001

Schmitz, C. L., Matyok, T., James, C. and Sloan, L. M. (2013). Environmental sustainability: Educating social workers for interdisciplinary practice. In M. Gray, J. Coates and T. Hetherington (Eds.), *Environmental social work*. Oxon, England: Routledge, pp. 260–279.

Smith, K., Hamerton, H., Hunt, S. and Sargisson, R. J. (2016). Local volunteers respond to the Rena oil spill in Maketū, New Zealand. *Kōtuitui: New Zealand Journal of Social Sciences Online*, 11(1): 1–10. doi:10.1080/1177083X.2015.1009474

Smith, L. T. (1999). *Decolonizing methodologies: Research and indigenous peoples*. London: Zed Books.

Statistics New Zealand. (2013). 2013 Census quickstats about a place: Maketū community. Available on www.stats.govt.nz/Census/2013-census/profile-and-summary-reports/quickstats-about-a-place.aspx?request_value=13860andamp;parent_id=13856andamp;tabname=

Tapaleao, V. (2011). Rena spill: Bay tourist industry braced for sharp summer slump. *New Zealand Herald*, Auckland, 13 October 2011. www.nzherald.co.nz/nz/news/article.cfm?c_id=1&objectid=10758673 [Accessed 18 October 2011].

Tauranga City Council. (2016). Tauranga City: Statistical information report. Tauranga: Tauranga City Council.

Tester, F. (2013). Climate change as a human rights issue. In M. Gray, J. Coates and T. Hetherington (Eds.), *Environmental social work*. Oxon, England: Routledge, pp. 102–118.

Thornley, L., Ball, J., Signal, L., Lawson-Te Aho, K. and Rawson, E. (2015). Building community resilience: Learning from the Canterbury earthquakes. *Kōtuitui: New Zealand Journal of Social Sciences Online*, 10(1): 23–35. doi:10.1080/1177083X.2014.934846

Urry, J. (2010). Consuming the planet to excess. *Theory, Culture and Society*, 27(2–3): 191–212.

Verity, F. (2007). *Community capacity building – A review of the literature*. South Australian Department of Health, Adelaide, Australia.

Voorhees, W. R. (2008). New Yorkers respond to the World Trade Center attack: An anatomy of an emergent volunteer organization. *Journal of Contingencies and Crisis Management*, 16(1): 3–13.

Waitangi Tribunal. (1989). *Report of the Waitangi Tribunal on the Kaituna River claim (Wai 4)*, 2nd ed. Available on www.waitangi-tribunal.govt.nz/reports/viewchapter.asp?reportID=32147734-26C7-4D5E-812C-2DA77AC2A578andchapter=5

Walsh-Tapiata, W. (2004). The past the present and the future. The New Zealand indigenous experience of social work. *Social Work Review*, 16(Summer): 30–37.

Winkworth, G., Healy, C., Woodward, M. and Camilleri, P. (2009). Community capacity building: Learning from the 2003 Canberra bushfires. *The Australian Journal of Emergency Management*, 24(2): 5–12.

35
Human-made disasters and social work
A Ukrainian perspective

Tetyana Semigina

Introduction

Since March 2014, a violent armed conflict has been taking place in Donetsk and Luhansk, densely populated regions in eastern Ukraine. At the time of writing of this chapter, despite all diplomatic peace efforts, the situation remains very tense and could be characterised as catastrophic in many ways. As of mid-2016, more than 1.8 million internally displaced persons (IDPs) who had to relocate to the safer regions of Ukraine had been registered by Ukrainian authorities (MSPU, 2016).

This chapter is based on the idea that human-created disasters stemming from war represent an equally important dimension of a disaster (Harding, 2007). The ideas of the 'green social work' model (Kemp, 2011; Dominelli, 2012a; Norton, 2012) are based on structural and interdisciplinary approaches whereby social workers can deal with the consequences of disasters. A valuable point in the application of such ideas is that the environmental agenda considers the mobilisation of people and resources as the basis for enhancing resilience among disaster survivors and communities. The other important theoretical frame for this study is the sustainable development model of social work (Lombard, 2016). It looks at ways of modernising practice and making social work more political in demanding the resources needed for ensuring social justice, including environmental justice. One question that needs to be asked, however, is how to utilise these modern approaches in a country where economic development is low, the level of corruption is high, and social work is underdeveloped.

Based on reflections, face-to-face semi-structured interviews with IDPs and service providers, as well as group discussions with leaders of NGOs and a desk review of the literature, this chapter explores the support provided to war-affected populations in Ukraine. It discusses existing challenges for social work interventions in the context of mass displacement caused by human-made disasters.

While this chapter is focused mainly on social work interventions for IDPs undertaken in 2014–2016, it also examines lessons from the post-Chornobyl displacement of populations. The analysis updates the knowledge about the nature of the social work paradigm in Ukraine and argues for a change towards implementation of the alternative views of post-disastrous interventions from the green social work prospective, as well as seeking solutions based on solidarity which green social workers also practice.

The nature of warfare and its immediate social consequences

In late 2013, the president of Ukraine, Viktor Yanukovych, resisted, quite unexpectedly, the signing of the long-anticipated Associate Agreement between the European Union and Ukraine. As a result, mass protests started in the Maidan, the central square of Kyiv (Kiev). Thus, the movement acquired the name of *Euromaidan* or the *Revolution of Dignity*. In three months, peaceful protests grew to the point when mass violence erupted in Kyiv (Kiev) and other Ukrainian cities. In February 2014, when security forces started shooting the protesters, Yanukovych lost support even of his own Party of Regions and fled to Russia (Haran, 2015).

As Kudelia (2015: 21) has pointed out, the ouster of Yanukovych provided 'a pretext for Russian interference with Ukrainian sovereignty, as Moscow disputed the legitimacy of his removal, seized control of the Crimean Peninsula, and promoted a violent separatist drive in the south and east [of Ukraine]'. The Provinces of Donetsk and Luhansk each declared itself a 'people's republic', being formally independent, but fully controlled and supplied by Russia (Mitrokhin, 2015). Ukraine had announced an 'anti-terrorist operation' to fight the separatists (President of Ukraine, 2014). However, clashes between Ukraine and 'people's republic' were so extensive that they were regarded as 'war' on both sides. It has been reported that by mid-2016 nearly 10,000 people have been killed in this conflict, while the number of wounded and disabled combatants, as well as non-combatants, is significant, yet officially unavailable.

In August 2014, there were 56,000 officially registered IDPs. In August 2015 this number rose to 1.4 million, and in 2016 it reached 1.8 million. IDPs from the eastern Ukraine now account for 98 per cent of the total number of displaced Ukrainians, while those from Crimea account for 2 per cent. In August 2014, IDPs were composed as follows: 32 per cent children; 14 per cent were older people or people with disabilities. By August 2016, around 60 per cent of IDPs were retirees, 4 per cent were people with disabilities, and 14 per cent were children. Half of all IDPS moved to the areas close to their previous homes; others moved to other regions (MSPU, 2016). Statistics show the tendency of IDPs to return, especially to Donetsk Oblast, including both governmentally controlled and uncontrolled areas (Demchenko et al., 2014). As the movement between the two areas is possible with minimal challenges, people actively cross the boundaries between them to get registration as IDPs and obtain pensions from the Ukrainian state, while in reality still being residents of the separatist controlled territories. So, official statistics of IDPs do not reflect the real situation regarding displacement. It is also worth mentioning that this migration was not organised by the state. It was a voluntary choice of the people forced to leave their homes in order to avoid shelling or because of their pro-Ukrainian position.

Guerrilla warfare, including the use of heavy weaponry and indiscriminate shelling in populated areas, was combined with economic, propaganda and cyber war, so the conflict turned into the 'hybrid war' (Polese et. al, 2016). This war evoked tremendous changes in the environment of the people and the country. The UN has stated, 'armed conflict [in Ukraine] has caused great damage to the economy, the social infrastructure is ruined, and people are suffering' (UN, 2014).

In September 2014 and in February 2015, two Minsk Trilateral Agreements were signed by Ukraine, Russia, and the OSCE (Organisation for Security and Co-operation in Europe), supported by the US and UN Security Council. The documents outlined the ceasefire, exchange of prisoners, withdrawal of foreign troops, removal of illegal military formations from Ukraine, and Ukraine's control of the border with Russia. As of mid-2016, the contradictory agreements have not been implemented, and only the 'ceasefire' is in place. However, with daily sporadic shelling and casualties among combatants, Ukraine still does not control over 400 kilometres of its borders and 3 per cent of its heavily populated and industrialised territory. The Annexation of Crimea is not a subject of the negotiations at all.

All in all, in spite of the disputable causes and multiple realities of the armed conflict on the territory of Ukraine, and the vague political consequences, it has to be regarded as a complex meta-problem as any violent warfare would be. It has inflicted wide-scale damage to civilian life in all parts of Ukraine, not only in the Donbas area, and worsened the humanitarian situation in the whole of the country.

Socio-political environment in Ukraine from 2014–2016

Ukraine, a former Soviet country, with current population of 45.5 million people, lies at the bottom threshold of middle-income jurisdictions (World Bank, 2011). Since proclaiming independence in 1991, Ukraine has experienced systemic crises, when numerous political, economic, social and cultural problems suddenly became urgent. Major political and social transformations were accompanied in Ukraine, as well as in other post-socialist countries, by dramatic growth in poverty, juvenile delinquency, drug and alcohol abuse, mental health issues and an HIV/AIDS epidemic, among other issues (Semigina and Boyko, 2014).

By 2014, the Ukrainian political context was characterised by the dominance of rich elite groups. They intend to preserve their own power position over that of developing the society. Meanwhile, the public discourse is focused on socialist political rhetoric: populist proclamations of helping poor people, the provision of social guarantees, and equality. It resulted in the ambivalent combination of state paternalism with intentions of the state regulating all areas of society, and neo-liberalisation. The Constitution adopted in 1997 proclaims Ukraine a welfare state. However, standards of living are rather low, the socialist-style system of privileges for elite groups has been preserved (Semigina and Gusak, 2015).

The 2014 Ukrainian 'Revolution of Dignity' was aimed at changing corrupt post-Soviet state governance structures. The election of Petro Poroshenko as the new president of Ukraine in May 2014 and the Verkhovna Rada (Parliament) of Ukraine in October 2014, as well as local elections in October 2015, created grounds for radical changes in the political landscape of the country and inspired hope for improvement of the overall situation in Ukraine.

However, no substantial reforms have been implemented in two years, while the overall economic situation and social conditions have dropped to critically low levels all over the country, not only in the regions where armed conflict had occurred, and people felt disillusioned. Mass perceptions of being poor among the populace, their mistrust of authorities, intolerance, xenophobia and regional divisions have been leading features of public opinion in Ukraine for years (KIIS, 2016). Additionally, as in many post-totalitarian countries, human dignity and human rights are still not valued, and the discrimination of people with any special needs is a common practice in the country. At the same time, more public discussions on tolerance and people's special needs have been taking place since 2014.

Social support during the armed conflict on the territory of Ukraine in 2014–2016

Communication with IDPs, service providers, leaders of NGOs, as well as review of the literature and various documents (UN, 2014; Balakiryeva, 2014; MLSP, 2016; OHCHR, 2014; Semigina and Gusak, 2015; Sereda, 2015) make it possible to define the key target groups for social work interventions during the ongoing armed conflict on the territory of Ukraine.

These are: (1) IDPs; (2) populations in conflict zone (especially vulnerable groups); (3) combatants (those with disabilities and veterans); and (4) relatives of combatants.

There is a strong possibility that not all IDPs are in need of social work interventions, as many 'local migrants' belong to wealthy groups who fled zones of armed conflict at the very beginning, bought apartments in other cities, transferred businesses to establish places of safety and so on. The remaining IDPs used opportunities provided by NGOs and the local authorities of other regions of Ukraine to escape. A study conducted in 2014 (Sereda, 2015) also demonstrates that IDPs actively exercised social capital (i.e. mutual support between neighbours, friends, community groups, and other social networks) to adapt to a new environment, whether temporary or permanent.

The main target group at the initial stage of the conflict was the population in pre-displacement, in the process of displacement and post-displacement situations. In the absence of a state assistance programme, most IDPs have been seeking assistance from grassroots civic or religious groups. The response from these groups has been tremendous, supported by private donations, active use of social media and a civic spirit (OHCHR, 2014).

International organisations responded quite fast to the new social challenges. For example, UNHCR, UNDP, The Red Cross and IOM created special aid programmes inside organisations. In partnership with national NGOs, they provide targeted humanitarian, medical, psychological and legal assistance. Moreover, they helped in finding housing and employment for IDPs. The study findings support the common belief that social workers from the statutory services were restrained by the formal procedures of their institutions and by the lack of skills and knowledge of how to tackle the problems, although activists from NGOs lack such skills as well. So, at the first stage of the conflict (March 2014–August 2014), only the basic needs of the war-affected population were met, and mainly by non-state actors.

By the end of 2014, almost each region gradually introduced its own system of rapid response to the internal displacement of people. This included hotlines (round-the-clock telephone lines), helplines, checkpoints of citizens, road and location maps that are available on the websites of regional state administrations, list of important phone numbers of public services and public organisations, latest statistics of IDPs in Ukraine and so on. Also, regions with a larger percentage of IDPs have assistance groups that include psychologists and social workers (Semigina and Gusak 2015). In 2015, the state adopted programmes to support IDPs and military veterans. The existing accounts from IDPs and providers demonstrate that so far, not many social services are available and their quality could be questioned.

In 2015, following the welfaristic approach that assumes that social workers should deal with 'clients' according to entitlement criteria which are not based an individual needs assessment, although payments of in-cash social assistance play an important role in social support, the state introduced the rigid, bureaucratic system of getting an official IDP status and minimum cash benefits. Additionally, the state launched a housing assistance programme, while putting to one side the psychological and numerous other social needs of the people. The cash and in-kind assistance for war veterans and their families was also set up by the state, while social and psychological rehabilitation implemented in other countries was not considered as tools required to overcome the consequences of post-war traumas (Cabinet of Ministries of Ukraine, 2015). Perhaps the most serious disadvantage of this approach is absence of livelihood enhancing, capacity rebuilding or empowering programmes. Such programmes are widely used to tackle both structural and individual issues among disaster-affected people and hosting communities within the green social work paradigm (Dominelli, 2012a). In interviews, leaders of NGOs were rather critical of the new governmental policies on IDPs and war-affected populations.

The study reveals the peculiarity of the divided society in Ukraine. Findings confirm that social workers were not able to influence the partially negative perceptions of IDPs within hosting communities. The data revealed the strength of the assumption that social workers might have their personal views that are different from the views of IDPs affected by pro-Russian propaganda or those with relatives serving in 'separatist' military units. Social workers confessed that it was extremely difficult for them to keep their neutral position and to overcome the ethical challenges inevitable in ambivalent politically based humanitarian disaster.

Based on these interviews it is possible to suggest that the lack of psychosocial assistance, combined with cumbersome and often fruitless effort to collect benefits, has created demand for greater political representation of and advocacy for war-affected populations. To date, no credible information about the efficacy of the undertaken interventions to solve the problems of the war-affected population is available. Conducted interviews and the desk review of the literature suggest that the current approaches have a number of serious drawbacks. This is evident from low level of re-employment among the IDPs reported by the Ukrainian government (MSPU, 2016). A shrinking economy, high unemployment rates and policies of austerity are not the only determinants of this situation. Some IDPs also expect that social workers solve all their problems and satisfy all their needs, urgent and long-term, a view that is in-line with the post-socialist paternalistic tradition (Semigina and Gusak, 2015). By way of an illustration, Belevsky's (2015) work exposes the inefficiency of the state housing programme for IDPs.

Turning now to the situation on the territories that are not controlled by the Ukrainian government it is worth stressing that no reliable information is available on activities of social services run by the 'authorities' of the self-proclaimed 'people's republics'. According to the Charity Fund 'Dobrota' (2016) operating in Donetsk, local and Russian humanitarian support is provided to people in need in the forms of both in-kind and cash benefits. To sum up, the findings from the study suggest that the interventions aimed to support the war-affected population in Ukraine have not been based on green social work ideas. They were undertaken in the framework of the traditional post-Soviet 'welfaristic approach' and were almost certainly ineffective in tackling the needs of people and their communities.

Lessons learnt from human-made disasters on the territory of Ukraine

Additionally, 30 years ago the Ukraine (Soviet Era name) had already experienced a horrific human-made disaster. In 1986, there was a terrible catastrophe at the Chornobyl nuclear plant (commonly used Chernobyl is the transliteration from Russian, while Chornobyl is the Ukrainian name for this city located not far from the capital of Ukraine, Kyiv). In the post-Chornobyl years, over 350,000 people were displaced as 'ecological refugees' (Brown, 2011: 32). The disaster had a huge 'sociological, economical and psychological effect' (Davies, 2015: 228) in Ukraine and beyond.

At the time of the Chornobyl catastrophe, professional social services did not exist in the country and the socio-political environment of Ukraine, then part of the Soviet Union, was different. In the case of the Chornobyl disaster, people were evacuated immediately by the state to the safer regions with no prospects of ever returning. No public attention was drawn to the displaced population as the Chornobyl catastrophe became a 'classified' issue. The IDPs were entitled to long-term, minimal in-cash assistance, and they received housing, sometimes in villages or specially built settlements, with no possibilities of finding employment. Bromet's and Havenaar's (2007) research shows that the psychological and social needs of the displaced people have never been met. This happened partly because professional social work did not exist in the country then, and neither did professional psychological help or civil society organisations. In the 1990s, when the Ukraine became independent, civil society organisations began to advocate for the rights of the IDPs from the Chornobyl zone and work directly with the IDPs' communities.

The comparison of the responses to two human-made disasters in Ukraine – a technological catastrophe and an armed conflict, with the international standards for such services (UN, 2004; IFSW, 2012), actual experience (Lai and Toliashvili, 2010; Kang, 2013; Lindgren, 2013; Petrini, 2014; Lavalette and Ioakimidis, 2016) and modern social work paradigms (Dominelli, 2014b; Pulla, 2014) provides a sketch of several quick lessons.

Despite the experience of the internal displacement in post-Chornobyl years, Ukraine was not ready for the new wave of mass forced migration that occurred in 2004. Ukrainian governance system and social workers were not prepared to deal with the wide-scale consequences of human-made disasters. A possible explanation for this might be that Ukraine had not been involved in any armed conflicts since WWII, and lacked experience of severe natural disasters.

In both cases – dealing with the Chornobyl catastrophe and armed conflict – social workers did not play crucial roles in solving the social needs of the affected populations in Ukraine. In the second case, the evacuation from the war-affected zones was voluntary and spontaneous with a lot of public attention and media discourses. A huge challenge to modern social work is that the Ukrainian state chose the same approaches in dealing with the IDS as those used during the post-Chornobyl period. In 2014–2016, Ukrainian social workers focused on meeting the immediate needs of people, mainly displaced persons. But, they ignored the structural factors of the disaster's aftermath, and did not move from the direct provision of basic services and crisis interventions to shaping an enabling environment for new vulnerable groups, overcoming the low resilience of the war-affected populations and hosting communities with their limited resources as advocated by green social work (Dominelli, 2012a).

This and other studies (Ground Truth Solutions, 2015) show that Ukrainian IDPs and ex-combatants sometimes face negative attitudes, because they were held partly responsible for the events that caused this hybrid warfare. Problems within the hosting communities occurred during the post-Chornobyl displacement as well (Davies, 2015). However, they were hidden from public view, and no interventions to overcome their problems or improve cohesion and tolerance were undertaken.

As discussed in the section on social support during the armed conflict on the territory of Ukraine in 2014–2016, Ukrainian social workers were unlikely be capable to work with the hosting communities. It is almost certain that the ideas of rebuilding sustainable caring relations and resilient communities (Dominelli, 2012b), economic livelihoods for disempowered populations and sustainable development (Drolet et al., 2015) were not used by Ukrainian practitioners. Up until now, no activities for rebuilding solidarities within communities or within the conflict-torn society are likely to be undertaken by social workers (Jones and Lavalette, 2013; Basic, 2015).

Taking into account the observed inefficiency of the social interventions undertaken, the shift from a welfaristic approach to the green social work practice and sustainable development paradigm could be the solution for Ukraine with its underdeveloped social services and lack of economic resources. The main limitation for green social work practices in Ukraine, however, is associated with lack of relevant knowledge and skills, and this would require capacity-building in both the field and academy.

Prospective innovations and steps for social work in Ukraine

The ongoing armed conflict as a complex humanitarian disaster alongside the lessons from the post-Chornobyl displacement are calling for the revision and updating of social workers' education and work practice. The following steps may be helpful to ensure a sustainable social work response to the current armed conflict, and any future disaster.

1 Social work interventions have to be more 'green'

In 2014–2016, innovative crisis services and long-term interventions for Ukraine were created step-by-step by NGOs and some municipal service providers. Focused on the therapeutic approaches aimed at elimination of the disaster consequences of conflict for an individual and society (Ramon and Maglajlic, 2012), they broadened the repertoire for social work with groups exposed to disaster. Ukraine began to learn new concepts and paradigms of eco-social approaches which were new for local social workers, but well known in many other countries. These included: help with the assessment of relationships and resources held by a person or a family, art-therapy interventions to deal with trauma, brief psychosocial behavioural interventions to restore self-efficacy, among others.

However, all these traditional approaches aimed at restoring the social and cultural environment, and are insufficient for effective social work responses to disasters that aggravate the vulnerability of people, communities and society. Green social work practice that helps people to understand better the connection between consumption, production and reproduction and the extent to which sustainable development can promote more enduring investments in their society (Dominelli, 2014) should be introduced. The focus of prospective long-term interventions has to be shifted from the provision of social welfare (humanitarian assistance) for the war-affected population to activities aimed at strengthening livelihoods and the development of the social entrepreneurship alongside social and psychological adaptions to the new environment, building individual and *community resilience*, community cohesion and tolerance.

2 Community interventions have to become a core of social work practice

IFSW (2012) stresses that social work with displaced persons should enhance autonomy and empower communities, not simply focus on their survival. Ukrainian experience supports the idea that long-term social work interventions with disaster-affected populations must focus on recovering the relations between a person and social systems, developing local support systems, involving community resources, including volunteers, to help people who find themselves outside their usual environment and relationships. Researchers claim that assistance could be effective only if it is based on the community development approach (Lai and Toliashvili, 2010; Dominelli, 2012b; Lavalette and Ioakimidis, 2016).

The research findings demonstrate that the same is true not only for IDPs, but for ex-combatants who need an enabling community environment to successfully transition home and adapt combat skills so that they are just as effective at home as they were in combat. Support will be effective when it incorporates not only soldiers but also their extended support system, including significant relationships, families, and external resources (Brusher, 2011).

More empowering strategies have to be used by Ukrainian social workers to avoid dependency and social exclusion of disastrous survivors within hosting communities. For example, social workers should advocate changes in housing assistance to eliminate social exclusion among those Ukrainian IDPs who were accommodated in special settlements. Ukrainian experience and studies from other countries (Arooj and Zubair, 2012) provide evidence of the negative psychological and social effects of such intervention causing segregation, unemployment and mental health problems.

It is important to bear in mind the fact that in Ukraine, community social work is practically undeveloped, with the minor exception of the community of people living with HIV/AIDS. This highlights an emerging prospect for scaling-up community social work in the country.

3 Social workers have to be ready to counter inequalities caused by disasters

In 2014–2016, Ukrainian social workers did not advocate for the rights of war-affected groups or use effective macro-practices. This can be explained by the lack of skills in political social work, the profession's marginal status in society, and the absence of a nationwide, strong professional organisation (Semigina and Boyko, 2014).

However, social workers must be ready to raise their voice on behalf of people in a disadvantaged position, uphold human and citizenship-based rights (Dominelli, 2012a). They should ensure that the state does all it can to mitigate the effects of any disaster (Drolet et al., 2015). Social workers can also pursue issues of cohesion and national reconciliation, and protest against war (Ioakimidis, 2015). As Bašić (2015) pointed out, educating for peace should also become part of community work and social work education.

4 Social work educational programmes need to be revised to incorporate the lessons of 2014–2016

Social work as an academic discipline was introduced in Ukraine in mid-1990s. Universities created their own programmes that are not always in line with international social work standards, but mostly based on its post-Soviet legacy as sort of indigenous knowledge. The evident challenges to social work caused by the armed conflict raise questions about the content and format of its social work education.

In 2016, the Taras Shevchenko National University of Kyiv launched a new Master's programme in social rehabilitation with a specific focus on supporting military personnel and IDPs. The Ukrainian League of Social Workers arranged training for state social workers and psychologists to improve their skills in tackling new challenges. Training on topics related to social interventions for IDPs were also arranged by the UNDP.

Nevertheless, lessons learnt from 2014–2016 social interventions to war-affected population point to the necessity of going beyond ad hoc trainings and the exemplary Master's programme. A more comprehensive approach would include reshaping the existing Bachelor's and Master's programmes in social work. They have to be enhanced with courses that provide students with the skills and knowledge in: (1) techniques to work with disaster survivors' traumas, and with people suffering from negative adaptation to high-stress emergency events; (2) up-to-date methods of community development, community education and community research, including environmental issues and preservation of resources; (3) work within conflict situations in communities using techniques from mediation, facilitation and methods of political advocacy (political social work); (4) social work in situations of emergencies and mass migration, including skills commonly utilised during survival situations; (5) techniques for building resilience and economic livelihoods. Social Work in Disaster Situations might be introduced as an optional course or even an academic concentration for a Master's programme in some universities, while the concepts of green social work and environmental justice have to be broadly promoted among academics and practitioners via exchange information and study visits

Concluding remarks

Some of the notable characteristics of Ukrainian social work responses to human-made disasters were: unpreparedness of public services in dealing with a new problem for the country, and low levels of professionalism in the newly emerged social services. These drawbacks related to the observed low efficiency of interventions undertaken to counter the consequences and challenges of 'hybrid' warfare.

While civil society groups, with the support of other actors, have already resolved the issues of evacuation and immediate post-evacuation intervention, Ukrainian social workers still need to develop long-term intervention strategies for IDPS and other war-affected groups. These strategies could follow more 'green' approaches than either classical therapeutic approaches or Soviet-style welfaristic programmes. To be efficient, the strategy has to be designed as multilevel and multidisciplinary, as advocated by green social workers. Thus, it has to include the following interventions: individual assistance for restoration of livelihoods; regaining access to resources; connection with the community; advocacy; and participation in collective political actions, including those aimed at reconciliation. To implement these strategies and be ready to deal with the aftermath of disasters, social workers must be equipped with relevant knowledge and skills. These include the methods and techniques of green social work model in situations of survival, emergency and mass migration, and enhancing community resilience (Dominelli, 2012a). These new courses and programmes have to be introduced within the universities.

The recent challenges experienced by Ukraine in 2014–2016 raised the issue of social solidarity, tolerance, and social values. They questioned the nature of the welfare policy and social services, social workers' responsibilities and the level of their professionalism. These challenges also created the ambivalent task of developing inclusive social services for the new types of people in need during of economic collapse and shifting them from 'welfaristic' approaches to a sustainable development model and green social work practice.

References

Arooj, M. and Zubair, A. (2012). Resilience, stress, anxiety and depression among internally displaced persons affected by armed conflict. *Pakistan Journal of Social and Clinical Psychology*, 10(2): 20–26.
Balakiryeva, O. (2014). *Spektr problem vymushenykh pereselentsiv v Ukrayini: shvydka otsinka sytuatsiyi ta potreb* [Spectrum of Problems of Displaced Persons in Ukraine: Rapid Appraisal of situation and needs]. Available on: www.uisr.org.ua/news/36/83.html
Bašić, S. (2015). Educating for peace in the aftermath of genocide: Lessons (not) learnt from Bosnia. *Social Dialogue*, 10: 22–25.
Belevsky, O. (2015). Osoblyvosti mechanizmy nadannya derzhanoyi zhytovoyi dopomogy vnytrishnyo peremishchenym osobam v Ukaini [Peculiarities of the mechanism for provision of state housing assistance to the internally displaced persons in Ukraine]. *Ukrainskiy Sotsium*, 3: 104–113.
Bromet, E. J. and Havenaar, J. M. (2007). Psychological and perceived health effects of the Chornobyl disaster: a 20-year review. *Health Physics*, 93(35): 516–521.
Brown, L. (2011). *World on the edge: How to prevent environmental and economic collapse*. London: W. W. Norton and Co Publishers.

Brusher, E. A. (2011). Combat and operational stress control. In E. C. Ritchie (Ed.), *Combat and operational behavioral health*. Falls Church, VA: Office of The Surgeon General United States Army, pp. 59–74.

Cabinet of Ministries of Ukraine (2015). On Approval of the Integrated State Program for Support, Social Adaptation and Reintegration of Ukrainian Citizens who moved from temporarily occupied territory of Ukraine and areas of anti-terrorist operation to other regions of Ukraine until 2017: Order #1094.

Charity Fund 'Dobrota' (2016). *Otchety* [Reports]. Available on: www.dobrota.donetsk.ua

Davies, T. (2015). Nuclear Borders: Informally Negotiating the Chernobyl Exclusion Zone. In Morris, J. and Polese, A. (eds.). *Informal Economies in Post-Socialist Space: Practices, Institutions and Networks*. Palgrave-Macmillan.

Demchenko, I. et al. (2014). *Resume of the analytical report on results of operational research 'HIV-Services for Displaced Persons out of Vulnerable to HIV Groups'*. Kyiv: International HIV/AIDS Alliance in Ukraine.

Dominelli, L. (2012a) *Green social work: From environmental crises to environmental justice*. Cambridge, UK: Polity Press.

Dominelli, L. (2012b). Mind the Gap: Built infrastructures, sustainable caring relations and resilient communities in extreme weather events. *Australian Social Work*, doi:10.1080/0312407X.2012.708764.

Dominelli, L. (2014b). Promoting environmental justice through green social work practice: A key challenge for practitioners and educators. *International Social Work*, 57: 338–345.

Drolet, J., Dominelli, L., Alston, M., Ersing, R., Mathbor, G. and Wu, H. (2015). Women rebuilding lives post-disaster: innovative community practices for building resilience and promoting sustainable development. *Gender and Development*, 23(3): 433–448, doi:10.1080/13552074.2015.1096040.

Ground Truth Solutions (2015). *Key Perceptions of Internally Displaced People in Ukraine*. Available on: http://groundtruthsolutions.org/wp-content/uploads/2015/07/Ukraine_R2_2015.pdf

Haran, O. (2015). Ukrainian-Russian conflict and its implications for Northeast Asia. *International Journal of Korean Unification Studies*, 24(3): 125–158.

Harding, S. (2007). Man-made disaster and development: The case of Iraq. *International Social Work*, 50(3): 295–306, doi:10.1177/0020872807076041.

IFSW (International Federattion of Social Workers) (2012). *Displaced Persons*. Available on: http://ifsw.org/policies/displaced-persons [Accessed 5 November 2017].

Ioakimidis, V. (2015). The two faces of Janus: Rethinking social work in the context of conflict. *Social Dialogue*, 10: 6–11.

Jones, C. and Lavalette, M. (2013). Two Souls of Social Work. *Critical and Radical Social Work*, 1(2): 147–165.

Kemp, S. P. (2011). Recentring the environment in social work practice: Necessity, opportunity, challenge. *British Journal of Social Work*, 41: 1198–1210.

Kang, H. K. (2013). Claiming Immigrant Cultural Citizenship: Applying Postcolonial Theories to Social Work Practice with Immigrants. *Critical and Radical Social Work*, 1(2): 233–245.

KIIS, Kyiv International Institute of Sociology (2016). *Data Bank*. Available on: www.kiis.com.ua/?lang=engandcat=data

Kudelia, S. (2015). The house that Yanukovych built. *Journal of Democracy*, 25(3): 19–34.

Lai, K. and Toliashvili, B. (2010). Community-based Programme for War-affected Children: the Case of Georgia. *Social Work and Social Policy in Transition*, 1(2): 92–118.

Lavalette, M. and Ioakimidis, V. (2016). Popular' Social Work In Extremis: Two case studies on collective welfare responses to social crisis situations. *Pradžia*, 3. Available on: www.zurnalai.vu.lt/socialine-teorija-empirija-politika-ir-praktika/article/view/10047

Lindgren, E. R. (2013). *The internally displaced people of Colombia*. Gotenburg: Goteborgs Universitet.

Lombard, A. (2016). Global agenda for social work and social development: A path toward sustainable social work. *Social Dialogue*, 14: 6–15.

Mitrokhin, N. (2015). Infiltration, instruction, invasion: Russia's War in the Donbass. *Journal of Soviet and Post-Soviet Politics and Society*, 1(1): 219–250.

MSPU, Ministry of Social Policy of Ukraine (2016). *Information for Internally Displaced People*. Available on: www.mlsp.gov.ua

Norton, C. L. (2012). Social work and the environment: An eco-social approach. *International Journal of Social Welfare*, 21: 299–308.

OHCHR (2014). *Report on the Human Rights Situation in Ukraine* (16 September).
Petrini, B. (2014). Employment and Livelihoods of Sudanese Refugees in Cairo. *Oxford Monitor of Forced Migration*, 4(1): 51–56.
Polese, A., Kevlihan, R. and Beacháin, D. O. (2016). Introduction: hybrid warfare in post-Soviet spaces, is there a logic behind? *Small Wars and Insurgencies*, 27(3): 361–366, doi: 10.1080/09592318.2016.1151660.
President of Ukraine (2014). On the decision of the National Security and Defense Council of Ukraine of April 13, 2014 "On urgent measures to overcome the terrorist threat and preserve the territorial integrity of Ukraine": Order #405/2014 issued on 14th of April, 2014.
Pulla, V. (2014). Towards the greening of social work practice. *International Journal of Innovation, Creativity and Change*, 1, 3. Retrieved from www.researchgate.net/publication/261798609_Towards_the_Greening_of_Social_Work_Practice
Ramon, S. and Maglajlic, A. (2012). Social work, political conflict and displacement. In (Eds.), *The SAGE handbook of international social work*, London: SAGE, pp. 311–324.
Semigina, T. and Boyko, O. (2014). Social work education in post-socialist and post-modern era: case of Ukraine. *Global social work education: Crossing borders Blurring boundaries*. Sydney: Sydney University Press, pp. 257–269.
Semigina, T. and Gusak, N. (2015). Armed conflict in Ukraine and social work response to it: What strategies should be used for internally displaced persons? *Social, Health, and Communication Studies Journal*, 1(2): 1–23.
Sereda, Y. (2015). Sotsialniy kapital vnytrishnyo peremishchenych osib yak chynnyk lokalnoyi integratsii v Ukraini [Social capital of internally displaced persons as a factor of local integration in Ukraine]. *Ukrainskiy Sotsium*, 3: 29–41.
UN (United Nations) (2004). *Guiding Principles of International Displacement*. Available on: www.unhcr.org/43ce1cff2.html
UN (2014). *UNDP-EU project will support recovery and help IDPs in Eastern Ukraine*. Available on: www.un.org.ua/en/information-centre/news/1919
World Bank (2011). *Middle Income Countries Overview*. Available on from: www.worldbank.org/en/country/mic/overview

36
Strategies used by activists in Israeli environmental struggles
Implications for the future green social worker

Ariella Cwikel and Edith Blit-Cohen

Introduction

The interdependency between humans and nature is the basis upon which humans rely for their physical existence (Dominelli, 2012). Another connection – an emotional and spiritual one – cannot be overestimated for human development, survival and well-being (Besthorn, 2003). Social work has been slow to enter the environmental field, in research, teaching and practice (Dominelli, 2011; 2013). Theorists and practitioners have called for the adoption of a new perspective for the 'person-in-environment' concept and the definition of a holistic approach to social work which utilised interdisciplinary discourses to promote practices and policies that take responsibility for the environment and those most vulnerable to changes in it (Dominelli, 2012). In this study, we identify the ways in which communities organised in local environmental struggles and examine what is, or could be, the role of green social work in such cases.

Context and description of the phenomenon

The State of Israel is a small country, with limited natural resources, a high population growth rate, and ongoing security needs. It will become increasingly crowded over time (Tal, 2006). Thus, clashes between the desire to preserve resources and habitats, uphold public health and adequate urban land-use standards, and needs for development, housing, infrastructure and waste management are expected (Shmueli, 2011).

Israel is an extreme example of pressures on the environment and many citizens face development plans that constitute an environmental threat (Tal, 2006). De-Shalit (2004) delineates the options in such cases: asking for compensation, or demanding that the hazard be relocated. Neither of these would solve the problem. The third option is to demand the cancellation of the plans. Because development involves economic interests of powerful people, such calls are usually rebuffed, leaving two choices: to give up or fight. This chapter elucidates those who choose to mobilise and fight an environmental threat to their health, income, quality of life and accessible natural habitats.

The method consisted of gathering information from 11 informants (six women, five men) by conducting in-depth semi-structured interviews. A review of documents and media stories was used to gain a broader picture of their struggles. The data was then content analysed to define main themes and categories of ideas. The findings were integrated using literature, to identify the methods of organisation and action strategies used. Conducted between the years 2013–2015, the research collected data from activists from three communities, who mobilised against environmental threats in the last decade in Israel's geographic and/or social periphery.

Those interviewed included three from the *Action Committee for Sasgon Valley*, who fought to preserve a unique natural habitat and prevent the building of a hotel complex in the Timna Canyon in south Israel; four activists from the *Action Committee for the Gazelle Valley in Jerusalem*, who fought to keep an urban nature preserve open to the public; and four activists from *We Want to Live Without Mines* (WWLWM), who fought to prevent the establishment of a phosphate mine at the Barir Field site, near the city of Arad in the south of Israel. All respondents requested the use of their real names.

Each of these conflicts extended over more than a decade, and had countless twists and turns to its plot. Therefore, in this chapter, we will present in detail only one of the three: the Barir Field struggle, the longest and most complicated one.

Fighting radioactive dust: Arad versus phosphate mine

Arad is a city in the Negev region in southern Israel, home to 23,400 residents and rated 5 out of 10 in the country's socio-economic scale. It was established in the early 1960s as a workers' town (Roded, 2016). In 1980, a vast deposit of phosphate ore, used in the chemical, agricultural and food industries, was accidentally discovered under the city. Mining of phosphate ore contains radioactive elements, such as radon, which accumulate as dust particles, which if inhaled, increase heart and lung disease morbidity (Shorman, 2013).

Two plans for phosphate mining in the site had been submitted and rejected in the past. In 2004, Rotem-Amfert Negev Ltd., controlled by Israel's biggest holding company, filed a plan to build a phosphate mine at Barir Field. The profit from the mine was estimated at $25 billion (Peled, 2014). The site consisted of 3,200 acres, and was planned less than 4 kilometres from Arad, 3.5 kilometres from Kseiffe and less than 1 kilometre from Al-Forah. Kseiffe and Al-Forah belong to Arab semi-nomadic ethnic groups or *Bedouin*. The mine would have devastating effects on these villages. However, political, economic and nationalist realities influenced their ability to participate in this struggle. They face immediate existential threats including expulsion and destruction of their homes, and a struggle for recognition, exerting pressure of limited resources remaining to resist the mine. However, its impact on the villages is integrated into their struggle narratives.

When the proposal was revealed, opposition to the mine was organised, out of concern for health, the city's economy and image. After years of Action Committee work, those involved founded WWLWM in 2011. This has achieved partial success in harnessing the Arad municipality. Despite a former mayor becoming a board member at ICL, the city's official position remained to oppose the mine.

The issue has been discussed repeatedly in the Social-Environmental Committee in the Knesset (legislative branch of Israel's government), with support from environmental groups, like the Coalition for Public Health (CPH), volunteers and professionals. Rulings on the matter were repeatedly postponed, partly due to disagreements between external experts and representatives of the Ministries of Environment and Health, regarding risks inherent in the mine's construction to 55,000 residents of Arad Valley. Health impact assessments found the mine to be hazardous and estimated that subsequent air pollution will lead to seven deaths each year. Radioactivity measurements, taken at a nearby abandoned mine and the phosphate-rich Barir Field were found to be between 2–8 times higher than the permissible exposure rate.

In 2010, Prime Minister Benjamin Netanyahu prevented the Regional Committee from discussing the case, and demanded a second opinion, kept under a cloak of 'national security', with help from the military secretary (who was later appointed chairman of ICL). A Supreme Court appeal by WWLWM and CPH revealed that the Report found nothing new and secrecy was unnecessary. In 2011, the Ministry of Health Committee commissioned an American expert whose report stated that there was a health hazard associated with the mine's construction. Consequently, the health minister opposed the plan in March 2014.

Rotem-Amfert began a high-profile public campaign to push the mine, stating that the plan's cancellation will result in layoffs and the plant's closure. It recruited the Ministries of Economy, Infrastructure, Finance and the Interior, and continued to promote the plan. The National Master Plan for Mining and Quarrying (NMP 14c) Committee decided to approve a mining area twice the original size. In the next Committee meeting, while protestors demonstrated outside, the Ministries of Health and Environment referred the issue back to the National Planning Council.

In December 2015, the Council approved the 'Policy Document for Mining and Quarrying of Industrial Minerals', primarily declaring Arad Valley the most suitable place for phosphate mining, and decreed a trial mine. Yet, a specialist had determined that this trial is irrelevant to the question of the mine's actual safety. In February 2016, the Arad municipality and 1,900 citizens filed a Supreme Court Appeal, claiming that permitting mining in Barir Field would threaten public health and that the Committee misinterpreted the 'Clean Air Act' 2008. In July 2016, the Regional Committee recommended to remove the mine from the NMP 14c. The Supreme Court discussed the Appeal in March 2017 and denied WWLWM and the City of Arad's petition, stating that there is still a place for such objections in the planning process itself.

What and how: organising for action

Strategy is required only if your goal is making a decision-maker or public servant do something he/she does not wish to do. Otherwise, you only need a plan. A plan defines the steps required to achieve a goal; a strategy addresses power relations between players of unequal power (Bobo et al., 2001).

In all three environmental conflicts there were powerful rivals: a wealthy, determined developer; the mayor of the municipality; ministers and even the prime minister; the fiercest financial force in the country; or all of the above. Therefore, 'unequal power' would be a huge understatement. In taking on the challenge, communities had to have a strategy, tactics and methods of operating.

But first, you need a 'Why?'

We asked the activists what brought them to take action. Some spoke of anger at the decision, or fear of its repercussions. The moment of realisation was usually powerful, and they used words like 'catastrophe', 'a bomb hitting me', 'danger', and 'shocking' to describe them. Eran said: 'Why did I join?! Well, because it blew my fuse!' That anger fuelled them, as Alinsky (1971) would say, and prevented them from sitting idly by while injustice got underway.

Some saw it as Israel did, 'a battle for life or death, a battle on the home front'. But most of them spoke more of the social responsibility, solidarity and a never-to-be-repeated chance to take action. Tal shared that she had once missed a chance to save a site where endangered flowers bloomed: 'I took my time, thinking what to do. By the time I got there it was ruined'. I said to myself, 'that mustn't happen again. I won't let it'. Timor spoke of a role he felt obligated to fulfil, as a part of an unspoken public land trust:

> If you live far away, you won't know there is a threat here. But here I'm a kind of emissary for others, as they are to me where they live. Without me having any more claims to the piece of nature that I am fighting for than they do.

In these struggles, the power structure was that of David vs. Goliath – the environment protectors challenging capitalist powers, contractors, and multimillionaires. Most activists felt it was time citizens fought back and spoke up for nature and future generations, feeling responsibility towards both.

Several activists spoke of a battle worth taking on, though prospects of succeeding are slim. But the feeling that *not taking action* would be worse than failing kept them going. Eran said:

> We started with the realisation that it's hopeless, but it's the right thing to do! I said to myself, 'F*** it! I don't care if this thing is unstoppable, I'm going to fight it'. I need to be able to look my kids in the eyes one day, and say, 'Daddy did what he could'.

For some, knowing they had nothing to lose was key to creating a strategy.

Organising strategies: getting ready to rumble

After forming an Action Committee, the activists had to learn to collaborate, communicate, assign formal roles and create a 'core' group. The core was the most active, a kind of inner circle; the outer circle came for mass support, such as demonstrations or email campaigns. While there were sometimes other circles, there were always at least these two.

They relied on the group's assets: knowledge, experience, connections, skills and talent. Some of the roles were formal: 'treasurer', 'spokesperson', 'copywriter'; others informal: 'peacemaker', 'anarchist', 'responsible adult'. Leadership roles developed naturally and were not decided upon officially. Simultaneously, they became experts in the details: statutory planning, environmental protection law, ecology, geology and history. They learnt thoroughly the plans they were fighting against.

Action strategies and tactics: getting things done

Strategies and tactics are defined differently by activists compared to the definitions given in the social change literature. One reason is the elusive nature of these definitions and differences in their interpretation. Furthermore, it is hard to separate tactics from strategies, since they are defined in the context of the strategy they serve (Bobo et al., 2001).

Social action. An approach aimed at redistributing power, a goal it has in common with the *Green Social Work Model*, which uses specific, locally adapted social action to confront 'structural inequalities including the unequal distribution of power and resources' (Dominelli, 2012: 25). Social action targets decision-makers and engages in creating policies and institutional practices. It is oppositional and uses confrontation, direct action and negotiation, harnessing the power of collective action for pressure, attention or disruption purposes. Social action movements, including environmental struggles, have to constantly reinvent their strategies, making them wider and more sophisticated (Rothman, 2001).

The strategies and tactics used were not always systematically planned. Rather, they were often a reaction to changing circumstances, in complex situations with multiple players. Therefore, activists were required to identify factors and forces at work, to determine which actions would bring desired results. Sarit explained:

> You cannot wage a struggle that is one-dimensional, it won't work. It must be 'multi' – community, media, government, court, district committee. There is something in the combination that helps the struggle … it must be all together, or it won't exist.

Eran recalled a metaphor used by their hired campaigner – the struggle as a leaf rake, where each tooth is a different front and all of them are necessary for the rake to work. Therefore, different strategies were used and sometimes the same tactic was employed to achieve several strategies.

Social action tactics assume that power derives from either money or people. Those who have little money must recruit as many people as possible to amass power (Alinsky, 1971). The activists spent valuable resources recruiting support for their cause. In environmental struggles, it is important to be able to claim to speak for the public. Thus, you need to demonstrate that you *actually* have public support.

Recruiting tactics. Staples (2012) describes tactics for gaining public support, all implemented in the three struggles: distributing pamphlets, public assemblies, going door to door, engaging school committees, networking, emailing campaigns, information stands, newspaper articles and collaborating with local organisations. In each action, they had to adapt the message to the audience. This was challenging since the situations were complex, and one needed to be accurate, but not tedious. Sometimes they only had one chance to get it right.

'… *But names will never hurt me*'. Another tactic used was naming, or giving names to the places they were fighting for. None had a formal name when they started out. 'Gazelle Valley' was named to emphasise the unique wildlife of the site. Similarly, 'Sasgon Valley' could not be found on any map before a developer thought of building a huge hotel there. But once the Action Committee was formed, they had to find something catchy, and named it after a mountain nearby. Soon everyone was using the new name. The developers protested, saying there is no such thing as 'Sasgon Valley'. The activists knew that the developers' attempts to uproot the name showed they were in trouble (Golan, 2010).

In the Arad case, it was the other way around. The mining company was the one doing the naming. There was no such place before, but now, whenever anyone mentions it, they call it Barir Field. Laksi recalled:

> The name appropriates the place before it's theirs. We shouldn't have fallen into that trap and used the name coined by the mining company. We tried using a different one, but it's too late, it's etched into the collective language.

Language is a significant component in environmental struggles, where the use of phrases such as 'wilderness' or 'untouched nature' is like a battle cry (Pickerill, 2008). Indeed, the findings show the conflicts studied used accurate and calculated messages and coined names with symbolic significance, creating identity and meaning.

Partnerships and coalitions

All the activists said that coalitions were critical for success. Like-minded local or national, institutionalised or grassroots organisations joined the different struggles based on their own agendas. The organisations brought their resources, disciplines and reputations. They could gain publicity by appealing to their constituencies, and adding expertise. The activists understood credit was one of few commodities they could barter with. Making sure all the partners' logos were on any publicity was a way to give them recognition and gain support.

At certain points, the organisations involved were leading the campaigns forward. Eran commented:

> We were always behind the scenes, making sure things moved. It became a real partnership . . . they considered our opinions. Many of our comments were incorporated in legal or statutory issues, of which we are by no account professionals. But they knew we are out there, on the ground, and know all the details. I guess they kind of needed us, too, in a way.

'Find a penny . . .'

Since all the struggles were community-based, this meant that resources were always scarce. The activists funded much of the expenses themselves: photocopies and letters, gas or travel expenses and even lawyers. They usually relied on small donations from citizens, funds or other organisations. Tova said:

> I told people even small change would help. They saw they weren't expected to contribute large sums, so they donated. I raised $300 in one day like this! Two months I kept it going. Our funds are mostly from those small donations.

Social action strategies

Once a campaign gains support, the next stage is to demand change by using social action and confrontation strategies (Homan, 2010). All the campaigns used mass petition signing, as a public show of support. One of the groups successfully pulled off an email-bombing campaign, targeting the mayor. Sarit told us with a grin: 'Finally he called and said, 'OK, you've convinced me, now *please* call off your guys. Tell them to stop flooding my e-mail box!' So, naturally, we called everyone and told them to keep sending e-mails. It was working!' Another group organised a mass public protest in the disputed valley. People showed up, but that day they learnt a humbling lesson, as Yaniv put it: 'If you want to look big, don't stand next to a mountain.' No matter how big the crowd, it looked dismal in comparison'.

Target practice

In all struggles, the threat was defined as the target (i.e. fighting against the threat, not the people behind it). The communities defined their objection carefully, opposing a specific, harmful location; the mining, not the company's workers. They wanted to protect the natural habitat, not tarnish the contractor's name. Mickey explained: 'We said our problem is the plan, not the contractor. What do I care *who* wants to build here? I want to protect this place, period. Why do I have to go after someone personally?'

This choice contradicts social action strategy models which emphasise that the target is the one with power to grant what you demand. It is always a person. The aim is to personalise the target (Homan, 2010). In light of this, this decision made by all three groups seems odd, but it is linked to the 'ethical code' that the different groups decided to abide by.

Polite green action machine

The next strategy identified was leading a positive, honest, decent, 'clean campaign'. Though it seems out of place in a struggle, many of the activists told us how they made conscious group decisions to uphold a certain moral standard. Timor claimed:

> We can't try to clean and fix the way things are, and at the same time be the ones ruining things, in the way we act. There has to be a correlation between the means and the end. Much of our strength depends on that.

Eran added: 'You can always attack; you could always take off the gloves, but then try putting them back on again! You don't slander. Because in the end, someone could do the same to you'. Another essential principle was being truthful and mindful of language. Timor explained:

> The gut reaction is always to lash back. But we really tried not to . . . even when we were harsh, we were never disrespectful . . . we also decided to never lie, *ever*. That was really important to us. There are moral sides to it, but also practical. Once you're caught bull★★★★ing, being dishonest, the one thing that you have, which is a bit of credibility, is gone.

Although these standards were not necessarily followed by their opponents, who were sometimes cynical, dishonest, and used every trick in the book. Powerful and simple (yet not always truthful) messages where used by opponents, while local activists had to strain to reach the public, with messages that encompassed the complexity of the struggle. The activists often became upset when adversaries used environmental figures and released misleading information, fabrications or just plain lies. Calling out lies and liars sometimes became necessary. In all three cases, tackling these instances during their struggles provided painful, low points, rather than victories.

In this case, we wondered as Alinsky (1971) did, whether playing clean in a dirty game is the right thing to do. Activists tried many times to alter the balance of power, including attempts to recruit local government, challenging opponents in court, using media to try and sway public opinion to their side, all carried out with caution. Homan (2010) emphasised the importance of preserving a moral code during community conflicts, as shown by the activists in this research, who chose truth over lies, to target threats rather than people, and play fair. Homan (2010) encourages activists to consider the moral implications of their actions, but also the consequences of avoiding them. He asks, whether ethical standards that dictate a 'polite' fight are still ethical, if they prolong wrongdoing and injustice.

Ready? . . . Steady . . . Stall!

Stalling, buying time and avoiding irreversible decisions was also useful. Laksi wondered:

> If we're facing the tractors, that's one step before losing. By stalling, I mean not getting to that point. We want to avoid statutory ruling. Stall, stall, stall. . . . Only come to the point where decisions are made, if we know for sure they will be in our favour.

Stalling bought time to organise, recruit more support or devise a plan. For this tactic, it became handy to cooperate with organisations with legal action capacities. In all three cases, taking a case to court was both the only way to get justice and a significant method of stalling, or preventing bad decisions from being made in statutory or other systems.

Mixing in the media

Print, broadcast and internet media were used in all three environmental struggles. These were usually the first tactics used, a way to tell people about the threat, gain support and place pressure on decision-makers. They used local and national (print and net-based) newspaper throughout the duration of their struggles. Prime-time television coverage was a sought-after accomplishment. This is not always a safe course of action. In one case, it backfired, when a reporter thought to be supportive aired a distorted portrayal of the conflict and the activists' motives for participating.

Given that the media is dominated by the power elites, and the fluctuating nature of media attention, it is not surprising that the need to continually raise awareness of the struggle was addressed by all the participants. They did their best to stay in touch with reporters, gave them 'exclusives' and used peaks in the conflicts to receive more coverage. A few of the activists reported creating 'image events' (Delicath and DeLuca, 2003) or powerful visual imagery, and the messages released to the media were always well thought out. Here, too, the ethical code decreed careful use of this tactic. In all three struggles, stories, messages or images that were deemed taboo were shelved, even if everyone agreed they could have been effective.

The three struggles in question made use of the internet and digital means of communication. As time went by and internet use disseminated, the digital presence increased. Most of the correspondence and decision-making within the groups was done by email. As Sima (2011) observed, here, too, activists feared that information would find its way to their adversaries, and that e-correspondence would be subjected to wiretapping. They were worried about being exposed, compromising the struggle, and even their own safety.

Confrontational strategies

In the conflicts studied, confrontation was used when there was hope of dealing with the asymmetrical power structures (Staples, 2012). Alinsky (1971) said that our actions are not what achieve change. However, reactions to our actions are what keeps the wheel of change in motion. In one such instance, the desired effect was achieved in an unexpected way. Tova explained:

> We were protesting outside the company's offices. We were few and it was going slow. The company sent busses full of employees! They did all our work for us! An argument started, we almost got beaten up. . . . Cars pulled over to see what was going on, it was a big show! If it wasn't for them, it would have been a total flop!

Generally speaking, direct action, disruptive or distractive tactics were seldom used, with only a few demonstrations to speak of over all the years studied except for the email campaign mentioned in the segment on social action strategies. But why is this? Apparently, confrontation strategies have become less common as struggles have become more sophisticated, the public less tolerant to disruptive methods, and power elites more skilful in responding to them (Rothman, 2001).

Perhaps these tactics are more suitable for large organisations. Greenpeace is one example of an organisation that has adhered to confrontational, non-violent direct action strategies since

1971. But there are many examples of small groups who previously resorted to extreme measures in environmental campaigns (Delicath and DeLuca, 2003).

Another possible reason for the absence of confrontational tactics may have something to do with the participants' ages. Yishai (2003) found that younger people take part in protest five times more than older people do. Batya commented:

> In one of the beach-saving campaigns, a group of young activists protested outside the Minister of Interior's home. He woke up to see a beach painted on his sidewalk. It was wonderful! When young people are involved, they're creative, bold, and innovative. They grew up with protests; it comes more naturally to them.

The price paid by activists

There were many costs for the activists. We identified five themes: time, money, exposure, professional, and personal life. Considering these conflicts lasted for more than a decade each, it is impossible to calculate how many volunteer hours were spent during all those years. We believe other areas are a derivative of time costs. Money spent was another cost the activists all agreed on.

Some activists pointed out that public exposure is a high price to pay. None were looking for celebrity going into the struggle, but some agreed to be in the spotlight, while for others, it was a 'necessary evil'. For several, whose privacy was extremely important personally, the need to be in the spotlight was almost unbearable, leaving them caught between their need for privacy and the goals of the campaign.

In terms of professional costs, this was mostly felt by those who held public positions, in the municipality, for instance, and who sometimes felt a conflict of interests between their loyalty to their workplace and their activism. Some passed up professional opportunities and others had been subjected to attempts at co-optation. All the activists told us about countless days they took time off work for campaign-related tasks or meetings.

Perhaps the most significant toll was taken on their personal life. Some found themselves in confrontation with friends who disagreed or were disappointed with friends who were indifferent to the struggle. Numerous days spent on the struggle often came at the expense of time with family. Several of them got divorced and some became chronically ill. This is not to say that their involvement was the sole reason for their strife, but some referred to activism-related stress as the culprit.

Define success. The activists were proud of many achievements: getting involved; raising awareness; receiving media coverage and telling the story, despite being in the periphery far from power centres; gathering support from people and organisations; and inspiring others. Some formal success was achieved in court or in planning committees. Sometimes, it was gained by influencing policy changes on a local or national scale, and those were high points in every struggle.

Another kind of success was achieving actual advance for the public good. In the case of Gazelle Valley, it ended in overwhelming success with the decision to grant the public their request, after a 13-year-long struggle. Michaella said she felt exuberant when the local committee declared the public would participate in planning a park, instead of a private housing project: 'We felt there is light at the end of the tunnel. After all these years . . . it's really happening!' Tal recalled: 'It was a real moment of joy. To choose what we want, and know the municipality would actually listen'. And Mickey told us: 'That was the most special and beautiful part. Because all of a sudden, they told us, "OK, we heard your objections. Now, tell us what you *do* want to do with the place."'

In the two other struggles that are still enduring, the threats still loom. But for the activists, every passing day is a small success. Batya recalled:

> Every time we prevailed I was amazed. To this day, there's no mine and no permit. That's a HUGE accomplishment! They're waging war against us with enormous forces. We have so little in comparison. In that respect, the struggle is a gigantic success.

Laksi, the veteran activist, who's been at it for more than 30 years, simply said: 'This interview is taking place in 2014. It's been 30 years now – and there's no mine. There's no mine! You don't need much more than that'.

Most activists we spoke to agreed that all the 'nice little achievements' are fine, but it ultimately comes down to a bottom line of whether they succeed or fail. Both Laksi and Timor – members of different groups – used the allegory of a man falling from a building to represent their stand on the matter. Timor said:

> A man falls from a building. While he's falling, someone shouts to him 'how's it going?' He answers: 'so far so good!' . . . Another way of putting it is that falling never killed anyone; it's hitting the ground that kills you. So . . . now we're in the air. And it's a philosophical question: is the fact that we haven't hit the ground yet, a success, or not?

Here is the bottom line: The more lasting success was achieved by legal means or when political situations changed and allowed new interests to be highlighted and fresh alliances to be formed. This corresponds with the 'multiple streams approach' (Kingdon, 1995), that posits policy changes are created because 'windows of opportunity' open when three streams – problems, policy and politics align. Similarly to other local environmental conflicts (Rootes, 1999), in these cases political opportunity played a major role in attaining success. With rigid power structures, usually not easily influenced by local communities, these groups had to identify changes in policy and political balances, taking advantage of opportunities to achieve successful outcomes.

Is there a professional in the crowd?

Throughout, the activists tried to involve professionals, along with those who were coalition members. These volunteer professionals came from legal, environmental and policy backgrounds, from academia and public service, giving their expertise and credibility to the claims. They gave tailwind through public support, lobbying, writing appeals and giving expert opinions.

We asked activists what professionals skills were needed in these struggles, and what could be the potential roles of community and/or social workers. The skills could be categorised into five groups:

a) Environmental justice, law and spatial planning.
b) Resource development and management.
c) Media, campaign and strategic planning.
d) Lobby and national/municipal politics.
e) Coalitions, coordination, organisational development, mediation.

This revealed the interdisciplinary world of environmental struggles of needing a lawyer-campaigner-resource-developer-organisational-lobby. Interdisciplinarity, recruiting and coordinating different professionals are highlighted by green social work (Dominelli, 2012. A community leader's role is to inspire by example (Staples, 2012), while green social workers mobilise, facilitate decision-making, advocate for and foster green community leadership in coproducing solutions (Dominelli, 2011).

Useful lessons: theory and practice implications

Green social workers constantly ask whether the interests of marginalised groups are represented in these conflicts; make a place for them at the table; and avoid their relegation to the side-lines or being foot-soldiers. They can promote policy that encourages citizen participation in planning, transparent decision-making, and independent assessments of social and environmental impacts. Green social workers can participate in public policy discourse, and push for funding to support community-led environmental struggles. Municipal or national governments targeted in conflicts are unlikely to support community struggles, but the not-for-profit sector could help fill this gap.

Finally, further research is needed to provide examples of what social workers have done, or can do as professionals in environmental conflicts. Social work education in Israel needs to include an interdisciplinary, broad knowledge-base, and methods for collaborating with other professions to respond to the growing environmental needs. Social workers further require interdisciplinary training in green social work to empower communities, negotiate with policymakers and contest policies that do not endorse a community's best interests. The current research also indicates the need for implementing green social work strategies in Israeli social work education.

References

Alinsky, S. D. (1971). *Rules for radicals*. New York, NY: Random House.
Besthorn, F. H. (2003). Radical ecologisms: Insights for educating social workers in ecological activism and social justice. *Critical Social Work*, 4(1). Available on http://www1.uwindsor.ca/criticalsocialwork/
Bobo, K., Kendall, J., and Max, S. (2001). *Organizing for social change: Midwest academy manual for activists*. Santa Ana, CA: Seven Locks Press.
Delicath, J.W. and DeLuca, K. M. (2003). Image events, the public sphere, and argumentative practice: The case of radical environmental groups. *Argumentation*, 17(3): 315–333. doi:10.1023/A:1025179019397
De-Shalit, A. (2004). *Red-Green: Democracy, Justice and Environment*. Tel-Aviv: Bavel (Hebrew).
Dominelli, L. (2011). Climate change: Social workers' roles and contributions to policy debates and interventions. *International Journal of Social Welfare*, 20(4): 430–438. doi: 10.1111/j.1468–2397.2011.00795.x
Dominelli, L. (2012). *Green social work: From environmental crises to environmental justice*. Cambridge, UK: Polity Press.
Golan, Y. (2010). *Last call for Sasgon Valley*. Israel: Dachpor (Hebrew).
Gray, M., Coates, J., and Hetherington, T. (Eds.). (2012). *Environmental social work*. New York, NY: Routledge.
Homan, M. S. (2010). *Promoting community change: Making it happen in the real world* (5th ed.). Belmont, CA: Brooks/Cole, Cangage Learning.
Kingdon, J.W. (1995). *Agendas, alternatives and public policy* (2nd ed.). Boston, MA: Little Brown.
Peled, M. (2014). *From Barir Field to the Political Field*. Available on www.calcalist.co.il/local/articles/0,7340,L-3628353,00.html
Pickerill, J. (2008). From Wilderness to Wild Country: The power of language in environmental campaigns in Australia. *Environmental Politics*, 17(1): 95–104. doi:10.1080/09644010701811681
Rootes, C. (1999). Environmental Movements: From the local to the global. *Environmental Politics*, 8(1): 1–12. doi:10.1080/09644019908414435
Roded, B. (2016). 'The Resource Curse': A phosphate mine near Arad. In *Corporate social responsibility in the renewing the City* (in print). Tel-Aviv: Rasling (Hebrew).

Rothman, J. (2001). Approaches to Community Intervention. In J. Rothman, J. L. Erlich, J. E. Tropman, J. Erlich, and J. Tropman (Eds.), *Strategies of Community Intervention: Macro Practice*. Itasca, IL: Peacock Publishers, 6th ed., pp. 27–64.

Shmueli, D. (2011). Environmental justice in the Israeli reality. In: Benstein (Ed.), *Sustainability: Vision, values, practice*. Tel-Aviv, Israel: Heshel Center and the Ministry of Environmental Protection (Hebrew), pp. 217–229.

Shorman, M. (2013). Estimating the risk of cancer and the hazardous index due to radiation from the phosphate mine in Russifa area. *Radiation Protection* Dosimetry, *156*(2): 125–130. doi: 10.1093/rpd/nct052

Sima, Y. (2011). Grassroots environmental activism and the internet: Constructing a green public sphere in China. *Asian Studies Review*, *35*(4): 477–497. doi:10.1080/10357823.2011.628007

Staples, L. (2012). Community organizing for social justice: Grassroots groups for power. *Social Work with Groups*, *35*(3): 287–296. doi:10.1080/01609513.2012.656233

Tal, A. (2006). *Environment in Israel: Natural resources, crises, struggles and policy – From early Zionism to the 21st century*. Tel Aviv: Am Oved (Hebrew).

Yishai, Y. (2003). *Between mobilization and reconciliation: Civil society in Israel*. Jerusalem: Carmel (Hebrew).

37
Working with children in disasters

Ines V. Danao

Introduction

Green social work as introduced by Dominelli (2012) is a holistic model of social work that offers an overarching framework in working with children in disasters. In her book entitled *Green Social Work: From Environmental Crises to Environmental Justice*, she defines green social work as

> that part of practice that intervenes to protect the environment and enhance people's wellbeing by integrating the interdependencies between people and their socio-cultural, economic and physical environments and among peoples within an egalitarian framework that addresses prevailing structural inequalities and useful distribution of power and resources.
>
> *Dominelli (2012: 8)*

When viewed through the lens of green social work, disasters risk reduction and management seek to harmonise human activities with the environment rather than subdue it. Given this perspective, social workers engaged in child protection in disasters will not only prevent children from being harmed but educate them to become carers of the environment. This chapter also covers the importance of understanding trauma and its implication to the well-being of children during disasters; the policies and implementing guidelines for child protection, mechanisms, programmes and interventions, as well as roles of social workers in this setting.

Christine Wamsler (2009:III) observed that the frequency of natural disaster has grown significantly worldwide. The number of disasters quadrupled during the last 30 years (UNISDR, 2006 cited by Wamsler, 2009). Among the major natural disasters that caught worldwide attention was the Indian Ocean Tsunami on 26 December 2004. In the Maldives, the Ministry of Planning and National Development (2006:6) reported that 82 citizens died; 1,313 were injured; and over 15,000 lost their homes during that Tsunami.

The Philippines, a disaster-prone country, is visited on average by 20 typhoons a year, five of which may be destructive, like Super Typhoon Yolanda or Haiyan, its international name. Super Typhoon Yolanda made history on 8 November 2013 at 4:00 in the morning, as one of the most devastating tropical cyclones in the world. This super typhoon affected at least

16 million people and displaced 4 million people. Just before the year 2016 ended, another super typhoon, Nina, hit the Southern Luzon Region on the evening of 25 December 2016. However, a feared imminent disaster expected to occur anytime is the 'Big One', a magnitude 7.2 earthquake from the West Valley Fault which could impact Metro Manila. The West Valley Fault is a 100-kilometer segment of an active fault line in the Valley Fault System, which tends to have a 400-year cycle between earthquakes. Those near the epicentre of an earthquake will first feel an up and down ground motion, followed by a horizontal ground motion (de la Cruz, 2014). Given the certainty of occurrence of disasters in the Philippines, like flash floods in major cities, the social workers' repertoire of skills must include working with children in disasters.

According to Dominelli (2010), the key aspects of professional social work interventions are orientated towards enhancing children's well-being. Moreover, protecting children from harm comprises the bulk of statutory social work. Promoting children's well-being and child protection occurs within an overarching perspective of emancipatory social work practice. This perspective is espoused by Dominelli (1997, 2009). This view is congruent with the social work belief in the inherent worth and dignity of every person. Emancipatory social work is one of the three key approaches of the profession (Dominelli, 2009). The other two are maintenance (Davies, 1985 cited by Dominelli, 2009) and therapeutic (Payne, 2005 cited by Dominelli, 2009). Maintenance practice assists service users to meet their basic needs. The therapeutic approach focuses on interpersonal relationship within and outside of the family, in the community, school and workplace. Neither the maintenance nor the therapeutic approach considers structural inequalities. The emancipatory social work practice, particularly the holistic variant, according to Dominelli (2009), seeks to address individual and structural problems because it views dealing with both as integral to enhancing individual and community well-being. Dominelli (2009: 158) added that 'promoting social work as both a political and moral profession means arguing for universal services, challenging taxation policies, addressing global interdependencies that have precipitated current crises for poor people like rising food and fuel prices and working to prevent diseases that have a global reach'. Emancipatory social work practice must underpin work with children in disasters, and it forms the basis for green social work which includes environmental hazards within its holistic approach as part of its commitment to enhance a social justice that incorporates environmental justice.

Understanding disaster, trauma, traumatic stress and their impact on survivors

There is wisdom in the adage, knowing the problem is half-solving the problem. Understanding disaster, trauma and traumatic stress prepares social workers in assisting service users to overcome the challenges brought about by disasters. James Lewis (1999) notes that disasters make news: floods in India, China or Bangladesh; earthquakes in Japan or Iran; and cyclones in the Philippines, Bangladesh or the Caribbean. He suggests that in disasters, reconstruction and development are simultaneous phenomena with each stage overlapping the others in the same or neighbouring places. This is opposed to the conventional way of viewing reconstruction and development in disasters as linear. Lewis (1999: 163) draws the following conclusions from the International Decade for Natural Disaster Reduction: 'There is wider realization that natural disasters are at least in part, man-made. There is a need for an active international platform to initiate the commitment, strength of purpose, resources, expertise and energy to merge palliative with preventive purpose into the next century'. El-Masri and Tipple (1997) explained that natural disasters are the outcome of interactions between natural events and human actions. Davis (1987 quoted in El-Masri and Tipple, 1997) opined that many of tragic impacts of natural disasters result from human misuse of resources, inappropriate actions, and lack of foresight. A tragic reminder of this observation is the trash slides due to heavy rains at Payatas, a solid waste dump in Quezon City, Metro Manila in 2000, where 288 people died and several hundred families were displaced (Co, 2010). Co cited that the Philippines' location within the Circum-Pacific Belt (with its associated high levels of risk from earthquakes and volcanoes) coupled with its position along the typhoon belt of the North Pacific Basin and susceptibility to the El Niño phenomenon, mean that the country is regularly affected by earthquakes, volcanic eruptions, typhoons, storm surges, landslides, floods and droughts. As I write about these natural and man-made disasters that the Philippines has to pro-actively manage, I am convinced more than ever that the Philippines' PSG (Policies, Standards and Guidelines for Bachelor of Science in Social Work and Master in Social Work) must be reviewed and revised to incorporate competencies for Social Work Practice in Disaster Risk Reduction and Management.

Disaster occurs when hazardous events strike vulnerable human settlements (Wamsler, 2009). The previous discussion on disasters shows that the tragic consequences of disasters are loss of life, properties, social and economic disruption, and physical destruction. Hence, disasters may lead to trauma, resulting in traumatic stress. Trauma is defined as

> an event, series of events, or set of circumstances that is experienced by an individual as physically or emotionally harmful or life threatening and that has lasting adverse effects on the individual's functioning and mental, physical, social, emotional, and spiritual well-being.
> *(SAMHSA, 2013 in Fact Sheet, 2016: 01)*

Stress is the body's alarm system while traumatic stress is the overwhelming of the body's alarm system. According to the Iowa Trauma Informed Care Project, trauma affects the individual, families and communities by disrupting healthy development, adversely affecting relationships and contributing to mental health issues including substance abuse, domestic violence and child abuse. The study of adverse childhood experiences (ACEs) showed that ACEs can affect the individual's physical and emotional health throughout the life span (Fact Sheet, 2016: 01). The impact of trauma (Hopper, 2009 in Michelfelder and Swoboda, 2012: 12) involves the activation of survival responses (fight, flight, freeze, or submit); shutting down of non-essential tasks; and potentially less rational thought at this time. Michelfelder and Swoboda (2012: 13) argued that prolonged exposure to trauma and/or repetitive traumatic events may result in emotional numbing, psychological avoidance and diminished sense of safety. The foregoing consequences of traumatic stress make it imperative to intervene in a timely manner to mitigate the adverse effects of disasters in children.

Child protection and the implications for the well-being of children in disasters

The evaluative study of long-term effects of psychosocial assistance and international solidarity work in Chile (Punamaki, 2000) enumerated three issues in recognising the ways in which children express their distress after traumatic events. First, the same symptoms may be adaptive and healthy at the acute stage of trauma but if symptoms persist, these become pathological. An example is a numbing of feelings that is initially helpful to cope with an overwhelming experience. Second, repetitive and ritualised expressions of distress tend to narrow and distort the child's sense of reality. It is natural for a four-year old to play funeral after a family member has died. This play activity becomes worrisome if repetitious and has no thematic change. Third, alongside psychological symptoms, trauma impacts on a child's beliefs and attitudes, learning abilities and interpersonal relationships.

The demolition of informal settlers' houses to remove them from hazardous areas or when legal land owners claim rights to their property exemplifies this. I recall my experience in social preparation work for the high-financed construction of a high-end commercial cum residential project. Children refused to go to school because the houses of their playmates had been demolished. Some clung to their mothers and cried whenever they were out of sight. A child who was left alone in the house was terrified of seeing their house being torn down. In the eyes of the child, the tearing apart of their house, a symbol of safety, is a violent scenario. Children showing symptoms of traumatic stress were also reported by mothers who were affected by the 7.8-magnitude earthquake that caused the collapse of a hotel in Baguio City, Philippines in 1990. During the psychological debriefing of survivors of the collapsed building, one mother reported that her six-month old baby became sensitive to noise. The baby was fretful and easily roused from sleep by any slight movement. A mother of a toddler observed that her child became afraid of the dark and started to bed wet.

Children, even in normal conditions, are vulnerable. This vulnerability is heightened during disasters. It was reported in *World News* (2010 cited by Dominelli, 2010) that paedophiles were abducting orphaned children in two disasters: the 2004 Asian Tsunami, and the 2010 Haitian earthquake. In the aftermath of Super Typhoon Haiyan, some evacuees were reported to have been lured into sexual activities in exchange for money. Unsupervised and unstructured daily situations in evacuation centres make children easy prey. Thus, in the Philippines, running child-friendly spaces (CFS) has become a valuable initiative among the international and local non-governmental organisations as well as faith-based institutions in collaboration with local government units.

International and national instruments of child protection

Selected legal instruments that set the standards for child protection are worth discussing briefly to provide the context in working with children in disasters. The *Hyogo Framework for Action* (2005–2015) shifted the global policy framework for disaster interventions from disaster response to disaster risk management and disaster risk reduction. This framework influenced the passage of the 2016 Philippine law that turned the National Disaster Coordinating Council (created by law in May 2010) into the National Disaster Risk Reduction and Management Council.

I also mention two relevant frameworks from the United Nations Children's Fund (UNICEF): Core Commitments for Children in *Humanitarian Action for Children* (2010:01) and the *Joint Statement on Advancing Child-Sensitive Social Protection* (2009:01). The core commitments for children in its *Humanitarian Action for Children* are a global framework for humanitarian work with children undertaken by UNICEF and its partners to protect the rights of children affected by humanitarian crisis. It defines a humanitarian situation as: 'any circumstance where humanitarian needs are sufficiently large and complex to require significant external assistance and resources and where a multi-sectoral response is needed, with the engagement of a wide range of international humanitarian actors (www.unicef.org/emergencies/index_68710.html).

The *Joint Statement on Advancing Child-Sensitive Social Protection* aims to build greater consensus on the importance of child-sensitive social protection. The initial signatories are: DFID UK, HelpAge International, Hope and Homes for Children, Institute of Development Studies, International Labour Organization, Overseas Development Institute, Save the Children UK, UNDP, UNICEF and the World Bank. In this *Joint Statement*, there are two principles of child-sensitive social protection that helping professionals and humanitarian workers must bear in mind. First, avoid the adverse impact of humanitarian crisis on children and reduce or mitigate social and economic risks that directly affect children's lives. Second, intervene as early possible where children are at risk to prevent irreversible impairment or harm (www.unicef.org/aids/files/CSSP joint statement 10.16.09.pdf).

In the Philippines, the 2007 definition of social protection included protection against hazards and improving people's capacity to manage risks. In 2012, the social protection operational framework of the Philippines was issued. Environmental and natural risks were among the four risks and vulnerabilities to be addressed. On 27 May 2010, Republic Act No. 10121 instituted the Philippine disaster risk reduction and management system and framework and appropriated funds for it (www.officialgazette.gov.ph/2016/05/18/republic-act-no-10821/). The child-sensitive law, Republic Act No. 10821 (passed on 18 May 2016), mandated the provision of emergency relief and protection for children before, during and after disasters. It describes disasters as a serious disruption of the functioning of the 'community or socially involving widespread human, material, eco-environmental losses and impacts which exceed the ability of the affected community or society to cope using its own resources' (www.ndrrmc.gov.ph/attachments/article/45/Republic_Act_10121.pdf). Among the salient features of Republic Act No. 10821 are the following:

- Child Protection Working Group (CPWG) that coordinates child protection efforts in humanitarian settings to ensure that girls and boys are protected from abuse, neglect, exploitation and violence. The National CPWG is chaired by the executive director of the Council for the Welfare of Children (CWC) with a UNICEF representative as co-chair. The CPWG brings together in one forum child protection actors and partners operational in areas affected by both natural and human-induced disasters and to facilitate the development and coordination of child protection strategies and responses, including advocacy with authorities and humanitarian actors as necessary. Given the big membership of the CPWG, the Core CPWG was constituted. I sit in the core group, representing academia. The CPWG operates at the national and regional levels. The Regional CPWG coordinates the cities, towns and provinces under its jurisdiction. The CWC is under the aegis of the Department of Social Welfare and Development, which is under the Office of the President of the Philippines. Among the significant accomplishments of the CPWG worth mentioning is the localisation of the Child- Friendly Space Implementation Guidelines after a series of consultations with various governmental and non-governmental organisations involved in child protection and welfare.

At this juncture, I will briefly describe two important documents of a CPWG member, an international non-governmental organisation that kindly shared with me their documents which demonstrate why they are among the key actors in the area of child protection in emergencies. The first document is the *Child Protection in Emergencies (CPiE) Results Framework* (Plan International, 2015). It contains the list of global outcome indicators organised around pre-designed outcome statements that link Plan International's Global Child Protection Strategy and current CPiE programming in an effort to standardise the monitoring of interventions and improve impact evaluations (by programme and globally). The framework provides guidance for country officers to frame their response and select quality indicators that focus on outcomes. The second document is the *Disaster Preparedness Protocol Plan Philippines*, Version Two, October 2014 (Plan International, 2014). This revised edition is a product of the extensive experience of Plan International Philippines' staff in responding to small, medium and large-scale disasters into a guide of processes and priority actions in child-centred community development and humanitarian work. In 2013, Plan International was involved in disaster response, recovery and rehabilitation of affected families during the Central Luzon flooding, displaced persons from the Zamboanga siege, the 7.2-magnitude quake of Bohol, and Typhoon Yolanda (Haiyan). The protocol is informed by the Philippines being ranked second for cyclones and earthquakes, fourth for landslides, fifth for tsunamis, and eighth for floods, among disaster-prone countries globally (Plan International, 2013).

- Comprehensive Emergency Programme for Children that takes into consideration humanitarian, inclusive, gendered and culturally sensitive standards for the protection of children, pregnant, and lactating mothers in emergencies.
- Psychological First Aid for Children.
- Establishment of Child-Friendly Spaces (CFS) to nurture the resilience and psychosocial well-being of children through community-organised structured activities and which are conducted in safe, child-friendly and stimulating environments to restore normalcy.
- Training emergency responders in child-focused emergency assessments, family tracing system/prevention of separation, mainstreaming child protection in other sectors, mental health and psychosocial support services, child friendly spaces, Inter-Agency Steering Committee (IASC) Guidelines on Gender-Based Violence (GBV) and Child Protection in Emergencies.

Social work interventions in disasters, particularly in the area of child protection: social workers' roles

Sheafor and Horesj (2008: 568–569) described the three stages in people's responses to disasters: impact, recoil and post-trauma; and highlighted social worker's roles in these. During the acute impact stage, one group may be calm, making sensible decisions and caring for themselves and others. Another group may be in state of emotional shock and disorientation but still able to communicate and follow instructions from others. The third one is a small number of groups who are hysterical or paralyzed by their fear. The third group runs the risk of taking action that may be harmful to themselves or to others. Among those who need special attention during the acute impact phase are young children, older people, persons with disabilities and those without social support networks. Some hours later the second, or recoil, phase occurs. Many people are emotionally exhausted and feel a strong need to talk about their experience. Sheafor and Horesj suggest mental health counselling and crisis intervention work at this stage, besides addressing people's immediate needs.

The third phase, post-trauma, may take months, years or a lifetime, depending on the adequacy of the crisis intervention services made available and used by each survivor. Survivors of disasters may experience the following: preoccupation with death and what they have lost, survivor guilt, and feelings of helplessness. Social workers' enabling roles will include facilitating survivors' adjustments to these challenges: accepting the reality of their loss (family members or material possessions); acknowledging the pain of the loss; adjusting to changes in their circumstances; and re-establishing their sense of identity, purpose and new meaning of life. These authors offer guidelines to social workers responding to disaster situations. Some portions of the guidelines are already being practiced in the Philippines as part of standard operating procedures by local and international organisations in their humanitarian activities. These include: securing proper authorisation from emergency response bodies; collecting accurate information (persons who are missing, have been killed or injured); location of survivors (to facilitate communication with relatives and reunification of families); information and referral services to avoid unnecessary worry and fear; mental health and social services that address increased need for these services and engage in case finding and outreach; children kept with their families; housing family members together; and ongoing self-care for the social workers to prevent vicarious trauma. This guidance has been developed due to repeated exposure to distressed persons (e.g. intrusive thoughts, sleeplessness, feelings of guilt, and rage). In my previous work with an international non-governmental organisation, the protocol that we followed included the schedule to rest, be debriefed within the team, collectively reflect on what worked, what did not work and why, draw out lessons, revise the plan as needed and map out contingency plans for the following days.

Psychosocial interventions

The Trauma Informed Care (TIC) framework offers service providers generic sets of knowledge applicable to any setting or organisation working with trauma survivors. Social workers who are not familiar with TIC may want to explore it to inform their practice. The projects with the following interventions that apply the Trauma Informed Care framework are:

- SAMHSA (Substance Abuse and Mental Health Services Administration), which has six key principles: safety; trustworthiness and transparency; peer support; collaboration and mutuality; empowerment, voice and choice; and cultural, historical and gender issues.
- Iowa TIC Project, sponsored by Orchard Place: TIC is an organisational structure and treatment framework that involves understanding, recognising and responding to the effects of all types of trauma.
- Evidence-based Trauma-Informed Philippine Psychotherapy (TIPP): TIPP is considered a 'journey toward healing' (Guirguis et al., n.d.).

Social work activities

Sheafor and Horesj (2008: 498) provide detailed guidelines for working with children under age 12. Before interviewing a child, plan for alternative action in case the child cries, will not want to be left alone by the parent, or will not talk. Use some form of play to make the child feel comfortable and able to communicate. Make available some art materials like clay and building blocks as well as dolls, puppets, doll's house and toy animals. For older children, use simple card or board games, toy telephones, puzzles and electronic games. Get started by placing yourself at the child's level physically by sitting or squatting. Give a simple description of yourself and assure the child that he or she is not in trouble. Begin with some friendly conversation. If the child refuses to talk, engage him or her in a parallel activity. Children tend to act out their thoughts and feelings. Ask the child to use the set of dolls or draw a picture of a person or family to make up a story. Sheafor and Horesj cautioned that sometimes children may incorporate some themes drawn from TV programmes, books and stories from their friends. Being aware of the possibility that children may garnish their stories with themes outside of their own personal experience can remind social workers not to be quick in judging people. The Child Friendly Space (CFS) Implementation Guidelines make the setting up and running of CFS in the Philippines easy even for novices. All focal persons of the Regional Child Protection Working Group have been trained in the more extensive adoption of the CFS on the ground.

The Child Friendly Space was inexistent as a concept when my colleague and I processed the traumatic experience of Filipino children affected by the 1991 eruption of Mount Pinatubo in Central Luzon, Philippines, three weeks after the terrifying event. 'It felt like it was the end of the world', was the description of the adults. Weeks before the eruption, the thick black smoke billowing from the mouth of the volcano was visible from provinces around Mount Pinatubo but the horrific experience that followed was beyond the imagination of the residents when the eruption buried many structures in the affected provinces. The parents of these children with ages ranging from two to eight narrated that at about 10:00 o'clock in the morning their surroundings were enveloped by dark ash-fall that quickly filled the rooftops and roads. Suddenly it was like night-time. Men had to shovel the ash-fall off the roofs and clear the roads. People had to regulate their food intake because they were unsure how long would the situation last. All stores were closed. In our session with the children, we used only crayons and paper for the children to draw what happened on that fearful day. What stood out most in my memory was the response of the two-year old boy whose vocabulary was very limited at that age. I showed him the photo of the church courtyard filled with ash-fall with what looked like snow capping the leaves of the plants. Immediately, he answered 'ilaw' (light) when I asked him what he wanted to draw. I drew a yellow speck. He repeated 'ilaw' many times. He seemed to be so dissatisfied with the number of specks of light I drew that he got the crayon from my hand and completely filled the paper with them. The mother who was within hearing distance explained that the boy had been scared of the dark since the eruption and wanted the lights on all the time.

My other experience is being a member of a crisis intervention team assigned to process the experience of a group of Vietnamese children who were stranded in the open sea for almost a month. They were pushed away from the shoreline of Thailand by the storm. Their food supply for a week ran out and they filled their stomach with anything available in the boat. They arrived in the Philippines, famished and grief-stricken. Half of the boat passengers had died. We welcomed them with bright smiles but no one reciprocated with a smile. There was no eye contact with us. They quietly obliged when we invited them to sit on the mat where pencils, crayons and papers were spread out. Some responded hesitantly, taking the paper and crayon in slow motion. Others were motionless. Initially, there were just scribbles of dark colours like black, grey and brown. In the afternoon, there were some forms. Mostly, pictures of boats. After mid-afternoon, some started talking to each other, followed by giggles. We quietly joined the conversation together with our interpreters. They were talking about their boat experience. Many drew the boat they rode in while others drew other boats that passed by. Some drew the sea creatures on the water that caused the giggles. They talked excitedly about them. Arts bring out the creative side of children that can be energising.

It brings to my mind another arts activity with Vietnamese asylum seekers that included children that demonstrated how a simple activity like drawing can help them express feelings of anxiety, giving way to clarity of mind to get out of the tunnel and expand their horizons. The expansion reveals opportunities and options that are liberating. To my mind, this is emancipatory social work practice. It is also consistent with green social work which focuses on listening to people, and using creative means to help them express their emotions and articulate their experiences. A 17-year old Vietnamese boy dreaded returning to Vietnam. He anticipated the horrible situations that awaited him and thought he would rather be dead than go back there. This was our conversation on the eve of his repatriation. The following day, the interpreter informed me of the bad news and handed me the boy's drawing. There was boy with a bubble enclosing the tall buildings, factory and a family. The interpreter explained that the boy visualised that when he returns home to his family, he will find a new Vietnam that is progressive. The boy was stimulated by the daily drawing activity to internally process his ambivalence and fear and come up with his own resolution to his internal conflict.

Traumatic memories, when narrated in a supportive environment, can be funny. I recall a psychological processing I carried out with survivors of a mud-flood brought about by torrential rains in Southern Luzon, Philippines. Everybody laughed as a 17-year old boy narrated how he saved himself from the rising flood water at 11:00 o'clock in the evening. When he reached the top of the coconut tree, he found a rooster that kept him company until he felt he was falling down slowly. In the nick of time, he was able to move to a mango tree. The mango began to tilt, so he quickly jumped to the nearby madre de cacao tree. He stayed there until 5:00 o'clock in the morning. Only when his feet touched the ground, did he realise that the flood had stripped him of his clothes, including his underwear. Fortunately underwear that had been swept by with the current was hanging on a fence. As he was walking home, he noticed people were laughing at him. He looked funny because he was fully covered with mud except for his eyes and nostrils.

Conclusion

Among the lessons that I extract from my work with children in disasters is an appreciation of the inner child. This may be tapped to connect the children with the practitioners that work with them. This gives way to the harmonious flow of energy that stimulates a healing engagement with the children. As the saying goes, 'we are ministered as we minister'.

The literature on children affected by traumatic stress, as in situations of disasters, underscores that early interventions with children should be mainstreamed in all policies and programmes concerned with disaster risk reduction and management at all levels. This is to prevent the long-lasting adverse effects of traumatic stress on children. Green social work and emancipatory social work practice skills include competencies in working with children in disasters. For Dominelli (2012), green social workers involved in child protection must realise that the needs of children are different from those of adults (e.g. keeping them safe from exploitation by adults and other children); getting them into school routines quickly; teaching them about how to restore their damaged environment; and becoming involved in preventative behaviours in looking after their environment to protect them and prevent further disasters from occurring. Children who have been involved in disasters must be helped back to normalcy; taught that human behaviour turns natural hazards into disasters; and be informed of their roles in safeguarding their futures.

References

Co, J. (2010). *Community-driven disaster intervention: Experiences of the Homeless People's Federation Philippines, Incorporated (HPFPI)*, Human Settlements Working Paper No. 25, Climate Change and Cities. September 2010. London: International Institute for Environment and Development.

de la Cruz, G. (2014). *Worst natural disasters in the Philippines.* www.rappler.com/move-ph/issues/disasters/64916-worst-natural-disasters-philippines [Accessed 2 January 2017].

Dominelli, L. (1997). *Sociology for social workers.* London: Macmillan.

Dominelli, L. (2009). *Introducing social work.* Cambridge: Polity Press.

Dominelli, L. (2010). *Social work in a globalizing world.* Cambridge: Polity Press.

Dominelli, L. (2012). *Green social work.* Cambridge: Polity Press.

El-Masri, S. and Tipple, G. (1997). Urbanization Poverty and Natural Disasters in A. Awotona (Ed.), *Reconstruction after disasters: Issues and practices.* England: Ashgate Publishing.

Fact Sheet (2016). *Understanding trauma: The effect of trauma on health.* November 2016. Centre for Health Care Strategies. www.chcs.org/media/understanding-trauma-fact-sheet-112216-final.pdf [Accessed 22 July 2017].

Guirguis, S., Putnam, K., Chang, T., Blair, R., Jun, A., Balderrama, N., Gurrero-Manalo, S., Sotto, J. and Steffen, A. (no date). *Handout for training in evidence-based trauma-informed Philippine psychotherapy.*

Lewis, J. (1999). *Development in disaster-prone places: Studies of vulnerability.* London: Intermediate Technology Publications, Ltd.

Michelfelder, M. and Swoboda, E. (2012). *Trauma 101.* Trauma Informed Care Stakeholders Group Training Subcommittee Power-point Presentation. www.traumainformedcareproject.org/resources/Trauma%20 101%20Powerpoint%20PresentationVI.pdf

Ministry of Planning and Development (2006). *The Maldives: Two years after the Tsunami.* Malé, Maldives: Ministry of Planning and National Development.

Plan International (2013). *Typhoon Haiyan response strategy: Child protection in emergencies thematic area brief.* Makati, Philippines: Plan International Philippines. December.

Plan International (2014). *Disaster preparedness protocol, Makati.* Manila: Plan International Philippines

Plan International (2015). *Child protection in emergencies: Results framework, Makati*, Philippines: Plan International Philippines.

Punamaki, R. (2000). *How to help children experiencing traumatic stress? An evaluation of long-term effects of psychosocial assistance and international solidarity work.* Helsinki: Stakes.

Republic Act No. 10821. 18 May 2016. Manila: Office of the President of the Philippines.

Sheafor, B. and Horesj, C. (2008). *Techniques and guidelines for social work practice*, 8th ed. Boston, MA.: Pearson Education.

United Nations Children's Fund (UNICEF) (2009). *Joint Statement on Advancing Child-Sensitive Social Protection* (2009:01). www.unicef.org/aids/files/CSSP joint statement 10.16.09.pdf. [Accessed 24 July 2017].

UNICEF (2010). *Core Commitments for Children in Humanitarian Action for Children* (2010:01) www.unicef.org/emergencies/index_68710.html [Accessed 24 July 2017].

UNICEF (2015). *Final Report. Typhoon Haiyan.* Manila: UNICEF.

Wamsler, C. (2009). *Urban risk reduction and adaptation.* Saarbrucken, Germany: VDM Verlaq.

Useful Websites

www.gov.ph/section/legis/republic-acts [Accessed 10 January 2017].
www.ndrrmc.gov.ph/attachments/article/45/Republic_Act_10121.pdf [Accessed 10 January 2017].
www.officialgazette.gov.ph/2016/05/18/republic-act-no-10821/ [Accessed 10 January 2017].
www.traumainformedcareproject.org/index.php [Accessed 10 January 2017].
www.unicef.org/ [Accessed 12 January 2017].

38

Persons with disabilities in the Great East Japan Earthquake

Lessons learnt and new directions towards evidence-based empowering just practices

Shigeo Tatsuki

Introduction

Disabled people's issues have seldom been discussed in the disaster policy literature and not until the UNISDR's Sendai meeting in 2015 were disabled people mentioned in international policy frameworks. This chapter provides empirical accounts of the social roots of disaster risks among persons with disabilities (PWD) following the 2011 Great East Japan Earthquake (GEJE). It considers the theoretical accounts of their difficulties, constraints and limitations from a social model of disabilities, and provides an action framework to deal with their root causes.

Multiple independent surveys reported that PWD died at a rate almost two times higher than the general population. The author argues that this mortality rate gap was observed only in Miyagi, one of the three heavily impacted regions in northeastern Japan. The root causes of PWD social vulnerability in Miyagi were attributed to decades-long normalisation practices in tsunami-prone areas. Second, those PWD who survived GEJE also experienced life functioning difficulties, which were mainly caused by sudden changes in the environment with disruptions of the lifeline and other essential services. Third, based on these empirical accounts, a three-layer action framework is proposed for disability inclusive disaster risk reduction (DiDRR).

Social roots of disaster risk among persons with disabilities

In *Risk Society*, the author, Ulrich Beck, asserts that risks in modern societies are not the products of the nature but rather are induced, introduced and, thus, manufactured by modernisation itself (Beck, 1992: 21). Critically examining Beck's writings, Dominelli (2012) from social work and Tierney (2014) from disaster research disciplines further advance his argument and agreed that the risks that modern world face are all manufactured. Floods, for example, may be considered as natural events after excess rainwater accumulates and overflows onto river banks and bordering floodplains. Floods as natural disasters, however, occur because of the rapid urbanisation pressure causing large numbers of new migrants to settle in unsafe flood-prone areas and thus making them more vulnerable to floods on the one hand, and because of the deforestation due to the modernisation demands from the urban areas as well as more intense rainfalls closely associated with climate change, on the other hand.

Disaster risks are manufactured by the interaction of the two factors, these are namely *hazards* and *vulnerability* (Wisner et al., 2004). *Hazard* is a trigger agent for a disaster. Natural hazards may include such physical phenomena as earthquakes, tsunamis, typhoons, heavy rainfalls, floods, landslides and other extreme natural events. Earthquake hazards occurring in a deserted island are a seismic phenomenon that does not cause any disaster because there is no damage or loss. It should be noted that it is not ground shaking itself, but rather the fact of people residing in seismically weak housing structures that causes human casualties in earthquakes. When buildings can no longer withstand the shaking, the subsequent collapse kills people inside. *Vulnerability* (in this case, people residing in seismically unfit housing) is the other predisposing factor of a disaster. In other words, disasters are induced and introduced when vulnerable parts of the society are exposed to hazards. This relationship may be expressed as the following equation:

$$Disaster\ Risk = f\ (hazards, vulnerability) \tag{1}$$

Vulnerability emerges in progression. At the most surface level, vulnerability is manifest as people living in unsafe conditions in the environment (e.g. dangerous locations, unprotected buildings), local economy (livelihoods at risk, low income), social relations (special groups at risk, lack of local institution) and public actions (lack of disaster preparedness, prevalence of endemic disease). Those unsafe conditions result from the dynamic pressures that operate within society. Those include the lack of local initiatives to counteract the disaster, appropriate skills, local investment, local market, press freedom and ethical standards in public life. Such societal macro-forces as rapid population growth, rapid urbanisation, deforestation, arms expenditure, debt repayment schedule, and decline in social productivity may also constitute dynamic pressures, as argued by green social workers (Dominelli, 2012). Finally, the causes of vulnerability at the root level include such structural constraints as limited access to power and resources, political and economic ideologies (Wisner et al., 2004). These root causes fundamentally determine the magnitude of the impact of a hazard on a society and, therefore, need to be critically addressed when any social change initiatives are attempted to reduce disaster damages and losses, and to enhance disaster resilience.

Disaster research and practice have long been treating categories of people such as frail older people and persons with disability (PWD) as 'vulnerable populations' due to their experiencing disproportionately more severe impacts from disasters. The term implies that the vulnerability is defined by their functional impairments and is treated as a trait of those individuals. Disability literature (e.g. Oliver, 1990; Twigg et al., 2011) calls this a 'medical model' of disability. It is not until the mid-2000s that an alternative 'social model' of disability (Oliver, 1990) became mainstream in disaster research and practice, which defined disability as a social construction caused by barriers, inaccessibility and exclusion by society (Twigg et al., 2011; Tatsuki, 2013). Disability emerges from the interaction between people's functional needs and the responsiveness/justice (or lack of it) of the environment and may be expressed as the following equation:

$$Disability = f\ (functional\ needs, environment) \tag{2}$$

The conceptual framework of this chapter on the disaster risk of persons with disabilities integrates with the well-established disaster research perspective on hazards and vulnerability, the social model of disability. By substituting disability in equation (2) for vulnerability in equation (1), the following model is proposed:

$$PWD\ Disaster\ Risk = f_1\ (hazards, f_2\ (functional\ needs, environment)) \qquad (3)$$

The disaster risk of PWD is defined as a function of *hazards* and *vulnerability*, the latter of which is now substituted for another function of life functional *needs* and *environmental (non)responsiveness/(in)justice*. The *hazards* factor may include exposure to such environmental threats as earthquake, tsunami, typhoon, heavy rainfalls, floods, landslides and other extreme natural events. *Functional needs* are assessed in such areas as communication, medical care, maintaining functional independence, supervision and transportation (Kailes and Enders, 2007). *Environmental (non) responsiveness/(in)justice* may consist of fragility, barriers and inaccessibility in the built environment as well as of societal inclusion/exclusion of PWD. The current conceptual framework of PWD disaster risk is thus very relevant to the green social work perspective (Dominelli, 2012).

Empirical data and evidence on PWD casualty due to the GEJE

Like preceding disasters, the 2011 Great East Japan Earthquake (GEJE) caused disproportionally more severe damage and casualties among older people and persons with disabilities. Unlike the preceding disasters, however, for the first time in disaster research history the numerical data on PWD casualties were collected by news media from all major GEJE-hit municipalities. For example, municipal direct death tolls of PWD (an official disability certificate holder), as well as those of all residents, were obtained by the Japan Broadcast Corporation (NHK) production team. This resulted in numerical data on all 31 municipalities that recorded more than 10 casualties from the 11 March 2011 disaster. The NHK surveys were conducted three times because municipalities kept updating PWD death tolls (Tatsuki, 2013).

Based on the NHK survey data, Tatsuki (2013) first examined the casualty gaps between the total and PWD populations for each of the three GEJE-hit prefecture municipalities by fitting simple regression lines as shown in Figure 38.1:

$$PWD\ mortality = casualty\ gap\ coefficient \times Total\ population\ mortality \qquad (4)$$

The above regression coefficient in equation (4) indicates the degree of the total-population-to-PWD casualty gap. The regression (casualty gap) coefficient for Miyagi municipalities was 1.92 suggesting that the PWD mortality rate was nearly twice that of the total population in Miyagi prefecture. In contrast, only a slightly higher (1.19 times) proportion of PWD died in Iwate. Likewise, the casualty gap coefficient for Fukushima was even smaller than that of Iwate (1.16 times). The casualty gaps were clearly observed in all three prefectures and that the gap was much bigger in Miyagi than in Iwate or Fukushima prefecture. The causes of the casualty gaps and of the PWD casualty prefectural differences, especially when comparing Miyagi with Iwate and Fukushima, were examined by multiple regression analyses by successively adding forensically explanatory variables (see Table 38.1). The selection of explanatory variables was partly based on the preceding studies of total population casualties (see Tatsuki, 2013 for more detail).

The final results are shown in Table 38.1. In model 1, only the total population mortality was entered as a baseline and its R^2 was already very high (.895). In model 2, a hazard factor of tsunami arrival time and a general municipality vulnerability factor of the proportion of older people (more precisely the sum of the proportions of those aged 65 or older and those in fishery and agriculture) were entered and its adjusted R^2 of about 1 per cent increased. Model 2

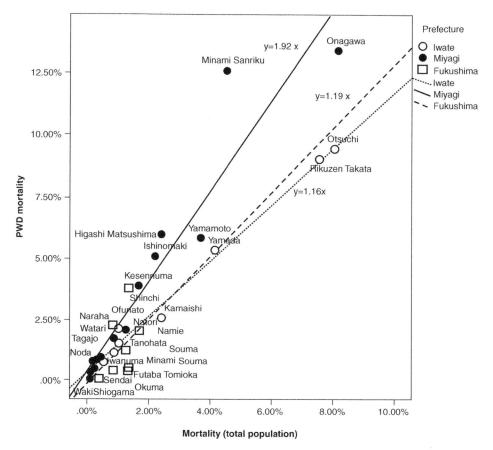

Figure 38.1 Regression of PWD mortality on total population mortality in Iwate, Miyagi, and Fukushima Prefectures

Source: Tatsuki (2013: S415)

Table 38.1 Multiple regression analyses of PWD casualty rates

Explanatory variables	Model 1	Model 2	Model 3	Partial ETA squared
Total population mortality	1.497*** (0.092)	1.279*** (0.137)	1.267*** (0.092)	0.883
Tsunami arrival time		-0.016 (0.010)	-0.019** (0.007)	0.207
Sum of the proportions of aged 65 or older and those in fishery and agriculture		0.371** (0.160)	0.658*** (0.125)	0.524
Proportion of institutionalised PWD			-0.929*** (.200)	0.463
Casualty rate of institutionalised elderly			0.206** (.081)	0.206
Adjusted R^2	0.895	0.906	0.961	

*** $p < .001$ ** $p < .05$

implies that the bigger the total population casualties, the older the people, and the more who were engaged in fishery and agriculture, and the sooner tsunami arrived, the more PWD died.

With the above three preceding predictors being treated as control variables, further forensic examinations were conducted to identify what hazards and/or vulnerability indicators were responsible for causing PWD mortality variabilities among tsunami hit municipalities. As a result (model 3), the two critical vulnerability indicators, the proportion of institutionalised PWD and the casualty rate of institutionalised older people, were found to be significant. The first of the two, the proportion of institutionalised persons with physical disabilities was found to be twice as effective (as evidenced by partial eta squared) as tsunami arrival time and its unstandardised coefficient was -0.929 ($p < .001$). This means that while controlling the effects of total population mortality, tsunami arrival time, the proportion of elderly and the other PWD vulnerability indicators of the casualty rate of institutionalised older people, a 1 per cent decrease in PWD institutionalisation or a 1 per cent increase in PWD living in communities caused 0.9 per cent higher PWD casualties. Rates of institutionalised people with physical disabilities were strikingly different among Iwate (3.1 per cent), Miyagi (0.7 per cent), and Fukushima (1.3 per cent). The considerably lower rate of institutionalisation in Miyagi, or a higher rate of social inclusion of PWD during normalcy seemed to be partly responsible for Miyagi's higher PWD casualties due mainly to tsunami hazards.

The second critical vulnerability indicator was the casualty rate for institutionalised older people whose institutions were directly exposed to tsunami hazards. The casualty rate of the institutionalised older people showed about the same effect size (partial eta squared) as tsunami arrival time and its coefficient was .206. This means that while controlling the effects of total population mortality, tsunami arrival time, the proportion of older people and PWD institutionalisation rate, a 1 per cent increase of the institutionalised older people's casualty implied that 20 per cent of this 1 per cent increase was counted as PWD casualties because the affected older people were also the holders of disability certificates. It is commonly known that the entrants to older people's nursing homes are usually encouraged to make an application for an official disability certificate to qualify for additional benefits. The casualty rate of institutionalised older people as reported by *Kahoku Shimpo* (2011) was again strikingly high in Miyagi (5.2 per cent) as opposed to Iwate (2.1 per cent) or Fukushima (0.4 per cent). This was due to social service institutions like nursing homes for older people tending to be in areas where land price is low. These cheap lands turned out to be scenic (tsunami-prone) seaside areas in Miyagi, while in Iwate and Fukushima, nursing homes tended to be on hillside and inland areas, respectively. This reasoning was commonly shared by politicians, administrators, and scholars in the field of disability policy practices and studies.

To sum up, the current disaster forensic investigations on PWD death and related data during GEJE revealed why PWD death tolls were higher compared with the total population statistics in general and even higher especially in Miyagi than in Iwate or Fukushima prefecture. First, the more social inclusion to and the less exclusion/institutionalisation of PWD from local community settings, the more PWD casualties were recorded. It should be noted that Miyagi was renowned for its normalisation initiatives before GEJE. The number of institutionalised PWD decreased and that of PWD residing in local communities increased. This became possible because a sizable number of Centres for Independent Living (CIL) started providing community living assistance services. Miyagi's normalisation policy and programmes, however, were locally optimised or compartmentalised only to normalcy when services necessary for reasonable accommodations for community living were arranged by local CILs and provided by the CIL personnel. There was a lack of coordination between everyday social services delivery and reasonable accommodation arrangements during disaster times in which informal neighbour supports are critical for evacuation and sheltering assistance. One root cause of social vulnerabilities was a lack of coordination between times of normalcy and disasters.

Second, unsafe locations mattered. Those Miyagi nursing homes for the older people along the seacoast were severely exposed to direct tsunami impacts. Many Miyagi nursing homes were in unsafe areas regarding tsunami hazards because nursing service providers usually are not able to afford higher-priced properties in inland residential or business district areas. Or, sometimes local land owners even invited the service providers to consider investing in their cheaper (but unsafe) land for possible construction of the nursing homes because they could not find any other buyers for their properties. The lack of appropriate zoning regulations may have prohibited the construction of any residential use properties in tsunami-prone areas. The other root cause, therefore, lay in the neoliberal economic and political ideology that underpinned the issues of the safety and security of social service institutions and their residents.

Empirical data and evidence on life functioning difficulties among surviving PWD

As a part of a community-based participatory research project, 41 GEJE surviving PWD and their supporters were invited to a grassroots assessment workshop held in Sendai city on 14 October 2013 to identify what difficulties PWD experienced in meeting their functional needs during the 2011 GEJE. The workshop participants were asked to report on post-it notes what challenges and difficulties they encountered in each disaster process phase after the 2011 disaster. Following the Total Quality Management (TQM) method (Nayatani, Eiga, Futami, and Miyagawa, 1994), the participants themselves sorted/grouped the difficulty and challenge cards according to their affinity. These empirical clustering processes led to the formation of a hypothesis that experienced difficulties could be understood according to, explained and measured by each major construct of the International Classification of Functioning, Disability and Health (ICF) as shown in Figure 38.2. Furthermore, the areas that drastically changed from before to after the GEJE concentrated on such constructs as environmental factors, activity and participation, while health condition, personal factors, body function and structure remained constant or dependent on the environmental responsiveness (or lack thereof) to newly arising needs for activity and participation that were caused by sudden disruption of services, goods and information from environments. This led to the operationalisation of the conceptual (i.e. social-model-based) definition of disability as shown in equation (2) into the empirical (i.e. ICF-based) definition of disability during a disaster as shown in equation (4).

$$Disability = f\,(Activities\ and\ participation,\ Environmental\ Factors) \qquad (4)$$

Based on the 2013 workshop findings, the ICF-based instrument was constructed and it was employed in a social survey conducted in Sendai city in 2015. The survey sample was randomly drawn from the city's disability certificate registry databases. From these population databases, 3,005 individuals or 5 per cent of those registered in each database were selected for the study. Because the age distribution of those with physical disability certificates is heavily skewed by those over 65 years of age, a 1:2 ratio sampling method was used to better represent those younger than 65 (Matsukawa and Tatsuki, 2016).

A checklist for functioning difficulties in times of disasters (the Checklist) was developed for the 2015 survey. The Checklist, a direct product of the 2013 workshop study, demonstrated that the participants' experiences of life difficulties during and after the GEJE could be better described and measured in terms of two selected ICF constructs ('Activities and Participation' and 'Environmental Factors') and their operational definitions. The Checklist consists of 31 ICF-like items, each of which asks a 'yes-no' question about whether a respondent experienced any difficulty in either five selected 'Activities and Participation' or all five 'Environmental Factors' domains. Hazard exposure items such as physical and house damage were also included in the questionnaire (see Table 38.2).

There were 3,005 questionnaires mailed to randomly sampled Sendai residents with disability in 2015 and 1,083 (36.0 per cent) valid responses were collected. The study sample showed an almost equal balance in gender (49.2 per cent for male, 48.8 per cent for female, 1.9 per cent unknown). The age of respondents varied from 1 to 101 with the mean age of 54.1

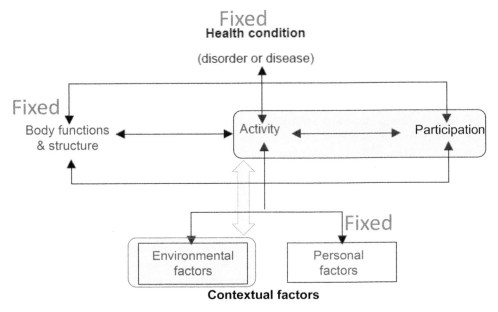

Figure 38.2 Disability and disaster in social context
Source: WHO (2002), p. 9

Table 38.2 Checklist for functioning difficulties in times of disasters

ICF Constructs	Chapter
ACTIVITIES AND PARTICIPATION	
	d2 GENERAL TASKS AND DEMANDS
	d4 MOBILITY
	d5 SELF-CARE
	d6 DOMESTIC LIFE
	d8 MAJOR LIFE AREAS
ENVIRONMENTAL FACTORS	
	e1 PRODUCTS AND TECHNOLOGY
	e2 NATURAL ENVIRONMENT AND HUMAN-MADE CHANGES TO ENVIRONMENT
	e3 SUPPORT AND RELATIONSHIPS
	e4 ATTITUDES
	e5–1 SERVICES, SYSTEMS AND POLICIES (Lifeline, Transportation & Communication Services)
	e5–2 SERVICES, SYSTEMS AND POLICIES (Formal & Informal Support Services)

(SD=20.1). Two-thirds (66.1 per cent) of responses were by PWD themselves and one-third (28.4 per cent) by family members. Based on the responses to hazard exposure items, respondents were classified as light (31 per cent), medium (53 per cent) and heavy (16 per cent) damage/exposure categories. The results were summarised as "ICF difficulties by damage/hazard exposure" for 100-to-1,000-hour phase after the GEJE. For more detailed explanations of the descriptive results, please see Matsukawa and Tatsuki (2016). To identify the characteristic associations of the ICF difficulties/needs and hazard exposure/damage levels, correspondence (dual scaling) analysis (Nishisato, 1980) was employed as shown in Figure 38.3.

In Figure 38.3, light, medium and heavy hazard exposure/damage categories (triangular markers) were plotted left to right on the horizontal axis while sets of activity and participation (ICF 'd' categories) as well as corresponding environmental factors (ICF 'e' categories) were plotted along a dome-shaped line. As for those with light damage/exposure, lifeline and other service disruptions (e5_1) were closely associated with self-care (d5) difficulties which seemed to demand more informal support from family and neighbours (e3). For those who experienced medium damage/exposure, disruptions in formal and informal support services (e5_2) seemed to have caused disruptions in, and produced new needs for work (d8), carrying out daily routines (d2), acquisition of necessities and conducting household tasks and care (d6), and mobility (d4). Finally, those with heavy damage/exposure seemed to have uniquely experienced severe environmental changes (e2), a lack of goods and products (e1), and, more seriously, prejudice and discrimination from formal and informal systems (e4).

Based on the empirical accounts as evidenced by Figure 38.3, this study proposed a three-layer action framework for disability inclusive disaster risk reduction (DiDRR). The first layer

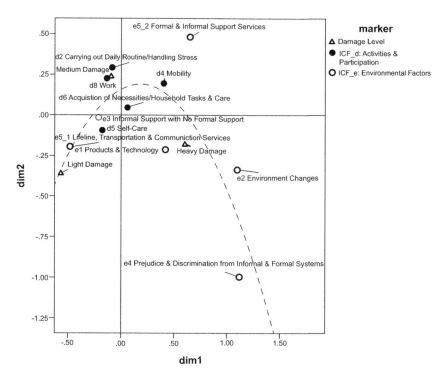

Figure 38.3 Corresponding analysis results of ICF-by-disaster damage cross-tabulated data, 100-to-1,000-hour phase

envisaged that *PWD shall be included*, emphasised the pre-disaster arrangements for the augmentation of reasonable accommodations in such areas as in the 'Activities and Participation' domain, and more specifically in its daily routines (d2), mobility (d4), self-care (d5), acquisition of necessities and conducting household tasks and care (d6) and work (d8) categories. The second layer requests that *everyone include PWD*, stressed strength building. Active engagement in community disaster drills and pre-disaster case management planning are good examples of ways not only to match functioning needs with community help but also to empower PWD through raising their DRR literacy. The third layer, which demanded that *social institutions include PWD*, aimed at statutory as well as emancipatory (Oliver, 1990) responses. Examples of such actions include the UN Convention on the Rights of Persons with Disabilities (UN, 2006), the *Sendai Framework for Disaster Risk Reduction 2015–2030* (UNISDR, 2015), enactments of national laws/local by-laws on the advancement of DiDRR, grassroots to national-level strength building and advocacy for and mainstreaming of PWD.

Evidence-based good practices

In this section, examples of evidence-based DiDRR practices are illustrated. It should be noted that evidence is not merely data. It is rather a fact about the causal relation between an intervention/treatment and its outcome. The first case (see Tatsuki, 2013, for a fuller description) focuses on the community-based provisions of reasonable accommodations during disaster. The case shows how community-based pre-disaster arrangements of reasonable accommodation augmentations saved lives of PWD and older people from the tsunami at the onset of GEJE. This is a good practice example of *'PWD shall be included'*. The second case illustrates *'everyone include PWD'* through the strength building of PWD. Empowerment of PWD was demonstrated through their active involvement in a community disaster drill and its partial effectiveness was empirically demonstrated. The third case pays attention to *'social institutions include PWD'* by examining the impacts of the Convention on the Rights of Persons with Disabilities (UN, 2006) on DiDRR practices among national and local governments alongside non-governmental organisations.

Case 1) Providing reasonable accommodations during disaster: Hachiman community response to GEJE tsunami attack

About 350 households, or 900 people, were residing in the Hachiman community in Ishinomaki city in Miyagi prefecture. In response to the city's initiative for organising community-based emergency response networks for people with functional needs in times of disasters (PFND), local *minsei-iins* (commissioned district welfare volunteers), resident association leaders, shop owners, housewives and retired residents decided to organise their own emergency response neighbourhood network in May of 2005. A list of nine Hachiman resident PFND was provided by the city because they were voluntarily registered in the city's PFND registry. Another eight persons were added to the network's list because the network members felt that they were also in need of neighbours' help for evacuation. The network recruited and assigned two local resident evacuation supporters (RES) for each PFND. The network members paid regular friendly visits to those 17 individuals, shared current situations with other network members, and kept updating the assignment of RES to each of the 17 people.

Almost six years after the community emergency network was formed, the 2011 tsunami attacked Hachiman community. At its onset, 14 individuals (12 households) were at their own residence, and the other three were temporarily in residential care facilities outside of the tsunami-inundated areas. Out of the 14 PFND who were at home, seven individuals in six households were assisted for emergency evacuation by their RES. Four RES dashed to the assigned PFND residence immediately after the earthquake and the other two RES (each of them was the PFND's own daughter) were with their mothers and drove them to the designated shelter. In contrast, no RES showed up to rescue six individuals in five households because their RESs were at work, out of town, or saving themselves from tsunami attacks. These six individuals with no RES assistance were saved either through self-help, a neighbour, or a home helper or acquaintance who happened to drive by the site. Finally, it is unknown if the RES came or not for two PFND because both died either from the tsunami or at the temporary housing unit.

In conclusion, Hachiman community's emergency response network functioned to help a half of the registered 14 PFND who were at their own homes and saved six lives, while self-help and informal mutual help from a neighbour or a friend saved about a third (six lives) of the people with frailties and/or disabilities in Hachiman community. It should be noted that at least about a half of the registered PFND might not be able to survive the tsunami attack without the network efforts. Note that one root cause of social vulnerabilities was attributed to the bureaucratic compartmentalisation between everyday social services delivery and reasonable accommodation arrangements during disaster times. The Hachiman community emergency response network initiatives seem to bridge augmentations of reasonable accommodations for PWD between these two phases and are hoped to be disseminated to other parts of the world.

Case 2) Strength-building through empowerment of DRR literacy: Beppu Disability-inclusive Disaster Risk Reduction Project

As a part of the strength building project for DiDRR, the evaluation study was conducted in Furuichi community, Beppu city, Oita prefecture in Fiscal Year (FY) 2016. The purpose of the study was to examine whether an active engagement and partnership with PWD in a community disaster drill was effective in terms of the empowerment of PWD. As the first step, a community-based participatory TQM-style (Nayatani et al., 1994) workshop with multiple stakeholders and a follow-up in-depth interview were conducted to define constructs that the stakeholders wished to empower in the project. Through this endeavour, disaster risk reduction literacy (DRR literacy) was identified as an outcome variable which consisted of 1) *understanding* of hazards and vulnerabilities, 2) *awareness* of preparedness measures and 3) *confidence* in immediate action. It was found that DRR literacy plays a key role for translating warning and alert into protective actions (Kawami, Hayashi and Tatsuki, 2016). Utilising the statements collected from the workshop and interview, sub-scales for the three constructs were developed and they were administered to the participants of the outcome effectiveness study. Each of the sub-scales showed acceptable internal consistency reliabilities of .88 for 12 items understanding sub-scale, .83 for 19 items awareness and .93 for 15 items confidence.

Twenty-two (14 male and eight female) PWD were involved in the study. Twelve (nine male and three female) participated in the disaster drill while 10 (five male and five female) PWD did not participate. Although the involved PWD were randomly assigned to either disaster drill participation or non-participation control groups, some PWD assigned to the control group showed strong interests in participating in the drill while others were very reluctant to go outside that day since there was strong wind and snowfall. Thus, the idea of randomisation was abandoned in the morning of the disaster drill. Instead, a statistical adjustment technique was employed to control the confounding factor of selection bias by matching participants and non-participants in terms of their propensities that seemed to have dictated their eagerness or reluctance to be part of the disaster drill.

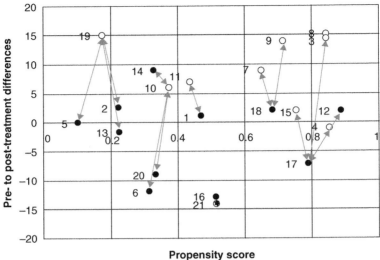

Figure 38.4 Result of matching treatment and control group participants based on their propensity scores

Figure 38.4 shows the result of the propensity score matching where the horizontal axis represents the propensity scores of the treatment (drill participation) or control (non-participation) group membership while the vertical axis indicates pre- to post-treatment difference in confidence sub-scale scores. Based on the matching, it was found that those who participated in the disaster drill showed about a 10-point increase (or average treatment effect) ($p < .001$) on the sub-scale of confidence in immediate actions. No significant treatment effect, however, was observed on the scores of understanding or awareness sub-scales. Apparently, more individualised consultation and awareness-raising are needed to empower DRR literacy on these two sub-scales, respectively. For FY 2017, the Beppu project will introduce case management processes for further empowerment of PWD so that the functional needs of each PWD can be properly assessed and matched with help from the neighbours and so that PWD themselves can learn more about surrounding hazards and vulnerabilities and become more aware of how to prepare for any upcoming disaster. The effectiveness of these endeavours will be tested by the end of March 2018.

Case 3) Statutory and institutional actions: social institutions shall include PWD

A statutory action may provide a basis for empowering just practices (Dominelli, 2012). One of the most influential sources for DiDRR in Japan is credited to a series of legislation processes and their products that finally led to the ratification of the Convention on the Rights of Persons with Disabilities (CRPD) in 2014, which has become the common base for bringing justice into potentially any imbalance that may exist between PWD functional needs and environmental unresponsiveness. Article 11 of the CRPD specifically deals with disaster risk information.

Since Japan signed the Convention in 2007, the ministerial board for disability policy reform was established and it began working collaboratively with civil society stakeholder organisations for and by PWD. In 2011, the parliament passed a major amendment to the Basic Act for Persons with Disabilities, in which the legal concept of 'reasonable accommodation' was stipulated in Japanese domestic laws for the first time. The amendment also included Article 26 that corresponded to CRPD Article 11 (safety and security during risk situation).

Furthermore, the Act on the Elimination of Discrimination against Persons with Disabilities (AED) passed Japan's parliament in 2013. This Act was formulated in response to calls from civil society. These interventions produced the principles of the Basic Act for Persons with Disabilities which legally forbids undue discrimination based on disability by the private sector and both the national and local governments. It further imposes an obligation on the government to provide reasonable accommodations. This Act came into effect on 1 April 2016.

The *Sendai Framework for Disaster Risk Reduction 2015–2030* (UNISDR, 2015) is the other major statutory basis for empowering just practice. It was during the Third United Nations World Conference on Disaster Risk Reduction (WCDRR) in 2015 that DiDRR for the first time was formally acknowledged as one of the most critical areas to be addressed. The conference adopted the *Sendai Framework* which included issues of inclusion. The PWD movement demanded 'Nothing about us, without us' which was incorporated into its guiding principles (UNISDR, 2015: 13).

What are the impacts of these statutory actions? About two months prior to AED being put into effect, an independent think tank conducted a nationwide survey on the current DiDRR state of affairs among all 1,740 municipal governments and 627 (36 per cent) of them responded (Shimazaki and Yamada, 2016). Of these, 12.9 per cent was considering and 17.9 per cent was planning to consider ways of adhering to the requirements stipulated by AED at the time of survey. The remaining two-thirds have not taken any such action. This relatively low rate of adherence to the Act may be due to the compartmentalised structure of the local government bureaucratic administration where it takes time for critical law changes in one area (e.g. disability) or adoption of a new international action framework (i.e. SF) to impact upon related areas of the local governments' everyday administration.

Provision of reasonable accommodations in times of disaster in the society is not a matter of 'if' but rather that of 'when'. There are other developments that are worth mentioning. Up until the present time, 26 local governments at both prefectural and municipal levels enacted by-laws that corresponded to the Act on the Elimination of Discrimination against Persons with Disabilities. Furthermore, 12 local governments have included an article on risk/disaster situations which can provide the basis for entitlements and disability inclusion during times of disaster.

One such good example is Beppu city. The city council passed their version of the discrimination elimination bylaw against PWD in September 2013, and this bylaw also included an article on risk/disaster situations. A network of local civil society organisations became a major locomotive for actualising this bylaw and the network worked collaboratively with the city administration and other community leaders. The network's final goal is to make all disaster risk management policies and programmes in the city disability inclusive. To meet this goal, the network, the city's various departments in charge of disaster risk management, social services for PWD and older people, service care providers and case managers, local community leaders and residents are currently working closely together to institutionalise proactive planning of care for PWD as well as to enrich emergency community help to PWD in times of disaster. The author is involved in conducting outcome evaluation studies that are to determine the scientific evidence for its effectiveness in empowering both PWD and community residents on DRR literacy. Upon the successful completion of this evaluation, the city plans to set a separate budget for proactive care planning and the mobilisation of community resources.

Conclusion

This chapter provided empirical accounts of the social roots of disaster risks among persons with disabilities (PWD) following the 2011 GEJE. Multiple independent surveys reported that PWD died at a rate almost two times higher than the general population. The author, however, argued that this mortality rate gap was observed only in Miyagi and that the root cause was attributed to decades-long normalisation practices in tsunami-prone areas, which have not been coordinated to countermeasures enacted during times of disaster. Second, those PWD who survived GEJE also experienced life functioning difficulties, which were mainly caused by sudden changes in the environment with disruptions of the lifeline and other essential services. Third, based on these empirical accounts, a three-layer action framework is proposed for disability inclusive disaster risk reduction (DiDRR). The first layer envisaged that *PWD shall be included*, and emphasises the augmentation of reasonable accommodations to meet life functioning needs that arise during disasters. The second layer requests that *everyone include PWD*, and stresses strength building. The third layer demands that *social institutions include PWD*. Green social workers demand PWD inclusion in statutory responses as integral to empowering just practices, and their work is also evidence based.

References

Beck, U. (1992). *Risk society: Toward a new modernity*. London, UK: Sage.
Dominelli, L. (2012). *Green social work: From environmental crises to environmental justice*. Cambridge, UK: Polity Press.
Kahoku Shimpo (2011). Focus: 59 elderly institutions hit by Tsunami and 578 people died or missing, 13 December.
Kailes, J. I. and Enders, A. (2007). A function-based framework for emergency management and planning, *Journal of Disability Policy Studies*, 17(4): 230–237.
Kawami, H., Hayashi, H. and Tatsuki, S. (2016). A study of nonlinear interaction effects of disaster risk reduction literacy with Seismic hazard risk, physical and human damages perception on risk avoidance behavior: Report of 2015 Hyogo Prefecture Survey on preparedness. *Journal of Social Safety Science*, 29: 135–142.
Matsukawa, A. and Tatsuki, S. (2016). The challenges and difficulties of people with disabilities from the perspective of the social model of disability: The 2014 ICF-based checklist survey of functioning difficulties in times of disasters in Sendai City in Miyagi prefecture. *Proceedings of the 4th ISSS Workshop on Great East Japan Earthquake Disaster*, 63–66.
Nayatani, Y., Eiga, T., Futami, R. and Miyagawa, H. (1994). *The seven new QC tools: Practical applications for managers*. Tokyo: 3A Corporation.
Nishisato, S. (1980). *Analysis of categorical data: Dual scaling and its applications*. Toronto: Univeristy of Toronto Press.
Oliver, M. (1990). *The politics of disablement*, London, UK: Palgrave Macmillan.
Shimazaki, K. and Yamada, M. (2016). Toward the creation of concrete measures for people requiring assistance during a disaster: An examination based on the results of a Questionnaire Survey of the local governments in Japan. *Quarterly Journal of Policy and Administration Studies*, 4: 159–185. Mitsubishi UFJ Research and Consulting.
Tatsuki, S. (2013). Old age, disability, and the Tohoku-Oki earthquake. *Earthquake Spectra*, 29: S403–S432.
Tierney, K. (2014). *The social roots of risk: Producing disasters, promoting resilience*. Stanford, CA: Stanford University Press.
Twigg, J., Kett, M., Bottomley, H., Tan, L. and Nasreddina, H. (2011). Disability and public shelter in emergencies. *Environmental Hazards*, 10: 248–261.
Wisner, B., Blaikie, P., Cannon, T. and Davis, I. (2004). *At risk: Natural hazards, people's vulnerability and disasters*. London: Routledge.

WHO (World Health Organization) (2002). *Towards a common language for functioning, disability and Health ICF.* Available on http://www.who.int/classifications/icf/icfbeginnersguide.pdf.

UNISDR (United Nations Office for Disaster Risk Reduction) (2015). *Sendai Framework for Disaster Risk Reduction 2015–2030.* Available on http://www.unisdr.org/files/43291_sendaiframeworkfordrren.pdf [Accessed 5 November 2017].

United Nations (2006). *Convention on the rights of persons with disabilities.* Available on www.un.org/development/desa/disabilities/convention-on-the-rights-of-persons-with-disabilities/convention-on-the-rights-of-persons-with-disabilities-2.html [Accessed 5 November 2017].

39
Social work and terrorism
Voices of experience

Marilyn Callahan

Introduction

A bomb is detonated in a railway station. A politician is assassinated. A sniper kills shoppers in a mall. The first question on the mind of everyone: Is this a terrorist attack? If so, it is considered much more frightening and significant than if it were an individual acting alone, no matter the damage inflicted.

In the last few decades, terrorism has gripped the attention of Europe and North America (the West) accustomed to feeling relatively safe from disasters befalling other 'less democratic' ones. In North America, this complacency ended abruptly on 11 September 2001 shattering the notion that terrorism happened somewhere else to someone else. I was at home on a small gulf island in British Columbia, Canada when my phone rang around 10:00. It was my eldest daughter quickly assuring me that my other daughter, the one living two blocks from the World Trade Centre in Manhattan, was safe. She had slept in that morning and, rather than take the subway at the WTC station, she had taken a taxi to work. She and the taxi driver felt this enormous shudder and assumed it was an earthquake. In a way it was. It awakened many in the West to the fear of terrorism and its presence within seemingly protected places called home and country.

The terrorist attacks in Madrid (2004), London (2005, 2017), Paris (2015), Brussels (2016), and Nice (2016) reinforced this recognition among Western countries. Interestingly, terrorists committed to causes unrelated to the aims of Al-Qaida and the so-called Islamic State (Da'esh) (ISIS) have killed many more people since 1970 than these Islamic groups (Schwartz, 2016). But because they attacked Western nations, they have become the enemy to be vanquished.

Western countries have responded by expending enormous efforts and resources to combat terrorism, a unifying priority on a scale rarely seen. 'The War on Terror', declared by President George W. Bush in 2002, has made some advances but has also fostered many missteps and created unforeseen challenges. The mandate of a 'War on Terror' rather than on terrorists or terrorism is very broad, and without boundaries. It is a war against 'both the dark forces that threaten civilisation and the fears they arouse' (Nunberg, 2004).

In the midst of this, the efforts of social workers to combat the effects of terrorism at home and abroad remain largely unrecognised. Yet, social work has a great deal to contribute to understanding and addressing international terrorism. This chapter aims to identify its contributions and amplify its voice.

To begin, I provide a critical analysis of the role of terrorism in shaping public policy, emphasising the central focus placed on dramatic problems compared to pervasive, yet relatively silent ones, such as poverty, a phenomenon familiar to social workers. The compromise of human rights and rise of prejudice and misinformation usually accompany such attention while more significant problems are ignored. Moreover, the collateral damage, not only to human life, the environment and ecology as featured in green social work, are rarely considered (Dominelli, 2012). Social work has a rich history with such analysis, albeit on problems of a different but related nature.

Further, social work has been at the forefront of addressing the kind of mayhem terrorist attacks create. While terrorism is viewed as a national and international issue, its immediate effects are local and it is here on the ground where social workers have made a significant contribution. However, responding to the complexities of terrorism is no simple task but fraught with contradictions, also familiar to social workers. Their rich experience in working with significant problems and their ambiguities is the focus of the remainder of the chapter.

Terrorism: critical perspectives

While terrorism is a slippery concept to define, there are some agreed characteristics (Hoffman, 2006). It is employed first and foremost as a political concept, the use of power to achieve political aims. It differs from war as it is not waged by nation-states against one another, nor does it follow the military or legal conventions of war. Instead, it relies upon random and covert acts of violence against symbolic targets, human or material. While random, it is not haphazard but employs carefully planned and selected sorties. It is often associated with those with less power as a way of disrupting dominant systems and avoiding capture. Like extremism it depends upon a strong bond among its adherents often forged through shared religious or ideological beliefs.

Terrorist acts feature specific strategies such as bombing, assassination, hijacking, kidnapping, extortion and the destruction of significant artefacts and lands. At its core, terrorism values actions above words. It is theatre, designed act by act, to inspire fear and disorganisation (Jenkins, 1985).

However, terrorism is a contested concept. Most recently in Europe and North America, it is used as shorthand to indicate organised fundamentalist Islamic group members insinuating themselves into societies, familiar or foreign, to carry out vicious attacks against these societies, all in the name of their mission (McCants, 2015).

However, what passes as terrorism depends on the eye of the beholder. When the Irish Republican Army bombed the Grand Brighton Hotel with the intention of killing Prime Minister Margaret Thatcher on 12 October 1984, many British citizens denounced this incident as another act of terrorism while those committed to an Irish Republic viewed it as a courageous strategy in the quest for Irish independence (English, 2013). Although this conflict was inspired in part by long-standing religious feuds (Catholic and Protestant) as well as geographical and political aims, Catholicism was not vilified in the same way that the Muslim religion has been in recent years. Defining terrorism depends upon one's vantage point and power to control the message. Is it revolution, criminal actions, self-defence or terrorism? Are they freedom fighters, outlaws, insurgents or terrorists?

While we generally consider terrorism to be a strategy of the less powerful against powerful state forces, states themselves can use terrorism against their citizens. Famously Stalin, Hitler, Gadhafi, and other tyrannical leaders have used the tools of terrorism to gain and maintain power. However, terrorism also occurs within states that are considered democratic or at least led by seemingly benign leaders. Miller (2013) notes how America marshalled legal and extra-legal systems in the 19th century to carry out terrorist acts against Indians including forced removal from ancestral lands, separation and murder of family members, incarceration, and the destruction of buffalo and horses, the economic base of the Cherokee and Crow. Much the same analysis has been applied to the experience of Afro Americans and other peoples colonised by democratic nations.

Another central misconception about terrorism committed by Al-Qaeda, ISIS and other similar groups is the focus upon 'us' versus 'them'. According to this popular belief 'us' is defined as Christian Westerners, and 'them', as members of particular militant Muslim groups. It is Westerners in their crosshairs. Yet, the essential target for ISIS and others is not the West, but Muslims, Christians and others living in their own countries, who must join the movement through fear or admiration if the terrorists' quest for a fundamental Islamic homeland is to be realised. The Global Terrorism Database estimates that in Iraq alone, from 2006 to 2015 there have been over 17,500 terrorist attacks resulting in over 52,000 deaths. In Western Europe during the same period, radical Islamic groups have killed less than 400 people (http://start.umd.edu/gtd/). However, by occasional attacks on the West and constantly striking within their own populations, radical Islamic groups hope to demonstrate both their power to those at home and their contempt for Western culture. Responses from the West such as civilian bombings and extralegal incarcerations fuel terrorists' causes.

Even though citizens have committed some terrorists' acts against their own Western countries, this notion of the terrorists as 'foreigners' serves several purposes. An external enemy is important for unifying a population through fear and centralising its power structures. Once there was no longer a threat from 'The Red Scare', a fear of communists and their use of nuclear weapons that lasted until the fall of the Berlin wall in November 1989, military spending in Western countries fell significantly. In the US, the cutback was a bipartisan effort begun under the presidency of George H W Bush and continued by Bill Clinton (Adair, 2008). The changes in former communist controlled countries of Eastern Europe were even more profound where old oligarchies disappeared and liberal market related ideas took hold in many. However, since the 'War on Terror' in Western nations, military spending has ramped up, not by government alone but in partnership with for profit companies. Political parties of all stripes have to pay at least lip service to security and safety as a result of the fears that have been engendered by terrorist talk. Diminishing resources for social and environmental issues as well as less commitment to democratic processes is the end result (Dancs, 2011).

The use of terrorism to achieve political aims is certainly not a recent phenomenon in human history. The concept gained purchase with the 'Regime de la Terreur' of 1793–94 in France, following the French Revolution and was ironically initiated to ensure the orderly transition to a more democratic form of government (Hoffman, 2006). From this, the word 'terror' was adopted into the English language with its meaning of 'fear so great as to overwhelm the mind' (http://etymonline.com). Many of the strategies employed by the leaders of the 'Regime de la Terreur' inform our ongoing definition of terrorism. Abualola (2013) provides an overview of the lengthy history of terrorism in Islamic countries, indicating its pervasive use among cultures and continents.

For social workers, a critical analysis of 'terrorism' has important implications. A focus on terrorism shifts the gaze away from the ongoing problems of local populations and the lack of resources to support improved conditions. Tensions within populations created by fear of terrorists introduce new problems that again distract from endemic ones. Assisting others to integrate into increasingly hostile environments is nothing new to social workers but made more daunting by unchallenged assumptions and chronic mistrust.

The response to terrorism: a multifaceted approach

In a show of international unity, the United Nations (UN) adopted a strategy to combat terrorism consisting of four pillars (United Nations Global Counter Terrorism Strategy, 2006):

- Addressing the conditions conducive to the spread of terrorism;
- Preventing and combatting terrorism;
- Building capacity and strengthening the role of the UN; and
- Ensuring human rights and the rule of law.

This framework serves as the guide for deploying efforts and measuring progress in the international struggle against all manifestations of terrorism. First, it includes broadly based strategies to change environmental factors conducive to promoting the terrorist narrative such as poverty, oppression and racial and religious intolerance. Next it focuses upon preventing terrorist activities by narrowing the gaze to those most likely to commit such acts and taking direct actions to prevent this occurrence. Third, it concentrates on ensuring that nation-states have the capacity to take independent actions. And finally, it requires that all actions take place within the framework of human rights and legal conventions.

This multifaceted strategy is a familiar approach to addressing large-scale problems such as poverty, addictions, HIV, criminal justice and others and has been widely used by many professionals including social workers. Applying theories based on ecology, oppression, systems, exclusion and others, the profession of social work has wrestled with a comprehensive approach to individual, group and social issues since its inception. Thus, from the outset, social workers have a mind-set and a knowledge and practice legacy to offer to the field of counter-terrorism (Itzhaky and York, 2005).

The ethical principles upon which social work is founded provide further support to the comprehensive strategy proposed by the UN (International Federation of Social Workers, 2012). The profession of social work condemns terrorism, given that it espouses violence, unlawful actions and intolerance among other characteristics. In their jointly owned ethical statement, the International Association of Schools of Social Work (IASSW) and International Federation of Social Workers (IFSW) include an explicit clause stating, 'Social workers should not allow their skills to be used for inhumane purposes, such as torture or terrorism' (www.IFSW.org). This statement also includes a commitment to several international agreements including civil and political rights, human rights, economic social and cultural rights, and the rights of indigenous and tribal peoples.

However, social work has always been positioned at the crossroads of many contradictions when seemingly comprehensive and ethical actions are applied in practice. The following section identifies some of these conundrums and the experience of social workers in tackling them.

Preventing and combatting terrorism while honouring the law and human rights

The development of the Guantanamo Bay detention camp by the US administration in 2002 is an example of the complications that occur when attempts to mitigate the spread of terrorism in fact betray the principles of human rights and other international agreements. At the camp, so-called terrorists have been detained indefinitely without trial and subjected to torture (Clark, 2006). The US National Association of Social Workers Legal Defence Fund joined with others in their successful application to the US Supreme Court arguing that detainees in Guantanamo who are not American citizens nonetheless have a right to challenge the legality of their detention in American courts of law (American National Association of Social Workers, 2004). In this case, the line between who are terrorists becomes blurred: those accused, or those on the other side who employ many of the tactics of terrorists in their fight against terrorism?

Similarly social workers have learned to struggle with their stance towards groups using terrorist methods in their fight for social justice (Ife, 2008). However, they have developed other approaches rather than transgress legal rights.

The African American Civil Rights Movement 1950–1970 provides a useful example. Social workers such as Whitney Young and Dorothy Height were prominent leaders in the movement and many other social workers, black and white, committed themselves to its goals and actions based on civil disobedience and non-violent actions. However, some within the movement argued for the use of arms for self-defence and challenged the commitment to non-violence. Malcolm X, a leader in the emerging Black Power movement, described the growing militancy: 'There's new strategy coming in. It'll be Molotov cocktails this month, hand grenades next month, and something else next month. It'll be ballots, or it'll be bullets' (Malcolm X, 12 April 1964). It is on this particular issue that movements often fracture. Indeed the American Civil Rights movement grappled with this tension throughout (Peniel, 2010).

The role of social work is not to abandon those advocating violence and lawlessness in their quest for social justice but to promote understanding of their position while not condoning unlawful actions. In this instance, social workers broadened the discussion, noting the use of terrorist tactics against Blacks over centuries and refocused on supporting the solutions advocated by the leaders in Black Power movement (Bell, 2014).

Those solutions focused on moving beyond the quest for equality in the 'White' world. Instead leaders sought recognition of the distinctive history and contributions of Black people and their capacity to provide for themselves as well as gain equal access to public programs. Advocates, including Black social workers, set up self-help measures such as school lunch programs, neighbourhood safety patrols and Black curricula (Bell, 2014). They also established the National Association of Black Social Workers with the aim of continuing Black solutions to Black issues (Reid-Merrit, 2010). Much was learned for other social movements. Militancy and non-violence can be powerful partners in creating social change.

Similarly, those seeking justice for Muslims living in the West and elsewhere have created their own ways of working alongside but separate from existing groups (Shamai, 2010). For instance the Islamic Social Services Association in Canada is similar to many other recently established groups, aiming to provide education and advocacy for those in the Muslim communities while at the same time offering social services (www.issacanada.com). Social workers working outside these groups seek to find spaces for them, provide links between them and mainstream services and work to reform mainstream services.

Standing with others while not condoning their behaviour

Social work has long played a role in promoting understanding of those who use violence against others, not only in their quest for social justice, but also for other unacceptable and unlawful reasons. Parents may murder their children and each other, a gang kills a gay person, people dealing drugs may kill one another or passers-by, a terrorist blows up a nightclub: all may be the clients of social workers.

The growth of social workers practicing as capital mitigating specialists in the US is a very dramatic example of the role that social workers play in standing for the least valued (Hughes, 2009). Hired as part of a legal team arguing for defendants who have committed often heinous crimes, social workers are charged with developing social histories to promote understanding of the defendants' behaviour. Their codes of ethics, focusing on social justice and the dignity and worth of the individual, as well as their perspectives on the individual within their personal, social and political context, provide social workers with particular competence (Berrigan, 2008).

Standing beside those such as murderers and terrorists who have committed highly unacceptable crimes against others without offering excuses for their behaviour remains a central task of social workers. As stated by the National Association of Social Workers in the US (2006) 'Increasingly we are challenged to stand up for the rights and liberties of the unpopular, so that rights and protections will remain available for all, and in recognition of our common humanity'.

Preventing and combatting terrorism without exacerbating conditions fostering terrorism

An irony of no small insignificance is the fact that efforts to tackle a problem can also increase its likelihood of continuing to be a problem. Once social and economic conditions that foster the development of terrorist behaviour have been identified, the next logical step is to drill down to those populations most affected by these conditions, and then further, to those who actually commit terrorist acts. The characteristics of those individuals can be used to identify others. Some form of profiling is the usual outcome.

Social work has extensive although not illustrious history with profiling in criminal justice, child welfare and mental health (Swift and Callahan, 2009). Practitioners apply risk assessment instruments to determine whether a particular individual is likely to commit further criminal acts or to abuse or neglect their child, or be a threat to those in the community because of their behaviour. However, the reliability of these instruments has been called into question, based as they are on the very small numbers of individuals committing these actions and the uncertainty of measuring the impact of larger social forces. What has happened instead is that large numbers of individuals are captured in the profilers' net, leading to wasted resources on needless investigations and stigmatisation of individuals with particular characteristics. Overall, these efforts can further the alienation of vulnerable groups, leading to their susceptibility to behaviour outside the law.

Most recently, this phenomenon has played out in the growth of Islamophobia, where those of the Muslim faith are stereotyped as tribal, dangerous and sexist (Lavalette and Penketh, 2014). The *Prevent* strategy in the UK is an example of an apparently laudable aim tied to a limited strategy with the distinct potential to harm those innocent of wrongdoing, particularly young Muslim men. Under Sections 36 to 41 of the new Counter-Terrorism and Security Act (2015) social workers among others are required to report individuals exhibiting particular characteristics first and then attempt to provide them with support. Not surprisingly this strategy places social workers in the position of quasi-police officers, making their offers of help a two-edged sword. Moreover many can be identified as 'potential' terrorists by virtue of their race, neighbourhood, or associations who have no such inclination. Social workers have argued that in the area of 'pre-crime' more effective strategies are not aimed primarily at the investigation of individuals. Instead, challenges to the discourse of terrorism based upon research and facts and community organising against hate and exclusion are more useful (Stanley, 2015).

Advocating for the human rights of terrorists while standing up for the rights and needs of their victims

One of the ongoing conundrums of crime prevention and criminal legal systems is that the resources spent on these activities vastly outweigh those directed at victims of crime. Indeed, the United Nations Global Terrorism Strategy, 2006) is silent on the victims of terrorism.

Estimates of the costs of the wars in Iraq, Syria, Afghanistan and Pakistan conclude that the US has spent US$4.8 trillion (about US$300 billion annually to 2016) with costs continuing to rise as veterans services and interest on the debt are factored in over time (Crawford, 2016). These wars were mounted with the stated aim of eliminating terrorist organisations and their governments. While there are no figures for the US expenditures on resettling the victims of these wars, an OECD report compares annual expenditures on refugee resettlement in 2015 among its members, with the US totalling US$1.56 billion (.01 per cent of GDP).

Social workers experiencing this reality in other fields of practice have taken leadership in the development of victim services, including those for battered women, sexual assault victims and others. Similarly, they are on the front lines of working with those most affected by terrorism and counter-terrorist efforts. For example, the President of the International Federation of Social Workers, Ruth Stark, reports on the role of social workers in the large refugee camps in Jordan, Lebanon and Turkey where meeting the very basic needs of survival such as clean water and food and even modest shelter are ongoing priorities (Hardy, 2016). Saeed (2013) portrays the arduous conditions in Syria where, in the years before the civil war, social workers worked in schools to offer individual and community services. Now those same schools are used for shelters and hospitals and are shuttered to education. Violence and sexual assault, children without parents or schools, chronic hunger and fear prevail within and outside the shelters.

Supporting victims of terrorism and other crimes requires action beyond immediate individual needs. Social workers have consistently argued for the broader rights of victim groups including reparations for loss of families, social systems, economic activities and environmental ruin (Dominelli, 2012).

While the millions of refugees fleeing countries decimated by terrorism such as Somalia, Syria and Afghanistan face untold hazards and reluctant receptions from other nations, the toll on social workers attempting to assist them is also heavy. The overwhelming and unremitting nature of the need without adequate resources to meet even basic requirements is professionally and personally debilitating. Perhaps most difficult of all for victim–survivors and social workers alike is dealing with the profound grief of those left behind and the uncertainty of the fate of friends, family and clients (Fraidlin and Rabin, 2006). That social workers are serving on the ground in spite of these appalling situations is a tribute to the profession and its members (British Association of Social Workers, 2013)

Addressing stereotypes and exclusion while settling newcomers

Vastly more persons have been displaced by the impact of terrorism than have been killed or injured (Global Terrorism Data Base, 2016). The more than 1 million Syrian refugees who came to Europe in 2015 have presented those countries with challenges of an almost unprecedented nature. European countries have not seen this level of migration since the years after World War Two and such an influx has provoked strenuous reactions of both support and rejection from residents.

Social work has a lengthy experience in dealing with stigma by employing individual, group and community approaches to force open the boundaries that deny membership to others (Shamai, 2010). One of the historical roots of Western social work, emanating in the slums of London during the 19th century, is the Settlement House Movement and the subsequent development of community organising (Healy, 2008). As waves of immigrants entered the US and Canada in the 19th and 20th centuries, social workers were at the forefront of developing community gathering places where newcomers and locals could collaborate. Over time, these efforts have developed into government and not-for-profit immigrant and refugee services still largely staffed by social workers.

This legacy continues. Social workers in those Western countries accepting the influx of refugees as a result of terrorist activities are taxed daily to provide quickly a wide range of refugee services, including community acceptance strategies and changes to mainstream social services (Australian Association of Social Workers, 2016, Islamic Social Services of Canada, 2017). They face dramatic attempts to limit entry of refugees to European and North American countries, none more notorious than that of the US where a failed Executive Order, issued by the president on 27 February 2017, aimed to limit entry to the US, in particular from seven predominantly Muslim countries. The National Association of Social Workers wasted no time in condemning this action, issuing a response on 1 March 2017 (Wilson, 2017). It states:

> Our national priority should be to find ways, within reasonable national security policies, to welcome refugees – not deny them sanctuary. We should also be reminded that many of the refugees from Muslim countries became displaced because of wars in which the United States has participated.

Questioning the importance of terrorism while not disregarding it: spectacular problems and chronic issues

Terrorism is one of these spectacular problems with little immediate effect within Western countries, yet with the capacity to commandeer vast resources and public attention. It speaks to a need for storytelling in the media with the narrative unfolding in daily missives and the intense desire for self-preservation among policymakers. At the root of this phenomenon is the appeal of narratives that combine a mixture of excitement and fear fed daily to the public waiting for the next instalment. As I write this on 25 February 2017, the newly appointed terrorist watchdog in Britain, Max Hill, is warning that the threat of terrorism in the UK is the highest that it has been since the IRA bombings of the 1970s and 1980s (Rily-Smith, 2017). The fact that there is a terrorist watchdog with a pulpit from which to make such pronouncements is evidence of the appeal of this narrative.

World hunger, appalling death rates from easily preventable diseases and other such calamities simply do not capture the same attention. While estimates vary, about one in nine persons worldwide do not have access to food for healthy development. Most of these people live in developing countries in Asia and Africa, with the highest percentage of hunger in Sub-Saharan Africa (one in four persons). It is estimated that about half of the children under five years who die each year (3.1 million) do so because of poor nutrition (World Hunger, 2016). Terrorism and its aftermaths simply add to the hunger of those geographical regions where agricultural lands are destroyed and farm workers are killed or have fled.

Social workers have long been aware that the most vexing problems confronting individuals are not necessarily the issues of most concern to policymakers and the general public. Child welfare illustrates visibly this anomaly. When a child is murdered or harmed at the hands of a parent or caregiver, a public uproar ensues and often blame is placed on social workers. Policy-makers quickly order public inquiries and tighten child protection policies, usually resulting in yet more administrative work for social workers and precious little improvements in the safety of children (Swift and Callahan, 2009). This phenomenon is evident in other areas. A person accused of a violent crime while on parole or after release from a mental health facility sparks similar reactions.

Yet these deaths or injuries, while horrifying, are rare. Daily, social workers confront the reality of children living in grim circumstances without adequate food, shelter, healthcare or guidance yet they can muster little attention for these conditions even when they try to make them a public issue.

Social workers have learned to act immediately and think long term in such circumstances. A terrorist bomb shatters a town square. Social workers and others must provide emergency aid and recovery operations. But second, they must consider the longer-term impact of that act: damage to the water supply, the loss of key leaders, the fleeing of citizens, the divisions that will be created within the community and so forth. The meaning of the act and the motivation of the terrorists both at an individual and community level must be explored and acted upon. And third, the focus on routing out terrorism in the community, while important, cannot overshadow the crucial issues long facing the community. Thinking and acting on these three dimensions is the professional skill of social work.

Conclusion

Terrorism may seem like a fairly recent phenomenon to those in Western countries, but in fact it has a lengthy history and shares much in common with other significant international problems. Social work has a long tradition and vast experience in dealing with complex and daunting problems, similar to the ones created by terrorists and has much to contribute to the field of counter-terrorism. A fundamental skill of social work is to look beyond currently held assumptions about any particular issue to provide critical analysis and new perspectives. Terrorism is one of those concepts that requires a thorough review, since it has been used as a foil for costly political and military misadventures. Critical analysis is one contribution that social work can make.

Social work has a rich tradition of viewing responses to social problems on an individual and larger social systems level, an approach used by the UN in developing its counter-terrorism response. As with any complex problem, counter-terrorism is fraught with contradictions and social work is no stranger to carrying out its work in the midst of cross currents, using as its touchstone a commitment to social justice and legal processes.

Addressing terrorism with action is another contribution. Social workers are active in the field of counter-terrorism in their own countries in the West offering emergency services to those affected by local terrorist attacks, concrete services to those fleeing terrorism in their homelands and confronting the misperceptions and prejudices that arise and that threaten the cohesion of their communities and nations. While less is known about the social workers who work in those countries torn apart by the terrorist activities, it is clear that they are struggling against all odds and that the resources of the West have been concentrated on military rather than humanitarian responses.

This chapter has focused on terrorism as an international issue that demands an analysis not only of its political, social and economic dimensions but on its destruction of the physical environment and the connections among all of these dimensions, the founding principle of green social work. Whole nations are destroyed and their populations scattered. Cultures are decimated. Untold environmental disasters are left unattended. Moreover, while narrow conceptions of terrorism prevail, significant problems like poverty worldwide and environmental catastrophes that existed long before terrorism caught the West's attention fall even further down the priority list. It is in these contexts that the voices and actions of social workers are crucial. Swimming against the stream is nothing new. The then-prime minister of Italy summed up succinctly the central message of this chapter: 'To fight terrorism, we need social workers as much as soldiers' (Renzi, 2016).

References

Abualola, T. (2013). *Social services in the field of terrorism*. Xlibris self-publishing service.

Adair, B. (2008). *He ignores bipartisan support for defense cuts*. 5 January. Available on www.politifact.com/truth-o-meter/statements/2008/jan/05/rudy-giuliani/he-ignores-bipartisan-support-for-defense-cuts/ [Accessed 27 July 2017].

American National Association of Social Workers (NASW) (2004). Social workers and international human rights. Available on www.socialworkers.org/ldf/legal_issue/200404.asp?back=yes/ [Accessed 27 July 2017].

Australian Association of Social Workers (2016). *Scope of social work practice with refugees and asylum seekers*, March. Available on www.aasw.asn.au/document/item/8529 [Accessed 27 July 2017].

Bell, J. (2014). *The black power movement and American social work*. New York: Columbia University Press.

Berrigan, H. (2008). *The indispensable role of the mitigation specialist in a capital case: a view from the federal bench*. Available on http://scholarlycommons.law.hofstra.edu/cgi/viewcontent.cgi?article=2619&context=hlr [Accessed 27 July 2017].

British Association of Social Workers (BASW) (2013). *The struggle to practise social work in Syria as the country collapses into war and retribution*. 18 March. Available on www.basw.co.uk/news/article/?id=464 [Accessed 19 April 2017].

Clark, P. (2006). Medical ethics at Guantanamo Bay and Abu Ghraib: The problem of dual loyalty. *Journal of Law, Medicine and Ethics*. http://onlinelibrary.wiley.com/doi/10.1111/j.1748-720X.2006.00071.x/ [Accessed 27 July 2017].

Crawford, N. (2016). *US budgetary costs of wars through 2016: $4.79 trillion and counting*. Available on http://watson.brown.edu/costsofwar/files/cow/imce/papers/2016/Costs of War through 2016 FINAL final v2.pdf [Accessed 26 July 2017].

Dancs, A. (2011). *Homeland security spending since 9/11*. Watson Institute. International and Public Affairs. Available on http://watson.brown.edu/costsofwar/files/cow/imce/papers/2011/Homeland%20Security.pdf [Accessed 27 July 2017].

Dominelli, L. (2012). *Green social work: From environmental crisis to environmental justice*. Cambridge: Polity Press.

English, R. (2013). Terrorist innovation and international politics: Lessons from an IRA case study? *International Politics*, 50: 496–511.

Fraidlin, M. and Rabin, B. (2006). Social workers confront terrorist victims: The interventions and difficulties. *Social Work and Health Care*, 43(2–3): 115–130.

Global Terrorism Data Base (2016). Available on www.start.umd.edu [Accessed 19 April 2017].

Hardy, R. (2016). The role of social work in the refugee crisis. *Social Care Network*, 15 March. Available on www.theguardian.com/social-care-network/2016/mar/15/social-work-refugee-crisis [Accessed 27 July 2017].

Healy, L. (2008). *International social work: Professional action in an interdependent world*. New York: Oxford University Press.

Hoffman, B. (2006). *Inside terrorism*. New York: Columbia University Press, 2nd Edition.

Hughes, E. (2009). Mitigating death. *Cornell Journal of Law and Public Policy*, 18: 337–388.

International Federation of Social Workers (IFSW) (2012). *Statement of ethical principles*, 3 March. Available on http://ifsw.org/policies/statement-of-ethical-principles/ [Accessed 27 July 2017].

Islamic Social Services of Canada. Available on www.issacanada.com [Accessed 27 July 2017].

Itzhaky, H. and York, A. (2005). The role of the social worker in the face of terrorism: Israeli community-based experience, *Social Work*, 50(2): 141–149.

Jenkins, B. (1985). *International terrorism: The other world war*. Santa Monica: Rand Corporation, November.

Ife, J. (2008). *Human rights and social work*. Cambridge: Cambridge University Press.

Lavalette, M. and Penketh, L. (Eds.) (2014). *Race, racism and social work*. Bristol: Polity Press.

Malcolm X. (1964). *The ballot or the bullet*. King Solomon Baptist Church, Detroit, Michigan. 12 April. Available on http://americanradioworks.publicradio.org/features/blackspeech/mx.html [Accessed 27 July 2017].

McCants, W. (2015). *The ISIS apocalypse*. New York: St. Martin's Press.

Miller, M. (2013). *The foundations of modern terrorism: State, society and the dynamics of political violence*. Cambridge: University Press.

National Association of Social Workers. (2006). *Social workers and international Human rights*. Available on www.socialworkers.org/ldf/legal_issue/200404.asp?back=yes&print=1/ [Accessed 27 July 2017].

Nunberg, G. (2004). *The -Ism schism; How much wallop can a simple word pack?* 11 July. Available on www.nytimes.com/2004/07/11/weekinreview/the-ism-schism-how-much-wallop-can-a-simple-word-pack.html [Accessed 27 July 2017].

Peniel, E. (2010). *Dark day, bright nights: From black power to Barack Obama*. New York: Basic Books.

Reid-Merritt, P. (2010). *Righteous self-determinism: The Black social work movement in America*. Baltimore: The Black Classic Press.

Renzi, M. (2016). To fight terrorism, we need social workers as much as soldiers. *The Guardian*, 27 March. Available on www.theguardian.com/commentisfree/2016/mar/22/terrorism-military-culture-matteo-renzi [Accessed 27 July 2017].

Rily-Smith, B. (2017). *Terror chief Max Hill warns risk of attacks in Britain is highest since dark days of IRA*, 25 February. Available on www.telegraph.co.uk/news/2017/02/25/terror-chief-max-hill-warns-risk-attacks-britain-highest-since/ [Accessed 27 July 2017].

Saeed, S. (2013). *The struggle to practise social work in Syria as the country collapses into war and retribution*. 18 March. Available on www.basw.co.uk/news/article/?id=464 [Accessed 27 July 2017].

Schwartz, B. (2016). *2015 Terrorism database*. Available on www.start.umd.edu/news/2015-global-terrorism-database-now-available/ [Accessed 27 July 2017].

Shamai, M. (2010). A sense of national belonging as a buffer against stress resulting from national terror. In Ruggiero, G., Sassaroli, S., Latzer, Y. (Eds.), *Perspectives on immigration and terrorism*. Amsterdam: IOSV Press, pp. 124–126.

Stanley, T. (2015). The idea that social workers can predict who will become terrorists is science fiction. *Community Care*, 25 August. Available on www.communitycare.co.uk/2015/08/25/idea-social-workers-can-predict-will-become-terrorists-science-fiction/ [Accessed 27 July 2017].

Swift, K. and Callahan, M. (2009). *At risk: Social justice in child welfare and other human services*. Toronto: University of Toronto Press.

United Nations global counter terrorism strategy. (2006). Available on www.un.org/counterterrorism/ctitf/en/united-nations-general-assembly-adopts-global-counter-terrorism-strategy/ [Accessed 27 July 2017].

Wilson, M. (2017). *NASW Statement. President Trump's immigration executive order is inhumane, De facto ban on Muslim immigrants*. 1 February, NASW, Social Work Blog in the US. On www.socialworkblog.org/advocacy/2017/01/nasw-statement-president-trumps-immigration-executive-order-is-inhumane-de-facto-ban-on-muslim-immigrants/ [Accessed 27 July 2017].

World hunger and poverty facts and statistics (2016). Available on www.worldhunger.org/2015-world-hunger-and-poverty-facts-and-statistics/ [Accessed 27 July 2017].

40
Personal reflections on the *Prevent* programme

Neil Denton and Kate Cochrane

Introduction

We write this chapter as practitioners, doers with more than 20 years' experience of working with individuals and communities that have endured harm motivated by hostility about the identity of the 'other'. This harm is caused by destructive conflict between groups and structures and systems that result in inequality and injustice. Our perspective draws on learning a lot by making mistakes, observing and learning from other professionals, listening and trying to remain vulnerable when in dialogue with individuals and communities.

We share some of that learning here by describing how human-created human harm motivated by politics or ideology aim to change a system/nation-state by using force against a civilian population, creating sufficient harm and fear to change the everyday. Such endeavours can provoke a nation-state into entering into a cycle of revenge and retribution that can exacerbate rather than ameliorate the culture of fear.

As practitioners we work to build and maintain the social fabric using a philosophy of universal human rights centred on a belief of the universal commonality of human need. We then ask who operates in the local and what does it mean for us personally and in our practice? What might it mean for you? What impact might these challenges have on those who work at an individual and community level? What can practitioners do to stay true to a value structure of human rights and human needs? How best can practitioners promote constructive change processes that reduce violence, increase justice in direct interaction and social structures, and respond to real-life problems in human relationships? What should practitioners be cautious about, and where are the opportunities for social growth that could be harnessed to aid progress towards a positive tomorrow?

We live in a closely connected world where the how and who of our communications is very different than it was a decade ago. Changes in technology and communication are happening at an exponential rate, in a context of world economic and political structures that are offering global accessibility and opportunity for the few, while leaving the majority to look on from increasingly disconnected and disenfranchised places. In this chapter we argue that economic and political globalisation has excluded the masses, while the globalisation of communication about conflict is more inclusive in its reach. Conflicts that were localised and somewhat hidden from those not directly affected are now evident anywhere at any time. Most people carry the receivers and transmitters of fear and hope in their pockets, a mere two clicks from real-time human conflict. 'Them' increasingly affects 'Us'. Proponents of ideologies that describe a world embroiled in a war of values, with the global Ummah of Islam under attack by an intolerant, aggressive and expansionist conspiracy of nation-states, have embraced the opportunities of global to personal communications more successfully than most. Thus, in value based conflict, the global is now local. And people need to adapt accordingly.

Understanding political perspectives

Compared with other European states, the United Kingdom (UK) has more experience of coping with and countering the impact of domestic terrorism. To understand the present, it is helpful to understand the past. Ever since Prime Minister Gladstone's self-declared 1868 mission to 'pacify Ireland', civil discord, violent strategies to address asymmetrical conflict, and discourse about domestic terrorism have been a part of governmental consciousness. Protecting citizens from violence, war and terror is a fundamental function of the nation-state. A century after Gladstone's declaration, the Provisional IRA was formed in response to the perceived failure of the Irish Republican Army to defend Catholic neighbourhoods and communities from harm during the 1969 Northern Ireland riots. The outcome was a progression and evolution of groups wishing to effect political change, and a developing and iterative pattern of government legislation and action to respond to the 'threat'. Volumes have been written about the 'Troubles' in Northern Ireland, making their insights accessible. However, the formation, development and activities of the Official Irish Republican Army, Provisional IRA, Ulster Defence Association, Ulster Volunteer Force, Irish National Liberation Army and the Real IRA provide the primary context within which the UK's counter-terrorism legislation should be understood.

What connects all of these actions and counter actions is the commonality of structure employed by the key players, where 'provocateur' and 'protector' operate hierarchically. This context of command and control helps to describe the rationale behind past solutions and the current lack of fit among purpose, policy, practice and potential that is crucial to understanding the present and the future.

In 1973, the Provisional IRA extended its campaign to mainland Britain, to increase the pressure on the UK's population, government and military capabilities to withdraw from Northern Ireland. On 21 November 1974, the Birmingham pub bombings killed 81 people and injured 182. According to the House of Commons Debates (Vol. 882 col. 743, 28 November 1974) then-Home Secretary Roy Jenkins described the actions of the IRA as 'the greatest threat [to the country] since the end of the Second World War'. Within eight days, the Prevention of Terrorism (Temporary Provisions) Act 1974 had become law. This legislation proscribed the IRA as an organisation, introduced greater police powers for the arrest and detention of those suspected of being involved in or supporting the IRA, and introduced powers of exclusion and removal from the UK for any individuals identified as being a member or supporter. Sequential and temporary legislation based on this Act culminated in the Northern Ireland (Emergency Provisions) Act 1998. This legislation had a common purpose: to disrupt and defeat the IRA. In 2000, the Terrorism Act was introduced to rationalise the previous temporary legislation. It contained the following.

A consolidated definition of terrorism to include action involving the use of firearms and explosives with the purpose of advancing a political, religious or other cause and designed to influence government, intimidate the public. This covered endangering life, violence against a person, serious damage to property, risks public health and/or safety, and disrupting electronic systems. The Act also identified proscribed groups and the concomitant police powers. Additionally, it broke from ordinary criminal law where suspects had to be charged within 24 hours of detention or be released (extended to 28 days in 2006); contained powers to 'stop and search' without suspicion; and a prohibition on collecting information that could be used by someone planning terrorist acts. Additionally, it endorsed bench trials instead of jury trials in Northern Ireland for scheduled offences, thereby continuing the system of Diplock courts established in 1973.

These measures were designed to combat the actions of a definable and hierarchical organisation, modelled on traditional military structures. This approach affirmed Fromkin's (1977) analysis of the nature of asymmetrical conflicts involving terrorism, that 'Terrorists don't win, states lose'. This was demonstrated by the significant groundswell of public support for the Provisional IRA following the government's adoption of internment without trail for those suspected of involvement in its activities.

Important lessons that remain universally relevant were learnt during this time of structural reactions to evolving threat. As social beings our evolutionary development and survival is based upon interdependence. However, these responses can have maladaptive consequences in the role they play in the escalation of inter-human conflict when these reinforce a sense of 'us' and intensify a sense of the differences that exist between 'us' and 'them'. Social identity theory, fundamental attribution error, dehumanisation, and the nature of prejudice are well-evidenced characteristics of the human condition that cannot be ignored. Signs of hostility, hatred and what these symbolise about a security strategy that fails to attend to social cohesion should have signposted new policy directions. In this chapter, we demonstrate their continuing importance in understanding the unintended consequences of current governmental and structural responses to the new terrorist threat on social cohesion and the potential implications of forgotten lessons, and replicated transgressions from such learning.

From a rigid hierarchy to a loose affiliation of like-minded individuals

On 11 September 2001, the perception and reality of the 'threat' changed. This change has been variously described as 'new terrorism', 'contemporary terrorism' (Laqueur, 2003), 'post-modern terrorism', 'super-terrorism', 'catastrophic terrorism' and 'hyper-terrorism' (Field, 2009). Whatever the adjectives and thinking behind these narratives, it is clear that those described as 'al Qaeda-inspired' operated differently from those of the Provisional IRA. The IRA's aim of minimising civilian casualties was replaced with an objective to maximise loss of life. Those promulgating the idea of the new global Jihad, perceived all citizens of nation-states opposed to the '(re)-establishment' of the Islamic Caliphate as active combatants, as legitimate targets.

The attacks on the World Trade Centre created a tsunami of fear and anger that engulfed the US and made waves that swiftly travelled across the Atlantic to the Houses of Westminster. We could feel the ripples in our small northern city. 'Why did they fly their planes into our buildings?!' were questions regularly asked on our physical and virtual streets. These ripples became a tangible sea change in interfaith and intercommunity relationships of trust and solidarity in the UK, and it did not feel like a change for the good.

As the US declared its 'War on Terror' (a war on an adverb). It superseded geographic and political boundaries and looked to its historic allies for support and solidarity. Millions opposed this war. The Second Gulf War, and Afghanistan, the genocide in Bosnia re-kindled anger and dismay at the death of innocent Muslims due to the action or inaction of the West and an impotent 'United Nations' (UN).

The 2001 Anti-terrorism, Crime and Security Act contained measures rejected from the 2000 Act as excessive when the British government found itself in an iterative pattern of reactive legislation in response to the new threat. The 'control orders' contained within the Prevention of Terrorism Act 2005 gave the police greater powers to restrict the freedoms of those suspected to be a security threat than any previously seen during peacetime.

Discourses about the 'enemy within' prevailed following the 7/7 bombings and signalled the return to out-group thinking. Voices on the street claimed that 'Not all Muslims are terrorists, but all terrorists are Muslims'. The resultant over-policing of Muslim communities – whether actual or perceived – perpetuates a legacy of resentment, mistrust and separation.

Newcastle is a city geographically and culturally far removed from 'that London'. Although greatly diminished due to the dual distances of where and who, the tsunami 350 miles away, reached it. Some keenly felt its ripples. A noticeable impact upon this most northerly city in England was that the Islamic Society of Newcastle University distributed clear plastic carrier bags for their members travelling on the Metro.

By 2003, government began to recognise that a new narrative and strategy was required. This gave rise to *CONTEST*, as the new counter-terrorism strategy. It combined the more traditional aspects of counter-terrorism (CT):

- Pursue – intelligence-led operations to detect and prosecute those actively planning to do harm.
- Protect – work to strengthen the physical and security infrastructures to make terrorist attacks more difficult to implement.
- Prepare – planning and preparation to mitigate the impact of any attack that occurred.

However, *Prevent* was an important new development designed to encompass the learning gained from the experiences of responding to the IRA. *Prevent* aimed to provide a:

- Programme of activity aimed at hearts and minds, attempting to reduce and ultimately eliminate the support base for terrorist activity and its supporting ideology, 'to stop people from becoming terrorists or supporting violent extremism'; and
- Coherent and accessible narrative that described how and why each of these elements coexisted and complemented each other to increase the safety of citizens.

Thus, *CONTEST*, and its constituent four 'Ps' of Pursue, Protect, Prepare and *Prevent* was born. When first published in 2006, those in charge clarified the importance placed on prevention.

Prevent: an either/or question in which the need to identify those at risk of causing harm took precedence

The *Prevent* programme aimed principally to affect hearts and minds, recognise 'the way in which some terrorist ideologies draw on and make use of extremist ideas which are espoused and circulated by apparently non-violent organisations'. It principally focused on 'challenging extremist ideas that are conducive to terrorism and also part of terrorist narrative' (Home Office 2011: 11). The stated objectives were to:

- Respond to the ideological challenge of terrorism and threat from those who promote it;
- Prevent people from being drawn into terrorism and ensure they are given appropriate advice and support; and

- Work with a wide range of sectors (including education, criminal justice, faith charities, the internet and health) where there are risks of radicalisation to be addressed.

Prevent has recently become a Statutory Duty for all public bodies under Section 29 of the Counter-Terrorism and Security Act 2015.

Despite clear statements of intention, this programme was designed to spot vulnerable individuals and acknowledge the need to address community grievances caused by foreign policy and experiences of Islamophobia. However, a disparity existed between the intention of the transmitter, and the emotional response of the receiver. Thus, work to engage hearts and minds was received by many in Muslim communities as a war on thought, and faith.

A needle in a haystack

The *Prevent* programme sought a unifying theory that explains why people do these things, identify those individuals, and stop them before they acted. Sadly, it is not that simple. There is no unifying explanatory theory about why people are moved to cause terrible harm to others (including themselves) by committing acts of terrorism. Research has not identified a single profile that can detect those most at risk of committing acts of terror. Different people connect with violent ideologies and groups for different reasons at different times.

How can these journeys to violence be understood? Many talk of these journeys as 'Pathways', 'a dialectical process that gradually pushed an individual toward a commitment to violence over time' (McCormick, 2003: 492). These pathways to, and motivations for, terrorism are varied and diverse. Individual, inter-personal, socio-cultural and interstate factors all play a part (Borum, 2011).

Instead of having huge numbers of front-line practitioners participating in 'WRAP' (Workshops to Raise Awareness of *Prevent*) training with a definitive list of indicators that would justify a referral to *Prevent* (all of which are subsequently screened by security services), a 'better safe than sorry' approach was advocated. Referrals into the *Prevent* process were encouraged for anyone who exhibited behaviour related to the relatively wide range of behaviours that correlate with vulnerabilities linked to identified pathways towards violent extremism. This has resulted in *Prevent* generating a large number of referrals, the vast majority of which become classified as not at risk of becoming violent extremists.

Government has responded to communities' and practitioners' concerns that the programme wrongly failed to include other forms of extremism, including the far right. While superficially positive, it has stigmatised more vulnerable individuals, and increased community resentment.

Securitised approaches to community development do not work

Prevent attempted to identify those individuals at risk of doing harm, and support Muslim communities in addressing grievances and strengthening their resolve against extremist narratives. These objectives are important and from an efficiency and delivery perspective there was logic to placing both programmes under one organisation.

However, this decision created a structural problem. From its inception to the present, *Prevent* has been funded, implemented and performance-managed by the Home Office, specifically the Office of Security and Counter-Terrorism (OSCT) which is also responsible for significant parts of the Pursue agenda. The Pursue model works by gathering information on and prosecuting individuals based on their *criminal* behaviour; communication with known terrorists, accessing information about potential targets or engaging in methods of causing harm, attempting to recruit others to a violent Islamist and hate-filled causes. Pursue has been successful as is shown by the rising number of convictions made within this process. Because these are criminal acts, the involvement of the police and security services is appropriate.

By contrast, *Prevent*, located in *pre-criminal* space, targets individuals engaging in behaviours that are not criminal, but of concern because they might indicate someone who possesses the 'pre-conditions' or 'vulnerabilities' that suggest they may move from thought to action. *Prevent* acknowledges that at this level, communities have the people best positioned to have a positive impact on these divisive narratives and identify 'at risk' individuals.

Significant resources allocated to *Prevent* shaped how Muslim communities perceived the programme. Specific funding to support Muslim communities (long justified from a fairness perspective), was a new phenomenon. As this funding was provided by OSCT to address 'grievances', this proved deeply problematic. Suddenly, after years of marginalisation and neglect, the government began to care about Muslims, not for their own sake, but to reduce the threat they posed. Yet, the vast majority of Muslims would describe the behaviours of extremists as entirely contrary to the core doctrines of their faith. 'You only care because you're scared that we might blow you up' was the message received.

Prevent was intended to build community capacity. But securitised approaches to community development do not work. Any attempt to: engage communities in open and robust debate about contentious issues; surface latent conflict; help communities work through feelings of anger and resentment, 'let the steam out', cannot happen if facilitated by the same part of government responsible for Pursue. Securitisation of this work pushes these difficult debates even further beneath the surface, and away from the safe spaces that those aiming to build cohesion and embrace the positive possibilities of conflict aim to create and support. More than at any other time, communities experiencing conflict and change need space and support to define and re-define their identities, express strong emotions free from judgement and blame, and identify strategies and requests that respond to unmet need. When public and private spaces are removed, only secret spaces remain. These secret shadows are where those advocating violence and hate feel most at home and operate most freely. Without meaning to, *Prevent* has pushed many of vulnerable young people towards the very individuals/groups they were being protected from (Open Society Justice Initiative, 2016).

State agencies' well-intentioned but clumsy approaches to promote equality by actively challenging prejudice and offensive language during their engagement with communities stifle honest debate, and leave many feeling unheard and unable to speak freely about important issues affecting them and their community. This continues to push latent community conflict beneath the surface. Because it is latent, it can be hard for state agencies to hear, but those operating at a local level are affected by these feelings of resentment and discontent. One author conducting private discussions with local marginalised groups, started each with the opening statement, 'I think people round here are scared of saying how they really feel for fear of being labelled racist/extremist/prejudiced'. Everyone concurred with this.

These factors, combined with a lack of a coherent and robust government programme to promote community cohesion means that many communities live the 'Parallel lives' first described by Cantle (2001), with even fewer opportunities to facilitate meaningful dialogue than existed then. From a counter-terrorism and cohesion perspective, this increasingly avoidant behaviour between communities of identity is problematic. Without meaningful contact, the opportunity to be curious about the other, and facilitate debate about 'difficult' issues, the void is filled with rumour and conjecture, stereotyping and prejudice. Communities will ascribe internal and moralistic explanations to the behaviour of those in the out-group (Heider 1958).

Allport (1958) shows in *The Nature of Prejudice*, this anti-locution and avoidance provides the foundations for discrimination, physical attack, and ultimately extermination as 'They' become less than human in our eyes, and appropriate targets for the 'creative evil', dynamics that Zimbardo (2004) observed as a consequence of this thinking.

Prevent has succeeded in some regards by raising awareness of these issues with a large number of front-line workers in the public and third sectors. These have ensured that those referred as at genuine risk of becoming violent extremists have received support to divert their behaviour to more positive paths. These positives have come at significant costs: a further erosion of trust from Muslim communities towards agencies of the nation-state; an additional loss of trust from other communities towards Muslim ones; a large number of vulnerable people being potentially further isolated due to being labelled as potential terrorists; and a suppression of open and safe debate about important issues of collective security and identity, particularly among disenfranchised and disadvantaged white communities. To this day, the *Prevent* strategy remains deeply controversial. Critics believe that *Prevent* is counter-productive and discriminates against Muslims, while others point to the lack robust measures of effectiveness. Many believe the brand to be toxic (Muslim Council of Britain, 2011). Given these negative consequences, is there a better way?

Conflict transformation: strengthening relationships and working towards a vision of a better tomorrow by embracing complexity and real-life problems

Approaching the issue from a conflict transformation perspective facilitates looking at the issue differently by promoting constructive change processes that reduce violence, increase justice in direct interaction and social structures, and respond to real-life problems in human relationships. Conflict can be viewed as neither inherently positive nor negative, but as energy for change. The strategies different parties involved in conflict adopt lead to constructive or destructive outcomes. In conflict transformation, process and outcome are indivisible because both the issue *and* the relationship between the parties involved are held in equal priority. Conflict transformation seeks to identify what lies at the heart of the matter to ascertain patterns from the past to help describe a better tomorrow. Contemporary socialisation encourages those faced with conflict to describe a situation by defining what is not wanted. From practitioners' earliest childhood experiences through to those in the Criminal Justice System, 'Good' invariably means not engaging in behaviours considered 'Bad'. Thus, conflict resolution does not focus on *asking 'What is wanted'?* What would a positive future look like?

We believe that a society where conflict is dealt with positively (not ignored or brushed under the carpet, or reliant on rules and punishments to obtain desired change) is a society that has compassion and kindness at its core. Conflict resolution offers a win/win alternative to the win/lose one. This can be achieved by attending to the needs of all parties involved in the situation. Acknowledging these dynamics indicates that *Prevent* can be similarly approached. The definition of extremism in the *Prevent* strategy is:

> Vocal or active opposition to fundamental British values, including democracy, the rule of law, individual liberty and mutual respect and tolerance of different faiths and beliefs. We also include in our definition of extremism calls for the death of members of our armed forces.
>
> *(Home Office Counter-terrorism Policy 2015:9)*

It describes what is not wanted

Conflict transformation reframes issues in terms of what is wanted. We would reframe the *Prevent* definition towards a positive tomorrow to sound like this:

> A society that values acceptance, understanding and diversity, where citizens are comfortable with British values including the opportunity to learn and improve from those with a different perspective; an active and inclusive democracy, a rule of law where everyone feels protected; self-actualised development of identity with a respect and curiosity for difference; and acceptance of the current need for armed forces, but engagement and dialogue about how they are used.

Additionally, it assists in shifting the emphasis of the work towards who delivers cohesion, integration and empowerment; facilitates the surfacing of latent conflict within and between communities; uses conflict as energy for change by encouraging dialogue about a new approach; and creates a process structure. Listening to language that judges and blames can identify real-life problems alongside unmet need and links emotional intelligence to belonging, identity, difference and positive contact (Allport, 1954).

Conflict transformation also attends to small and local concerns e.g. parking, places for children to play, saying hello, day-to-day acts of kindness that improve human relationships. This involves moving away from judging and blaming towards need and request, creating safe spaces wherein people can be deeply honest with themselves and others about their fears and hopes, hurts and responsibilities. For (re)defining identity(ies), asking questions, 'Who am I, who are you, who are we?' and using sport, music, arts, rituals, shared work, fun and laughter as dialogue. This can promote understandings of how perceptions of identity are linked to power, systems and structures which organise and govern relationships. This approach can also foster a new politics that also engages todays insecure majority in reducing inequality(ies) for all, as advocated by green social workers (Dominelli, 2012).

The characteristics of conflict transformational practice, also inherent within green social work, are:

1. Developing the capacity to see presenting issues as an opportunity to look through the issues and focus on the scene that lies beyond the immediate situation.
2. Having the capacity to integrate multiple time frames including short-term responses and long-term change.
3. Posing the energies of conflict as dilemmas for avoiding binaries such as 'human rights versus terrorist threats' to consider their complexity which requires 'both/and' thinking that holds issues in a situation together as interdependent goals.
4. A capacity to see complexity as a friend, not a foe. '[T]he capacity to live with apparent contradictions and paradoxes lies at the heart of transformation' (Lederach 2003: 52). Abraham Lincoln observed, 'I destroy my enemies when I make them my friends'.
5. A capacity to hear and engage with the voices of identity which often underpins most conflicts because identity protects the sense of self and group survival. Identity is lodged deep in the narratives of how people see themselves, who they are, where they have come from, and what they fear they will become or lose. Identity is dynamic and under constant definition and redefinition, especially during conflicts. Identity is also relational, and not all about inter-identity exchanges. Thus, the most critical parts of the process are about creating internal, self, or intra-group spaces, where safe and deep reflection about the nature of the situation, responsibility, hopes and fears can be perused.

There is no agreed understanding of what drives people to commit acts of terror, but widely accepted theories of what needs to be done to promote cohesive communities, and firm evidence about factors that support the development of emotionally intelligent, well-socialised and connected humans that conflict transformation can utilise.

Everything to lose, nothing to gain

Ideology, although important, is insufficient in moving people to act. This requires mobilisation (Zald and McCarthy, 1987) that increases perceived benefits and minimises perceived costs. Conflict transformation offers alternative strategies for mobilisation and connection with others through good socialisation and encouraging belonging to the wider community. This helps increase perceived costs whereby people realise that they have important things to lose. Practitioners and activists must, therefore, provide incentives and remove disincentives.

Reducing psychological costs uses diffusion of responsibility, de-individualisation, obedience, and social identity. Diffusion of responsibility is a socio-psychological phenomenon whereby individuals feel less responsible (culpable) for transgressive behaviour when committed in the presence of, or on behalf of a group (Darley and Latane, 1968). De-individualisation is a state or situation in which the focus of judgement is collective rather than individual. This reduces an individual's inhibition or restraints by reducing self-awareness or by facilitating conformity to situation-specific norms (Silke, 2003). Obedience to authority also diminishes personal responsibility by transferring an actor's moral agency from the self to the authority (Milgram, 1978). Finally, social identities (Tajfel and Turner, 1986), viewing the self in relation to social groups or categories, can also weaken individual responsibility by boosting the salience of group norms.

Such transference also blames and dehumanises potential victims. People with a sense of belonging to social groups that have positive agendas to do good can diminish the influence of a terror group. They become self-actualised and gain a wider understanding of Islam, accept race as a false construct and strengthen their capacity to resist and question authority. When seeing the other as human, they can retain extreme views but are less likely to act on them. Ensuring that these views can be discussed in private enables secret space to facilitate mainstream prevention, expression and dialogue. As J. S. Mill opined:

> The peculiar evil of silencing the expression of an opinion is, that it is robbing the human race; posterity as well as the existing generation; those who dissent from the opinion, still more than those who hold it. If the opinion is right, they are deprived of the opportunity of exchanging error for truth. If wrong, they lose, what is almost as great a benefit, the clearer perception and livelier impression of truth, produced by its collision with error.
> *(1859, Chapter 2 online)*

Responding to those with an actualised self/those not yet ready/able or willing to renounce violence/ideology of violence and harm

Protective force and restorative approaches that encourage non-violence and dialogue have to be aligned to existing structures, particularly those building community(ies) and not securitised services. This is to facilitate a rethinking of the narrative that securitised services protect the public from those already actively engaged in causing harm. Achieving this aim requires communication, the development of trust between them and analytical tools that go beyond the securitised threshold. It also needs reflection upon taken-for-granted concepts and the fit (or not) with other programmes and priorities if the militarisation of the streets and restrictions on universal freedoms and rights including free movement, free speech, and free association are to be avoided.

Emergency planning and recovery can be linked to social work's responsibility to meet social need. Doing so means reframing analytical models that assess risk through security to refocus on everyday compassion, community courage and promoting political neutrality when coping with disasters. Additionally, targeting resources and moving towards sustainability and green social work would end residualist approaches to 'problem families'. A change in paradigm and perspective could mainstream inter-group communication, community development and human rights and concentrate efforts upon what is wanted, rather than what is not wanted.

Conclusion

Robust research that explains what is happening, creates 'a profile' or single unifying theory to identify terrorists is unavailable beyond identifying some general pathways or vulnerabilities that many who have perpetrated terrorist acts have in common. However, from a conflict transformation perspective, identifying individuals is not especially helpful because investigation reveals many 'false positives' – that is, people who possess these vulnerabilities, or express extremist views, are deemed at low risk of translating thought into action. Moreover, their numbers are too great, the resources too costly and the delivery body inappropriate for organisations to encompass these effectively. A simple focus on what is not wanted is of limited use. It can impact negatively on cohesion, and push vulnerable individuals and their extremist views away from the public space of open and honest debate about difficult and contentious issues, into shadows beyond reach – the spaces where violent extremists operate without scrutiny and become the unopposed voice.

A paradigm shift towards what is wanted, where conflict transformation is s a valuable piece of the jigsaw and the majority of the pieces are not securitised, is more promising. An interconnected strategy, where practitioners understand how the pieces fit together to make the whole, where pieces remain separate and distinct, can promote a positive future, provide guiding principles of navigating the journey, and a proportionate and compassionate response to those who have fallen victim to those peddling hate, division and violence. This holistic approach can promote the harmonious society sought by green social workers (Dominelli, 2012). Moreover, it enables practitioners to respond to these individuals and groups while providing clarity about socially acceptable behaviour and offering a path back to rehabilitation and re-integration into society. Moreover, those who have been helped along this path can become trusted guides for others who have lost their way.

The current War on Terror is a conflict without a peace process and risks being trapped in a cycle of ever-increasing violence and fear of retribution and retaliation, as polarisation constantly increases. These polarised positions gather gravitational force, pulling diverse communities further away from each other – from avoidance to discrimination, to physical attack and ultimately extermination. This direction of travel is taking society away from a positive horizon, but it is not yet too late to pause, to breathe, to re-consider this trajectory and help each other along the difficult, yet important, road back to each other and towards a safe place for all children. This journey will not be made through great leaps, nor inventing new technologies, but by acknowledging the value and contribution of many thousands of small steps. Steps that are made every day by social workers and those invested in maintaining and building our social fabric, of responding to individual human need from a universal human rights perspective. Steps that lead to a world where patterns of coercive violence are being replaced with respect, creative problem-solving, individual and social capacities for dialogue, and non-violent systems for assuring human security and social change. Reaching this requires a complex web of change processes guided by a transformational understanding of life and relationships and courage. Keep your eyes on the prize, hold on, and remember, 'Los Buenos, Somos Más' (The good, there are more of us).

References

Allport, G. W. (1958). *The nature of prejudice*. Reading, MA: Addison-Wesley.
Borum, R. (2011). Radicalization into violent extremism II: A review of conceptual models and empirical research. *Journal of Strategic Security*, 4: 37–62.
Cantle, T. (2001). *Report of the community cohesion review team*. London: Home Office.
Dominelli, L. (2012). *Green social work*. Cambridge: Polity Press.
Field, A. (2009). The 'New Terrorism': Revolution or evolution? *Political Studies Review*, 7: 195–207.
Fromkin, D. (1977). Die Strategie des Terrorismus. In M. Funke (Ed.), *Terrorismus: Untersuchungen zur Struktur und Strategie revolutionärer Gewaltpolitik* (pp. 83–99). Düsseldorf.
Government (UK) Policy (2015). *Counter-terrorism policy*. Available on www.gov.uk/government/publications/2010-to-2015-government-policy-counter-terrorism/2010-to-2015-government-policy-counter-terrorism#appendix-2-prevent [Accessed 23 July 2017].
Heider, F. (1958). *The psychology of interpersonal relations*. New York: Wiley. Home Office (2011). *CONTEST: The United Kingdom's Strategy for Countering Terrorism*. Cm 8123, July. London: TSO.
Home Office (2015). *Counter-extremism strategy*. London: HM Government.
Laqueur, W. (2003). *No end to war: Terrorism in the twenty-first century*. London: Continuum.
Latané, B. and Darley, J. M. (1968). Group inhibition of bystander intervention in emergencies. *Journal of Personality and Social Psychology*, 10: 215–221.
Lederach, J. P. (2003). Conflict Transformation. In G. Burgess and H. Burgess (Eds.), *Beyond intractability*. Boulder, CO: Conflict Information Consortium, University of Colorado.
McCormick, G. H. (2003). Terrorist decision making. *Annual Review of Political Science*, 6: 473–507.
Milgram, S. (1978). *Obedience to authority: An experimental view*. New York: Harper and Row.
Mill, J. S. (1859). *On liberty*. London: John W. Parker and Son, West Strand. Available on www.utilitarianism.com/ol/two.html [Accessed 23 July 2017].
Muslim Council of Britain. (2011). Available on http://archive.mcb.org.uk/stigmatising-muslim-civil-society-wont-avert-terrorism-prevent-strategy-still-flawed/ [Accessed 23 July 2017].
Open Society Justice Initiative (OSJI) (2016). *Eroding trust: The UK's prevent counter-extremism strategy in health and education*. New York: Open Society Foundation.
Silke, A. (2003). Deindividuation, anonymity and violence: Findings from Northern Ireland, *Journal of Social Psychology*, 143: 493–499.
Tajfel, H. and Turner, J. C. (1986). The social identity theory of intergroup behaviour. In S. Worchel and W. G. Austin (Eds.), *Psychology of intergroup relations*, 2nd ed. Chicago: Nelson-Hall, pp. 7–24.
Zald, J., Mayer, N. and McCarthy, J. D. (Eds.) (1987). *Social movements in an organizational society: Collected essays*. London: Transaction Publishers.
Zimbardo, P. G. (2004). A situationist perspective on the psychology of evil: Understanding how good people are transformed into perpetrators. In A. G. Miller (Ed.), *The social psychology of good and evil*. New York: Guilford Press, pp. 21–50.

41

Reflecting on the 2015 Gorkha earthquake, tread carefully

Hanna A. Ruszczyk

Introduction

I write this chapter from the perspective of a social scientist, a human geographer who was investigating community resilience to earthquakes, as well as a practitioner who had worked for the United Nations (UN) in different countries for over a decade. First, I reflect on my experiences during and after the 2015 Gorkha earthquake in Nepal as well as on my role as a privileged foreign researcher who could leave for safety. Briefly, I reflect on what the earthquake allowed to happen in Nepal in the subsequent two years. The Gorkha earthquake sequence (including the 12 May earthquake) killed almost 9,000, injured 22,000 and devastated almost 800,000 homes (GofN, Ministry of Home Affairs et al., 2015). Most homes remain to be rebuilt over two years later due to delays in government handling of the disaster. Second, I consider ethical issues in relation to being a foreign researcher in a disaster. I consider how to approach settings, which are vastly different from one's own, and how to consider providing support to people in difficult and trying times. Natural hazard events occur with regularity but humans turn them into disasters. Over 40 years ago, O'Keefe et al. (1976) put forward the argument that there is no such thing as a 'natural disaster'. Society does not seem to have learnt the significance of this statement.

An earthquake

Bharatpur, Nepal, only 38 miles south of the 25 April epicentre in Gorkha, is where I was conducting my long-term research on urban disaster community resilience when the earthquake began. These excerpts are from my Durham University (UK), Department of Geography PhD researcher blogs (Ruszczyk 2015: a, b):

> The earthquake started at 11:56 a.m. on the day of rest (Saturday), therefore there were few vehicles traveling, the shops were still closed and few people were out in Bharatpur. My research assistant and I were walking on New Road in the industrial area of town where the India bound trucks get serviced, where buses are made etc. It is a wide unpaved road near the river. The metal was shaking on the commercial building near me. I asked

R what he thought was going on. He said, 'earthquake'. I felt faint and not stable on the ground, there was a yellow haze and it appeared as if waves were coming from the ground and the ground was shaking horizontally. It lasted around a minute and a half. I swayed but did not fall. The city's infrastructure was intact and only a few buildings were damaged. The 6.7 magnitude aftershock on Sunday, April 26, was especially grim and felt almost as powerful as the Saturday earthquake. In the first 72 hours, we experienced 68 aftershocks. It was, quite simply, terrifying.

Within five to seven days after the earthquake, Bharatpur (in Chitwan district bordering India) was a transit point for people fleeing the Kathmandu Valley by overcrowded buses. The Kathmandu Valley was perceived as dangerous; people were fleeing to temporarily relocate and live with extended families in the plains of Nepal. According to the Sub-Metropolitan City of Bharatpur (SMCB) authorities, Bharatpur provided food and water to over 100,000 people who were travelling onward to southeastern and southwestern parts of Nepal.

The aftershocks continued for many long months. On 12 May 2015 a particularly strong aftershock (almost as devastating as the 25 April earthquake) shook Nepal. According to the local authorities, the 12 May earthquake caused structural damage in the city: 100 buildings were totally destroyed and 300 buildings were partially collapsed. The SMCB staff struggled with the volume of requests for structural integrity assessments of earthquake damage. Subsequently, the SMCB trained 38 volunteer engineer consultants who assessed 3,000 reported damaged buildings out of a building stock of 40,000 in Bharatpur.

I wrote an article for the US-based *Natural Hazards Observer* in August 2015 and this is the concluding paragraph:

> I will return to Bharatpur in late September 2015 to continue my [PhD] fieldwork. I look forward to learning how people and the government have incorporated the earthquake experience into their lives and professional work and if the experience will change more than natural hazards mitigation, preparation and response in Nepal. I wonder if there will be changes in the political sphere, the creation of a constitution and possible municipal elections.

I sought to learn how my professional colleagues, Bharatpur residents and also key stakeholders for the PhD research had incorporated the earthquake experience in their lives and how important the earthquake continued to be to them. The anthropologist, Edward Simpson, in his *Political Biography of an Earthquake: Aftermath and Amnesia in Gujarat, India* describes earthquakes as a special kind of a hazard. A hazard that creates ruptures in physical, social, political and economic spheres and from which a new kind of a future can be imagined and created by people and governments.

Terror and trauma

There is an image on the cover of *Lapham's Quarterly* on the subject of disaster (Lapham, 2016) of an ancient king's theatre mask in stone (with eyebrows raised and the mouth in the shape of the number 0). This theatre mask reminds me of the terror of the quaking and the fear of time – the unknown future. My physical geography colleagues told me the possibility of aftershocks was very high. Knowing there would be aftershocks and that some of those aftershocks could be worse than Saturday's 11:56 earthquake terrified me. I was also fleetingly terrified that some of Bharatpur's residents would think I had caused the earthquake by asking the city's residents questions about their earthquake knowledge and preparedness. In my Master of Arts research, I found some urban dwellers in the Kathmandu Valley were hesitant to talk about possible earthquakes for fear they would come (Ruszczyk, 2014).

After my initial email/blogs in the hours and days after the earthquake and some non-academic articles I penned, I have written very little about the earthquake and my experience (over two years after the event). Other academics have written eloquently, but I have needed to keep my experiences to myself. I did not lose anyone or anything in the earthquake except my centring. For this book, I had written a draft of this chapter in a scholarly fashion, with minimal emotion, stressing the points I thought relevant. I could already envision the yawn of the reader and the reader's eyes begin to close. I was not being honest regarding what the earthquake meant to me and what the earthquake possibly did and did not do to Bharatpur's residents whom I had been interviewing when the earthquake occurred. I decided to try again with this chapter.

It has taken me much time to process the experience and to make sense of it in some way. My reading of disasters and natural hazards has changed after the earthquake experience. I look more carefully at the tone and the concept of time in disaster literature. It is only when I read some disaster scholars or some scientists wearily discuss why is it people do not learn from earthquakes and why are the same mistakes repeated after earthquake experiences that I feel the urge to interrupt and explain. 'It is because people need to forget the earthquake and all of the accompanying feelings and occurrences that manifest themselves during a crisis that is triggered by nature and helped by man to create a disaster'. People cannot worry about something they cannot control. That is the role of governments and unfortunately, many governments have short attention spans. So we may be destined to repeat some of the same errors, year after each year, decade after decade and century after century. Unless, we link our efforts post-disaster to what people view as important – everyday *economic security* and *stability* in their everyday lives. Often, this link is not made during the post-hazard event.

There is a tremendous amount left unsaid and unacknowledged between those who were there and those who come after the earth stops quaking. I think it bears repeating and stressing that people were exhausted by the earthquake, we functioned at diminished capacity, we had sleepless nights and our memory was very short. The continued shaking of the earth and the not knowing when it would shake again and how intensely was a time full of terror. An earthquake is not experienced in the same way as a reoccurring hazard or a slow-onset event such as flooding. An earthquake changes everything and everyone in some way (Simpson, 2013). There are lessons to be learnt about the national building code, earthquake resistant construction, good governance, aid being distributed fairly, empowering communities to rebuild in the way they desire, building the capacity of government to assess where landslides might occur, how to distribute relief and reconstruction material in the quickest and most cost-effective manner and the list of lessons goes on.

What is imperative to also understand post the Gorkha earthquake – is what and how the earthquake changed the environment for those who did not lose their homes, their families or friends, their livelihoods, or those who were not displaced. The earthquake allowed other things to happen and, other topics are more important than the earthquake itself to millions of people in Nepal. In some cases, the earthquake itself is not the most important issue, as hard as this may be to believe (similar to Hyndman's (2011) findings post-tsunami in 2004). The approved constitution in September 2015 with its promise of stability and end of 'transition' for the country's inhabitants and the unexpected economic turmoil and devastation of the unofficial economic blockade at the border crossings with India (through which 85 per cent of all goods enter the landlocked country of Nepal) were much more relevant to the majority of Nepalis. Four months after leaving, I returned to Nepal. This coincided with the constitution being suddenly promulgated and the enactment of Indian unofficial economic blockade at all India-Nepal border crossings. Livelihoods were significantly impacted and uncertainty over future systems prevailed. Shock after shock for Nepali residents. Different traumatic events for different groups.

The earthquake and me

The earthquake experience changed me as a person and as a researcher. I now know that in time of crisis, a paradise is built in hell (paraphrasing Rebecca Solnit's title of her 2009 book detailing the extraordinary communities that arise in disaster). Solnit describes societies after a natural hazard-induced disaster as utopian for a brief time. Societies are 'more flexible and improvisational, more egalitarian and less hierarchical, with more room for meaningful roles and contributions from all members – and with a sense of membership' (Ibid: 308). In Bharatpur, people looked out for each other and created a collective spirit of resilience, which manifested itself in a variety of ways to the survivors. I witnessed a collective spirit where class, caste and gender were ignored. For a certain amount of time, a focus on the greater common good prevailed. Then the dust settled, everyday life returned and everyday coping strategies returned with all of their difficulties and limitations.

Through Blanchot's (1995) book, *The Writing of the Disaster*, survivors understand the difficulties of describing something that happened to those who were not present. There are words that are used among those who witnessed and participated in the event that those who were not there cannot understand. We, those who were there, talk about being a survivor (rather than a victim), time after the earthquake is considered in very long seconds, minutes and hours, rather than 'the first days'. Four days after the earthquake, I wrote:

> It is fascinating to witness the various stages that come after the hazard. Saturday was shock and everyone continued with their organised activities (I conducted a focus group and went to a scheduled interview), the second day (24 hours later) people were numb and nervous and were processing what had happened the day before and continued to happen with the too regular aftershocks. Monday, 48 hours later, people are emotional/tearful and needed to talk about where they were when the earthquake happened or 'attacked'.

Through the months of May and June 2015, I struggled to understand how to accommodate the earthquake event into my life and research. The trauma of the earthquake experience had a dramatic impact on my understandings of personal resilience and what constitutes community resilience in a crisis event. The word community no longer proved useful, rather, the word collective more appropriately reflected what I heard, saw and felt during and in the days after the earthquake. My understanding of concepts has changed (time, trauma, survivors, hope, compassion, uncertainty, security, sense of loss, communal, cooperative, upheavals, fractures, rifts). I found a more nuanced, deeper connection had been created between research informants and myself. When I returned four months later, people introduced me as 'one of us'. The local community knew I had experienced the earthquake in their city, felt the terror and uncertainty they had felt in the minutes, hours, and days after the quaking started. Everyone had a story about the earthquake but they were left unspoken for the most part. The silence, the lull in conversation when we thought back to the tremors and terror, was pregnant with emotion. What was surprising for me was how people had incorporated the earthquake into their lives and the continuing aftershocks; people had moved on with their lives, their worries and priorities. My research tried to reflect this.

The French philosopher Blanchot (1995, 1) proposes 'the disaster ruins everything, all the while leaving everything intact'. He also argues that (Ibid, 3) 'the disaster is related to forgetfulness – forgetfulness without memory, the motionless retreat of what has not been treated – the immemorial, perhaps. To remember forgetfully'. Survivors need to forget but it is always there in their memory. Survivors must move on in a way. In the weeks after the earthquake, my UK and American friends and colleagues suggested I seek counselling support if I thought I needed it. They said I needed to be aware of possible post-traumatic stress syndrome, to consider taking a break from the PhD research. My Asian friends and colleagues (both female and male) from Pakistan, India, Nepal and Bangladesh gave different advice – they told me to move on. To forget it. My Asian friends reminded me that everyday life is full of hardship (open defecation, intermittent access to municipal piped water, intermittent access to electricity, the problematic caste system, a 10-year internal conflict in Nepal which recently finished and killed 13,000 people, everyday hazards such as air pollution and road traffic accidents and the list goes on). The earthquake is just one of many hardships and disasters. This difference in attitude is very relevant to the discussion of how to support survivors. I do not have a clear answer except to suggest exercising caution when exporting coping mechanisms from one culture to another culture. This utilises the ethos of green social work (Dominelli, 2012) where a grounded understanding of the interdependencies between people and their environment and local contexts is considered before support is offered to those in need.

Ethical considerations

In the second part of this chapter I discuss ethical issues in relation to being a foreign researcher in a disaster. I consider how to approach settings, which are vastly different from one's own, and how to consider providing support to people in difficult and trying times. There were differences between my situation and those of the people I was engaging with during the earthquake sequence. I only had myself and my colleagues to worry about. My family was safe, far away. I could access expert knowledge about earthquakes and landslides from colleagues at Durham. They answered my questions and gave a level of comfort. On the other hand, I was heavily dependent on networks I created that are not based on family networks; in a way I was a burden or an additional obligation for them. After the Indian government relaxed entry procedures on the border crossings overland, I was able to depart at Raxual, the closest border crossing to Bharatpur (three hours away). Durham organised everything for me to evacuate except for the car that I organised. Once in India, again I was supported by high-ranking Indian government officials who generously gave their precious time which could have been utilised elsewhere in relation to the earthquake. Due to my privileged situation as a foreign researcher who had access to technical expertise, formal systems that functioned, money and connections, I was removed from a problematic situation.

Naturally, this left me feeling particularly guilty in relation to my friends, colleagues and key informants that I left behind. I was the special foreigner who could depart when she wanted to. I had to leave behind in a continuing dangerous situation people with whom I had shared a terrifying experience. It was highly problematic for me. I planned on staying and continuing my fieldwork, but Durham University required me to be evacuated or I risked losing the insurance coverage for my fieldwork trip. If I did not have the insurance, I was particularly vulnerable and would have had much greater difficulties if the situation worsened and I was hurt. I promised to return as soon as I could and when I would not be an additional burden to the people I interacted with.

The issue of risk assessments and insurance warrants further reflection. Who wields the power? Who makes the decisions on safety, protocols to be utilised, evacuating, to what extent is the student researcher involved? Whose knowledge is most valued in extreme situations, whose safety is most important? Also, UK universities provide insurance coverage for their staff and students, but not local team members who are part of research fieldwork trips. My research assistant was a long distance from his family and had to make his own way back to safety. Duffield (2014: 77) suggests that due to the 'growth of research-related risk aversion within UK universities', research maybe inhibited or curtailed in the future due to fear of terrorism, rioting and protests, flying and also malaria. I find that in addition to this list, we could realistically add everyday life where most of the world's population lives (motorcycles, power outages, quality of water and solid waste management). Only these items are not high on a Western risk register. So should we stop engaging with most of the world's population in their 'risky' reality? I should hope not.

Nepali culture is significantly different to mine and I am acutely aware of the differences in terms of religion, caste and class, gender roles, and the conditions lingering in a post-conflict state. Mohanty criticises individuals from the world's minority who speak on behalf of the world's majority. I acknowledge this as a significant risk although attempts were made to enter the 'space and vision of, and in solidarity with, communities in struggle in the Two-Thirds World' (2003: 507). I was aware of my status as a foreigner, as a woman who had much freedom of movement compared to some Nepali women, my level of education, my access to foreign healthcare and the relative ease in earning money compared to most Nepalis I engaged with.

My fieldwork and the study were conducted in accordance with the ethical principles set out by the Graduate Committee of the Geography Department, Durham University. I strove to be aware of my reflexivity and the role I played as a researcher as well as the research process as noted by England (1994). Following England's suggestion (1994: 81), I attempted to utilise 'a more reflexive and flexible approach to fieldwork [that allowed me] to be more open to any challenges to [my] theoretical position that fieldwork almost inevitably raises'. England (Ibid: 82) suggests, 'Reflexivity is self-critical sympathetic introspection and the self-conscious analytical scrutiny of the self as researcher'. The questions of why are you doing this as a social worker, and of what benefit will you be to the people you want to engage with warrants reflection. Will you be requiring resources that could be utilised more effectively elsewhere post-disaster? Virtual helplines may be an alternative tool to utilise to support those on the ground (Dominelli, 2012). Do you require too much education about the local condition and norms in order to make yourself useful? Proceed with caution, I would advise in a disaster context. Green social workers would concur.

Culture and disaster

Bankoff's research (2007: 338) in the Philippines highlights informal and formal community groups, forms of social capital, which have existed for hundreds of years in different forms. He believes this is due in part to the devastation that regularly hits the Philippines in the form of natural hazards. 'Perhaps the important role hazard has played in the daily life of its peoples encourages forms of mutual dependence and cooperative activity'. In the everyday of urban Nepal, there can also be dangers to going it alone. Formal and informal associations and networks devoted to mutual assistance allow people to withstand and prepare for unexpected misfortunes. The nature of informal associations and networks as well as social services defies easy definition as I learnt through my research. Who is excluded from local support mechanisms is not always clear. These issues are problematic for an external person to understand. For example, tenants in the city are particularly vulnerable, they are often excluded from the urban social support systems organised on a neighbourhood level. Even the more affluent tenants may be excluded. Social support systems are based on home ownership to a large extent in cities. Homeowners do not want to invest their time and energy to support tenants who are or may not be living there long-term.

Only action that places the community at the centre and supports the community's coherence will be of long-term benefit to people post-disaster (Wisner et al., 2004; Wisner et al., 2012; Crabtree, 2015). Aldrich (2012) found similar evidence regarding social capital and the benefits to the long-term redevelopment of communities based not necessarily on outside intervention, but on local people leading the efforts and receiving support, which they requested. Crabtree (2015) discovered in Bihar, India (bordering Nepal) after the 2008 Kosi Floods that dignity, safety, loss of livelihoods and also a loss of hope for the future were frequently mentioned by survivors as issues they were facing. The word disaster 'comes from the Latin compound of *dis-*, or away, without, and *astro*, star or planet; literally, without a star' (Solnit 2009, 10). This may be interpreted as being lost, or losing a guiding light. In his writing about nature, Clark (2011: 68) suggests, 'Those who endure disasters large or small tend to feel estranged from others who have not shared what they have been through'. This is highly relevant. I struggled to explain to my family and friends what had happened and how it had felt. I felt most comfortable with those who had experienced it. But since I was evacuated out of Nepal, I was disconnected from those with whom I had spent the first 72 hours of the earthquake and the tens of aftershocks. Upon my return to the United Kingdom (UK), I found comfort with colleagues and friends who had a bond with Nepal and its people. Together, over a period of days and weeks, we reflected on the events and considered how to proceed or not.

Describing disasters, Hewitt (2015: 30) suggests, 'Disaster images are mostly of spectacular destruction and heroic rescue: maps, experts and spokespersons in distant metropolitan and agency headquarters; lorries, planes and ships bringing modern goods and expertise from donor countries and by dedicated agencies'. Years earlier, Hewitt (1998: 87) argued against such disaster pornography. 'Letting those in hazard speak for and of themselves, is one of the few possibilities for keeping the faces and pain in the foreground of interpretation and response; as part of the social evaluation of problems and responses, not merely as advertisements on the front cover'. This warning related to disaster pornography should be heeded post-disaster as well. As a foreign researcher or social worker, one has the luxury of being able to leave and return home. Fighting against voyeurism (England, 1994; Rigg et al., 2005) is essential. Power relations need to be explicitly considered; although reflecting upon them and 'being sensitive to these power relations does not remove them' (England 1994: 85). Considering who we are accountable to when we seek to provide help from a different cultural framing is worthy of reflection before embarking to provide support in a different cultural setting to one's own.

The role of first responders must not be undervalued. They are not the foreigners who are flown in. First responders post-hazard event are everyday people, the neighbours, the family members, the local government or military. In his discussion of survivors, Hewitt argues that

> inhabitants who are at risk or disaster victims are commonly portrayed as dysfunctional or panic-stricken, even though they typically carry out most of the immediate, life-saving actions, bear the brunt of the loses, hardships and disruptions, and are often side-lined in reconstruction efforts.
>
> *(2015: 28)*

Over and over again, there are instances of outsiders disrupting social systems and imposing their own ways of working on the first responders and the communities overall. Solnit (2009) had similar reflections based on her research in New York City, Hurricane Katrina, Mexico City Earthquake, and other places. It is critical to understand that many survivors have carried out acts of courage and supported their fellow humans. This has been repeatedly been documented by scholars. For example, Ride and Bretherton suggest,

> community resilience may seem to be stronger in response to natural disasters than to other types of crisis such as a violent conflict. The perception that the disaster cause comes from outside the community helps to consolidate bonds between members to respond collectively to the crisis.
>
> *(2011: 15)*

National residents are the first responders and their role should be not forgotten.

For those who have not been directly engaged by the natural hazard, there is an immediate desire to help, to act in some way. Clark (2011: 61) in his discussion of the response post the 26 December 2004 Indian Ocean Tsunami (in which almost 230,000 died in 11 countries) describes it as a rushing through the response. Rather, there should be a need to stay in the moment and to feel the ground-swelling of emotions that accompany the devastation. 'A kind of surge, a fast-spreading intensity of feeling that swept up distant others into relations of attentiveness, care and giving. A wave of affect, we might say, at once global and very local'. Sometimes the need to 'do something' should remain as a need. Immediate action is not always the best response. Solnit (2005) explains that we cannot disregard natural occurrences such as tsunami waves and the movement of tectonic plates. As humans, we need to make the space to be shocked, to consider and to grieve for what others and we have witnessed and lost. We need to be cognisant of our desire to help and how best to provide this care. Ride and Bretherton (2011: 9) argue forcefully that 'the root of culture is in meaning. The need to interpret and make sense of events will be evident in a disaster situation, and the different cultural groups will bring different frames of reference to this task'. This is very important to consider as an outsider to the disaster. The imperative should be to listen, and to be there as support is required again. This follows the green social work ethos.

To do no harm. This is an aspiration of all those who work with disadvantaged groups or individuals. Kellehaer (2002: 66) argues 'the ethic [principle] 'do no harm' is alarmingly simplistic'. To consider what this means for survivors and how to engage with people post-disaster event requires significant reflection, consideration and research into the context, culture and society and environment. Possibly, no action is the best action. Kellehaer also suggests that researchers (and I would suggest social workers both foreign and in-country are in this category as well) are also 'merely' travellers. 'We enter other people's territories' (Ibid: 71) with social, political, economic, environmental, governance and power structures that may be different to ours and ones that we cannot or possibly should not change due to our engagement. In *Green Social Work*, Dominelli (2012) argues also for doing no harm and being acutely aware of social and environmental issues at play. Schipper (2015) argues for the necessity to understand the importance of religion, socio-cultural traditions and belief systems in their role of influencing perceptions and attitudes as well as behaviours and response to hazards. There are differences in perceptions of different cultures. Learning how different they are is important for an outsider.

Krüger et al.'s (2015) book, *Cultures and Disasters: Understanding Cultural Framings in Disaster Risk Reduction*, is a valuable resource in attempting to understand the role of culture in disasters. There is also research about the 'tyranny of Western expertise' (Marsella, 2010), arguing for locally based, culturally appropriate forms of social support and coping mechanisms. I have heard of Western psychosocial support being offered in Nepal post-earthquake. This is a new

Western intervention in Nepal. Anecdotally, people are uncertain what to make of it. They are unsure if it is useful or not. 'Local knowledge regarding coping methods' (Crabtree 2015: 171) is essential to understand before Western forms of support are introduced. Research is needed to assess the benefits or damage caused by Western psychosocial support interventions post-earthquake. Summerfield (2005) strongly argues psychosocial interventions have been appropriately criticised for their cultural insensitivity and insufficient consideration of people who are focusing on the future and rebuilding their lives. Crabtree (2015: 171–172) explains that post-flooding in Bihar; displaced people living in camps received psychosocial support including yoga. 'Counselling, a western form of intervention, was both given and received by the villagers; those who did not receive psychosocial help stated that they would have appreciated it'. In Nepal, research is needed to assess its appropriateness and effectiveness.

After a devastating earthquake such as the one in Nepal, compassion is easily felt. In her book, *Regarding the Pain of Others*, Sontag suggests:

> Compassion is an unstable emotion. It needs to be translated into action, or it withers. . . . The question is what to do with the feelings that have been aroused, the knowledge that has been communicated. If one feels that there is nothing 'we' can do – but who is that 'we'? – and nothing 'they' can do either – and who are 'they'? – then one starts to get bored, cynical, apathetic.
>
> *(2003: 79)*

From my experience, I would say to tread carefully. Following the principles of green social work (Dominelli, 2012) there is a necessity to understand nuance, the context in which the natural hazard occurred, and which subsequently became a disaster. In conclusion, the word disaster signifies a loss of guiding star. If there is any guidance from this chapter, it is this: Tread carefully. Sometimes no immediate response is the best response. Sometimes, reaching out and listening is best. People need to find their guiding star again on the basis of their culture, belief systems, support systems and lastly, in the midst of the uncertain earth.

References

Aldrich, D. P. (2012). *Building resilience: Social capital in post-disaster recovery*. Chicago, The University of Chicago Press.

Bankoff, G. (2007). Dangers to going it alone: social capital and the origins of community resilience in the Philippines. *Continuity and Change*. [Online] 22(2), 327. doi:10.1017/S0268416007006315

Blanchot, M. (1995). *The writing of the disaster: L'écriture du désastre*. Lincoln, University of Nebraska Press.

Clark, N. (2011). *Inhuman nature: sociable life on a dynamic planet*. London, SAGE.

Crabtree, A. (2015). Deep roots of nightmares. In F. Krüger, G. Bankoff, T. Cannon, B. Orlowski, and E.L.F. Schipper (Eds.). *Cultures and disasters: understanding cultural framings in disaster risk reduction*. Abingdon, Routledge. pp. 155–176.

Dominelli, L. (2012). *Green social work*. Cambridge, Polity Press.

Duffield, M. (2014). From immersion to simulation: Remote methodologies and the decline of area studies. *Review of African Political Economy*. [Online] 41 (sup1), S75–S94. doi:10.1080/03056244.2014.976366

England, K. V. L. (1994). Getting personal: Reflexivity, positionality, and feminist research. *Professional Geographer*, 46(1): 80–89.

Government of Nepal, Ministry of Home Affairs and Disaster Preparedness Network-Nepal (2015). *Nepal disaster report 2015*. [Online]. Ministry of Home Affairs (MoHA), Government of Nepal; and Disaster Preparedness Network-Nepal (DPNet-Nepal). Available on www.drrportal.gov.np/uploads/document/329.pdf [Accessed 9 February 2017].

Hewitt, K. (1998). Excluded perspectives in the social construction of disaster. In E. L. Quarantelli (Ed.), *What is a disaster? Perspectives on the question*. London, Routledge. pp. 75–92.

Hewitt, K. (2015). Framing disaster in the 'global village': cultures of rationality in risk, security and news. In F. Krüger, G. Bankoff, T. Cannon, B. Orlowski, and E.L.F. Schipper (Eds.). *Cultures and disasters: understanding cultural framings in disaster risk reduction*. Abingdon, Routledge. pp. 19–36.

Hyndman, J. (2011). *Dual disasters: Humanitarian aid after the 2004 Tsunami*. Sterling, VA, Kumarian Press.

Kellehaer, A. (2002). Ethics and Social Research. In J. G. Perry (Ed.). *Doing fieldwork: eight personal accounts of social research*. Sydney, Australia, University of New South Wales Press. pp. 61–73.

Krüger, F., Bankoff, G., Cannon, T., Orlowski, B., and Schipper, E.L.F. (Eds.) (2015). *Cultures and disasters: understanding cultural framings in disaster risk reduction*. Abingdon, Routledge.

Lapham, L. H. (Ed.) (2016). *Lapham's quarterly, disaster*. New York, American Agora Foundation.

Marsella, A. J. (2010). Ethnocultural aspects of PTSD: an overview of concepts, issues, and treatments. *Traumatology*, 16(4): 17–26.

Mohanty, C. T. (2003). *Feminism without borders: decolonizing theory, practicing solidarity*. Durham; London, Duke University Press.

O'Keefe P., Westgate K. and Wisner B. (1976). Taking the naturalness out of natural disasters. *Nature*, 260, 566–567.

Ride, A. and Bretherton, D. (Eds.) (2011). *Community resilience in natural disasters*. New York, Palgrave Macmillan.

Rigg, J., Lawt, L., Tan-Mullins, M. and Grundy-Warr, C. (2005). The Indian Ocean Tsunami: socio-economic impacts in Thailand. *The Geographical Journal*, 171(4): 374–379.

Ruszczyk, H. A. (2015a). Nepal earthquake *Durham Geography Postgraduates*. [Online]. Available on http://community.dur.ac.uk/geopad/nepal-earthquake-day-1/ [Accessed 17 March 2017].

Ruszczyk, H. A. (2015b). Returning home from Nepal *Durham Geography Postgraduates*. [Online]. Available on http://community.dur.ac.uk/geopad/2015/04/ [Accessed 17 March 2017].

Ruszczyk, H. A. (2014). *Local understandings of community resilience in earthquake prone Nepal*. Master of Arts by Research. Durham University.

Schipper, E. L. F. (2015). Religion and Belief Systems: drivers of vulnerability, entry points for resilience building? In F. Krüger, G. Bankoff, T. Cannon, B. Orlowski, and E.L.F. Schipper (Eds.). *Cultures and disasters: understanding cultural framings in disaster risk reduction*. Abingdon, Routledge. pp. 145–154.

Simpson, E. (2013). *The political biography of an earthquake: aftermath and amnesia in Gujurat, India*. London, C. Hurst and Co.

Solnit, R. (2009). *A paradise built in hell: the extraordinary communities that arise in disaster*. New York, Penguin Books.

Solnit R. (2005). Sontag and Tsunami *Sontag and Tsunami*. [Online]. Available on www.tomdispatch.com/post/2095/ [Accessed 27 September 2016].

Sontag, S. (2003). *Regarding the pain of others*. New York, Picador.

Summerfield D. (2005). What exactly is emergency or disaster 'mental health'? *Bulletin of the World Health Organization*, 8376.

Wisner, B., Blaikie, P. M., Cannon, T. and Davis, I. (2004). *At risk: natural hazards, people's vulnerability, and disasters*. 2nd ed. Abingdon, Routledge.

Wisner, B., Gaillard, J. C. and Kelman, I. (Eds.) (2012). *The Routledge handbook of hazards and disaster risk reduction*. Abingdon, Routledge.

Part XI
Education

42
Making connections with survivors of a catastrophic flood in West Virginia
A green social work approach to climate change adaptation

Willette F. Stinson and Larry D. Williams

Introduction

A catastrophic flood in West Virginia was an extreme weather event that presented an unprecedented advocacy opportunity for social workers who saved many lives that were endangered by this event. Thus, this chapter provides social workers with a good example of what persons are going to do when responding actively to an environmental crisis. The main argument is that green social work is progressive, has a moral compass pointing towards justice (Dominelli, 2016), and holds potential to do a lot more. This chapter intends to help persons define and redefine their current and future roles in preventing environmental injustice(s). This catastrophic flood is viewed as a time for community involvement and support in which social workers were able to participate. As authors, our aim in this chapter is to broaden and deepen understanding of the climate change adaptation process, and support the development of better disaster preparedness planning and response measures to improve livelihoods, human health and well-being (Howard, 2012). We advocate incorporating storytelling into crisis intervention to facilitate social welfare and social justice in green social work practice and thereby contribute to the intellectual and political substance of the green social work model.

Description of the phenomenon of a particular disaster or environmental crisis

Historically, the cornerstone of social work practice is the person in the environment (PIE) or the ecological perspective (Wieck, 1981). However, recent trends in global warming, the effects of greenhouse gasses, extreme changes in weather patterns, massive earthquakes, tsunamis, urban unrest, and hurricanes (Collins, 2015) have resulted in environmental disasters that have displaced thousands, if not millions of people globally. This has led to what Cohn (2011) termed environmental refugees. Those considered environmental refugees tend to be from developing countries, racial and ethnic minorities, and those most vulnerable to social injustices (Cohn, 2011; Malonenbeach and Zuo, 2013). Crumbling infrastructures and egregious neglect by policymakers are very likely to increase their risk of exposure to contaminated air, water and food supplies (Vardoulakis, Dear and Williamson, 2016; Dwyer, 2009) during man-made and environmental disasters.

The state of West Virginia in the US found itself on the national media stage. From 23 to 24 June 2016, there was extreme precipitation and flooding that forced West Virginians into the role of storyteller, and they showed the world the Mountaineer spirit, namely the philosophy of getting knocked down and getting back up on your feet. The Salvation Army and the American Red Cross arrived with volunteers in response to the call for help from all over the country. The American Red Cross, in partnership with the Southern Baptist Convention and AmeriCorps, helped plan and manage the multitude of resources needed to support a natural disaster of this large scope and scale. Between 23 June 2016 and 18 July 2016, the American Red Cross of West Virginia responded to people in homes hit by the devastating and historic West Virginia flooding. Their endeavours resulted in 13 shelters being opened, over 2,300 overnight stays, over 198,300 meals and snacks served, nearly 133,000 relief items distributed and more than 8,500 mental health contacts made. Also, over 1,700 cases were opened to help individuals and families in need; this process engendered a systems-wide response.

On social media Duracell Batteries posted, 'West Virginia, we're on the way'. Also, famous West Virginians such as Brad Paisley, Jennifer Garner, Coach Jimbo Fisher, Coach Rick Trickett, and Coach Nick Saban came together to support schools affected by the devastating flood waters. For persons who wanted to contribute to ongoing flood relief efforts, the websites, www.volunteerwv.com and www.wvflood.com were established. Also, Jim Justice, CEO of the Greenbrier Resort, created 'The Greenbrier's Neighbors; Loving Neighbors' campaign to collect food and money for flood victims. More information about the campaign and how to make donations can be found on the Resort's website.

The Greenbrier Resort, which has 710 rooms and employs about 1,800 people, was set to host the PGA (Professional Golfers Association) tour in July, but cancelled it due to the flooding. Ensuing fires engulfed homes, and for some there was very little to return to. As roads were cleared, many residents, in parts of the state, cautiously returned to their homes to salvage whatever belongings they could find. In the heat and mud, the media set out to document this historic disaster through interviews, photographs and videos. Newspapers reported that more than 10 inches of rain – one-quarter of West Virginia's yearly rainfall, had fallen in a single day. It was evident that the nation was observing West Virginians battling high waters.

As the waters receded, people made sacrifices for people they had not known before. And, stories of rescue and clean-up arose, as did stories of loss of homes, vehicles, businesses, schools and, most tragically, lives. The flooding was especially deadly due to a phenomenon that the meteorologist called 'training', which means repeated rain, associated with thunderstorms, line up over the same location like the cars of a freight train. Torrential rain inundated parts of southern and central West Virginia. This was an exceptional meteorological incident that had damaging results. Part of the worst flooding occurred in Greenbrier County, and the National Weather Service described rainfall there as 'historic' and 'an extremely rare' occurrence. According to Jason Samenow of *The Washington Post*, the flood was a once-in-a-1000-year-event. The National Weather Service concurred, saying: 'Return period data suggest this would be nearly a one in a thousand year event'. The torrential rain and high water destroyed more than 100 homes, washed out scores of bridges and roads and knocked out power to 66,000 properties and trapped 500 people in a shopping centre when a bridge was washed out. Also, it forced the shutdown of gas in the town of White Sulphur Springs, according to Governor Ray Earl Tomblin. This historic disaster was called, 'the worst in a century in some parts of the state'. Governor Tomblin declared a state of emergency in 44 of West Virginia's 55 counties on Friday, 24 June 2016. He deployed 150 members of the National Guard to help emergency responders. President Obama declared the flooding a 'major disaster', making funding obtainable for residents of Greenbrier, Kanawha, and Nicholas counties, all profoundly affected by the flooding. Specifically in the hardest-hit county, Greenbrier, in excess of 10 inches fell and as much as seven inches fell in three hours. While this event is one of the worst in some parts of the state, it is the third deadliest flood on record in state history. Also, the death toll is recorded as the highest from flash floods in the United States (US) since May 2010, when CNN reported the death of 27 people in flooding in Kentucky, Mississippi and Tennessee.

The socio-economic, political and cultural contexts

Dominelli (2013) reported that the context for social work guidance that can help legitimise the rationale for the social work profession to address environmental issues is social justice. This lies at the heart of green social work and includes disaster mitigation, preparedness and prevention as well as socio-economic issues, alongside geological and meteorological aspects. For instance, the rebuilding of the new Herbert Hoover High School and the Clendenin Elementary schools is projected to cost US$68 million. According to Ryan Quinn of the *Charleston Gazette-Mail* newspaper (16 September 2016), Charlie Wilson, Kanawha County Schools' executive director of facilities planning, gave the US$68 million figure on 15 September 2016, saying 'the Federal Emergency Management Agency is expected to fund at least 75 per cent of that cost, if not 90 per cent, and the public school system plans to ask the SBA for the remaining 25 per cent or 10 per cent this year'. Also, in the same newspaper publication, Laura Haight wrote that nearly four

> months after the 23 June 2016 floods, the Crossing Mall in Elkview remains empty, with no signs of construction to replace the culvert that was swept away by raging flood waters. A hotel, restaurants, gas stations, stores, and other businesses in the shopping centre, including Kmart and Kroger, still are inaccessible, with no connection to Little Sandy Road.

Other problems in these contexts involve such tasks as designing waste collection routes, forecasting the demand for natural energy sources such as coal, deciding whether new schools for displaced students should be portable, rented or purchased, and determining how many of each type of vaccination should be distributed to a given pharmacy. Such problems are addressed in an attempt to increase efficiency in a situation where it is clear what efficiency means (Carlisle and Hanlon, 2014). Green social workers can assist in assessing needs and ensuring that medicines reach the people who need them.

Flooding is one of life's most difficult challenges, even in the most lowly and secluded places. It develops a sense of urgency around the need for water, its access, management and control. The fundamental reason that flooding occurs more or less in some geographic areas has practical, geological and other physical explanations, although some explain it primarily in cultural terms including 'religion' and 'race'. However, another factor is climate change. According to the Francis, Oreskes, Bramhall and Korn (2014) Report, climate change is likely to aggravate pre-existing inequalities by increasing the levels of frequency and severity of floods. Climate is connected to human action and beliefs. People like to attribute troubles precipitated by floods to such things as science or the economy, yet the adverse effects of changing ecology lie within human behaviour. For instance, a goal of climate assessments for the purpose of mitigating a client's/service user's social vulnerability to climate change must include that of helping people adapt to climate change for a sustainable future (Rust, 2004).

Such an environmental crisis is an opportunity for social workers to help others in sustaining their health, safety and well-being. In particular, social work's role is to counsel individuals, families and groups and enhance their capacity for social functioning and to cope more effectively with the vicissitudes of everyday life. Social work has a compass that points towards justice, and its practitioners strive to help persons of all backgrounds improve their situations holistically (Dominelli, 2016), and feel better as the shadows of despair begin to disappear from their faces.

According to the National Association of Social Workers (NASW, 2006: 141), 'Social workers have a professional obligation to become knowledgeable and educated about the precarious position of the natural environment, to speak out and take action on behalf of it, and to help their clients act in an environmentally responsible manner'. Even though NASW has precisely worded this environmental policy statement, Shaw (2006) reported that only 10 per cent of Californian social workers who answered his survey were aware that NASW has an environmental policy. Nonetheless, social workers have, at least, a moral responsibility to help clients/service users with climate change adaptation (DiMento and Doughman, 2007) and mitigation (Dominelli, 2012). Consistent with green social work values, the social work profession's core value of creating a just world and empowering underserved and underrepresented populations can be exemplified in climate change adaptation work and should be achieved within a time frame sufficient to allow societies to sustain themselves while recognising that all nations, especially developing countries, need access to resources for reaching the goal of sustainable social and economic development.

The United Nations (1992), through the Parties (government delegates of UN member states) to the United Nations Framework Convention on Climate Change (UNFCCC) acknowledges that, 'change in the Earth's climate and its adverse effects are a common concern of human kind'. Article 1.1 of the UNFCCC asserts that climate change not only affects adversely the natural and supervised ecosystems, but also has 'significant deleterious effects' on the 'operation of socio-economic systems or on human health and welfare'. Therefore, community responders including social workers should not only consider climate change in monetary and environmental terms, but also 'take climate change into account' in their relevant 'social [. . .] policies and actions' to minimise the 'adverse effects of mitigation and adaptation projects on societies' public health and welfare (Article 4.1 (f)). Considering that social workers have this environmental policy for social work intervention, storytelling on social vulnerability to climate change will help to broaden and deepen their understanding of social vulnerabilities and minimise threats to social welfare and environmental justice.

This commentary was written to pay respect and consider the service of social work professionals and lay people who literally went out on the limb despite the risk of compassion fatigue (Adams et al., 2002) that can occur when helping survivors left homeless and traumatized in the aftermath of what was a major disaster for West Virginia. We, as authors, argue strongly for the realisation of social workers' potential to empower communities in the future, with knowledge of the importance of the role that social work has to play in being an integral part of the team(s) working with survivors of a natural catastrophe such as a flood. This view concurs with Dominelli's (2011) arguments for green social workers' involvement in disasters.

What was done in practice interventions, why and how?

A strategy or a planned choice in handling the effects, of this 2016 West Virginia flooding disaster, has been to determine what the residents wanted to do. How to go about it; the issue of how much money would be allocated to the effort came later. For example, before funds can be appropriately allocated to facilities, decision-makers have to decide what approach to take. But it is difficult to decide what one should attempt without some fairly good idea of feasibility and cost. Public policy analysis or political mapping can make a huge contribution to answering such questions. Our view, however, is that for the analysis of the practice of social work in the middle of public policy decisions, the methods of other disciplines, particularly those of the political and social sciences may have an equally important role to play.

Some crisis intervention methods to help persons affected by flooding, that do not have an economic origin and are at most quasi-quantitative, have come in use in socio-economic, political and cultural contexts. What are those methods for mental and emotional support? And, why and how were they carried out in practice or an intervention? Take notice of disaster services and logistics enabling a community to prepare for, respond to and help people recovering from floods big and small!

In what follows, we as authors conducted a review of the literature to produce outcomes and recommendations for practice in responding to the effects of flooding on mental health (Murray et al., 2012). A crisis intervention approach may constitute a synthesis of two trends in previous work on the general problems for survivors of flooding disasters. One trend may have dealt with the guidance on emergency planning for the impacts of flooding on psychosocial and mental health needs (Crabtree, 2013). The other trend focused on the pre-disaster characteristics of people coping with stress and their length of stay in treatment (Adams et al., 2006) or recovery. The findings of Murray et al. (2012) suggest that a fusion of these two main trends into systematic emphasis upon length-by-outcome groupings is now required. More generally, it is necessary to predict both the amount and rate of coping that constitutes improvement (Benveniste, 2000). Murray et al.'s (2012) review of the literature published from 2004 to 2010 made a beginning in this direction. However, much more needs to be done when such disasters occur. There is a dearth of literature pertaining to assessments of communities to determine the need for long-range local health service support when disasters take place and the lack of evidence-based support for school guidelines addressing the needs of students for future events. This has led us as authors to recommend that to address the aftermath of disasters, social workers worldwide review community structured crisis interventions, in a consultative manner, with local health services, first responders, school and government officials, church representatives, urban planners and others with experiences in natural disaster emergencies to propose ways forward. This is in keeping with the principles of green social work.

We know a community collectively and individually needs its residents to help one another survive and nurture positive ways of behaving. This chapter aims to acknowledge that they know that, and to ignite passion for more persons entering the field of social work, and to showcase that West Virginians managed to achieve the cooperation and crisis intervention needed after a major natural disaster like that of 2016. Survivor stories can usefully communicate and value each resident's recovery from their catastrophic loss. Storytelling is an effective procedure to follow in getting impressive results from a community-based responder team (Harrison, 2009). Social work must go beyond being tangentially involved in green social work practice that involves lack of water and other challenges imposed by climate change or unsustainable urban development, to be intrinsically involved in both in-country and international community-based responder systems to develop a holistic systems-based understanding of urban environments and/or complex environmental health challenges (Vardoulakis et al., 2016), as advised in the green social work model.

This chapter is intended to acquaint professionals in various disciplines with what social workers think, value, and argue about as being critically important in the advent of an environmental crisis (McKinnon, 2008). Its other aim is to help social workers respect their own traditions and values while they are learning new ones within rapidly changing environmental, societal and institutional contexts.

Self-evaluation: what lessons can be useful for others?

This chapter is useful in teaching about the West Virginia Flood of 2016 as a natural disaster to talk about and learn from. Hopefully, readers will rise to the occasion and conduct their own assessments of their usual responses to and feelings after a major natural disaster and juxtapose these with new ideas generated by discourses on crisis interventions and encourage the thought that the social responsibility of unburdening one another after a major natural disaster is a duty that can be accomplished.

Assessments that reflect reality impart tangible evidence of what are the most important lessons that can be useful for others. When catastrophic things beyond one's control (e.g. floods or earthquakes) happen, people may learn that their usual behaviours or feelings may not be relevant after a major natural disaster.

One lesson to start serving others is by telling an effective story. Throughout this crisis in Charleston, WV, the media reminded people who social work changes lives. This reminder endorses the value of the services provided by social workers. Amazing success stories can explain things in ways that facilitate profound understandings. The big question to answer is what are key messages for green social work? Then, to explore what tips will tell an effective green social work story for social workers who want to engage with sustainability and want to succeed and achieve their goals so that they do not leave anyone behind (or to avoid guess work)?

How do social workers determine their own key messages? News releases, letters-to-the-editor and other skilful communications can create useful perceptions. One goal of such messages could be to spark a feeling (e.g. of compassion, concern, happiness or anger). But, the practitioner should be him/herself and take the time to observe human qualities in communities.

Another goal should be to communicate the difference that a social worker brings. Dreaming of a world where living safely and crisis prevention would have the same meanings for all people, green social workers should continue this work and investigate why the number of people at risk of an environmental disaster has been growing each year, while the majority of people live in areas with high poverty levels that make them more vulnerable to disasters (Landry et al., 2016).

Flooding has distinctly different impacts on the emotional and mental health of individuals. The ensuing lessons are interesting, and are identified in the following list:

1. Telling an effective story that speaks to the adaptive capacity of individuals, families and communities to emerge stronger after a flood disaster is encouraging.
2. For talking points to support key messages, practitioners may need to change their talking points based on the needs and interests of the audience or clients/service users.
3. Feelings motivate people to act.

As authors reflecting on our experiences, we advocate storytelling and recording oral histories about social risks and social vulnerability to climate change (Bowman and Bowman, 2010) through a multidimensional approach that facilitates social welfare and social justice as advocated in green social work practice. Making sense of social work through storytelling is a method for modelling critical reflective practice (Harrison, 2009), and effectively to inform others of what they should know and how you feel. Another possible benefit of reading this chapter includes feeling empowered to enable environmental refugees to move forward in a sustainable manner.

New questions for research

The primary purpose of this chapter is to provide knowledge of a specific environmental crisis and raise awareness that understanding and direct responses to a disaster survivor's expectations are fundamental to developing a counselling relationship that may result in the ultimate realisation of the goals of coping with the situation, adjusting to the new reality, and returning to a previous or balanced level of functioning.

Counselling is usefully regarded as a learning phenomenon. In developing an effective counselling relationship, including the personalities of both the client/service user and counsellor forms an important part of the content in the sessions. Counselling satisfaction for survivors of a natural disaster is a variable that is dependent upon many other variables in the overall evaluation of the impact of the counselling process.

Crisis intervention by counsellors should help persons who have developed the symptoms of an Acute Stress Disorder, because they have been exposed to a traumatic situation that overwhelmed their ability to cope with it in a way that they are accustomed to. Furthermore, counsellors and emergency responders generally agree on helping patients/clients/service users to:

- Tell their story.
- Get some detachment from the overwhelming experience to understand what happened.
- Put into words the experience of trauma.
- Return to a previous or balanced level of functioning.

Social workers' knowledge of others' values with respect for the integrity of the patient/client/service user, especially those that are incompatible, supports ethical practice. Clinical and practical knowledge can go so far, but social workers have to be qualified in terms of personality, attitude and demeanour. Practices that are in the best interest of the client/service user stem from:

1. The altruism of the professional worker as expressed in community actions in the interest of others, and selfless efforts of courage regardless of maintenance of security and status;
2. Better judgment, due in part at least to experience in crisis intervention;
3. Knowing one's own values to distinguish those values from that of clients/service users;
4. Skill in expressing ideas clearly and concisely and working effectively with staff and clients/service users; and
5. Knowledge of medical terminology, disease processes, as they relate to clinical interventions and appropriate therapies based on medical or psychological treatment modalities.

Thorough knowledge of social work research, practice, protocols and processes, conversations, interviews with legislators or stakeholders, and public decisions can provide answers to the following questions, so that a main point of green social work can be conveyed to legislators:

- What is the impact of floods on the socio-economic livelihoods of people in your respective community?
- What are the demographics of the most vulnerable groups to floods and what are their coping strategies?
- What are the sustainable policy options for dealing with the problem of floods?

Conclusion

The questions, derived by inductions from the experiences of many, justify the following conclusion. Greater emphasis in training programs on the use of crisis intervention in community-wide disasters could expedite assistance (McKnight and Zack, 2007; Schein, 2016) and provide greater security of public servant administrators and their staff. Regard for the well-being of families and children is relevant to having a service mission that includes protecting public water supplies and fostering stewardship of this natural resource for use by current and future generations of citizens.

This writing will be useful to social workers wanting justification for the significance of answering three questions raised for further exploration. Those questions were: 'What is the impact of floods on the socio-economic livelihoods of people in your respective community'? 'What are the demographics of the most vulnerable groups to floods and what are their coping strategies'? 'What are sustainable policy options for dealing with the problem of floods'? Those three questions, formulated on the basis of work currently being done in the field of green social work, pose questions for future research.

Also, this work can help enlarge social workers' philosophies and their pedagogies (Dominelli, 2006; Dominelli and Ioakimidis, 2015). Moreover, a targeted use of optimism may be more effective than simply reaching safety or shelter for survivors of the West Virginia flooding of 2016. This was a major natural catastrophe in which social work proved its societal and institutional value and that augmented lay people's knowledge of crisis interventions afterward. Through reporting such events, the authors offer support for the social worker(s) striving to achieve the cooperation needed to form a more disciplined, non-threatening atmosphere and maximise each individual's productivity.

References

Adams, R.E., Boscarino, J.A. and Figley, C. (2006). Compassion fatigue and psychological distress among social workers: A validation study. *American Journal of Orthopsychiatry*, 76(1): 103–108.

Benveniste, D. (2000). Intervencion en crisis despues de grandes desastres. (Intervention in crisis after major disasters). *Tropicos: La Revista del sociedad psicoanalitica de Caracas*. Año VIII, Vol. I, Spanish translation by Adriana Prengler.

Bowman, M.S. and Bowman, R.C. (2010). Telling Katrina stories: Problems and opportunities in engaging disaster. *Quarterly Journal of Speech*. 96(4): 455–461.

Carlisle, S. and Hanlon, P. (2014). Connecting food, well-being, and environmental sustainability: towards and integrative public health nutrition. *Critical Public Health*, 24(4): 405–417.

Cohn, W. A. (2011). Environmental refugees and humanity. *Our Modern Identity*. TNP autumn, pp. 18–28.

Collins, S. D. (2015). War-making as an environmental disaster. *New Labor Forum*, 24(2): 25–30.

Crabtree, A. (1983). Questioning psychological resilience after and the consequences for disaster risk reduction, *Social Indicators Research*, 113(2): 711–728.

Cree, V. E. (2009). The changing nature of social work. In Adams, R., Dominelli, L. and Payne, M. (eds), *Social Work: Themes, issues and critical debates* (Third edition), Basingstoke: Palgrave Macmillan. pp. 26–36.

Cree, V. E. (2011). Introduction: Reading social work. In V. E. Cree (Ed.), *Social work: A reader*. Abingdon: Routledge. pp. 1–8.

DiMento, J. F. C. and Doughman, P. (Eds.) (2007). *Climate change: What it means for us, our children, and our grandchildren*. Cambridge, MA: MIT Press.

Dominelli, L. (2006). Globalization and social work: International and local implications. *The British Journal of Social Work*, 36(3): 365–380, April.

Dominelli, L. (2011). Climate change: Social workers' contributions to policy and practice debates. *International Journal of Social Welfare*, 20(4): 430–439. doi:10.1111/j.1468-2397.2011.00795.x

Dominelli, L. (2012). *Green social work: From environmental crises to environmental justice*. Cambridge: Polity Press.
Dominelli, L. (2016). Social work challenges in the second decade of the 21st century: Against the bias, *Affilia*, December.
Dominelli, L. and Ioakimidis, V. (2015). Social work on the frontline in addressing disasters, social problems and marginalization. *International Social Work*, 58(1): 3–6.
Dwyer, T. (2009). How to connect bioethics to environmental ethics, health, sustainability, and justice. *Bioethics*, 23(9): 497–502.
Figley, C. R. (1995). *Compassion fatigue: Coping with secondary traumatic stress disorder*. New York: Brunner/Mazel.
Figley, C. R. (2002). *Treating compassion fatigue*. New York: Brunner-Routledge.
Francis, P., Oreskes, N. and Bramhall, M. (2014). *The encyclical on climate change and inequality: On care for our common home*. New York: Random House.
Harrison, K. (2009). Listen: This really happened: Making sense of social work through story-telling. *Social Work Education*, 28(7): 750–764, October.
Howard, J. (2012). Storm damage at NYU library offers lessons for disaster planning in the stacks. *Chronicle of Higher Education*, 59(13): A18-A19, 23 November.
Malonenbeach, E. E. and Zuo, Q. (2013). Environmental sustainability in the US assisted living facilities. *Journal of Housing for the Elderly*, 27: 255–277.
McKinnon, J. (2008). Exploring the nexus between social work and the environment. *Australian Social Work*, 61(3): 256–268.
McKnight M. and Zach, L. (2007). Choices in chaos: Designing research into librarians' information services improvised during a variety of community-wide disasters in order to produce evidence-based training materials for librarians, *Evidence Based Library and Information Practice*, 2(3): 50–75. Edmonton, AB, Canada: EBLIP.
NASW (National Association of Social Workers) (2006). *Social work speaks: National Association of Social Workers Policy Statements 2006–2009*. 7th ed. Washington, DC: NASW Press, pp. 136–143.
Rust, M. J. (2004). Creating a psychotherapy for a sustainable future. *Psychotherapy and Politics International*, 2(1): 50–63.
Schein, E. (2016). *Humble consulting: How to provide real help faster*. Oakland, CA: Berrett-Koehler Publishers, Inc.
Shaw, T. V. (2006). *Social workers knowledge and attitude toward the ecological environment. University of California at Berkeley, Doctoral Dissertation*, 68(3): 1162.
Stanke C., Muray, V. and Amlot, R. (2012). The effects of flooding on mental health: Outcomes and recommendations from a review of the literature. *PLOS Currents Disasters*, 30 May Edition 1, pp. 1–17. doi: 10.1371/4f9f1fa9c3cae.
United Nations (1992). *United Nations convention framework convention on climate change*. Available on https://unfccc.int/files/essential_background/background_publications_htmlpdf/application/pdf/conveng.pdf
Vardoulakis, S., Dear, K. and Williamson, P. (2016). Challenges and opportunities of urban health sustainability: the HEALTHY-Polis initiative. *Environmental Health*, 15(Supp. 1): 30.
Wieck, A. (1981). Social Work and the environment: understanding people and place, *Social Work*, 26(2): 140–143.

43
Towards a curriculum in disaster risk reduction from a green social work perspective

Carin Björngren Cuadra and Guðný Björk Eydal

Introduction

The social work curriculum needs serious development to cover disasters. In this chapter, we argue for the systematic inclusion of disaster risk reduction in it. We build upon what green social work (Dominelli, 2012) and other scholars emphasise when demanding the inclusion of environmental issues in social work (Dominelli, 2011; Kemp, 2011; Gray et al., 2013). We suggest that developing disaster risk reduction as embedded in green social work has strong potential to impact on mainstream disaster risk reduction because it strengthens interventions in the very processes that lead to disasters.

Disaster risk reduction in both policy and research (Baez and Becker, 2016) involves the:

> practice of reducing disaster risks through systematic efforts to analyse and manage the causal factors of disasters, including through reduced exposure to hazards, lessened vulnerability of people and property, wise management of land and the environment, and improved preparedness for adverse events.
>
> *(UNISDR, 2009: 10)*

The strength of the construct is its recognition of the ongoing nature of disaster risks and potential to reduce these (ibid). Disaster risk reduction aims to analyse and manage the causal factors of disasters (Rapeli et al., 2017) and respond adequately when risks become manifest in crises, during disasters and in their aftermath. We note that all such tasks are integrated into green social work.

This broad and encompassing approach to disaster risk ties it to transdisciplinary conversations on environmental concerns, making disaster risk reduction a salient aspect of social work's contribution to sustainable development, ecologically, economically and socially. From a social work perspective, disaster risk reduction addresses socio-ecological risks including global injustices and threats to the environment. Thus, disaster risk reduction can be considered a part of the global sustainability agenda (Chmutina et al., 2015). This agenda leans on the concept of sustainable development understood as meeting 'the needs of the present without compromising the ability of future generations to meet their own' (World Commission on Environment and Development, 1987: 16). As pointed out in this Commission's Report, the concept of sustainable development implies limitations imposed by the present state of technology and social organisation on environmental resources and the ability of the biosphere to absorb the effects of human activities (ibid).

For this chapter, we draw upon information obtained through a web-based questionnaire sent to the European Schools of Social Work (EASSW) in June 2016. This limits the discussion to the European scene. The project sought to map the extent to which disasters as a topic were covered in the social work curriculum and whether any school had an interest in participating in the possible development of a joint European course.

The questions consequently asked to what extent the schools of social work teach topics connected to disasters. Courses, for example, could be labelled disaster social work, disaster interventions or have alternative names in the area of disasters such as disaster preparedness or disaster management, or green or environmental social work. The questionnaire was distributed via email to all members, 310 in total. After two reminders were sent out, 38 questionnaires were returned, making the response rate 12.2 percent. This low response rate may mirror a low interest in the topic and could imply that member schools chose not to answer the questionnaire as they did not deem themselves affected by the subject. The low response rate can also be ascribed to gaps in the internal communication within respective member schools and the administrative distribution chain, or a heavy workload, a well-known reason for not answering questionnaires.

Based on these findings, we argue and show in Table 43.2 on page 530 that the schools of social work in EASSW do not include much about disaster risk reduction in their curricula. This implies that neither practitioners nor educators can utilise the basic competences in this domain of social work and assume an active role in disaster risk reduction. We will join the call for the better acknowledgement of social workers as vital partners regarding disasters (Alston, 2007; Dominelli, 2012). This plea is based on an appreciation of the general knowledge domain of social work alongside its orientation towards social risks and vulnerability which have always been part of the field of knowledge of social workers (Soliman and Rogge, 2002). Social work involves theoretical and practical field questions regarding processes that create and counteract social vulnerability as well as how social work interventions can be organised and implemented to prevent and reduce social vulnerability (Cuadra et al. 2013). Furthermore, the individuals and communities that primarily pay for the implications of environmental degradation and ecological crisis in terms of the destruction of lives and livelihood (Fotopoulos, 2007; UNDP, 2016) are the same people whom social workers have engaged with traditionally. However, we suggest that to enhance a qualitative engagement in addressing disasters, there is a need for a comprehensive curriculum that is firmly linked to environmental issues in disaster risk reduction and gives social workers a solid knowledge-base for their interventions in disaster settings. As suggested by Kemp (2011: 1200), the base involves a conceptual framework, research and practice. To this knowledge-base green social work adds policy formulation and implementation (Dominelli, 2011, 2012).

The tasks of social workers in times of disasters

Social workers have been recognised as important resources both before disasters in mitigation and preparedness; and after disasters in response and recovery (Desai, 2007; IASSW, 2010; Gillespie and Danso, 2010). This is regardless of the causes of disasters. The focus of social workers in disaster management is usually the local scene, at municipal and community level (Cuadra, 2015). In an international systematic review of the literature, Eydal et al. (2016) with reference to Rapeli (2016) identified 30 different tasks that social workers perform.

In the immediate response phase, their tasks involve outreach services, alongside the identification of victim–survivors and those most exposed to hazards, and referral to relevant services including healthcare. Tasks cover the provision of shelter and housing, water, medicine, food and clothing, and other practical help such as providing channels for information. They also coordinate various actors in civil society and the voluntary sector (Eydal et al. 2016).

In the aftermath of disasters, social work can be involved in the reconstruction of communities and coordination of actors in channelling the distribution of resources. It can also involve the reconstruction of social functions and development of new possibilities for livelihoods alongside supporting victim–survivors in insurance issues (ibid). Other tasks in the aftermath involve psychosocial support to individuals, families and communities to recover from any trauma, bereavement counselling, helplines and contributions to family reunion (ibid). Additionally, social workers have a crucial role in supporting decision-makers and management in advocating for the needs of the most vulnerable people (ibid).

Regardless of their multiple tasks, social workers can play important roles in disaster management and advocacy as identified by Dominelli (2011, 2012), Adamson (2014) and the *United Nations Office for Disaster Risk Reduction* (UNISDR). In line with green social work the latter is particularly keen to promote social worker engagement in disasters (UNISDR, 2015a). UNISDR stresses that the role of social workers in disaster risk reduction is far more than simply helping communities cope with the impacts of events like floods or earthquakes. It also connects to social workers' engagement in the causes relevant to vulnerable peoples, such as poverty, poor health, housing, environmental challenges or, as occurs frequently, a combination of such factors (ibid). When responding to these, social workers act as a 'transmission chain' (ibid) or, as we would put it, adopt a mediating position between policymakers at government levels and various communities. This position can promote unheard voices to broaden the understanding of 'the human dimensions of environmental issues' (Kemp 2011: 1200). It also entails a re-examination of the interconnectedness between people, the physical environment and their impact on human well-being (Dominelli, 2012; Kennedy 2016).

The endeavour to strengthen social work's engagement in disaster risk reduction is underpinned by a global consensus regarding very problematic future scenarios that encompass a growing number of disasters (Manyena, 2011; UNISDR, 2016; UNISDR, 2015b). The numbers of natural disasters, especially climate-related ones, have more than doubled since the 1980s (Munich Re, 2015). *The Intergovernmental Panel on Climate Change* (IPCC) (2014) concurs that a growing number of severe negative events due to climate changes are very likely. Furthermore, the *Global Risk Report*, places extreme weather events, involuntary migration, and natural disasters (in that order) among the top 10 global risks most likely to occur (World Economic Forum, 2017). Also, the impacts of extreme weather events and natural disasters are ranked high, only topped by weapons of mass destruction and water crises (ibid). It is noteworthy that the risk of failure of climate change mitigation and adaptation are considered interconnected not only to weather events but also to water crises and large-scale involuntary migration. The latter can be due to environmental degradation such as draught as currently in East Africa and Horn of Africa (IOM, 2017) as well as due to warfare, which is currently witnessed in Syria (IOM, 2016). From the European perspective, the highest ranked risks are increasing polarisation and the intensification of national sentiments over large-scale unemployment (World Economic Forum, 2017) that are largely interlinked with involuntary migration.

With this problematic situation encompassing risks that can be framed as socio-ecological, humanity faces a 'daunting double challenge' in how to support equitable human development while preserving the bio-physical integrity of Earth systems (Gerst et al., 2013: 123). If humanity follows the path of ongoing conventional development, it will transgress more than five out of seven planetary boundaries by 2025 (ibid). The planetary boundaries are: climate change, ocean acidification, nitrogen cycle, phosphorus cycle, global freshwater use, change in land use, and rate of biodiversity loss. Thus, planetary boundaries refer to the safe operating space for humanity to respect environmental processes that regulate the stability of Earth (ibid). Successfully staying in Earth's operating space would require that resource-efficient and renewable technologies are more equitably distributed global income alongside social and cultural changes (ibid). Green social work asks social workers to address those issues.

Climate change has been labelled as perhaps the greatest global crisis which humanity has faced and can result in a global long-term disaster (Chmutina et al., 2015). The problems are targeted through a large number of legally binding and voluntary international and national frameworks (Chmutina et al., 2015). However, the current frameworks have not involved any significant change in basic institutional structures or values (Gerst et al., 2013). These frameworks have evolved rapidly, and in many cases their focus has shifted from mitigation of present and anticipated climate change through to reductions in energy consumption to reduce anthropogenic greenhouse gas emission, to adaptation (Chmutina et al., 2015) implying that efforts geared towards coping with its effects ignore the causes. From the perspective of social work, the difference between adaptation and mitigation to climate change is interesting. We return to it later because it bears upon disasters as an area of teaching and what to include in the universities' social work curricula.

According to Earth sciences and resilience research, the global situation calls for a re-assessment and change of lifestyle, values, and what is considered to be human well-being on a global scale as well as the involvement of social agencies and democratic movements (Gerst et al., 2013). This provides the context for arguing that a social work that addresses disaster risk reduction with a long-term mitigation approach is necessary. Further, as upheld by green social work its practice would by definition be rooted in social justice and respect of nature (see Dominelli, 2012).

Resilience as a prerequisite for sustainable development

During the last few decades, there has been a shift in approaches to disasters (Baez and Becker, 2016). This shift, which has been observed internationally (ibid.) involves a change of focus from reaction to prevention (Manyena et al., 2011), is of interest to social work. It also involves a transition from disaster management – trained experts dealing with actual events when they occur, to disaster risk management (Baez and Becker, 2016). The *Sendai Framework for Disaster Risk Reduction 2015–2030* confirms this development (ibid). It widens the scope of the actions needed in prevention, preparedness, response to and recovery from disasters (Rapeli et al., 2017).

This approach implies new linkages between policy areas. Policy dealing with disasters connects to areas like the environment, and urban and rural development (Dominelli, 2012; Baez and Becker, 2016). Thus, a firm linkage between disaster risk reduction and both global and national goals for sustainable development are essential. The approach thus implies that disaster risk reduction is understood with sustainability as an overarching framework (Manyena, 2016), and addresses people's vulnerabilities alongside their capacities in the long run (Rapeli et al., 2017). This development suggests that traditional disaster management organisations are no longer the only ones expected to take an active part. Instead, disaster risk reduction concerns all sectors of society – private and public actors, business, civil society and communities as well as households and individuals (Dominelli, 2012; Baez and Becker, 2016).

This shift calls for a wider understanding of how to enhance communication and co-operation between individuals, families, communities, and organisations in the public, private and voluntary sectors (ibid). It demands new knowledge and methods centred on how to enhance the participation of all potential partners (Rowlands, 2013; Danielsson et al., 2015), as also required by green social work (Dominelli, 2012). For us, this shift calls upon social workers not only to act as a 'transmission chain' or in mediating and supporting roles, but also to re-examine the interconnectedness between people, their environment and its impact on human well-being (Dominelli, 2012, 2017; Kennedy, 2016). We term this a 'prodding role' most needed in exploring important drivers of planetary change and involve economic, social, cultural, institutional, technological and environmental drivers (Gerst et al., 2013).

A concept that intends to grasp this broad approach to disasters is *resilience*. We see resilience as a goal oriented umbrella concept for disaster risk reduction. It addresses:

> the ability of a system, community or society exposed to hazards to resist, absorb, accommodate, adapt to, transform and recover from the effects of a hazard in a timely and efficient manner, including through the preservation and restoration of its essential basic structures and functions through risk management.
>
> *(UNISDR, 2009: 24)*

In short, resilience highlights an ability to 'bounce back' or learn from experiences to 'bounce forward' and move on following a disaster (Manyena et al., 2011). As disasters can be a catalyst for change, the 'bounce forward' notion encapsulates change processes within the context of new realities brought about by a disaster (ibid). Thus, resilience as a concept implies elements of continuity over time. This has implications for pre- and post-disaster planning, including community continuity recovery planning (ibid). It involves pre-disaster planning that recognises the importance of adjusting to new post-disaster realities (ibid).

However, from our perspective it is important to acknowledge that the concept of resilience has been critiqued extensively (Emilson, 2015) inter alia bases on a concern that continuity might conserve unjust social relations (Dominelli, 2012). Resilience theory has been criticised for being apolitical, building on consensus, neglecting power issues, being abstract, and presented through an engineering perspective (Emilson, 2015). The concept has also been linked to the neoliberal policy agenda (Dominelli, 2012; Joseph, 2013) which gives primacy to de-regulation, marketisation, privatisation and individualisation (Klein, 2007). The latter emphasises the individual's responsibility and 'free choice' (ibid). Interestingly, 'free choice' has been castigated for forming a normative base that has facilitated the introduction of resilience as a concept (Bergström, 2016). This element has played out in numerous information campaigns that target individuals and households and urge them to cope during disasters for at least 72 hours (ibid). We return to this point for its bearing upon the role of social workers.

For social workers, these criticisms become relevant when establishing resilience as a concept and engaging in disaster risk reduction in the field. In social work, resilience is most familiar as a concept aiming at individuals and underpinned by psychology and health sciences in constructs such as 'born survivors'. In the UNISDR definition, resilience is conceptually understood and applied at many levels. It describes organisations, enterprises, and technological and ecological systems. In the latter sense, the concept addresses nature's ability to respond to climate changes, albeit slowly. The concept is also applied at an overarching societal level. There, resilience is understood as a societal ability. While disaster risk reduction is understood as a contribution to a resilient society, the resilient society is deemed a prerequisite for sustainable development.

With these criticisms in mind, a major and valuable point about resilience from a social work perspective is that it highlights disaster risk reduction within a broad multi-sectorial and preventive approach. As not only traditional disaster management organisations are involved, it also implies anticipated engagement by individuals, households and communities. The development of resilience is a societal issue (Baez and Becker, 2016). Resilience also captures the interaction between structural and individual prerequisites (Dominelli, 2012). Another point is that the concept's broad sweep opens up the potential for responding to unknown and complex hazards. Where there is resilience, there is an ability to respond to unpredictable, unexpected and dynamic processes and events (Bergström, 2016). The concept also introduces long-term reflection, over years and generations to come (Sparf, 2016), which in the context of planetary changes is a valuable consideration.

Social work developing resilience

Societal resilience is influenced by a range of factors that involving economies, infrastructures, environments, governments and social systems (Eydal et al., 2016). Social services and social work generally aim to increase the resilience of people (Zakour and Gillespie, 2013). Social workers play an important role at the local level in enhancing the resilience of individuals and communities as their competences involve factors that influence resilience, whether to strengthen households' socio-economic status through income support, education, support of older people in managing a long-lasting heat wave (Eydal et al., 2016) or enhancing service accessibility for those who are functionally impaired.

The everyday strengthening of resilience is highly relevant for disaster situations (Gillespie and Danso, 2010). Everyday resilience constitutes a fundamental prerequisite for disaster resilience. Given the expected engagement by individuals and households, we want to underline that social workers can perform mediating and supporting roles in relation to those who cannot fulfil current expectations about taking an active part in disaster management (Cuadra, 2017). Another contribution to overall societal resilience are social workers' disaster preparedness activities and service continuity planning in their own organisation to uphold societal functions (Cuadra, 2017). Competence to interact with policymakers at governing levels adds to their contribution to societal resilience. The value in this latter engagement lies in the knowledge created through social workers' encounters with individuals and communities.

The identified tasks and contributions to disaster risk reduction and resilience that have been discussed thus far represent a short-term perspective that addresses disasters, when and if, they occur and during their aftermath. The problematic future scenarios that we outlined earlier require engagement through a long-term mitigating approach. Therefore, simply preparing for and responding to disasters through short-term strategies and practices are insufficient. Social workers need to do more, given the current perilous state of planet Earth, a concern of green social work (Dominelli, 2012).

When it comes to climate change, complementary strategies that mitigate current development through energy consumption and greenhouse gas emission reductions need to be applied over the next few decades (IPCC, 2014). As stated by the IPCC, without mitigation efforts beyond those in place today, and even with adaptation, global warming by the end of the 21st century will lead from high to very high risk of severe, widespread and irreversible impacts globally (ibid.). Dominelli (2012) has argued that successful management of environmental crises and climate change require social workers to address structural inequalities, socio-economic disparities and resource distribution, patterns of consumption and production as well as the use of resources which also includes the utilisation of plants, animals and the physical environment. These form part of the *Green Social Work Model* that addresses the interactions between people (humans) and their environments within socio-ecological systems. Green social work contributes to developing resilience in socio-ecological systems as well as people and communities (Dominelli, 2012). For disasters, this involves a long-term mitigating approach based on analysing and addressing the causal factors of disasters connected to climate change and other environmental crises. This constitutes part of the disaster risk reduction initiatives supported by green social workers.

Against this background, we have underlined the 'daunting double challenge' (Gerst et al., 2013: 124) involving equitable human development while preserving the bio-physical integrity of Earth. For our suggestion regarding the involvement of social workers, we return to our initial interest in mapping the extent to which disaster interventions are included in the curriculum. We supplement this interest with our understanding of the different emphases that come to the fore in schools' accounts of disasters as an area of teaching.

Getting an overview

The questionnaires EASSW sent to the European schools of social work raised questions about both current curriculum content and willingness to take part in developing a joint European course. These asked whether disasters were covered within a specific course or integrated into overarching subjects, the level of the courses, and if these were elective or compulsory. We will now present the results, though with a caution about the low response rate that limits the generalisability of the conclusions, but which leaves room for suggestions.

Among the 38 schools that responded the questionnaires, five stated that they had no interest in the subject. Out of the remaining 33 schools, 17 expressed an interest to take an active part in developing a joint course. However, as illustrated in Figure 43.1, only nine of the interested schools currently include disasters in the curriculum.

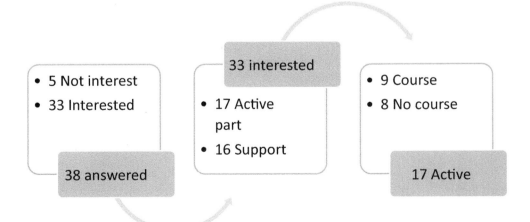

Figure 43.1 Overview of the responses and interest in developing the topic of disasters in a joint European course

Table 43.1 Categorisation of courses given by members of EASSW

Course			Integrated	Topic	Total
	Non-graduate				
		Elective		4	4
		Non-elective	4	2	6
	Graduate				
		Elective	3	3	6
		Non-elective	2		2
	PhD level			2	2
	Practitioner				4
Total			9	11	24

The total number of current courses is higher because schools that expressed that they could not take an active part in a joint course, but still supported the idea, accounted for some of these courses. Their total number is 24 (Table 43.1).

As can be read from the Table 43.1, there are courses dealing with disasters being taught both at non-graduate and graduate levels, and there are both non-elective and elective courses. Further, the topics of disaster are covered both by being integrated in a course within an overarching subject, and in courses dedicated specifically to disasters. The balance between these two pedagogical approaches (integrated or specialist) is fairly even. Practitioners (i.e. persons with or without qualifying degrees active in social work) are also targeted to some extent. According to this mapping there are currently two PhD courses that cover disasters.

Table 43.2 gives an overview of the courses. In the categorisation of the courses we relate to the four phases of disasters – mitigation, preparation, response and recovery (Quarantelli 1997; Alexander, 2015), though questionnaire participants have not covered preparation in their replies. The courses whose overarching subject provides room for dealing with the topics of disasters regardless of the phase are put in a group which we call General. In this group, there are courses introducing fundamental concepts in social work and courses introducing international perspectives. While dealing with the general competences of social work, the content of General courses includes topics about disasters, but it is impossible to tell to what extent coverage occurs based on the responses received.

The next identified group deals with the Mitigation of disasters as the perspective of long-term prevention. Only one of the schools of social work that answered the questionnaire gave a course covering this subject. In this case, it is a course dedicated to social work and sustainable development.

We call the next group Response. Judging by their names, we placed courses and topics that dealt with immediate responses in times of disasters in this group. This included courses such as social work in emergencies and extreme events, as well as crises interventions. In the Response group there were also courses that addressed grief and psychological first aid, trauma, and post-disaster trauma. This latter theme can also be considered an aspect of the subsequent phase, recovery. This phase gave name to the last identified group, Recovery. Here, there was one specialist course dealing with social work with children and families in the aftermath of disasters (Table 43.2).

Table 43.2 Topics covered in courses grouped according to the phases of disasters

Topics	Approach	Dedicated course	Integrated	Country
	General		International social work	Israel, Portugal, Ukraine
			International organisations (incl. social policy of such organisations)	Italy, Ukraine
			Professional concepts of SW	Ukraine
	Mitigation	SW and sustainable development		Sweden
	Response			
		Social work in extreme situations		Slovenia
			SW in emergency	Italy
		Psychosocial interventions on emergencies and strong emotional impact		Spain
		Crisis interventions	Crisis interventions	Austria, Portugal, Israel, Czech Republic
		Stress, trauma, post-trauma		Israel
			Crisis, grief and psychological first aid	Iceland
			Psychology of crisis	Hungary
	Recovery	SW with children and families in the aftermath of disasters		Denmark

Some observations

This chapter approaches an issue that might be helpful to the future development of the social work curriculum. In this we join forces with scholars whose endeavours preceded us (see Gray et al., 2013). However, our underlying research suffers from considerable weaknesses. Its limitations include a small group of respondents and material that does not cover the syllabus for each course. Bearing these cautions in mind, we want to share some observations.

The first observation concerns the low number of courses currently dealing with disasters. Second, only one course covers disasters with sustainability as an overarching framework. This implies that the course addresses environmental issues. A third observation concerns a certain bias towards the response phase. Fourth, the individual level seems to be the most common level of intervention. This is the level targeted by courses we classified as pertaining to the response and the recovery phases, namely social work in the aftermath of disasters. This neglects other levels that involve community and structural matters.

Taken together, the observations indicate that current curricula among schools of social work in Europe do not engage much with disasters regardless of phase. This indicates a need for the development of a social work curriculum in disaster risk reduction. Although such development can benefit from existing engagement with interventions at the individual level in the response phase, these would need a broadening of approaches to cover all phases of disasters, and long-term mitigation.

Closing up: towards a critical curriculum in disaster risk reduction

The roles of social work that are given primacy according to this mapping exercise are indeed very important in relation to social workers' engagement in disasters. The importance of targeting individuals who have been victim–survivors of a disaster crisis, resonates with Pyles (2007: 321) who points out that 'social work has been less involved in rebuilding and community development than in traumatic stress intervention and the coordination of relief efforts'. This tendency might mirror a certain tension between the importance of working on the individual level with psychosocial support and counselling, and emphasising community work that has been observed in the literature (Pyles, 2007; Dominelli, 2012; Rowlands, 2013). Such tension is a recurring theme in the history and traditions of social work (Cuadra, 2015) and is unproductive. Both orientations and their respective competencies are equally important in the daily practices of social workers. And as green social work emphasises, both are necessary in all disasters (Dominelli, 2012).

Social services and social work in various countries have played extensive and important roles in disasters. Their involvement could become larger if the full potential of social work were applied pre- and post-disasters and across the multiplicity of roles that they can assume (Dominelli, 2012; Rapeli et al., 2017). A comprehensive approach would enhance the resilience of individuals, communities and societies as it engages with the interface between structural and individual prerequisites (Dominelli, 2012).

We suggest a curriculum based on green social work that covers all phases of disasters: mitigation, preparation, response and recovery, and reconstruction, for its content and learning outcomes. We argue that social work's contribution to disaster risk reduction needs to encompass a strong long-term preventive perspective and develop resilience in social-ecological systems besides being engaged in the other phases of disasters. Rooted in social justice and respecting nature, a social work that addresses the interaction between people and environment in social-ecological systems prepares it to assume the transformative approach necessary to address, re-assess, and change lifestyles, values, and human well-being (Gerst et al., 2013). In short, the development of a disaster risk reduction curriculum should be embedded in the venture of green social work.

We are not positioned to outline a complete curriculum but can make an input that keeps the perilous state of Earth in mind. As suggested by Kemp (2011), a curriculum on environmental issues needs to involve giving the students both conceptual frameworks and knowledge-based practice. As the state of planet Earth calls for a re-assessment and change in human lifestyles, values, and well-being (Gerst et al., 2013), the curriculum has to include issues on energy usage, patterns of consumption, and production alongside the use and distribution of resources (Dominelli, 2012). A social work curriculum could engage all those involved in a transdisciplinary exploration of alternative production forms on the borders of capitalist, industrial mass-production together with the commons that promote sharing and collaboration (Seravalli, 2014). Such engagement implies conceptualisation of the involvement of social agencies and democratic movements as enacted in community work. This can provide opportunities for community-led, renewable forms of energy consumption and sustainable development that can drive local economies in new directions and enhance community resilience (Dominelli, 2012, 2017).

The curriculum could also engage with urban and rural development at local, national and international levels, underpinned by locally grounded knowledges and experiences. This competence requires conceptual frameworks and practice for interventions including advocacy and mobilisation aiming at policy-level changes leading to structural development. In this venture, the student would need conceptual tools to explore the drivers of planetary change (Gerst et al., 2013), the processes that lead to disasters and leave room to develop collaborative transdisciplinary practices.

Developing such a curriculum might be easier said than done. Social workers are optimally positioned to respond to the human implications of environmental change (Kemp 2011), their existing competences could facilitate this being done. But, it would take a widening of the understanding of the person-in-the environment to include concerns for the physical environment and ensure that social and environmental justice become integral to any environmental involvement by social workers (Dominelli, 2012, 2017).

References

Adamson, C. (2014). A social work lens for a disaster-informed curriculum. *Advances in Social Work and Welfare Education*, 16(2): 7–21.

Alexander, D. E. (2015). Evaluation of civil protection programmes, with a case study from Mexico. *Disaster Prevention and Management*, 24(2): 263–283.

Alston, M. (2007). It's really not easy to get help. *Social Work*, 60(4): 421–435.

Baez U. and Becker P. (2016). Katastrofriskreducering. In Baez, U. and Becker, P. (Eds.) *Katastrofriskreducering*. pp. 23–58. Lund: Studentlitteratur.

Bergström, J. (2016). Vem bär ansvaret för samhällets katastrofriskreducering. In Baez, U. and Becker, P. (Eds.). *Katastrofriskreducering*. pp. 81-104. Lund: Studentlitteratur.

Chmutina, K., Bosher, L. and Dainty, A. (2015). *Securitization of climate change and natural hazards in the UK*. Presentation at First Needs Conference, Copenhagen, December.

Cuadra, C. B., Lalander, P. and Righard, E. (2013). Socialt arbete i Malmö. Perspektiv och utmaningar. *Socialvetenskaplig tidskrift*, 20(1): 4–12.

Cuadra, C. B. (2015). *Disaster social work in Sweden*. Nordiska Ministerrådet, The Nordic Welfare Watch – in Response to Crisis. Working Paper No. 1:2015.

Cuadra, C. B. (2017). *Stärkt roll för socialtjänsten i kommunal krisberedskap*. Kunskapsunderlag för socialtjänstens delaktighet i kommunala risk-och sårbarhetsanalyser (Sorsa). Lund: School of Social Work, Lund University.

Danielsson, E., Sparf, J., Karlsson, R. and Oscarsson, O. (2015). *Sektorsövergripande samverkan vid med frivilliga*. Östersund: Mittuniversitet (RCR Working Paper Series 2015: 2).

Desai, A. (2007). Disaster and social work responses. In L. Dominelli (Ed.). *Revitalising communities in a globalising world*. pp. 297-314 Aldershot: Ashgate.

Dominelli, L. (2011). Climate change: Social workers' roles and contributions to policy debates and interventions' *International Journal of Social Welfare*, 20(4): 430–438.

Dominelli, L. (2012). *Green social work*. Cambridge: Polity Press.

Dominelli, L. (2016). Greening social work. In Meeuwisse, A., Swärd, H., Sunesson, S., and Knutagård, M. *Socialt Arbeite: En Grundbok*. Stockholm: Natur & Kultur, pp. 445–462.

Eydal, G. B., Ómarsdóttir, I. L., Björngren Cuadra, C., Dahlberg, R., Hvinden, B., Rapeli, M. and Salonen, T. (2016). *Local Social Services in Nordic countries in Times of Disaster*. Report for the Nordic Council of Ministers. Ministry of Welfare, Reykjavík, Iceland.

Emilson, A. (2015). *Design in the space between stories*. Malmö: Malmö University. Doctoral thesis.

Fotopoulos, T. (2007). Is degrowth compatible with a market economy? *The International Journal of Inclusive Democracy*, 3: 1, January. Available on http://www.inclusivedemocracy.org/journal/vol3/vol3_no1_Takis_degrowth.htm [Accessed 21 September 2017].

Gerst, M. D., Raskin, P. D. and Rockström, J. (2013). Contours of a resilient global future. *Sustainability*, 6(1): 123–135.

Gillespie, D. F. and Danso, K. (Eds.) (2010). *Disaster concepts and issues.* Alexandria, VA: CSWE Press.

Gray, M., Coates, J. and Hetherington, Y. (2013). *Environmental social work.* London: Routledge.

IASSW (International Association of Schools of Social Work) (2010). *Policy Document on Disaster Intervention* for Consideration by IASSW Board, Jan 2010.

Sustainability, Climate Change, Disaster Intervention Committee. https://www.iassw-aiets.org/sustainability-climate-change-disaster-intervention-committee/ [Accessed 16 October 2017].

IOM (2016). *Global migration trends 2015 factsheet.* Available on www.iom.int/news/iom-releases-global-migration-trends-2015-factsheet [Accessed 19 July 2017].

IOM (2017). *UN migration agency appeals for USD 60 million to aid victims of East Africa's worst drought in decades.* Available on www.iom.int/news/un-migration-agency-appeals-usd-60-million-aid-victims-east-africas-worst-drought-decades [Accessed 19 July 2017].

IPCC (Intergovernmental Panel on Climate Change) (2014). *Climate change 2014. Synthesis report. Summary for policymakers.* Available on https://www.ipcc.ch/pdf/assessment-report/ar5/syr/AR5_SYR_FINAL_SPM.pdf [Accessed 1 October 2017].

Joseph, J. (2013). Resilience as embedded neoliberalism. *Resilience*, 1(1): 38–52.

Kemp, S. P. (2011). Recentring environment in social work practice. *British Journal of Social Work*, 41(6): 1198–1210.

Kennedy, E. (2016). *Unpublished manuscript.* Presented 31 March 2016, School of Social Work, Lund University.

Klein, N. (2007). *The shock doctrine.* Toronto: Alfred A. Knopf.

Manyena, B. (2011). Disaster resilience, *Local Environment*, 16(5): 417–424.

Manyena, B. (2016). After Sendai. *International Journal of Disaster Risk Science*, 7: 41–53.

Munich, R. (2015). *2014 Natural catastrophe year in review.* Available on www.iii.org/sites/default/files/docs/pdf/munichre-010715.pdf [Accessed 5 May 2017].

Pyles, L. (2007). Community organizing for post-disaster social development. *International Social Work*, 50(3): 321–333.

Quarantelli, E. L. (1997). Ten criteria for evaluating the management of community disasters. *Disasters*, 21(1): 39–56.

Rowlands, A. (2013). Disaster recovery management in Australia and the contribution of social work. *Journal of Social Work in Disability and Rehabilitation*, 12(1–2): 19–38.

Seravalli, A. (2014). *Making commons.* Malmö: Malmö University. Doctoral Thesis.

Soliman, H. H. and Rogge, M. E. (2002). Ethical considerations in disaster services: A social work perspective. *Electronic Journal of Social Work*, 1(1): 1–23.

Sparf, J. (2016). Kunskap och övningar för resiliens. In U. Baez and P. Becker (Eds.). *Katastrofriskreducering.* Lund: Studentlitteratur.

UNDP (2016). Overview. *Human Development Report 2016.* Available on http://hdr.undp.org/sites/default/files/HDR2016_EN_Overview_Web.pdf [Accessed 19 July 2017].

UNISDR (2009). *Terminology on disaster risk reduction.* Available on www.unisdr.org/we/inform/terminology [Accessed 5 November 2017].

UNISDR (2015a). *Social workers are keyplayers i disaster risk reduction.* European Association of Schools of Social Work, 30 June. Available on www.unisdr.org/archive/45008 [Accessed 5 November 2017].

UNISDR (2015b). *The Sendai framework for disaster risk reduction 2015–2030.* Available on www.unisdr.org/files/43291 [Accessed 5 November 2017]. www.preventionweb.net/files/43291_sendaiframeworkfordrren.pdf [Accessed 5 May 2017].

UNISDR (2016). *Poverty and death: Disaster mortality 1996–2015.* Centre for Research on the Epidemiology of Disaster (CRED). www.unisdr.org/files/50589_creddisastermortalityallfinalpdf.pdf [Accessed 19 July 2017].

World Commission on Environment and Development (1987). *Report of the world commission on environment and development.* Available on www.un-documents.net/our-common-future.pdf [Accessed 5 May 2017].

World Economic Forum (2017). *The Global Risks Report 2017.* 12th Edition. Geneva: World Economic Forum. Available on http://www3.weforum.org/docs/GRR17_Report_web.pdf. [Accessed 16 October 2017].

Zakour, M. J. and Gillespie, D. F. (2013). *Community disaster vulnerability practice.* New York: Springer.

44
Greening social work education in Aotearoa/New Zealand

Lynsey M. Ellis, Ksenija Napan and Kieran O'Donoghue

Introduction

Temperature and sea level rises, extreme weather events, food and water insecurity and loss of biodiversity are gaining notoriety in popular and social media, with the evidence of their presence all around us. Associated impacts can be seen not only in the physical worlds with droughts, rising seas, wild weather and extreme temperatures, but also in the social and economic world. Secondary impacts (Butler and Harley, 2010) on food and water security and human health (Adlong and Dietsch, 2014; McMichael, 2013; Franchini and Mannucci, 2015; Friel, 2010) will affect not only governments, corporate profits and the economy but also job security for communities across the world. The changing climate will bring with it both risks and opportunities. It seems that the threat of disaster as a consequence of climate change offers an opportunity to develop a socially just, culturally respectful and sustainable world with indigenous wisdom paving the way. According to Teixeira and Krings:

> The communities most affected by environmental injustices are often the same communities where social workers are entrenched in service provision at the individual, family, and community level.
>
> *(2015: 1)*

People with limited financial resources are often victims of discrimination, inequity and potentially most vulnerable to the impacts of an unsustainable world. These groups often have established relationships with both statutory and non-government agencies and particularly social workers (Drolet and Sampson, 2014; Gray and Coates, 2015; Grise-Owens, Miller, and Owens, 2014). They will also be further disadvantaged by the impacts of climate change (Lawler, 2011; New Zealand College of Public Health Medicine, 2013). Paradoxically, some of these groups have incredible resilience and resourcefulness demonstrated in a range of creative solutions, movements and communities across the globe that offer alternative approaches to living outside of the mainstream (Tigger-Ross et al., 2015). Social work, being the only profession with social justice embedded in its definition needs to creatively offer support in building resilience and adaptation to impacts of climate change and globalisation (Appleby et al., 2015).

This chapter presents a simple yet relevant approach of introducing a *Sustainable Social Work* workshop to social work programmes and as professional development opportunities offered for practicing social workers in Aotearoa/New Zealand. The workshop introduces current knowledge related to climate change and sustainability focusing on its relevance to social and community work while preparing social workers for action in being part of the solution to the environmental challenges. Aiming at increasing awareness on the issues and relevance of impacts of climate change to social work while supporting students through their own journey of acceptance, by harnessing the skills they already have, building resilience in communities and understanding how this work aligns not only with ethics of social work but also social and environmental justice.

Social justice and green social work

In order to be able to think globally and act locally, social workers need to understand the risks and relevance that climate change has to their clients (and themselves) and develop strategies to address these through policy development and effective community and social work practices (Dominelli, 2014; Hoffand and Polack, 1993; Lombard, 2015). There is a clear connection between social and environmental justice (Nesmith and Smyth, 2015; The Earth Charter Initiative, 2009). As social workers are fundamentally concerned with social justice, the extension of the well-known practice of understanding the person within their context can be extended to encompass not only social but also environmental justice (Besthorn, 1997; Weick, 1981; Zapf, 2009).

Environmental justice emerged from the US in the early 1980s in response to environmental destruction and concern that 'toxic facilities were disproportionately located in low-income communities of colour' (Philip and Reisch, 2015: 476). It emerged due to concern with the quality of the environment in which people live and the effect it was and is having on local people's well-being. Social justice can essentially be explained as a concern with the equality of opportunity for people to fulfil their potential (Friesen, 2007). This concept fits well and can include not only social opportunity but also environmental opportunities available to people. Green social work (Dominelli, 2012) has argued that environmental justice now comprises an essential component of social justice.

The person-in-environment perspective has been traditionally only concerned with the environment from the perspective of how it functions to service the social needs of human beings. It does not take into consideration more fundamental rights of the planet and all of its inhabitants, as does green social work. Social work scholars are arguing that to be truly socially just we need to take on a broader and deeper ecological perspective (Besthorn and Canda, 2002; Besthorn, 2014; Coates, 2003; Dominelli, 2012) by being concerned with the well-being of all flora and fauna on the planet and their rights to live well and safe from destruction and abuse. This idea was developed by scientist James Lovelock and his Gaia theory (Lovelock, 2006), in which he acknowledged that humans are part of and not adjunct to the planet and its ecology, acknowledging that Earth is a living ecosystem. Similar ideas are the foundation to many indigenous beliefs (Roberts et al., 1995). Of particular relevance to the Aotearoa/New Zealand context is the role of holistic thinking in Māori culture, which will be discussed later in the chapter.

From a macro-ecological practice perspective, it can be argued that all who live on the planet (both human and non-human) have a right to co-exist and flourish. However, the responsibility for this destruction lies squarely at the feet of humans (IPCC, 2007). Humans are thus obliged to take action. 'Green social work' (Dominelli, 2012) combines these two perspectives:

social workers' macro-practice and ecological thinking – to take action in a local space while acknowledging the integrated interaction between the global and the local. Well-educated social workers have the ability to use their skills in advocacy, influence on policy and challenge power dynamics to support those being affected by environmental degradation and injustices. The ability of social workers to bring people together across disciplines, cultures and geographical locations are important features in green social work practice (Dominelli, 2012). Community development as an essential aspect of social work will have its merited place in promotion of a sustainable 'globalised' world.

Aotearoa/New Zealand social work education

Aotearoa/New Zealand prides itself on being a bicultural country founded on Te Tiriti o Waitangi/The Treaty of Waitangi a document that promises partnership and sovereignty to both Māori and non-Māori. In this country, the primary competence of becoming a social worker includes being able to practise social work with Māori (Social Work Registration Board, 2014). This requires the understanding and appreciation of a worldview based on the values summarised in Table 44.1.

Table 44.1 Māori values of significance to social work

Value	Description (as Māori language is a contextual language this side of the table only gives the general idea about the meaning of the term; true meaning is dependent of the context in which it is used)
Whanaungtanga	A sense of belonging, reciprocal relationships
Manakitanga	It is a measurement of people's ability to extend aroha (love in its widest sense), hospitality, generosity, welcoming
Kotahitanga	Oneness, unity, solidarity, collective action
Rangatiratanga	Self-governance, chieftainship, right to exercise authority, ownership, leadership
Mohiotanga	Sharing of information, knowledge, knowing, understanding, comprehension, intelligence, awareness, insight, perception
Maramatanga	Understanding, enlightenment, insight, understanding, light, meaning, significance, brainwave
Tuakana/Teina	Older/younger relationships reciprocity: older looking out for younger and younger looking out for older
Kaitiakitanga	Guardianship, stewardship, trusteeship, protection of natural resources
Whakapapa	Genealogy in a widest possible sense that extends blood lineage Connections, to be in contact
Wairuatanga	Spiritual well-being
Tikanga	Correct procedure, custom, habit, lore, method, manner, rule, way – the customary system of values and practices that have developed over time and are deeply embedded in the social context
Hakari	Celebration
Atuatanga	Paying respect to divinity Respecting diversity of beliefs
Mauri	Life principle, vital essence, special nature, a material symbol of a life principle, source of emotions – the essential quality and vitality of a being or entity. Also used for a physical object, individual, ecosystem or social group in which this essence is located

The Māori worldview is deeply connected to sustainability and assumes people as guardians who are responsible to their ancestors and descendants, and must protect and live in harmony with nature (Kawharu, 2000). There are plenty of examples around earth stewardship and the practice of kaitiakitanga interwoven in Aotearoa/New Zealand's indigenous history (Harmsworth, 2002). Unfortunately, despite this rich bicultural heritage, Non-Māori New Zealand social work has not been quick to answer the call to action made by environmental and climate scientists. The connections between social work sustainability and climate change have not been adequately addressed in social work education in Aotearoa/New Zealand.

In response to the growing environmental concerns facing this and future generations. The School of Social Work at Massey University supported the development of a workshop addressing the relevance of sustainability and climate change looking at the risks and the opportunities the current environmental predicament brings. Concepts of sustainability, environmental justice and climate change were introduced into the field education training in 2013 and are increasingly offering fieldwork placements in community development settings to widen the skills and understanding of the importance of community in addressing issues related to climate change to encourage sustainable practice in social work. The aim is to provoke and engage to educate and enlighten students and social work practitioners by developing knowledge, attitudes and skills that will mobilise them into action. Following a comprehensive overview of the risks and opportunities felt by the impacts of climate change and the contribution social work can make, the workshop was developed for the teaching curriculum in the field education programme and later extended into a PhD action research project.

A place in the curriculum

We have chosen to add in sustainability and climate change into the field education curriculum under the learning goal of social justice due to the parallels with environmental justice. This introduction was led by the first author having an interest in environmental social work, which from the literature, seems to be common way of introducing environmental issues into the social work curriculum (Mary, 2008; Nesmith and Smyth, 2015). The structure of the teaching prior to placement encourages students to start developing their own practice which is informed by a range of perspectives, theories including ecological systems, radical, strengths-based, green social work and a range of postmodern and indigenous models.

Green social work is taught in the field education programme when preparing students for placement in the final years of BSW and MASW programmes within the context of the wider social work curriculum, where other core social work knowledge, values and skills have previously been covered. Studies of the environment can be interpreted as an area of 'macro-practice' in social work (Reisch, 2016).

Workshop development, content and the process of continuous improvement

The workshop has been running as part of the field education programme since 2013. To date, 15 workshops have been delivered to 293 students 31 were social work practitioners in the field as delivered as professional development opportunity. As part of a PhD research project a further six workshops with 66 participants was also delivered totalling 359 participants (at time of writing). The workshop was developed via an action research process using transformative learning theory to inform and improve the design using Mezirow's journey of transformation (Mezirow, 1997, 2003). Participants are taken on a three-hour experiential journey, starting with the facts including distressing information about the precarious future of humanity, though a process of discussion and activities leading them to solutions and finally action (Harre, 2012).

Workshop content

The three-hour workshop is in two sections. The first section starts by introducing the science and facts around the issue of climate change and the current and predicted impacts on the physical environment and human well-being. This is interspersed with exercises to give participants time to talk, reflect and draw conclusions for their personal and professional life. The aim of this section of the workshop is to encourage participants to see the connections between the environment and human activity (especially their own activity) and understand that the science around anthropogenic climate change is now clear. This section concludes with a video clip that brings intended learning points together.

After a break, the second section looks at sustainable solutions with the aim of giving participants hope and tools to take action. The definition of sustainability is discussed and participants get involved in an exercise focusing on a basic life cycle assessment (Strachan, 2008) to help them bring items and resources they use in everyday life into the context of carbon emissions. Current literature is presented to support the importance of environmental justice and social work, drawing links with social justice goals and those of the third generation rights in the international definition of social work jointly agreed by the International Association of Schools of Social Work (IASSW) and International Federation of Social Workers (IFSW) (IFSW, 2014). These issues are discussed further in the context of the Global Agenda for Social Work which was originally scoped by IASSW and IFSW, but is now held jointly owned by IASSW, IFSW and ICSW (International Council on Social Welfare) (IFSW, 2012). Some examples from practice in Aotearoa/New Zealand and overseas are offered as showcasing a range of ways how green social work can be put into practice.

The workshop concludes by inviting the participants to draw a picture of their sustainable future followed by a *Traffic Light Exercise* where they as asked to circle in green, orange and red around the things they think are:

- easy to do (green);
- possible, but will require some effort (orange); and
- possible, but will require a lot of work or transformation on many levels (red).

This concluding exercise was chosen for several reasons. It includes:

- drawing which utilises a creative part of the brain;
- allows the participants to have creative, solution-focused conversations with peers around their sustainable future;
- allows them to see the future in a positive way;
- allows them to see where they may be able to take action; and
- is the final part of the session, so they can leave with short- and long-term action plans.

The feedback from this exercise is very positive with participants reporting leaving with a feeling of hope and inspired to take action.

Workshop evaluations

Evaluations were conducted after each workshop and used to inform the design and changes for the following workshop which is the part of the action–reflection approach to the workshop development. One of the observations over this time has been the acceptance of climate change as a reality by participants. Back in 2013, students were still debating about whether climate change was real, many thinking that impacts would not be evident this century. Since the Intergovernmental Panel on Climate Change (IPCC) Assessment Reports Four and Five were released, the findings indicate that these issues are able to be resolved (IPCC, 2007, 2014b). Social and popular media appear to have taken on board that climate change impacts are real and that these are gradually becoming more widely understood. Therefore, the workshop no longer lists climate change impacts but participants are asked to chart impacts (in groups) according to their understanding of it locally. While not always exact, this engages participants better and builds on filling the gaps in knowledge in order to undertake an informed action. It seems that students are getting this information through social media as environmental issues in their social work education have not been explicitly discussed until they participate in this workshop.

As the debate has now moved towards how the impacts will be felt, students are understandably concerned with much of the current evidence suggesting that their generation will bear the brunt of climate change impacts. They are especially interested in consequences for Aotearoa/New Zealand as well has having an interest in global perspectives. Their views are expressed in Table 44.2.

A major theme in the early feedback was that participants wanted to know what to do with the information they had learnt, what could they do to make a difference to the environmental crisis? How would it apply in actual social work practice? As the workshop has been continuously developed over years on the basis of feedback and rapid changes in the environment, the focus has shifted from information sharing to social action relevant to social and community work considering current circumstances.

The sustainability check as a tool for practice

Social work has a range of fields of practice and therefore it would not be useful to prescribe particular interventions for each context. It is not the role of social work to prescribe interventions for clients and communities but to highlight issues by asking questions and inviting people to find solutions for themselves. This approach lies at the heart of green social work (Dominelli, 2012). Transformative learning theory suggests that if the client/service user (or in this case workshop participant) comes up with their own solutions, they are more likely to be successful

Table 44.2 Participants' evaluation data

Evaluation data:	N	%
Participants felt workshop content was relevant to social work	198	84.3
Participants said they intended to change their behaviour as a result of attending the workshop	214	91.1
Participants said they would like to hear more about climate change and sustainability	183	77.9
Participants said they would like to learn more about how climate change and sustainability is applied in practice	147	62.6
Total participants in student workshops 2013 to 2016 = 235		

(Taylor, 1998). The same style of intervention can be used here with the social work role being to facilitate transformative reflection into action.

The sustainability check was developed from a need to have a tool that can be used across all areas of practice that would invite participants to ask questions about their own practice. A simple exercise in the workshop taken from Strachan (2008) teaches participants about their connection to environmental sustainability using a basic life cycle assessment (Dresner, 2008). The exercise (used in the workshop) asked participants (in small groups) to take any item and ask the following questions:

1   What is it made of?
2   Where has it come from?
3   Who made it?
4   What need does it fulfil?
5   Is it necessary?
6   What will happen to it in the future? (Strachan, 2008: 2)

This encourages the participants to reflect on the sustainability of the resources they are using, how they are connected to carbon emissions, themselves and the earth. As Strachan claims:

> This approach enables learners to discover an understanding of systems thinking for themselves and this can be reinforced if they are given the opportunity to apply that understanding to a context with which they are familiar. In so doing they can become more at ease with the inter-connected nature of the world and less overwhelmed with its complexity.
> (2008: 2)

Workshop participants are encouraged to use the *sustainability check* as a tool in their social work practice in the same way they use the code of ethics, anti-oppressive or bicultural practice, as a filter when making practice decisions (Aotearoa New Zealand Association of Social Workers, 2013). By using the sustainability check within their practice participants assess how sustainable they are being and are encouraged to be more mindful about the resources they are choosing to use, this does not relate to objects only, but to processes and interventions as well.

This exercise can modify questions to address social work processes instead of just products, engendering critical reflection and encouraging meaningful actions. These questions are:

1   What is the core purpose of this intervention?
2   Where has it come from and is it culturally appropriate?
3   Who created it?
4   What need does if fulfil?
5   Is it necessary?
6   What will happen to my clients/service users, their families and communities if we follow through with it?

This simple, yet deep exercise can also enable social workers to critically reflect on unsustainable assessment processes, endless form filling, adoption of tools imported but not contextualised within a local context and lack of action to address causes of poverty and physical and mental health within the community. It can also promote the use of current research and indigenous wisdom to address chronic community problems instead of resorting to short-term 'band aid' interventions.

How to awaken the sense for social and environmental justice in social work students

From the years of teaching green social work, we have learnt that the impacts of climate change are issues of concern for many social workers. Its relevance to the context of social work practice, however, is something new. For educators wanting to teach environmental social work, the reflections and learning from our experience so far would be, to allow plenty of time for discussion during teaching. Once given the opportunity to reflect on the practicalities of climate change, particularly the health social and economic impacts, the relevance to the social world and the clients of social work, becomes apparent.

The intention of the workshops is to educate and evoke awareness of environmental justice enabling participants to take action. For this to happen, some form of transformation has to take place therefore, transformational learning theory was used to design and inform the workshop process. Mezirow's 10 stages of transformation (Cranton, 2006) were used to chart people's transformation at all the stages, concluding with what Mezirow (1991) describes a 'perspective transformation' (Mezirow, 1991: 145), where new learning leads to a change in perspective through critical reflection. The transformation happens in the reflection undertaken by the participants themselves. As with all transformative learning, once the person makes the connections for themselves, they are more likely to be compelled to take action. In this case, participants develop the connection between the use of resources, the current political system, their place in a consumer society and their power to have an impact by the choices they make. This may mobilise them to transform the way they live within their community and move towards more liveable, more engaging and more proactive participants. Simply informing them of this does not have the same impact on their willingness to take action.

Contrary to perceptions, teachers do not need to know lots of climate science to teach this subject. To know that climate change is anthropogenic (and have data to justify it) is enough in our experience. Social workers have not been too interested in the scientific details, there is plenty available online if people want further reading on the topic (Hansen et al., 2008; IPCC, 2014a). There is now also an array of social work literature on the subject so a few articles including: Zapf (2009), Dominelli (2012, 2014), Peeters (2012), Jeffery (2014), Gray and Coates (2015), Teixeira and Krings (2015) and many more can be found in the references to this chapter. It seems that critical reflexivity (so essential for social work practice) is a most important skill needed. Once the initial concepts and connections have been made between climate, use of resources, and physical, social, health and economic impacts, and when participants realise that they have the agency to make a meaningful contribution to create resilient and sustainable communities, it is more likely that they will spring into action.

The literature supports an integrated rather than a 'bolt on' approach as identified by green social work (Dominelli, 2012) and others (Mann, 2011; Boetto and Bell, 2015; Gray and Coates, 2015), and thus can be a critique of this style of bespoke teaching. However, given that we are only in the developing awareness stage, the 'bolt on' approach seemed to be a good place to start. Integration will become the long-term aim of teaching sustainability and green social work throughout the curriculum content.

Questions and future developments

Main questions that have arisen while developing this curriculum innovation have been:

- How to integrate indigenous knowledge without exploiting the indigenous community?
- How to create a sustainable world within an intrinsically unsustainable neoliberal system which owes its existence on widening the gap between rich and poor people?

- Is it ethical to educate students to be agents of social change when the majority of them end up in jobs where they are asked and required to be agents of social control?
- How can disempowered communities contribute to the creation of a more sustainable and just world when they are struggling for mere survival?
- How to educate communities to grow their own food especially in neighbourhoods where this is perceived as another sign of poverty where fast food and packaged food are considered a symbol of wealth?
- How to redevelop trust when trust has been broken, when social workers have been perceived as an extended arm of an unsustainable and oppressive system?

The work at Massey University School of Social Work continues with a deeper look into the value of green social work education. The author team are supporting an in-depth action research PhD study, critically evaluating what has been done and attempting to find out how social workers can develop tools and strategies to realise social and environmental justice within the neoliberal context and contribute to the development of an environmentally just system. Indigenous knowledge and the power of the oppressed can be allies in building a respectful and appreciative world where social and community workers truly support individuals, groups and communities to realise their full potential. It is our hope that by analysing in-depth evaluations of workshops, conducting interviews with interested social workers and capturing transformations that happen during the process will help us highlight both the risks and opportunities for the future social work generations in Aotearoa/New Zealand and beyond.

References

Adlong, W. and Dietsch, E. (2014). Environmental education and the health professions: framing climate change as a health issue. *Environmental Education Research*, 1–23. http://doi.org/10.1080/13504622.2014.930727

Anthony, J. M. (2013). Globalization, climate change, and human health. *The New England Journal of Medicine*, 368: 1335–1343. Retrieved from www.nejm.org/doi/full/10.1056/NEJMra1109341

Aotearoa New Zealand Association of Social Workers. (2013). *The code of ethics of ANZASW*.

Appleby, K., Bell, K. and Boetto, H. (2015). Climate change adaptation: Community action, disadvantaged groups and practice implications for social work. *Australian Social Work*, 1–14. http://doi.org/10.1080/0312407X.2015.1088558

Besthorn, F. (1997). *Reconceptualizing social work's "person in environment" perspective: Explorations in radical social work thought*. University of Kansas. Available on http://search.proquest.com.ezproxy.massey.ac.nz/docview/304345578?accountid=14574

Besthorn, F. and Canda, E. (2002). Revisioning environment: Deep ecology for education and teaching in social work. *Journal of Teaching in Social Work*, 22(1/2): 79–101.

Besthorn, F. H. (2014). Ecopsychology, meet ecosocialwork: What you might not know – a brief overview and reflective comment. *Ecopsychology*, 6(4): 199–206. http://doi.org/10.1089/eco.2014.0024

Boetto, H. and Bell, K. (2015). Environmental sustainability in social work education: An online initiative to encourage global citizenship. *International Social Work*, 58(3): 448–462. http://doi.org/10.1177/0020872815570073

Butler, C. D. and Harley, D. (2010). Primary, secondary and tertiary effects of eco-climatic change: The medical response. *Postgraduate Medical Journal*, 86(1014): 230–234. http://doi.org/10.1136/pgmj.2009.082727

Coates, J. (2003). *Ecology and social work: Towards a new paradigm* (1st ed.). Halifax: Fernwood.

Cranton, P. (2006). *Understanding and promoting transformative learning: A guide for educators of adults*. Available on www.amazon.com/Understanding-Promoting-Transformative-Learning-Educators/dp/0787976687 [Accessed 17 February 2016].

Dominelli. (2012). *Green social work: From environmental crises to environmental justice*. Cambridge: Polity Press.

Dominelli, L. (2014). Promoting environmental justice through green social work practice: A key challenge for practitioners and educators. *International Social Work*, 57(4): 338–345. http://doi.org/10.1177/0020872814524968

Dresner, S. (2008). *The principles of sustainability*, 2nd ed. London: Earthscan. Available on https://books.google.co.nz/books/about/The_Principles_of_Sustainability.html?id=SE2QisFYYkgCandpgis=1

Drolet, J. L. and Sampson, T. (2014). Addressing climate change from a social development approach: Small cities and rural communities' adaptation and response to climate change in British Columbia, Canada. *International Social Work*, 1–13. http://doi.org/10.1177/0020872814539984

Franchini, M. and Mannucci, P. M. (2015). Impact on human health of climate changes. *European Journal of Internal Medicine*, 26(1): 1–5. http://doi.org/10.1016/j.ejim.2014.12.008

Friel, S. (2010). Climate change, food insecurity and chronic diseases: sustainable and healthy policy opportunities for Australia. *New South Wales Public Health Bulletin*, 21(5–6): 129–133. http://doi.org/10.1071/NB10019

Friesen, M. (2007). Perceptions of social justice in New Zealand. In R. Porter (Ed.), *Pursuing social justice in New Zealand* (1st ed., pp. 143–158) Auckland: Maxim Institute.

Gray, M. and Coates, J. (2015). Changing gears: Shifting to an environmental perspective in social work education. *Social Work Education*, 34(5): 1–11. http://doi.org/10.1080/02615479.2015.1065807

Grise-Owens, E., Miller, J. J. and Owens, L. W. (2014). Responding to global shifts: Meta-practice as a relevant social work practice paradigm. *Journal of Teaching in Social Work*, 34(1): 46–59. http://doi.org/10.1080/08841233.2013.866614

Hansen, J., Sato, M., Kharecha, P., Beerling, D., Masson-delmotte, V., Pagani, M., Raymo, M., Royer, D. L. and Zachos, J. C. (2008). Target Atmospheric CO_2: Where Should Humanity Aim? Pleistocene Epoch. *The Open Atmosheric Science Journal*, (2): 217–231.

Harmsworth, G. (2002). *Indigenous concepts, values and knowledge for sustainable development: New Zealand case studies*. Presentation at the 7th Joint Conference, April 22–24. Available on www.landcareresearch.co.nz/publications/researchpubs/harmsworth_indigenous_concepts.pdf

Hennessy, K., Fitzharris, B., Bates, B.C., Harvey, N., Howden, S.M., Hughes, L., Salinger, J. and Warrick, R. (2007). *Australia and New Zealand. Climate Change 2007: Impacts, Adaptation and Vulnerability*. Contribution of Working Group II to the Fourth Assessment Report of the Intergovernmental Panel on Climate Change involving M.L. Parry, O.F. Canziani, J.P. Palutikof, P.J. van der Linden and C.E. Hanson (Eds.) Cambridge: Cambridge University Press, pp. 507-540.

Harre, N. (2012). *Psychology for a better world: Strategies to inspire sustainability*. Auckland: Auckland University.

Hoffand, M. D. and Polack, R. (1993). Social dimensions of the environmental crisis: Challenges for social work. *Social Work*, 38(2): 204–211.

IFSW (International Federation of Social Workers) (2012). *The Global Agenda: For Social Work and Social Development: Commitment to Action* (for International Association of Schools of Social Work (IASSW), International Council of Social Welfare (ICSW) and International Association of Social Workers). Available online at: http://www.globalsocialagenda.org [Accessed 5 November 2017].

IFSW (2014). *Global definition of social work*. http://ifsw.org/get-involved/global-definition-of-social-work/ [Accessed 26 January 2016].

IPCC (Intergovernmental Panel on Climate Change) (2014). *Working Group II Fact Sheet Climate Change 2014: Impacts, Adaptation, and Vulnerability*. Retrieved August 20, 2014, from http://ipcc-wg2.gov/AR5/images/uploads/IPCC_WG2AR5_FactSheet.pdf [Accessed 5 November 2017].

IPCC (Intergovernmental Panel on Climate Change) (2014). Summary for policymakers. In: *Climate Change 2014: Impacts, Adaptation, and Vulnerability*. Part A: Global and Sectoral Aspects. Contribution of Working Group II to the Fifth Assessment Report of the Intergovernmental Panel on Climate Change [Field, C.B., V.R. Barros, D.J. Dokken, K.J. Mach, M.D. Mastrandrea, T.E. Bilir, M. Chatterjee, K.L. Ebi, Y.O. Estrada, R.C. Genova, B. Girma, E.S. Kissel, A.N. Levy, S. MacCracken, P.R. Mastrandrea and L.L. White (Eds.)]. Cambridge: Cambridge University Press, pp. 1–32.

Jeffery, D. (2014). Environmentalism in social work: What shall we teach? *Affilia*, 29(4), 492–498. http://doi.org/10.1177/0886109914533697

Kawharu, M. (2000). Kaitiakitanga: A Maori anthropological perspective of the Maori socio-environmental ethic of resource management. *The Journal of the Polynesian Society*, 109(4): 349–370. Retrieved from www.jstor.org/stable/20706951?seq=1#page_scan_tab_contents

Lawler, J. (Unicef). (2011). *Children's vulnerability to climate change and disaster impacts in East Asia and the Pacific*. Available on www.unicef.org/media/files/Climate_Change_Regional_Report_14_Nov_final.pdf [Accessed 5 November 2017].

Lombard, A. (2015). Global agenda for social work and social development: A pathway towards sustainable social work. *Maatskaplike Werk*, 50(2).

Lovelock, J. (2006). *The revenge of Gaia. Earth's climate crisis and the fate of humanity*. New York: Basic Books.

Mann, S. (2011). *The Green graduate: Educating every student as a sustainable practitioner*. Wellington, NZ: NZCER Press.

Mary, N. (2008). *Social work in a sustainable world*. Chicago: Lyceum Books.

Mezirow, J. (1991). *Transformative dimensions of adult learning*. Wiley. Available on https://books.google.com/books?id=4xmfAAAAMAAJandpgis=1 [Accessed 5 November 2017].

Mezirow, J. (1997). Transformative learning: Theory to practice. *Fostering Critical Reflection in Adulthood*, 48(3): 214–216. http://doi.org/10.1002/ace.7401

Mezirow, J. (2003). Transformative learning as discourse. *Journal of Transformative Education*, 1(1): 58–63. http://doi.org/10.1177/1541344603252172

Nesmith, A. and Smyth, N. (2015). Environmental justice and social work education: Social workers' professional perspectives. *Social Work Education*, August: 1–18. http://doi.org/10.1080/02615479.2015.1063600

New Zealand College of Public Health Medicine. (2013). *Climate Change*.

Peeters, J. (2012). Sustainable development: A mission for social work? *Journal of Social Intervention: Theory and Practice*, 21(2): 5–22.

Philip, D. and Reisch, M. (2015). Rethinking social work's interpretation of 'Environmental Justice': From local to global. *Social Work Education*, 34(5): 471–483. http://doi.org/10.1080/02615479.2015.1063602

Reisch, M. (2016). Why macro practice matters introduction: The changing environment of social work practice. *Journal of Social Work Education*, 523: 258–268. http://doi.org/10.1080/10437797.2016.1174652

Roberts, M., Norman, W., Minhinnick, N., Wihongi, D. and Kirkwood, C. (1995). Kaitiakitanga: Maori perspectives on conservation. *Pacific Conservation Biology*. Available on www.scopus.com/inward/record.url?eid=2-s2.0-0029500512andpartnerID=tZOtx3y1

Social Work Registation Board. (2014). *Core competence standards – social workers registration board*. Available on www.swrb.govt.nz/competence-assessment/core-competence-standards [Accessed 21 October 2015].

Strachan, G. (2008). Systems thinking: The ability to recognize and analyse the inter-connections within and between systems. In *The handbook of sustainability literacy: Multimedia version* (1st ed., pp. 1–4). Totnes, UK. http://doi.org/10.1109/TNSRE.2008.929253

Taylor, E. (1998). Transformative learning theory – an overview. In *The Theory and Practice of Transformative Learning A Critical Review Information Series No. 374* (pp. 5–20). Washington, DC.: ERIC Clearinghouse on Adult, Career, and Vocational Education Center on Education and Training for Employment College of Education The Ohio State University 1900 Kenny Road Columbus, Ohio 43210–1090. Available on www.calpro-online.org/eric/docs/taylor/taylor_02.pdf [Accessed 5 November 2017].

Teixeira, S. and Krings, A. (2015). Sustainable social work: An environmental justice framework for social work education. *Social Work Education*, August: 1–15. http://doi.org/10.1080/02615479.2015.1063601

The Earth Charter Initiative (2009). *A guide for using the Earth Charter in Education* (No. 0). Available on http://www.unesco.org/education/tlsf/mods/theme_a/img/02_earthcharter.pdf [Accessed 5 November 2017].

Tigger-Ross, C., Brooks, K., Papadopoulou, L., Orr, P., Sadauskis, R., Coke, A. and Walker, G. (2015). *Community resilience to climate change: an evidence review*. York. Available on www.researchgate.net/profile/Neil_Simcock/publication/301765645_Community_resilience_to_climate_change_an_evidence_review/links/5726593308aef9c00b88f7f8.pdf [Accessed 5 November 2017].

Weick, A. (1981). Reframing the person-in-environment perspective. *Social Work*, 26(2): 140–143.

Zapf, M. (2009). Social work and the environment: Understanding people and place. *Critical Social Work*, 11(October), 30–46. Available on http://books.google.com/books?hl=enandlr=andid=LuF71mNltJEC andoi=fndandpg=PP1anddq=Social+Work+and+the+Environment+:+Understanding+People+and+Placeandots=85ws-UGBIuandsig=T9r_lud7AdHcIMGWaZIsxwRJVLo [Accessed 5 November 2017].

45
Greening Australian social work practice and education

Sharlene Nipperess and Jennifer Boddy

Introduction

Australia's environment is unique and diverse. It is renowned for its extraordinary wildlife and spectacular landscapes. But Australia's environment is also at great risk. Mining, logging, land clearing and the impacts of climate change threaten habitats and all that live within these environments. Australian social workers have long considered environmental issues in their practice and within social work education. However, it is only relatively recently that a commitment to environmental justice has begun to influence mainstream social work.

This chapter will provide an overview of Australian social work's responses to environmental issues in social work education and practice. It begins with an analysis of the environmental context in which social work is practised in Australia. It then explores the key themes that Australian social work practitioners and academics have focused on including practice in relation to climate change-induced disasters, place-based green social work, the relationship between gender and environmental issues, the role of eco-social transitions, eco-spiritual perspectives, ecological living in social work practice and education, and social work education and the environment. The chapter concludes with a number of recommendations for Australian social work to further embrace green social work practice and education.

Background

Australia, the sixth largest country in the world measured by total area, is diverse in climate, geology, flora and fauna. Its habitats include the tropics of northern Australia, alpine heaths of central Victoria and New South Wales, semi-arid and desert habitats of central Australia and rich marine environments around its coastline. It is one of the oldest, driest, flattest continents in the world and because of its relative geographic isolation, a high proportion of Australia's flora and fauna is unique. Consequently, there are numerous and well-known United Nations Educational, Scientific and Cultural Organisation (UNESCO) World Heritage listed sites including the Great Barrier Reef, the Tasmanian Wilderness and Kakadu National Park (UNESCO, 2016). Despite the incredible biodiversity of Australia, many of these World Heritage Sites and other significant areas of Australia are at risk. Mining, land clearing for large-scale agricultural development and logging are destroying many of these natural habitats (The Wilderness Society, 2016) and climate change continues to have a significant and deleterious effect on the environment and all that live within in it.

Climate change is the most serious environmental threat to Australia. Indeed the most significant environmental event of 2016 was caused by climate change. After two of the hottest years on record in 2015 and 2016, the Great Barrier Reef experienced its worst bleaching event with researchers finding that two-thirds of the northern corals have died (Hughes et al., 2016). This bleaching could not have occurred without climate change and increases in water temperature caused by global warming (King et al., 2016). Extreme weather has always occurred in Australia – cyclones, droughts, bushfires, floods, but climate change has been shown to make these extreme weather events more frequent and more severe (Hope et al., 2016). In the last 10 years, Australia has experienced a number of sudden and catastrophic weather events that have destroyed lives, homes, crops and habitats including: the 2009 Black Saturday bushfires that killed 173 people and damaged over 2000 homes; numerous Category 5 tropical cyclones; widespread damaging floods; and heat waves. Drought, which is less sudden, but no less catastrophic, continues to have a significant impact on the Australian environment, and the wildlife and people living within affected areas.

Social workers in Australia have long been interested in the relationship between the natural environment and social work (e.g. Bull, 1976; Penton, 1993; Ife, 1995; Lane, 1997; McKinnon, 2001; Alston and Kent, 2004), though arguably it has been marginal in social work practice and education until relatively recently. The Australian literature on environmental social work has increased exponentially in the last 10 years, and especially since 2012, with the development of a significant body of literature that explores environmental social work generally (e.g. McKinnon, 2001, 2008, 2012, 2013; Molyneux, 2010; Boetto, 2016a, 2016b; Bowles, Boetto et al., 2016; Alston, 2017; Ramsay and Boddy, 2017a). There is also a large body of Australian literature focused on specific themes including practice in relation to climate change-induced disasters, place-based green social work, the relationship between gender and environmental issues, the importance of eco-social transitions, eco-spirituality, ecological living, and social work education and the environment. We will discuss each of these themes in detail, although this body of Australian literature has not developed in isolation. It has developed alongside and in collaboration with the significant scholarship on social work and the environment in the international context (e.g. Dominelli, 2011, 2012, 2013; Alston and Besthorn, 2012; Gray and Coates, 2012, 2016).

Practice in relation to climate change-induced disasters

Australian social workers have considered the practice implications of climate change-induced disasters for a number of years. Margaret Alston has been a pioneer in this work and has drawn particular attention to the impacts of slow-onset climate changes on rural communities (Alston and Kent, 2004, 2008; Alston, 2006; 2007; 2010a; 2010b; 2012; 2013). Slow-onset disasters include droughts and climate change, which can last for several years.

Australia is particularly vulnerable to droughts. Historical climate records show that Australia has experienced droughts regularly but the worst recorded drought was the recent Millennium Drought, where well below normal rainfall was recorded for several years from 2001 to 2009 (Trewin, 2013). The Millennium Drought affected all Australians as water storages were reduced and there were severe water restrictions experienced across Australia. Cities and towns responded by introducing new and innovative measures to save water. However, it was the rural areas, and particularly the Murray-Darling River Catchment Area that were particularly badly affected because significantly reduced or even no rainfall over subsequent years had a severe impact on crops, livestock and peoples' livelihoods. Entire families and communities found themselves in perilous financial situations with crop after crop failing due to lack of rain.

After such a dry period it is unsurprising that the countryside is particularly vulnerable to bushfires. In the last year of the Millennium Drought, the state of Victoria experienced the Black Saturday bushfires, which killed 173 people, destroyed over 2000 homes and hectares of forests and untold wildlife. Although bushfires have always been part of the Australian landscape, with some species of plants requiring fire for their seeds to germinate, research has shown that bushfires have increased in frequency by 40 per cent in the last five years (Dutta, 2016). Droughts are often broken by flooding rains and over the past 10 years, Australia has experienced a number of damaging floods including the Queensland floods in 2011 which killed 37 people and destroyed vast swathes of the environment causing millions of dollars in property damage. In the last 10 years, five Category 5 cyclones have lashed Australia's coast, again causing millions of dollars of property damage and significantly impacting on the natural environment.

Much of the Australian literature on environmental social work has explored the impacts of these disasters on people and communities affected, and the implications of this for social work practice and social work education. Australian researchers have explored the impact of drought on rural communities (Alston and Kent, 2004; Alston, 2006; Alston, 2007; Stehlik, 2013), bushfires (Alston et al., 2016; Hickson and Lehmann, 2014), floods (Shevaller and Westoby, 2014), and climate change and disaster social work generally (Alston, 2010a, 2013, 2017; Appleby et al., 2017; Hetherington and Boddy, 2013). The literature identifies three phases following a catastrophic disaster: the immediate crisis period, the medium-term recovery stage and long-term social work responses (Dominelli, 2012; Alston, 2013; Alston, Hazeleger and Hargreaves, 2016). However, social work practice in climate disasters of slow onset such as drought looks somewhat different to social work practice following catastrophic events. Stehlik (2013: 138) argues that 'what is unique and unusual about drought in Australia, and the social work response, is that it is *not* a named "disaster" and is, therefore, *not* dealt with under emergency management framework' (emphasis in original). This is in stark contrast with the way catastrophic events are managed. In an emergency, Australian governments are very quick to respond and this includes ensuring that social workers are available to work with people affected by the disaster in the immediate crisis period, through to long-term recovery. The nature of the crisis is, therefore, somewhat different.

Climate change–induced disasters are not the same as other environmental disasters such as earthquakes and tsunamis, which have been experienced in the Pacific region and have caused such devastation. However, in relation to climate change, Alston argues:

> that social workers have the capacity, experience and skills to build new knowledge of people and place and to bring to global forums their understanding of the social consequences of climate and environmental challenges in different locations and circumstances.
>
> *(2017: 102)*

It is clear that as climate change makes the likelihood of such disasters occurring more frequent, social work is in a good place to act both locally and globally to work towards a more socially and environmentally just future.

Place-based green social work

The concept of place is increasingly being understood as a key concept for social work and is particularly relevant for environmental social work. While social work has arguably always understood the importance of the connection between people and communities, it has been slow to understand the connection between people and their physical environment, although highlighted in earlier literature unlinked to environmental social work, such as Dominelli (2002). Alston et al. (2016: 159) note the 'importance of the physical environment in which people live, as being equally significant to a person's understanding of self'. When the physical environment is lost, such as in bushfires and floods, there are significant implications for a person's sense of self and well-being.

In relation to the particular places where social work is practised, social work in Australia has long grappled with the particular challenges faced by people living in rural, regional and remote parts of Australia (see Maidment and Bay, 2012). Australia has a relatively small population of 24 million and although it has one of the lowest population densities in the world, given that most of the population lives around the coast predominantly in the southeast corner, it is also one of the most urbanised (see Australian Government, 2015). Nevertheless, there is a substantial population that live in rural, regional and remote areas of the country and these areas are particularly vulnerable to disasters. Perhaps due to this, much of the environmental social work literature originated from social workers practicing and researching in rural, regional and remote areas of Australia. This has focused largely on the impact of drought (Alston and Kent, 2004; Alston, 2006; Alston, 2007; Stehlik, 2013) as discussed in the section on practice in relation to climate change-induced disasters. Also, the Australian literature explores how rural communities respond to broader issues of climate change and sustainability, advocating that these issues should be incorporated into social work practice (Alston, 2012; Alston et al., 2016; Mason, 2011; see also Dominelli, 2012, 2013 from the United Kingdom) and social work education (Dominelli, 2012; Crawford et al., 2015).

The relationship between gender and environmental issues

Like others (Dominelli, 2012), Australian authors have highlighted how climate change and environmental degradation affects those most marginalised (Hetherington and Boddy, 2013), and they have focused extensively on the gendered impacts of climate change. Alston (2000) for example has consistently argued that because women in Australia and globally are less likely than men to own land and other resources, it is more difficult for them to recover from environmental disasters. Further, they are less able to be involved in decision-making and thus have greater difficulty expressing their needs (Alston, 2000, 2013). Women working on family farms are particularly disadvantaged. They often work on the farm as well as away from the farm to generate income for the family. They engage extensively in household and non-paid caring work, they often manage the household finances, and will undertake volunteer work within the community to support others (Alston, 2000, 2006, 2007, 2010b; Alston and Kent, 2004). The strain placed on families as a result of climate change has resulted in increased incidences of domestic violence, business decline, increases in the costs of living and increased workloads (Boetto and McKinnon, 2013). It is also compounded by cultural norms that encourage women to prioritise the emotional and physical health and well-being of family members and the community at their own expense, and has led many women to become the 'guardian of men's health' (Alston, 2010b: 66).

Such issues not only adversely affect women, but also men. Alston (2012; Alston and Kent, 2008) and Pease (2014) argue that dominant hegemonic masculinity prevents positive adaptation to climate change and disasters. It damages men's sense of self-worth when they are no longer the primary income earner; invites men to remain stoic and prevents them from seeking help; and focuses on individualism resulting in many men blaming themselves for their struggles rather than seeing them in the wider context of climate change (Alston, 2012). While men's privileged positioning has traditionally allowed them to preserve their power and influence, in times of stress resulting from climate change, it is grossly unhealthy and leaves many men isolated (Alston, 2012; Pease, 2014) with poor physical and mental health and much higher rates of suicide than those living in urban areas (Alston, 2012).

Australian social workers, among others (e.g. Dominelli, 2012; 2013), have proposed a number of approaches to address gender inequalities and unhelpful gender role norms. These approaches have tended to be grounded in a commitment to gender equality, social justice, human rights, democracy and empowerment of oppressed peoples. For instance, Alston argues for an ecological and ecofeminist approach so that social workers can build knowledge of environmental and climate crisis work (Alston, 2013; see also Lane, 1997). She also advocates a rights-based framework that is sensitive to gender (Alston, 2010b; see also Ife, 2012). Pease (2014) stipulates that knowledge of feminist theory and critical masculinity studies is essential for disaster management and prevention, while Boetto and McKinnon (2013) suggest that collective action within a community-based approach would be useful. Irrespective of the theoretical framework, there is consensus in Australian literature (Alston, 2013; Pease, 2014) and beyond (Dominelli, 2012) that gender analysis must be central to social work practice and policy development.

Eco-social transition, ecological living and eco-spiritual perspectives

Traditionally Australian social workers have been influenced by eco-social approaches such as Besthorn (2000, 2002) and more recently by green social work and its commitment to environmental justice (see Dominelli, 2012). Australian social workers have sought to promote eco-social transition and sustainability through community development initiatives and advocacy. Lane (1997) points out that social workers have been involved in local area planning and community action over pollution and development. This is more likely to be successful when social workers understand that community development is a long-term process and not an emergency response to disasters (Shevallar and Westoby, 2014). Further, it must be supported by colleagues and managers (McKinnon, 2013), where practitioners have good supervision and peer support networks, undertake comprehensive training, recognise the power of discourses, and challenge therapeutic language (Shevallar and Westoby, 2014).

Recently, the focus of Australian social work academics has been on the importance of holistic practice and the benefits of connecting with nature (Boetto, 2016a; Heinsch, 2012; Ryan, 2013). Heinsch (2012) encourages social workers to engage in a nature-based approach to practice. She suggests that social workers should include connection with the natural environment and with pets in their assessments, adopt nature-based activities in practice, introduce nature in everyday surroundings, provide opportunities for clients to view and interact with nature while visiting services, and promote environmental awareness, among other things. Boetto (2016a) extends the work in this field by encouraging social workers to adopt a distinct philosophical base that includes a holistic worldview, recognises the interdependence of all life, seeks global citizenship within the profession, values cultural diversity, and adopts values related to sustainability and de-growth. She also suggests that as a profession social work must reconceptualise what well-being means so that it includes sustainable and relational attributes (Boetto and Bowles, 2017). Finally Ryan (2013) has written extensively about social work, animals and the natural world.

Australian social workers, among others such as Coates (Coates et al., 2006), Hart (2002), Bruyere (2001), and Dominelli (2010) have also begun to explore how Indigenous perspectives can be embedded in environmental social work, particularly in relation to eco-spiritual perspectives. Aboriginal and Torres Strait Islander peoples have lived in Australia for many thousands of years. During this time, Australia's First Nation peoples have cared for this land using ecological knowledge passed on from generation to generation. Gray and Coates (2013) argue that Indigenous eco-spiritual approaches can provide useful insights, as well as innovations, that can be used to address climate change and other global challenges (see also Coates et al., 2006). They also note that 'the eco-spiritual perspective recognises human interests are inextricably bound with planetary well-being' (Gray and Coates, 2013: 356).

In recognition of the importance of promoting sustainability, eco-social transition, and connection with the natural environment, there has been a very recent focus in Australian social work literature on drawing from and collaborating with diverse knowledge bases and initiatives (Bay, 2013; Boddy and Ramsay, 2017; Green and McDermott, 2010; Boetto, 2016a). Bay (2013), for instance, examined a transition town movement within a rural Australian town, while Boddy and Ramsay (2017) explored the practice of permaculture in a metropolitan region of Australia. Both found that the skills and values adopted in these initiatives aligned well with social work. For example, skills and knowledge in community work, group work, leadership and relationship building were important in both studies. Participants from both studies valued social justice and living sustainably. As part of adopting diverse approaches to eco-social transition and sustainability it is important for social workers to draw knowledge from both the natural and social sciences (Green and McDermott, 2010) and, as advocated in a green social work approach (Dominelli, 2012), incorporate art, music, poetry, videos, animations and other means to communicate and create knowledge.

Social work education and the environment

Twenty-nine Australian universities offer qualifying social work degrees. There has traditionally been limited engagement with environmental content in these degrees (Jones, 2010; Boetto and Bell, 2015; Harris and Boddy, 2017). However, Australian authors have long argued for the incorporation of ecological literacy (Jones, 2006, 2008, 2010, 2013; McKinnon, 2013; Gray and Coates, 2015). Fortunately, positive change is occurring. Crawford et al. (2015: 586) have noted, 'this topic is making a transition from being on the margins of social work to becoming mainstream' with just over half of all Australian schools of social work appearing to offer units that include some – albeit sometimes cursory, information on the natural environment and sustainability (Harris and Boddy, 2017).

There are an increasing number of examples in Australian literature on units and activities that incorporate principles and practices of green social work (Jones, 2010; Pack, 2014; Boetto and Bell, 2015; Ramsay and Boddy, 2017b), a trend evident internationally (Besthorn, 2003; Dominelli, 2012; Melekis and Woodhouse, 2015). Although diverse in delivery, these focused on transformative learning, using critical reflection and experiential learning processes. Ramsay and Boddy (2017b), for example, describe an experiential learning approach to assist students to understand their relationship with the non-human world and the natural environment through exercises that inform students about the natural environment, responsibilities to protect it, and the impacts on people and others if we fail to do so. Jones (2008, 2010) describes a compulsory on-campus unit that brings together social and environmental concerns within a framework of community development. Such an approach is consistent with green social work that advocates for working at both a community and individual level (Dominelli, 2012). As part of this, Jones describes two trigger activities where students assess their carbon footprint and are invited to walk around their community to reflect on their understanding of the interconnectedness of humans with their environments. Boetto and Bell (2015) describe a six-week voluntary online course for social work students, which is focused on promoting global citizenship, covering content related to: global warming, global citizenship; gender, social justice and human rights; carbon footprints; glocalisation; and ecological social work. Consistent with an embedded and transformative approach, Pack (2014) describes an intensive course that uses an extended simulation of a disaster to prepare students for practice in emergency and disaster situations. Other Australian authors, similar to Dominelli (2012), have identified the importance of greening not only social work education within the university setting, but also within field education (Crawford et al., 2015; Boetto et al., 2015) through the development of new learning goals related to the environment and sustainability (Crawford et al., 2015) and practice settings focused on food relief (Boetto et al., 2015).

Some authors have commented on particular theories and content areas that could be covered in social work education (Jones, 2013; Pease, 2014; Gray and Coates, 2015). Green social work advocates for the integration of scientific expertise with local, Indigenous knowledges. In Australia, Gray and Coates (2015) argue that greater links could be made with macro-practice and the role of social workers in conducting community assessments which draw on local and 'traditional knowledge' of the environment, a practice advocated by green community workers. Units which focus on social policy, human rights, social justice, community development and practice, and global and international social work could all be easily adapted to include environmental content in Australian universities (Gray and Coates, 2015; Nipperess, 2016; Harris and Boddy, 2017). As part of this, it is important that students develop eco-literacy, informed by spirituality, Indigenous perspectives, and critical theory (Jones, 2013; Pease, 2014).

Futures

Australian literature related to the environment has typically focused on disaster relief (Alston, 2013; Shevaller and Westoby, 2014; Alston, et al., 2016; Appleby et al., 2017), rural and drought affected regions of Australia (Alston and Kent, 2004; Alston, 2006; Alston, 2007; Stehlik, 2013), and social work education to promote eco-literacy (Jones, 2010; Pack, 2014; Boetto and Bell, 2015). More recently there has been a focus on eco-social transitions and ecological living (Boetto, 2016a; Boetto, 2016b; Boddy and Ramsay, 2017). This literature has made an important contribution to greening social work practice and education.

In order to advance green social work further, we would argue that Australian social workers must:

1. Use an intersectional approach to examine the effects of climate change not only on women, but also on diverse and marginalised populations experiencing multi-faceted disadvantage.
2. Transform the social work curriculum, with both embedded content and discrete courses on ecology, environmental justice, and the natural environment, to ensure that green social work is central to all Australian social work degrees.
3. Adopt a structural analysis of social and economic systems that are adversely affecting people and their environments.
4. Advocate to policymakers and politicians calling for urgent action to mitigate further climate changes.
5. Learn from Indigenous eco-spiritual perspectives and recognise the interdependence of human health and well-being and that of the natural environment.
6. Undertake research to evaluate green social work practice initiatives.
7. Examine how green social work can be adopted within metropolitan contexts where much of the Australian population is located.

We endorse the argument that it is imperative that green social work becomes mainstream social work practice, where social and environmental justice are valued and ecosystems are at the centre of practice (Dominelli, 2012).

Conclusion

Australia has seen an increasing number of extreme and ongoing weather events particularly since the start of the millennium, including bushfires, flooding, and seemingly unending extreme drought. Many Australian social workers have drawn attention to the impacts of these events on marginalised and disadvantaged people, with a particular focus on women and people living in rural and remote areas. As part of this, Australian social workers have highlighted the interdependence of human health and the natural environment. Numerous initiatives and articles have emerged in the last five to 10 years that have described social work practice in Australian rural areas in response to disasters. This literature has also highlighted the importance of eco-social transition and ecological living. Further, a number of examples have emerged of social work education that promotes global citizenship, environmental justice and knowledge of ecosystems. Given the extent of mining, logging and land clearing in Australia, coupled with more numerous and frequent extreme weather events, Australian social workers must do more to advocate for the protection of ecosystems not only through direct practice, but also through activism, research and education. Green social work offers a model and a practice for doing this.

References

Alston, M. and Besthorn, F. (2012). Environment and sustainability. In K. Lyons, T. Hokenstad, M. Pawar, N. Huegler and N. Hall (Eds.), *The SAGE handbook of international social work*. London, UK: SAGE Publications, pp. 56–69.

Alston, M. and Kent, J. (2004). Coping with a crisis: Human services in times of drought. *Rural Society*, 14(3): 214–227.

Alston, M and Kent, J. (2008). The big dry: Exacerbating the link between rural masculinities and poor health outcomes for rural men. *Australian Journal of Sociology*, 44(2): 133–147.

Alston, M. (2000). *Breaking through the grass ceiling: Women, power and leadership in rural Australia*. Churr, Switzerland: Harwood Publishers.

Alston, M. (2006). 'I'd just like to walk out of here': Women's experiences of drought. *Sociologia Ruralis*, 46(2): 154–170.

Alston, M. (2007). 'It's not easy to get help': services to drought affected families. *Australian Social Work*, 60(4): 421–435.

Alston, M. (2010a). *Innovative human services practice: Australia's changing landscape*. South Yarra: Palgrave Macmillan.

Alston, M. (2010b). Gender and climate change in Australia. *Journal of Sociology*, 47(1): 53–70.

Alston, M. (2012). Addressing the effects of climate change on rural communities. In J. Maidment and U. Bay (Eds.), *Social work in rural Australia: Enabling practice*. Crows Nest, NSW: Allen and Unwin, pp. 204–217.

Alston, M. (2013). Social work in the context of climate change and disasters. In M. Connolly and L. Harms (Eds.), *Social work: contexts and practice*, 3rd ed. South Melbourne, VIC: Oxford University Press, pp. 315–26.

Alston, M. (2017). Ecosocial work: Reflections from the global south. In A-L Matthies and K. Närhi (Eds.), *The ecological transition of societies: The contribution of social work and social policy*. Abingdon: Routledge, pp. 91–104.

Alston, M., Hazeleger, T., and Hargreaves, D. (2016). Social work in post-disaster sites. In J. McKinnon and M. Alston (Eds.), *Ecological social work: Towards sustainability*. London: Palgrave Macmillan, pp. 158–74.

Alston, M., Whittenbury, K., and Western, D. (2016). Rural community sustainability and social work practice. In J. McKinnon and M. Alston (Eds.), *Ecological social work: towards sustainability*. London: Palgrave Macmillan, pp. 94–111.

Appleby, K., Bell, K. and Boetto, H. (2017). Climate change adaptation: Community action, disadvantaged groups and practice implications for social work. *Australian Social Work*, 70(1): 78–91.

Australian Government (2015). *State of Australian cities 2014–2015*. Department of Infrastructure and Regional Development. Available on https://infrastructure.gov.au/infrastructure/pab/soac/ [Accessed 26 July 2017].

Bay, U. (2013). Transition town initiatives promoting transformational community change in tackling peak oil and climate change challenges. *Australian Social Work*, 66(2): 171–186.

Besthorn, F. H. (2000). Toward a deep-ecological social work: Its environmental, spiritual and political dimensions. *The Spirituality and Social Work Forum*, 7(2): 2–7.

Besthorn, F. H. (2002). Is it time for a new ecological approach to social work: What is the environment telling us? *The Spirituality and Social Work Forum*, 9(1): 2–5.

Besthorn, F. H. (2003). Radical ecologisms: Insights for educating social workers in ecological activism and social justice. *Critical Social Work*, 4(1). Available on http://www1.uwindsor.ca/criticalsocialwork/

Boddy, J. and Ramsay, S. (2017). Promoting ecosocial transition through permaculture. In A. L. Matthies and K. Närhi (Eds.), *Ecosocial transition of societies: Contribution of social work and social policy*. Surrey: Ashgate, pp. 206–216.

Boetto, H. and Bell, K. (2015). Environmental sustainability in social work education: An online initiative to encourage global citizenship. *International Social Work*, 58(3): 448–462.

Boetto, H. and Bowles, W. (2017). Ecosocial transitions – exploring the wisdom of our elders. In A. L. Matthies and K. Närhi (Eds.), *Ecosocial transition of societies: Contribution of social work and social policy*. Surrey: Ashgate, pp. 190–205.

Boetto, H. and McKinnon, J. (2013). Rural women and climate change: A gender-inclusive perspective. *Australian Social Work*, 66(2): 234–47.

Boetto, H. (2016a). A transformative eco-social model: Challenging modernist assumptions in social work. *British Journal of Social Work*. 47(1): 48–67. doi:10.1093/bjsw/bcw149

Boetto, H. (2016b). Developing ecological social work for micro-level practice. In J. McKinnon and M. Alston (Eds.), *Ecological social work: Towards sustainability* (pp. 59–77). London: Palgrave.

Boetto, H., Inch, J., Lloyd, S. and Barber, N. (2015). Exploring food security in social work field education: Analysis of a food relief program. *Advances in Social Work and Welfare Education*, 17(1): 52–67.

Bowles, W., Boetto, H., Jones, P., and McKinnon, J. (2016). Is social work really greening? Exploring the place of sustainability and environment in social work codes of ethics. *International Social Work*. doi: 10.1177/0020872816651695

Bruyere, G. (2001). First nations approaches to social work. In L. Dominelli, W. Lorenz and H. Soydan (Eds.), *Beyond racial divides*. Aldershot: Ashgate.

Bull, M. (1976). Habitat – home comments on UN (or United Nations). Habitat Forum on Human Settlements, Vancouver, 1976. *Australian Social Work*, 29(40): 33–39.

Coates, J., Gray, M. and Hetherington, T. (2006). An ecospiritual perspective: Finally a place for indigenous approaches. *British Journal of Social Work*, 36(3): 381–399.

Crawford, F., Agustine, S., Earle, L., Kyuyini-Abubakar, A., Luxford, Y. and Babacan, H. (2015). Environmental sustainability and social work: A rural Australia evaluation of incorporating eco-social work in field education. *Social Work Education*, 34(5): 586–599.

Dominelli, L. (2002). *Anti-oppressive social work theory and practice*. London: Palgrave Macmillan.

Dominelli, L. (2010). *Social work in a globalizing world*. Cambridge: Polity.

Dominelli, L. (2011). Climate change: Social workers' roles and contributions to policy debates and interventions. International Journal of Social Welfare, 20(4): 430-438.

Dominelli, L. (2012). *Green social work: From environmental degradation to environmental justice*. Cambridge: Polity Press.

Dominelli, L. (2013). Mind the gap: Built infrastructures, sustainable caring relations and resilient communities in extreme weather events. *Australian Social Work*, 66(2): 204–217. doi:http://dx.doil.org/10.1080/0312407X.2012.708764

Dutta, R. (2016). Fires are increasing in warming world, but a new model could help us predict them', *The Conversation*. Available on https://theconversation.com/fires-are-increasing-in-warming-world-but-a-new-model-could-help-us-predict-them-54466 [Accessed 29 December 2016].

Gray, M. and Coates, J. (2012). Environmental ethics for social work: Social work's responsibility to the non-human world. *International Journal of Social Welfare*, 21(3): 239–247.

Gray, M., and Coates, J. (2013). Changing values and valuing change: toward an ecospiritual perspective in social work. *International Social Work*, 56(3): 356–368. doi:10.1177/0020872812474009

Gray, M. and Coates, J. (2015). Changing gears: Shifting to an environmental perspective in social work education. *Social Work Education*, 34(5): 502–512.

Gray, M. and Coates, J. (2016). Environmental social work as critical, decolonising practice. In B. Pease, S. Goldingay, N. Hosken and S. Nipperess (Eds.), *Doing critical social work: Transformative practices for social justice*. Crows Nest: Allen and Unwin, pp. 271–285.

Green, D. and McDermott, F. (2010). Social work from inside and between complex systems: Perspectives on person-in-environment for today's social work. *The British Journal of Social Work*, 40(8): 2414–2430.

Harris, C. and Boddy, J. (2017). The natural environment in social work education: A content analysis of Australian social work courses. *Australian Social Work*, 70(3): 337–349.

Hart, M. A. (2002). Seeking mino-pimatisiwin (the good life): An aboriginal approach to social work practice. *Native Social Work Journal*, 2(1): 91–112.

Heinsch, M. (2012). Getting down to earth: Finding a place in nature in social work practice by. *International Journal of Social Welfare*, 21(3): 309–318.

Hetherington, T. and Boddy, J. (2013). Ecological work with marginalised populations: time for action on climate change. In M. Gray, J. Coates and T. Hetherington (Eds.), *Environmental social work*. Routledge: Abingdon, pp. 46–61.

Hickson, H. and Lehmann, J. (2014). Exploring social workers' experience of working with bushfire-affected families. *Australian Social Work*, 67(2): 256–273.

Hope, P., King, A., Wang, G., Arbaster, J. and Grose, M. (2016). Climate change played a role in Australia's hottest October and Tasmania's big dry in 2015. *The Conversation*. Available on https://theconversation.com/climate-change-played-a-role-in-australias-hottest-october-and-tasmanias-big-dry-in-2015-70389 [Accessed 29 December 2016].

Hughes, T., Schaffelke, B. and Kerry, J. (2016). How much coral has died in the Great Barrier Reef's worst bleaching event? *The Conversation*. Available on https://theconversation.com/how-much-coral-has-died-in-the-great-barrier-reefs-worst-bleaching-event-69494 [Accessed 29 December 2016].

Ife, J. (1995). *Community development: Creating community alternatives – vision, analysis and practice*. Melbourne: Longman.

Ife, J. (2012). *Human rights and social work: Towards rights-based practice*. Cambridge: Cambridge University Press.

Jones, P. (2006). Considering the environment in social work education: Transformations for eco-social justice. *Australian Journal of Adult Learning*, 46(3): 364–382.

Jones, P. (2008). Expanding the ecological consciousness of social work students: Education for sustainable practice. In: *Proceedings of EDU-COM 2008 International Conference*, pp. 285–292. From Sustainability in Higher Education: Directions for Change, 19–21 November 2008, Khon Kaen, Thailand.

Jones, P. (2010). Responding to the ecological crisis: Transformative pathways for social work education. *Journal of Social Work Education*, 46(1): 67–84.

Jones, P. (2013). Transforming the curriculum: Social work education and ecological consciousness. In M. Gray, J. Coates and T. Hetherington (Eds.), *Environmental social work*. Abingdon: Routledge, pp. 213–230.

King, A., Karoly, D., Black, M., Hoegh-Guidberg, O. and Perkins-Kirkpatrick, S. (2016). Great Barrier Reef bleaching would be almost impossible without climate change. *The Conversation*. Available on https://theconversation.com/great-barrier-reef-bleaching-would-be-almost-impossible-without-climate-change-58408 [Accessed 29 December 2016].

Lane, M. (1997). Community work, social work: Green and postmodern? *British Journal of Social Work*, 27(3): 319–341.

Maidment, J. and Bay, U. (Eds.) (2012). *Social work in rural Australia: Enabling practice*. Crows Nest, NSW: Allen and Unwin.

Mason, R. (2011). Confronting uncertainty: Lessons from rural social work. *Australian Social Work*, 64(3): 377–394.

Melekis K. and Woodhouse V. (2015). Transforming social work curricula: Institutional supports for promoting sustainability. *Social Work Education*, 34(5): 573–585.

McKinnon, J. (2001). Social work, sustainability, and the environment. In M. Alston and J. McKinnon (Eds.), *Social work: Fields of practice*, Oxford University Press, South Melbourne, Vic, pp. 225–236.

McKinnon, J. (2008). Exploring the nexus between social work and the environment. *Australian Social Work*, 61(3): 256–268.

McKinnon, J. (2012). Social work and changing environments. In K. Lyons, T. Hokenstad, M. Pawar, N. Huegler and N. Hall (Eds.), *The SAGE handbook of international social work*, London, UK: SAGE Publications, pp. 265–78.

McKinnon, J. (2013). The environment: a private concern or a professional practice issue for Australian social workers. *Australian Social Work*, 66(2): 156–170.

Molyneux, R. (2010). The practical realities of ecosocial work: a review of the literature. *Critical Social Work*, 11(2): 61–69.

Nipperess, S. (2016). *Human rights and green social work: Implications for social work education*. Paper presented to ANZSWWER Symposium: Advancing our critical edge in social welfare research, education and practice, Townsville, September 29–30.

Pack, M. (2014). Northern exposure: integrating disaster management in a humanitarian and community studies program in the Northern Territory of Australia. *Advances in Social Work and Welfare Education*, 16(2): 73–85.

Pease, B. (2014). Hegemonic masculinity and the gendering of men in disaster management: implications for social work education. *Advances in Social Work and Welfare Education*, 16(2): 60–72.

Penton, K. (1993). Ideology, social work and the Gaian connection. *Australian Social Work*, 46(4): 41–48.

Ramsay, S. and Boddy, J. (2017a). Environmental social work: A concept analysis. *British Journal of Social Work*, 47(1): 68–86.

Ramsay, S. and Boddy, J. (2017b). Greening social work through an experiential learning framework. In M. Rinkel and M. Powers (Eds.), *Promoting community and environmental sustainability: A workbook for global social workers and educators*. Berne, Switzerland: International Federation of Social Workers, pp. 74–88.

Ryan, T. (2013). Social work, animals and the natural world. In M. Gray, J. Coates and T. Hetherington (Eds.), *Environmental social work*. Abingdon: Routledge, pp. 156–171.

Shevaller, L. and Westoby, P. (2014). 'Perhaps?' and 'Depends!' The possible implications of disaster related community development for social work. *Advances in Social Work and Welfare Education*, 16(2): 23–35.

Stehlik, D. (2013). Social work practice with drought-affected families. In M. Gray, J. Coates and T. Hetherington (Eds.), *Environmental social work*. Abingdon: Routledge, pp. 135–155.

The Wilderness Society (TWS) (2016). Protect nature. *TWS*. Available on www.wilderness.org.au/campaigns/protect-nature [Accessed 28 December 2016].

Trewin, B. (2013). Drought conditions return to Australia's eastern states. *The Conversation*, Available on https://theconversation.com/drought-conditions-return-to-australias-eastern-states-21149 [Accessed 29 December 2016].

United Nations Educational, Scientific and Cultural Organisation (UNESCO) (2016). Australia. *UNESCO*. Available on http://whc.unesco.org/en/statesparties/au [Accessed 28 December 2016].

46

Greening social work education

Transforming the curriculum in pursuit of eco–social justice

Peter Jones

Introduction

Despite stubborn resistance from some quarters, the public is beginning to recognise that anthropogenic climate changes pose enormous challenges for humanity and the planet. While climate change is certainly not the only environmental issue facing the earth today, it has emerged as the most urgent and pressing of issues, both overarching and clearly linked with a long list of environmental concerns including deforestation, biodiversity loss, food and water security, pollution and waste. There is now clear evidence of the ways in which anthropogenic climate change is already impacting upon both natural systems and human well-being (IPCC, 2014; CSIRO, 2015; Wahlquist, 2017). It is becoming increasingly obvious that these negative impacts are not being distributed equally, but fall disproportionately on those already in situations of disadvantage (Dominelli, 2012; Wade, 2015; Worland, 2016).

As social work begins the process of expanding its professional worldview to encompass more fully a concern with the natural environment, and recognition that human well-being is fundamentally and inextricably linked with environmental well-being, the role of social work education is brought into focus. It has been argued that the shift required by the profession if it is to truly embrace a green or eco-social paradigm will be dramatic and transformative (Besthorn, 2012; Dominelli, 2012; Peeters, 2012). While such change will require shifts in all aspects of the profession, a fundamental rethinking of the nature and purpose of social work education will be crucial to this transformation.

This chapter discusses the increasingly visible movement to expand social work's connection to the environment and the calls for greater professional engagement in this area. Recent literature exploring this issue within social work education is presented and the role that social work education might play in promoting engagement with environmental issues and in facilitating a wider professional transformation is then discussed before exploring some of the pedagogical approaches and curriculum challenges that should be considered as part of this process. Ideas are then presented outlining what a truly transformed eco-social curriculum might look like.

A note about terminology

A number of authors have noted the challenges of language when attempting to describe a social work approach which is concerned with the natural environment and its relationship to human well-being (see for example, Gray and Coates, 2015; Melekis and Woodhouse, 2015; Boetto, 2016). The terms 'green', 'environmental', 'ecological' and 'eco-social' have all been suggested and all have limitations associated with them. In reflecting upon these limitations, this chapter uses the phrase 'eco-social' to describe an approach to social work which encompasses an understanding of ecology (i.e. recognition of the interconnected nature of all living and non-living elements) and society, and which sees human well-being as inherently and inextricably linked to a healthy and sustainable natural environment, and thus giving it green credentials.

Social work, social work education and the environment

A relatively small, but rapidly growing, body of academic writing addressing issues of social work and the natural environment now exists. A number of authors have usefully reviewed this body of existing literature (McKinnon, 2008; Besthorn, 2012; Narhi and Matthies, 2016), highlighting a consistent call for the profession to expand its concerns beyond a narrow social orientation to include recognition of the importance of the non-human environment, both inherently and in relation to human well-being. Gray et al. (2013) provide a particularly valuable overview of this material, identifying key authors and central themes emerging from the literature. Ramsay and Boddy (2016) also offer an interesting concept analysis of environmental social work, examining published work in this field to identify its attributes and characteristics and to develop a definition of this approach to practice. Given the coverage of this body of work elsewhere, this chapter will not reproduce such a general review here.

However, a number of writers have also advanced the argument that social work education, as a critical component of the wider profession, needs to better integrate the natural environment into its core concerns (Jones, 2010; Dominelli, 2012, 2013, 2014; Gray and Coates, 2015). Hayward et al. (2013) noted that despite research indicating social work students and practitioners were indeed interested in issues of the environment, their actual experience of education and practice still reflected an individualistic or humanistic perspective. This orientation was confirmed by Harris and Boddy (2017: 10) who conducted a content analysis of Australian social work courses and concluded that 'there is an overall lack of engagement in Australian social work education with content related to the natural environment'.

For some authors, the inclusion of 'environmental justice' as a key professional consideration has framed their ideas about revising social work education (Dominelli, 2012; Beltran, Hacker and Begun, 2016). Philip and Reisch (2015), for example, review the environmental justice movement in the United States (US) and argue that integrating a global perspective on environmental justice into social work education would help to expand the profession's currently narrow understanding of 'person-in-environment'. Teixeira and Krings (2015) present a framework designed to guide the integration of environmental justice principles into traditional social work education, bringing together insights from the global standards for social work education and environmental justice perspectives. There is evidence that this greater inclusion of environmental justice concerns in social work education would be welcomed by the profession (Miller and Hayward, 2014). Nesmith and Smyth (2015: 497) surveyed American social workers and found that participants 'believed that addressing environmental injustices was relevant to the profession, that they received inadequate training on it, and that it should be integrated more intentionally into social work education'.

A number of examples have also now been reported of practical attempts to integrate environmental concerns into professional education (e.g. Schmitz, Matyok, James and Sloan, 2013; Dominelli, 2013; Jones, 2014). Drolet et al. (2015), for instance, present an account of the development of a new course on social work and sustainable social development, arising from the authors' recognition of the need to play a role in responding to environmental as well as social and economic crises. Kaiser, Himmelheber, Miller and Hayward (2015) describe using the specific issue of food justice as a lens through which social work students can learn about environmental issues and their relevance. Focusing on this issue allows the authors to make connections with a number of different fields of practice, methods and practice levels throughout the social work programme. In another example, Boetto and Bell (2015) developed an online unit on ecological social work as a way of addressing their concern that social work students had few opportunities to make connections between the profession, the natural environment and global citizenship.

Ways in which greater environmental awareness might be introduced into social work education via field education and service-learning activities has also been explored. Lucas-Darby (2011) included 'greening concepts' in a community practice course with a service-learning component, where students worked with a chosen community to identify an environmental need or concern and develop a plan for addressing it at the community level. Crawford et al. (2015) also describe developing field education curricula to include a focus on environment and sustainability. The impetus for this initiative was their recognition of the significant threat to human well-being posed by climate change and their immediate experience of the impact of drought in their rural location. Boetto et al. (2015: 62) similarly report on an initiative to integrate content on the environment and climate change into a social work programme by providing a field education placement in a local food relief programme and found that for the students involved, the placement expanded their 'perspectives about the complex interplay between climate change, food insecurity and vulnerability'.

This emerging literature on social work education and the integration of environmental content provides useful discussion and examples of the ways in which an expanded ecological orientation might be embedded within the existing structures and concerns of social work education. However, there are calls for a deeper and more profound transformation of social work education itself (Besthorn and Canda, 2002; Dominelli, 2012; Besthorn, 2013; Jones, 2012). Gray and Coates (2015) provide a useful example of this view in their argument for a transformative shift in social work education towards an environmental perspective. Rather than simply looking for opportunities to insert environmental content into the traditional curriculum, Gray and Coates (2015: 507) identify the need for 'a fundamental rethinking of the humanistic values and theories informing social work'. These authors suggest that as well as this values shift, a transformed curriculum would encompass a theoretical framework inclusive of environmental issues, highlight a macro-role for social workers, and link these elements with a critical understanding of policy development and implementation.

The recent literature on social work education and the environment, therefore, leads to a number of important observations. First, there is a clear and growing call for social work education to integrate environmental perspectives into the curriculum. Second, there is evidence that educators are beginning to explore how this might happen in a practical sense, with new courses being developed and embedded in existing programmes and approaches. And finally, there is an argument that while such initiatives are valuable and necessary, a more fundamentally transformative approach is needed – that simply 'adding in' the environment to existing approaches to social work education is unlikely to produce the type of profound change required if the profession is to make a meaningful and effective contribution to moving towards a more sustainable world.

Pathways to change

Given the nature and scale of the environmental crisis, the argument for change in social work education seems very clear. The analysis of Australian social work courses conducted by Harris and Boddy (2017) is, therefore, deeply concerning, indicating that there is very little content relating to the natural environment in such courses (0.43 percent of all social work subjects). The authors note that some of the barriers to the integration of environmental content include the issues of curriculum lag, a lack of mandated environmental content from accrediting bodies and the impacts of neo-liberal ideology on universities in general. Harris and Boddy (2017) argue that in the face of the environmental crisis, social work educators must prioritise rapid curriculum change. However, the question remains as to how such change might be practically implemented, and what the scope of such change should be. Social work struggles with the issue of a 'crowded curriculum' (Jones, 2012; Boetto and Bell, 2015) as new and emerging social issues, practice approaches, theories and demands from the field jostle for space within existing programmes. Simultaneously, the higher education context in many countries is one characterised by the imposition of an increasingly stark neo-liberal, managerialist agenda, leaving educators and practitioners feeling under-resourced and overwhelmed (Lawson et al., 2015; Pease and Nipperess, 2016). In such a context, the prospect of needing to 'add in' another topic may be unappealing to many social work educators.

It has previously been argued (Jones, 2013) that a number of different pathways exist for changing the social work curriculum to reflect better an expanded professional ecological consciousness. The first of these can be referred to as the 'bolt-on' approach, whereby new content is 'bolted-on' to the existing curriculum by adding new units or content to a degree programme. The example provided by Beltran et al. (2016) illustrates this approach. The second option could be referred to as the 'embedding' approach. This pathway involves looking to embed or integrating a new content focus throughout the existing curriculum. In the case of eco-social work this means looking for opportunities within an existing programme and across the curriculum to integrate material on the values, knowledge and skills required for an eco-social approach. Kaiser et al.'s (2015) use of food justice as a lens to connect environmental issues with a wide range of curriculum areas is an example of this approach.

The third approach is the 'transformative' option. Rather than seeking to add the eco-social perspective into the existing curriculum, this approach advocates using the foundation concepts of an eco-social approach as the fundamental basis for social work education. In other words, this approach asks what understandings, knowledge and skills are needed to live sustainably, before exploring how the answers to this question might inform and shape the social work curriculum.

An eco-social foundation for social work education

While all three approaches discussed in the pathways to change section have the potential to improve social work education's engagement with environmental issues, there is a significant philosophical difference between the first two options and the transformative approach. Curriculum design initiatives that seek to 'bolt-on' or 'embed' environmental content in social work programmes assume that the current philosophical foundation of those programmes, and indeed of the profession, is sound and adequate. In other words, they assume that a 'business as usual' approach, with the simple addition of environmental content, will be sufficient in equipping students, and hence the profession, with the knowledge and skills required for addressing climate change and other environmental issues. However, as Coates (2003) and others have argued, the roots of social work as a profession lay in the very values and beliefs of modernity which themselves underpin the causes of the current ecological crisis. The critique of this foundation lies at the heart of Dominelli's (2012) articulation of green social work and underpins her concern to ensure that environmental justice is holistic, and not an 'add-on' but integral to the reconceptualisation of social justice in the profession. In this manner the approach articulated by Dominelli (2012) argues that green social work should be integrated into the curriculum and that doing so creates the potential for the curriculum to be truly transformative.

Similarly, Boetto's (2016) development of a transformative eco-social model for social work makes a compelling argument for fundamental change based on recognition of this problematic philosophical foundation. Boetto (2016: 16) argues that 'the profession's ontological foundations, based on modernist assumptions, are incongruent with an eco-social approach that aims to protect the natural environment'. Therefore, she (2016: 5) advocates for a fundamental shift of social work's current ontological and epistemological assumptions, placing recognition of 'identity as interconnectedness with nature' at the centre of a transformed consideration of professional knowledge, values, ethics and practice methods, as did Dominelli (2012) previously.

Dominelli and Boetto's arguments have direct relevance for the development of a transformed eco-social work education. The holistic, ecological foundation from which such a curriculum might be developed must be seen as beginning with a set of eco-social concepts, from which appropriate values, knowledge and skills can be extrapolated. While there is no clear consensus on what such a core set of concepts might include, a number of good starting points have been identified. Ife (2016), for example, nominates the basic concepts of ecology as guiding principles for an ecological approach. These include holism, sustainability, diversity, equilibrium, and interdependence, again points made by green social workers (Dominelli, 2012). Similarly, Coates (2003) describes a set of five 'integrative guidelines' representing the core aspects of the transformative worldview required if we are to move towards a sustainable future: wisdom in nature, becoming, diversity, relationship in community, and change. Dominelli (2012) drew on indigenous and ecofeminist worldviews and transdisciplinarity to shift the discourses in social work's repertoire. Gray and Coates (2015) suggest that a transformed social work curriculum would be guided by a set of eco-centric environmental values relating to conservation, de-growth, diversity, sustainability, spirituality and restoration. Boetto (2016) draws on eco-feminism and deep ecology as the ontological foundations for a new set of values with a focus on sustainability, including values of de-growth, collectivism, ecological justice and global citizenship.

There will no doubt be discussion and disagreement about what exactly a core set of eco-social concepts and values for a transformed social work education might include or look like. However, the direction in which the profession needs to head is becoming increasingly clear. The movement required is away from a traditional, modernist and anthropocentric orientation towards a set of concepts and values which are grounded in recognition of the interdependent nature of humans' relationship with the environment and oriented towards sustainability. From this transformed foundational consideration, a number of pedagogical approaches might arise to support and inform the development of eco-social work education as well as the actual content that such curricula might include.

Looking forward – towards an eco-social curriculum

With a foundation of eco-social concepts, principles and values, attention can be turned to the pedagogical approaches and content which could be developed and utilised in an eco-social work programme. Such a shift would involve four dimensions: a fundamental shift in core foundations and orientation; the adoption of alternative pedagogical approaches; the addition of new core content; and the expansion of existing approaches and content.

Alternative pedagogies: transformative learning and education for sustainability

Transformative learning theory represents an approach to adult learning which has clear congruencies with social work values and methods (Jones, 2010; Witkin, 2014) and which has proven effective in efforts to expand ecological consciousness (see, for example, Kovan and Dirkx, 2003; D'Amato and Krasney, 2011; Chen and Martin, 2015). Based on an initial theoretical development by Mezirow (1991, 2012), the theory argues that, through processes of socialisation and acculturation, people construct 'meaning perspectives' that act as perceptual filters through which new experiences are mediated. Transformative learning occurs when a new experience leads to critical reflection on the foundations of a person's frame of reference, revealing its inadequacies or limitations. As a consequence of this critical reflection, the person takes action to create a new, more open, inclusive and flexible perspective. A transformative learning approach would argue that people's understanding of humans' relationship with, and place in, the natural world is often limited as a consequence of their socio-cultural context and dominant discourses (anthropocentric, individualised, patriarchal, and so on). By facilitating reflection on these existing frames of reference the potential for transformation is created. An extensive body of literature exists on how such transformative learning can be fostered in the classroom (see, for example, Kasworm and Bowles, 2012; Taylor and Laros, 2014).

A second broad pedagogical approach appropriate for a transformed eco-social work education is 'education for sustainability', or EfS (Bedi and Germein, 2016; Sharma and Monteiro, 2016). Education for sustainability refers to an approach to education that is concerned with what we need to know, across all fields of human knowledge and action, in order to live sustainably. The Australian Research Institute for Environment and Sustainability (ARIES) states that

> Education for Sustainability . . . is an internationally recognised educational approach that moves beyond just imparting knowledge about the environment – educating *about* sustainability – to building people's capacity for transformational change – educating *for* sustainability. It focuses on motivating and engaging people to help create a better future.
> *(ARIES, 2014–2017)*

In this sense, EfS critically explores existing assumptions about the content and delivery of education and the values that underpin it. A number of sources have attempted to articulate the features of an EfS approach, demonstrating the broad scope that it entails (see, for example, Department of the Environment, Water, Heritage and the Arts, 2009). Bedi and Germein (2016: 127) capture a sense of this breadth in noting that through 'embodying transformative, constructivist, and social approaches to learning, EfS aims to develop higher order thinking modes such as reflective, critical, relational, whole-of-systems, or ecological thinking'. The significance and urgency attached to implementing an EfS approach in higher education, as well as the barriers to doing so, have now been well surveyed in the literature (e.g. Gale et al., 2015; Higgins and Thomas, 2016).

New content: environmental education and eco-literacy

A transformed eco-social curriculum would also include some significant new areas of content. In particular, students would be expected to develop deep understandings of the natural environment, the operation of natural systems and humans' place in, and relationship with, the non-human world. This is a significant departure from traditional social work content. However, it is essential in a transformed eco-social approach, laying the foundation for the ontological shift described by Boetto (2016), among others, away from modernist, anthropocentric perspectives and towards recognition of fundamental human interdependence with nature. This content could be introduced and supported using insights and experience from the fields of environmental education and education for eco-literacy. Environmental education (Kopnina, 2015; Bodor, 2016) has been a feature of mainstream education systems in many Western countries for decades. Using a wide range of approaches, it involves equipping students with knowledge of nature and the operation of natural systems (Flowers et al., 2015; Mitchell et al., 2015).

Clearly connected to environmental education, but arguably manifesting a stronger critical analysis, is the approach of eco-literacy (Orr, 1992; Reynolds et al., 2010; Goleman et al., 2012). Recognising the interdependent relationship between humans and the non-human world, and the urgency of the current ecological crisis, eco-literacy advocates argue that a deeper understanding of the environment, and the operation of natural systems and people's place within them, is essential if we are to move towards social and environmental sustainability. It is the loss of such fundamental understanding, or literacies, and the ensuing ecological alienation, which is a major contributing factor to the crisis that we now confront. As with environmental education a wealth of scholarship and practical resources exists in the field of eco-literacy which could be drawn on by social work educators looking to introduce this new content into social work programmes (Turner and Donnelly, 2013; Madden and Dell'Angelo, 2016).

Sustainability itself will also need to be a key aspect of new content in a transformed curriculum. Aspects of sustainability as a concept are almost certainly touched on in many existing social work programmes but would entail a much more focused and specific consideration in a transformed approach. Social work programmes would need to commit to focused engagement with the concept of sustainability itself – the origins and meanings of the concept, how it might be measured and facilitated, and the range of dimensions related to it, including social, economic, cultural and environmental sustainability (see, for example, Robertson, 2014; Blewitt, 2015).

Expanding and revising: integrating eco-social concepts

In addition to the introduction of new content, some expansion and revision of existing curriculum areas would also be required, to reflect the new eco-social foundation. In this aspect of the transformation, opportunities to integrate eco-social content into existing curriculum material and/or to amend existing material to more fully reflect the new value-base, would be explored. In some content areas this expansion will be relatively obvious and straightforward, for example, integrating material on ecological justice into an existing unit examining values and ethics in social work. In other areas, the connections may be less obvious but, nonetheless, important and valuable. Revising a unit on child protection issues to reflect the eco-social value of holism could exemplify this. Content on practice methods, such as community development, may be expanded to include attention to specific issues such as disaster management work. The area of mental health could be expanded to explore the mental health implications of people's relationships with the environment, the biophilia hypothesis – which argues that humans have an inbuilt drive to connect with nature – and environmentally based interventions such as nature therapy. Dominelli (2012), Gray, Coates and Hetherington (2013) and Boetto (2016) all provide examples of environmental issues and related social work practice strategies that serve to highlight areas where existing approaches to education and practice might be expanded, as indicated in Figure 46.1.

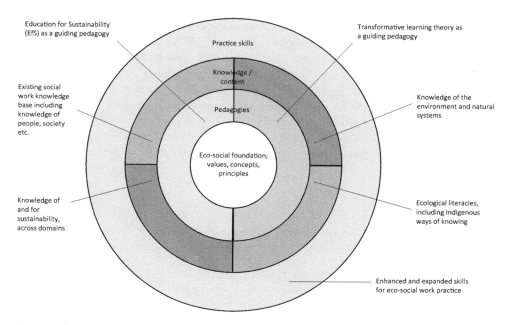

Figure 46.1 A green, eco-social curriculum for social work education

A transformed eco-social approach to social work education would allow much of the existing focus of social work education to be retained. For example, education about specific fields of practice such as disability, mental health, youth, families and children will not be replaced, but rather transformed through the use of a new conceptual lens. The current domains of practice, at micro-, mezzo- and macro-levels will also remain relevant, with new opportunities, strategies and methods appearing at each of these (Dominelli, 2012). The transformation does, however, open up the potential for important new areas of social work practice including around issues such as pollution, toxic waste disposal, food security and climate change (see Gray et al., 2013) as well as giving increased prominence to existing areas such as disaster management and response. Most significantly, shifting the foundational concepts and values for the profession creates the opportunity to look at traditional issues and practices through a new lens, one that is not shackled to old paradigm thinking, but which starts with recognising what will be required to move towards a society characterised by greater sustainability across all dimensions.

Conclusion

The urgency attached to the current ecological crisis, and to the scale and impacts of climate change in particular, has not been matched by change within social work as a profession. While there is a rapidly growing body of literature calling for the profession to expand its traditional person-in-environment perspective better to include consideration of the natural environment, there are fewer signs of this call producing actual changes at the frontlines of practice and education. Curriculum transformation within social work education programmes presents an opportunity to rapidly respond to this crisis in a way that would have significant knock-on effects throughout the profession. Such transformation will of necessity mean moving away from social work's traditional ontological and epistemological foundations and towards a set of core eco-social concepts and values that place humans' relationships with the natural world at their centre. This transformed foundation, supported by appropriate pedagogical approaches, provides a basis for introducing new core content on the environment and sustainability as well as revising and expanding existing content to better reflect an eco-social orientation. Most importantly, a transformed eco-social curriculum will help to equip future social workers with the values, knowledge and skills required to respond effectively to what is emerging as the single biggest threat to human and environmental well-being. Green social workers are working to achieve this objective.

References

Australian Research Institute for Environment and Sustainability (ARIES) (2014–2017). *Education for sustainability*. Available on http://aries.mq.edu.au/about/education_for_sustainability_processes/ [Accessed 23 November 2017].

Beltran, R., Hacker, A. and Begun, S. (2016). Environmental justice is a social justice issue: Incorporating environmental justice into social work practice curricula. *Journal of Social Work Education*, 52(4): 493–502.

Bedi, G. and Germein, S. (2016). Simply good teaching: Supporting transformation and change through education for sustainability. *Australian Journal of Environmental Education*, 32(1): 124–133.

Besthorn, F. (2012). Deep ecology's contributions to social work: A ten-year retrospective. *International Journal of Social Welfare*, 21: 248–259.

Besthorn, F. (2013). Radical equalitarian ecological justice: A social work call to action. In M. Gray, J. Coates, and T. Hetherington (Eds.), *Environmental social work*. Abingdon: Routledge, pp. 31–45.

Besthorn, F. and Canda, E. (2002). Revisioning environment: Deep ecology for education and teaching in social work. *Journal of Teaching in Social Work*, 22: 79–101.

Blewitt, J. (2015). *Understanding sustainable development*. Abingdon: Routledge.

Bodor, S. (2016). Environmental education: Understanding the world around us. *The Geography Teacher*, 13(1): 15–16.

Boetto, H. (2016). A transformative eco-social model: Challenging modernist assumptions in social work. *British Journal of Social Work*. Advance online publication. doi: 10.1093/bjsw/bcw149

Boetto, H. and Bell, K. (2015). Environmental sustainability in social work education: An online initiative to encourage global citizenship. *International Social Work*, 58(3): 448–462.

Boetto, H., Inch, J., Lloyd, S. and Barber, N. (2015). Exploring food security in social work field education: Analysis of a food security relief program. *Advances in Social Work and Welfare Education*, 17(1): 52–66.

Chen, J. and Martin, A. (2015). Role-play simulations as a transformative methodology in environmental education. *Journal of Transformative Education*, 13(1): 85–102.

Coates, J. (2003). *Ecology and social work: Toward a new paradigm*. Halifax: Fernwood Publishing.

Crawford, F., Augustine, S., Earle, L., Kuyini-Abubakar, A., Luxford, Y. and Babacan, H. (2015). Environmental sustainability and social work: A rural Australian evaluation of incorporating eco-social work in field education. *Social Work Education*, 34(5): 586–599.

Commonwealth Scientific and Industrial Research Organisation (CSIRO) (2015). *Climate change in Australia: Projections for Australia's NRM regions*. Canberra: CSIRO.

D'Amato, G. and Krasny, M. (2011). Outdoor adventure education: Applying transformative learning theory to understanding instrumental learning and personal growth in environmental education. *The Journal of Environmental Education*, 42(4): 237–254.

Department of the Environment, Water, Heritage and the Arts (2009). Living sustainably: The Australian government's national action plan for education for sustainability. Canberra: DEWHA.

Dominelli, L. (2012). *Green social work: From environmental crises to environmental justice*. Cambridge: Polity Press.

Dominelli, L. (2013). Social work education for disaster relief work. In M. Gray, J. Coates, and T. Hetherington (Eds.), *Environmental social work*. Abingdon: Routledge, pp. 280–297.

Dominelli, L. (2014). Promoting environmental justice through green social work practice: A key challenge for practitioners and educators. *International Social Work*, 57(4), 338–345.

Drolet, J., Wu, H., Taylor, M. and Dennehy, A. (2015). Social work and sustainable social development: Teaching and learning strategies for 'green social work' curriculum. *Social Work Education*, 34(5): 528–543.

Flowers, A., Carroll, J., Green G. and Larson, L. (2015). Using art to assess environmental education. *Environmental Education Research*, 21(6): 846–864.

Gale, F., Davison, A., Wood, G., Williams, S. and Towle, N. (2015). Four impediments to embedding education for sustainability in higher education. *Australian Journal of Environmental Education*, 31(2): 248–263.

Goleman, D., Bennett, L. and Barlow, Z. (2012). *Eco-literate: How educators are cultivating emotional, social, and ecological intelligence.* San Francisco: Jossey-Bass.

Gray, M. and Coates, J. (2015). Changing gears: Shifting to an environmental perspective in social work education. *Social Work Education*, 34(5): 502–512.

Gray, M., Coates, J. and Hetherington, T. (2013). Introduction: Overview of the last ten years and typology of ESW. In M. Gray, J. Coates, and T. Hetherington (Eds.), *Environmental social work*. Abingdon: Routledge, pp. 1–28.

Harris, C. and Boddy, J. (2017). The natural environment in social work education: A content analysis of Australian social work courses. *Australian social work*. Advance online publication. doi: 10.1080/0312407X.1263352

Hayward, R., Miller, S. and Shaw, T. (2013). Social work education on the environment in contemporary curricula in the USA. In M. Gray, J. Coates, and T. Hetherington (Eds.), *Environmental social work* (pp. 246–259). Abingdon: Routledge.

Higgins, B. and Thomas, I. (2016). Education for sustainability in universities: Challenges and opportunities for change. *Australian Journal of Environmental Education*, 32(1): 91–108.

Ife, J. (2016). *Community development in an uncertain world: Vision analysis and practice*, 2nd ed. Port Melbourne: Cambridge.

Intergovernmental Panel on Climate Change (IPCC) (2014). *Climate change 2014 synthesis report: Summary for policy makers.* Available on www.ipcc.ch/pdf/assessment-report/ar5/syr/AR5_SYR_FINAL_SPM.pdf [Accessed 5 August 2016].

Jones, P. (2010). Responding to the ecological crisis: Transformative pathways for social work education. *Journal of Social Work Education*, 46(1): 67–84.

Jones, P. (2012). Transforming the curriculum: Social work education and ecological consciousness. In M. Gray, J. Coates and T. Hetherington (Eds.), *Environmental social work* (pp. 213–230). Abingdon: Routledge.

Jones, P. (2014). Ecological literacy in social work education: Using a scenario-based approach to bring community spaces into the classroom. In *Proceedings of the XI international transformative learning conference*, pp. 365–370. New York, NY, USA: Teacher's College.

Kaiser, M., Himmelheber, S., Miller, S. and Hayward, A. (2015). Cultivators of change: Food justice in social work education. *Social Work Education*, 34(5): 544–557.

Kasworm, K., and Bowles, T. (2012). Fostering transformative learning in higher education settings. In E. Taylor, P. Cranton, and Associates (Ed.), *The handbook of transformative learning: Theory, research, and practice.* San Francisco, CA: Jossey-Bass, pp. 388–407.

Kopnina, H. (2015). Future scenarios and environmental education. The *Journal of Environmental Education*, 45(4): 217–231.

Kovan, J. and Dirkx, J. (2003). 'Being called awake': The role of transformative learning in the lives of environmental activists. *Adult Education Quarterly*, 53(2): 99–118.

Lawson, S., Sanders, K. and Smith, L. (2015). Commodification of the information profession: A critique of higher education under neoliberalism. *Journal of Librarianship and Communication*, 3(1): eP1182. doi:10.7710/2162–3309.1182

Lucas-Darby, E. (2011). The new color is green: Social work practice and service learning. *Advances in Social Work*, 12(1): 113–125.

Madden, L. and Dell'Angelo, T. (2016). Using photojournals to develop ecoliteracy in a blended environmental science course. *Journal of College Science Teaching*, 46(1): 26–31.

McKinnon, J. (2008). Exploring the nexus between social work and the environment. *Australian Social Work*, 61(3): 268–282.
Melekis, K. and Woodhouse, V. (2015). Transforming social work curricula: Institutional supports for promoting sustainability. *Social Work Education*, 34(5): 573–585.
Mezirow, J. (1991). *Transformative dimensions of adult learning*. San Francisco: Jossey-Bass.
Mezirow, J. (2012). Learning to think like an adult: Core concepts of transformation theory. In E. Taylor and P. Cranton (Eds.), *The handbook of transformative learning: Theory, research and practice* (pp. 73–95). San Francisco, CA: Jossey-Bass.
Miller, S. and Hayward, S. (2014). Social work education's role in addressing people and a planet at risk. *Social Work Education*, 33(3): 280–295.
Mitchell, I., Ling, C., Krusekopf, C. and Kerr, S. (2015). Pathways toward whole community transformation: A case study on the role of school engagement and environmental education. *Environment, Development and Sustainability*, 17(2): 279–298.
Narhi, K. and Matthies, A. (2016). The eco-social approach in social work as a framework for structural social work. *International Social Work*. Advance online publication. doi: 10.11770020872816644663
Nesmith, A. and Smyth, N. (2015). Environmental justice and social work education: Social workers' professional perspectives. *Social Work Education*, 34(5): 484–501.
Orr, D. (1992). *Ecological literacy: Education and the transition to a postmodern world*. Albany: State University of New York Press.
Pease, B. and Nipperess, S. (2016). Doing critical social work in the neoliberal context: Working on the contradictions. In B. Pease, Goldingay, S., Hosken, N. and Nipperess, S. (Eds.), *Doing critical social work: Transformative practices for social justice* (pp. 3–24). Crows Nest, NSW, Australia: Allen and Unwin.
Peeters, J. (2012). The place of social work in sustainable development: Towards eco-social practice. *International Journal of Social Welfare*, 21(1), 105–107.
Philip, D. and Reisch, M. (2015). Rethinking social work's interpretation of 'environmental justice': From local to global. *Social Work Education*, 34(5): 471–483.
Ramsay, S. and Boddy, J. (2016). Environmental social work: A concept analysis. *British Journal of Social Work*. Advance online publication. doi:10.1093/bjsw/bcw078
Reynolds, H., Brondizio, E. and Robinson, J. (2010). *Teaching environmental literacy: Across campus and across the curriculum*. Bloomington: Indiana University Press.
Robertson, M. (2014). *Sustainability: Principles and practice*. Abingdon: Routledge.
Schmitz, C., Matyok, T., James, C. and Sloan, L. (2013). Environmental sustainability: Educating social workers for interdisciplinary practice. In M. Gray, J. Coates, and T. Hetherington (Eds.), *Environmental social work*. Abingdon: Routledge, pp. 260–279.
Sharma, R. and Monteiro, S. (2016). Creating social change: The ultimate goal of education for sustainability. *International Journal of Social Science and Humanity*, 6(1): 72–76.
Taylor, E. and Laros, A. (2014). Researching the practice of fostering transformative learning: Lessons learned from the study of andragogy. *Journal of Transformative Education*, 12(2): 134–147.
Teixeira, S. and Krings, A. (2015). Sustainable social work: An environmental justice framework for social work education. *Social Work Education*, 34(5), 513–527.
Turner, R. and Donnelly, R. (2013). Case studies in critical eco-literacy: A curriculum for analyzing the social foundations of environmental problems. *Educational Studies*, 49(5): 387–408.
Wade, K. (2015). *Climate change and the global economy: Regional effects*. Available on www.schroders.com/nl/nl/institutioneel/nieuws-narktinformatie/economie/climate-change-and-the-global-economy-regional-effects/ [Accessed 5 November 2016].
Wahlquist, C. (2017). Climate change: 90 percent of rural Australians say their lives are already affected. *The Guardian*, 16 January. Available on www.theguardian.com/environment/2017/jan/16/climate-change-90-of-rural-australians-say-their-lives-are-already-affected [Accessed 20 January 2017].
Witkin, S. (2014). Change and deeper change: Transforming social work education. *Journal of Social Work Education*, 50(4): 587–598.
Worland, J. (2016). How climate change unfairly burdens poorer countries. *Time*, 5 February. Available on http://time.com/4209510/climate-change-poor-countries/ [Accessed 10 February 2016].

Conclusions
Towards a green society and mainstreaming green social work in social work education and practice

Lena Dominelli, Bala Raju Nikku and Hok Bun Ku

Introduction

Green social work has transformative potential. It can encourage community residents to change their behaviour and develop more resilient and sustainable pathways to sustainability. Working together with those inhabiting communities assists in the transformation of social work theory, education and practice. In this chapter we consider how green social work can be mainstreamed so that all social work students and practitioners can become aware of environmental issues and environmental justice and incorporate it into their daily work. Such action can contribute to the development of a green society.

Mainstreaming green social work in social work education and practice

The increasing complexities of global environmental crises in terms of numbers affected, frequency and impact on people's physical, social, cultural and political environments have challenged professional social work practice (Dominelli, 2012). However, environmental issues languish largely on the periphery of social work discourses, practice and education (Coates, 2005). Much social work literature on disasters ignores the physical environment (Jones, 2010), focusing instead on what social workers do or should do; for example, a number of manuals published through the United Nations (UN), humanitarian agencies like the Red Cross, the Red Crescent Societies or American Federal Emergency Management Agency (FEMA). The question of why social work remains in a disadvantaged position with regards to addressing these needs warrants further reflection and scholarly scrutiny. Given this context, the development of green social work scholarship is not only timely, but crucial.

Dominelli (2011) suggests five key processes of practice areas that social workers can undertake in carrying out their tasks during disaster interventions. These are relevant across the disaster cycle including preventive and mitigation activities during the pre-disaster period, recovery and reconstruction stages. These activities include the following:

1. *Consciousness-raising* to highlight the interdependencies between people and planet Earth by discussing scenarios that might mitigate the hazards causing concern and promote an equitable and sustainable world.
2. *Advocating and lobbying* for equal access to green technologies and an equitable sharing of Earth's resources locally, nationally and internationally.
3. *Mobilising communities* to devise strategies for forms of development that promote solidarity and sustainability while caring for other people, and the Earth's flora, fauna and mineral resources.
4. *Dialoguing with residents, policymakers, and the media* to transform policies at the local, national and international levels into more life-enhancing ones that the planet can sustain. Developing curricula that cover disasters ranging from poverty to climate change and promote interventions that build individual and community resilience, capabilities and sustainability among people and the biosphere (Dominelli, 2011: 437).
5. *Challenging* social work educators to equip students with the knowledge and skills to become effective practitioners while also providing opportunities for students to transform abstract concepts into practical actions (Dominelli, 2013; Drolet et al. 2015; Jones, 2013: Steinemann, 2003).

To nurture social work students, green social work concepts, theory and practice examples should be integrated into the core modules of social work programmes. Once integration into the curriculum takes place, social work students can be assisted to respond to the interrelationships between human beings and the natural environment (Dominelli, 2013; Boetto and Bell, 2015) and communicate best practices with their peers and exchange materials with schools of social work across the globe. Social work educators and practitioners have an important role to play in developing and sustaining environmental justice in a way that respects the inherent dignity and worth of all persons (Dominelli, 2014).

Social work curriculum development, like any other, is a political process. The social work curriculum may be a prescriptive statement, specified by the professional association or a government body in a particular country. These rarely cover education for risk/disaster and emergency management, a situation evident in most curricula across the world. Nonetheless, as the contributions to Section 11 have indicated, schools of social work that do cover these topics have found that much of the core content and mainstream skills can be directly used when working in emergency response sites.

However, practitioners' professional education has few elements that prepare them for specific disaster management roles and activities (Cooper and Briggs, 2014). Social workers all over the globe should play important roles beyond those they already play disaster rescue, recovery and preparation for future disasters. They should become involved in strategic thinking and policy-making tables. Hence, further advancements in green social work scholarship and research are warranted. Developing green social work is a humble effort in filling the gap that exists between these aspirations and contemporary realities. Courses that address disaster social work in the classroom and e-learning mode are currently rare. There are general courses on disaster and management, usually not run by social work educators, available through various institutions and agencies involved in disaster management. These are variable and often exist outside universities and their quality management procedures and structures. More use should be made by humanitarian workers of social work qualifications that are subject to regulatory bodies and scrutiny.

Social workers have historically contributed to disaster management in four major and overlapping areas. These are: working with individuals and families, accessing resources, managing complex interagency co-ordination, and working with communities (Zakour 1996; Quarantelli, 1985). There is a need for further efforts to integrate green social work in the social work curricula in schools of social work globally. The International Association of Schools of Social Work (IASSW) and its regional organisations can make crucial contributions to these efforts, but it requires additional organisational capacity to do so.

Green social work has successfully introduced neglected issues into environmental debates and increased understanding of its centrality to social work practice, as indicated by Dominelli and Ku (2017). Green social work (Dominelli 2012) has been significant in introducing new issues into professional social work's debates about the environment. These have included: the mainstreaming of environmental considerations so that the physical environment becomes firmly embedded within ecological perspectives and professional preoccupations; a widening of the theoretical and practice base to ensure that social and environmental justice are considered integral to any environmental (in its widest sense) involvement by social workers; highlighting the need to think of innovative approaches to socio-economic development to meet human needs without destroying physical environments; and making disaster interventions core elements in the social work repertoire of knowledge, skills, capacity-building and curriculum. The curriculum should cover green social work's commitment to: holistic views of the world; a structural analysis of human and social development; integrating social and environmental justice; challenging neoliberal forms of social development; and highlighting interdependencies among peoples and between peoples and their physical and social environments (Dominelli, 2012; Dominelli and Ku, 2017:8).

In addition to these suggestions, green social work calls for transdisciplinary collaboration involving natural scientists, social and human scientists, and local people in responding to environmental disasters and promoting the coproduction of knowledge. Transdisciplinary collaboration is extremely important for mainstreaming green social work because it allows social workers to overcome their lack of skills in different aspects (e.g. in economic and financial, environmental and physical, chemical and biological disciplines). Social workers work hand-in-hand with other professions and residents to coproduce new models of green social work practice that will move disaster-prone societies towards more sustainable green ones.

Towards a green society

Social work, as a human rights-based profession, cannot take on every global issue alone. Alliances with others are essential in achieving transformative change. Global movements of power, politics, technology-driven capital flows and human resources are increasingly affecting human lives. To support a green social work curriculum, a green society is necessary. Greening society is the cornerstone for the survival of the Earth and everything within it. As the profession responsible for people's well-being, social workers have a powerful mandate to find sustainable ways to save the planet. To achieve this reality, green social workers can provide meaningful strategies for the profession to adopt. The contributions in this *Handbook* provide the evidence that green social work initiatives are being implemented across the world and are producing positive changes already. However, so much more needs to be done by every human being, individually and collectively. Let us work together locally and globally to realise this goal.

References

Boetto, H. and Bell, K. (2015). Environmental sustainability in social work education: An online initiative to encourage global citizenship. *International Social Work*, 58: 448–462.

Coates, J. (2005). The environmental crisis. *Journal of Progressive Human Services*, 16: 25–49.

Cooper, L. and Briggs, L. (2014). Do we need specific disaster management education for social work? *The Australian Journal of Emergency Management*, 29(4): 38–42.

Dominelli, L. (2011). Climate change: Social workers' roles and contributions to policy debates and practice interventions. *International Journal of Social Welfare*, 20(4): 430–438.

Dominelli, L. (2012). *Green social work: From environmental crises to environmental justice*. Cambridge: Polity Press.

Dominelli, L. (2013). Environmental justice at the heart of social work practice: Greening the profession. *International Journal of Social Welfare*, 22: 431–439.

Dominelli, L. (2014). Promoting environmental justice through green social work practice: A key challenge for practitioners and educators. *International Social Work*, 57: 338–345.

Dominelli, L and Ku, H. B. (2017). Green social work and its implications for social development in China. *China Journal of Social Work*, 10(1): 3–22.

Drolet, J., Wu, H., Taylor, M. and Dennehy, A. (2015). Social work and sustainable social development: Teaching and learning strategies for a 'Green Social Work' Curriculum. *Social Work Education*, 34(5): 528–543.

Jones, P. (2010). Responding to the ecological crisis: Transformative pathways for social work education. *Journal of Social Work Education*, 46(1): 67–84.

Jones, P. (2013). Transforming the Curriculum: Social work education and ecological consciousness. In Gray, M., Coates, J., and Hetherington, T. (Eds.), *Environmental social work* (pp. 213–230). London: Routledge.

Quarantelli, E. L. (1985). *Organizational behaviour in disaster and implications for disaster planning*. New York-Delaware: Disaster Research Center, University of Delaware.

Steinemann, A. (2003). Implementing sustainable development through problem-based learning: Pedagogy and practice. *Journal of Professional Issues in Engineering Education and Practice*, 129: 216–224.

Zakour, M. J. (1996). Disasters and social work. *Journal of Social Services Research*, 22(1): 7–25.

Name index

Abdelnabi, R. 347
Abel, N. D. 118
Abualola, T. 480
Acker J. 255
Ackerly, B. A. 88
Adair, B. 480
Adams, R. E. 516, 517
Adamson, C. 426, 524
Addams, J. 75, 412
Addy, C. L. 338
Adger, W. N. 18, 65, 118, 123, 268, 269
Adlong, W. 535
Adusumalli, M. 122
AES Home Page 224
Aftandilian, D. 185, 187
Agrawal, A. 276
Agarwal, B. 255
Agrawal, R. 112
Ahmadi, F. 246
Alcamo, J. 249
Aldrich, D. P. 506
Aldunce, P. 92
Alexander, D. E. 26, 53, 58, 529
Algemene Rekenkamer Curaçao (ARC) 348, 354
Alinsky, S. D. 444, 446, 448, 449
Allouche, J. 57
Allport, G. W. 495, 496
Almeida, P. 403
Alston, M. 12, 18, 65, 88, 89, 96, 234, 235, 236, 237, 293, 297, 386, 523, 548, 548, 549, 550, 551, 553
American Counselling Association 328
American National Association of Social Workers (NASW) 482, 483
Amin, A. 175
Amin, S. 221
Amnesty International 310
Anand, S. 316
Ananias, J. 299
Anderko, L. 335
Anderson, S. 111
Anfasa, F. 348
Anthony, J. M. no ref c44

Aotearoa New Zealand Association of Social Workers 541
Appleby, K. 235, 535, 549, 553
Apu'u Kaaviana 136
Araya Jarquín, M. 220, 225
Arnall, A. 272
Arooj, M. 438
Ashiabi, G. S. 198, 199
Atkinson, J. 421, 423
Austin, R. 400
Australian Association of Social Workers (ASSW) 485
Australian Government 550
Australian Research Institute for Environment and Sustainability (ARIES) 563
Awatere, S. 423
Awi, M. 138
Azman, A. 112

Baard, P. 238
Backhouse, M. 420
Baez U. 522, 525, 527
Bahadu, A. 26
Baird, S. 328
Balakiryeva, O. 433
Bankoff, G. 505
Banks, S. 325
Barbados Statistical Service 244
Bargh, M. 425
Barrett, C. 263
Basher, R. 74
Bašić, S. 436, 438
Baum, F. 339
Baxamusa, M. H. 401
Bay, U. 386, 550, 552
Bazerghi, C. 183
BBC 207
BBC documentary 53
BBC News 53, 55, 57
Beck, U. 464
Becker, J. 423, 425
Becker, P. 522, 525, 527
Bedi, G. 563

Name index

Been, V. 398
Belevsky, O. 435
Bell, B. 88
Bell, J. 197, 482
Bell, K. 426, 535, 542, 552, 560, 561, 570
Bell, S. M. 339
Beltran, R. 559, 561
Benessh, E. C. 337
Benjamin, S. 56
Benveniste, D. 517
Berger, R. M. 75
Bergström, J. 526, 527
Berlinger, J. 64
Berrigan, H. 483
Besthorn, F. H. 2, 12, 74, 75, 159, 197, 199, 236, 238, 244, 249, 250, 426, 427, 442, 536, 548, 551, 552, 558, 559, 560
Besthorn, M. A. 244, 249, 250
Bettini, G. 321, 322, 323
Betz, L. 337
Bhatia, R. 354
Bhawra, J. 182
Biddinger, P. D. 55
BIS 21
Bisset, S. 182, 184
Bizzarri, M. 426
Blanchot, M. 503, 504
Blewitt, J. 564
Blocher, J. 321
Bobo, K. 444, 445
Boddy, J. 548, 549, 550, 552, 553, 559, 561
Bodor, S. 564
Boetto, H. 426, 542, 548, 550, 551, 552, 553, 559, 560, 561, 562, 564, 570
Bonafasia, M. F. 353
Borum, R. 493
Bossart, G. D. 342
Boulanger, G. 59
Bowen, K. J. 335, 340
Bowles, T. 563
Bowles, W. 548, 551
Bowman, M. S. 518
Bowman, R. C. 518
Boyko, O. 433, 438
Bradshaw, S. 223
Bragin, M. 51
Brand, R. 232, 234, 239
Braun, V. 388
Bretherton, D. 507
Bride, B. E. 328
Briggs, L. 65, 570
Briskman, L. 424
Brisson, D. 198
British Association of Social Workers (BASW) 484
Broadbent, N. 90
Brodnig, G. 123
Brofenbrenner, U. 12

Bromet, E. J. 435
Bronfenbrenner, U. 152, 413
Brown, B. 233
Brown, D. 255, 256
Brown, L. 435
Brown, S. D. 57
Brownson, R. C. 338, 339
Brundiers, K. 276
Brundtland, G. H. 423
Brusher, E. A. 437
Bruyere, G. 551
Bryant, B. 398
Brydon-Miller, M. 270
Bryman, A. 349
BTI 243
Bulkeley, H. 269
Bull, M. 548
Bullard, R. D. 18, 74, 198, 199, 386, 398
Bunyavanich, S. 339
Burger, J. 339
Busby, E. 423
Butler, C. D. 535

Cabinet Office 26, 52, 53
Cabinet of Ministries of Ukraine 434
Caglioti, C. 347
Cain, C. 399, 400
Cajas Albán, M. L. 224
Calais Migrant Solidarity 324
Callahan, M. 14, 483, 485
Canda, E. 536, 560
Cantle, T. 494
Caribbean 360 147
Caribbean Community (CARICOM) 216
Carlisle, S. 515
Carlson, K. 65
Carmichael, S. 245
Carney, D. 246
Caro, R. 401
Carruthers, D. 18
Carr-West, J. 363
Carson, R. 12
Cary, J. 88
Cassadou, S. 347
Castleden, M. 26
Catto, K. D. 55
Center for Disease Control and Prevention (CDC) 353
Central Bureau of Statistics(CBS) 112
Cerdas Guntanis, L. 220, 225
Chagutah T. 255, 256
Chambers, R. 246, 267
Chan, K. L. 90
Chan, S. S. 59
Chapin-Hogue, S. 182, 188
Charity Fund 'Dobrota' 435
Charrel, R. N. 348

Chase, C. 102
Chattopadhyay, S. 353
Chavis, B. 398
Checker, M. 400
Cheetamun, A. 250
Che Guevara 236
Chen, H. M. 138
Chen, J. 563
Chen, M. 90
Chen, Y. L. 138, 140
Cheng, W. N. 138
Cheung, C. K. 113
Cheung, W. K. 90
Chiang, B. 132, 133
China Daily 169, 206
China Soybean Industry Association (CSIA) 207
Chiwara, P. 299
Chmutina, K. 522, 525
Chou, Y. C. 285, 286
Chow, D. L. 347
Christensen, T. 52, 59
Christian Aid 254
Christopher, C. 374
CIA 144, 244
Clark, N. 506, 507
Clark, P. 481
Clarke, L. 102
Clarke, V. 388
Clay, P. M. 342
Climate and Migration Coalition 321
Co, J. 456
Coates, J. 12, 51, 63, 65, 74, 75, 117, 200, 235, 236, 237, 293, 377, 386, 414, 415, 417, 422, 427, 535, 536, 542, 548, 551, 552, 553, 559, 560, 562, 564, 569
Cocking, C. 57
Coghlan, D. 270
Cohn, W. A. 513, 514
Colditz, G. A. 337
Cole, D. 303
Colegio de Trabajadores Sociales de Chile 225
Coleman-Jensen, A. 198
Collins, S. D. 513
Colten, C. E. 425
Combs-Orme, T. 398
Comim, F. 269
Comisión Económica para América Latina y el Caribe (CEPAL) 219
Comisión Nacional de Verdad y Reconciliación 100
The Commonwealth 144
Commonwealth Scientific and Industrial Research Organisation (CSIRO) 558
Connor, A. 339
Conrad, D. 328
Consejo Nacional de Trabajo Social 225
Constanza, R. 342

Conway, G. 246, 267
Cooke, M. 285
Coombs-Orme, T. 18
Cooper, L. Z. 65, 570
Corbin, C. A. 147, 148, 151, 245
Corbin, J. 66
Corfe, S. 51
Correspondent, S. 281
Council on Social Work Education (CSWE) 75
Cox, D. 325
Coyle, M. 398
Crabtree, A. 506, 508, 517
Cranton, P. 542
Crask, P. 144
Crawford, F. 550, 552, 553, 560
Crawford, N. 484
Cree, V. E. not found in c42
Creswell, J. W. 294
Cronin, M. 51, 58, 59
Cuadra, C. B. 523, 527, 531
Cui, K. 81
Curtis, S. 364, 366, 368
Cutter, S. R. 113

D'Afflitti, J. 339
Daley, K. 339
D'Amato, G. 563
Dancs, A. 480
Danielsson, E. 526
Danso, K. 87, 88, 523, 527
Darley, J. M. 497
Darlington, S. M. 337
Dart, L. 185, 187
Davies, T. 30, 435, 436
Davis, D. E. 403
Davis, M. 2
Declaration of Nyeleni 201
DeCosse, D. 87
Deepak, A. C. 196, 197, 201
De Garza Talavera, R. 220
Degeling, C. 340
De Haan, L. 247
De Lamballerie, X. 347
Delgado, M. 175
Delicath, J. W. 449, 450
Dell'Angelo, T. 564
Delport, C. S. L. 294
DeLuca, K. M. 449, 450
Demchenko, I. 432
Demick, B. 90
Densmore, A. 26, 30
Department for Environment, Food and Rural Affairs (DEFRA) 363, 364, 368
Department for International Development 297
Department of Social Work, Madras Christian College 285

575

Name index

Department of the Environment, Water, Heritage and the Arts 563
Desai, A. S. 295, 523
De-Shalit, A. 442
Devereux, S. 261, 263
Dewane, C. 195, 198, 199, 376
DFID 246
Dhemba, J. 262
Dictionary.com 148
Dietsch, E. 535
Dimdam E. 234
DiMento, J. F. C. 516
Dirkx, J. 563
Dodds, S. 285
Dominelli, L. 1, 2, 5, 10, 11, 12, 13, 15, 16, 23, 26, 35, 38, 51, 58, 59, 63, 64, 65, 71, 74, 75, 81, 87, 88, 89, 90, 92, 94, 96, 107, 108, 110, 113, 117, 118, 121, 122, 123, 124, 126, 128, 129, 133, 138, 139, 140, 141, 145, 146, 147, 149, 151, 152, 153, 159, 164, 167, 168, 169, 175, 179, 181, 195, 206, 207, 208, 210, 211, 212, 214, 220, 221, 224, 225, 232, 233, 234, 235, 236, 237, 238, 242, 244, 246, 247, 248, 249, 250, 251, 254, 255, 257, 264, 268, 269, 270, 276, 285, 286, 289, 290, 293, 295, 298, 299, 300, 301, 302, 303, 309, 318, 321, 322, 325, 326, 329, 336, 337, 338, 343, 348, 355, 360, 361, 362, 365, 367, 376, 381, 386, 387, 394, 398, 400, 401, 402, 403, 410, 411, 413, 416, 417, 418, 422, 423, 424, 425, 426, 427, 431, 434, 436, 437, 438, 439, 442, 445, 451, 452, 454, 455, 457, 462, 464, 465, 466, 474, 479, 484, 496, 498, 504, 505, 507, 508, 513, 515, 516, 520, 522, 523, 524, 525, 526, 527, 528, 531, 532, 536, 537, 540, 542, 548, 549, 550, 551, 552, 553, 554, 558, 559, 560, 562, 564, 565, 569, 570, 571
Dominica News Online 145
Donnelly, R. 564
Doughman, P. 516
Douglas, M. 413
Dow, K. 64
Downing, T. E. 64
Draper, C. 184, 185, 186
Dresner, S. 541
Drolet, J. 12, 64, 65, 89, 365, 395, 436, 438, 560, 570, 535
Drury, J. 57
Dryzek, J. S. 269
Duffield, M. 505
Dufka, C. L. 285
Duggan, J. 210
Du Plessis, P. 303
Durie, M. 423, 425, 427
Dutta, R. 549
Dwyer, T. 514

Earle, S. A. 343
The Earth Charter Initiative 536

Earth Justice 224
Earthquake Report 223
Easthope, L. 56
Ebi, K. L. 335, 340
Economic Commission for Latina America and the Caribbean 223
The Economic Times 207
Edmonds-Cady, C. 81
Edwards, A. 318
Edwards, P. 78
Edwards, S. W. 339
EEFIT 30
Ehrenreich, J. H. 151
Eikenberry, A. M. 175
Ellemor, H. 426
Ellis, R. 64
El-Masri, S. 455, 456
Eltaiba, N. 318
Elvir, O. 224
Emilson, A. 526
Enarson, E. 64, 65, 254, 290
Enders, A. 466
England, K. V. L. 505, 506
England, N. 363
England, P. 28, 29
English, P. B. 339
English, R. 479
Engstrom, D. 107
Ennia 355
Environment Agency 365
Environment Bay of Plenty 422
Erickson, C. L. 244, 249
Erlich, J. 82
Estes, R. 75
Evans, S. 363
EwF 28, 29, 31, 32
Eydal, G. B. 523, 524, 527

Fact Sheet 456
Fagerholm, K. 325
Fan, M. F. 133
FAO 183
Fara, K. 295, 298, 299
Featherston, D. 234
Federal Emergency Management Agency (FEMA) 70
Federation of Environmental Organizations Sri Lanka 374
Fendt, L. 222
Ferguson, K. M. 175
Ferreira, S. B. 179
Ferris, J. 185
Field, A. 491
Figley, C. R. 328
Figueroa, R. M. 269
Firth, C. 185, 187, 189
Fish, J. 338

Fisher, M. 339
Fisher, R. 182
Fisman, D. N. 340
Fleming, L. E. 342
Fletcher, H. 422
Flores Dewey, O. 403
Flowers, A. 564
Food and Agriculture Organization of the United Nations (FAO) 196, 254, 256, 257, 261, 295
Fordham, M. 254
Fossi, M. C. 342
Foster, J. 55
Fotopoulos, T. 523
Fraidlin, M. 484
Franchini, M. 535
Francis, P. 515
Fraser, B. 421
Freedman, D. 184, 185, 186
Freeman, A. 197
Freire, P. 202, 203, 257
Frieden, T. R. 338
Friel, S. 335, 340, 535
Friesen, M. 536
Fromkin, D. 491

Gabriel, J. C. 146
Gale, F. 563
Gangsei, D. 107
Garasky, S. 198
Garnaut, R. 234
Gates, J. D. 55
Gee, G. 398
Gemenne, F. 321, 321
Géradin, P. 348
Germain, C. 75
Germain, C. B. 152, 386
Germain, C. N. 414
Germein, S. 563
Gerst, M. D. 524, 525, 526, 528, 531, 532
Ghojavand, K. 285
Giddens, A. 254
Gilchrist, R. 24, 324
Gillespie, D. F. 87, 88, 523, 527
Gilliland, B. 147
Gioli, G 321, 322, 323
Giroux, H. 231, 232, 234
Gitterman, A. 75, 152, 414
Glaser, B. S. 66
Global Agenda 212
Global Agenda for Social Work and Social Development Commitment to Action 301
Global Justice Now 322
Global Post 207
Global Terrorism Data Base 484
Global Witness 222, 223
Golan, Y. 446
Goldman Environmental Prize 226

Goleman, D. 564
Goodman, B. 335, 338
Google Maps 123
Gorin, S. H. 338
Gotchfeld, M. 339
Gotham, K. F. 403
Gould, E. A. 348
Government of Barbados 244
Government of Nepal, Ministry of Home Affairs and Disaster Preparedness Network-Nepal c41
Government of the Commonwealth of Dominica 147
Government of Zimbabwe 255
Goździak, E. M. 310, 317
Granadam, M. 348
Grande, S. 18
Grant, K. 327
Gray, M. 12, 51, 65, 117, 159, 232, 233, 236, 237, 293, 376, 422, 424, 427, 535, 542, 548, 552, 553, 559, 560, 562, 564, 565
Green, D. 552
Greenberg, M. R. 339
Gregory, C. 198
Gregory, S. 403
Grenfell Tower Inquiry 56
Grewal, I. 315, 317
Grise-Owens, E. 535
Gross, J. 401
Grossman, R. L. 400
Ground Truth Solutions 436
Guha, R. 124
Guirguis, S. 460
Gundersen, C. 183, 199
Guo, P.Y. 140
Guo, Y. 208
Gusak, N. 433, 434, 435

Haidula, T. 294
Haines, A. 335, 340, 362
Hamerton, H. 422, 423
Hamilton, L. C. 400
Hammon, W. M. 348
Han, Y. 90, 91
Hancox, D. 239
Handl, G. 219
Hanlon, P. 515
Hansen, J. 542
Haran, O. 432
Harding, S. 431
Hardy, R. 325, 484
Harley, D. 535
Harling, K. 294
Harmsworth, G. 423, 538
Harre, N. 539
Harris, C. 552, 553, 559, 561
Harris, M. 327
Harrison, K. 517

Name index

Harrison, S. 54
Hart, M. A. 551
Hartsfield, K. 187
Harvey, D. 234, 238, 417
Harvey, G. 337
Haug, F. 133
Havenaar, J. M. 435
Hay, I. 247
Hayward, B. M. 118
Hayward, R. A. 199, 202, 426
Hayward, S. 559, 560
He, C. 89
Healy, L. M. 74, 75, 327, 484
Heider, F. 494
Heinsch, M. 551
Helsloot, I. 421
Henderson, B. R. 187
Hennessy, K. no ref c44
Hens, L. 335, 337, 340
Hernández, P. 107
Hetherington, T. 117, 137, 549, 550, 552
Hewitt, K. 506
Hickson, H. 549
Higa, Y. 348
Higgins, B. 563
Hikkaduwa, H. N. 374
Hilary, B. 210
Hillsborough Independent Panel 54
Hirsch Hadorn, G. 23, 24
HM Government Committee on Climate Change 362, 364, 368
Ho, S. J. 141
Hoefer, R. 301
Hoff, M. D. 2, 74, 75, 398, 400
Hoffand, M. D. 536
Hoffman, B. 479, 480
Hoffmann-Riem, H. 23
Holden, R. 267
Holland, B. 269
Hollis, F. 1
Homan, M. S. 447, 448
Hope, P. 548
Hopkins, E. 90
Horesj, C. 459, 460
Hoskins, A. 57
Hossain, M. A. 281, 291
Hou, C. 89, 90
Houghton, A. 339
Houle, C. 99
Houtart, F. 221
Howard, J. 513
Hoy, D. 335, 340
Hsieh, W. C. 133
Hu, S. 89
Huang, Y. Y. 142
Hudson, J. 423
Hughes, E. 423, 482

Hughes, T. 548
Hugman, R. 159, 247
Human Development Report (HDR) 112
Hung, H. L. 139
Hunt, J. 316
Hunt, S. 422, 423, 426
Hurricane Otto 224
Hurst, W. 90
Hyde, C. 201
Hyndman, J. 309, 502

IASC 13
Ibrahim, F. 232, 234, 235
IFAD 183
Ife, J. 232, 236, 482, 548, 551, 562
IFRC 18, 282
Intergovernmental Panel on Climate Change (IPCC) 76, 255, 361, 536, 540, 542, 558
Internal Displacement Monitoring Centre (IDMC) 64, 87
International Association of Schools of Social Work (IASSW) 58, 75, 88, 89, 244, 293, 523
International Council on Social Welfare (ICSW) 58, 75, 89, 244
International Federation of Social Workers (IFSW) 58, 75, 89, 195, 244, 246, 322, 326, 436, 437, 481, 539
International Fund for Agricultural Development 295
International Strategy for Disaster Reduction 295
Ioakimidis, V. 88, 436, 437, 438, 520
IOM 524
Ip, D. 211
Iravani, M. R. 285
Isbister, J. 300
Islamic Social Services of Canada 485
Ismail, I. 374
Itzhaky, H. 481
Izasa, M. 225

Jackson, J. 28, 29
Jaggar, A. M. 315, 316, 317, 317
James, C. (2015) 147
James, L. 299
James, R. (2013) 147
Jamrozik, A. 232, 233
Janardhanan, A. 281
Jani, J. S. 386
Jansen, G. G. 310
Jarvis, D. 386
Javadian, R. 151, 153
Jayaraman, N. 282
Jayne, T. 262
Jeffs, T. 24, 324
Jenkins, B. 479
Jenkins, S. R. 328
Johnson, D. 151

Johnson, G. 398
Jones, C. 436
Jones, D. N. 51, 58, 59
Jones, P. 75, 236, 276, 552, 553, 559, 560, 561, 563, 569, 570
Joseph, D. 152
Joseph, J. 526

Kahoku Shimpo 468
Kailes, J. I. 466
Kaiser, M. 560, 561
Kang, H. K. 436
Kapolo, I. N. 296, 299
Kapucu, N. 51, 138
Karban, K. 338
Kaseke, E. 262
Kasworm, K. 563
Kaufman, P. R. 198
Kawami, H. 473
Kawas, N. 224
Kawharu, M. 538
Kazis, R. 400
Kellar-Guenther, Y. 328
Kellehaer, A. 507
Keller, J. 234
Kelley, F. 75
Kelley, P. C. 322
Kelly, J. J. 75
Kelly, P. M. 65, 123, 268
Kemp, S. P. 75, 410, 411, 413, 414, 415, 416, 417, 431, 522, 523, 524, 531, 532
Kennedy, E. 524, 526
Kent, J. 548, 549, 550
Keohane, N. 51
Kesby, M. 210
Kim, S. 201
King, A. 548
King, L. 327
King, R. 54
Kingdon, J. W. 451
Kiper, T. 302
Kite-Powell, H. L. 342
Klein, B. W. 200
Klein, J. T. 24
Klein, N. 231, 232, 234, 237, 238, 526
Kluver, J. D. 175
Knickman, J. R. 338
Knutsson, P. 246
Kondrat, M. E. 58
Kopnina, H. 564
Kornbluh, P. 100
Koutroulis, G. 133
Kovan, J. 563
Kovner, A. R. 338
Krantz, L. 247
Krasney, M. 563
Krieger, N. 338

Krings, A. E. 401, 402, 403, 535, 542, 559
Krüger, F. 507
Ku, H. B. 90, 206, 207, 209, 211, 213, 571
Kudelia, S. 432
Kuo, H. J. 140
Kurmalineva, R. 263
Kyiv International Institute of Sociology (KIIS) 433
Kyoto Protocol- United Nations framework convention on climate change 235
Kythreotis, A. P. 235

Lafferty, K. D. 342
Lagos, J. 103
Lai, K. 436, 437
LaMore, R. L. 94
Lane, M. 548, 551
Lane, S. N. 12, 23
Lanier, J. 184, 186
Lapham, L. H. 501
Laqueur, W. 491
Laros, A. 563
Larson, G. 54
Latane´, B. 497
Laupland, K. B. 340
Lavalette, M. 237, 436, 437, 483
Lavelle, M. 398
Lavine, A. 399, 401
Lawler, J. 535
Laws, E. A. 342
Lawson, L. 184
Lawson, S. 561
Least Developed Countries Expert Group 255
Lederach, J. P. 496
Lee, C. Y. 132
Lee, M. C. not in c14
Lee, V. J. 347
Lehmann, J. 549
Leonard, P. 232
Leparc-Goffart, I. 348
Lerner, S. 398
Leung, T. T. F. 58, 90
Lewis, J. 455
Li, F. 207
Libby, P. 202
Liebenthal, A. 18
Lightfoot, E. 299
Lin, J. J. 140
Lin, J. R. 137
Lin, W. I. 140
Lind, J. 57
Lindell, M. 282
Lindgren, E. R. 436
Liu, F. 403
Liu, P. 206
Livelaw news network 126
Lobb, R. 337

Name index

Lockie, S. 243
Lockwood, S. 423
Logan, J. R. 400
Lombard, A. 431, 536
London Assembly 55
Long, J. 56
Long, K. C. 310, 317
Loopstra, R. 182
Lovell, M. 151
Lovelock, J. 536
Lu, H. 65, 209
Lu, L. T. 140
Lucas-Darby, E. 560
Luk, T. 161, 164, 165, 169
Lysack, M. 239

Ma, L. 206
Macchi, M. 123
MacGregor, S. 123
Macias, T. 198
Madden, L. 564
Madhavan, D. 289
Mafico, M. 263
Maglajlic, A. 437
Maidment, J. 550
Majori, G. 353
Malcolm X. 482
Malone, D. 112
Malonenbeach, E. E. 514
Mandiberg, J. 175
Mann, S. 542
Mannucci, P. M. 535
Manyena, B. 524, 525, 526
Mararike, C. 262
Marlow, C. 58
Marques, A. 342
Marsella, A. J. 507
Marston, G. 233
Martin, A. 563
Martin, C. E. 88
Martin-Brown, J. 402
Martinez-Alier, J. 169
Mary, N. 75, 538
Maskrey, A. 36
Mason, R. 550
Masters, S. 54
Mathbor, G. M. 65, 423
Mathias, J. 80
Matondi, P. B. 255
Matsukawa, A. 469, 471
Matthies, A, L. 75, 559
Maxwell, D. 263
McCants, W. 479
McCarthy J. G. 497
McCormick, G. H. 493
McCormick, S. 65
McDermott, F. 552

McDonald, C. 233
McFadden, L. 243
McGurty, E. M. 398
McIlvaine-Newsad, H. 188
McKibben, B. 233, 238
McKinlay, J. B. 338
McKinnon, J. 12, 17, 74, 75, 235, 237, 244, 248, 386, 426, 518, 548, 550, 551, 552, 559
McKittrick, D. 55
McKnight M. 520
McMichael, A. J. 335, 340
McNiff, J. 275
McTaggart, R. 210
Mearns 269
Meggitt, C. 327
Meizen-Dick, R. 256
Melekis K. 552, 559
Menjivar Ochoa, M. 221
Mercer, J. 423, 425, 426
Mermelstein, J. 285
Merzel, C. 339
Meyer, C. H. 411, 414, 416, 418
Meyer, E. 12
Meyer, E. E. 12, 74
Mezirow, J. 539, 542, 563
Michelfelder, M. 456
Midgley, J. 160, 300
Miles, D. 236
Milgram, S. 497
Miljenović, A. 387
Mill, J. S. 497
Miller, M. 480
Miller, S. 560
Miller, S. E. 422, 559
Ministry of Environment 247, 248, 250
Ministry of Health, the Environment and Nature (MHEN) 354, 355
Ministry of Planning and Development 454
Ministry of Social Policy of Ukraine (MSPU) 431, 432, 435
Mitchell, I. 564
Mitchell, J. 323
Mitchell, T. 336
Mitrokhin, N. 432
MOEF 122
Mohai, P. 398
Mohan, A. 347
Mohan, G. 168
Mohanty, C. T. 315, 317, 505
Mollenkopf, J. 399
Molotch, H. L. 399, 400
Molyneux, R. 548
Moniz, C. 338
Monteiro, S. 563
Moore, S. K. 342
Moosa-Mitha, M. 315
Morley, M. 100, 101

Morrow, B. 65, 290
Morse, S. 246
Morton, D. 293
Moth, R. 293
Movimiento por la Paz 221
MTPDRC 133
Muldoon, A. 152, 153
Mullaly, B. 232, 236
Mullaly, R. 326
Muller, L. 238
Munich, R. 524
Mupedziswa, R. 274
Murty, S. A. 63
Mushunje, M. T. 256, 262, 263
Muslim Council of Britain 495
Musson, R. M. W. 28
Myers, R. M. 348

Naidoo, P. 247
Namibia Red Cross Society (NRCS) 293, 294, 297
Narain, J. P. 354
Närhi, K. 75, 559
Narváez, L. 219, 220
Nasci, R. S. 354
Nash, S. L. 321, 322, 323
NASW 281
National Association of Social Workers (NASW) 483, 516
National Botanical Research Institute 303
National Drought Mitigation Centre 295
National Security Archive 100
National Statistics Agency 294
Nayatani, Y. 469, 473
Neamtan, N. 208
NERC 22, 24, 26, 28, 29, 31, 32
Nesmith, A. 87, 536, 538, 559
Nevo, I. 328
New Era Newspaper 298
The New Indian Express 282, 287
News 373
News First 378
New Zealand College of Public Health Medicine 535
NHS England 363
Nichenametla, P. 130
NIDM no ref in c23
Nikku, B. R. 112, 113, 118
Nilsson, M. 340
Nipperess, S. 553, 561
Nishisato, S. 471
Nixon, R. 74
Noble, C. 232, 236, 237
Nordrum, A. 374
Norman, C. 185
Norris, F. H. 275, 421, 425, 426
Norton 269

Norton, A. 254, 255
Norton, C. L. 431
Norwood, G. 53
NTD TV 207
Ntseane, D. 274
Nuehring, E. 285
Nunberg, G. 478
Nunes, A. R. 65
Nurse, L. A. 242
Nussbaum, M. C. 269
Nyers, P. 323

O'Connor, J. 400
Offer, A. 199
Office of the Prime Minister (OPM) 294, 295
Oficina Regional para América Latina y el Caribe 219, 223
Ofosu-Amaah, W. 402
O'Keefe P. 500
OHCHR 433, 434
Oliver, M. 465, 472
Oliveria, G. de L. T. 207
Oliver-Smith, A. 87
Olivier, M. P. 262
Olson, J. 342
O'Neal, K. K. 199
ONS 44, 45
Opasa, C. no ref in c8
Open Society Justice Initiative (OSJI) 494
Orr, D. 564
Ostrander, N. 182, 188
Oven, K. J. 32, 360, 362, 364, 365
Oxfam 1, 235
Oxfam Australia 235
Oxford Innovation 25, 26, 27
Ozanne, E. 232, 233

Paavola, J. 269
Pacholok, S. 65
Pack, M. 552, 553
Padilla, C. M. 338
Palinkas, L. A. 75
Panti, C. 342
Park, P. 210
Parks, V. 401
Parry, N. 289
Partido Verde Ecologista Costa Rica no ref c18
Pash, R. 144, 145, 147
Paul, J. A. 197
Pawar, M. 325
Payne, M. 325
Payne-Sturges, D. C. 398
Pease, B. 257, 550, 551, 561
Peeters, J. 75, 376, 426, 542, 558
Peled, M. 443
Pellot, A. S. 347
Pellow, D. N. 400, 403

Name index

Pencheon, D. 362
Peniel, E. 482
Penketh, L. 483
Penny, A. 144, 145, 147
Penton, K. 548
Peterson, P. E. 399
Petras, J. 100, 101
Petrini, B. 436
Philip, D. 276, 394, 536, 559
Physicians for social responsibility 224
Pialoux, G. 347
Pickerill, J. 446
Picou, J. S. 421
Piketty, T. 400
Pinto, J. 100
Pittaway, E. 18, 54, 290
Plan International 458, 459
Pocket, R. 338
Polack, R. 536
Polese, A. 432
Pope Francis 380
Portal de Vicerrectoría de Acción Social 220
Porter, R. 188
Potvin, L. 182, 184
Powers, M. C. F. 75
Prasad, V. 123
President of Ukraine 432
Proctor, E. M. 423, 425
Professional Social Work 54
Programa de las Naciones Unidas para el Medioambiente 222
Public Health England (PHE) 363
Public Safety Canada 63
Pulido, L. 403
Pulla, V. 436
Pun, N. 209
Punamaki, R. 456
Purifoy, D. M. 201
Purohit, B. M. 335
Pyle, J. L. 317
Pyles, L. 150, 386, 531

QSR International 92
Quarantelli, E. L. 113, 139, 539, 571
Quinn, A. 322
Quisumbing, A. 256

Rabin, B. 484
Rainey, S. 398
Rambaree, K. 243, 246, 247, 248, 249, 250
Ramon, S. 59, 437
Ramsay, S. 548, 552, 553, 559
Raphael, S. 145
Rawlinson, K. 55
RCUK 21
Reason, P. 210, 270, 274
Rebuilding Lives Post-Disaster (RLPD) 63

Red Latinoamericana de Mujeres Defensoras de los Derechos Sociales y Ambientales 222
Rehn, E. 310
Reichert, E. 326
Reid-Merritt, P. 482
Reisch, M. 276, 386, 394, 536, 538, 559
Reisen, W. K. 354
Renzi, M. 487
Republic Act No. 10821 458
Republic of Namibia 294, 297, 298, 299, 302
Reynolds, H. 564
Rezza, G. 348, 353
Ride, A. 507
Rigg, J. 506
Rily-Smith, B. 485
Ring, K. A. 245
Riva, M. 364
Rivera, F. G. 82
Roberts, M. 536
Robertson, M. 564
Robin, M. 254, 255
Robinson, M. C. 347
Robinson, T. 196, 197, 198
Roche, J. 322
Rock, L. F. 147, 148, 151, 245
Rockloff, S. F. 243
Roded, B. 443
Rodriguez, P. 18
Roelvink, G. 231, 239
Rogers, P. 53
Rogge, M. E. 2, 12, 18, 74, 398, 400, 523
Romao, F. L. 400
Roncarolo, F. 182, 184
Rootes, C. 451
Rooyen, C. V. 58
Rose, D. 232, 233
Rosen, S. 197
Rosenberg, D. 113
Rosner, D. 339
Ross, A. 55
Ross-Sheriff, F. 310, 315, 317, 318
Rothman, J. 446, 449
Rowlands, A. 526, 531
Rudd, K. 235
Rudnick, A. 348
Ruitenberg, A. 421
Rust, M. J. 516
Ruszczyk, H. A. 500, 502
Ruwanpura, K. N. 64
Ryan, D. 58
Ryan, T. 551
Rygiel, K. 317, 318

Sabates-Wheeler, R. 261
Sabia, D. 258
Sabry, H. 375, 376
Sachan, N. 335, 340

Name index

Saeed, S. 484
Saez, E. 400
Said, M A. 289
Salazar, G. 100
Saleebey, D. 414
Salkin, P. 399, 401
Salverda, T. 247, 249
Samarasundera, E. 339
Sampson, T. 535
Samuels, G. M. 318
Sandifer, P. A. 249
Sargisson, R. J. 422, 422, 423
Scheerhout, J. 54
Schein, E. 520
Schill, M. 400
Schipper, E. L. F. 65, 507
Schlechter D. 298, 299
Schlosberg, D. 140, 269
Schmitz, C. L. 74, 427, 560
Schneider, M. 207
Scholberg, G. 376
Schuffenecker, I. 347, 348
Schuldt, J. P. 65
Schumacher, E. F. 289
Schwartz, B. 478
Science Daily 207
Scoggins, H. L. 187, 189
Scraton, P. 54
Seager, J. 309
Seballos, T. 12
Sem, G. 242
Semigina, T. 433, 434, 435, 438
Sempik, J. 185
Sen, A. 269
Seravalli, A. 531
Sereda, Y. 433, 434
Serres, D. 239
Sewpaul, V. 257, 264
Shahar, I. B. 151, 153
Shamai, M. 482, 484
Shao, P. C. 133
Shapouri, S. 197
Sharma, R. 563
Sharpley, R. 247
Shaw, T. V. 516
Sheafor, B. 459, 460
Sherwood, H. 56
Shevaller, L. 549, 551, 553
Shi, L. 269
Shieh, J. C. 133
Shimazaki, K. 475
Shmueli, D. 442
Shorman, M. 443
Shortell, S. 363
Shrestha, N. R. 112
Siemens, L. 182, 187, 188
Silke, A. 497

Silva, M. Das G. 222, 224
Sim, T. 13, 90, 92
Sima, Y. 449
Simpson, E. 501, 502
Singer, P. 234
Singh, A. 335
Singh, R. V. 271
Singh, V. P. 335, 340
Sirleaf, E. J. 310
Slonim-Nevo, V. 328
Small, S. A. 210
Smith, K. 424, 425
Smith, L. T. 425
Smyth, N. 536, 538, 559
Social Work Registration Board 537
Soine, L. 75
Solas, J. 119
Soliman, H. H. 523
Solnit, R. 99, 101, 102, 103, 106, 108, 503, 506, 507
Somerset County Council 53
Sontag, S. 508
Sparf, J. 527
Srinivasan, S. 398
Stake, R. E. 294
Stalin, J. 282
Stanke, C. 45
Stanley, T. 483
Staples, L. 446, 449, 452
Statistics New Zealand 423
Stearns, L. 403
Steen, R. 54
Stehlik, D. 549
Stein, I. 327
Steinemann, A. 570
Steiner, H. 242
Stewart, J. R. 342
Stiglitz, J. 231
Stoecker, R. 399
Stokke, K. 168
Stone, C. N. 399
Storey, K. 400
Stoyanov, S. 335, 337, 340
Strachan, G. 539, 541
Strauss, A. 66
Streeter, C. L. 63
STREVA 22
Strydom, H. 294
Sudmeier-Rieux, K. 64
Suhrbier, A. 347
Sulleh, A. 238
Summerfield D. 508
The Sun 145, 146
Sundet, P. 285
Sustainability, Climate Change, Disaster Intervention Committee c43
Sustainable Development Unit (SDU) 367

Name index

Sutter, J. D. 64
Sweifach, J. 56
Swift, K. 14, 483, 485
Swoboda, E. 456
Sze, J. 403

Tadesse, T. 298, 302
Taiban, S. 133
Tajfel, H. 497
Tal, A. 442
Tam, C. H. L. 90
Tang, K. L. 113
Tansey, G. 197
Tapaleao, V. 422
Tatsuki, S. 465, 466, 467, 469, 471, 472, 473
Taubman, A. 94
Tauranga City Council 421
Taylor, A. 182
Taylor, E. 541, 563
Taylor, S. A. 343
Tedeschi, P. 386
Teixeira, S. 401, 402, 535, 542, 559
Tester, F. 418, 424
Thirberville, S. D. 347, 353
Thomas, D. S. G. 64
Thomas, I. 563
Thomas, M. 299
Thompson-Dyck, K. 65, 87
Thornley, L. 426
Thywissen, K. 26
Tickwell, D. no ref in c19
Tierney, K. 99, 102, 106, 464
Tigger-Ross, C. 535
Tipple, G. 455, 456
Toliashvili, B. 436, 437
Townsend, M. 141
Townsend, P. 315
Trading Economics 244
Travis, D. A. 340
Trewin, B. 548
Truell, R. 58, 59
Tseng, S. C. 138
Tsetsarkin, K. A. 347
Tulloch, J. 57
Turbett, C. 327, 329
Turje, M. 196, 197, 201
Turner, J. C. 497
Turner, R. 564
Twigg, J. 465
Twigger-Ross, C. 53
Twiss, J. 189
Twynam, C. 64

Unga, M. 12
Ungar, M. 386
United Nations (UN) 64, 87, 219, 360, 362, 432, 433, 436, 472, 516

United Nations Children's Fund (UNICEF) 321, 457, 458
United Nations Development Program (UNDP) 244, 523
United Nations Development Programme 256
United Nations Disaster Relief Organization (UNDRO) 117
United Nations Economic and Social Council 293
United Nations Education, Scientific and Cultural Organization (UNESCO) 159, 169
United Nations Educational, Scientific and Cultural Organisation (UNESCO) 547
United Nations Environmental Program 221, 225
United Nations Framework Convention on Climate Change (UNFCCC) 64
United Nations General Assembly (UNGA) 35, 36, 37, 41, 42, 44
United Nations Global Counter Terrorism Strategy 481
United Nations High Commission for Refugees (UNHCR) 322
United Nations International for Disaster Reduction (UNISDR) 35, 37, 38, 39, 40, 41, 42, 43
United Nations Office for Disaster Risk Reduction (UNISDR) 1, 65, 89, 472, 475, 522, 524, 526
United Nations Statistics Division (UNSTATS) 44
Universidad de Costa Rica, Escuela de Trabajo Social 220
University of Denver Graduate School of Social Work 376
Urry, J. 234, 427
U.S. Environmental Protection Agency (EPA) 398
U.S. Poverty Guidelines 184

Van Dillen, S. 247
van Schalkwyk, A. 337
Vardoulakis, S. 514, 517
Venugopal, V. 288
Verdugo, P. 100
Verheul, R. 325
Verity, F. 421
Vervaeck, A. 90
Vickers, M. 210
Vitale, L. 100
von dem Knesebeck, O. 339
Voorhees, W. R. 422

Wade, K. 558
Wahlberg, K. 197
Wahlquist, C. 558
Wahlström, M. 96
Waitangi Tribunal 422, 426
Walker, R. 340
Walkup, R. B. 339
Wallace, M. I. 337
Wallulis, J. 258

Walsh-Tapiata, W. 424
Walter, C. L. 201
Wamsler, C. 454, 456
Wang, K. 207
Wang, M.Y. (2014) 138
Wang, S. 207
Wang, T.Y. (2010) 140
Warner, K. D. 87
Warner, R. 175
Warren, D. 401
Weaver, S. C. 347, 354
Webb, S. 232, 233, 236, 237
Weerasuriya, R. 141
Weick, A. 75, 94, 536
Welbourne, P. 326
Westoby, P. 549, 551, 553
WFP 183
Whittaker, J. 327
WHO 43, 46
Wieck, A. 513
Wiek, A. 276
The Wilderness Society (TWS) 548
Willett, J. 74, 76
Williams, J. 54
Williams, J. H. 386
Wilson, M. 485
Winkler, H. 254
Winkworth, G. 421
Winn, P. 100
Wisner, B. 142, 268, 465, 506
Wistow, J. 11, 365, 366
Witkin, S. 563
Women Refugee Commission 322
Woodhouse V. 552, 559
Worland, J. 558
World Bank 112, 254, 256, 293, 295, 315, 433
World Café participant 416
World Commission on Environment and Development 87, 523
World Conference on Natural Disaster Reduction 36, 37
World Economic Forum 324

World Food Programme 201, 293
World Health Organization (WHO) 347, 353, 354, 355, 360, 362, 470
World Population Review 243
World Social Forum (WSF) 221
Worldwatch Institute 221
Wright, E. O. 208, 214
Wroe, L. 323, 324
Wu, D. 348
Wu, H. 87, 88, 89, 90, 91

Xiang, R. 169

Yamada, M. 475
Yan, H. 206
Yan, M. C. 90
Yanay, U. 56
Yang, J. 164
Yishai, Y. 450
York, A. 481
Younghusband, E. 12
Yuan, L. 207

Zach, L. 520
Zakour, M. J. 63, 88, 324, 527, 571
Zald, J. 497
Zapf, M. K. 74, 75, 536, 542
Zavirsek, D. 59
Žganec, N. 387
Zhang, H. (2008) 213
Zhang, J. (2011) 206
Zheng, L. 90, 91
Zhou, L. 208
Zibechi, R. 101
Ziliak, J. P. 183
Zimbabwe National Statistical Agency (ZIMSTATS) 256
Zimbardo, P. G. 495
Zinsstag, J. 340
Zubair, A. 438
Zuber-Skerritt, O. 210
Zuo, Q. 514

Subject index

7/7 bombings 55, 492
9 Minimum Characteristics of a Disaster-Resilient Community 33
921 earthquake 67, 71, 171, 180; *see also* Nantou earthquake

action plan 5, 10, 13–15, 24, 27–28, 126, 539
action research 23, 159, 161, 154, 206, 210–211, 214, 267–270, 274–276, 356, 394, 538, 543
advisor 24, 25, 302
Advisory Board 75–77, 220, 225
affected populations, disaster 41, 203, 431, 434–437
Africa 18, 32, 78, 198, 250, 254, 256, 293, 298, 324, 336, 347, 349, 485, 524
Agenda for Sustainable Development 64, 244
agriculture 112, 124, 127, 129, 134, 141, 144, 147–478. 151, 183, 196, 202, 206–207, 209, 211–213, 239, 242, 244, 254–261, 268, 273, 295, 297, 389, 466–468
Agüita de la Perdiz 105–106
Allende Gossens, Salvador 100
Almaty 29, 31
American Academy of Social Work and Social Welfare 75
Aotearoa 5, 238, 420, 425–427, 535–541, 543
architects 88–89, 91, 93–96, 103, 177, 238
asylum seeker 233, 321, 324, 461
Atayal people 171–172, 176, 180
Australia 5, 63–64, 66, 67–71, 232, 235, 238, 382, 485, 547–554, 559, 561, 563
autonomy 68, 119, 177, 179, 180, 225, 236, 326, 363, 437

Barbados 4, 242–245, 248–251 255
Bataclan 55
bauxite mining in Jamaica 77
Bhopal 12, 234
Bodin District of Sindh flood 69
Boston Marathon 55, 94, 115, 126–127, 146–147, 149, 177, 224, 282, 514
British Geological Survey 28, 32

built environment 19, 51, 88, 96, 116, 466
Built Infrastructure for Older People's Care in Conditions of Climate Change (BIOPICCC) 364–366, 368
bushfires 63, 67–69, 234, 548

Calais (refugee camp, also known as 'The Jungle') 323–329
Canadian Association for Social Work Education (CASWE) 66
capabilities 4, 53, 246, 250, 267, 269, 272, 275, 318, 414, 423, 425, 490, 570
capability 269, 275, 415
Caribbean 77, 144, 147–149, 151, 153, 219, 222–223, 243–244, 347–348, 455
Caribbean Disaster Emergency Management Agency (CDEMA) 153
Caribbean island 347
caste system 122, 129, 504
category 1 responders 52
category 2 responders 52
charity 106–108, 130, 435
Chennai Floods 281, 284–285, 287–288, 290
Chernobyl, nuclear disaster 12, 431, 435–437
chikungunya 347–355
child protection 454–462, 485, 564
children's rights 13, 326
Chile 18, 88–108, 225, 456
China 4, 23, 25, 29, 30–32, 64, 87, 89, 90, 92–93, 95, 110–114, 159–162, 165, 169, 206–214, 340, 348, 415, 418, 455
Christchurch 29
Civil Contingencies Act 2004 (CCA) 52–53
Civil Contingencies Committee 52
climate change 2–4, 11–12, 16, 23–25, 37, 51, 53, 64–65, 69, 72, 75–77, 82, 87–89, 96, 110, 124, 132, 139, 141–142, 153, 169, 197–199, 202–203, 225, 234–236, 239, 242–251, 254–263, 267–272, 281–282, 286–287, 293, 298–300, 322, 335–337, 339–340, 342, 348, 359, 361–362, 364, 366, 368–369, 387, 409–411, 416–418, 465, 513, 515–518,

524–528, 535–536, 538–540, 542, 547–551, 553, 558, 562, 565, 570
climate change adaptation 65, 72, 250, 269, 270, 272, 340, 513, 516
climate change planning 65, 96
climate justice 222, 267, 269, 270, 273
cloud burst 110, 113
coastal water management 222, 267–273
coastal zone management 4, 242–244
Cockpit Country 77–78
collaboration 21, 23, 27, 29, 32, 43, 45, 66–67, 71, 74, 79, 80–82, 130, 134, 136–138, 140–141, 161–165, 182, 188, 250–251, 258, 336–337, 340, 360, 364–369, 410, 457, 460, 531, 548, 571
collaboration between physical and social scientists 21
communities 3, 4, 9–19, 23, 25, 27–32, 35–38, 40, 51, 63–71, 75–78, 81–82, 87, 89, 90–96, 99, 103, 107–108, 110–111, 113–119, 121–126, 128–130, 134, 137–142, 145–150, 152–153, 159–169, 171–173, 175, 177–182, 187, 195–199, 201, 209–210, 213–214, 220–221, 223–226, 232, 236–239, 243–245, 248–250, 262, 264–265, 267–270, 273, 276, 285, 287–290, 294–298, 300–302, 326, 332, 338, 342, 355–356, 364–365, 369, 374–377, 380, 386–387, 392, 394–395, 397–398, 400–404, 412–413, 415–426, 431, 434–438, 442–444, 447, 451–452, 456, 468, 482, 486, 489–490, 492–498, 502–503, 506, 516–518, 523–528, 531, 535–536, 540–543, 548–550, 569, 570–571
community 2, 4–5, 10–17, 23, 25–27, 29–30, 33, 35, 37–39, 43–46, 51–53, 63–71, 74–82, 87–96, 99–103, 105–106, 108, 112, 114–118, 121, 123–127, 129–130, 132, 134–142, 144–146, 148–149, 151–152, 154, 160–169, 171–181, 182–190, 196–203, 206, 208–210, 212–214, 220, 223, 225, 236, 239, 240, 242–245, 248, 250, 254, 260–262, 264–265, 267, 268–276, 281–282, 285, 287, 289, 290, 296–297, 299, 301–303, 309, 311, 313–314, 319, 324, 327–328, 337, 339, 342–343, 348, 355–356, 376–382, 385–395, 397–404, 409, 412, 414, 416, 420, 422–423, 425–427, 434, 437–439, 446–448, 451–452, 455, 458–459, 468–469, 472–473, 483, 485–486, 489, 491, 493–494, 497–498, 500, 502, 505–507, 513, 516–517, 519–520, 523, 526, 530–531, 535–538, 540–543, 550–553, 560, 562, 564, 569, 570
community action 12, 17, 53, 118, 324, 519, 551
community based risk reduction 16–17, 29, 30, 33
community benefits agreements (CBAs) 397, 400–403
community building 100, 134, 164–167, 201, 203, 382, 423

community development 23, 68, 82, 90, 129–130, 136, 160, 165, 172, 177–178, 185, 188, 206, 244–245, 303, 380, 393–395, 437–438, 459, 493–494, 498, 531, 537–538, 551–553, 564
community empowerment 67, 135, 138–140
community garden 182–190, 197, 201, 239
community group 52, 77–78, 103, 164, 166–168, 220, 225, 274, 378, 380, 400–401, 434, 505
community practices 63, 75
community social work 13–14, 171, 182, 438
Community Supporting Agriculture (CSA) 206, 212, 214
community work 15, 51, 71, 136, 164, 167–168, 176–177, 180, 220, 223, 245, 298, 438, 531, 536, 540, 552
community workers 139, 163–164, 166–167, 543, 553
Concepción 105
continuity 52, 53, 359–361, 366, 526–527
Costa Rica 220–225
Council for Aboriginal Affairs (Taiwan) 174–175
Council on Social Work Education (CSWE) (USA) 66, 75
critical role of social work 51
critical theory 2–5, 14–15, 17–18, 32, 41, 43–45, 51–52, 54, 64, 67–68, 71, 82, 87, 116–117, 124, 128–130, 137–139, 147, 151, 160, 165, 179, 197–199, 202–203, 212, 231, 249, 251, 257, 270, 276, 287, 336–337, 342, 355, 362, 365, 373, 383, 393–395, 402, 414, 422, 433–434, 447, 464–465, 468, 475, 479–480, 486, 496, 505–507, 517–518, 531, 541–543, 551–553, 559–560, 563–564
Croatia 385–387, 392, 395
cross-sectoral 359–362, 364, 366
crowd disasters 54
CSA movement 206
cultural contexts 2, 66, 75, 81, 295, 515, 517, 563
cultural heritage 39, 64, 87, 141, 337, 425, 538
Curaçao 347–356
curriculum 1, 3, 5, 10, 15–18, 59, 65, 115, 117–118, 182, 188, 224, 286, 298, 303, 338, 343, 348, 355, 373, 382, 403, 426–427, 482, 522–532, 538, 542, 553, 558–566, 570–571

Dakanua 133, 136–137, 139, 141
definition of green social work 9–12, 35, 74, 89, 124, 145, 175–176, 195, 206–207, 220, 236–237, 242–243, 254, 288–289, 300, 321, 336–337, 348, 376, 386–387, 403, 414–416, 422–423, 431, 434–435, 445, 454, 465, 513, 523, 536, 549–550, 558, 569–570
Department for International Development (DfID) 24, 32, 33, 246, 297, 457
desertification 76, 244
development 1, 3, 10, 11, 12, 14–18, 21

587

Subject index

dictatorship 100, 101, 103, 104, 108, 221
disaster 2–5, 9–19, 24–30, 32–33, 35–46, 51–59, 63–72, 87–96, 99–108, 110–109, 121–130, 132–142, 144–153, 162, 172, 174, 176–179, 208–209, 219–220, 222–225, 231, 233–237, 239, 245, 249–250, 272, 281–290, 293–295, 299–304, 309–310, 319, 324–327, 337–338, 348, 360–361, 365, 373, 375, 378, 382–383, 387–410, 418, 420–427, 431, 435–439, 454–459, 462, 464–466, 468–476, 478, 486, 498, 500–508, 513–520, 522–532, 535, 547–554, 564, 565, 569–571
disaster cycle 10, 13, 33
disaster intervention 2, 10, 11, 16–18, 68, 250, 283, 289, 290, 299, 348, 457, 523, 528, 569, 571
disaster preparedness 17, 38–39, 46, 52, 59, 63, 121–122, 126, 128–130, 136–137, 281, 289–290, 458, 465, 513, 523, 527
disaster recovery 46, 63, 65, 66–69, 70–71, 285
disaster relief 63, 116, 129, 139, 140, 142, 151, 281, 285, 286–287, 324, 418, 553
disaster resilience 67, 118, 235, 465, 527
disaster response 2, 10–11, 16–18, 68, 250, 283, 289, 290, 299, 348, 457, 523, 528, 569, 571
disaster risk management 37, 40, 42–43, 96, 457, 475, 525
disaster risk reduction 4, 5, 16–17, 29–30, 32–33, 35–46, 64–65, 87–89. 94, 96, 219–220, 224–225, 272, 288, 290, 360–361, 456–458, 462, 464, 471–473, 475, 507, 522–531
disaster social work 67, 71, 89–91, 114–119, 145–146, 153, 289, 337, 523, 549, 570
disaster survivors 19, 54, 71, 88, 94–95, 132, 149, 431, 438
Dominica 144–154, 349
Donetsk (Ukraine) 431–432, 435
DRR 472–475
Duona Tribal Village 135, 139

earthquake 14, 22–33, 67, 71, 87–96, 99–108, 110, 113, 116–117, 159–160, 171, 174, 176–180, 220, 223–225, 284–286, 455, 457, 464–466, 473, 478, 500–508
earthquake survivors 93, 96
Earthquakes without Frontiers (EwF) 21–22, 28
ecological justice 133, 141, 159, 164, 269, 293, 562, 564, 566
ecological systems theory 152
Economic and Social Science Research Council (ESRC) 11, 22, 24, 26, 33
Eco-Sensitive Zone (ESZ) 122
eco-social 5, 90, 409, 413–418, 551–554, 547, 558–559, 561–566
eco-tourism 67, 115, 166, 302
elite panic 99, 101–102, 106
emergency services 19, 54, 56, 69, 365, 486

empowerment 15, 37–39, 43, 67, 77, 81, 108, 135, 137–138, 140–142, 146, 164, 167, 172, 175–177, 180, 184, 186, 195, 201, 237, 246–250, 264, 290, 301–304, 318, 366, 426, 437, 452, 460, 472–474, 496, 551, 576
Engineering and Physical Sciences Research Council (EPSRC) 11, 24, 364
environment 1–5, 9–19, 22–23, 25, 35, 37–39, 42, 51–53, 58–59, 63–65, 67–68, 71–72, 74–82, 87–96, 112–113, 116–119, 121–122, 131–138, 140–142, 144–147, 149, 151–155, 159, 161–165, 167–169, 172, 175–177, 179–181, 185, 195–199, 201–203, 206, 208–214, 219–226, 231, 233–239, 242–251, 254, 257, 264, 267–270, 275–276, 282–283, 286–290, 293–295, 297–304, 314, 321–324, 326–327, 329, 335–340, 342–343, 348–350, 352–356, 361–366, 368, 373–383, 385–388, 394–395, 397–407, 409–418, 420, 422–427, 431–439, 442–452, 454–455, 458–459, 461, 462, 464–466, 469–471, 474, 476, 479–481, 484, 486, 502–504, 507, 513–519, 522–528, 530–532
environmental crisis 65, 220, 223, 269, 513, 516, 519, 560–561
environmental degradation 2, 9, 11, 16, 65, 67, 74, 81, 117, 132, 162, 196, 211, 236–237, 243–244, 248, 250–251, 283, 287–288, 321, 327, 336–337, 373, 375, 382, 386, 426–427, 523–524, 537, 550
environmental disasters 4, 5, 18, 65, 140, 208, 220, 234–235, 237, 239, 410, 486, 513–514, 549–550, 571
environmental exploitation 4, 195–198, 203
environmental injustice 19, 74, 76–77, 81, 159, 199, 242, 250, 324, 376, 397, 403, 410, 513
environmental justice 1–2, 10–11, 15, 18–19, 74–75, 77–82, 87, 96, 121, 131, 138, 140, 142, 149, 153, 169, 195–196, 201, 203, 211, 222, 237, 245, 248–249, 251, 268–269, 276, 287, 290, 293, 300–301, 303, 321–322, 329, 337–382, 386–388, 392–403, 410, 413, 416–417, 422, 426, 431, 439, 451, 454–455, 516, 532, 536–539, 442, 543, 547, 551–554, 559, 562, 569, 570–571
environmental paradigm 9
environmental racism 18, 198–199, 386, 398
environmental rights 10, 15, 222, 251
environmentally friendly reconstruction 132, 134
Erika 144–153
ethics 5, 66–67, 199, 225, 237, 281, 326, 422, 483, 536, 541, 562, 564
EwF 21–33; *see also* Earthquakes without Frontiers
external cladding 56
Eyjafjallajökull eruption 28

farmer 297
first tier responders *see* category 1 responders

Subject index

Fishery Association 163, 166–168
floods 53, 63, 69, 113, 281, 283–284, 287–288, 290, 365, 464, 506, 515–518
food banks 183, 188, 201
food insecurity 76, 182, 183, 184, 187, 195–203, 254–264, 296, 560
food security 4, 39, 43, 122, 183, 185, 188, 190, 198, 200, 206–214, 246, 255–257, 262, 264, 294, 298–299, 303, 410, 565
forced migration 74, 254, 310, 316–317, 322–323, 436
forest rights 121, 125, 128, 130–131
Fort McMurray wildfires 63
Francis Bacon 23
Fukushima 234, 466–468

Gaga 172–173, 178, 180
Gandhamur factory campaign 79–81
garbage recycling 189, 225, 350, 356, 373–382, 409, 411–412
gelatine factory 79
globalisation 136, 179, 212, 226, 238, 249, 317, 489, 535
Gorkha earthquake 32–33, 500–507
Goromonzi (Zimbabwe) 4, 254, 257–259, 262
Gram Sabha 125–131
Great East Japan Earthquake (GEJE) 464, 466
green agricultural practices 3–4
green politics 231, 237, 239–240
green social work 1–5, 9–19, 23–24, 26, 35–42, 44–46, 51, 58–59, 63–66, 71, 74–82, 87–96, 106–108, 110, 113, 114, 116–119, 121–122, 124–129, 131–135, 138–142, 145, 152–153, 159–161, 163, 167–169, 171–172, 175–182, 188, 195–199, 201–203, 206–208, 210–214, 220, 223–226, 231, 234, 236–238, 240, 242, 246–247, 254–255, 264, 267–270, 273–274, 276, 281–282, 287–290, 293–294, 300–304, 318–319, 321, 323, 326, 328–329, 336–338, 342–343, 348–349, 355–356, 359–364, 367, 369, 373–383, 386–387, 392–395, 397–399, 401–404, 409–410, 413, 415–416, 419, 422–427, 431–432, 434–437, 439, 442, 445, 451–452, 454–455, 461–462, 465–466, 476, 479, 486, 496, 498, 504–505, 507–508, 513, 515–520, 522–529, 531, 536–540, 542–543, 547–549, 551–554, 562, 566, 569–571
green social work curriculum 16–18, 46, 522–532, 571
green social work framework 10, 13, 119
green social work intervention 90, 94
green social work model 14, 38, 113, 117, 121–122, 125, 188, 293, 300, 304, 355, 402–403, 431, 434–435, 513, 417, 428
green social work perspective 78, 81–82, 116, 132, 145, 168, 175, 180, 211, 348, 356, 466, 522

green social work practice 17, 159–169, 206, 208, 211–212, 214, 289, 329, 382, 401–402, 427, 436–437, 439, 513, 517–518, 537, 547, 553, 571
green social work theory 1, 4, 24, 203
green social work theory and practice 1, 24
green social worker 3, 4, 10–11, 13–19, 40, 59, 63, 76, 81–82, 89–96, 106–108, 118–119, 127, 131, 133, 135, 139–140, 142, 152, 169, 178–180, 196, 198–199, 201–203, 207, 213–214, 220, 223, 226, 240, 247, 267, 269–270, 274, 276, 289, 318–319, 323, 342–343, 348–349, 355, 359–363, 367, 369, 386, 397–399, 401–403, 432, 439, 442, 452, 462, 465, 476, 496, 498, 505, 515–516, 518, 528, 562, 566, 571
Green Watershed 159, 161–167, 169
greening social work 5, 118, 535, 553, 558
greening social work education 118, 535, 558
Grenfell Tower 51, 53, 55, 56–57
grounded theory 66

Haiti 28, 457
health and social care 11, 18, 359–365, 368
health care 36, 39, 43
health impact of disasters 4, 35, 39, 42–43, 398, 401, 403, 444
Hillsborough disaster 54
Himalayan disaster 110–111, 113, 121
human rights 11, 38, 58, 66, 89, 91, 105, 113, 119, 185, 188, 195, 198, 201, 203, 220–221, 225, 232, 236, 246, 287, 325, 386–388, 392, 395, 433, 479, 481, 483, 489, 495, 498, 551, 553, 571
hydro-electricity 114, 122
hydropower 111, 127, 144, 161, 163, 223

immediate relief 10, 116, 299, 387
immigrant 70, 101, 106, 183, 233, 317, 484–485
immigration 70–71, 317, 323–325, 329
Increasing Resilience to Natural Hazards (IRNH) 22–24, 27–28, 33
independence from Spain 100
India 4, 10, 12, 31–32, 63–64, 75, 79, 80–82, 110–115, 118, 121–124, 130, 234
Indian Ocean Tsunami 10, 64, 110, 284, 290, 454, 507
indigenous communities 4, 159, 168–169, 171, 180, 238, 421, 423, 425–426
indigenous people 18, 133, 135, 138, 140, 144, 160, 171–180, 221–222, 225, 236, 238, 316, 421, 426
innovation 1, 3, 5, 25, 26, 27, 65, 69, 118, 130, 142, 145, 151, 152, 289, 337, 387, 395, 402, 409, 437, 542, 552
innovative community practices 63
Integrated Coastal Zone Management (ICZM) 4, 242–244, 249–251
Inter-Agency Standing Committee (IASC) 13, 459
interdisciplinary 21–22, 26–27, 67, 74, 91, 118, 153, 337–338, 343, 410, 416, 431, 442, 451–452

589

Subject index

internally displaced persons (IDPs) 431–439
international social work 74–78, 91, 172, 203, 283, 438, 530, 553
international social workers 74, 76, 78
intersectionality 309, 335
Internal Displacement Monitoring Centre (IDMC) 64, 87
International Association of Schools of Social Work (IASSW) 10, 12, 16, 58, 66, 75, 88, 110, 114, 244, 264, 293, 307, 325, 387, 481, 523, 539, 571
International Council on Social Welfare (ICSW) 75, 244, 264, 386, 539
International Decade for Natural Disaster Reduction (IDNDR) 36, 44, 284, 455
International Disaster Database 64
International Federation of Social Workers (IFSW) 58, 195, 244, 383, 386, 481, 484, 539
International Health Regulations (IHR) 43, 46
International Monetary Fund (IMF) 77, 235, 238
Irish Republican Army (IRA) 54–55, 57, 479, 485, 490–492
Israel 5, 442–423, 445, 452, 530

Jamaica 75, 77–78, 82
Jerusalem 56, 443
Jiasian Community Association (JCA) 134, 139, 141
just practice 237, 269, 286, 293, 464, 474–476

Kaohsiung City 132, 135, 137
Karadiyana garbage dump 374–380
Kathmandu 32, 114, 116, 118, 501, 502
Kazakhstan 29–32
Kenya 75–77, 82, 310, 312, 318
Kerala 79–81
Koudmen 145–146, 151

La Pincoya 103–106, 108
lahars 28
landslide 28–30, 32, 51, 110–111, 124–127, 132, 135, 139, 145–148, 159, 234, 283, 361, 456, 459, 465–466, 502, 504
Lashi Lake 159–167
Latin America 219–220, 225
left-behind children 94, 178
Lijiang 159–162, 167, 169
livelihoods 16, 26–27, 29, 38, 39, 41–43, 45, 46, 63–64, 67–69, 71, 76, 78, 87, 95, 111–118, 121–130, 133, 136, 141–142, 144–153, 161, 165, 180, 209, 211, 213–214, 221, 238–239, 242–251, 255–257, 260–264, 267–276, 288, 293–295, 297–298, 300–303, 311, 361, 422, 434–437, 439, 465, 502–503, 506, 513, 519–520, 523–524, 549
locally undesirable land uses (LULUs) 397–398, 400–403

Luhansk (Ukraine) 431–432
Lushan earthquake 88–92

Mahakali River 114
mainstreaming green social work 15, 569, 571
Manchester Arena 55
Mandakini 113, 115, 121
Māori 421–427, 536–538
marginalisation 2–3, 10–11, 15, 18, 23, 35–36, 45, 63, 67, 71, 74, 76, 81–82, 87, 89, 125, 140, 151, 153, 177, 179, 195, 210, 237–238, 243, 246–248, 250–251, 264, 267–269, 276, 287–290, 295, 300, 310, 315, 317–318, 329, 348, 438, 452, 494, 548, 550, 553–554
Maroon tribal territory 78
Mauritius 4, 242–251
mental health 13, 43, 68, 136, 141, 146–150, 199, 245, 249, 316, 318, 336–337, 339–340, 360, 376, 394, 398, 399, 401, 403, 433, 438, 456, 459–460, 483, 485, 514, 517–518, 541, 551, 564, 565
migrant 5, 70–71, 76, 90, 95, 101, 106, 122, 183, 209, 233, 309, 316–319, 321–322, 325, 329, 339, 434, 464, 484–485
mudslide 144, 161–162
multidisciplinary 51, 243, 249–251, 269, 298, 336–337, 339, 355, 439
Mutito, (Kenya) 76

Namibia 4, 293–304
Nantou earthquake 67
natural disaster 3–4, 36–37, 40, 44, 51–52, 63, 67, 71, 100–101, 106, 110, 117, 133, 138, 144, 146–147, 151–152, 174, 179, 209, 223–226, 231, 234, 239, 243, 245, 284, 286, 295, 299, 300, 436, 454–456, 464, 500, 507, 514, 517–519, 524
Natural Environment Research Council (NERC) 22, 24–29, 31–33
Natural Hazards Advisory Group (NHAG) 25–27
Natural Hazards Theme Action Plan 24, 28
Naxi people 159–163, 166
neoliberal 2–3, 9–10, 105, 113, 133, 139, 141, 168, 175, 179, 196–197, 199, 203, 212, 220, 231–240, 254, 329, 386, 400, 402, 424, 427, 469, 526, 542–543, 571
Nepal 4, 29, 31–33, 110–118, 122, 239, 284–285, 500–508
Nepal Earthquake Virtual Helpline 116
Nepal Red Cross 32, 116
Nepal School of Social Work (NSSW) 116–117, 119
new environmental paradigm 9
new environmental paradigm, green social work 9–19
New Zealand 5, 238, 276, 420–427, 535–543
nuclear waste 5, 385, 387–392, 395
nuclear waste disposal 5, 385, 387–392, 395

Subject index

Pakistan 32, 63–64, 66, 69, 71, 110–101, 113–114, 313, 316, 484, 504
Panchayati Raj Act 130
PAR 23, 206, 210
Paris Agreement 64, 235
participation 64, 71, 77, 80–81, 88–90, 92–93, 95, 121, 123, 130–131, 136, 138, 140, 166–168, 172–173, 178, 180, 185, 189–190, 200 203, 210–212, 219, 220–221, 225, 243, 256, 260–261, 269–272, 275, 289–290, 348, 356, 381–382, 393, 397, 401–403, 412–414, 439, 469, 471, 473–474, 526
participatory 24, 40, 65, 69, 76, 81, 88, 90, 91, 122–124, 127, 129–130, 134, 154, 162, 164, 165, 167, 206, 210, 214, 220, 225, 250–251, 269, 270, 273, 356, 364, 388, 394, 469, 473
participatory action research 206, 210, 214, 220, 225, 359, 394
Participatory Small Watershed Management Programme (PWM) 159, 161–169
pathway 29, 116, 121, 127, 129, 136, 148, 214, 300, 342, 416–417, 493, 498, 561, 569
patriarchy 122, 131, 238
persons with disabilities (PWD) 459, 464–466, 469, 472, 474–476
Petite Savanne 145–147, 149–150
Philippines 454–460, 505
Pinochet Ugarte, Augusto 100
plastic (bag) waste 373–381, 383
post-Morakot 132
post-Ya'an earthquake 87
Prevent programme 489, 492–494
Prevent strategy 483, 489, 492–496
profession 1–4, 9, 75, 88, 107, 113, 151–153, 175–177, 195, 199, 201–203, 220, 224–225, 246, 251, 254, 270, 281, 286, 299, 321–322, 324–325, 327, 356, 385–387, 393, 395, 411–418, 427, 455, 481, 484, 515, 535, 551, 558–562, 565–566, 571
professional practice 9, 10–12, 16–17, 23, 25–26, 45, 51–56, 66–69, 88–96, 106–107, 117–118, 138, 145–148, 150–151, 159–160, 172, 175–180, 185, 202, 225, 231, 233–234, 237–238, 242, 244–245, 248–250, 271–272, 281, 285–287, 289–290, 303–304, 318, 323, 325–329, 337–338, 342–343, 355–356, 360–365, 373, 383, 386–387, 390, 394, 411, 435–436, 438–439, 443, 447, 450–452, 455, 458, 481, 484–501, 514, 516–519, 530, 536–539, 558–562, 569–571
professional social work 23, 54, 66–67, 90, 113, 117–118, 145, 175, 238, 242–249, 285, 287, 289, 373, 386, 411, 436, 455, 469, 471
public interest design (PID) 87–95

rebuilding people's lives post-disaster 63
Rebuilding Lives Post-Disaster (RLPD), partnership 10, 63–66
Recognition of Forest Rights Act (FRA) 125–126, 130
reconstruction 10, 13, 15, 17–19, 33, 38–39, 63–64, 67, 71, 87–96, 117, 119, 126, 132–142, 147, 149, 159–160, 209, 220, 223, 387, 453, 502, 524, 531, 570
recovery 10, 17, 27, 33, 37–39, 43, 46, 52, 58–59, 63–71, 87–92, 94, 95–96, 114, 118, 121, 135, 137–139, 147–150, 239, 285, 288, 385, 387, 459, 486, 498, 517
recycling waste 5, 337, 373, 375, 378, 412
Red Crescent 33, 223, 569
Red Cross 32–33, 56, 116, 223, 245, 293, 317, 434, 514
reflection 3, 25, 51, 55–57, 71, 115–117, 132, 139, 141, 169, 171, 176–177, 181, 210, 255, 272, 275, 378, 431, 481, 496–497, 505–507, 527, 540–542, 552, 563, 569
reflective practice 326, 518
refugee 309–319, 321–329, 435, 484–485, 513, 519
respondents, research 25, 68, 69, 200, 257–260, 286–287, 329, 349–256, 389, 443, 471, 530
responders, emergency 19, 28, 52–54, 66, 322, 327, 363, 423, 426, 459, 506–507, 515–519
RIPL (Rebuilding People's Lives After Disasters Network) 10
Rudraprayag District 111, 113, 115, 121

second tier responder *see* category 2 responders
Sendai Framework (Sendai Framework for Disaster Risk reduction 2015–2030) 16, 17, 35–46, 64, 87–88, 94, 360–361, 472, 475, 525
Sichuan 87, 91, 93
Small Island Developing States (SIDS) 151, 242
social enterprise 174–175, 181, 214, 271–275, 214, 271–272
social injustice 88, 96, 195–196, 203, 235, 289, 376, 416, 514
social protection 4, 29, 88, 90, 233, 254–255, 257, 259, 261–264, 270–272, 274–275, 457–458
Social Workers Without Borders 321, 323; *see also* SWWB
solidarity 80, 99–108, 136, 168, 179, 180, 221, 223, 238–239, 324, 328, 386, 432, 439, 445, 456, 481, 505, 537, 570
soup kitchens 184, 188, 299
South Africa 336
Sri Lanka 107, 373–383
Storm Charley 70
Storm Frances 70
Storm Jeanne 70
Strengthening Resilience in Volcanic Areas (STREVA) 22
suicide bomber 55, 57
sustainable development 16, 35, 37–42, 45–46, 63–64, 87–88, 90–91, 94, 95–96, 129, 152–153,

591

Subject index

159, 164–168, 172, 178, 183, 208–209, 214, 219–225, 242–247, 250–251, 264, 276, 281, 293, 340, 362, 367, 423, 431, 436–439, 522–523, 525–531
sustainable livelihoods 115, 238, 242–243, 246–247, 267, 298, 302–304
SWWB 321–329; *see also* Social Workers Without Borders

Taiwan 4, 63, 64, 66–67, 113, 132, 139, 142, 160–181, 286
Taiwan Indigenous Dmavun Development Association (TIDDA) 171–173, 176–180
Tamil Nadu 281, 286
terrorism 52, 54–55, 57, 100, 196, 478–487, 490–494, 505
Tian Shan mountains 29, 30
Tohoku earthquake 28, 30
Toro, Luzmenia 104, 105, 108
tourism 67, 95, 115, 121–122, 135, 141, 144, 147, 151, 159, 161, 166–167, 169, 174, 179, 242–244, 248, 302, 381, 420, 422
tourism city 159, 161
transdisciplinary 1–5, 9, 12–15, 17, 21–28, 32–33, 88, 246, 285, 335–338, 340, 343, 359–360, 362, 364, 368, 522, 531–532, 571
transdisciplinary collaboration 21, 337, 571
Tribal Kitchen Project 171–174, 178
Tropical Storm Erika 144–146
tsunami 10, 28, 54, 63–64, 101–102, 104–105, 107–108, 110, 113, 283–284, 289, 290, 373, 454, 457, 459, 464–469, 472–473, 476, 491–492, 502, 507, 513, 549
typhoon 132–142, 454–457, 459, 465–466
Typhoon Morakot 132–142

Ukraine 5, 431–439
United Kingdom (UK) 51, 52, 363, 490, 506, 550
United Nations Climate Change Conference (COP21) 64
United Nations Development Programme (UNDP) 69, 117, 159, 161, 256, 434, 457
United Nations Framework Convention on Climate Change (UNFCCC) 12, 64, 516
United Nations International Strategy for Disaster Reduction (UNISDR) 16, 26, 37, 40, 526
Uttarakhand 110–114, 118, 121, 126, 130

Victoria bushfires 67–69, 549
Volusia County, Florida, Hurricane 69–70

Wamunyu, Kenya 76
waste 5, 22, 75, 138, 153, 198, 210, 222, 234–235, 287, 352, 354, 362, 373–375, 379, 381, 385–398, 402–403, 411–412, 442, 456, 505, 515, 558, 565
waste reduction project 373–383
watershed management system 159–168, 271–276, 342
Wenchuan earthquake 89–90, 113
West Virginia 513–520
women farmers 4, 254, 258, 261, 264
World Bank 77, 112, 130–131, 165, 243, 264, 315, 403, 457
World Health Organization (WHO) 43, 339, 360

Ya'an earthquake 87
Yi community 159–160, 162–163, 166
Yokohama Strategy and Plan of Action for a Safer World 36
Yunnan Province 161, 206, 210, 214

Zimbabwe 4, 254–256, 259, 261–262, 264